3 75/N
4/5

CoinWorld

Guide to U.S. Coins, Prices & Value Trends

By William T. Gibbs
and
Coin Values Market Analyst
Mark Ferguson, contributor

Seventeenth Edition
2005

A SIGNET BOOK

SIGNET
Published by New American Library, a division of
Penguin Group (USA) Inc., 375 Hudson Street,
New York, New York 10014, USA
Penguin Group (Canada), 10 Alcorn Avenue, Toronto,
Ontario M4V 3B2, Canada (a division of Pearson Penguin Canada Inc.)
Penguin Books Ltd., 80 Strand, London WC2R 0RL, England
Penguin Ireland, 25 St. Stephen's Green, Dublin 2,
Ireland (a division of Penguin Books Ltd.)
Penguin Group (Australia), 250 Camberwell Road, Camberwell, Victoria 3124,
Australia (a division of Pearson Australia Group Pty. Ltd.)
Penguin Books India Pvt. Ltd., 11 Community Centre, Panchsheel Park,
New Delhi - 110 017, India
Penguin Group (NZ), Cnr Airborne and Rosedale Roads, Albany,
Auckland 1310, New Zealand (a division of Pearson New Zealand Ltd.)
Penguin Books (South Africa) (Pty.) Ltd., 24 Sturdee Avenue,
Rosebank, Johannesburg 2196, South Africa

Penguin Books Ltd., Registered Offices:
80 Strand, London WC2R 0RL, England

Published by Signet, an imprint of New American Library,
a division of Penguin Group (USA) Inc.

First Signet Printing, November 2004
10 9 8 7 6 5 4 3 2 1

Printed in the United States of America

Foreword

The information included in The *2005 Coin World Guide to U.S. Coins, Prices & Value Trends* has been compiled by William T. Gibbs, *Coin World* news editor, and Beth Deisher, *Coin World* editor, with assistance from Paul Gilkes, senior staff writer, and Fern Loomis, editorial assistant. Price guide values have been researched by Mark Ferguson, *Coin World's Coin Values Market* analyst, who also wrote Chapter 4. Johanna L. Peters designed the book and the cover.

For more than 44 years, since 1960, *Coin World* has reported on people, laws, new issues, auctions, pricing trends and other elements that affect the hobby and business of collecting coins and related items.

In the *Coin World Price Guide*, the *Coin World* editors present in an easy-to-use format a wealth of information and insights. The retail value guide included in the *Coin World Price Guide* is from *Coin World's Coin Values*, a monthly price guide magazine included as part of a *Coin World* subscription and shipped with the first issue of each month and available in a newsstand edition. The value of the information included in this section has been proven over time.

To contact the editors of *Coin World* or request subscription information, write to *Coin World*, P.O. Box 150, Dept. 02, Sidney, Ohio 45365-0150. Visit *Coin World Online* at **www.CoinWorld.com**. Get the latest information on the State quarter dollars program at **www.StateQuarters.com**. Check out the latest coin values at **www.CoinValuesOnline.com**.

Contents

Introducing the guide

1

Welcome to the world of coins. *Coin World's 2005 Guide to U.S. Coins, Prices and Value Trends,* the largest edition of our annual price guide ever, is designed for the collector, whether neophyte or advanced. However, it should also be useful to the noncollector who has inherited some old coins or who has just become interested in coins, and to the history buff interested in facets of American history virtually ignored in most history textbooks.

This year's annual feature, "Treasure from the Sea," focuses on treasure coins and ingots recovered from three 19th century shipwrecks: the *SS Central America,* the *SS Brother Jonathan* and the *SS Republic.* Humans have long been fascinated by gold and by treasure, in works of fiction such as Robert Louis Stevenson's *Treasure Island* and through broadcast documentaries on television. We will examine each of these shipwrecks and the treasure each carried in its cargo hold, which has now entered or begun entering the collector market.

This year's edition also contains illustrations of all State quarter dollars through 2004 and the preliminary designs for the 2005 coins.

We also illustrate the 2004 Jefferson, Westward Journey 5-cent coins. These coins commemorate the bicentennials of the Louisiana Purchase (1803) and the Lewis and Clark Expedition (1804 to 1806).

Our comprehensive analysis of the rare coin market during the period from July 2003 to August 2004, written by Coin Values Analyst Mark Ferguson, follows the annual feature and State quarter dollars chapter, and then we get right into what you buy this book for—the retail price guide of U.S. coins, which has been expanded (more grades and more values) this year, especially in the ever-more popular "modern" U.S. coins. Within the pricing section, we also present the technical specifications for each series, such as size, weight, composition, etc.

Following the pricing section are chapters devoted to mintages, Proof and Uncirculated Mint sets and commemorative coins. Then you'll find a chapter about the art and science of grading (determining a coin's level of preservation and ultimately its value), a background history of U.S. coins, and a look at Mint marks and why they are important.

We then discuss the history and latest techniques of coin manufacturing, followed by an illustrated guide to error and die variety coins, including the news that despite the U.S. Mint's claims to the contrary since 1996 and 1997, some forms of doubled die varieties are still occurring even with changes to the die production process. You'll also find a glossary of often-encountered terms and an index.

Why do people collect coins?

People collect coins for many different reasons. You may want to collect coins because of their historical significance. Coins reveal much about a nation. For example, the word LIBERTY, appearing on every United States coin, says volumes about Americans' love of freedom. The motto E PLURIBUS UNUM, Latin for "out of many, one," defines the nation's character, forged from 50 states and the many peoples who make up such a diverse country. The motto IN GOD WE TRUST was introduced during the Civil War, and while at first optional, became mandatory after Theodore Roosevelt, facing strong public criticism, backed down on his insistence the motto *not* be used on new gold coins introduced in 1907 (he thought the motto's use sacrilegious).

You may collect coins for their artistic beauty. The country's greatest sculptor at the beginning of the 20th century, Augustus Saint-Gaudens, sculptured classical designs for gold $10 and $20 coins.

You may, like some people, collect for financial reward. This book is not an investment advisory; *Coin World* has always promoted coin collecting, not coin investing. Many authors are willing to give you their personal recommendations. However, we would be remiss if we did not point out that many individuals have profited from collecting U.S. coins. As is true for any investment, investing in rare coins is a calculated risk. It is essential that the investor knows exactly what he is buying and understands the risks. The risks may be great, but so may be the rewards.

You may collect simply for the love of collecting. A true collector can't explain to the uninitiated the inner joy that comes from owning a 160-year-old half cent that costs less than $40, or a unique misstruck coin pulled from circulation at face value, or an 1861 half dollar that may have been struck by the Confederate States of America after it took control of the three U.S. Mints located south of the Mason-Dixon Line.

Regardless of your vantage, we hope you will find this book useful, educational and entertaining.

Tips for new collectors

Beginning collectors soon learn that there are no "wrong" ways or "right" ways to collect coins and related numismatic items. No one way or method of collecting is objectively better than another.

However, there are right and wrong ways to do many things collectors routinely do.

Here are some useful tips any collector, beginning or experienced, can benefit from:

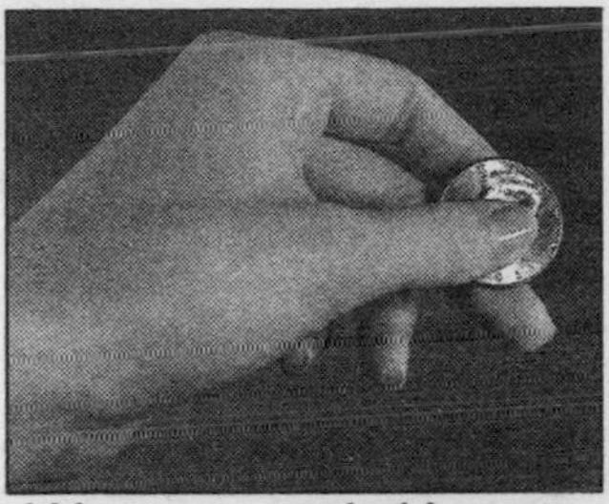

Wrong way to hold a coin.

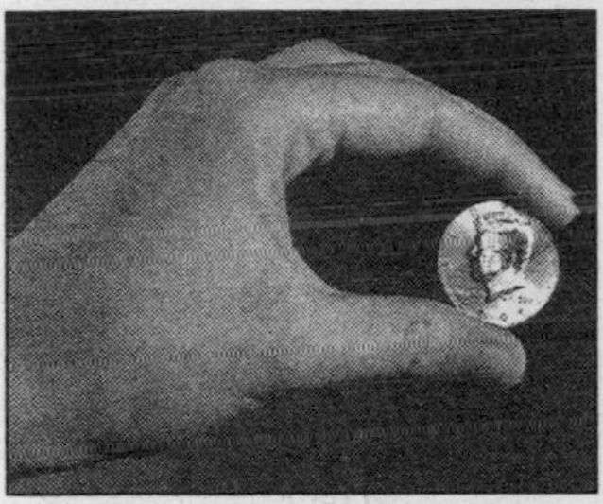

Right way to hold a coin.

• Never hold a coin by placing your fingers on the coin's surfaces. Instead, hold the coin by its edge. The human skin contains oil and contaminants that can damage a coin's surfaces.

• Never speak or sneeze while bending over a coin. While this advice may sound silly, it's practical. Saliva and mucus can also damage a coin's surfaces if contact is made.

• Avoid the impulse to clean your coins. Experienced hobbyists use chemicals to safely remove undesirable toning from a coin, and dirt and other substances can be removed without harming the coin; however, these techniques are best left to the expert. Cleaning coins with abrasive cleaners like scouring powder or pencil erasers will damage them; never use an abrasive cleaning method. As for the impulse to clean naturally toned coins, they usually should be left alone. A patina—the film that builds up on the surfaces of the coin—forms on copper and silver coins as a natural result of the chemical reaction of the coinage metal to the environment. This film actually helps protect the metal from further reactions. In addition, many collectors and dealers find natural toning attractive, and will even pay a premium for pleasingly toned coins.

• Store your coins properly. Hobbyists have found that certain types of plastic used in coin holders and flips (plastic holders creased in the middle, with the coin housed on one side) actually damage the coins placed in them. Avoid storage materials made of polyvinyl chloride (PVC); ask your dealer what is safe. In addition, some forms of paper envelopes and albums contain high amounts of sulfur, a substance that will cause copper and silver coins to tone. Do not leave your coins exposed to sunlight, high heat or high humidity for very long; all can damage a coin.

• Learn about grading. Chapter 7 discusses grading in more detail. Even a basic knowledge of what grading represents is important if you begin to buy coins from others. That's because the higher the grade or condition a coin is in, the more it is worth. However, if a collector does not know whether a coin's grade is represented accurately, he can end up paying more than the coin is worth if the coin grades lower than indicated by the seller.

Getting started

Collecting can be fun for the individual and for the entire family. It can be as easy as getting a couple of rolls of coins from a bank and placing the coins into folder-style albums (one of *Coin World's* most popular columns is "Found in Rolls," written by a collector who searches through dozens of rolls every week), or a family trip to a local coin show (there are coin shows every weekend in some part of the United States.

State quarter dollars and Jefferson 5-cent coins are good places to start since their designs have changed (ending the original series for each denominations). It takes little effort to go to the bank, buy several rolls of quarters or 5-cent coins and put individual dates and Mint marks into the holes of an inexpensive album or holder. Most coin stores carry some sort of album or holder for the State quarter dollars or Jefferson 5-cent coins. After going through the rolls and saving the coins needed, take the unwanted coins back to the bank and get some more, or just spend them. If you have duplicates of some coins, trade them with other collectors for the dates you need.

Sorting pocket change and searching new rolls from the bank brings enjoyment to many beginners. It's inexpensive and doesn't take a lot of time or effort. You may want to substitute Roosevelt dimes for the quarter dollars or 5-cent coins, or maybe the Lincoln cent, but the goal is still the same—collecting an example of each date and Mint mark for any given series.

Coin collecting opens many doors: economics, history, art and technology, both old and new. Welcome to the world of collecting and U.S. coins!

Treasure from the Sea

2

The sea is a harsh mistress: unpredictable, unforgiving, deadly. The seafloors are littered with the dreams of mankind: the wrecks of ships, from the earliest Viking cogs to the most modern of passenger liners, the vessels lost on missions of exploration and commerce, peace and war, their hulls rotting and rusting away, many completely disintegrated. Scattered about wrecks and locked away in holds that remain intact are their contents, waiting for someone to come along and pluck the scattered relics from the ocean floor: pottery, bottles, personal items of passengers and crew, and what many consider the most desirable sunken treasure of all, gold coins and bars.

During the last decade of the 20th century and the first years of the 21st, collectors have had opportunities to buy U.S. gold coins and ingots worth well in excess of $100 million that were salvaged from just three 19th century U.S. shipwrecks: the *SS Central America*, lost Sept. 13, 1857; the *SS Brother Jonathan*, sunk July 30, 1865; and the *SS Republic*, sunk Oct. 25, 1865.

Until the late 20th century and the early 21st century, the locations of these ships were lost; the treasures they carried in their holds when they sank, unobtainable. However, the sea has finally given up its secrets.

The *Central America's* location in the Atlantic Ocean off the North Carolina coast was unknown for more than 130 years. The Columbus-America Discovery Group, founded by an Ohio-based team of researchers, scientists, historians and investors, found the wreck in 1987, 8,000 feet down.

The exact location of the *Brother Jonathan* off the coast of Oregon was unknown as well, although ship's captains and others repeatedly claimed to have found and lost the site throughout the 19th century and into the 20th century. It wasn't until 1993 that the wreck was confirmed found, just 250 feet below the surface. Salvors recovered about 1,260 U.S. gold coins, most of them $20 double eagles.

The *Republic*, the last vessel to sink, by coincidence was the last vessel found, discovered in the summer of 2003 off the Georgia coast in the Atlantic Ocean by Odyssey Marine Exploration, a Florida-based firm. The wreck lies nearly 1,700 feet down and as this book was being prepared, continued to give up some of the $400,000 in specie (gold and silver coins) believed aboard the ship.

Finding sunken treasure ships is tough, dangerous work. Many tasks wait each shipwreck: finding it, locating its cargo, bringing that cargo to the surface and establishing legal ownership to the recovered artifacts under maritime law. Each task is expensive (with no guarantees of finding anything of value even if one does find the ship sought) and dangerous.

Finding the shipwreck is the first test, of course, made difficult by the nature of the sea. Because the ocean is so featureless, for most of maritime history seafarers at best had only a vague understanding of their location at sea once they left sight of land. While the principles of marine navigation had been mastered by the mid-19th century when these three treasure ships sank, all went down in bad weather. Two were lost during hurricanes of days duration, well out to sea, with weather conditions prohibiting accurate readings on the navigational equipment available to their crews; at best, 20th century maritime historians had only vague ideas of where each vessel's final resting spot lay. The third vessel, sunk during a gale, was within sight of land when it went down, but its final location was lost for 130 years.

The second and third tasks were largely impossible to achieve when the three ships sank. Even had the ships' locations been known when they were lost, 19th century diving technology had not reached a level that would have ensured recovery of the treasure.

Diving bells and diving suits, two of the mainstays of modern deep-water recovery, date to the 16th century but were still primitive by today's technology. The first submarines date to the late 18th century and even though a Confederate submarine successfully attacked and sank a Union warship during the American Civil War, the undersea vessel itself sank during its attack. While submarine technology slowly improved during the remainder of the 19th century, it had not reached a level where submarines could be used for treasure hunting and recovery efforts.

Thus the *Central America*, the *Brother Jonathan* and the *Republic* remained beyond reach for more than a century.

In the meantime, insurers of the lost cargo, including the gold, paid the claims of the clients and registered their payments in their records. The cargo now belonged to the insurers, at least on paper. In reality, it belonged to the sea.

At sea, on the ocean floor in three locations, the wood and iron that formed the decks, hulls and other parts of each ship slowly decayed and rusted, until little of each vessel remained intact. Deposits formed by biological processes present on the ocean bottom began encrusting many of the coins open to the elements.

For decades, each vessel remained undisturbed, save by the sea's natural denizens.

Then came the scientists and the historians, the hunters and their futuristic equipment that the 19th century's Jules Verne, who wrote about undersea treasure himself in his *20,000 Leagues Under the Sea,* still would have recognized as the real counterparts to his famous fictional submarine, the *Nautilus.*

SS Central America

The gold carried aboard the *Central America* when it sank came from California goldfield yields, tons of which were shipped eastward every year by sea. California until 1848 barely registered on the collective American mind. Then carpenter John Marshall found several gold nuggets in a ditch at the site of a newly constructed sawmill owned by John Sutter on the American River. By that summer, some 4,000 men were pulling from the ground every day gold worth $30,000 to $40,000. In December, President James K. Polk opened his address to Congress with official confirmation that reports of an abundance of gold being found in California had been corroborated by U.S. Army officers there, notes *America's Lost Treasure,* a book about the *Central America* treasure.

Newspapers reported the president's remarks and California suddenly became the destination for thousands seeking to make their fortunes wrestling gold from the riverbeds and hillsides.

Not everyone found fortunes in gold. Many found it profitable, instead, to support the miners. An industry sprang up in California to assay the gold and prepare it for coinage production. Private minters struck pioneer gold coins in denominations as high as $50, until a new federal Branch Mint was opened in San Francisco in 1854 to turn the gold into federal coinage.

Gold ingot weighing nearly 17 ounces was found amidst the wreckage of the *SS Central America.*

Gold ingots, coins (both federal and private) and even nuggets were among the treasure found at the wreck site of the *Central America.*

Before and after the Branch Mint was opened, millions of dollars in new gold coins and bars were shipped eastward. A common route was by ship along the west coast of North America and Central America to the Panamanian Isthmus, where the gold and passengers disembarked and crossed the narrow strip of land joining the two continents. As the amount of gold being shipped increased to staggering amounts, Eastern financiers built a 47-mile-long railroad across the isthmus in the early to mid-1850s to facilitate the transportation of the gold and passengers from the city of Panama on the Pacific Ocean north to Aspinwall on the Atlantic side. At Aspinwall, the gold and passengers would embark on another ship that would take them north, with the gold often transported to New York City.

One ship plying the Caribbean Sea and Atlantic Ocean route was the *SS Central America.*

The *Central America* was a sidewheel steamship (it also carried sails used to supplement the ship's engines). The vessel, launched in October 1852, was originally named the *George Law* after the founder of the United States Mail Steamship Co., which operated the vessel. It began plying the Panama-New York route in October 1853, rated to carry nearly 500 passengers in cabins and steerage.

In June 1857, while being overhauled, the ship was renamed the

Central America; it twice steamed the New York-Panama-New York circuit under that name, carrying passengers, crew and cargo, before arriving at Aspinwall for the last time on Sept. 2, 1857. There, commercial shipments of gold valued at $1.2 million to $1.3 million and weighing tons were loaded. Some of the nearly 500 passengers who boarded the vessel carried their own gold. The *Central America* was literally a treasure ship.

Much of the gold in the commercial shipments was in the form of newly struck 1857-S Coronet $20 double eagles, struck at the San Francisco Branch Mint. The ship also carried ingots, large, small and in between, assayed and cast by various private businesses in California, and privately struck gold coins in denominations as high as $50. Gold nuggets and dust also rested in the ship's hold and in the possession of the passengers.

The *Central America* steamed from Aspinwall Sept. 3 and made for Havana, where it arrived Sept. 7 after an uneventful voyage. It left Cuba Sept. 8 for New York City, carrying a fortune in gold and more than 600 passengers and crew. It never made its destination.

On Sept. 9, the wind began to pick up as the ship made its way north. By the next day, the weather had developed into a full hurricane. Despite the weather, the ship continued to steam northward.

From Sept. 11 to 13, the ship and its crew fought the seas and the wind, but lost the battle. Other ships happened on the scene and were able to rescue the women and children among the passengers (the age-old rule, women and children first, applied), but just a few of the men. The ship sank beneath the waves on Sept. 13, with more than 430

Gold coins of various denominations were recovered from the *Central America.* Some of the pieces shown were struck privately; others were struck at the San Francisco Branch Mint.

The gold ingots found in the wreckage of the *Central America* were of various weights and fineness, typical for ingots made of California gold.

men on board. A few were rescued, but more than 400 men drowned. And except for a small amount of gold carried by a few rescued passengers, all of the gold went to the ocean bottom.

The loss of so much gold made an already bad financial situation worse in the East. The nation was in the midst of a financial crisis brought about by excessive debt, chiefly from the financing of railroad construction. The loss of the *SS Central America* gold forced a temporary suspension of specie payments to prevent a run on the banks, according to Normand E. Klare's *The Final Voyage of the* Central America *1857.*

The book notes that insurance companies (nine in all) assured the public that they would pay the claims on the more than $1 million in losses. Of the insured gold, $550,000 was insured in New York, $950,000 in London (destination for some of the gold) and $100,000 in Philadelphia, according to Normand Klare's book.

The total amount of gold lost by individual passengers was uncertain, but estimates at the time put it near $1.2 million. The total value of all gold believed on board the vessel totaled more than $2.4 million.

Not surprisingly, a commercial diving firm made plans to retrieve the treasure, but abandoned the operation when it determined the ship had been lost in waters too deep for the level of diving gear technology available. The exact position of the vessel was unknown, which would have made finding the wreck close to impossible in an era predating sonar.

The sinking of the *SS Central America* was as infamous in the 19th century as the sinking of the *Titanic* in the 20th. The loss of life was the greatest of any commercial passenger vessel wreck in the 19th century. The loss of the gold was also the greatest of its kind during the century. And yet, as decades passed, the *Central America* faded out of the collective American memory. For well over a century, the gold lay on the ocean bottom, lost, remembered only by maritime enthusiasts and treasure hunters, and beyond retrieval.

In the late 1970s, a talented ocean engineer from Ohio, Tommy Thompson, became interested in treasure ships. He had worked for legendary maritime treasure hunter Mel Fisher after Thompson graduated from college in the 1970s and thus had gained a practical knowledge of treasure hunting. However, Thompson did not consider himself a treasure hunter. He wanted to document everything he found for its historical importance, not simply dredge all of the gold up with no regard for the history and science of the wreck site.

In 1978, Thompson met Bob Evans, a geologist who, Gary Kinder writes in *Ship of Gold in the Deep Blue Sea,* seemed to remember everything he learned. The two became friends and discussed many things, eventually turning to Thompson's months with Fisher and Thompson's desire to find a treasure ship. In 1983, Thompson began studying historical records for the right treasure ship, and identified a possible target: the *Central America.* Evans researched the environment of the ocean bottom where the ship was thought to have sunk and found that the bottom consisted of hard sediment, ideal for search and recovery efforts. (Sinking into soft sediment, if deep enough, could prevent discovery of a wreck, and preclude recovery of any treasure.)

Some gold ingots and coins in this image are discolored, bearing deposits from being underwater for more than a century.

The two began to gather investors, and the Columbus America Discovery Group, based in Columbus, Ohio, was formed. They began to gather resources, including a ship and equipment for conducting the search for the *SS Central America.* They developed the technology to search the ocean floor 8,000 feet down and to recover artifacts from that depth. Among their tools was the *Nemo,* a remotely operated

This "brick" is gold, worth a fortune in 1857 when the *Central America* sank and worth even more today (both in terms of gold content and collector value).

submersible named after the fictional captain of Jules Verne's *Nautilus.*

Beginning in 1987, Thompson, Evans and their team searched the area they thought the *Central America* rested in, and in September, found a promising site, where debris and coal scattered about the ocean floor suggested a shipwreck. However, the team found nothing conclusive that proved the vessel the *Central America.*

They returned to the site the next year, found more debris, and on Sept. 11, 1988, 131 years to the day when the *Central America* began taking on water from the hurricane, the team found the vessel, including one of the ship's giant paddlewheels. They recovered the ship's bell, allowing them to confirm the vessel's identity. A few weeks later, they discovered gold: stacks and stacks of coins and bars, lying exposed on the ocean floor, sticking out of the sediment, some in towers many coins thick. (The photograph on the cover of this book is from the *Central America,* showing just a small fraction of the gold that awaited the team.)

Geologist Bob Evans helped find the *SS Central America* and retrieve the treasures it held. He poses with a huge gold ingot, standing well above smaller pieces.

The *Nemo* began recovering the gold in late September, and by the time the season ended (winter weather made recovery efforts difficult), had brought to the surface hundreds of coins and bars.

The Columbus-America Discovery Group recovered an almost unimaginable fortune in gold over the next few years. Many of the coins were Mint State 1857-S Coronet $20 double eagles, struck at the San Francisco Branch Mint. The ingots bore the names of many famous and some not-so-famous private assayers working in California in 1857. The study of these ingots has added greatly to the understanding of California assayers.

However, it would be another decade before any of the gold reached the market.

The insurers who had paid claims in the 1850s still had the records of payment in their archives more than 13 decades later. The Columbus-America Discovery Group had already filed legal claims with the court, but the insurers went to court to claim they owned the gold. The legal case lasted nearly a decade and was argued all the way to the U.S. Supreme Court. Eventually, the court with jurisdiction ruled that 92.4 percent of the gold would go to the finders and 7.6 percent to the insurers.

However, before the coins and ingots could be sold, many of them had to be "conserved," a word used by the owners to describe the removal of the natural deposits found on the coins and ingots, some resulting from chemical and biological processes, including deposits from the rusting of the iron parts of the ship. Bob Evans developed a method of removing the encrusted materials from the coins that the owners said left the gold surfaces undamaged. (The "conserving" of the coins brought some controversy, since many considered the process "cleaning" and wondered how Professional Coin Grading Service, the grading service hired to grade many of the coins, could encapsulate them when its own policies kept it from encapsulating "cleaned" coins.)

When it came time to sell the coins, the insurers and Columbus-America Discovery Group took different approaches.

The insurers sold their portion – gold coins and assay bars – in a Dec. 14, 2000, auction conducted in New York City by Christie's in association with Spink. The sale, totaling just 169 lots, realized more than $2.2 million.

Columbus-America chose to sell its portion of the treasure to a consortium of coin dealers and investors in January 2000 for more than $100 million. Sales of the coins to the public began March 1, 2000. Since that time, the coins and ingots have been sold into the market for millions of dollars.

The *SS Central America* may not have given up all of its gold yet. According to Kinder, declassified U.S. Army records indicate the *SS Central America* carried another 30,000 pounds of gold aboard when it sank: a secret shipment of gold to shore up the northeastern economy.

At current bullion prices, that shipment, if found and recovered, would be worth more than $12 million, but its collector value could be much higher.

SS Brother Jonathan

The discovery of almost unimaginable quantities of gold in California beginning in 1848 brought about immense changes to the western reaches of the United States, but only accelerated the changes already occurring.

During the 1840s, the nation's borders and settlers began moving westward, beyond the states that had been formed west of the Mississippi River from 1821 (Missouri) to 1846 (Iowa) and beyond the lands purchased from France in 1803 as the Louisiana Purchase.

Great Britain controlled the disputed northern regions west of the Louisiana Purchase territory, known as the Oregon Country, while Mexico owned the southern regions. That did not stop Americans from moving into these still foreign lands in small numbers in the 1830s and thousands from populating the regions in the 1840s before Great Britain and Mexico bowed to the inevitable and transferred ownership to the United States.

The Texas annexation came in 1845, when that former Mexican state and independent republic became an American state. Great Britain's cession of the Oregon Country in 1846 and the Mexican cession of 1848 extended the U.S. national borders to the Pacific Ocean for the first time. With both regions officially part of the United States by the time of the California gold discoveries in 1848, populations swelled, especially in California and Oregon. California became a state in 1850, with Oregon achieving the same status in 1859.

Commerce between the two states became increasingly important as each state's population grew, but transportation between the most important cities, San Francisco and Portland, remained difficult. Stagecoach service between the two was established in the 1860s and a railroad line was constructed between California and Oregon in the

This beautifully preserved 1865-S Coronet gold $10 eagle was found in the wreckage of the *SS Brother Jonathan*.

1880s. Until then, however, sea transportation was the most efficient means of shipping large cargos and numbers of passengers from one state to the other.

Among the ships that began plying the regular San Francisco to Portland route in the 1850s was the *SS Brother Jonathan,* a steam-powered side-wheeler that, like the *Central America,* also carried sails.

The *Brother Jonathan* carried cargoes of both goods and passengers, not only between California and Oregon but to British Columbia as well.

When the vessel steamed northward from San Francisco on July 28, 1865, among the cargo it carried onboard was ore-crushing equipment for the Owyhee District in Idaho, site of additional gold finds, two cases of playing cards, a billiard table, two camels and 50 cases of cigars. Its passenger compliment was uncertain because of last-minute arrivals not carried on the ship's manifest; the estimated numbers range from 170 to 200, according to Q. David Bowers in *The Treasure Ship* S.S. Brother Jonathan*: Her Life and Loss 1850-1865.* Crewmembers numbered about 60.

Also onboard was an unknown quantity of gold coins (the amount was unpublished), at least some certainly carried as passenger property. Some of the gold was left with the purser for storage during the journey.

The voyage was not a comfortable one. The seas quickly became rough and most of the passengers spent the voyage in bed, seasick. It made a scheduled stop at Crescent City, Calif., July 29, according to Bowers. It continued its northward voyage the morning of July 30, plowing back into seas even rougher than when the vessel stopped at Crescent City.

Several hours after it left Crescent City, the *Brother Jonathan* slammed into a rocky reef, breaking the ship's keel. Water began pouring into the ship and the waves pounded it against the rocks until the foremast dropped through the bottom of the ship, worsening the flooding.

The wind and rough waters made launching lifeboats almost impossible. Since most passengers were confined to bed with seasickness and because the ship quickly filled with water and rested at a tilt, getting to the upper deck proved difficult. Of the more than 200 passengers and crew aboard, contemporary records indicate that about 20 made it to shore safely, and most of those saved were crewmembers (the only passengers to survive were women and children; none of the adult male passengers apparently survived).

The cargo, including the gold, sank with the ship.

Efforts to recover the ship's cargo began not long after it sank and continued for decades after. The location of the wreck became lost, although ships' captains passing through the area claimed to have found the wreck site numerous times. Despite these claims, according to Bowers, no accounts exist of anyone ever salvaging gold coins from the wreckage.

That changed in 1988.

Donald G. Knight, founder of Sea-Epics Research Inc., was fascinated by the shipwreck and sought, and was granted, a permit by the California State Lands Commission to search for the *Brother Jonathan,* writes Bowers in his book. However, the company was unable to obtain funding to engage in the search and the project was shelved.

Knight, however, did not give up his dreams of finding the vessel. In 1991, he and several partners founded a new firm, Deep Sea Research Inc., with the goal of finding the vessel and salvaging its treasure.

Deep Sea Research began its search for the *Brother Jonathan* in 1991, with operations continuing through 1992 and 1993. At first, the search was unsuccessful, as the team seeking the wreckage focused on its supposed location, searching the sea floor for weeks in September 1993. On Oct. 1, 1993, the team shifted its search south of the original search area. It found the wreckage of the *Brother Jonathan* within hours of shifting to the new site!

The salvors who located the *Brother Jonathan* found more 1865-S Coronet gold $20 double eagles than any other coin located at the wreck site.

The team recovered a few artifacts from the remains of the wreck, located 250 feet beneath the surface, to use in filing a court claim to legal ownership of the wreck and anything recovered from the site.

In 1994, however, state officials sought to claim possession of the wreck on various grounds. DSR lawyers successfully fought all claims by the state, Bowers writes. The state appealed to the Ninth District Circuit Court, which in March 1995 ruled in favor of DSR on all counts. The state then appealed to the U.S. Supreme Court, which agreed to hear the case. The Supreme Court April 22, 1998, ruled 9-0 to clear the way for a federal maritime court to hear and decide the case, with a decision written by Justice Sandra Day O'Connor that said the court was "rooting for the treasure seekers, whose bold adventurers spark the imagination and inspire dreams."

While attorneys for the state and for DSR argued in one court after another, DSR was searching for the iron safe known to have been aboard the vessel and thought the likely repository for the gold the ship's purser held. One of the most intensive searches began in late August 1996.

On the fourth day of the search, Aug. 30, the crew aboard the two-man submarine used by DSR saw several stacks of gold coins, the first found at the wreck site, but lost the exact location in the "sea dust" kicked up from the ocean floor. They regained the site later that day after the murky water cleared somewhat and recovered 564 gold coins, most of them double eagles: single pieces, stacks of two to four stuck together by natural underwater biological processes and even a stack of about 25 coins massed together. Some of the 1865-S Coronet double eagles—struck at the San Francisco Branch Mint—were said to be as brilliant as they were the day they were struck.

The coins rested in what had probably been the location of the purser's office aboard the vessel.

The team continued operations into September, recovering additional gold totaling 875 pieces. The safe was recovered Sept. 6, but when opened, anticlimactically was found to contain no gold or anything else of value.

When operations resumed in August 1997, the salvors used a diving bell—descendant of the first diving bells from the 16th century. The divers aboard the bell found 332 gold coins during the 1997 operations, again most of them double eagles, bringing the total to 1,207 coins.

In 1999, with the case still before a maritime court, DSR and state officials reached a private agreement: DSR would retain ownership of 1,007 of the recovered coins, with 200 coins and other artifacts going to the state. The state agreed to keep its coins off the market for 15 years.

DSR, however, could sell its coins at any time.

In preparation for their dispersal into the marketplace, DSR hired Robert Johnson to conserve the coins. As with the *SS Central America* gold coins, the residues deposited on the coins were removed by a technique that the auction house hired to sell the coins said left the "majority of the coins ... no different in appearance than they might be if they had been stored in a bank vault for these many years."

DSR consigned 1,006 of the coins to Auctions by Bowers and Merena, to offer at public auction. The remaining coin, bearing coral incrustations, was given to Del Norte County Museum in Crescent City. The auction firm at that time was a Collectors Universe company, which owns Professional Coin Grading Service, a third-party grading service.

Among the coins found during the first two years of recovery were 620 1865-S Coronet double eagles, which until the time of the discovery had been extremely rare in Mint State (about eight pieces grading Mint State were previously known). Of the *Brother Jonathan* 1865-S Coronet double eagles, all but 45 were Mint State (and the circulated specimens were mostly graded About Uncirculated)!

The coins were sold at auction May 29, 1999. They brought more than $5.3 million.

DSR conducted its last diving operations on the wreckage of the *Brother Jonathan* from Sept. 1 to Oct. 10, 2000, during which it recovered 52 more gold coins, most double eagles. Those gold coins, 38 of which were graded and encapsulated by Numismatic Guaranty Corporation of America, began entering the marketplace in 2003.

SS Republic

On Aug. 16, 2003, a marine exploration firm claimed it had found a 19th century shipwreck, said to be carrying 20,000 gold $20 double eagles, at the bottom of the Atlantic Ocean.

The *SS Republic* was lost at sea Oct. 25, 1865. The firm that found the *Republic*, Odyssey Marine Explorations Inc., Tampa, Fla., said contemporary accounts indicated that the ship carried aboard $400,000 in specie, bound from New York City to New Orleans to help shore up the Southern city's sagging economy in the post-Civil War era.

The *SS Republic* left New York Oct. 18, bound to New Orleans with 56 passengers and its cargo, including the specie. On the morning of Oct. 23, the ship encountered an east-northeasterly gale. By evening, the gale had become a "perfect hurricane," according to Odyssey.

The next day, the ship's paddlewheels stalled; the ship began to drift in the hurricane.

On the morning of Oct. 25, the *Republic's* donkey boiler, used to power the pumps that pumped water from the hold overboard, failed. As the ship continued to take in water, the ship's crew began to prepare to abandon ship on the vessel's four lifeboats and a makeshift raft constructed from spars and boards.

All but one passenger made it to one of the lifeboats or raft. Eventually, other ships rescued all 62 individuals aboard the lifeboats and two of the 18 who had been on the raft.

According to Odyssey's Web site, "When news of the *Republic's* sinking reached Charleston, the *Daily Herald* reported on October 30th, 'Her cargo was valuable, and in addition she had on board some $400,000 in treasure, which went down with the ship.'"

According to the company's Web site, "During the last 12 years, over 1,500 total square miles have been devoted to the search for this elusive target, with Odyssey searching over 1,000 square miles during the past two years alone," according to the firm. "Odyssey investigated 24 targets in 2002 and 2003. ..."

While Odyssey officials were certain the wreck they had found represented the *Republic*, it was not until the ship's bell was brought to the surface in October 2003 that they had the proof they sought: The bell bore the name *Tennessee*, the original name of the *Republic*.

Odyssey Marine found its first gold coins amongst the wreckage in the fall of 2003. By Jan. 27, 2004, Odyssey reported it had recovered more than 17,000 coins. Of those, it had recovered 2,950 gold coins and 14,230 silver coins.

As of April 2004, the firm reported recovering 51,212 coins: two silver quarter dollars, 47,094 half dollars, 1,496 $10 eagles and 2,620 $20 double eagles. All of the coins date from the 1840s to 1865.

The *SS Republic* coins also require conservation. To that end, in December 2003, Odyssey Marine hired Numismatic Conservation Services to conserve the coins and Numismatic Guaranty Corporation of America to encapsulate them (and grade those meeting coin market standards).

The diversity of the coins recovered to date has surprised professional numismatists who have seen the coins.

Donald H. Kagin, a California dealer who is a specialist in pioneer gold coins and a consultant to Odyssey, is among them. He told *Coin World* that he believes collectors will be "pleasantly surprised" by the diversity of the coins.

According to an NGC press release: "Among the coins already retrieved are numerous gold eagles, gold double eagles and silver half dollars, nearly all dating between the early 1850s and 1865. Unlike other recently salvaged shipwrecks, a wide variety of dates and Mints have been noted in this find."

The quality of the coins being recovered is also generating surprise and excitement among those who have seen the coins already recovered, including Kagin.

According to the NGC press release, "Based on the pieces recovered thus far that have been professionally conserved by Numismatic Conservation Services and graded and encapsulated by Numismatic Guaranty Corporation, this collection may already include several finest-known examples of United States gold and silver coins from the period."

Among those pieces is an 1854-O Coronet double eagle that NGC has graded About Uncirculated 58, tying it with three other examples for finest known. The coin is a classic rarity of the New Orleans Mint; no more than 30 examples are believed to have survived.

Two other low-mintage gold coins have been found aboard the *SS Republic*, according to NGC officials.

One is an 1865-S Coronet, Inverted Date $10 eagle, graded MS-62. The 186 of the date was punched into the die upside down, then punched into the die correctly. The other is an 1857-O Coronet double eagle, graded MS-62 prooflike. Of coins with their respective dates and Mint marks, both coins received the highest grade ever assigned by NGC.

Another rarity found at the wreck site is an 1860 Coronet double eagle, graded MS-65. According to NGC, the coin is rarely found in Mint State.

Not all of the coins found at the *SS Republic* wreck site can be graded by NCG. Many of the silver half dollars bear the signs of having been submerged in seawater for a nearly 140 years. After NCS conserves them, NGC is encapsulating these pieces attributed to the *Republic* but leaving them ungraded.

Odyssey Marine began selling these coins through the Shop at Home television network in May 2004, the first public offering of coins from the *SS Republic.*

Coins characterized as coming from the "numismatic collection" were to be offered at an uncertain future date, after Odyssey had recovered enough coins to determine a population. Those pieces will be offered at a yet-to-be-determined numismatic value, according to Odyssey officials.

State quarter dollars 3

More than 139 million Americans can't be wrong—collecting State quarter dollars is fun.

As 2005 dawns, the United States will be entering the seventh year of a 10-year program of circulating commemorative quarter dollars honoring each of the 50 states. The first State quarter dollars entered circulation in January 1999. The last will enter circulation near the end of 2008. Between those two dates, more new coinage designs will enter circulation than in any previous 10-year period in U.S. coinage history.

The United States Mint is producing five different quarter dollars each year for 10 years, until each state is represented by a quarter dollar with a commemorative reverse design. Congress, spurred by spirited lobbying by the coin collecting community, authorized the 10-year program in 1997. Most collectors are joyous over the opportunity to collect something new from circulation after so many decades of coins of numbing sameness.

While the portrait on the obverse remains that of George Washington, another change should be immediately obvious on the State quarter dollars other than the new reverse designs. The date and denomination have changed sides, with the date now located on the reverse and the denomination QUARTER DOLLAR now on the obverse where the date used to be.

Changing our change

Until the State quarter dollars program was introduced, most Americans did not give the coins in their change a second glance. Coinage designs, after all, had been a static, unchanging force in our daily lives. For many Americans, until the State quarters and the new Westward Journey 5-cent coins, the quarter dollar they were familiar with previously always depicted George Washington and an eagle; the cent, Abraham Lincoln; the dime, Franklin D. Roosevelt; the half dollar, John F. Kennedy; and the 5-cent coin, Thomas Jefferson.

To collectors, that was a problem.

Coinage designs used to change with regularity, sometimes to the point of absurdity from a modern viewpoint. For example, three distinctly different design types were used in 1793 for the nation's first cents: a Flowing Hair Liberty, Chain cent obverse-reverse combination; a Flowing Hair Liberty, Wreath cent; and a Liberty Cap, Wreath cent. Public and official dissatisfaction over these coinage designs resulted in rapid changes in less than 12 months, the first change being made after just 36,103 cents were struck over the period of a few weeks!

While the pace of design change during the next century wasn't always that hectic, Mint officials changed designs for most denominations on a routine basis. Congress finally put the brakes on unrestricted design changes in 1890. It passed a new law requiring the Treasury Department to seek congressional approval to change coinage designs unless the designs had been in use for at least 25 years.

Happily for collectors, Mint officials during the early decades of the 20th century interpreted the 1890 regulation as *requiring* design changes every 25 years. For example, new designs for the dime, quarter dollar and half dollar had been introduced in 1891; 25 years later, in 1916, Mint officials felt compelled to introduce new designs for each of those three denominations.

By the 1960s, however, Mint officials' bureaucratic thought processes had changed: Change was bad. Keeping the status quo was good.

After the introduction of the Kennedy half dollar in 1964, changes to U.S. coin designs were few and short-lived: Two new dollar coins were introduced in 1971 and 1979, giving collectors some new designs to collect. However, the only changes to existing coinage denominations came in 1975 and 1976 when new reverses were created for the quarter dollar, half dollar and dollar to celebrate the nation's Bicentennial. In 1977, the celebration over, Mint officials returned the original designs to the three coins and the Bicentennial coins soon passed from general circulation (the half dollar and dollar rarely circulated anyway).

Changing coinage designs simply to put a new face on them became a concept largely foreign to Mint and congressional officials from the 1960s until the end of the 20th century. However, led by the popularity of the State quarter dollars program, government officials now embrace design changes. Two new Jefferson, Westward Journey 5-cent coin designs were introduced in 2004, two more are planned in 2005 and new renditions of Jefferson and his home at Monticello will likely be introduced in 2006. As this edition is being edited in mid-2004, Congress was considering a plan that would put every president's portrait on a circulating dollar coin, released at the rate of four every year until all of the former presidents have been honored.

Which leads us to why coin collectors are so excited about the ongoing changes to the Washington quarter dollar. Collectors are tired of seeing the same old designs in circulation day after day, year after year, decade after decade. After all, the Washington quarter dollar has been around for a long time.

Washington's birth

The Washington quarter dollar was introduced in 1932 as a circulating commemorative coin to celebrate Washington's 200th birthday, just 16 years after the then current design had been introduced. Under the 1890 law, congressional approval was required, sought and given for the change since the existing Standing Liberty-Flying Eagle designs had been in use for less than the required 25 years. And there the Washington designs remained, fixed in time for 66 years.

The decision to depict Washington on a legal tender coin likely would have horrified the man being honored. Back before Congress devised the U.S. coinage system in 1792, our Founding Fathers began debating a national coinage. Some suggested that the nation's coins should depict the current president, then George Washington. The scion of Mount Vernon rejected this suggestion, indicating that to place his image on U.S. coinage would be to follow Europe's lead, where many nations at the time placed the portrait of their reigning sovereign on their coinage. Congress in its wisdom acceded to Washington's view and instead required each coin to depict on its obverse an allegorical representation of Liberty.

For all of the 18th and 19th centuries, and the first decades of the 20th century, various images of Liberty dominated most U.S. coinage designs. (A few coins produced during the 19th century depict such subjects as a shield, flying eagle or large star rather than Liberty.) Then, in 1892, government policy changed. That year represented the 400th anniversary of Christopher Columbus' first voyage to what became known as the Western Hemisphere. Many nations celebrated, including the United States, which staged the World's Columbian Exposition in 1893 (the expo was supposed to start in 1892, but the exposition grounds were not ready until 1893).

Many numismatic collectibles resulted from the U.S. celebration, including the attractive admission tickets, many privately and government-issued medals, and two noncirculating commemorative coins, the first such coins issued by the United States. The government issued an 1893 commemorative quarter dollar and 1892 and 1893 commemorative half dollars. Not only were these the first U.S. commemorative coins, they were the first U.S. coins to depict actual individuals instead of allegorical figures of Liberty (other than a few pattern pieces, or experimental coins, issued just after the Civil War but never issued for circulation or general production).

The legislation authorizing the coins required that Columbus' portrait be placed on the half dollar and Queen Isabella's portrait on the quarter dollar. (Isabella was Columbus' chief sponsor, although it is a myth that she sold her jewels to finance his first voyage.) One other commemorative coin was issued during the 19th century, the 1900 Lafayette silver dollar, which depicts George Washington and the Frenchman who rallied to America's cause during the Revolutionary War. Congress authorized other commemorative coins depicting actual persons during the first decade of the 20th century.

It was not until 1909, the centennial celebration of Lincoln's birth, that the first circulating coin to depict an actual person was produced. A portrait of Lincoln was placed on the cent to replace the aging Liberty portrait on the Indian Head cent, attracting only minor objections to the change in policy. Editors at *The Numismatist*, considered by many the leading coin collector magazine of the day, said, "Let us have a Lincoln portrait coin for circulation and not be hampered by the time-worn objection to placing a citizen's portrait upon our coins." One wonders what they might have said had they known that more than 95 years later, the same portrait would still be in use (a record for any U.S. coinage design).

Portraits became the rule rather than the exception once the Lincoln cent opened the floodgates for changes to circulating coinage. Washington followed in 1932 on the quarter dollar; Thomas Jefferson in 1938 on the 5-cent coin (replacing an American Indian); Franklin Roosevelt in 1946 (replacing the Winged Liberty Head); Benjamin Franklin (replacing the Walking Liberty); and John F. Kennedy on the half dollar, in 1948 and 1964, respectively. New dollar coins have depicted Dwight D. Eisenhower (introduced in 1971), Susan B. Anthony (1979) and Sacagawea (2000).

The changes that have occurred since 1999 did not come easy. Before then, official policy used to state that there was no public support for changes in coinage designs. While collectors argued that point, lobbying efforts at the Treasury Department and on Capitol Hill were largely fruitless. Collectors got close several times, with one legislative effort derailed when conservative elements claimed, incorrectly, that the effort to change coinage designs was directed at removing from the coins the motto IN GOD WE TRUST. Furthermore, many in Washington, D.C., would find it difficult to remove from our circulating coinage such icons as George Washington, Thomas Jefferson and Abraham Lincoln. Lawmakers also might find it daunting to select a racially diverse five Americans for portrayal, if the policy of depicting actual persons were continued.

However, coin collectors finally gained a sympathetic ear when Rep. Michael Castle, R-Del., was named chairman of the House subcommittee in charge of coinage legislation in the mid-1990s. Rep. Castle listened and acted when collectors told Congress that too many expensive commemorative coins were being struck merely to raise funds for various special-interest groups. For example, consider two coins issued while his predecessor, Rep. Joseph P. Kennedy II, D-Mass., served as chairman of the subcommittee. Two commemorative coins were authorized (with little or no opportunity for public comment) that depict Kennedy's relatives: a silver dollar depicting his father, Robert F. Kennedy, and a second silver dollar depicting an aunt, Eunice Kennedy Shriver (who is still living), as a founder of the Special Olympics.

To answer coin collectors' cries that too many programs were being approved, many with inappropriate subjects, Castle got Congress to approve legislation limiting commemorative programs to no more than two a year (although Congress has violated that law already). He also forced changes that call for greater accountability from those organizations and foundations receiving funds from commemorative coin sales. And he indicated he was open to the idea of requiring the Treasury Department to change some of the circulating coins' designs.

Coins for states

During Castle's commemorative coin hearing July 12, 1995, he asked New York City coin dealer Harvey Stack, representing the Professional Numismatists Guild, for any other recommendations after Stack read his prepared statement on commemorative programs. Stack is an opponent of multiple noncirculating commemorative coin programs, which can be very expensive (especially if collectors buy one of everything being offered) and which very often drop in value after collectors buy the coins from the Mint. Stack suggested a circulating commemorative quarter dollar program honoring each of the 50 states as a means of introducing a broader audience to coin collecting, and at low cost (at face value from circulation!). While Stack may not have been the first to suggest the idea publicly, he was the first to do so publicly to someone in government who could act on the proposal. The Citizens Commemorative Coin Advisory Committee, then chaired by the director of the U.S. Mint, unanimously endorsed the idea, as did other hobby leaders testifying at the hearing. Castle warmed to the idea and introduced legislation that passed both houses and was signed into law. Even Treasury officials backed the program, but not until completing a congressionally mandated study and asking Congress to order the program to be implemented. At Castle's instigation, Congress did.

Over the 10 years of the program, five quarter dollars will be issued each year at roughly 10-week intervals in the order the states entered the Union. Each coin will have a design reflective of the state being commemorated. Each state's governor may recommend up to five design concepts, with each state determining the process by which its design concepts are selected. The secretary of the Treasury approves the proposed designs after consultation with two government-appointed committees empowered to comment on coinage designs. The state's governor selects the final design from those approved by the secretary of the Treasury.

Congress avoided any controversy over removing Washington from the design by mandating changes to the reverse only. The 1932 Washington portrait will remain in place on the obverse of each quarter dollar, although some surprising changes have taken place that involve the obverse and reverse. Mint officials studied the placement of existing inscriptions on both sides, the space available on the reverse for the individual state designs, and the need for additional space for new reverse legends. Officials concluded that in order to incorporate the new designs and inscriptions, they needed authority to reposition existing legends. Since the positioning of such elements as the date and QUARTER DOLLAR are mandated by law, Treasury officials had to get congressional authority to move them. Congress again moved remarkably quickly; President Clinton signed the legislation into law in May 1998. Mint officials also had to make the Washington portrait smaller to make space for the additional inscriptions.

The most jarring changes involve the date and the denomination. Mint officials moved the date from the obverse to the bottom of the reverse. (These coins are not the first U.S. coins with dates on the reverse; gold dollars and $3 coins have reverse dates.) The denomination QUARTER DOLLAR was moved from the reverse to the obverse, beneath Washington's portrait (where the date is located on pre-1999 quarter dollars). Officials moved UNITED STATES OF AMERICA from the reverse to the obverse, and some of the obverse legends were moved into different positions on that side.

The Mint has struck State quarter dollars at both the Philadelphia and Denver Mints for circulation, and collector-only versions at those two facilities and the San Francisco Mint. Collectors wanting to collect an example of each coin from circulation will need a specimen from the Philadelphia and Denver Mints, or 100 coins over 10 years. According to Mint officials, no special effort is being made to place a particular state's coins into circulation in that state. As with all coins, distribution is under the control of the Federal Reserve Bank, which buys coins from the Mint at face value and sells them to commercial banks when requested. It's anyone's guess as to how widely the State coins will circulate, and for how long. (The Mint has struck millions of each quarter dollar, and for some issues, more than 1 billion pieces. Mintage figures are found in Chapter 6.)

Consider, for example, the 1776-1976 Bicentennial quarter dollars, half dollars and dollars—the only other circulating commemorative coins produced by the U.S. government in recent decades. The Mint struck and circulated more than 1.67 billion 1976 Washington quarter dollars, each—like the State coins—bearing a commemorative reverse design (a Colonial drummer and Liberty torch). Despite the large quantity produced, few are seen in circulation today, probably because individuals pull the coins from circulation when they encounter them, just because their designs are a little different. Even today, nearly three decades after the coins entered circulation (in 1975), circulated specimens are worth face value only. Still, they're fun to collect.

Collectors have provided some insight into the circulation patterns of the State quarters. *Coin World* has been tracking distribution since the program began, through its First Reports and Circulation Reports page at its State quarter dollars Web site (**www.statequarters.com**). *Coin World* tracks when a newly issued State quarter is reported for each of the 50 states. So far, each coin has shown up in each state within a few months of release. However, that does not mean the State quarters are circulating everywhere.

For example, Philadelphia Mint and Denver Mint strikes are not distributed evenly throughout the country. Denver Mint coins tend to circulate more in the West, with Philadelphia Mint coins found in larger quantities in the East. There is some broader distribution, but for the most part, collectors tend to find coins from one Mint more often than those of the other Mint. Informal tracking by *Coin World* readers who record what they find over short periods tends to confirm the regional distribution by Mint mark through the Federal Reserve Banks.

Some collectors tell *Coin World* that they have difficulty finding any State quarters locally. That might be because the banks and other commercial businesses in their locale have little need to order new coins from the Federal Reserve and thus are not getting quantities of the State quarters. The few pieces that show up probably do so through normal commercial channels as they are spent in circulation. While it has been fun for those finding the coins, those who cannot find the coins in circulation are forced to pay retailers premiums, which they find frustrating.

To help collectors, *Coin World* established a trading forum that can be reached through its Web site (**www.coinworld.com/forum.asp**). Once registered, a collector is permitted to offer to trade State quarter dollars in his possession for State quarters he needs.

How to collect

Why are most collectors happy about the State quarter dollar program? It gives them something to collect from circulation that's different from all of the other coins. And that's fun.

In fact, the ranks of coin collectors have grown immensely since the introduction of the State quarters. United States Mint officials report as many as 139 million adult Americans are saving the State quarter dollars from circulation. *Coin World* staff members encounter many people collecting the quarters who never collected coins before. Many of these new collectors are constantly asking, "When's the next quarter due?"

So how should collectors collect the new State quarter dollars?

A basic approach would be to collect one coin for each state, regardless of issuing Mint, for 50 coins, from Delaware (the first state) to Hawaii (the 50th state). Collectors can pull the coins from circulation, which is the most fun. Most of these coins will exhibit circulation wear and damage, unless collectors acquire fresh rolls of coins directly from their local banks.

A second approach would double the number of coins to 100

pieces, by seeking examples of each coin struck at the Denver and Philadelphia Mints. This approach will be even more fun for collectors, although collectors again are finding most coins in their area are predominately from one Mint or the other. Since most collectors collect by date and Mint mark, this approach will probably be the most common.

A third approach is to buy the coins directly from the Mint. The Mint offers the copper-nickel clad circulating coins and special silver versions in a variety of packaging. Benefits to this approach include getting all of the coins being produced in a higher level of condition than likely to be encountered in circulation. The drawbacks will be cost (collectors will pay much more than face value for the coins) and a lower "fun" threshold (collectors who buy directly from the Mint will miss the thrill of the hunt from circulation).

Another approach would be to add a single example to one's collection of quarter dollars by type. A type collection would include one of each major design within a specific denomination or century. For example, a 20th century type set of quarter dollars would include a Barber quarter dollar, a Standing Liberty coin, silver composition Washington quarter dollars from 1932 to 1964 and 1992 to 1998 (the latter were struck not for circulation but for the Silver Proof sets), a copper-nickel clad specimen from 1965 to date, a Bicentennial reverse specimen, and one or more specimens of the new State coins (a true type coin collection would require one coin from each state, since each has its own reverse design and thus is a separate type).

The following list records the year when each quarter dollar of the 50 states has been or will have been issued into circulation. Following each state is the date it ratified the Constitution (for the first 13 states) or entered the Union.

2005

California	Sept. 9, 1850
Minnesota	May 11, 1858
Oregon	Feb. 14, 1859
Kansas	Jan. 29, 1861
West Virginia	June 20, 1863

2006

Nevada	Oct. 31, 1864
Nebraska	March 1, 1867
Colorado	Aug. 1, 1876
South Dakota	Nov. 2, 1889
North Dakota	Nov. 2, 1889

2007

Montana	Nov. 8, 1889
Washington	Nov. 11, 1889
Idaho	July 3, 1890
Wyoming	July 10, 1890
Utah	Jan. 4, 1896

2008

Oklahoma	Nov. 16, 1907
New Mexico	Jan. 6, 1912
Arizona	Feb. 14, 1912
Alaska	Jan. 3, 1959
Hawaii	Aug. 21, 1959

Coin market analysis 4

The period from August 2003 to July 2004 was marked by a continuing brisk coin market. Demand remained high in all collecting sectors, continuing to grow throughout the market and pushing up values across the board during 2004. In fact, it's been difficult to identify areas of the coin market that have not been hotly sought after, in all grades.

Expanding demand primarily came from new collectors entering the coin market, existing collectors expanding their collections, big collector-investor money purchasing major rarities, and dealers expanding their inventories through profits and increased business capitalization from many sources.

During the early summer of 2004, no signs of a slowdown in the coin market were visible. The past couple of years have, without a doubt, seen the greatest bull market the hobby has ever experienced, and it's been rooted in the best market fundamental possible—a sincere collecting interest. The previous bull markets of 1979 to 1980 and again during 1989 were primarily driven by fickle investment money, interested mainly in short-term profits, not long-term holding.

But these days genuine hobby interest is at an all time high. Growing numbers of people are buying a variety of specialty books about specific collecting areas in the coin market, according to major numismatic supply houses. Internet traffic has been rising for coin dealers, and other private traders, as well as auction businesses, because of the ease of doing transactions over the Internet, and for use in ferreting out information.

In general, as we moved into the summer of 2004, the coin market remained very bullish in virtually all segments. Higher coin values enticed major collections into the sales arena, where the market continued to soak them up like a dry sponge. And the big money was "trickling down" into buying up quantities of lesser priced coins.

Auctions

Prior to 2004 there was a critical shortage of fresh coins entering the market. Dealer inventories were depleted and their customers had ready cash to spend on coin purchases, but the coins they wanted were either very difficult to find or perceived as being overpriced. It took courage for both dealers and collectors to step up and pay those higher prices for coins, often exceeding published values.

Escalating coin values moved so fast during 2004 that it was difficult for value guides to keep up with these rising values. Market analysts "report" the market trend, we don't "set" the trend. Therefore, a short reporting lag often develops in a quickly rising market, and conversely could also happen if the market goes the other way. But again, no signs of a reversal are on the horizon; quite the contrary—positive fundamentals primarily are dominating today's coin market.

Sellers have recognized these positive signs and, of course, are aware of the elevated coin values. So they seem to have surfaced with collections to sell. Several large collections traded hands privately and quietly during 2004, but we've also seen some very impressive holdings consigned to auctions and selling, as well.

Typical auctions seemed to be bringing in less than $5 million each in total just a few years ago. But in 2004 we saw these totals often reach the $5 million to $10 million range, and sometimes higher. This can be attributed partly to higher coin values, but also to more coins coming onto the market.

It's become a concern by many whether the coin market can absorb all these coins. Experience has shown that cumulative auction sales of $50 million to $100 million within a week to 10 days can fairly easily be absorbed into the current market climate. However, runs of these amounts of sales by groups of major auction houses, scheduling the same sales venue, and coordinating auction sessions so they don't compete, is becoming more common, often preceding major shows.

Too many of these back-to-back sales in a short time span often result in opportunities for buyers. Dealers routinely make auction purchases on credit, and when their auction bills come due they are sometimes in a generous selling mood. Collectors can often drive hard bargains when this situation is encountered.

Precious metals

After experiencing a rather steady price climb during 2003, the three precious metals most popular in the coin market, gold, silver and platinum, took more of a bumpy ride during 2004. Prices were soft during the winter of 2003 to 2004; however, all three metals rallied in price during spring 2004. Gold peaked at more than $427 per ounce on April 1, 2004; silver at $8.29 on April 2; and platinum reached the lofty level of $936 on April 19. All three metals softened quickly after this point, but by mid- to late May 2004 began recovering, and thereafter began an irregular upward trend.

Of course, these precious metal price changes directly affect values for bullion coins, such as the American Eagle series of coins. Bulk circulated silver coins are also directly affected because they are traded by their silver content, which is often translated into a value per dollar of face value, like three or four times face value. Because 90 percent silver coins, dated 1964 or earlier, are traded in bulk, grading seems to make no difference as to this price factor. Of course, if a $1,000 face value bag of nearly slick Walking Liberty half dollars would be offered for sale to a bullion dealer, I'm sure the price would be discounted because worn coins weigh less than lightly circulated pieces (and thus contain less silver).

The values of many Coronet and Indian Head gold coins of various denominations and Saint-Gaudens $20 double eagles rise and fall with changing precious metal prices as well. Although these coins are traded by their grades or grade ranges, such as Extremely Fine to About Uncirculated (EF to AU), the values of these coins are so close to their bullion content values that significant enough changes in precious metal prices impact trading in these coins. This is probably an indication that the premiums over the bullion value for these coins are low and destined to rise, if demand rises sharply.

A great number of American Eagle bullion coins have been graded and encapsulated ("slabbed," in collector slang) by third-party grading services. High grades of Mint State 69 and 70 and Proof 69 and 70, with "70" being perfect, are becoming quite common. Caution is recommended when thinking of purchasing these coins for profit. Instead, these coins graded so highly may better be considered novelty items, or inexpensive examples of high-grade types and dates of these coins. It may be financially risky to load up on bulk purchases of such coins.

Registry collections

However, ultra high-grade regular issue coins, in both Mint State and Proof strikings, have been extremely popular as "registry collections," established by two leading coin grading services, Numismatic Guaranty Corporation of America (NGC) and Professional Coin Grading Service (PCGS). In these systems, collectors can "register" their collections, anonymously if desired, and in doing so enter into a competitive "sport" in an attempt to collect the highest graded sets.

For many collectors this has become a fun and profitable, but often challenging, way to collect. The competitions have also had an effect on the market.

Registry competitions have driven coin values, especially for the highest-graded modern coins (those minted after 1933) to new levels—higher than reasonable logic permits for some market analysts to feel comfortable.

And not all grading standards between grading services are the same. Therefore, values for "registry" coins have varied enormously for coins graded identically between different grading services. In general, "registry" style coins graded by PCGS have been bringing the most money, often by multiples of the prices where coins graded by other services are selling. This could be a factor of the perception of this company's grading standards, but more than likely, it has to do with PCGS allowing only PCGS-graded coins into its registry program. NGC, on the other hand, allows both PCGS- and NGC-graded coins into its official registry collections.

Several of the top registry sets have already been sold into the market. Many of them have been consigned to major auctions and are promoted as top registry sets. It seems that either these collectors reached the pinnacle of their collecting endeavors for these sets, becoming bored, or wanted to "dump" them while prices were still high, or of course sell for other personal reasons.

For many collectors the thrill of owning or having something diminishes as time advances beyond its acquisition. And often the thrill of collecting is in the chase, rather than in the having. After completing a set, many people still have that "itch" or collecting bug in their blood and need to begin again in another area. So some sellers are parting with their collections simply to begin again on another series. Others wait until their collections are complete before registering their sets.

Market overview

Advancing through the various series and denominations of U.S. coins, the following provides a 2004 coin market overview beginning with early copper coins: half cents and large cents, which were minted between 1793 and 1857. Early copper is a very serious collecting area, attracting a range of collectors, from advanced specialists who collect prized minor varieties to novices who collect the basic design type coins of the various issues.

The early copper collecting area is heavily influenced by the Early American Coppers (EAC) club, an established group of fun-spirited but astute students of this area of the hobby. This influence makes its presence known in grading early copper coins, which translates to values that differ between coins graded the same by EAC standards and "commercial" grading standards used by today's grading services. There's nothing wrong with these two-tier grading systems, in which EAC standards are admittedly much more strict than the commercial standards, it's just the way it is. However, in valuing early copper coins, it's important to know about this difference. *Coin World* values lean toward reflecting the commercial grading standards, although we respect the "EAC system."

Values for early copper coins have remained strong and steady to advancing during 2004. Collectors of type coins of other series, but including early copper coins, have helped push values much higher for common design types, especially the very early copper pieces. Two important auctions of early copper coins will be held at the end of 2004 and the beginning of 2005, so in following the current trend of the general coin market, these sales can be expected to draw out the specialist collectors, boosting competition, and hence, values.

Generally, coins from all series and denominations have experienced strong demand during 2004. Type coin collectors have had an impact on higher values for every series, especially short series like 2- and 20-cent coins. Low-grade coins have been in demand, meaning About Good coins with incomplete rims, as well as the crème de la crème of quality rarities.

All four 5-cent coin series, usually referred to as "nickels," attracted interest in 2004 with the introduction into circulation of two new coins with commemorative reverses, honoring the Louisiana Purchase and explorers Meriwether Lewis and William Clark. The Indian Head 5-cent series is the most difficult to collect, but the Shield series, which began in 1866, and the Liberty Head series, which took its place in 1883 and ran through 1912, are shorter and much easier to collect. The current series, Jefferson 5-cent coins, is by far the longest series to collect. Many Jefferson 5-cent coins are weakly struck with the steps leading up to the Monticello building on the reverse merging into one another without distinct separations.

Among silver series, all Seated Liberty denominations sustained a strong boost in values in the fall of 2003 in all grades. This surge in values continued throughout 2004 and was even given another boost in early summer with the sale of a major, virtually complete, collection of high-grade circulated and Mint State Seated Liberty coins of all denominations. Rarities, often taking years to locate, showed their true desirability through the values they attracted.

Earlier U.S. coins have exhibited their importance through higher values and disappearance from the market. A supply of these coins is very much lacking to satisfy the pent up demand for early coins. The only area where sellers feel price resistance is in the Draped Bust silver dollar series. Several specialists have made similar comments about this early series.

On the other hand, Morgan silver dollars are hot in all areas, such as ultra-high grades, circulated grades, key dates, prooflikes and deep-mirror prooflikes (DMPLs), attractively toned dollars, certified Carson City Mint coins in Government Services Administration holders and more. The market for Peace dollars is strong also, but more stable, rather than with quickly escalating values as found for the Morgan dollars, except for the keys in the Peace series.

In all series, key coins have been experiencing unprecedented demand. Many collectors are buying up multiple examples, because they know these coins have kept rising in value over the long-term. Dealers are having trouble keeping key coins in stock and are driving wholesale bid prices higher and higher.

Rare gold is an area that's expensive to collect, but has nevertheless been one of the hottest series during 2004. Rare dates in all U.S. gold series have been sought after in high and low grades, but without a doubt "registry" style collecting of rare gold has been going on for years, especially in the Coronet $20 double eagle series. Collectors want the finest graded coins, and the lower the graded population for each, the better. Well-healed rare gold collectors have been vying for finest knowns for many years before registry sets began, and many of these gold sets are being quietly held, out of the limelight.

On the other hand, numerous budget-minded collectors have been forced to reduce their expectations because of rising values. Collectors are asking for valuations for early About Good coins, where current listings typically begin with Good. Others are dropping their requirements for value-adding characteristics, like full bands on Winged Liberty Head dimes, full heads on Standing Liberty quarter dollars and full bell lines on Franklin half dollars.

Market trend

The coin market was in a very bullish state through the summer of

2004 with continually rising values in most collecting areas. This was a definite departure from the usual trend in which there's a market lull during spring tax time, and then another lull during the summer. The market instead has charged ahead at full speed all year long. In fact, some dealers reported that July was their best month for numismatic business, ever!

Traditionally the late summer American Numismatic Association convention and show kicks off a new season of trading, establishing the market trend for the rest of the year. However, the 2004 ANA show, held in Pittsburgh, was a continuation of the same hot market trend experienced all year long.

At that point in the 2004 market, dealers had become fatigued from all the hard work and the busy travel schedules they'd maintained by attending major shows and auctions from coast to coast every few weeks, with little rest. And without skipping a beat, the major Long Beach, Calif., show followed right on the heels of the ANA convention, being held just a couple of weeks later. Usually there's at least a month or so between these two major shows.

While business was brisk at the ANA show, a few major rarities were put on display, attracting awe-inspired attention. Two of the five 1913 Liberty 5-cent coins struck were displayed together. However, they didn't attract the long lines of viewers seen the previous year at the Baltimore convention at which the long lost fifth example was found and displayed with the other four pieces.

Instead, two other major rarities stole the limelight, one a double eagle, the other a silver dollar.

Upon entering the show attendees were greeted by a very attractive display of the better of the two known Philadelphia minted 1861 Coronet, Paquet Reverse gold $20 double eagles. This one was graded Mint State 67, the other having seen light circulation. The owner said the coin was not for sale, but valued it at $10 million, which, if it ever sold at that price, would eclipse the $7.59 million brought at auction by the only 1933 Saint-Gaudens double eagle the federal government allows to be privately owned.

In July 1989, the Dexter example of the 15 known 1804 Draped Bust dollars was the market's first coin to sell near the $1 million dollar level at $990,000. As we near the end of 2004, several coins have now exceeded the million-dollar mark.

The other showstopper displayed was the finest known 1794

Flowing Hair silver dollar, thought by many to be the first silver dollar ever struck by the U.S. Mint. It's called a Specimen example, believed to have been struck for presentation. Just 125 to 150 or so 1794 Flowing Hair dollars are known to still exist, and most have weakly struck areas on them. But this coin is very sharp in almost all its details and possesses beautiful prooflike surfaces. Again, it's valued at a similar multi-million dollar level as the gold coins mentioned above.

These coins are leading the trend of the coin market. Money spent on high-end rarities like these flows throughout the coin market, supporting values of lower priced coins. Private sales of such coins often remain out of the limelight, but public auction transactions have shown us the general direction of coin values. The three 2004 pre-ANA auctions brought in more than $18 million, while the official ANA auction realized in excess of $20 million.

In short, the 2004 coin market was awash with cash and short of supply. There was no sign of a reversal as the summer market closed, and generally, coin values were still rising throughout the market.

Values of U.S. coins

5

Rare coin prices rise and fall based upon the interest of collectors, investors and dealers, the overall economy, changes in precious metals prices and a host of other factors.

We make no predictions in these pages about what the future may bring for rare coins. We provide the reader with information. The *Coin Values* listings that follow give a guide as to retail value. However, users of this book should note that the price information included here was compiled in July 2004, and while many of the values given will not change substantially, some may. Users seeking the latest pricing information should consult the information published in *Coin World's Coin Values,* a glossy magazine published as a supplement to the first issue of *Coin World* every month and in an expanded newsstand edition, or the weekly updates at Coin World Online (**www.CoinValuesOnline .com**), which is available free to subscribers.

We will note that historically, the rare coin market appears to move in cycles. Q. David Bowers, a longtime and well-respected dealer, was one of the first in the hobby to write about price cycles. The overall market moves in cycles, with peaks in 1973 to 1974, 1979 to 1980 and 1989, and slumps in 1975 and 1976 and 1981 to late 1987 (the market as this edition was edited had been rising for a year or more). Bowers writes about this in much more detail in the seventh edition of the *Coin World Almanac,* now available. (See Chapter 4 for *Coin Values* analyst Mark Ferguson's examination of the market, characterized as very strong, from August 2003 to August 2004.)

Individual series also experience cyclical movements, with gold coins popular in some years, Proof sets and rolls in other years, and high-grade "modern" U.S. coins at other times.

How coins become rare

The first factor that makes a coin rare is its mintage. The term mintage is the number of specimens struck for any given date at a specific Mint. However, mintage figures are often deceptive. For example, the United States Mint struck 312,500 1933 Indian Head gold $10 eagles. However, price records indicate that the coin is much rarer than the mintage would indicate; perhaps as few as 30 to 40 pieces exist.

What happened? The coins were struck shortly before President Franklin D. Roosevelt signed an executive order forbidding Americans to own certain gold coins. The only gold coins not banned from private ownership were those with numismatic value held by collectors and dealers. Only a few of the 1933 Indian Head eagles struck were released into circulation; the rest were melted before they ever left the Mint.

Another case of how mintage figures can be misleading is raised by the two 1883 Liberty Head 5-cent subtypes. Two distinct subtypes were struck that year. The first bears the denomination on the reverse in the form of the Roman numeral V; the word CENTS does not appear. After larcenous individuals began gold-plating the Liberty Head, No CENTS 5-cent coin and passing it off as the similarly sized $5 gold half eagle, a new subtype was struck. The second subtype bears the word CENTS in addition to the Roman numeral V.

Approximately three times as many of the second, With CENTS variety were struck (mintage: 16 million) as the first, No CENTS variety (mintage: 5.5 million). However, prices for the more "common" variety are much higher than for the lower mintage piece. Why is that so? a new collector might ask.

The sudden replacement of the 1883 Liberty, No CENTS 5-cent variety led to the quick withdrawal of the coin by the public, certain they had a rarity. The much more common subtype entered circulation and stayed there, with many more pieces eventually consigned to the melting pot as they became too worn and were withdrawn by banks. Thus, collectors saved many more specimens of the first version than the second version.

Most coins end up in the melting pot. As coins circulate, they become worn, scratched and damaged. Eventually, they are returned to the Mint for melting. Gold and silver coins have been melted in large quantities by the government and by private individuals. When gold surpassed $800 an ounce and silver reached $50 an ounce in January 1980, millions of common-date gold and silver coins were melted for their precious metal content. A worn 1964 quarter dollar, for example, worth a dollar or less to a collector in 1978 had a bullion value of $9.04 when silver hit $50 an ounce! Recent coins considered common are probably much scarcer than thought because of the widespread melting.

Many coins are otherwise removed from circulation, through loss or deliberate destruction or disposal. Think of all the coins you have seen on the ground in parking lots or on the street. Some people throw low-denomination coins like cents away as worthless. Damaged coins may be tossed into the garbage without being redeemed.

Researchers study survival rates by degree of preservation. One author traced the appearances of all U.S. gold coins sold at auction by grade. At least three grading services publish population reports of the coins they grade, another indicator of the survival rate for a particular coin in a particular condition. These population reports can be misleading, however, in that a single coin may be submitted to a grading service (or services) many times by an owner hoping to get a higher grade for the piece at some point. A coin submitted a half dozen times may be listed in the firm's population report a half dozen times, thus artificially inflating the number of coins with that grade.

Unexpected supplies of coins turning up on the market can also have an impact on the rare coin market. A 1903-O Morgan silver dollar in Uncirculated was listed in a popular price guide published in 1962 as being valued at $1,500, and a 1904-O Morgan dollar, also in Uncirculated condition, was priced at $350. A year later, in the next edition of the same price guide, the 1903-O Morgan dollar was priced at $30 in the same grade, a loss of more than $1,400, and the 1904-O dollar was worth just $3.50, 1 percent of its value a year earlier!

What happened? The Treasury Department emptied some of its vaults as citizens turned in ever-increasing numbers of silver certificates in exchange for silver dollars. Numerous bags of the 1903-O and 1904-O Morgan dollars, in storage for nearly 60 years, were suddenly dumped onto the market at face value. Prices plummeted.

It is unlikely that such extreme examples will occur again. The Treasury Department sold the last of its silver dollar holdings beginning in 1972 in a series of seven sales, through the General Services Administration. However, some private hoards of certain coins still exist.

Demand and dealer promotion can also affect the price of a coin. For example, certain types of error coins are promoted as part of the regular series although in actuality, they are not. For example, the 1955 Lincoln, Doubled Die Obverse cent is heavily promoted, as is the 1972 Lincoln, Doubled Die Obverse cent. Activity is high for both coins, collector albums often have a space reserved for them, and dealers heavily promote them. However, other doubled die cents, much rarer than the 1955 and 1972 coins, are promoted only by a few dealers specializing in error and die variety coins. Their prices are often much lower than the heavily promoted pieces because their existence is known only to a few specialists and the supply is greater than the demand.

About the Coin Values

The values in this price guide were compiled by Mark Ferguson for *Coin World*. Many different sources are used in determining the values, including dealer price lists (both buy and sell), prices quoted on several dealer trading networks, Internet transactions, public auction prices, realistic (and confirmed) private transactions and any additional information acquired by the staff. In addition, demand and rarity are key considerations in compiling *Coin Values*. Values are for properly graded, problem-free, original coins with attractive color. Values given here are generally for sight-seen coins (coins that dealers demand to see before bidding on them), as opposed to sight-unseen coins (which dealers offer to buy without looking at them first, although at considerably lower bids than sight-seen coins). A sight-seen coin is generally acknowledged to be of higher value than a sight-unseen coin, even if the two coins bear the same grade.

The values section in this year's edition continues the expansion introduced in the 2004 edition, with many new grades and values added to some sections. Many of the additions will be found among the "modern" coins—roughly those coins struck since 1934, including all of the series currently still in production. The interest in ultra high-grade examples of these coins has resulted in some incredible prices being paid for "common" coins in "uncommon" high grades. Much of this increased interest is being driven by collectors building "registry sets." Professional Coin Grading Service and Numismatic Guaranty Corporation of America, two major grading services, maintain databases at their Web sites where collectors can register the coins in their collections. Points are awarded for every coin, with higher-grade coins awarded more points. The competition to own the highest-graded set of a particular series of coins has helped drive prices for even common coins to incredible levels. While many collectors are paying high prices for high-grade but otherwise common coins, other, more traditional collectors believe the market for such coins will eventually collapse and the values of these coins will drop. Time will tell who is right.

Coin World neither buys nor sells coins. This values section is published as a reader service and may or may not be the same as an individual's or a firm's buy or sell prices.

Unless otherwise noted, condition (grade) designations are for the lowest possible level of each grade range.

Users should also be aware that coins that have been graded by some third-party grading services may not meet market standards for that grade, and thus would bring lower prices than coins graded by another grading service. The values that follow are for coins accurately graded to market grading standards. Coins assigned the "same" grade but by a lower-tier "grading standard" may be worth less money, either because they grade below market standards or because the upper tier services have more "name recognition" among buyers.

Buyers are advised to consult with experienced and knowledgeable collectors and dealers for advice on a coin's grade and whether a particular grading service is judged to meet market standards.

See **Chapter 7** for additional information concerning grading.

Reading a values listing

It is not possible to configure each line of values to the market peculiarities of each date and variety of every series of U.S. coin. Therefore, gaps may appear in the listing.

A dash listed among the values usually indicates a coin for which accurate market information is not available due to rarity or lack of activity in the marketplace. An asterisk indicates no coins issued.

Also, the letter C following a numerical grade for a Proof coin stands for "cameo," while the letters DC stand for "deep cameo." Cameo coins have contrasting surface finishes: mirror fields and frosted devices (raised areas). Deep cameo coins are the ultimate level of cameo, with deeply frosted devices. Cameo and deep cameo coins bring premiums.

Liberty Cap, Left half cent

Date of authorization: April 2, 1792
Dates of issue: 1793
Designer/Engraver: Adam Eckfeldt
Diameter: 23.50 mm/0.93 inch
Weight: 6.74 grams/0.22 ounce
Metallic content: 100% copper
Edge: Lettered (TWO HUNDRED FOR A DOLLAR)
Mint mark: None

	G-4	VG-8	F-12	VF-20	VF-30	EF-40	EF-45
1793	2000.	3000.	4500.	6000.	8000.	18500.	20000.

Liberty Cap, Right half cent

Date of authorization:	April 2, 1792
Dates of issue:	1794-1797
Designers:	(Large Head): Robert Scot (Small Head): Scot-John Gardner
Engraver:	Robert Scot
Diameter:	23.50 mm/0.93 inch
Weight:	1794-1795: 6.74 grams/0.22 ounce 1795-1797: 5.44 grams/0.18 ounce
Metallic content:	100% copper
Edge:	1794-1795: Lettered (TWO HUNDRED FOR A DOLLAR) 1795 (Type of 1796): Plain 1796: Plain 1797: Most Plain, Some Lettered, Some Gripped
Mint mark:	None

	AG-3	G-4	VG-8	F-12	VF-20	VF-30	EF-40	EF-45
1794	300.	400.	650.	1000.	1500.	2500.	3500.	4500.
1795 Lettered Edge, Pole	150.	300.	550.	900.	1700.	2250.	3250.	4000.
1795 Plain Edge, Pole, Punctuated Date	175.	350.	650.	950.	1500.	2500.	3750.	5000.
1795 Plain Edge, No Pole	150.	350.	500.	700.	1100.	2100.	2750.	3750.
1795 Lettered Edge, Pole, Punctuated Date	175.	350.	675.	1000.	2000.	3000.	4500.	5500.
1796 With Pole	5500.	9000.	13500.	16500.	20500.	24500.	30000.	37500.
1796 No Pole	8500.	19000.	27500.	38500.	65000.	-		-
1797 Plain Edge	200.	350.	500.	1000.	1800.	2500.	4500.	5500.
1797 Pl. Edge,1 above 1	175.	325.	450.	800.	1500.	2000.	3000.	3500.
1797 Lettered Edge	600.	1500.	2750.	5000.	—	—	—	—
1797 Gripped Edge	—	—	—	—	—	—	—	—

—— = Insufficient pricing data

Draped Bust half cent

Date of authorization: April 2, 1792
Dates of issue: 1800-1808
Designers: Obverse: Gilbert Stuart-Robert Scot
Reverse: Scot-John Gardner
Engraver: Robert Scot
Diameter: 23.50 mm/0.93 inch
Weight: 5.44 grams/0.18 ounce
Metallic content: 100% copper
Edge: Plain
Mint mark: None

	G-4	VG-8	F-12	VF-20	VF-30	EF-40	AU-50	MS-60B
1800	50.	75.	150.	250.	400.	600.	800.	1500.
1802/0 1802 Reverse	700.	1400.	2500.	8000.	—	—	—	—
1802/0 1800 Reverse	13500.	25000.	35000.	—	—	—	—	—
1803	50.	75.	150.	250.	400.	700.	1500.	3000.
1804 Plain 4, Stemless	50.	60.	80.	150.	300.	500.	700.	1200.
1804 Plain 4, Stems	60.	100.	200.	300.	800.	1250.	—	—
1804 Crosslet 4, Stemless	50.	60.	80.	150.	300.	450.	650.	1300.
1804 Crosslet 4, Stems	50.	60.	80.	150.	250.	400.	600.	1500.
1804 Spiked Chin	50.	60.	80.	200.	250.	450.	700.	2000.
1805 Med. 5, Stemless	50.	60.	80.	125.	175.	350.	600.	1250.
1805 Large 5, Stems	50.	60.	80.	150.	300.	400.	700.	—
1805 Small 5, Stems	750.	1500.	3500.	—	—	—	—	—
1806 Small 6, Stemless	50.	60.	80.	125.	175.	250.	400.	1000.
1806 Large 6, Stems	50.	60.	80.	125.	150.	250.	450.	1000.
1806 Small 6, Stems	200.	400.	700.	1250.	1500.	2650.	—	—
1807	50.	60.	80.	150.	250.	450.	800.	2100.
1808	50.	60.	90.	175.	400.	500.	1200.	2400.
1808/7	200.	350.	600.	1000.	2250.	3750.	9500.	—

—— = Insufficient pricing data

Classic Head half cent

Date of authorization: April 2, 1792
Dates of issue: 1809-1835
Designer/Engraver: John Reich
Diameter: 23.50 mm/0.93 inch
Weight: 5.44 grams/0.18 ounce
Metallic content: 100% copper
Edge: Plain
Mint mark: None

	G-4	VG-8	F-12	VF-20	VF-30	EF-40	AU-50	MS-60B
1809	35.	40.	55.	75.	100.	200.	350.	850.
1809 Circle in 0	35.	50.	75.	100.	200.	400.	700.	—
1809/6	35.	50.	75.	100.	125.	200.	500.	1100.
1810	40.	50.	100.	250.	400.	700.	1000.	2100.
1811	125.	350.	600.	1100.	2100.	4500.	7500.	—
1825	35.	40.	55.	80.	100.	140.	350.	750.
1826	35.	40.	55.	70.	75.	125.	225.	450.
1828 13 Stars	35.	40.	55.	70.	75.	125.	175.	300.
1828 12 Stars	35.	40.	55.	85.	110.	225.	400.	1050.
1829	35.	40.	55.	70.	75.	100.	160.	300.
1831 Originals and Restrikes: Original VF-25 $8600; VF-30 $10250; PF-65 Br $22500; Restrike PF-64 R&B $12500; PF red $24500.								
1832	35.	40.	55	70	75.	80.	200.	300.
1833	35.	40.	55.	70.	75.	80.	200	300.
1834	35.	40.	55.	70.	75.	80.	200.	300.
1835	35.	40.	55.	70.	75.	80	200.	300.
1836 Originals and Restrikes Original PF-15 $1500; PF-60 $3500; PF-63 $5500; PF-64 $12000; 2nd Restrike PF-64 $12500; PF-65 red $45000.								

—— - Insufficient pricing data

Coronet half cent

Date of authorization: April 2, 1792
Dates of issue: 1849-1857
Designers: Obverse: Robert Scot-Christian Gobrecht
Reverse: John Reich-Gobrecht
Engraver: Christian Gobrecht
Diameter: 23.50 mm/0.93 inch
Weight: 5.44 grams/0.18 ounce
Metallic content: 100% copper
Edge: Plain
Mint mark: None

Note: For copper-alloy coins, the letter B following a numerical grade (as in MS-63B) is shorthand for brown, RB represents red and brown, and R stands for red. It is common practice for grading services to qualify copper coins. In addition to a Mint State grade, a copper coin is assigned as brown, red and brown, or red. Generally, full red coins are valued higher than red and brown coins, which in turn are valued higher than brown coins, all else being equal.

	G-4	VG-8	F-12	VF-20	VF-30	EF-40	AU-50	MS-60B
1840-49 Originals and Restrikes VF-20 $1500; AU-50 $2750; PF-60 $3800; PF-63 $5500; PF-64 $8250; PF-65 red $15000.								
1849 Large Date	40.	45.	60.	75.	85.	125.	200.	325.
1850	40.	45.	60.	75.	85.	125.	225.	500.
1851	35.	45.	60.	75.	85.	100.	150.	300.
1852 Restrikes: 1st Restrike Small Berries PF-60 $2600; PF-62 $4000; PF-63 $4500; PF-64 Br $4750; PF-65 R&B $11500; Large Berries PF-63 Br $90000.								
1853	35.	45.	60.	75.	85.	100.	150.	300.
1854	35.	45.	60.	75.	85.	100.	150.	300.
1855	35.	45.	60.	75.	85.	100.	150.	300.
1856	35.	45.	60.	75.	85.	100.	150.	350.
1857	45.	50.	70.	85.	100.	125.	200.	400.

Flowing Hair, Chain cent

Date of authorization: April 2, 1792
Dates of issue: 1793
Designer/Engraver: Henry Voigt
Diameter: 28.50 mm/1.13 inches
Weight: 13.48 grams/0.43 ounce
Metallic content: 100% copper
Edge: Vine and bars, or lettered (ONE HUNDRED FOR A DOLLAR)
Mint mark: None

	AG-3	G-4	VG-8	F-12	VF-20	VF-30	EF-40	AU-50
1793 AMERICA	2000.	5000.	7500	10000.	16000.	20000.	25000.	45000.
1793 AMERICA, Periods	2000.	5500.	7500.	12000.	18000.	23000.	30000.	50000.
1793 AMERI.	2500.	6000.	8000.	14000.	20000.	25000.	35000.	60000.

Flowing Hair, Wreath cent

Date of authorization: April 2, 1792
Dates of issue: 1793
Designers: Obverse: Henry Voigt-Adam Eckfeldt
Reverse: Eckfeldt
Engraver: Adam Eckfeldt
Diameter: 28.50 mm/1.13 inches
Weight: 13.48 grams/0.43 ounce
Metallic content: 100% copper
Edge: Vine and bars, lettered (ONE HUNDRED FOR A DOLLAR)
Mint mark: None

	AG-3	G-4	VG-8	F-12	VF-20	VF-30	EF-40	AU-50
1793 Vine and Bars	1000.	2000.	2500.	4000.	6000.	7500.	10000.	16000.
1793 Lettered Edge	1400.	2000.	2500.	4000.	6000.	7500.	11000.	20000.
1793 Strawberry Leaf	100000.	175000.	275000.	—	—	—	—	—

—— = Insufficient pricing data

Liberty Cap cent

Date of authorization:	April 2, 1792
Dates of issue:	1793-1796
Designers:	(1793-1794): Joseph Wright (1794-1796): Wright-John Gardner
Engravers:	(1793-1794): Joseph Wright (1794-1796): Robert Scot
Diameter:	28.50 mm/1.13 inches
Weight:	1793-1795: 13.48 grams/0.43 ounce 1795-1796: 10.89 grams/0.35 ounce
Metallic content:	100% copper
Edge:	Plain, or lettered (ONE HUNDRED FOR A DOLLAR)
Mint mark:	None

	AG-3	G-4	VG-8	F-12	VF-20	VF-30	EF-40	AU-50
1793	1500.	2500.	6000.	8500.	20000.	25000.	40000.	80000.
1794 Head of 1793	700.	1400.	2500.	3500.	7500.	10000.	18000.	—
1794 Head of 1794	125.	400.	500.	700.	1400.	1800.	3000.	5000.
1794 Head of 1795	150.	500.	600.	800.	1500.	2000.	3500.	5500.
1794 Starred Reverse	5000.	10000.	20000.	35000.	60000.	75000.	110000.	—
1795 Plain Edge	100.	400.	500.	750.	1500.	2000.	3000.	5000.
1795 Lettered Edge	125.	500.	600.	800.	1800.	2500.	4500.	6500.
1795 Jefferson Head, Plain Edge	4000.	7500.	14000.	22000.	45000.	75000.	—	—
1796	125.	400.	500.	1000	2000	2500.	4000.	9000.

—— = Insufficient pricing data

Draped Bust cent

Date of authorization: April 2, 1792
Dates of issue: 1796-1807
Designers: Obverse: Gilbert Stuart-Robert Scot
Reverse: Joseph Wright-Scot
Engraver: Robert Scot
Diameter: 28.50 mm/1.13 inches
Weight: 10.89 grams/0.35 ounce
Metallic content: 100% copper
Edge: Plain, lettered (ONE HUNDRED FOR A DOLLAR), gripped
Mint mark: None

	AG-3	G-4	VG-8	F-12	VF-20	VF-30	EF-40	AU-50
1796 Reverse of 1794	100.	200.	600.	1200.	2000.	2400.	3500.	7250.
1796 Reverse of 1796	100.	150.	400.	1000.	2000.	2500.	3000.	5000.
1796 Reverse of 1797	100.	150.	300.	700.	1000.	1400.	2300.	4000.
1796 LIHERTY	200.	300.	800.	1200.	2500.	4000.	7500.	—
1797 Reverse of 1797, Stems	75.	150.	250.	400.	600.	900.	1400.	3000.
1797 Reverse of 1796, Gripped Edge	75.	150.	250.	400.	800.	1200.	2500.	4000.
1797 Reverse of 1796, Plain Edge	75.	150.	250.	450.	850.	1400.	3000.	4500.
1797 Reverse of 1797, Stemless	100.	200.	350.	600.	1300.	2300.	4000.	8500.
1798 1st Hair Style	50.	100.	200.	350.	800.	1100.	2100.	4000.
1798 2nd Hair Style	50.	100.	200.	350.	800.	1200.	2000.	3500.
1798 Reverse of 1796	60.	150.	300.	600.	1500.	3300.	6600.	9000.
1798/7 1st Hair Style	100.	200.	350.	600.	1500.	2500.	4000.	9500.
1799	1200.	2000.	3500.	8000.	18000.	25000.	60000.	—
1799/8	1200.	2100.	4500.	9500.	20000.	28000.	—	—
1800 Normal Date	50.	80.	150.	250.	600.	900.	1800.	4750.
1800/798 1st Hair Style	40.	80.	175.	550.	1250.	2650.	4000.	8000.
1800/79 2nd Hair Style	50.	100.	150.	350.	750.	1500.	2000.	6000.
1801	30.	75.	100.	200.	400.	700.	1000.	2500.
1801 3 Errors	75.	150.	400.	800.	1800.	4250.	6000.	12000.

—— = Insufficient pricing data

DRAPED BUST CENT (CONTINUED)

	AG-3	G-4	VG-8	F-12	VF-20	VF-30	EF-40	AU-50
1801 1/000	40.	80.	100.	250.	500.	900.	2000.	5000.
1801 100/000	40.	90.	175.	300.	600.	1000.	2000.	4000.
1802	40.	75.	100.	250.	300.	500.	1000.	2000.
1802 Stemless	40.	75.	150.	250.	350.	500.	1000.	2250.
1802 1/000	40.	80.	175.	300.	500.	800.	1600.	3000.
1803	40.	75.	100.	200.	350.	500.	1000.	2000.
1803 Large Date, Small Fraction	3000.	6000.	11000.	18000.	40000.	80000.	—	—
1803 Large Date, Large Fraction	50.	90.	225.	400.	1000.	2000.	3000.	5500.
1803 Stemless S-243	40.	75.	100.	225.	550.	650.	1200.	2300.
1803 100/000 S-249	40.	75.	125.	250.	650.	1000.	1500.	3000.
1804	400.	800.	1400.	2500.	3500.	5500.	8000.	19000.
1804 restrike (c. 1860)	—	—	—	450.	500.	600.	700.	1000.
1805 Pointed 1	40.	75.	100.	200.	400.	500.	1000.	2500.
1805 Blunt 1 S-267	40.	75.	100.	200.	400.	500.	1000.	2500.
1806	50.	80.	125.	250.	450.	650.	1500.	3500.
1807 Large Fraction	40.	75.	100.	200.	350.	450.	1000.	2000.
1807 Small Fraction	40.	75.	100.	250.	550.	1200.	2750.	—
1807 Small Fraction, Comet	40.	75.	100.	250.	750.	1400.	3000.	5500.
1807/6 Large 7	60.	100.	125.	200.	400.	500.	1000.	2250.
1807/6 Small 7	1600.	2750.	4500.	9000.	17500.	—	—	—

—— = Insufficient pricing data

Classic Head cent

Date of authorization: April 2, 1792
Dates of issue: 1808-1814
Designer/Engraver: John Reich
Diameter: 28.50 mm/1.13 inches
Weight: 10.89 grams/0.36 ounce
Metallic content: 100% copper
Edge: Plain
Mint mark: None

Note: For copper-alloy coins, the letter B following a numerical grade (as in MS-63B) is shorthand for brown, RB represents red and brown, and R stands for red. It is common practice for grading services to qualify copper coins. In addition to a Mint State grade, a copper coin is assigned as brown, red and brown, or red. Generally, full red coins are valued higher than red and brown coins, which in turn are valued higher than brown coins, all else being equal.

	AG-3	G-4	VG-8	F-12	VF-20	VF-30	EF-40	AU-50	AU-55	MS-62RB
1808	30.	60.	175.	325.	600.	1000.	2000.	3500.	4700.	11000.
1809	75.	150.	300.	500.	1100.	1750.	3000.	5000.	6000.	14000.
1810	30.	60.	125.	300.	650.	900.	1400.	2200.	2800.	7000.
1810 10/09	30.	60.	125.	300.	700.	1000.	1500.	3250.	4000.	9000.
1811	50.	100.	200.	400.	1000.	1400.	2500.	4000.	5000.	12000.
1811/0	50.	100.	225.	500.	1300.	2100.	4000.	10000.	12000.	—
1812	30.	60.	125.	300.	600.	800.	1100.	2500.	3000.	7000.
1813	40.	75.	150.	300.	600.	900.	1500.	3000.	4000.	7500.
1814 Plain 4	50.	80.	125.	300.	600.	800.	1200.	2500.	3000.	9000.
1814 Crosslet 4	40.	75.	125.	300.	600.	850.	1300.	2000.	2500.	6000.

—— = Insufficient pricing data

Coronet cent

Date of authorization: April 2, 1792
Dates of issue: 1816-1857
Designers: (1816-1835)
Obverse: Robert Scot
Reverse: John Reich
(1835-1839)
Obverse: Scot-Christian Gobrecht
Reverse: Reich
(1839-1857)
Obverse: Scot-Gobrecht
Reverse: Reich-Gobrecht
Engravers: (1816-1835) Obverse: Scot
Reverse: Reich
(1835-1839) Obverse: Gobrecht
Reverse: Reich
(1839-1857) Obverse: Gobrecht
Reverse: Gobrecht
Diameter: 28.50 mm/1.13 inches
Weight: 10.89 grams/0.35 ounce
Metallic content: 100% copper
Edge: Plain
Mint mark: None

	G-4	VG-8	F-12	VF-20	EF-40	AU-50	AU-55	MS-62RB	MS-63RB
1816	16.	25.	40.	100	225.	350.	400.	800.	1200.
1817 13 Stars	16.	22.	30.	70.	175.	250.	300.	600.	750.
1817 15 Stars	18.	27.	45.	150.	500.	1000.	1500.	—	—
1818	16.	22.	35.	100.	150.	225.	300.	500.	650.
1819	16.	22.	30.	75.	150.	225.	300.	550.	800.
1819/8	19.	30.	45.	100.	300.	500.	600.	1600.	2250.
1820	16.	23.	30.	80.	175.	250.	350.	600.	750.
1820/19	18.	25.	45.	120.	400.	800.	1250.	2000.	2500.
1820 Small Date, Curled 2	16.	23.	30.	80.	425.	700.	1100.	—	—
1820 Large Date, Curled 2	18.	27.	60.	110.	750.	1950.	—	—	—
1820 Large Date, Plain 2	16.	23.	30.	80.	200.	250.	350.	550.	650.

—— = Insufficient pricing data

	G-4	VG-8	F-12	VF-20	EF-40	AU-50	AU-55	MS-62RB	MS-63RB
1821	30.	60.	150.	550.	1400.	3000.	4000.	12000.	18000.
1822	16.	23.	50.	125.	300.	600.	800.	2000.	3500.
1823	80.	200.	400.	900.	3000.	7500.	10000.	—	—
1823/2	75.	150.	350.	800.	2500.	4500.	6500.	—	—
1823 restrike	—	—	—	—	500.	600.	750.	1200.	1500.
1824	16.	30.	60.	200.	500.	1250.	1750.	3000.	3750.
1824/2	18.	35.	80.	350.	1100.	2500.	3000.	12000.	25000.
1825	16.	25.	50.	150.	400.	850.	1400.	3000.	4500.
1826	16.	25.	50.	125.	300.	400.	600.	1800.	2800.
1826/5	30.	75.	200.	400.	900.	1600.	2100.	4500.	9000.
1827	16.	25.	50.	125.	275.	450.	550.	1100.	1500.
1828 Large Date	16.	25.	35.	100.	250.	350.	400.	900.	1300.
1828 Small Date	18.	30.	65.	135.	300.	600.	700.	1500.	2100.
1829 Large Letters	16.	25.	40.	125.	250.	600.	700.	1300.	1700.
1829 Small Letters	30.	75.	150.	500.	1250.	3000.	—	—	—
1830 Large Letters	16.	25.	35.	100.	200.	300.	400.	800.	1250.
1830 Small Letters	20.	40.	125.	400.	1000.	2500.	4000.	17500.	—
1831	16.	25.	35.	80.	175.	300.	400.	800.	1100.
1832	16.	25.	35.	80.	200.	300.	400.	750.	1000.
1833	16.	25.	35.	80.	150.	250.	300.	600.	800.
1834 Small 8, Large Stars, Medium Letters	16.	25.	35.	80.	225.	350.	450.	1100.	1400.
1834 Large 8, Small Stars, Medium Letters	16.	25.	35.	80.	225.	350.	450.	1100.	1400.
1834 Large 8, Large Stars, Medium Letters	125.	200.	350.	600.	2100.	4500.	—	—	—
1835	16.	25.	35.	80.	150.	250.	300.	500.	600.
1835 Small 8, Small Stars	16.	25.	35.	80.	250.	400.	500.	—	—
1835 Large 8, Large Stars	16.	25.	35.	80.	400.	700.	800.	—	—
1835 Type of 1836	16.	25.	35.	80.	150.	250.	350.	600.	800.
1836	16.	25.	35.	80.	150.	250.	350.	600.	800.
1837 Plain Cord, Large Letters	16.	25.	35.	80.	150.	250.	350.	600.	800.
1837 Plain Cord, Small Letters	16.	25.	35.	80.	150.	250.	350.	1200.	—
1837 Beaded Cord	16.	25.	35.	80.	150.	250.	350.	700.	—
1838	16.	25.	35.	80.	150.	250.	350.	700.	800.
1839 Head of 1838	16.	25.	35.	80.	150.	300.	400.	1100.	1500.
1839/6	300.	500.	1400.	2500.	6000.	13000.	—	—	—
1839 Silly Head	16.	25.	35.	80.	250.	400.	500.	1600.	3000.
1839 Booby Head	16.	25.	35.	80.	200.	500.	700.	1500.	2500.

—— = Insufficient pricing data

Modified Portrait

Mature Head

	G-4	VG-8	F-12	VF-20	EF-40	AU-50	AU-55	MS-62RB	MS-63RB
MODIFIED PORTRAIT									
1839 Type of 1840	15.	20.	25.	40.	90.	250.	300.	600.	800.
1840 Large Date	15.	20.	25.	40.	80.	200.	250.	500.	700.
1840 Small Date	15.	20.	25.	40.	80	200.	250.	500.	700.
1840 Small Date, Large 18	20.	25.	30.	75.	150.	300	350.	600.	800.
1841	15.	20.	30.	75.	125.	300.	350.	450.	600.
1842	15.	20.	25.	40.	80.	200.	250.	400.	500.
1843 Petite Head, Small Letters	15.	25.	30.	50.	100.	250.	300.	500.	800.
1843 Mature Head , Large Letters	15.	25.	30.	50.	125.	300.	350.	500.	600.
1843 Petite Head, Large Letters	20.	35.	50.	150.	350.	600.	800.	1400.	2000.
1844	15.	25.	25.	35.	100.	200.	300.	450.	500.
1844/81	20.	30.	50.	150.	400.	750.	900.	—	—
1845	15.	25.	30.	35.	80.	200.	250.	350.	400.
1846 Medium Date	15.	25.	30.	35.	80.	150.	200.	350.	800.
1846 Small Date	15.	25.	30.	40.	100.	250.	300.	600.	1000.
1846 Tall Date	15.	25.	30.	45.	125.	300.	350.	—	—
1847	15.	25.	30.	60.	80.	150.	200.	400.	600.
1847 7/Small 7	20.	30.	50.	80.	175.	300.	400.	—	—
1848	15.	25.	30.	40.	75.	150.	200.	350.	400.
1849	15.	25.	30.	40.	75.	150.	200.	350.	500.
1850	15.	25.	30.	40.	75.	150.	200.	300.	350.
1851	15.	25.	30.	40.	75.	150.	200.	300.	350
1851/81	18.	30.	40.	75.	150.	250.	350.	900.	1400.
1852	15.	25.	30.	35.	75.	150.	200.	300.	350.
1853	15.	25.	30.	35.	75.	150.	200.	300.	350.
1854	15.	25.	30.	35.	75.	150	200.	300.	350.
1855	15.	25.	30.	35.	75.	150.	200.	300.	350.
1855 Knob Ear	15.	25.	35.	60.	100.	250.	300.	750.	1200.
1856	15.	25.	30.	40	75.	150.	200.	300.	350.
1857	50.	100.	150.	200.	250.	300.	350.	600.	700.
1857 Large Date	40.	80.	100.	150.	200.	250.	300.	500.	600.

—— = Insufficient pricing data

Flying Eagle cent

Date of authorization: Feb. 21, 1857
Dates of issue: 1856-1858
Designers: Obverse: Christian Gobrecht-James B. Longacre
Reverse: Longacre
Engraver: James B. Longacre
Diameter: 19.30 mm/0.76 inches
Weight: 4.67 grams/0.15 ounce
Metallic content: 88% copper, 12% nickel
Edge: Plain
Mint mark: None

Note: Mint State 65 and Proof 65 copper values are for coins with full red original color; lower Mint State and Proof grades reflect specimens that are red and brown.

	G-4	VG-8	F-12	VF-20	EF-40	AU-50	MS-60	MS-63	MS-64	MS-65	MS-66
1856	6000.	7000.	7500.	8500.	9000.	11000.	12000.	20000.	30000.	55000.	175000.
1857	25.	30.	35.	50.	135.	200.	300.	1000.	1650.	4000.	7500.
1858 Large Letters	25.	30.	35.	50.	135.	200.	300.	1000.	1650.	4000.	6000.
1858 Small Letters	25.	30.	35.	50.	135.	200.	300.	1000.	1650.	4000.	10000.
1858/7 early die state	75.	100.	200.	400.	800.	1600.	3500.	10000.	25000.	50000.	—

—— = Insufficient pricing data

Indian Head cent

Shield Added

Date of authorization:	Feb. 21, 1857
Dates of issue:	1859-1909
Designer/Engraver:	James B. Longacre
Diameter:	1859-1864: 19.30 mm/0.76 inch
	1864-1909: 19.05 mm/0.75 inch
Weight:	1859-1864: 4.67 grams/0.15 ounce
	1864-1909: 3.11 grams/0.10 ounce
Metallic content:	1859-1864: 88% copper, 12% nickel
	1864-1909: 95% copper, 5% tin and zinc
Edge:	Plain
Mint mark:	1908-1909, reverse under wreath

Note: For copper-alloy coins, the letter B following a numerical grade (as in MS-63B) is shorthand for brown, RB represents red and brown, and R stands for red. It is common practice for grading services to qualify copper coins. In addition to a Mint State grade, a copper coin is assigned as brown, red and brown, or red. Generally, full red coins are valued higher than red and brown coins, which in turn are valued higher than brown coins, all else being equal.

INDIAN HEAD CENT (CONTINUED)

	G-4	VG-8	F-12	VF-20	EF-40	AU-50	MS-60	MS-63	MS-64	MS-65	MS-66	PF-63	PF-64	PF-65	PF-66
COPPER-NICKEL															
1859	14.	16.	20.	50.	125.	200.	250.	500.	1500.	3500.	6000.	1600.	3000.	5000.	7500.
SHIELD ADDED															
1860 Broad Bust T 2	9.00	12.	15.	20.	60.	100.	150.	225.	600.	1000.	5000.	1000.	2100.	4000.	8500.
1860 Narrow Bust	12.	15.	25.	50.	100.	150.	250.	500.	1500.	11000.	-	*	*	*	*
1861	20.	30.	40.	50.	110.	175.	200.	250.	350.	1500.	2500.	800.	4500.	8500.	32000.
1862	9.00	10.	12.	20.	35.	60.	100.	175.	350.	1100.	2500.	750.	1300.	2500.	4000.
1863	9.00	10.	12.	18.	30.	60.	100.	175.	350.	1100.	2500.	800.	1500.	3500.	8500.
1864	20.	25.	35.	50.	75.	100.	150.	225.	400.	1400.	11500.	800.	1500.	3500.	7500.

	G-4	VG-8	F-12	VF-20	EF-40	AU-50	MS-60B	MS-63RB	MS-64RB	MS-64R	MS-65RB	MS-65R	MS-66R	PF-63RB	PF-64RB	PF-65R
BRONZE																
1864 Initial L	55.	65.	125.	175.	250.	300.	350.	550.	750.	2200.	1500.	3750.	30000.	-	53000.	70000.
1864	7.00	13.	20.	35.	60.	75.	100.	200.	300.	450.	350.	1000.	3000.	1500.	3000.	14500.
1865	7.00	11.	18.	21.	37.	50.	85.	150.	225.	500.	850.	1600.	21000.	550.	1200.	7500.
1866	45.	50.	65.	100.	200.	225.	250.	500.	800.	3125.	1300.	9500.	-	500.	800.	5000.
1867/7	65.	80.	125.	175.	250.	350.	450.	750.	1350.	-	-	-	-	*	*	*
1867	45.	55.	75.	110.	200.	225.	250.	400.	700.	2500.	1300.	10000.	-	525.	800.	4750.
1868	40.	45.	65.	85.	175.	200.	250.	450.	800.	1750.	1000.	6000.	7500.	675.	875.	5800.
1869	60.	85.	225.	300.	375.	450.	500.	700.	1000.	2200.	1500.	5000.	20000.	385.	900.	2700.
1869/9	125.	175.	300.	400.	550.	600.	700.	800.	1200.	-	1800.	-	-	*	*	*
1870	50.	75.	225.	300.	375.	450.	475.	550.	750.	2000.	1500.	5000.	18500.	375.	875.	2500.
1871	60.	85.	300.	350.	400.	450.	500.	950.	1300.	5000.	3500.	12500.	-	375.	850.	2100.
1872	75.	125.	300.	350.	400.	500.	600.	850.	1500.	12500.	4000.	25000.	75000.	450.	1000.	4000.
1873 Closed 3	35.	50.	75.	100.	175.	250.	325.	650.	1200.	3750.	3250.	12000.	17000.	300.	465.	3000.
1873 Doubled LIBERTY Die 1 bold	150.	400.	850.	1500.	2500.	4000.	6500.	15000.	35000.	-	-	-	-	*	*	*

—— = Insufficient pricing data

INDIAN HEAD CENT (CONTINUED)

	G-4	VG-8	F-12	VF-20	EF-40	AU-50	MS-60B	MS-63RB	MS-64RB	MS-64R	MS-65RB	MS-65R	MS-66R	PF-63RB	PF-64RB	PF-65R
1873 Open 3	20.	30.	50.	75.	150.	200.	250.	350.	550.	2500.	1400.	10000.	-	-	-	-
1874	18.	20.	30.	50.	100.	150.	175.	250.	400.	2000.	750.	5000.	7500.	200.	310.	2300.
1875	18.	30.	50.	60.	100.	135.	175.	300.	500.	1600.	900.	3750.	-	300.	700.	4000.
1876	30.	40.	65.	125.	225.	275.	300.	400.	750.	1600.	1200.	4500.	10000.	260.	600.	2600.
1877	550.	750.	1300.	1700.	2000.	2500.	3000.	3700.	6000.	9000.	10000.	20000.	78000.	4000.	5000.	10000.
1878	30.	45.	75.	125.	225.	275.	300.	375.	650.	1200.	1000.	5000.	4000.	180.	500.	1200.
1879	8.00	12.	15.	30.	65.	75.	85.	125.	225.	400.	400.	1400.	2500.	200.	250.	1050.
1880	4.00	5.00	6.00	10.	25.	40.	60.	110.	200.	375.	400.	1000.	3250.	180.	240.	1600.
1881	4.00	5.00	6.00	8.00	18.	25.	40.	150.	200.	350.	425.	1000.	1750.	170.	230.	1000.
1882	4.00	5.00	6.50	10.	18.	25.	40.	90.	175.	350.	375.	1200.	2000.	170.	230.	1600.
1883	4.00	4.50	5.00	8.00	17.	25.	40.	75.	175.	400.	375.	1400.	2000.	170.	230.	725.
1884	4.00	5.00	7.00	12.	25.	35.	60.	125.	225.	500.	500.	2200.	-	170.	230.	1100.
1885	6.00	7.00	12.	25.	60.	75.	100.	200.	350.	750.	750.	2000.	-	160.	245.	1700.
1886 Feather between I and C	4.00	7.00	20.	50.	140.	175.	225.	275.	425.	1300.	1500.	3100.	7500.	265.	350.	2250.
1886 Feather between C and A	8.00	15.	30.	75.	175.	200.	300.	525.	1250.	6000.	2750.	15000.	50000.	-	-	-
1887	2.00	2.50	3.50	5.50	18.	25.	50.	150.	300.	400.	400.	1000.	6000.	200.	400.	6000.
1888/7	1200.	2000.	4500.	8000.	12000.	17500.	20000.	30000.	40000.	-	-	-	-	*	*	*
1888	2.00	2.50	4.50	5.50	18.	28.	42.	150.	350.	1000.	900.	3600.	8500.	225.	325.	6000.
1889	2.00	2.50	3.00	4.75	10.	22.	30.	65.	225.	700.	500.	3125.	17500.	165.	200.	1700.
1890	2.00	2.50	3.00	3.75	10.	21.	30.	65.	225.	450.	375.	1650.	5500.	180.	240.	2000.
1891	2.00	2.50	3.00	3.75	10.	20.	30.	65.	225.	450.	375.	1100.	-	165.	400.	3400.
1892	2.00	2.50	3.00	3.75	12.	20.	30.	65.	225.	425.	375.	1200.	3500.	150.	190.	1050.
1893	2.00	2.50	3.00	3.75	10.	20.	29.	65.	225.	400.	500.	1400.	2000.	150.	200.	1125.
1894	4.00	5.00	9.00	12.	45.	60.	75.	100.	225.	400.	375.	900.	2250.	150.	215.	1550.
1894/94	20.	30.	75.	150.	250.	400.	700.	1700.	2500.	6500.	7500.	10000.	-	*	*	*
1895	2.00	2.50	3.00	4.00	12.	20.	30.	50.	150.	200.	200.	1100.	2000.	150.	275.	1125.

—— = Insufficient pricing data

INDIAN HEAD CENT (CONTINUED)

	G-4	VG-8	F-12	VF-20	EF-40	AU-50	MS-60B	MS-63RB	MS-64RB	MS-64R	MS-65RB	MS-65R	MS-66R	PF-63RB	PF-64RB	PF-65R
1896	2.00	2.50	3.00	4.00	10.	22.	35.	50.	150.	225.	225.	900.	2500.	220.	385.	2000.
1897	2.00	2.50	3.00	3.50	10.	20.	30.	50.	150.	200.	250.	900.	3000.	150.	200.	1500.
1898	2.00	2.50	3.00	3.50	10.	18.	25.	45.	100.	350.	250.	600.	3000.	150.	200.	1000.
1899	2.00	2.50	2.75	3.50	12.	18.	25.	45.	90.	150.	200.	600.	1500.	185.	225.	1000.
1900	2.00	2.50	2.75	3.50	14.	18.	25.	40.	90.	225.	250.	900.	3300.	135.	200.	1000.
1901	2.00	2.50	2.75	3.50	8.00	17.	25.	40.	90.	150.	175.	500.	1050.	135.	205.	1000.
1902	2.00	2.50	2.75	3.50	8.00	17.	25.	40.	90.	125.	175.	500.	1050.	135.	200.	1000.
1903	2.00	2.50	2.75	3.50	8.00	17.	25.	40.	90.	125.	175.	500.	1050.	135.	400.	1000.
1904	2.00	2.50	2.75	3.50	8.00	17.	25.	40.	90.	125.	175.	600.	1250.	185.	250.	1400.
1905	2.00	2.50	2.75	3.50	8.00	17.	25.	40.	90.	125.	175.	500.	1050.	175.	225.	1000.
1906	2.00	2.50	2.75	3.50	8.00	17.	25.	40.	90.	125.	175.	500.	1150.	170.	200.	1000.
1907	2.00	2.50	2.75	3.50	8.00	17.	25.	40.	90.	125.	175.	750.	1250.	175.	300.	1450.
1908	2.00	2.50	2.75	3.50	8.00	17.	25.	40.	90.	125.	175.	700.	2000.	135.	200.	1100.
1908-S	70.	80.	90.	110.	175.	200.	250.	400.	550.	1000.	750.	3000.	4000.	*	*	*
1909	3.50	4.00	4.50	5.00	16.	25.	35.	60.	85.	150.	175.	600.	1500.	190.	285.	1600.
1909-S	325.	350.	400.	450.	550.	600.	750.	1000.	1300.	2000.	1800.	5000.	8500.	*	*	*

—— = Insufficient pricing data   * = None issued

Lincoln, Wheat cent

Date of authorization:	Feb. 21, 1857
Dates of issue:	1909-1958
Designer:	Victor D. Brenner
Engraver:	Charles Barber
Diameter:	19.05 mm/0.75 inch
Weight:	1909-1942, 1944-1958: 3.11 grams/0.10 ounce 1943: 2.69 grams/0.09 ounce; 2.75 grams/0.09 ounce
Metallic content:	1909-1942: 95% copper, 5% zinc and tin 1942: 95% copper, 5% zinc 1943: zinc-coated steel 1944-1946: 95% copper, 5% zinc 1947-1958: 95% copper, 5% zinc and tin
Edge:	Plain
Mint mark:	Obverse under date

Note: For copper-alloy coins, the letter B following a numerical grade (as in MS-63B) is shorthand for brown, RB represents red and brown, and R stands for red. It is common practice for grading services to qualify copper coins. In addition to a Mint State grade, a copper coin is assigned as brown, red and brown, or red. Generally, full red coins are valued higher than red and brown coins, which in turn are valued higher than brown coins, all else being equal.

Also, the letter C following a numerical grade for a Proof coin stands for "cameo," while the letters DC stand for "deep cameo." Cameo coins have contrasting surface finishes: mirror fields and frosted devices (raised areas). Deep cameo coins are the ultimate level of cameo, with deeply frosted devices. Cameo and deep cameo coins bring premiums.

LINCOLN, WHEAT CENT (CONTINUED)

	G-4	VG-8	F-12	VF-20	EF-40	AU-50	MS-60B	MS-63RB	MS-64RB	MS-64R	MS-65RB	MS-65R	MS-66R	MS-67R	MS-68R	PF-63RB	PF-64RB	PF-65C	PF-65R	PF-66	PF-66DC	PF-66R	PF-67DC	PF-67R	PF-68DC	PF-69DC
BRONZE ALLOY																										
1909 VDB	4.00	4.50	5.00	5.50	6.00	7.00	10.	14.	23.	50.	30.	110.	220.	—	—	5000.	6000.	—	12000.	—	—	—	—	—	—	—
1909-S VDB	550.	575.	700.	750.	1100.	1300.	1400.	1500.	2500.	4000.	4000.	6000.	11000.	—	—	*	*	*	*	*	*	*	*	*	*	*
1909	2.00	2.50	3.00	3.50	4.00	10.	14.	20.	22.	25.	35.	100.	360.	—	—	500.	700.	—	2500.	—	—	3500.	—	—	—	—
1909-S	75.	85.	100.	175.	225.	250.	275.	325.	350.	500.	650.	1600.	2600.	—	—	*	*	*	*	*	*	*	*	*	*	*
1909-S over Horizontal S	100.	125.	150.	200.	300.	350.	450.	500.	650.	800.	850.	2000.	3000.	—	—	*	*	*	*	*	*	*	*	*	*	*
1910	0.50	0.75	1.00	1.50	3.00	7.00	15.	25.	30.	40.	75.	175.	450.	—	—	400.	500.	—	3000.	—	—	—	—	—	—	—
1910-S	8.00	9.00	10.	15.	25.	60.	75.	85.	125.	200.	200.	1000.	2000.	—	—	*	*	*	*	*	*	*	*	*	*	*
1911	0.40	0.60	1.00	1.50	4.00	8.00	19.	32.	55.	75.	150.	460.	650.	—	—	400.	500.	—	2500.	—	—	8000.	—	—	—	—
1911-D	6.00	7.00	10.	15.	45.	65.	85.	125.	325.	550.	475.	1000.	2750.	—	—	*	*	*	*	*	*	*	*	*	*	*
1911-S	17.	20.	25.	30.	50.	100.	175.	250.	275.	475.	510.	2000.	3500.	—	—	*	*	*	*	*	*	*	*	*	*	*
1912	1.50	1.75	2.00	4.50	9.00	18.	30.	40.	60.	95.	90.	400.	1350.	—	—	400.	800.	—	7500.	—	—	—	—	—	—	—
1912-D	7.00	7.50	8.00	20.	50.	80.	140.	200.	300.	475.	450.	1500.	3000.	—	—	*	*	*	*	*	*	*	*	*	*	*
1912-S	12.	15.	20.	25.	50.	75.	125.	200.	300.	575.	660.	2000.	6000.	—	—	*	*	*	*	*	*	*	*	*	*	*
1913	1.00	1.25	1.50	3.50	14.	16.	28.	40.	65.	75.	100.	250.	1600.	—	—	400.	500.	—	2000.	—	—	3000.	—	—	—	—
1913-D	3.50	4.00	5.00	10.	30.	60.	100.	135.	300.	450.	375.	1250.	3000.	—	—	*	*	*	*	*	*	*	*	*	*	*
1913-S	7.00	8.00	9.00	14.	35.	70.	140.	225.	300.	650.	700.	3000.	8000.	—	—	*	*	*	*	*	*	*	*	*	*	*
1914	0.60	1.00	1.75	4.00	10.	27.	40.	50.	65.	75.	100.	325.	625.	—	—	400.	500.	—	2500.	—	—	5000.	—	—	—	—
1914-D	125.	200.	250.	350.	550.	1200.	1500.	2500.	3500.	6500.	5000.	17000.	30000.	—	—	*	*	*	*	*	*	*	*	*	*	*
1914-S	10.	12.	14.	25.	50.	140.	250.	450.	1250.	1750.	1750.	8500.	20000.	—	—	*	*	*	*	*	*	*	*	*	*	*
1915	2.00	2.50	4.50	12.	40.	65.	80.	110.	130.	200.	255.	750.	1200.	—	—	500.	600.	—	3500.	—	—	—	—	—	—	—
1915-D	2.50	3.00	3.50	5.00	14.	30.	60.	90.	145.	200.	260.	1000.	3000.	—	—	*	*	*	*	*	*	*	*	*	*	*
1915-S	7.00	7.50	8.00	13.	38.	70.	150.	250.	400.	1000.	775.	3500.	—	—	—	*	*	*	*	*	*	*	*	*	*	*
1916	0.50	1.00	1.50	2.00	4.00	10.	14.	25.	45.	50.	52.	125.	935.	—	—	500.	700.	—	9000.	—	—	20000.	—	—	—	—

—— = Insufficient pricing data   * = None issued

LINCOLN, WHEAT CENT (CONTINUED)

	G-4	VG-8	F-12	VF-20	EF-40	AU-50	MS-60B	MS-63RB	MS-64RB	MS-64R	MS-65RB	MS-65R	MS-66R	MS-67R	MS-68R	PF-63RB	PF-64RB	PF-65C	PF-65R	PF-66	PF-66DC	PF-66R	PF-67DC	PF-67R	PF-68DC	PF-69DC
1916-D	1.00	1.50	2.00	3.50	10.	24.	60.	100.	140.	250.	630.	2800.	—	—	—	*	*	*	*	*	*	*	*	*	*	*
1916-S	1.50	2.00	2.50	3.00	12.	30.	70.	110.	350.	700.	1250.	4500.	10000.	—	—	*	*	*	*	*	*	*	*	*	*	*
1917	0.50	1.00	1.50	2.00	4.00	9.00	12.	25.	30.	40.	55.	275.	1350.	—	—	*	*	*	*	*	*	*	*	*	*	*
1917 Doubled Die	70.	100.	240.	400.	900.	1100.	1500.	2250.	3500.	—	—	15000.	—	—	—	*	*	*	*	*	*	*	*	*	*	*
1917-D	0.50	1.00	1.75	4.00	10.	24.	60.	130.	200.	450.	370.	2000.	5000.	—	—	*	*	*	*	*	*	*	*	*	*	*
1917-S	0.50	1.00	1.50	2.50	9.00	20.	65.	150.	260.	1200.	750.	5000.	15000.	—	—	*	*	*	*	*	*	*	*	*	*	*
1918	0.50	1.00	1.50	2.00	4.00	8.00	12.	30.	65.	80	175.	600.	350.	—	—	*	*	*	*	*	*	*	*	*	*	*
1918-D	0.50	1.00	1.50	3.00	9.00	20.	65.	120.	165.	500	410.	2200.	4250.	—	—	*	*	*	*	*	*	*	*	*	*	*
1918-S	0.50	1.00	1.50	2.50	9.00	30.	60.	150.	475.	1200	1100.	5250.	10000.	—	—	*	*	*	*	*	*	*	*	*	*	*
1919	0.50	1.00	1.50	2.00	2.50	5.00	9.00	25.	30.	60	50.	100.	585.	—	—	*	*	*	*	*	*	*	*	*	*	*
1919-D	0.50	1.00	1.50	2.50	5.00	30.	50.	100.	175.	250.	335.	1600.	5475.	—	—	*	*	*	*	*	*	*	*	*	*	*
1919-S	0.50	1.00	1.50	2.50	4.00	15.	40.	80.	350.	700.	750.	4000.	20000.	—	—	*	*	*	*	*	*	*	*	*	*	*
1920	0.50	1.00	1.50	2.00	2.50	5.00	13.	20.	26.	40.	30.	120.	1075.	—	—	*	*	*	*	*	*	*	*	*	*	*
1920-D	0.50	1.00	1.50	2.50	[illegible]	25.	60.	100.	140.	300.	325.	1000.	3700.	—	—	*	*	*	*	*	*	*	*	*	*	*
1920-S	0.50	1.00	1.50	2.50	8.00	30.	90.	200.	350.	1250.	1075.	7500.	6500.	—	—	*	*	*	*	*	*	*	*	*	*	*
1921	0.50	1.00	1.50	2.00	6.00	18.	40.	70.	75.	90.	75.	250.	1425.	—	—	*	*	*	*	*	*	*	*	*	*	*
1921-S	2.00	2.50	3.00	4.00	20.	75.	100.	200.	375.	2300.	825.	4500.	—	—	—	*	*	*	*	*	*	*	*	*	*	*
1922 Missing D, Die Pair 2	450.	600.	800.	1200.	2500.	3500.	6500.	30000.	35000.	50000.	45000.	125000.	—	—	—	*	*	*	*	*	*	*	*	*	*	*
1922-D	10.	12.	14.	16.	25.	45.	80.	100.	160.	250.	350.	2000.	7500.	—	—	*	*	*	*	*	*	*	*	*	*	*
1923	0.50	1.00	1.50	2.00	3.50	8.00	15.	25.	70.	90.	160.	500.	935.	—	—	*	*	*	*	*	*	*	*	*	*	*
1923-S	2.50	3.00	4.00	6.00	25.	75.	200.	400.	675.	1700.	1250.	4500.	—	—	—	*	*	*	*	*	*	*	*	*	*	*
1924	0.50	1.00	1.50	2.00	3.50	10.	21.	45.	60.	75.	75.	230.	720.	—	—	*	*	*	*	*	*	*	*	*	*	*
1924-D	13.	16.	20.	35.	90.	175.	250.	350.	525.	1000.	1250.	5000.	18000.	—	—	*	*	*	*	*	*	*	*	*	*	*

—— = Insufficient pricing data * = None issued

LINCOLN, WHEAT CENT (CONTINUED)

	G-4	VG-8	F-12	VF-20	EF-40	AU-50	MS-60B	MS-63RB	MS-64RB	MS-64R	MS-65RB	MS-65R	MS-66R	MS-67R	MS-68R	PF-63RB	PF-64RB	PF-65C	PF-65R	PF-66	PF-66DC	PF-66R	PF-67DC	PF-67R	PF-68DC	PF-69DC
1924-S	1.50	2.00	2.50	4.00	15.	60.	100.	225.	650.	1500.	1500.	7000.	—	—	—	*	*	*	*	*	*	*	*	*	*	*
1925	0.50	1.00	1.50	2.00	2.50	7.00	10.	20.	30.	35.	35.	100.	225.	—	—	*	*	*	*	*	*	*	*	*	*	*
1925-D	0.50	1.50	1.50	2.00	9.00	25.	50.	80.	175.	325.	300.	2400.	10000.	—	—	*	*	*	*	*	*	*	*	*	*	*
1925-S	0.50	1.00	1.50	2.00	7.00	25.	60.	150.	650.	1600.	2050.	6500.	—	—	—	*	*	*	*	*	*	*	*	*	*	*
1926	0.50	1.00	1.50	2.00	2.50	5.00	8.00	15.	20.	25.	22.	65.	430.	—	—	*	*	*	*	*	*	*	*	*	*	*
1926-D	0.50	1.00	1.50	2.00	8.00	25.	60.	90.	300.	425.	575.	3000.	—	—	—	*	*	*	*	*	*	*	*	*	*	*
1926-S	3.00	4.00	5.00	7.00	15.	60.	125.	275.	925.	5000.	6500.	65000.	—	—	—	*	*	*	*	*	*	*	*	*	*	*
1927	0.50	1.00	1.50	2.00	2.50	4.00	9.00	15.	27.	35.	35.	90.	825.	—	—	*	*	*	*	*	*	*	*	*	*	*
1927-D	0.50	1.00	1.50	2.00	4.00	16.	55.	85.	140.	250.	325.	1300.	—	—	—	*	*	*	*	*	*	*	*	*	*	*
1927-S	1.50	2.00	2.50	4.00	12.	30.	65.	125.	275.	550.	1375.	5000.	—	—	—	*	*	*	*	*	*	*	*	*	*	*
1928	0.50	1.00	1.50	2.00	2.50	4.00	9.00	15.	27.	38.	32.	85.	425.	—	—	*	*	*	*	*	*	*	*	*	*	*
1928-D	0.50	1.00	1.50	2.00	4.00	12.	30.	55.	75.	150.	165.	775.	4000.	—	—	*	*	*	*	*	*	*	*	*	*	*
1928-S	1.00	1.50	2.50	3.00	5.00	15.	65.	85.	165.	300.	460.	3000.	—	—	—	*	*	*	*	*	*	*	*	*	*	*
1929	0.50	1.00	1.50	2.00	2.50	5.00	7.00	14.	25.	35.	60.	225.	475.	—	—	*	*	*	*	*	*	*	*	*	*	*
1929-D	0.50	1.00	1.50	2.00	4.00	9.00	20.	30.	45.	65.	100.	825.	1850.	—	—	*	*	*	*	*	*	*	*	*	*	*
1929-S	0.50	1.00	2.00	2.00	3.50	5.00	20.	19.	28.	40.	45.	225.	600.	—	—	*	*	*	*	*	*	*	*	*	*	*
1930	0.50	1.00	1.50	2.00	2.50	3.00	5.00	7.00	10.	16.	25.	40.	100.	—	—	*	*	*	*	*	*	*	*	*	*	*
1930-D	0.50	1.00	1.50	2.00	3.00	4.50	13.	25.	28.	35.	45.	90.	250.	—	—	*	*	*	*	*	*	*	*	*	*	*
1930-S	0.50	1.00	1.50	2.00	2.50	6.00	12.	13.	25.	30.	30.	50.	180.	—	—	*	*	*	*	*	*	*	*	*	*	*
1931	0.50	1.00	2.00	2.00	2.50	7.00	19.	30.	38.	45.	50.	100.	725.	—	—	*	*	*	*	*	*	*	*	*	*	*
1931-D	4.00	5.00	6.00	7.00	12.	40.	60.	85.	110.	135.	225.	800.	2500.	—	—	*	*	*	*	*	*	*	*	*	*	*
1931-S	65.	75.	85.	100.	110.	120.	130.	140.	150.	350.	200.	750.	1500.	—	—	*	*	*	*	*	*	*	*	*	*	*
1932	1.50	2.00	3.00	3.00	4.00	12.	20.	20.	25.	35.	40.	70.	200.	—	—	*	*	*	*	*	*	*	*	*	*	*
1932-D	1.00	2.00	3.00	3.00	3.50	9.00	17.	30.	34.	38.	45.	80.	215.	—	—	*	*	*	*	*	*	*	*	*	*	*
1933	1.50	2.00	3.00	3.00	4.00	9.00	18.	25.	27.	35.	40.	70.	140.	—	—	*	*	*	*	*	*	*	*	*	*	*

—— = Insufficient pricing data * = None issued

LINCOLN, WHEAT CENT (CONTINUED)

	G-4	VG-8	F-12	VF-20	EF-40	AU-50	MS-60B	MS-63RB	MS-64RB	MS-64R	MS-65RB	MS-65R	MS-66R	MS-67R	MS-68R	PF-63RB	PF-64RB	PF-65C	PF-65R	PF-66	PF-66DC	PF-66R	PF-67DC	PF-67R	PF-68DC	PF-69DC
1933-D	2.00	2.50	3.00	4.00	6.00	15.	20.	23.	24.	30.	35.	70.	155.	—	—	*	*	*	*	*	*	*	*	*	*	*
1934	—	—	0.25	0.40	1.25	4.00	8.00	9.00	12.	—	—	35.	65.	220.	—	*	*	*	*	*	*	*	*	*	*	*
1934-D	—	—	0.35	0.55	5.00	8.75	12.	28.	35.	—	—	65.	150.	850.	—	*	*	*	*	*	*	*	*	*	*	*
1935	—	—	0.22	0.40	0.75	1.00	1.25	6.00	9.00	—	—	30.	50.	150.	—	*	*	*	*	*	*	*	*	*	*	*
1935-D	—	—	0.40	0.45	0.85	2.00	3.25	5.00	10.	—	—	25.	55.	135.	—	*	*	*	*	*	*	*	*	*	*	*
1935-S	—	—	0.55	1.50	2.50	4.25	6.50	25.	30.	—	—	50.	150.	8000.	—	*	*	*	*	*	*	*	*	*	*	*
1936	—	—	0.22	0.40	0.70	0.90	1.25	2.00	4.00	—	—	20.	45.	100.	—	—	—	—	—	—	—	—	—	—	—	—
1936-D	—	—	0.30	0.40	0.85	1.00	1.85	4.00	8.00	—	—	15.	40.	150.	—	*	*	*	*	*	*	*	*	*	*	*
1936-S	—	—	0.32	0.50	1.50	2.00	2.65	5.00	8.00	—	—	23.	70.	250.	—	*	*	*	*	*	*	*	*	*	*	*
1936 Satin Proof	*	*	*	*	*	*	*	*	*	*	*	*	*	*	*	300.	600.	—	2000.	—	—	3500.	—	—	—	—
1936 Brilliant Proof	*	*	*	*	*	*	*	*	*	*	*	*	*	*	*	450.	700.	—	2500.	—	—	6000.	—	10000.	—	—
1937	—	—	0.20	0.30	1.00	1.50	2.00	2.00	4.00	—	—	20.	70.	110.	—	75.	200.	—	300.	—	—	1500.	—	3500.	—	—
1937-D	—	—	0.25	0.40	0.65	1.00	2.25	3.00	5.00	—	—	25.	45.	100.	—	*	*	*	*	*	*	*	*	*	*	*
1937-S	—	—	0.25	0.40	0.65	1.00	2.00	4.00	5.00	—	—	28.	45.	125.	—	*	*	*	*	*	*	*	*	*	*	*
1938	—	—	0.20	0.30	0.60	1.00	1.25	3.00	5.00	—	—	15.	45.	150.	—	50.	150.	—	250.	—	—	800.	—	2500.	—	—
1938-D	—	—	0.40	0.75	0.85	1.00	1.85	4.00	8.00	—	—	15.	60.	135.	—	*	*	*	*	*	*	*	*	*	*	*
1938-S	—	—	0.35	0.55	0.80	1.00	2.50	3.50	6.00	—	—	23.	50.	100.	—	*	*	*	*	*	*	*	*	*	*	*
1939	—	—	0.15	0.25	0.30	0.40	0.50	1.50	4.00	—	—	15.	40.	130.	—	50.	150.	—	500.	—	—	1800.	—	4000.	—	—
1939-D	—	—	0.40	0.75	1.00	1.30	1.75	3.00	6.00	—	—	18.	45.	100.	—	*	*	*	*	*	*	*	*	*	*	*
1939-S	—	—	0.25	0.40	0.75	1.00	1.30	2.50	5.00	—	—	20.	40.	100.	—	*	*	*	*	*	*	*	*	*	*	*
1940	—	—	0.20	0.30	0.40	0.45	0.60	1.00	3.00	—	—	18.	40.	175.	—	40	150.	—	250.	—	—	500.	—	—	—	—
1940-D	—	—	0.30	0.50	0.60	0.70	0.90	2.00	4.00	—	—	15.	32.	125.	—	*	*	*	*	*	*	*	*	*	*	*
1940-S	—	—	0.30	0.50	0.60	0.90	1.25	2.00	4.00	—	—	10.	38.	160.	—	*	*	*	*	*	*	*	*	*	*	*
1941	—	—	0.23	0.40	0.50	0.55	0.80	1.50	3.00	—	—	18.	32.	150.	—	40	150.	—	250.	—	—	500.	—	2000.	—	—

—— = Insufficient pricing data   * = None issued

LINCOLN, WHEAT CENT (CONTINUED)

	G-4	VG-8	F-12	VF-20	EF-40	AU-50	MS-60B	MS-63RB	MS-64RB	MS-64R	MS-65RB	MS-65R	MS-66R	MS-67R	MS-68R	PF-63RB *	PF-64RB *	PF-65C *	PF-65R *	PF-66 *	PF-66DC *	PF-66R *	PF-67DC *	PF-67R *	PF-68DC *	PF-69DC *
1941-D	—	—	0.40	0.60	0.90	1.45	1.65	3.00	4.00	—	—	18.	35.	150.	—	*	*	*	*	*	*	*	*	*	*	*
1941-S	—	—	0.50	0.70	0.80	1.00	1.75	3.00	5.00	—	—	27.	45.	125.	—	*	*	*	*	*	*	*	*	*	*	*
1942	—	—	0.20	0.30	0.40	0.45	0.65	1.00	2.50	—	—	18.	42.	100.	—	40.	125.	—	250.	—	—	600.	—	—	—	—
1942-D	—	—	0.25	0.35	0.40	0.45	0.60	1.00	2.50	—	—	16.	40.	100.	—	*	*	*	*	*	*	*	*	*	*	*
1942-S	—	—	0.55	0.75	1.00	1.50	2.50	6.00	12.	—	—	30.	40.	100.	—	*	*	*	*	*	*	*	*	*	*	*
ZINC-COATED STEEL																										
1943	—	—	0.20	0.30	0.40	0.65	0.80	1.50	3.00	—	—	18.	30.	80.	—	*	*	*	*	*	*	*	*	*	*	*
1943-D	—	—	0.25	0.45	0.60	0.75	1.00	2.50	5.00	—	—	13.	30.	80.	—	*	*	*	*	*	*	*	*	*	*	*
1943-S	—	—	0.35	0.55	0.75	1.00	2.00	4.00	9.00	—	—	20.	40.	100.	—	*	*	*	*	*	*	*	*	*	*	*
SHELL-CASE BRASS																										
1944	—	—	0.10	0.15	0.20	0.35	0.42	1.00	1.50	—	—	10.	21.	100.	—	*	*	*	*	*	*	*	*	*	*	*
1944-D	—	—	0.20	0.25	0.30	0.35	0.40	1.00	1.50	—	—	15.	30.	100.	—	*	*	*	*	*	*	*	*	*	*	*
1944-D/S Variety 1	—	—	75.	150.	200.	250.	350.	450.	750.	—	—	2000.	4000.	—	—	*	*	*	*	*	*	*	*	*	*	*
1944-D/S Variety 2	—	—	32.	48.	90.	100.	145.	275.	350.	—	—	750.	—	—	—	*	*	*	*	*	*	*	*	*	*	*
1944-S	—	—	0.15	0.20	0.25	0.35	0.40	1.00	1.50	—	—	10.	25.	80.	—	*	*	*	*	*	*	*	*	*	*	*
1945	—	—	0.10	0.15	0.24	0.40	0.55	1.00	1.50	—	—	12.	35.	125.	—	*	*	*	*	*	*	*	*	*	*	*
1945-D	—	—	0.15	0.20	0.25	0.40	0.45	1.00	1.50	—	—	10.	30.	100.	—	*	*	*	*	*	*	*	*	*	*	*
1945-S	—	—	0.15	0.20	0.25	0.30	0.40	1.00	1.50	—	—	10.	30.	65.	—	*	*	*	*	*	*	*	*	*	*	*
1946	—	—	0.10	0.15	0.20	0.25	0.30	1.00	1.50	—	—	11.	30.	90.	—	*	*	*	*	*	*	*	*	*	*	*
1946-D	—	—	0.15	0.18	0.20	0.25	0.30	1.00	1.50	—	—	10.	25.	100.	—	*	*	*	*	*	*	*	*	*	*	*
1946-S	—	—	0.20	0.25	0.30	0.35	0.40	1.00	1.50	—	—	15.	30.	150.	—	*	*	*	*	*	*	*	*	*	*	*
1946-S/D	—	—	—	—	—	—	175.	300.	400.	—	—	600.	750.	—	—	*	*	*	*	*	*	*	*	*	*	*

—— = Insufficient pricing data * = None issued

LINCOLN, WHEAT CENT (CONTINUED)

	G-4	VG-8	F-12	VF-20	EF-40	AU-50	MS-60B	MS-63RB	MS-64RB	MS-64R	MS-65RB	MS-65R	MS-66R	MS-67R	MS-68R	PF-63RB	PF-64RB	PF-65C	PF-65R	PF-66	PF-66DC	PF-66R	PF-67DC	PF-67R	PF-68DC	PF-69DC
BRONZE ALLOY																										
1947	—	—	0.05	0.05	0.05	0.10	—	1.50	—	—	—	10.	50.	135.	—	*	*	*	*	*	*	*	*	*	*	*
1947-D	—	—	0.05	0.05	0.05	0.10	0.10	0.40	—	—	—	9.00	30.	40.	—	*	*	*	*	*	*	*	*	*	*	*
1947-S	—	—	0.05	0.05	0.05	0.10	0.10	0.75	—	—	—	11.	30.	125.	—	*	*	*	*	*	*	*	*	*	*	*
1948	—	—	0.05	0.05	0.05	0.10	0.10	0.50	—	—	—	10.	100.	250.	—	*	*	*	*	*	*	*	*	*	*	*
1948-D	—	—	0.05	0.05	0.05	0.10	0.10	0.50	—	—	—	6.00	35.	400.	—	*	*	*	*	*	*	*	*	*	*	*
1948-S	—	—	0.05	0.05	0.05	0.10	0.10	1.35	—	—	—	5.50	30.	125.	—	*	*	*	*	*	*	*	*	*	*	*
1949	—	—	0.05	0.05	0.05	0.10	0.10	0.65	—	—	—	15.	150.	250.	—	*	*	*	*	*	*	*	*	*	*	*
1949-D	—	—	0.05	0.05	0.05	0.10	0.10	0.65	—	—	—	17.	30.	40.	—	*	*	*	*	*	*	*	*	*	*	*
1949-S	—	—	0.05	0.05	0.05	0.10	0.10	1.25	—	—	—	11.	40.	60.	—	*	*	*	*	*	*	*	*	*	*	*
1950	—	—	0.05	0.05	0.05	0.10	0.10	0.75	—	—	—	15.	80.	500.	—	35.	50.	70.	60.	—	8900.	120.	—	720.	—	—
1950-D	—	—	0.05	0.05	0.05	0.10	0.10	0.65	—	—	—	7.50	40.	250.	—	*	*	*	*	*	*	*	*	*	*	*
1950-S	—	—	0.05	0.05	0.05	0.10	0.10	0.85	—	—	—	10.	35.	45.	—	*	*	*	*	*	*	*	*	*	*	*
1951	—	—	0.05	0.05	0.05	0.10	0.10	0.65	—	—	—	14.	75.	95.	—	25.	50.	310.	60.	—	—	145.	—	270.	—	—
1951-D	—	—	0.05	0.05	0.05	0.10	0.10	0.35	—	—	—	10.	30.	95.	—	*	*	*	*	*	*	*	*	*	*	*
1951-S	—	—	0.05	0.05	0.05	0.10	0.10	0.55	—	—	—	12.	35.	45.	—	*	*	*	*	*	*	*	*	*	*	*
1952	—	—	0.05	0.05	0.05	0.10	0.10	0.55	—	—	—	18.	45.	75.	—	13.	35.	—	50.	—	—	90.	—	210.	—	—
1952-D	—	—	0.05	0.05	0.05	0.10	0.10	0.25	—	—	—	11.	30.	50.	—	*	*	*	*	*	*	*	*	*	*	*
1952-S	—	—	0.05	0.05	0.05	0.10	0.10	1.75	—	—	—	10.	25.	50.	—	*	*	*	*	*	*	*	*	*	*	*
1953	—	—	0.05	0.05	0.05	0.10	0.10	0.20	—	—	—	16.	70.	90.	—	10.	30.	70.	35.	—	—	40.	—	155.	—	—
1953-D	—	—	0.05	0.05	0.05	0.10	0.10	0.20	—	—	—	11.	25.	35.	—	*	*	*	*	*	*	*	*	*	*	*
1953-S	—	—	0.05	0.05	0.05	0.10	0.10	0.50	—	—	—	10.	25.	125.	—	*	*	*	*	*	*	*	*	*	*	*
1954	—	—	0.05	0.05	0.05	0.10	0.10	0.40	—	—	—	15.	35.	100.	—	5.00	12.	—	18.	—	—	40.	—	90.	—	—
1954-D	—	—	0.05	0.05	0.05	0.10	0.10	0.35	—	—	—	12.	25.	40.	—	*	*	*	*	*	*	*	*	*	*	*
1954-S	—	—	0.05	0.05	0.05	0.10	0.10	0.20	—	—	—	14.	22.	85.	—	*	*	*	*	*	*	*	*	*	*	*

—— = Insufficient pricing data   * = None issued

LINCOLN, WHEAT CENT (CONTINUED)

	G-4	VG-8	F-12	VF-20	EF-40	AU-50	MS-60B	MS-63RB	MS-64RB	MS-64R	MS-65RB	MS-65R	MS-66R	MS-67R	MS-68R	PF-63RB	PF-64RB	PF-65C	PF-65R	PF-66	PF-66DC	PF-66R	PF-67DC	PF-67R	PF-68DC	PF-69DC
1955	—	—	0.05	0.05	0.05	0.10	0.10	0.15	—	—	—	18.	45.	55.	—	5.00	13.	—	18.	—	230.	20.	—	55.	—	—
1955 Doubled Die	—	—	1000.	1200.	1300.	1400.	1700.	2500.	5000.	9000.	—	35000.	—	—	—	*	*	*	*	*	*	*	*	*	*	*
1955-D	—	—	0.05	0.05	0.05	0.10	0.10	0.15	—	—	—	15.	40.	100.	—	*	*	*	*	*	*	*	*	*	*	*
1955-S	—	—	0.05	0.05	0.05	0.10	0.10	0.50	—	—	—	15.	30.	60.	—	*	*	*	*	*	*	*	*	*	*	*
1955	—	—	—	—	—	—	—	—	—	—	—	—	—	—	—	4.75	—	—	12.	—	—	—	—	—	—	—
1956	—	—	0.05	0.05	0.05	0.10	0.10	0.15	—	—	—	11.	125.	175.	—	2.00	3.00	—	5.00	—	—	25.	—	60.	—	—
1956-D	—	—	0.05	0.05	0.05	0.10	0.10	0.15	—	—	—	10.	25.	55.	—	*	*	*	*	*	*	*	*	*	*	*
1957	—	—	0.05	0.05	0.05	0.10	0.10	0.15	—	—	—	11.	90.	125.	—	2.00	3.00	35.	5.00	—	—	20.	—	30.	—	—
1957-D	—	—	0.05	0.05	0.05	0.10	0.10	0.15	—	—	—	10.	35.	75.	—	*	*	*	*	*	*	*	*	*	*	*
1958	—	—	0.05	0.05	0.05	0.10	0.10	0.15	—	—	—	12.	30.	40.	—	2.50	4.00	—	6.00	—	—	20.	950.	30.	—	—
1958-D	—	—	0.05	0.05	0.05	0.10	0.10	0.15	—	—	—	11.	20.	75.	—	*	*	*	*	*	*	*	*	*	*	*

—— = Insufficient pricing data   * = None issued

Lincoln, Memorial cent

Date of authorization:	Feb. 21, 1857
Dates of issue:	1959-present
Designers:	Obverse: Victor D. Brenner Reverse: Frank Gasparro
Engravers:	Obverse: Charles Barber Reverse: Gilroy Roberts
Diameter:	19.05 mm/0.75 inch
Weight:	1959-1982: 3.11 grams/0.10 ounce 1982-present: 2.50 grams/0.08 ounce
Metallic content:	1959-1962: 95% copper, 5% zinc and tin 1962-1982: 95% copper, 5% zinc 1982-present: 97.5% zinc, 2.5% copper (99.2% zinc, 0.8% copper planchet plated with pure copper)
Edge:	Plain
Mint mark:	Obverse under date

Note: For copper-alloy coins, the letter B following a numerical grade (as in MS-63B) is shorthand for brown, RB represents red and brown, and R stands for red. It is common practice for grading services to qualify copper coins. In addition to a Mint State grade, a copper coin is assigned as brown, red and brown, or red. Generally, full red coins are valued higher than red and brown coins, which in turn are valued higher than brown coins, all else being equal.

Also, the letter C following a numerical grade for a Proof coin stands for "cameo," while the letters DC stand for "deep cameo." Cameo coins have contrasting surface finishes: mirror fields and frosted devices (raised areas). Deep cameo coins are the ultimate level of cameo, with deeply frosted devices. Cameo and deep cameo coins bring premiums.

LINCOLN, MEMORIAL CENT (CONTINUED)

	G-4	VG-8	F-12	VF-20	EF-40	AU-50	MS-60B	MS-63RB	MS-64RB	MS-64R	MS-65RB	MS-65R	MS-66R	MS-67R	MS-68R	PF-63RB	PF-64RB	PF-65C	PF-65R	PF-66	PF-66DC	PF-66R	PF-67DC	PF-67R	PF-68DC	PF-69DC
MEMORIAL REVERSE																										
1959	—	—	—	—	—	—	—	0.15	—	10.	—	20.	40.	175.	—	—	1.00	—	12.	—	60.	25.	375.	40.	—	—
1959-D	—	—	—	—	—	—	—	0.15	—	8.00	—	16.	40.	150.	—	*	*	*	*	*	*	*	*	*	*	*
1960 Large Date	—	—	—	—	—	—	—	0.15	—	5.00	—	10.	20.	175.	—	1.00	1.00	—	12.	—	—	14.	—	19.	—	—
1960 Small Date	—	—	—	—	—	—	—	2.00	—	8.00	—	17.	40.	200.	—	14.	14.	—	20.	—	—	30.	—	70.	—	—
1960-D Large Date	—	—	—	—	—	—	—	0.15	—	5.00	—	10.	21.	50.	—	*	*	*	*	*	*	*	*	*	*	*
1960-D Small Date	—	—	—	—	—	—	—	0.20	—	6.00	—	12.	25.	75.	—	*	*	*	*	*	*	*	*	*	*	*
1961	—	—	—	—	—	—	—	0.15	—	5.00	—	10.	100.	125.	—	0.60	0.60	—	10.	—	—	14.	170.	40.	—	—
1961-D	—	—	—	—	—	—	—	0.15	—	10.	—	20.	100.	125.	—	*	*	*	*	*	*	*	*	*	*	*
BRASS ALLOY																										
1962	—	—	—	—	—	—	—	0.15	—	5.00	—	10.	40.	100.	—	0.60	0.60	—	10.	—	30.	14.	50.	40.	—	—
1962-D	—	—	—	—	—	—	—	0.15	—	10.	—	20.	110.	140.	—	*	*	*	*	*	*	*	*	*	*	*
1963	—	—	—	—	—	—	—	0.15	—	7.00	—	15.	150.	225.	—	0.60	0.60	—	10.	—	40.	14.	—	70.	—	—
1963-D	—	—	—	—	—	—	—	0.15	—	7.00	—	15.	150.	225.	—	*	*	*	*	*	*	*	*	*	*	*
1964	—	—	—	—	—	—	—	0.15	—	5.00	—	10.	35.	75.	—	1.00	2.00	—	10.	—	30.	14.	50.	40.	—	—
1964-D	—	—	—	—	—	—	—	0.15	—	6.00	—	12.	40.	100.	—	*	*	*	*	*	*	*	*	*	*	*
1965	—	—	—	—	—	—	—	0.15	—	5.00	—	10.	25.	35.	—	*	*	*	*	*	*	*	*	*	*	*
1966	—	—	—	—	—	—	—	0.25	—	5.00	—	10.	15.	25.	—	*	*	*	*	*	*	*	*	*	*	*
1967	—	—	—	—	—	—	—	0.15	—	5.00	—	10.	20.	25.	—	*	*	*	*	*	*	*	*	*	*	*
1968	—	—	—	—	—	—	—	0.15	—	6.00	—	12.	30.	50.	—	*	*	*	*	*	*	*	*	*	*	*
1968-D	—	—	—	—	—	—	—	0.15	—	6.00	—	12.	30.	50.	—	*	*	*	*	*	*	*	*	*	*	*
1968-S	—	—	—	—	—	—	—	0.15	—	7.00	—	14.	25.	75.	—	1.00	2.00	—	6.00	—	25.	7.00	45.	8.00	—	—

—— = Insufficient pricing data * = None issued

	G-4	VG-8	F-12	VF-20	EF-40	AU-50	MS-60B	MS-63RB	MS-64RB	MS-64R	MS-65RB	MS-65R	MS-66R	MS-67R	MS-68R	PF-63RB	PF-64RB	PF-65C	PF-65R	PF-66	PF-66DC	PF-66R	PF-67DC	PF-67R	PF-68DC	PF-69DC
1969	—	—	—	—	—	—	—	0.25	—	7.00	—	7.50	250.	—	—	*	*	*	*	*	*	*	*	*	*	*
1969-D	—	—	—	—	—	—	—	0.15	—	5.00	—	10.	100.	150.	—	*	*	*	*	*	*	*	*	*	*	*
1969-S	—	—	—	—	—	—	—	0.15	—	6.00	—	12.	25.	75.	—	1.00	2.00	—	6.00	—	20.	7.00	35.	8.00	—	—
1969-S Doubled Die	—	—	—	—	—	—	—	—	—	—	—	20000.	—	—	—	*	*	*	*	*	*	*	*	*	*	*
1970	—	—	—	—	—	—	—	0.25	—	5.00	—	10.	35.	65.	—	*	*	*	*	*	*	*	*	*	*	*
1970-D	—	—	—	—	—	—	—	0.15	—	5.00	—	6.00	50.	75.	—	*	*	*	*	*	*	*	*	*	*	*
1970-S Low 7	—	—	—	—	—	—	—	0.15	—	9.00	—	19.	50.	—	—	0.75	—	—	6.00	—	18.	7.00	27.	8.00	—	—
1970-S Level 7	—	—	—	—	—	—	—	24.	—	30.	—	62.	80.	—	—	50.	—	—	55.	—	160.	90.	—	100.	—	—
1970-S Doubled Die	—	—	—	—	—	—	—	5000.	—	*	—	20000.	*	*	—	*	*	*	*	*	*	*	*	*	*	*
1971	—	—	—	—	—	—	—	0.25	—	15.	—	30.	50.	75.	—	*	*	*	*	*	*	*	*	*	*	*
1971-D	—	—	—	—	—	—	—	0.25	—	5.00	—	7.00	30.	60.	—	*	*	*	*	*	*	*	*	*	*	*
1971-S	—	—	—	—	—	—	—	0.15	—	5.00	—	6.00	50.	75.	—	1.50	2.50	—	6.00	—	—	15.	700.	45.	—	—
1972	—	—	—	—	—	—	—	0.15	—	5.00	—	5.00	35.	65.	—	*	*	*	*	*	*	*	*	*	*	*
1972-D	—	—	—	—	—	—	—	0.15	—	6.00	—	13.	30.	60.	—	*	*	*	*	*	*	*	*	*	*	*
1972-S	—	—	—	—	—	—	—	0.20	—	15.	—	30.	60.	125.	—	1.50	2.50	—	6.00	—	—	7.00	—	8.00	—	—
1972 Doubled Die	—	—	—	—	—	—	—	205.	—	—	—	405.	800.	—	—	*	*	*	*	*	*	*	*	*	*	*
1973	—	—	—	—	—	—	—	0.15	—	5.00	—	9.00	32.	50.	—	*	*	*	*	*	*	*	*	*	*	*
1973-D	—	—	—	—	—	—	—	0.15	—	6.00	—	12.	40.	75.	—	*	*	*	*	*	*	*	*	*	*	*
1973-S	—	—	—	—	—	—	—	0.25	—	5.00	—	10.	60.	100.	—	1.00	2.00	—	6.00	—	—	8.00	—	10.	—	—
1974	—	—	—	—	—	—	—	0.15	—	5.00	—	10.	20.	40.	—	*	*	*	*	*	*	*	*	*	*	*
1974-D	—	—	—	—	—	—	—	0.15	—	5.00	—	10.	40.	75.	—	*	*	*	*	*	*	*	*	*	*	*
1974-S	—	—	—	—	—	—	—	0.25	—	5.00	—	10.	25.	45.	—	1.00	2.00	—	6.00	—	—	8.00	—	10.	—	—
1975	—	—	—	—	—	—	—	0.15	—	5.00	—	9.00	14.	35.	—	*	*	*	*	*	*	*	*	*	*	*

—— = Insufficient pricing data   * = None issued

LINCOLN, MEMORIAL CENT (CONTINUED)

	G-4	VG-8	F-12	VF-20	EF-40	AU-50	MS-60B	MS-63RB	MS-64RB	MS-64R	MS-65RB	MS-65R	MS-66R	MS-67R	MS-68R	PF-63RB	PF-64RB	PF-65C	PF-65R	PF-66	PF-66DC	PF-66R	PF-67DC	PF-67R	PF-68DC	PF-69DC
1975-D	—	—	—	—	—	—	—	0.15	—	7.00	—	15.	60.	110.	—	*	*	*	*	*	*	*	*	*	*	*
1975-S	*	*	*	*	*	*	*	*	*	*	*	*	*	*	*	4.00	5.00	—	6.00	—	10.	7.00	21.	8.00	—	—
1976	—	—	—	—	—	—	—	0.15	—	10.	—	20.	18.	40.	—	*	*	*	*	*	*	*	*	*	*	*
1976-D	—	—	—	—	—	—	—	0.15	—	10.	—	20.	20.	60.	—	*	*	*	*	*	*	*	*	*	*	*
1976-S	*	*	*	*	*	*	*	*	*	*	*	*	*	*	*	3.00	4.00	—	12.	—	—	15.	—	20.	—	—
1977	—	—	—	—	—	—	—	0.15	—	10.	—	20.	35.	150.	—	*	*	*	*	*	*	*	*	*	*	*
1977-D	—	—	—	—	—	—	—	0.15	—	10.	—	20.	65.	125.	—	*	*	*	*	*	*	*	*	*	*	*
1977-S	*	*	*	*	*	*	*	*	*	*	*	*	*	*	*	2.00	3.00	—	6.00	—	10.	7.00	15.	8.00	—	—
1978	—	—	—	—	—	—	—	0.15	—	10.	—	20.	65.	100.	—	*	*	*	*	*	*	*	*	*	*	*
1978-D	—	—	—	—	—	—	—	0.15	—	7.00	—	15.	70.	110.	—	*	*	*	*	*	*	*	*	*	*	*
1978-S	*	*	*	*	*	*	*	*	*	*	*	*	*	*	*	2.50	4.00	—	6.00	—	10.	7.00	15.	8.00	—	—
1979	—	—	—	—	—	—	—	0.15	—	7.00	—	15.	40.	100.	—	*	*	*	*	*	*	*	*	*	*	*
1979-D	—	—	—	—	—	—	—	0.15	—	5.00	—	10.	60.	125.	—	*	*	*	*	*	*	*	*	*	*	*
1979-S Filled S	*	*	*	*	*	*	*	*	*	*	*	*	*	*	*	3.00	4.00	—	7.00	—	—	10.	—	30.	—	—
1979-S Clear S	*	*	*	*	*	*	*	*	*	*	*	*	*	*	*	3.00	4.00	—	10.	—	—	—	—	—	—	—
1980	—	—	—	—	—	—	—	0.15	—	5.00	—	9.00	15.	40.	—	*	*	*	*	*	*	*	*	*	*	*
1980-D	—	—	—	—	—	—	—	0.15	—	6.00	—	13.	60.	200.	—	*	*	*	*	*	*	*	*	*	*	*
1980-S	*	*	*	*	*	*	*	*	*	*	*	*	*	*	*	1.50	2.50	—	6.00	—	10.	7.00	14.	8.00	—	—
1981	—	—	—	—	—	—	—	0.15	—	5.00	—	10.	40.	95.	—	*	*	*	*	*	*	*	*	*	*	*
1981-D	—	—	—	—	—	—	—	0.15	—	6.00	—	12.	50.	60.	—	*	*	*	*	*	*	*	*	*	*	*
1981-S	*	*	*	*	*	*	*	*	*	*	*	*	*	*	*	2.50	4.00	—	7.00	—	12.	8.00	22.	10.	—	—
1982 Large Date	—	—	—	—	—	—	—	0.20	—	5.00	—	8.00	30.	60.	—	*	*	*	*	*	*	*	*	*	*	*
1982 Small Date	—	—	—	—	—	—	—	0.30	—	5.00	—	10.	35.	70.	—	*	*	*	*	*	*	*	*	*	*	*

—— = Insufficient pricing data   * = None issued

	G-4	VG-8	F-12	VF-20	EF-40	AU-50	MS-60B	MS-63RB	MS-64RB	MS-64R	MS-65RB	MS-65R	MS-66R	MS-67R	MS-68R	PF-63RB	PF-64RD	PF-65C	PF-65R	PF-66	PF-66DC	PF-66R	PF-67DC	PF-67R	PF-68DC	PF-69DC
1982-D Large Date	—	—	—	—	—	—	—	0.20	—	5.00	—	8.00	20.	50.	—	*	*	*	*	*	*	*	*	*	*	*
1982-S	*	*	*	*	*	*	*	*	*	*	*	*	*	*	*	2.50	4.00	—	2.00	—	—	—	14.	—	18.	35.
COPPER-PLATED ZINC																										
1982 Large Date	—	—	—	—	—	—	—	0.25	—	5.00	—	8.00	50.	70.	—	*	*	*	*	*	*	*	*	*	*	*
1982 Small Date	—	—	—	—	—	—	—	0.75	—	5.00	—	10.	50.	70.	—	*	*	*	*	*	*	*	*	*	*	*
1982-D Large Date	—	—	—	—	—	—	—	0.30	—	5.00	—	9.00	25.	50.	—	*	*	*	*	*	*	*	*	*	*	*
1982-D Small Date	—	—	—	—	—	—	—	0.25	—	5.00	—	7.00	20.	30.	—	*	*	*	*	*	*	*	*	*	*	*
1983	—	—	—	—	—	—	—	0.15	—	5.00	—	8.00	30.	60.	—	*	*	*	*	*	*	*	*	*	*	*
1983-D	—	—	—	—	—	—	—	0.15	—	5.00	—	7.00	20.	70.	—	*	*	*	*	*	*	*	*	*	*	*
1983 Doubled Die	—	—	—	—	—	—	—	170.	—	—	—	300.	500.	725.	—	*	*	*	*	*	*	*	*	*	*	*
1983-S	*	*	*	*	*	*	*	*	*	*	*	*	*	*	*	2.50	4.00	—	3.50	—	—	—	14.	—	18.	35.
1984	—	—	—	—	—	—	—	0.15	—	5.00	—	7.00	25.	50.	—	*	*	*	*	*	*	*	*	*	*	*
1984-D	—	—	—	—	—	—	—	0.30	—	5.00	—	7.00	25.	35.	—	*	*	*	*	*	*	*	*	*	*	*
1984 Doubled Die	—	—	—	—	—	—	—	155.	—	—	—	190.	240.	360.	—	*	*	*	*	*	*	*	*	*	*	*
1984-S	*	*	*	*	*	*	*	*	*	*	*	*	*	*	*	4.00	5.00	—	3.00	—	—	—	18.	—	25.	55.
1985	—	—	—	—	—	—	—	0.50	—	5.00	—	6.00	14.	80.	—	*	*	*	*	*	*	*	*	*	*	*
1985-D	—	—	—	—	—	—	—	0.15	—	5.00	—	6.00	10.	25.	—	*	*	*	*	*	*	*	*	*	*	*
1985-S	*	*	*	*	*	*	*	*	*	*	*	*	*	*	*	4.00	5.00	—	3.50	—	—	—	14.	—	18.	35.
1986	—	—	—	—	—	—	—	0.75	—	5.00	—	6.00	11.	25.	—	*	*	*	*	*	*	*	*	*	*	*
1986-D	—	—	—	—	—	—	—	0.20	—	5.00	—	9.00	20.	50.	—	*	*	*	*	*	*	*	*	*	*	*
1986-S	*	*	*	*	*	*	*	*	*	*	*	*	*	*	*	6.00	8.00	—	6.00	—	—	—	15.	—	19.	40.

—— = Insufficient pricing data * = None issued

LINCOLN, MEMORIAL CENT (CONTINUED)

	G-4	VG-8	F-12	VF-20	EF-40	AU-50	MS-60B	MS-63RB	MS-64RB	MS-64R	MS-65RB	MS-65R	MS-66R	MS-67R	MS-68R	PF-63RB	PF-64RB	PF-65C	PF-65R	PF-66	PF-66DC	PF-66R	PF-67DC	PF-67R	PF-68DC	PF-69DC
1987	—	—	—	—	—	—	—	0.50	—	5.00	—	6.00	12.	50.	65.	*	*	*	*	*	*	*	*	*	*	*
1987-D	—	—	—	—	—	—	—	0.15	—	5.00	—	6.00	12.	50.	175.	*	*	*	*	*	*	*	*	*	*	*
1987-S	*	*	*	*	*	*	*	*	*	*	*	*	*	*	*	3.00	4.00	—	3.50	—	—	—	15.	—	19.	40.
1988	—	—	—	—	—	—	—	0.15	—	5.00	—	6.00	22.	50.	200.	*	*	*	*	*	*	*	*	*	*	*
1988-D	—	—	—	—	—	—	—	0.15	—	5.00	—	6.00	10.	35.	130.	*	*	*	*	*	*	*	*	*	*	*
1988-S	*	*	*	*	*	*	*	*	*	*	*	*	*	*	*	9.00	12.	—	2.00	—	—	—	15.	—	20.	95.
1989	—	—	—	—	—	—	—	0.15	—	5.00	—	6.00	17.	60.	200.	*	*	*	*	*	*	*	*	*	*	*
1989-D	—	—	—	—	—	—	—	0.15	—	5.00	—	6.00	17.	35.	200.	*	*	*	*	*	*	*	*	*	*	*
1989-S	*	*	*	*	*	*	*	*	*	*	*	*	*	*	*	9.00	12.	—	2.50	—	—	—	14.	—	18.	35.
1990	—	—	—	—	—	—	—	0.15	—	5.00	—	6.00	15.	40.	150.	*	*	*	*	*	*	*	*	*	*	*
1990-D	—	—	—	—	—	—	—	0.15	—	5.00	—	6.00	10.	40.	125.	*	*	*	*	*	*	*	*	*	*	*
1990-S	*	*	*	*	*	*	*	*	*	*	*	*	*	*	*	4.50	6.00	—	4.00	—	—	—	15.	—	19.	40.
1990-S No S	*	*	*	*	*	*	*	*	*	*	*	*	*	*	*	3400.	3500.	—	4000.	—	—	—	—	—	5000.	—
1991	—	—	—	—	—	—	—	0.15	—	5.00	—	7.00	17.	35.	175.	*	*	*	*	*	*	*	*	*	*	*
1991-D	—	—	—	—	—	—	—	0.15	—	5.00	—	6.00	11.	45.	100.	*	*	*	*	*	*	*	*	*	*	*
1991-S	*	*	*	*	*	*	*	*	*	*	*	*	*	*	*	20.	25.	—	6.00	—	—	—	14.	—	18.	35.
1992	—	—	—	—	—	—	—	0.15	—	5.00	—	6.00	10.	35.	170.	*	*	*	*	*	*	*	*	*	*	*
1992-D	—	—	—	—	—	—	—	0.15	—	5.00	—	6.00	10.	35.	125.	*	*	*	*	*	*	*	*	*	*	*
1992-S	*	*	*	*	*	*	*	*	*	*	*	*	*	*	*	3.00	4.00	—	5.00	—	—	—	14.	—	19.	40.
1993	—	—	—	—	—	—	—	0.15	—	5.00	—	6.00	20.	40.	290.	*	*	*	*	*	*	*	*	*	*	*
1993-D	—	—	—	—	—	—	—	0.15	—	5.00	—	6.00	9.00	35.	160.	*	*	*	*	*	*	*	*	*	*	*
1993-S	*	*	*	*	*	*	*	*	*	*	*	*	*	*	*	5.00	6.00	—	7.00	—	—	—	14.	—	18.	35.
1994	—	—	—	—	—	—	—	0.15	—	5.00	—	9.00	17.	20.	75.	*	*	*	*	*	*	*	*	*	*	*
1994-D	—	—	—	—	—	—	—	0.15	—	5.00	—	6.00	11.	60.	200.	*	*	*	*	*	*	*	*	*	*	*
1994-S	*	*	*	*	*	*	*	*	*	*	*	*	*	*	*	5.00	6.00	—	6.50	—	—	—	15.	—	19.	40.

—— = Insufficient pricing data * = None issued

LINCOLN, MEMORIAL CENT (CONTINUED)

	G-4	VG-8	F-12	VF-20	EF-40	AU-50	MS-60B	MS-63RB	MS-64RB	MS-64R	MS-65RB	MS-65R	MS-66R	MS-67R	MS-68R	PF-63RB	PF-64RB	PF-65C	PF-65R	PF-66	PF-66DC	PF-66R	PF-67DC	PF-67R	PF-68DC	PF-69DC
1995	—	—	—	—	—	—	—	0.15	—	5.00	—	6.00	12.	50.	175.	*	*	*	*	*	*	*	*	*	*	*
1995 Doubled Die, early die state	—	—	2.00	3.50	5.00	7.50	10.	18.	—	—	—	50.	70.	35.	190.	*	*	*	*	*	*	*	*	*	*	*
1995-D	—	—	—	—	—	—	—	0.15	—	5.00	—	6.00	10.	55.	135.	*	*	*	*	*	*	*	*	*	*	*
1995-S	*	*	*	*	*	*	*	*	*	*	*	*	*	*	*	6.00	7.00	—	7.00	—	—	—	14.	—	18.	30.
1996	—	—	—	—	—	—	—	0.15	—	5.00	—	6.00	8.00	25.	75.	*	*	*	*	*	*	*	*	*	*	*
1996-D	—	—	—	—	—	—	—	0.15	—	5.00	—	6.00	14.	55.	140.	*	*	*	*	*	*	*	*	*	*	*
1996-S	*	*	*	*	*	*	*	*	*	*	*	*	*	*	*	3.00	4.00	—	4.50	—	—	—	15.	—	19.	40.
1997	—	—	—	—	—	—	—	0.15	—	5.00	—	6.00	12.	70.	150.	*	*	*	*	*	*	*	*	*	*	*
1997-D	—	—	—	—	—	—	—	0.15	—	5.00	—	6.00	12.	40.	100.	*	*	*	*	*	*	*	*	*	*	*
1997-S	*	*	*	*	*	*	*	*	*	*	*	*	*	*	*	8.00	10.	—	7.00	—	—	—	12.	—	15.	40.
1998	—	—	—	—	—	—	—	0.15	—	5.00	—	6.00	14.	50.	125.	*	*	*	*	*	*	*	*	*	*	*
1998-D	—	—	—	—	—	—	—	0.15	—	5.00	—	6.00	12.	50.	75.	*	*	*	*	*	*	*	*	*	*	*
1998-S	*	*	*	*	*	*	*	*	*	*	*	*	*	*	*	7.00	3.00	—	6.00	—	—	—	12.	—	15.	25.
1999	—	—	—	—	—	—	—	0.15	—	5.00	—	6.00	10.	25.	100.	*	*	*	*	*	*	*	*	*	*	*
1999-D	—	—	—	—	—	—	—	0.15	—	5.00	—	6.00	10.	25.	100.	*	*	*	*	*	*	*	*	*	*	*
1999-S	*	*	*	*	*	*	*	*	*	*	*	*	*	*	*	5.00	6.00	—	6.00	—	—	—	12.	—	15.	25.
2000	—	—	—	—	—	—	—	0.15	—	5.00	—	6.00	9.00	25.	80.	*	*	*	*	*	*	*	*	*	*	*
2000-D	—	—	—	—	—	—	—	0.15	—	5.00	—	6.00	9.00	25.	80.	*	*	*	*	*	*	*	*	*	*	*
2000-S	*	*	*	*	*	*	*	*	*	*	*	*	*	*	*	2.50	4.00	—	6.00	—	—	—	12.	—	15.	25.
2001	—	—	—	—	—	—	—	0.15	—	5.00	—	6.00	9.00	25.	80.	*	*	*	*	*	*	*	*	*	*	*
2001-D	—	—	—	—	—	—	—	0.15	—	5.00	—	6.00	20.	45.	150.	*	*	*	*	*	*	*	*	*	*	*
2001-S	*	*	*	*	*	*	*	*	*	*	*	*	*	*	*	3.00	4.00	—	7.50	—	—	—	15.	—	18.	60.
2002	—	—	—	—	—	—	—	0.15	—	5.00	—	6.00	9.00	25.	80.	*	*	*	*	*	*	*	*	*	*	*
2002-D	—	—	—	—	—	—	—	0.15	—	5.00	—	6.00	9.00	25.	80.	*	*	*	*	*	*	*	*	*	*	*

—— = Insufficient pricing data * = None issued

	G-4	VG-8	F-12	VF-20	EF-40	AU-50	MS-60B	MS-63RB	MS-64RB	MS-64R	MS-65RB	MS-65R	MS-66R	MS-67R	MS-68R	PF-63RB	PF-64RB	PF-65C	PF-65R	PF-66	PF-66DC	PF-66R	PF-67DC	PF-67R	PF-68DC	PF-69DC
2002-S	*	*	*	*	*	*	*	*	*	*	*	*	*	*	*	3.00	4.00	—	—	—	—	—	15.	—	17.	42.
2003	—	—	—	—	—	—	—	0.15	—	5.00	—	6.00	9.00	25.	80.	—	—	—	—	—	—	—	—	—	—	—
2003-D	—	—	—	—	—	—	—	0.15	—	5.00	—	6.00	9.00	25.	80.	—	—	—	—	—	—	—	—	—	—	—
2003-S	—	—	—	—	—	—	—	—	—	—	—	—	—	—	—	3.00	4.00	—	—	—	—	—	15.	—	17.	42.
2004	—	—	—	—	—	—	—	0.15	—	5.00	—	6.00	9.00	25.	80.	—	—	—	—	—	—	—	—	—	—	—
2004-D	—	—	—	—	—	—	—	0.15	—	5.00	—	6.00	9.00	25.	80.	—	—	—	—	—	—	—	—	—	—	—
2004-S	—	—	—	—	—	—	—	—	—	—	—	—	—	—	—	3.00	4.00	—	—	—	—	—	15.	—	17.	42.

—— = Insufficient pricing data * = None issued

2 cents

Date of authorization: April 22, 1864
Dates of issue: 1864-1872
Designer/Engraver: James B. Longacre
Diameter: 23.00 mm/0.91 inch
Weight: 6.22 grams/0.20 ounce
Metallic content: 95% copper, 5% zinc and tin
Edge: Plain
Mint mark: None

Note: For copper-alloy coins, the letter B following a numerical grade (as in MS-63B) is shorthand for brown, RB represents red and brown, and R stands for red. It is common practice for grading services to qualify copper coins. In addition to a Mint State grade, a copper coin is assigned as brown, red and brown, or red. Generally, full red coins are valued higher than red and brown coins, which in turn are valued higher than brown coins, all else being equal.

	F-12	VF-20	EF-40	AU-50	MS-60B	MS-63RB	MS-64RB	MS-65R	PF-63RB	PF-65R
1864 Small Motto	200.	350.	600.	700.	800.	1000.	1300.	3000.	18000.	75000.
1864 Large Motto	25.	30.	40.	75.	100.	165.	275.	1500.	650.	4000.
1865	25.	30.	40.	75.	100.	165.	275.	1500.	450.	3000.
1866	25.	35.	40.	75.	100.	165.	275.	2000.	450.	2100.
1867	35.	45.	50.	100.	125.	175.	300.	2000.	450.	2600.
1868	35.	45.	60.	110.	140.	200.	300.	2500.	450.	2100.
1869	35.	45.	60.	125.	175.	200.	400.	2000.	450.	2100.
1870	35.	50.	90.	150.	250.	300.	600.	2500.	450.	2300.
1871	40.	60.	125.	175.	250.	425.	800.	2500.	475.	2100.
1872	400.	700.	800.	900.	1000.	1300.	2000.	3500.	550.	2300.
1873 Closed 3 Proofs Only	1400.	1500.	1600.	1700.	*	*	*	*	2000.	3000.
1873 Open 3 Restrike Proofs Only	—	—	—	—	*	*	*	*	2500.	6000.
1873 Open 3 Restrike Proofs Only	—	—	—	—	—	—	—	—	2500.	6000.

—— = Insufficient pricing data

Copper-nickel 3 cents

Date of authorization: April 22, 1864
Dates of issue: 1865-1889
Designer/Engraver: James B. Longacre
Diameter: 17.90 mm/0.71 inch
Weight: 1.94 grams/0.06 ounce
Metallic content: 75% copper, 25% nickel
Edge: Plain
Mint mark: None

	F-12	VF-20	EF-40	AU-50	MS-60	MS-63	MS-64	MS-65	MS-66
1865	18.	23.	30.	50.	100.	175.	300.	700.	1500.
1866	18.	23.	30.	50.	100.	175.	300.	700.	—
1867	18.	23.	30.	50.	100.	175.	300.	900.	—
1868	18.	23.	30.	50.	100.	175.	300.	700.	1500.
1869	18.	23.	30.	60.	125.	200.	300.	800.	1700.
1870	18.	23.	30.	60.	125.	200.	300.	800.	2000.
1871	20.	25.	35.	60.	125.	200.	300.	850.	1700.
1872	20.	25.	35.	60.	125.	250.	350.	1200.	2000.
1873 Closed 3	20.	30.	50.	85.	175.	275.	450.	2000.	—
1873 Open 3	20.	30.	50.	85.	200.	350.	750.	3000.	—
1874	20.	25.	35.	60.	125.	200.	400.	1400.	2500.
1875	20.	30.	40.	75.	165.	200.	350.	900.	1700.
1876	22.	35.	40.	90.	185.	300.	600.	2000.	3000.
1877 (Proofs only)	1100.	1200.	1300.	1500.	*	*	*	*	*
1878 (Proofs only)	500.	550.	600.	700.	*	*	*	*	*
1879	80.	90.	100.	135.	250.	350.	500.	900.	1500.
1880	100.	125.	140.	180.	300.	400.	450.	900.	1500.
1881	18.	23.	30.	50.	100.	200.	300.	750.	1400.
1882	100.	125.	140.	175.	250.	450.	600.	1200.	2000.
1883	225.	275.	325.	400.	500.	1000.	2000.	5000.	8500.
1884	500.	600.	700.	800.	1000.	1500.	2500.	6500.	—
1885	600.	650.	750.	900.	1100.	1200.	1500.	3000.	—
1886 (Proofs only)	350.	400.	450.	500.	*	*	*	*	*
1887/6 (Proofs only)	400.	450.	500.	550.	*	*	*	*	*
1887	300.	350.	400.	600.	750.	900.	1200.	1500.	2000.
1888	75.	85.	100.	150.	300.	400.	500.	900.	1200.
1889	110.	125.	140.	175.	300.	450.	600.	900.	1500.

—— = Insufficient pricing data * = None issued

Silver 3 cents

Date of authorization: March 3, 1851
Dates of issue: 1851-1873
Designer/Engraver: James B. Longacre
Diameter: 14.00 mm/0.55 inch
Weight: (1851-1853): 0.80 grams/0.03 ounce
(1854-1873): 0.75 grams/0.02 ounce
Metallic content: (1851-1853): 75% silver, 25% copper
(1854-1873): 90% silver, 10% copper
Weight of pure silver: (1851-1853): 0.60 grams/0.02 ounce
(1854-1873): 0.67 grams/0.02 ounce
Edge: Plain
Mint mark: 1851-O only, reverse right field

	VG-8	F-12	VF-20	EF-40	AU-50	MS-60	MS-63	MS-64	MS-65	MS-66	PF-65
1 OUTLINE OF STAR											
1851	30.	35.	40.	65.	150.	200.	300.	500.	1000.	2000.	—
1851-O	50.	60.	100.	150.	300.	400.	500.	1200.	2500.	8500.	*
1852	30.	35.	40.	65.	150.	200.	300.	500.	1000.	2000.	*
1853	30.	35.	40.	75.	175.	250.	350.	650.	1200.	2500.	*
3 OUTLINES OF STAR											
1854	30.	35.	50.	125.	300.	400.	800.	2000.	3500.	6000.	40000.
1855	75.	90.	125.	200.	350.	750.	1500.	3000.	11000.	—	18000.
1856	30.	35.	50.	100.	225.	350.	800.	1800.	3700.	9000.	18000.
1857	30.	35.	50.	100.	250.	375.	800.	1800.	3500.	—	15000.
1858	30.	35.	50.	100.	225.	350.	800.	1800.	3500.	7500.	8000.
2 OUTLINES OF STAR											
1859	30.	35.	40.	75.	150.	200.	325.	500.	1200.	2500.	2500.
1860	30.	35.	40.	85.	150.	200.	375.	500.	1200.	2500.	4500.
1861	30.	35.	40	75.	150.	200.	300	500.	1000.	1800.	2100.
1862	30.	35.	40.	75.	150.	200.	300	500.	1000.	1800.	2000.
1862/1	35.	40.	50.	85.	175.	250.	375.	800.	1000.	1800.	—
1863	350.	400.	450.	500.	600.	700.	1200.	1500.	2500.	3500.	1500.
1863/2 (Proofs only)	500.	600.	700.	900.	1100.	*	*	*	*	*	6000.
1864	350.	400.	450.	500.	600.	700.	1200.	1500.	2000.	3000.	1500.
1865	350.	400.	450.	500.	600.	700.	1200.	1500.	2000.	3500.	1500.
1866	350.	400.	450.	500.	600.	700.	1200.	1500	2000.	3000.	1500.
1867	350.	400.	450.	500.	600.	700.	1400.	1800.	3000.	6500.	1500.
1868	350.	400.	450.	500.	600.	700.	1400.	2500.	6000.	8500.	1500.
1869	350.	400.	450.	500.	600.	700.	1200.	1600.	3000.	6000.	1500.

—— = Insufficient pricing data * = None issued

SILVER 3 CENTS (CONTINUED)

	VG-8	F-12	VF-20	EF-40	AU-50	MS-60	MS-63	MS-64	MS-65	MS-66	PF-65
1869/8 (Proofs only)	—	—	—	—	625.	*	*	*	*	*	6000.
1870	350.	400.	450.	500.	600.	800.	1200.	1500.	5000.	6500.	1500.
1871	350.	400.	450.	500.	600.	700.	1200.	1500.	2000.	3000.	1500.
1872	400.	425.	450.	500.	750.	1000.	1600.	2500.	6000.	11000.	1800.
1873 Closed 3 (Proofs only)	700.	750.	800.	850.	900.	*	*	*	*	*	2000.

Enlarged to show detail

One outline of star

Three outlines Two outlines

—— = Insufficient pricing data * = None issued

Shield 5 cents

Rays removed

Date of authorization:	May 16, 1866
Dates of issue:	1866-1883
Designer/Engraver:	James B. Longacre
Diameter:	20.50 mm/0.81 inch
Weight:	5.00 grams/0.16 ounce
Metallic content:	75% copper, 25% nickel
Edge:	Plain
Mint mark:	None

SHIELD 5 CENTS (CONTINUED)

	G-4	VG-8	F-12	VF-20	EF-40	AU-50	MS-60	MS-63	MS-64	MS-65	MS-66	PF-63	PF-64	PF-65	PF-66
1866	25.	35.	45.	60.	175.	225.	250.	400.	800.	2500.	6000.	2500.	3500.	5000.	6500.
1867	35.	45.	60.	85.	200.	300.	350.	500.	1100.	4000.	7500.	35000.	50000.	80000.	—
RAYS REMOVED FROM REVERSE															
1867	18.	20.	25.	30.	40.	75.	100.	200.	350.	900.	2500.	700.	1800.	4000.	5000.
1868	18.	20.	25.	30.	40.	75.	100.	200.	350.	900.	2500.	400.	800.	1500.	2500.
1869	18.	20.	25.	30.	40.	75.	100.	200.	350.	900.	2500.	500.	700.	1500.	2500.
1870	20.	25.	35.	45.	70.	125.	150.	300.	500.	1500.	3000.	400.	700.	1500.	2500.
1871	55.	65.	85.	125.	200.	250.	300.	600.	900.	1500.	2500.	400.	700.	1500.	2000.
1872	20.	25.	35.	50.	65.	110.	175.	325.	700.	1200.	2500.	400.	700.	1200.	1800.
1873 Closed 3	25.	30.	40.	75.	125.	150.	250.	500.	1000.	2000.	3500.	400.	700.	1200.	1800.
1873 Open 3	20.	25.	35.	50.	65.	100.	175.	300.	500.	1500.	2500.	*	*	*	*
1874	25.	35.	50.	60.	80.	110.	175.	325.	550.	1700.	3000.	400.	750.	1500.	2000.
1875	30.	35.	60.	90.	125.	150.	200.	400.	600.	2000.	3500.	400.	900.	2000.	2500.
1876	25.	30.	55.	70.	100.	125.	185.	300.	400.	1200.	3000.	400.	700.	1200.	1800.
1877 (Proofs only)	1300.	1400.	1500.	1800.	2000.	2300.	*	*	*	*	*	2500.	3000.	3500.	5000.
1878 (Proofs only)	600.	650.	700.	850.	1000.	1100.	*	*	*	*	*	1200.	1500.	2000.	2500.
1879	350.	450.	500.	600.	700.	800.	900.	1100.	1400.	2000.	2500.	500.	800.	1200.	1800.
1880	400.	500.	600.	750.	1200.	1800.	3500.	7500.	15000.	25000.	—	400.	500.	700.	1200.
1881	250.	300.	350.	450.	700.	800.	900.	1100.	1400.	2000.	2500.	400.	500.	700.	1200.
1882	18.	20.	25.	30.	40.	75.	125.	200.	300.	750.	2000.	400.	500.	700.	1200.
1883/2	135.	200.	250.	300.	450.	600.	700.	1000.	1500.	5000.	7500.	*	*	*	*
1883	18.	20.	30.	35.	50.	80.	125.	200.	300.	750.	2000.	400.	500.	700.	1200.

—— = Insufficient pricing data * = None issued

Liberty Head 5 cents

No CENTS — With CENTS

Date of authorization:	May 16, 1866
Dates of issue:	1883-1912
Designer/Engraver:	Charles Barber
Diameter:	21.21 mm/0.84 inch
Weight:	5.00 grams/0.16 ounce
Metallic content:	75% copper, 25% nickel
Edge:	Plain
Mint mark:	1912 only, reverse left of CENTS

LIBERTY HEAD 5 CENTS (CONTINUED)

	VG-8	F-12	VF-20	EF-40	AU-50	MS-60	MS-63	MS-64	MS-65	MS-66	PF-63	PF-64	PF-65	PF-66
1883	6.00	7.00	8.00	10.	14.	30.	50.	75.	250.	750.	350.	600.	1200.	2000.
CENTS ADDED BELOW WREATH ON REVERSE														
1883	15.	25.	35.	65.	75.	100.	150.	300.	700.	1200.	300.	400.	700.	1500.
1884	25.	30.	40.	75.	100.	175.	250.	400.	2500.	4000.	250.	400.	700.	1500.
1885	500.	700.	800.	1000.	1200.	1400.	2000.	2500.	5000.	7000.	1000.	1500.	2000.	2500.
1886	300.	400.	500.	650.	800.	900.	1200.	1700.	5000.	8500.	500.	600.	800.	1800.
1887	15.	30.	40.	75.	90.	125.	200.	350.	1200.	2500.	200.	400.	700.	1500.
1888	30.	45.	85.	125.	175.	250.	300.	400.	1800.	5000.	200.	400.	700.	1500.
1889	12.	25.	35.	65.	100.	125.	200.	350.	1000.	2500.	200.	400.	700.	1500.
1890	18.	25.	35.	65.	110.	175.	250.	500.	2000.	3000.	200.	400.	700.	1500.
1891	9.00	20.	25.	50.	100.	150.	200.	300.	1400.	2000.	200.	400.	700.	1500.
1892	9.00	20.	25.	50.	100.	140.	175.	300.	1400.	2500.	200.	400.	700.	1500.
1893	9.00	20.	25.	50.	100.	140.	175.	300.	1400.	2500.	200.	400.	700.	1500.
1894	20.	90.	125.	200.	250.	300.	400.	700.	1800.	2500.	200.	400.	700.	1500.
1895	6.00	25.	40.	65.	100.	140.	200.	350.	2000.	3000.	200.	400.	700.	1500.
1896	15.	35.	45.	75.	125.	150.	250.	400.	2000.	3500.	200.	400.	700.	1500.
1897	5.00	12.	20.	40.	75.	100.	175.	350.	1500.	2500.	200.	400.	700.	1500.
1898	5.00	12.	20.	40.	75.	140.	200.	250.	1400.	2000.	200.	400.	700.	1500.
1899	3.00	8.00	14.	30.	60.	100.	135.	250.	750.	1500.	200.	400.	700.	1500.
1900	3.00	8.00	14.	30.	75.	100.	135.	250.	750.	1500.	200.	400.	700.	1500.
1901	3.00	5.00	14.	30.	55.	80.	125.	250.	750.	1800.	200.	400.	700.	1500.
1902	3.00	5.00	14.	30.	55.	80.	125.	250.	750.	1800.	200.	400.	700.	1500.
1903	3.00	5.00	14.	30.	55.	80.	125.	250.	750.	1800.	200.	400.	700.	1500.
1904	3.00	5.00	12.	30.	55.	80.	125.	250.	750.	1800.	200.	400.	700.	1500.
1905	3.00	5.00	12.	30.	55.	80.	125.	250.	750.	1800.	200.	400.	700.	1500.
1906	3.00	5.00	12.	30.	55.	80.	125.	250.	750.	2500.	200.	400.	700.	1500.
1907	3.00	5.00	12.	30.	55.	80.	125.	300.	1000.	2500.	200.	400.	700.	1500.
1908	3.00	5.00	12.	30.	55.	80.	125.	250.	1000.	2500.	200.	400.	700.	1500.

—— = Insufficient pricing data * = None issued

LIBERTY HEAD 5 CENTS (CONTINUED)

	VG-8	F-12	VF-20	EF-40	AU-50	MS-60	MS-63	MS-64	MS-65	MS-66	PF-63	PF-64	PF-65	PF-66
1909	3.00	5.50	12.	30.	65.	90.	150.	300.	1000.	2000.	200.	400.	700.	1500.
1910	3.00	5.00	12.	25.	50.	65.	125.	250.	800.	2500.	200.	400.	700.	1500.
1911	3.00	5.00	12.	25.	50.	65.	125.	250.	750.	1800.	200.	400.	700.	1500.
1912	3.00	5.00	12.	25.	50.	65.	125.	250.	750.	1800.	200.	400.	700.	1500.
1912-D	4.00	8.00	30.	75.	150.	300.	400.	600.	1800.	3000.	*	*	*	*
1912-S	200.	300.	500.	800.	1300.	1500.	1800.	2500.	5000.	7500.	*	*	*	*
1913	Eliasberg Specimen Proof 66 (NGC) sold for $3 million in August 2003.													

—— = Insufficient pricing data * = None issued

Indian Head 5 cents

Bison on Mound Bison on Plain

"Buffalo nickel"

Date of authorization:	May 16, 1866
Dates of issue:	1913-1938
Designer:	James Earle Fraser
Engraver:	Charles Barber
Diameter:	21.21 mm/0.84 inch
Weight:	5.00 grams/0.16 ounce
Metallic content:	75% copper, 25% nickel
Edge:	Plain
Mint mark:	Reverse below FIVE CENTS

—— = Insufficient pricing data

INDIAN HEAD 5 CENTS (CONTINUED)

	G-4	VG-8	F-12	VF-20	EF-40	AU-50	MS-60	MS-63	MS-64	MS-65	MS-66	PF-63	PF-64	PF-65	PF-66
BISON STANDING ON MOUND															
1913	8.00	11.	13.	15.	20.	25.	35.	50.	75.	150.	350.	1200.	2500.	4000.	5000.
1913-D	12.	15.	20.	25.	35.	50.	60.	75.	125.	350.	1000.	*	*	*	*
1913-S	35.	40.	45.	55.	75.	85.	100.	150.	500.	1000.	2000.	*	*	*	*
BISON STANDING ON PLAIN															
1913	9.00	10.	12.	14.	20.	25.	35.	60.	100.	350.	1500.	1200.	2000.	3000.	4000.
1913-D	90.	125.	150.	175.	200.	250.	300.	400.	600.	1300.	4500.	*	*	*	*
1913-S	250.	325.	350.	400.	450.	500.	600.	1000.	2000.	5000.	10000.	*	*	*	*
1914	18.	20.	25.	30.	35.	40.	50.	100.	250.	550.	1500.	1200.	2000.	3000.	4000.
1914/3	200.	350.	450.	700.	1000.	2000.	3500.	10000.	20000.	35000.	—	*	*	*	*
1914-D	75.	100.	125.	150.	250.	300.	400.	500.	1500.	3000.	4000.	*	*	*	*
1914-S	20.	30.	40.	50.	75.	125.	200.	500.	1000.	3000.	7500.	*	*	*	*
1915	5.00	6.00	7.00	11.	20.	40.	50.	85.	140.	350.	1000.	1000.	2000.	2500.	3500.
1915-D	15.	20.	35.	50.	125.	150.	250.	350.	600.	4000.	8000.	*	*	*	*
1915-S	30.	40.	75.	140.	250.	400.	500.	800.	1500.	3500.	7500.	*	*	*	*
1916 Doubled Die	2000.	4000.	6500.	9000.	15000.	30000.	45000.	135000.	275000.	300000.	—	*	*	*	*
1916-D	10.	15.	20.	35.	85.	110.	175.	300.	750.	3500.	15000.	*	*	*	*
1916-S	6.00	10.	15.	30.	65.	110.	200.	300.	600.	3500.	6000.	*	*	*	*
1916	4.00	5.00	6.00	7.00	10.	18.	45.	75.	125.	750.	1500.	1500.	2500.	4000.	5500.
1917	4.00	5.00	6.00	8.00	15.	30.	60.	150.	250.	750.	1500.	*	*	*	*
1917-D	15.	20.	35.	75.	150.	250.	400.	800.	2000.	4500.	20000.	*	*	*	*
1917-S	20.	35.	65.	100.	200.	300.	400.	1500.	2500.	6000.	14000.	*	*	*	*
1918	4.00	5.00	6.00	12.	30.	50.	100.	500.	1000.	2000.	4000.	*	*	*	*
1918/7-D	1200.	2000.	3000.	6000.	10000.	13000.	30000.	60000.	125000.	250000.	—	*	*	*	*
1918-D	15.	25.	40.	125.	250.	350.	400.	1200.	2000.	5000.	10000.	*	*	*	*
1918-S	12.	25.	40.	100.	200.	300.	650.	3000.	8500.	30000.	50000.	*	*	*	*

—— = Insufficient pricing data   * = None issued

INDIAN HEAD 5 CENTS (CONTINUED)

	G-4	VG-8	F-12	VF-20	EF-40	AU-50	MS-60	MS-63	MS-64	MS-65	MS-66	PF-63	PF-64	PF-65	PF-66
1919	2.00	2.50	3.00	6.00	12.	30.	45.	100.	250.	750.	1800.	*	*	*	*
1919-D	15.	25.	50.	125.	300.	400.	600.	1800.	3000.	8500.	12000.	*	*	*	*
1919-S	8.00	20.	40.	125.	300.	400.	600.	2500.	5000.	20000.	40000.	*	*	*	*
1920	2.00	2.50	3.00	6.00	12.	30.	50.	150.	400.	1200.	3000.	*	*	*	*
1920-D	7.00	15.	30.	125.	300.	400.	600.	2000.	3500.	8500.	25000.	*	*	*	*
1920-S	4.00	7.00	20.	100.	200.	300.	500.	1800.	6000.	32500.	45000.	*	*	*	*
1921	3.00	4.00	6.00	20.	50.	75.	125.	300.	500.	1000.	2000.	*	*	*	*
1921-S	65.	125.	200.	600.	1000.	1400.	1800.	2500.	4000.	12000.	20000.	*	*	*	*
1923	2.00	2.50	3.00	6.00	15.	35.	50.	150.	250.	750.	1200.	*	*	*	*
1923-S	6.00	8.00	18.	150.	300.	350.	500.	1000.	3500.	15000.	45000.	*	*	*	*
1924	2.00	3.00	5.00	10.	20.	45.	75.	250.	1000.	2500.	3500.	*	*	*	*
1924-D	6.00	8.00	30.	85.	250.	350.	400.	1500.	2000.	6000.	25000.	*	*	*	*
1924-S	14.	30.	100.	500.	1400.	2000.	2500.	4500.	6000.	15000.	40000.	*	*	*	*
1925	3.00	3.50	4.00	7.00	15.	35.	50.	125.	250.	750.	2500.	*	*	*	*
1925-D	10.	20.	40.	100.	200.	300.	450.	800.	2000.	7500.	25000.	*	*	*	*
1925-S	5.00	10.	20.	100.	200.	300.	500.	2000.	5000.	45000.	—	*	*	*	*
1926	1.00	1.50	2.50	4.00	10.	20.	35.	70.	100.	200.	700.	*	*	*	*
1926-D	6.00	12.	25.	100.	200.	275.	350.	600.	2000.	6000.	12000.	*	*	*	*
1926-S	18.	35.	75.	500.	1000.	3000.	4500.	8000.	15000.	100000.	—	*	*	*	*
1927	1.00	1.50	2.50	4.00	10.	20.	35.	75.	100.	300.	800.	*	*	*	*
1927-D	3.00	5.00	10.	30.	80.	125.	175.	300.	1000.	9000.	—	*	*	*	*
1927-S	2.00	3.00	5.00	35.	100.	175.	500.	3000.	9000.	20000.	—	*	*	*	*
1928	1.50	2.00	3.00	5.00	10.	25.	35.	75.	150.	500.	2000.	*	*	*	*
1928-D	2.00	3.00	4.00	18.	45.	50.	60.	100.	150.	1000.	6500.	*	*	*	*
1928-S	2.00	2.50	3.00	12.	30.	100.	250.	700.	1500.	7000.	25000.	*	*	*	*
1929	1.00	1.50	2.50	4.00	10.	20.	35.	75.	125.	400.	2500.	*	*	*	*
1929-D	1.50	2.00	3.00	8.00	35.	45.	65.	125.	350.	2000.	4500.	*	*	*	*

—— = Insufficient pricing data   * = None issued

INDIAN HEAD 5 CENTS (CONTINUED)

	G-4	VG-8	F-12	VF-20	EF-40	AU-50	MS-60	MS-63	MS-64	MS-65	MS-66	PF-63	PF-64	PF-65	PF-66
1929-S	1.00	1.50	2.00	2.50	12.	25.	50.	85.	200.	600.	2000.	*	*	*	*
1930	1.00	1.50	3.00	4.00	10.	20.	35.	75.	100.	250.	600.	*	*	*	*
1930-S	1.00	2.00	3.00	4.00	15.	30.	50.	125.	300.	800.	2500.	*	*	*	*
1931-S	14.	16.	18.	20.	25.	40.	50.	80.	125.	400.	1800.	*	*	*	*
1934	1.00	2.00	3.00	4.00	10.	20.	50.	65.	125.	400.	700.	*	*	*	*
1934-D	1.00	2.00	3.00	6.00	15.	45.	75.	100.	400.	1200.	7000.	*	*	*	*
1935	1.00	1.50	2.00	2.50	3.00	9.00	20.	40.	65.	125.	300.	*	*	*	*
1935 Doubled Die	40.	50.	100.	200.	500.	1500.	3000.	7000.	20000.	35000.	—	*	*	*	*
1935-D	1.00	1.50	2.50	6.00	15.	40.	65.	75.	150.	1000.	3500.	*	*	*	*
1935-S	1.00	1.50	2.00	2.50	4.00	17.	50.	75.	100.	200.	800.	*	*	*	*
1936	1.00	1.50	2.00	2.50	3.00	9.00	35.	45.	50.	100.	150.	—	—	—	—
1936-D	1.00	1.50	2.00	2.50	4.00	12.	40.	50.	55.	100.	250.	*	*	*	*
1936-S	1.00	1.50	2.00	2.50	3.00	12.	40.	50.	55.	125.	250.	*	*	*	*
1936 Satin Proof	*	*	*	*	*	*	*	*	*	*	*	1500.	2000.	2700.	3500.
1936-D 3 and one half legs	300.	500.	600.	1000.	1200.	—	—	—	—	—	—	*	*	*	*
1936 Brilliant Proof	*	*	*	*	*	*	*	*	*	*	*	1800.	2500.	3000.	4000.
1937	1.00	1.50	2.00	2.50	3.00	9.00	18.	35.	40.	60.	100.	1200.	1700.	2500.	3500.
1937-D	1.00	1.50	2.00	2.50	3.00	10.	30.	40.	45.	70.	125.	*	*	*	*
1937-D 3 Legs	300.	500.	600.	700	800.	1200.	2000.	6000.	10000.	30000.	80000.	*	*	*	*
1937-S	1.00	1.50	2.00	2.50	3.00	10.	30.	40.	40.	75.	150.	*	*	*	*
1938-D	2.00	2.50	3.00	3.50	4.00	10.	20.	30.	40.	50.	100.	*	*	*	*
1938-D/D	2.00	3.00	5.00	7.00	10.	15.	30.	45.	60.	75.	—	*	*	*	*
1938-D/S	5.00	8.00	12.	15.	18.	30.	50.	75.	135.	200.	500.	*	*	*	*

—— = Insufficient pricing data   * = None issued

Jefferson 5 cents

Date of authorization:	May 16, 1866; March 27, 1942; April 23, 2003
Dates of issue:	1938-present
Designer:	Felix Schlag; Peace Medal reverse, Norman E. Kenneth; Keelboat reverse, Al Maletsky
Engraver:	John R. Sinnock
Diameter:	21.21 mm/0.84 inch
Weight:	5.00 grams/0.16 ounce
Metallic content:	(1938-1942): 75% copper, 25% nickel (1942-1945): 56% copper, 35% silver, 9% manganese (1946-present): 75% copper, 25% nickel
Weight of pure silver:	(1942-1945): 1.75 grams/0.06 ounce
Edge:	Plain
Mint mark:	(1938-1942, 1946-1964): Reverse right of building (1942-1945, silver): Reverse above dome (1968-present): Obverse below Jefferson's ponytail

The letters FS following a numerical grade stand for Full Steps. They refer to fully formed, undamaged steps on Monticello on the reverse of 1938 to 2003 Jefferson 5-cent coins.

Also, the letter C following a numerical grade for a Proof coin stands for "cameo," while the letters DC stand for "deep cameo." Cameo coins have contrasting surface finishes: mirror fields and frosted devices (raised areas). Deep cameo coins are the ultimate level of cameo, with deeply frosted devices. Cameo and deep cameo coins bring premiums.

Peace Medal reverse

Keelboat reverse

	VG-8	F-12	VF-20	EF-40	AU-50	MS-60	MS-63	MS-64	MS-65	MS-65FS	MS-66	MS-66FS	PF-63	PF-64	PF-65	PF-65DC	PF-66	PF-66C	PF-66DC	PF-67	PF-67C	PF-67DC	PF-68DC	PF-69DC
COPPER-NICKEL																								
1938	0.15	0.35	0.45	0.65	0.90	2.25	2.75	5.00	30.	200.	65.	—	60.	110.	125.	—	225.	—	—	450.	—	—	—	—
1938-D	0.65	0.70	1.00	1.75	2.25	3.50	5.00	7.00	15.	—	40.	110.	*	*	*	*	*	*	*	*	*	*	*	*
1938-S	1.35	1.75	2.05	2.75	3.50	4.00	5.00	8.00	16.	250.	45.	—	*	*	*	*	*	*	*	*	*	*	*	*
1939	0.08	0.18	0.25	0.45	0.75	1.35	2.50	5.00	20.	40.	25.	140.	45.	100.	125.	—	375.	—	—	2415.	—	—	—	—
1939 Doubled Monticello	24.	40.	60.	70.	125.	165.	300.	400.	575.	—	800.	—	*	*	*	*	*	*	*	*	*	*	*	*
1939-D	3.50	4.00	5.00	9.00	20.	35.	45.	55.	80.	—	125.	—	*	*	*	*	*	*	*	*	*	*	*	*
1939-S	0.75	1.00	1.75	3.25	8.50	15.	22.	25.	35.	335.	150.	—	*	*	*	*	*	*	*	*	*	*	*	*
1939	—	—	—	—	—	—	—	—	—	—	—	—	45.	—	70.	—	—	—	—	—	—	—	—	—
1940	0.08	0.10	0.20	0.25	0.60	0.75	1.35	5.00	12.	90.	17.	200.	45.	90.	115.	—	175.	—	—	550.	—	—	—	—
1940-D	0.13	0.20	0.30	0.50	1.45	2.25	2.75	5.00	15.	40.	27.	70.	*	*	*	*	*	*	*	*	*	*	*	*
1940-S	0.14	0.20	0.35	0.55	1.00	1.90	3.35	5.00	10.	60.	25.	275.	*	*	*	*	*	*	*	*	*	*	*	*
1941	0.08	0.10	0.20	0.30	0.40	0.65	1.25	7.00	12.	60.	20.	105.	40.	75.	110.	—	175.	—	—	500.	—	—	—	—
1941-D	0.10	0.15	0.30	0.55	1.40	2.15	3.00	6.00	8.00	40.	35.	80.	*	*	*	*	*	*	*	*	*	*	*	*
1941-S	0.10	0.15	0.30	0.60	1.75	2.75	4.00	5.00	13.	60.	25.	—	*	*	*	*	*	*	*	*	*	*	*	*
1942	0.10	0.15	0.20	0.45	0.70	1.25	4.25	6.00	30.	100.	50.	—	45.	90.	115.	—	150.	—	—	250.	—	—	—	—
1942-D	0.35	0.45	1.25	2.75	7.00	14.	17.	19.	35.	60.	60.	90.	*	*	*	*	*	*	*	*	*	*	*	*
1942-D/Horizontal D	—	30.	45.	—	—	475.	750.	1550.	2850	—	—	—	*	*	*	*	*	*	*	*	*	*	*	*
SILVER																								
1942-P	0.35	0.65	0.75	1.10	3.00	5.25	8.00	9.00	12.	60.	22.	120.	125.	175.	225.	—	250.	1850.	—	400.	—	—	—	—
1942-S	0.45	1.00	1.45	2.00	2.75	5.00	9.00	14.	25.	200.	50.	235.	*	*	*	*	*	*	*	*	*	*	*	*
1943/2-P	35.	42.	65.	90.	160.	250.	300.	425.	650.	1150.	850.	—	*	*	*	*	*	*	*	*	*	*	*	*
1943-P	0.35	0.60	0.75	1.10	1.75	2.75	4.00	7.00	16.	35.	26.	125.	*	*	*	*	*	*	*	*	*	*	*	*

—— = Insufficient pricing data * = None issued

JEFFERSON 5 CENTS (CONTINUED)

	VG-8	F-12	VF-20	EF-40	AU-50	MS-60	MS-63	MS-64	MS-65	MS-65FS	MS-66	MS-66FS	PF-63	PF-64	PF-65	PF-65DC	PF-66	PF-66C	PF-66DC	PF-67	PF-67C	PF-67DC	PF-68DC	PF-69DC
1943-P Doubled Eye	17.	24.	30.	49.	88.	115.	150.	250.	400.	—	750.	—	*	*	*	*	*	*	*	*	*	*	*	*
1943-D	0.55	0.75	1.00	1.50	2.10	2.50	4.00	11.	10.	50.	25.	75.	*	*	*	*	*	*	*	*	*	*	*	*
1943-S	0.35	0.60	0.75	1.10	1.75	2.90	5.00	10.	13.	45.	26.	120.	*	*	*	*	*	*	*	*	*	*	*	*
1944-P	0.40	0.65	0.80	1.15	2.00	2.75	4.00	6.00	25.	60.	52.	—	*	*	*	*	*	*	*	*	*	*	*	*
1944-D	0.50	0.85	1.00	1.80	3.00	6.50	9.00	10.	20.	40.	30.	60.	*	*	*	*	*	*	*	*	*	*	*	*
1944-S	0.60	0.90	1.25	1.90	3.00	3.75	4.75	7.00	16.	75.	40.	—	*	*	*	*	*	*	*	*	*	*	*	*
1945-P	0.40	0.65	0.80	1.50	2.00	2.65	4.75	7.00	20.	125.	35.	380.	*	*	*	*	*	*	*	*	*	*	*	*
1945-P Doubled Die	—	15.	20.	30.	48.	75.	120.	200.	450.	—	700.	—	*	*	*	*	*	*	*	*	*	*	*	*
1945-D	0.60	1.00	1.35	1.75	2.35	2.65	4.00	7.00	20.	40.	30.	75.	*	*	*	*	*	*	*	*	*	*	*	*
1945-S	0.35	0.55	0.70	1.25	1.50	2.15	3.75	6.00	16.	150.	25.	—	*	*	*	*	*	*	*	*	*	*	*	*
COPPER-NICKEL																								
1946	0.08	0.07	0.15	0.20	0.30	0.50	0.70	5.00	10.	215.	20.	—	*	*	*	*	*	*	*	*	*	*	*	*
1946-D	0.07	0.10	0.15	0.30	0.45	0.55	0.80	7.00	14.	25.	35.	120.	*	*	*	*	*	*	*	*	*	*	*	*
1946-D/Horizontal D	42.	65.	80.	140.	225.	275.	400.	650.	1350.	—	—	—	*	*	*	*	*	*	*	*	*	*	*	*
1946-S	0.10	0.20	0.25	0.35	0.40	0.50	0.55	5.00	11.	125.	30.	350.	*	*	*	*	*	*	*	*	*	*	*	*
1947	0.08	0.07	0.15	0.20	0.30	0.55	0.95	5.00	10.	45.	15.	185.	*	*	*	*	*	*	*	*	*	*	*	*
1947-D	0.06	0.08	0.15	0.40	0.60	0.70	1.20	5.00	20.	25.	25.	115.	*	*	*	*	*	*	*	*	*	*	*	*
1947-S	0.06	0.08	0.15	0.25	0.30	0.35	0.45	10.	18.	100.	25.	800.	*	*	*	*	*	*	*	*	*	*	*	*
1948	0.07	0.07	0.10	0.20	0.32	0.40	0.55	5.00	10.	20.	12.	1000.	*	*	*	*	*	*	*	*	*	*	*	*
1948-D	0.07	0.10	0.30	0.45	0.60	0.85	1.35	7.00	8.00	70.	13.	90.	*	*	*	*	*	*	*	*	*	*	*	*
1948-S	0.10	0.20	0.35	0.40	0.45	0.50	0.60	5.00	10.	25.	20.	175.	*	*	*	*	*	*	*	*	*	*	*	*

—— = Insufficient pricing data   * = None issued

	VG-8	F-12	VF-20	EF-40	AU-50	MS-60	MS-63	MS-64	MS-65	MS-65FS	MS-66	MS-66FS	PF-63	PF-64	PF-65	PF-65DC	PF-66	PF-66C	PF-66DC	PF-67	PF-67C	PF-67DC	PF-68DC	PF-69DC
1949	0.08	0.15	0.20	0.30	0.45	0.65	0.75	5.00	10.	125.	20.	—	*	*	*	*	*	*	*	*	*	*	*	*
1949-D	0.07	0.10	0.25	0.45	0.55	0.75	1.50	5.00	5.00	30.	23.	115.	*	*	*	*	*	*	*	*	*	*	*	*
1949-D/S	—	—	35.	70.	105.	150.	200.	300.	600.	—	—	—	*	*	*	*	*	*	*	*	*	*	*	*
1949-S	0.35	0.45	0.60	0.75	0.90	1.15	1.45	5.00	8.00	200.	20.	—	*	*	*	*	*	*	*	*	*	*	*	*
1950	0.15	0.20	0.30	0.45	0.70	0.80	0.90	5.00	18.	150.	57.	—	35.	60.	70.	—	75.	485.	—	95.	1125.	—	—	—
1950-D	4.75	5.00	5.15	5.25	6.00	6.75	7.50	15.	40.	50.	58.	75.	*	*	*	*	*	*	*	*	*	*	*	*
1951	0.07	0.07	0.15	0.30	0.35	0.75	1.40	5.00	12.	475.	15.	1500.	25.	45.	50.	—	60.	125.	—	125.	275.	—	—	—
1951-D	0.07	0.07	0.25	0.45	0.55	0.65	1.00	5.50	6.50	35.	28.	250.	*	*	*	*	*	*	*	*	*	*	*	*
1951-S	0.25	0.30	0.45	0.70	1.00	1.50	2.25	5.00	10.	40.	35.	1200.	*	*	*	*	*	*	*	*	*	*	*	*
1952	0.07	0.07	0.08	0.10	0.50	0.70	0.95	5.00	18.	—	25.	—	13.	35.	40.	—	45.	65.	—	55.	150	—	—	—
1952-D	0.08	0.10	0.15	0.25	0.75	1.00	1.25	5.00	20.	—	25.	575.	*	*	*	*	*	*	*	*	*	*	*	*
1952-S	0.07	0.10	0.15	0.25	0.35	0.60	1.00	5.00	20.	350.	40.	—	*	*	*	*	*	*	*	*	*	*	*	*
1953	0.07	0.07	0.08	0.10	0.20	0.22	0.35	5.00	10.	—	42.	—	7.00	35.	40	—	45.	85.	—	50.	300.	—	—	—
1953-D	0.07	0.07	0.10	0.15	0.18	0.21	0.35	5.00	23.	260.	42.	—	*	*	*	*	*	*	*	*	*	*	*	*
1953-S	0.08	0.15	0.20	0.25	0.30	0.38	0.75	5.00	10.	—	42.	—	*	*	*	*	*	*	*	*	*	*	*	*
1954	0.07	0.07	0.08	0.10	0.15	0.19	0.35	5.00	8.00	400.	14.	—	4.00	20.	25.	—	30.	50.	—	45.	80.	—	—	—
1954-D	0.07	0.07	0.08	0.10	0.15	0.19	0.35	5.00	12.	—	—	2250.	*	*	*	*	*	*	*	*	*	*	*	*
1954-S	0.07	0.07	0.08	0.10	0.20	0.23	0.40	4.00	15.	—	35.	—	*	*	*	*	*	*	*	*	*	*	*	*
1954 S/D	—	—	9.00	16.	22.	30.	45.	60.	215.	—	—	—	*	*	*	*	*	*	*	*	*	*	*	*
1955	0.15	0.22	0.25	0.30	0.35	0.40	0.75	5.00	6.00	475.	27.	—	3.00	12.	15.	—	20.	25.	—	30.	50.	900.	—	—
1955-D	0.07	0.07	0.08	0.10	0.15	0.19	0.30	4.00	6.00	—	27.	—	*	*	*	*	*	*	*	*	*	*	*	*
1955 D/S Variety 1	—	—	10.	17.	26.	30.	50.	75.	110.	130.	—	—	*	*	*	*	*	*	*	*	*	*	*	*
1956	0.05	0.05	0.05	0.05	0.05	0.16	0.25	4.00	40.	60.	25.	—	1.00	2.00	4.00	—	12.	95.	—	23.	180.	1000.	—	—
1956-D	0.05	0.05	0.05	0.05	0.05	0.16	0.25	4.00	35.	425.	80.	—	*	*	*	*	*	*	*	*	*	*	*	*

—— = Insufficient pricing data   * = None issued

	VG-8	F-12	VF-20	EF-40	AU-50	MS-60	MS-63	MS-64	MS-65	MS-65FS	MS-66	MS-66FS	PF-63	PF-64	PF-65	PF-65DC	PF-66	PF-66C	PF-66DC	PF-67	PF-67C	PF-67DC	PF-68DC	PF-69DC
1957	0.05	0.05	0.05	0.05	0.05	0.17	0.25	8.00	15.	—	60.	—	1.00	1.50	2.50	—	15.	—	—	20.	—	—	—	—
1957-D	0.05	0.05	0.05	0.05	0.05	0.16	0.25	4.00	14.	400.	20.	—	*	*	*	*	*	*	*	*	*	*	*	*
1958	0.06	0.08	0.12	0.17	0.20	0.25	4.00	7.00	50.	—	—	—	1.00	1.50	4.00	—	20.	30.	—	25.	50.	—	—	—
1958-D	0.05	0.05	0.05	0.05	0.05	0.16	0.25	7.00	15.	50.	25.	55.	*	*	*	*	*	*	*	*	*	*	*	*
1959	0.05	0.05	0.05	0.05	0.05	0.16	0.25	4.00	10.	—	35.	—	1.00	1.50	2.50	—	12.	20.	—	20.	35.	1300.	—	—
1959-D	0.05	0.05	0.05	0.05	0.05	0.16	0.25	4.00	7.00	375.	50.	1850.	*	*	*	*	*	*	*	*	*	*	*	*
1960	0.05	0.05	0.05	0.05	0.05	0.16	0.25	4.00	7.00	—	12.	—	1.00	1.50	2.50	—	12.	20.	—	20.	35.	—	—	—
1960-D	0.05	0.05	0.05	0.05	0.05	0.16	0.25	7.50	40.	—	50.	—	*	*	*	*	*	*	*	*	*	*	*	*
1961	0.05	0.05	0.05	0.05	0.05	0.16	0.25	4.00	8.00	—	15.	—	1.00	1.50	2.50	—	12.	20.	—	20.	25.	—	—	—
1961-D	0.05	0.05	0.05	0.05	0.05	0.16	0.25	10.	45.	—	75.	—	*	*	*	*	*	*	*	*	*	*	*	*
1962	0.05	0.05	0.05	0.05	0.05	0.16	0.25	3.00	7.00	90.	15.	—	1.00	1.50	2.50	—	12.	20.	—	20.	35.	—	65.	—
1962-D	0.05	0.05	0.05	0.05	0.05	0.16	0.25	3.50	55.	—	75.	—	*	*	*	*	*	*	*	*	*	*	*	*
1963	0.05	0.05	0.05	0.05	0.05	0.16	0.25	3.00	30.	250.	40.	—	1.00	1.50	2.50	—	12.	20.	—	20.	25.	—	—	—
1963-D	0.05	0.05	0.05	0.05	0.05	0.16	0.25	3.00	45.	—	65.	—	*	*	*	*	*	*	*	*	*	*	*	*
1964	0.05	0.05	0.05	0.05	0.05	0.16	0.25	3.00	35.	760.	275.	—	1.00	1.50	2.50	—	12.	20.	—	20.	25.	—	—	—
1964-D	0.05	0.05	0.05	0.05	0.05	0.16	0.25	8.50	22.	—	100.	—	*	*	*	*	*	*	*	*	*	*	*	*
1965	—	—	—	—	—	0.13	0.25	3.00	10.	—	20.	—	*	*	*	*	*	*	*	*	*	*	*	*
1966	—	—	—	—	—	0.13	0.25	3.00	12.	—	25.	—	*	*	*	*	*	*	*	*	*	*	*	*
1967	—	—	—	—	—	0.13	0.25	3.00	12.	—	25.	—	*	*	*	*	*	*	*	*	*	*	*	*
1968-D	—	—	—	—	—	0.13	0.25	3.00	5.00	—	16.	—	*	*	*	*	*	*	*	*	*	*	*	*
1968-S	—	—	—	—	—	0.13	0.25	8.00	12.	—	20.	—	1.00	2.00	3.00	—	5.00	—	8.00	9.00	—	16.	35.	—
1969-D	—	—	—	—	—	0.13	0.25	3.00	6.00	—	11.	—	*	*	*	*	*	*	*	*	*	*	*	*
1969-S	—	—	—	—	—	0.13	0.25	8.00	15.	—	30.	—	1.00	2.00	3.00	—	5.00	—	13.	8.00	—	30.	65.	—
1970-D	—	—	—	—	—	0.13	0.25	4.00	12.	—	25.	—	*	*	*	*	*	*	*	*	*	*	*	*

—— = Insufficient pricing data * = None issued

	VG-8	F-12	VF-20	EF-40	AU-50	MS-60	MS-63	MS-64	MS-65	MS-65FS	MS-66	MS-66FS	PF-63	PF-64	PF-65	PF-65DC	PF-66	PF-66C	PF-66DC	PF-67	PF-67C	PF-67DC	PF-68DC	PF-69DC
1970-S	—	—	—	—	—	0.13	0.25	7.50	12	—	35.	—	1.00	2.00	3.00	—	5.00	—	12.	8.00	—	20.	40.	—
1971	—	—	—	—	—	0.45	0.75	3.00	5.00	—	25.	—	*	*	*	*	*	*	*	*	*	*	*	*
1971-D	—	—	—	—	—	0.20	0.50	3.00	10	60.	27.	125.	*	*	*	*	*	*	*	*	*	*	*	*
1971-S	*	*	*	*	*	*	*	*	*	*	*	*	2.50	3.50	5.00	—	6.00	—	15.	15.	—	35.	75.	700.
1971-S No S	*	*	*	*	*	*	*	*	*	*	*	*	900.	1000.	1100.	—	—	—	—	—	—	—	500.	4500.
1972	—	—	—	—	—	0.13	0.25	3.00	8.00	—	25.	—	*	*	*	*	*	*	*	*	*	*	*	*
1972-D	—	—	—	—	—	0.13	0.25	3.00	10.	—	25.	—	*	*	*	*	*	*	*	*	*	*	*	*
1972-S	*	*	*	*	*	*	*	*	*	*	*	*	2.00	3.00	4.00	—	5.00	—	10.	8.00	—	15.	25.	—
1973	—	—	—	—	—	0.13	0.25	3.00	5.00	—	15.	—	*	*	*	*	*	*	*	*	*	*	*	*
1973-D	—	—	—	—	—	0.13	0.25	3.00	10.	28.	35.	—	*	*	*	*	*	*	*	*	*	*	*	*
1973-S	*	*	*	*	*	*	*	*	*	*	*	*	1.50	2.50	4.00	—	5.00	—	12.	10.	—	20.	45.	100.
1974	—	—	—	—	—	0.13	0.25	3.00	5.00	—	15.	—	*	*	*	*	*	*	*	*	*	*	*	*
1974-D	—	—	—	—	—	0.15	0.27	3.00	10.	—	25.	—	*	*	*	*	*	*	*	*	*	*	*	*
1974-S	*	*	*	*	*	*	*	*	*	*	*	*	1.50	2.50	4.00	—	5.00	—	10.	11.	—	15.	18.	—
1975	—	—	—	—	—	0.25	0.40	3.00	5.00	20.	30.	—	*	*	*	*	*	*	*	*	*	*	*	*
1975-D	—	—	—	—	—	0.20	0.35	3.00	5.00	—	30.	—	*	*	*	*	*	*	*	*	*	*	*	*
1975-S	*	*	*	*	*	*	*	*	*	*	*	*	2.00	3.00	4.00	—	5.00	—	10.	11.	—	14.	17.	—
1976	—	—	—	—	0.14	0.25	0.45	3.00	10.	—	25.	—	*	*	*	*	*	*	*	*	*	*	*	*
1976-D	—	—	—	—	—	0.30	0.45	3.00	5.00	—	30.	—	*	*	*	*	*	*	*	*	*	*	*	*
1976-S	*	*	*	*	*	*	*	*	*	*	*	*	1.50	2.50	4.00	—	5.00	—	10.	11.	—	25.	17.	—
1977	—	—	—	—	—	0.13	0.25	3.00	9.50	—	25.	—	*	*	*	*	*	*	*	*	*	*	*	*
1977-D	—	—	—	—	—	0.28	0.40	3.00	12.	20.	30.	—	*	*	*	*	*	*	*	*	*	*	*	*
1977-S	*	*	*	*	*	*	*	*	*	*	*	*	1.50	2.50	4.00	—	5.00	—	11.	10.	—	15.	25.	45.
1978	—	—	—	—	—	0.13	0.25	3.00	10.	—	25.	—	*	*	*	*	*	*	*	*	*	*	*	*

—— = Insufficient pricing data   * = None issued

JEFFERSON 5 CENTS (CONTINUED)

	VG-8	F-12	VF-20	EF-40	AU-50	MS-60	MS-63	MS-64	MS-65	MS-65FS	MS-66	MS-66FS	PF-63	PF-64	PF-65	PF-65DC	PF-66	PF-66C	PF-66DC	PF-67	PF-67C	PF-67DC	PF-68DC	PF-69DC
1978-D	—	—	—	—	—	0.15	0.35	3.00	10.	95.	25.	—	*	*	*	*	*	*	*	*	*	*	*	*
1978-S	*	*	*	*	*	*	*	*	*	*	*	*	1.50	2.50	4.00	—	5.00	—	11.	10.	—	14.	20.	—
1979	—	—	—	—	—	0.13	0.25	3.00	5.00	—	30.	—	*	*	*	*	*	*	*	*	*	*	*	*
1979-D	—	—	—	—	—	0.13	0.27	3.00	10.	50.	25.	—	*	*	*	*	*	*	*	*	*	*	*	*
1979-S Filled S	*	*	*	*	*	*	*	*	*	*	*	*	1.00	2.00	3.00	—	5.00	—	10.	9.00	—	12.	14.	45.
1979-S Clear S	*	*	*	*	*	*	*	*	*	*	*	*	2.00	3.00	4.00	—	5.00	—	11.	10.	—	13.	25.	—
1980-P	—	—	—	—	—	0.13	0.25	3.00	5.00	195.	15.	—	*	*	*	*	*	*	*	*	*	*	*	*
1980-D	—	—	—	—	—	0.13	0.25	3.00	5.00	—	25.	—	*	*	*	*	*	*	*	*	*	*	*	*
1980-S	*	*	*	*	*	*	*	*	*	*	*	*	1.00	2.00	3.00	—	5.00	—	12.	9.00	—	18.	25.	—
1981-P	—	—	—	—	—	0.13	0.25	3.00	5.00	—	20.	—	*	*	*	*	*	*	*	*	*	*	*	*
1981-D	—	—	—	—	—	0.13	0.25	3.00	10.	95.	20.	—	*	*	*	*	*	*	*	*	*	*	*	*
1981-S Filled S	*	*	*	*	*	*	*	*	*	*	*	*	1.50	2.50	4.00	—	5.00	—	10.	9.00	—	12.	14.	45.
1981-S Clear S	*	*	*	*	*	*	*	*	*	*	*	*	2.00	3.00	4.00	—	5.00	—	10.	9.00	—	12.	14.	—
1982-P	—	—	—	—	—	0.14	0.75	3.00	15.	—	25.	—	*	*	*	*	*	*	*	*	*	*	*	*
1982-D	—	—	—	—	—	0.25	1.25	3.00	15.	—	25.	—	*	*	*	*	*	*	*	*	*	*	*	*
1982-S	*	*	*	*	*	*	*	*	*	*	*	*	3.00	4.00	5.00	—	6.00	—	10.	9.00	—	14.	20.	25.
1983-P	—	—	—	—	—	0.87	0.90	3.00	5.00	—	20.	—	*	*	*	*	*	*	*	*	*	*	*	*
1983-D	—	—	—	—	—	0.80	0.90	3.00	5.00	—	20.	—	*	*	*	*	*	*	*	*	*	*	*	*
1983-S	*	*	*	*	*	*	*	*	*	*	*	*	3.00	4.00	5.00	—	6.00	—	10.	9.00	—	12.	20.	30.
1984-P	—	—	—	—	—	0.10	0.45	3.00	5.00	—	15.	—	*	*	*	*	*	*	*	*	*	*	*	*
1984-D	—	—	—	—	—	0.15	0.45	3.00	5.00	—	15.	—	*	*	*	*	*	*	*	*	*	*	*	*
1984-S	*	*	*	*	*	*	*	*	*	*	*	*	5.00	6.00	7.00	—	8.00	—	10.	9.00	—	12.	14.	25.
1985-P	—	—	—	—	—	0.13	0.45	3.00	5.00	100.	15.	—	*	*	*	*	*	*	*	*	*	*	*	*
1985-D	—	—	—	—	—	0.15	0.45	3.00	5.00	—	15.	—	*	*	*	*	*	*	*	*	*	*	*	*

—— = Insufficient pricing data   * = None issued

	VG-8	F-12	VF-20	EF-40	AU-50	MS-60	MS-63	MS-64	MS-65	MS-65FS	MS-66	MS-66FS	PF-63	PF-64	PF-65	PF-65DC	PF-66	PF-66C	PF-66DC	PF-67	PF 67C	PF-67DC	PF-68DC	PF-69DC
1985-S	*	*	*	*	*	*	*	*	*	*	*	*	2.50	3.50	5.00	—	6.00	—	10.	9.00	—	12.	25.	35.
1986-P	—	—	—	—	—	0.10	0.45	3.00	5.00	—	15.	—	*	*	*	*	*	*	*	*	*	*	*	*
1986-D	—	—	—	—	—	0.15	0.85	3.00	5.00	—	15.	—	*	*	*	*	*	*	*	*	*	*	*	*
1986-S	*	*	*	*	*	*	*	*	*	*	*	*	8.00	9.00	10.	—	12.	—	10.	9.00	—	12.	14.	—
1987-P	—	—	—	—	—	—	0.25	3.00	5.00	18.	12.	30.	*	*	*	*	*	*	*	*	*	*	*	*
1987-D	—	—	—	—	—	—	0.25	3.00	5.00	—	12.	—	*	*	*	*	*	*	*	*	*	*	*	*
1987-S	*	*	*	*	*	*	*	*	*	*	*	*	2.00	3.00	4.00	3.00	5.00	—	7.00	6.00	—	9.00	15.	30.
1988-P	—	—	—	—	—	—	0.25	3.00	5.00	12.	12.	—	*	*	*	*	*	*	*	*	*	*	*	*
1988-D	—	—	—	—	—	—	0.25	3.00	5.00	—	12.	—	*	*	*	*	*	*	*	*	*	*	*	*
1988-S	*	*	*	*	*	*	*	*	*	*	*	*	5.00	6.00	7.00	3.00	8.00	—	7.00	9.00	—	9.00	15.	25.
1989-P	—	—	—	—	—	—	0.25	3.00	5.00	—	12.	18.	*	*	*	*	*	*	*	*	*	*	*	*
1989-D	—	—	—	—	—	—	0.25	3.00	5.00	—	12.	—	*	*	*	*	*	*	*	*	*	*	*	*
1989-S	*	*	*	*	*	*	*	*	*	*	*	*	4.00	5.00	6.00	3.00	7.00	—	7.00	8.00	—	9.00	15.	35.
1990-P	—	—	—	—	—	—	0.25	3.00	5.00	—	10.	—	*	*	*	*	*	*	*	*	*	*	*	*
1990-D	—	—	—	—	—	—	0.25	3.00	5.00	—	10.	—	*	*	*	*	*	*	*	*	*	*	*	*
1990-S	*	*	*	*	*	*	*	*	*	*	*	*	4.00	5.00	6.00	3.00	7.00	—	7.00	8.00	—	9.00	20.	50.
1991-P	—	—	—	—	—	—	0.30	3.00	5.00	—	10.	—	*	*	*	*	*	*	*	*	*	*	*	*
1991-D	—	—	—	—	—	—	0.30	3.00	5.00	—	10.	—	*	*	*	*	*	*	*	*	*	*	*	*
1991-S	*	*	*	*	*	*	*	*	*	*	*	*	4.00	5.00	6.00	4.00	7.00	—	7.00	8.00	—	9.00	15.	20.
1992-P	—	—	—	—	—	—	0.35	3.00	5.00	10.	10.	—	*	*	*	*	*	*	*	*	*	*	*	*
1992-D	—	—	—	—	—	—	0.25	3.00	5.00	11.	10	—	*	*	*	*	*	*	*	*	*	*	*	*
1992-S	*	*	*	*	*	*	*	*	*	*	*	*	2.00	3.00	4.00	3.00	5.00	—	7.00	6.00	—	9.00	15.	25.
1993-P	—	—	—	—	—	—	0.25	3.00	5.00	—	10.	10.	*	*	*	*	*	*	*	*	*	*	*	*
1993-D	—	—	—	—	—	—	0.25	3.00	5.00	—	10.	14.	*	*	*	*	*	*	*	*	*	*	*	*

—— = Insufficient pricing data * = None issued

JEFFERSON 5 CENTS (CONTINUED)

	VG-8	F-12	VF-20	EF-40	AU-50	MS-60	MS-63	MS-64	MS-65	MS-65FS	MS-66	MS-66FS	PF-63	PF-64	PF-65	PF-65DC	PF-66	PF-66C	PF-66DC	PF-67	PF-67C	PF-67DC	PF-68DC	PF-69DC
1993-S	*	*	*	*	*	*	*	*	*	*	*	*	2.50	3.50	5.00	3.00	6.00	—	7.00	7.00	—	9.00	15.	20.
1994-P	—	—	—	—	—	—	0.25	3.00	5.00	—	10.	—	*	*	*	*	*	*	*	*	*	*	*	*
1994-D	—	—	—	—	—	—	0.25	3.00	5.00	—	10.	—	*	*	*	*	*	*	*	*	*	*	*	*
1994-S	*	*	*	*	*	*	*	*	*	*	*	*	2.50	3.50	5.00	3.00	6.00	—	7.00	7.00	—	9.00	15.	25.
1994-P Matte Finish	—	—	—	—	—	—	65.	80.	100.	—	125.	—	—	—	—	—	—	—	—	—	—	—	—	—
1995-P	—	—	—	—	—	—	0.25	3.00	5.00	—	10.	—	*	*	*	*	*	*	*	*	*	*	*	*
1995-D	—	—	—	—	—	—	0.30	3.00	5.00	35.	12.	—	*	*	*	*	*	*	*	*	*	*	*	*
1995-S	*	*	*	*	*	*	*	*	*	*	*	*	4.00	5.00	6.00	4.50	7.00	—	7.00	8.00	—	9.00	15.	20.
1996-P	—	—	—	—	—	—	0.25	3.00	5.00	—	10.	—	*	*	*	*	*	*	*	*	*	*	*	*
1996-D	—	—	—	—	—	—	0.25	3.00	5.00	20.	10.	33.	*	*	*	*	*	*	*	*	*	*	*	*
1996-S	*	*	*	*	*	*	*	*	*	*	*	*	2.50	3.50	5.00	3.00	6.00	—	7.00	7.00	—	9.00	20.	46.
1997-P	—	—	—	—	—	—	0.25	3.00	5.00	—	10.	—	*	*	*	*	*	*	*	*	*	*	*	*
1997-D	—	—	—	—	—	—	0.25	3.00	5.00	—	10.	10.	*	*	*	*	*	*	*	*	*	*	*	*
1997-S	*	*	*	*	*	*	*	*	*	*	*	*	4.00	5.00	6.00	3.00	7.00	—	7.00	8.00	—	9.00	15.	26.
1997-P Matte Finish	—	—	—	—	—	—	175.	225.	275.	—	—	—	—	—	—	—	—	—	—	—	—	—	—	—
1998-P	—	—	—	—	—	—	0.25	3.00	5.00	—	10.	—	*	*	*	*	*	*	*	*	*	*	*	*
1998-D	—	—	—	—	—	—	0.25	3.00	5.00	—	10.	—	*	*	*	*	*	*	*	*	*	*	*	*
1998-S	*	*	*	*	*	*	*	*	*	*	*	*	3.00	4.00	5.00	3.00	6.00	—	7.00	7.00	—	9.00	15.	25.
1999-P	—	—	—	—	—	—	0.20	3.00	5.00	16.	10.	65.	*	*	*	*	*	*	*	*	*	*	*	*
1999-D	—	—	—	—	—	—	0.20	3.00	5.00	—	10.	50.	*	*	*	*	*	*	*	*	*	*	*	*
1999-S	*	*	*	*	*	*	*	*	*	*	*	*	3.00	4.00	5.00	3.00	6.00	—	7.00	7.00	—	8.00	10.	20.
2000-P	—	—	—	—	—	—	0.20	3.00	5.00	14.	10.	50.	*	*	*	*	*	*	*	*	*	*	*	*
2000-D	—	—	—	—	—	—	0.20	3.00	5.00	5.50	10.	20.	*	*	*	*	*	*	*	*	*	*	*	*
2000-S	*	*	*	*	*	*	*	*	*	*	*	*	1.50	2.50	3.50	3.00	5.00	—	7.00	6.00	—	8.00	10.	25.

—— = Insufficient pricing data   * = None issued

	VG-8	F-12	VF-20	EF-40	AU-50	MS-60	MS-63	MS-64	MS-65	MS-65FS	MS-66	MS-66FS	PF-63	PF-64	PF-65	PF-65DC	PF-66	PF-66C	PF-66DC	PF-67	PF-67C	PF-67DC	PF-68DC	PF-69DC
2001-P	—	—	—	—	—	—	0.20	3.00	5.00	—	10.	100.	*	*	*	*	*	*	*	*	*	*	*	*
2001-D	—	—	—	—	—	—	0.20	3.00	5.00	15.	10.	100.	*	*	*	*	*	*	*	*	*	*	*	*
2001-S	*	*	*	*	*	*	*	*	*	*	*	*	2.00	3.00	4.00	3.00	5.00	—	7.00	6.00	—	9.00	15.	30.
2002-P	—	—	—	—	—	—	0.20	3.00	5.00	—	10.	—	*	*	*	*	*	*	*	*	*	*	*	*
2002-D	—	—	—	—	—	—	0.20	3.00	5.00	—	10.	—	*	*	*	*	*	*	*	*	*	*	*	*
2002-S	*	*	*	*	*	*	*	*	*	*	*	*	1.50	2.50	3.50	3.00	5.00	—	7.00	6.00	—	9.00	15.	25.
2003-P	—	—	—	—	—	—	0.20	3.00	5.00	—	10.	—	—	—	—	—	—	—	—	—	—	—	—	—
2003-D	—	—	—	—	—	—	0.20	3.00	5.00	—	10.	—	—	—	—	—	—	—	—	—	—	—	—	—
2003-S	—	—	—	—	—	—	—	—	—	—	—	—	2.50	3.50	5.00	3.00	5.00	—	7.00	6.00	—	9.00	15.	25.
2004-P Peace Medal reverse	—	—	—	—	—	—	0.20	3.00	5.00	—	10.	—	—	—	—	—	—	—	—	—	—	—	—	—
2004-D Peace Medal reverse	—	—	—	—	—	—	0.20	3.00	5.00	—	10.	—	—	—	—	—	—	—	—	—	—	—	—	—
2004-S Peace Medal reverse	—	—	—	—	—	—	—	—	—	—	—	—	—	—	—	—	5.00	—	7.00	6.00	—	9.00	15.	25.
2004-P Keelboat reverse	—	—	—	—	—	—	0.20	3.00	5.00	—	10.	—	—	—	—	—	—	—	—	—	—	—	—	—
2004-D Keelboat reverse	—	—	—	—	—	—	0.20	3.00	5.00	—	10.	—	—	—	—	—	—	—	—	—	—	—	—	—
2004-S Keelboat reverse	—	—	—	—	—	—	—	—	—	—	—	—	—	—	—	—	5.00	—	7.00	6.00	—	9.00	15.	25.

—— = Insufficient pricing data   * = None issued

Flowing Hair half dime

Half disme pattern   Flowing Hair

Date of authorization: April 2, 1792
Dates of issue: 1792 (half disme); 1794-1795
Designer/Engraver: Robert Scot
Diameter: 16.50 mm/0.65 inch
Weight: 1.348 grams/0.04 ounce
Metallic content: 89.25% silver, 10.75% copper
Weight of pure silver: 1.20 grams/0.04 ounce
Edge: Reeded
Mint mark: None

HALF DISME PATTERN

	AG-3	G-4	VG-8	F-12	VF-20	EF-40	AU-50	MS-60	MS-63
1792	7500.	12000.	20000.	35000.	40000.	50000.	75000.	125000.	175000.

FLOWING HAIR HALF DIME

	AG-3	G-4	VG-8	F-12	VF-20	EF-40	AU-50	MS-60
1794	800.	1200.	1500.	2000.	3000.	5000.	7500.	14000.
1795	600.	1000.	1200.	1700.	2500.	4000.	6500.	10000.

Draped Bust half dime

Small Eagle

Heraldic Eagle

Date of authorization: April 2, 1792
Dates of issue: 1796-1805
Designer: Obverse: Gilbert Stuart-Robert Scot
Reverse:
(1796-1797): Robert Scot-John Eckstein
(1800-1805): Robert Scot
Engraver: Robert Scot
Diameter: 16.50 mm/0.65 inch
Weight: 1.35 grams/0.04 ounce
Metallic content: 89.25% silver, 10.75% copper
Weight of pure silver: 1.20 grams/0.04 ounce
Edge: Reeded
Mint mark: None

	AG-3	G-4	VG-8	F-12	VF-20	EF-40	AU-50	MS-60
DRAPED BUST, SMALL EAGLE HALF DIME								
1796/5	800.	1400.	1800.	2500.	4000.	6500.	12000.	25000.
1796 LIBERTY	600.	1000.	1400.	2000.	3500.	6000.	9000.	15000.
1796 LIKERTY	600.	1000.	1400.	2000.	3500.	6000.	9000.	18000.
1797 15 Stars	600.	1000.	1400.	2000.	3500.	6000.	9000.	15000.
1797 16 Stars	600.	1000.	1400.	2000.	3500.	6000.	9000.	15000.
1797 13 Stars	1000.	2000.	2500.	3000.	4000	8000	15000.	25000.

	AG-3	G-4	VG-8	F-12	VF-20	EF-40	AU-50	MS-60
DRAPED BUST, HERALDIC EAGLE HALF DIME								
1800	400.	700.	1000	1800	2500.	4000.	7500.	12000.
1800 LIBEKTY	400.	700.	1000.	1800.	2500.	4000.	7500.	12000.
1801	500.	800.	1200.	2000.	2500.	4000.	8000.	15000.
1802	10000	17000.	25000.	35000.	60000.	80000.	125000.	—
1803	500.	900.	1200.	1800.	3000.	5000.	8000.	15000.
1805	600.	900.	1400.	1800.	3000.	5000.	12000.	25000.

—— = Insufficient pricing data

Capped Bust half dime

Date of authorization:	April 2, 1792
Dates of issue:	1829-1837
Designers:	John Reich-William Kneass
Engraver:	William Kneass
Diameter:	15.50 mm/0.61 inch
Weight:	1.35 grams/0.04 ounce
Metallic content:	89.25% silver, 10.75% copper
Weight of pure silver:	1.20 grams/0.04 ounce
Edge:	Reeded
Mint mark:	None

CAPPED BUST HALF DIME (CONTINUED)

	G-4	VG-8	F-12	VF-20	EF-40	EF-45	AU-50	AU-55	MS-60	MS-62	MS-63	MS-64	MS-65	MS-66
1829	25.	35.	40.	75.	125.	150.	200.	250.	300.	550.	800.	1600.	2800.	4000.
1830	25.	35.	40.	75.	125.	150.	200.	250.	300.	550.	800.	1600.	3500.	5000.
1831	25.	35.	40.	75.	125.	150.	200.	250.	300.	550.	800.	1600.	2500.	4000.
1832	25.	35.	40.	75.	125.	150.	200.	250.	300.	550.	800.	1600.	2500.	4000.
1833	25.	35.	40.	75.	125.	150.	200.	250.	300.	550.	800.	1600.	2500.	4000.
1834	25.	35.	40.	75.	125.	150.	200.	250.	300.	550.	800.	1600.	2500.	4000.
1835 all varieties	25.	35.	40.	75.	125.	150.	200.	250.	300.	550.	800.	1600.	2500.	4000.
1836 all varieties	25.	35.	40.	75.	125.	150.	200.	250.	300.	550.	800.	1600.	2500.	4000.
1837 Small 5c	30.	40.	50.	100.	200.	250.	350.	500.	1000.	1500.	2500.	5000.	12000.	—
1837 Large 5c	25.	35.	40.	75.	125.	150.	200.	250.	300.	700.	1000.	2000.	4000.	6000.

—— = Insufficient pricing data   * = None issued

Seated Liberty, half dime

Date of authorization: April 2, 1792
Dates of issue: 1837-1873
Designers: (1837-1840): Christian Gobrecht
(1840-1859):
Obverse: Gobrecht-Robert B. Hughes
Reverse: Christian Gobrecht
(1860-1873):
Obverse: Christian Gobrecht-Robert B. Hughes-James B. Longacre
Reverse: James B. Longacre
Engraver: (1837-1840): Christian Gobrecht
(1840-1859): Christian Gobrecht
(1860-1873): James B. Longacre
Diameter: 15.50 mm/0.61 inch
Weight: (1837-1853): 1.34 grams/0.04 ounce
(1853-1873): 1.24 grams/0.04 ounce
Metallic content: 90% silver, 10% copper
Weight of pure silver: (1837-1853): 1.20 grams/0.04 ounce
(1853-1873): 1.12 grams/0.04 ounce
Edge: Reeded
Mint mark: Reverse within or below wreath

	G-4	VG-8	F-12	VF-20	EF-40	AU-50	MS-60	MS-62	MS-63	MS-64	MS-65
NO STARS											
1837 Large or Small Date	40.	50.	85.	150.	300.	500.	900.	1000.	1200.	1800.	3500.
1838-O	125.	200.	300.	500.	1000.	1500.	4000.	6500.	10000.	18000.	—
NO DRAPERY											
1838	20.	25.	30.	40.	100.	200.	400.	500.	600.	1000.	2500.
1838 Small Stars	30.	40.	50.	125.	250.	400.	700.	900.	1200.	2000.	5000.
1839	20.	25.	30.	40.	100.	200.	400.	500.	600.	1000.	2500.
1839-O	25.	35.	45.	65.	100.	200.	800.	1200.	2000.	3500.	4500.
1839-O Large O	325.	625.	1100.	1750.	3000.	4500.	—	—	—	—	—
1840	20.	30.	40.	50.	80.	150.	400.	500.	600.	1000.	2500.
1840-O	25.	35.	45.	65.	100.	300.	900.	1500.	2500.	5000.	8000.
DRAPERY											
1840	25.	40.	80.	125.	250.	400.	600.	750.	1000.	1350.	4000.

—— = Insufficient pricing data * = None issued

SEATED LIBERTY, HALF DIME (CONTINUED)

	G-4	VG-8	F-12	VF-20	EF-40	AU-50	MS-60	MS-62	MS-63	MS-64	MS-65
1840-O	40.	65.	125.	200.	500.	1200.	3500.	5000.	9000.	—	—
1841	20.	25.	30.	40.	75.	150.	300.	400.	500.	800.	1500.
1841-O	20.	25.	30.	65.	150.	350.	800.	1000.	1500.	2500.	—
1842	20.	25.	30.	40.	75.	150.	300.	400.	500.	800.	2000.
1842-O	30.	50.	75.	250.	600.	1500.	3000.	3500.	5000.	8000.	15000.
1843	20.	25.	30.	40.	75.	150.	300.	400.	500.	800.	1500.
1844	20.	25.	30.	40.	75.	150.	300.	400.	500.	800.	1500.
1844-O Small O	60.	130.	250.	515.	850.	1700.	4900.	9000.	—	—	—
1844-O Large O	65.	110.	175.	350.	700.	—	4000.	—	—	—	26500.
1845	20.	25.	30.	40.	75.	150.	300.	400.	500.	800.	1500.
1846	300.	500.	700.	1000.	2500.	3500.	—	—	—	—	—
1847	20.	25.	30.	40.	75.	150.	300.	400.	500.	850.	1500.
1848 Medium Date	20.	25.	30.	40.	75.	150.	350.	500.	700.	1500.	3000.
1848 Large Date	25.	30.	50.	75.	200.	350.	700.	1200.	1800.	3000.	5000.
1848-O	20.	25.	35.	65.	150.	300.	500.	600.	800.	1500.	2000.
1849/6	25.	30.	40.	65.	125.	250.	600.	900.	1400.	1800.	3000.
1849/8	35.	50.	65.	80.	150.	300.	1000.	1400.	2000.	2500.	3000.
1849	20.	25.	30.	65.	100.	150.	300.	400.	600.	1200.	2000.
1849-O	30.	40.	100.	250.	500.	1200.	2500.	3500.	6000.	9000.	12000.
1850	20.	25.	35.	50.	75.	150.	300.	400.	500.	800.	1500.
1850-O	20.	30.	40.	75.	150.	350.	1000.	1200.	1800.	3000.	5000.
1851	20.	25.	30.	40.	75.	150.	300.	400.	500.	800.	1500.
1851-O	20.	25.	30.	50.	125.	250.	600.	700.	900.	1400.	4500.
1852	20.	25.	30.	40.	65.	150.	300.	400.	500.	800.	1500.
1852-O	35.	50.	75.	150.	300.	500.	1200.	1500.	2500.	3500.	—
1853	35.	50.	75.	150.	250.	400.	800.	1000.	1200.	1500.	2500.
1853-O	200.	300.	400.	700.	1500.	3000.	7000.	9000.	12000.	22500.	—
ARROWS											
1853	20.	25.	30.	40.	75.	150.	250.	300.	400.	700.	2000.
1853-O	20.	25.	30.	40.	75.	200.	400.	700.	1200.	2000.	4500.
1854	20.	25.	30.	40.	65.	150.	300.	400.	500.	700.	2000.
1854-O	20.	25.	30.	40.	100.	200.	350.	600.	1000.	2500.	5000.
1855	20.	25.	30.	40.	65.	150.	250.	300.	400.	700.	2500.
1855-O	20.	25.	40.	75.	200.	300.	700.	1000.	1500.	2500.	5500.
NO ARROWS											
1856	20.	25.	30.	40.	65.	150.	300.	350.	400.	800.	1600.
1856-O	20.	25.	30.	65.	125.	300.	400.	700.	1200.	1800.	3000.
1857	20.	25.	30.	40.	65.	150.	250.	300.	400.	800.	1500.
1857-O	20.	25.	30.	50.	75.	250.	400.	500.	600.	1000.	2000.
1858	20.	25.	30.	40.	65.	150.	250.	300.	400.	800.	1500.
1858/Inverted Date	28.	45.	55.	115.	200.	300.	475.	525.	750.	2000.	—
1858/1858	35.	50.	75.	155.	245.	325.	675.	775.	1300.	1975.	3000.
1858-O	20.	25.	30.	50.	100.	200.	300.	400.	500.	1000.	2000.

—— = Insufficient pricing data * = None issued

	G-4	VG-8	F-12	VF-20	EF-40	AU-50	MS-60	MS-62	MS-63	MS-64	MS-65
1859	20.	25.	30.	50.	100.	150.	300.	350.	400.	1000.	1500.
1859-O	20.	25.	35.	50.	200.	300.	400.	450.	500.	1200.	2000.
1860 Transitional	—	—	—	—	—	—	1800.	2250.	3250.	4750.	8000.
LEGEND OBVERSE											
1860	20.	25.	30.	35.	65.	100.	200.	250.	300.	500.	1200.
1860-O	20.	25.	30.	35.	65.	125.	300.	350.	400.	600.	1500.
1861	20.	25.	30.	35.	65.	100.	200.	250.	300.	500.	1200.
1861/0	30.	40.	75.	200.	400.	500.	800.	1000.	1200.	1800.	4000.
1862	25.	35.	50.	65.	80.	125.	250.	300.	400.	600.	1200.
1863	200.	250.	300.	400.	600.	700.	1000.	1200.	1500.	1800.	2500.
1863-S	30.	50.	65.	75.	200.	350.	800.	1000.	1200.	2000.	3000.
1864	400.	500.	600.	900.	1200.	1500.	2000.	2200.	2500.	3000.	3500.
1864-S	65.	85.	125.	200.	300.	500.	800.	1000.	1500.	2500.	4500.
1865	400.	500.	600.	700.	800.	900.	1100.	1200.	1500.	1800.	2500.
1865-S	35.	50.	65.	100.	200.	600.	1000.	1400.	2000.	5000.	—
1866	400.	500.	600.	700.	800.	900.	1100.	1200.	1500.	1800.	3000.
1866-S	35.	50.	65.	100.	200.	400.	700.	800.	1000.	1800.	5000.
1867	600.	700.	800.	900.	1000.	1100.	1300.	1400.	1500.	1800.	2500.
1867-S	35.	50.	65.	100.	200.	400.	800.	1000.	1200.	2000.	4000.
1868	65.	85.	125.	200.	500.	600.	800.	900.	1000.	1500.	2500.
1868-S	20.	25.	35.	50.	65.	150.	400.	800.	800.	1500.	3500.
1869	20.	25.	35.	50.	65.	150.	400.	600.	800.	1000.	2500.
1869-S	20.	25.	35.	50.	65.	150.	400.	600.	1000.	2000.	4500.
1870	20.	25.	35.	50.	65.	100.	250.	300.	400.	600.	1200.
1870-S Unique - Graded (PCGS) MS-63											
1871	20.	25.	35.	50.	65.	100.	250.	300.	400.	600.	1200.
1871-S	20.	30.	50.	75.	100.	200.	400.	500.	700.	1000.	3000.
1872	20.	25.	35.	50.	65.	100.	250.	300.	400.	600.	1200.
1872-S S in Wreath	20.	25.	35.	50.	65.	100.	250.	300.	400.	600.	1200.
1872-S S Below Wreath	20.	25.	35.	50.	65.	100.	250.	300.	400.	600.	1200.
1873	20.	25.	35.	50.	65.	100.	250.	300.	400.	600.	1200.
1873-S	20.	25.	35.	50.	65.	100.	250.	300.	400.	600.	1200.

—— = Insufficient pricing data * = None issued

Draped Bust dime

Small Eagle Heraldic Eagle

Date of authorization:	April 2, 1792
Dates of issue:	1796-1807
Designer:	Obverse: Gilbert Stuart-Robert Scot Reverse: (1796-1797): Robert Scot-John Eckstein (1800-1805): Robert Scot
Engraver:	Robert Scot
Diameter:	18.80 mm/0.74 inch
Weight:	2.70 grams/0.09 ounce
Metallic content:	89.25% silver, 10.75% copper
Weight of pure silver:	1.20 grams/0.04 ounce
Edge:	Reeded
Mint mark:	None

	G-4	VG-8	F-12	VF-20	EF-40	AU-50	AU-55	MS-60	MS-62
1796	1500.	2000.	2500.	3500.	5000.	7500.	10000.	15000.	20000.
1797 16 Stars	1500.	2000.	2500.	3500.	6000.	8500.	10000.	15000.	20000.
1797 13 Stars	1500.	2000.	2500.	3500.	6000.	8500.	10000.	15000.	20000.
1798/97 16 Stars	750.	1000.	1500.	2000.	3500.	4000.	5000.	7500.	12000.
1798/97 13 Stars	2000.	3000.	4500.	6500.	9000.	—	—	—	—
1798	600.	900.	1200.	1800.	2500.	3000.	4000.	7000.	12000.
1798 Small 8	900.	1200.	1800.	2500.	4500.	7500.	8500.	12000.	15000.
1800	600.	900.	1200.	2000.	3000.	4000.	5000.	6000.	10000.
1801	600.	900.	1500.	2500.	5000.	8000.	9000.	15000.	25000.
1802	1000.	1400.	1800.	3000.	6000.	10000.	18000.	28000.	—
1803	600.	900.	1200.	2000.	4500.	8000.	9000.	12000.	—
1804 13 Star	1200.	1800.	3000.	4500.	12000.	30000.	40000.	—	—
1804 14 Star	1500.	2000.	3500.	5000.	15000.	35000.	45000.	—	—
1805 4 Berries	500.	750.	1000.	1400.	2000.	3000.	4000.	5000.	7500.
1805 5 Berries	600.	850.	1200.	1800.	2500.	4500.	6000.	—	—
1807	500.	750.	1000.	1400.	2000.	3000.	4000.	5000.	7500.

—— = Insufficient pricing data

Capped Bust dime

Date of authorization: April 2, 1792
Dates of issue: 1809-1837
Designer/Engraver: John Reich
Diameter: (1809-1828): 18.80 mm/0.74 inch
(1828-1837): 17.90 mm/0.71 inch
Weight: 2.70 grams/0.09 ounce
Metallic content: 89.25% silver, 10.75% copper
Weight of pure silver: 2.41 grams/0.08 ounce
Edge: Reeded
Mint mark: None

	G-4	VG-8	F-12	VF-20	EF-40	AU-50	AU-55	MS-60	MS-63	MS-64	MS-65
OPEN COLLAR STRIKE											
1809	125.	200.	350.	600.	1200.	1800.	2500.	4500.	6500.	10000.	17000.
1811/09	125.	200.	300.	500.	1000.	1500.	2000.	3000.	6000.	10000.	25000.
1814 Small Date	40.	65.	110.	225.	500.	1000.	1300.	2000.	4500.	7000.	14000.
1814 Large Date	30.	40.	55.	140.	400.	600.	700.	1000.	2500.	6000.	12000.
1814 STATESOFAMERICA	40.	65.	110.	225.	500.	1000.	1300.	2000.	4500.	7000.	15000.
1820 Large 0	25.	35.	50.	110.	375.	600.	700.	1000.	2000.	4000.	9000.
1820 Small 0 Office Boy Reverse	30.	40.	60.	150.	400.	650.	750.	1100.	2250.	4500.	7850.
1820 STATESOFAMERICA	35.	50.	75.	200.	450.	850.	1200.	1800.	3500.	6000.	10000.
1821 Small Date	25.	35.	60.	125.	400.	700.	900.	1400.	3000.	4000.	—
1821 Large Date	25.	35.	50.	125.	400.	600.	750.	1000.	2200.	4500.	9500.
1822	350.	550.	900.	1400.	2400.	4500.	6000.	9500.	16000.	—	—
1823/2 Large E reverse	25.	30.	45.	110.	400.	550.	700.	1100.	2500.	4000.	8500.
1823/2 Small E reverse	25.	30.	45.	110.	400.	550.	700.	1100.	3150.	7250.	—
1824/2	30.	50.	100.	350.	600.	1100.	1400.	1800.	5000.	—	—
1825	25.	35.	50.	110.	400.	550.	650.	900.	2500.	4000.	9000.
1827	25.	35.	50.	110.	400.	550.	650.	900.	2200.	4000.	9000.
CLOSE COLLAR STRIKE											
1828 Large Date	75.	100.	175.	300.	600.	1000.	1500.	2500.	4000.	—	—
1828 Small Date	35.	45.	75.	150.	350.	600.	800.	1200.	2500.	4000.	—
1829 Curl Base 2	4000.	6000.	8000.	16000.	—	—	—	—	—	—	—
1829 Small 10c	25.	30.	50.	85.	300.	350.	500.	800.	1700.	2800.	6000.

—— = Insufficient pricing data

	G-4	VG-8	F-12	VF-20	EF-40	AU-50	AU-55	MS-60	MS-63	MS-64	MS-65
1829 Medium 10c	25.	30.	50.	85.	300.	350.	550.	900.	1800.	2800.	6000.
1829 Large 10c	35.	50.	100.	200.	400.	600.	750.	1000.	2000.	3500.	6500.
1830	25.	30.	35.	75.	250.	325.	450.	650.	1500.	2500.	6000.
1830/29	35.	60.	100.	200.	350.	600.	800.	1200.	3500.	5500.	—
1831	25.	30.	35.	60.	250.	325.	450.	650.	1500.	2500.	6000.
1832	25.	30.	35.	60.	250.	325.	450.	650.	1500.	2500.	6000.
1833	25.	30.	35.	60.	250.	325.	450.	650.	1500.	2500.	6000.
1834	25.	30.	35.	60.	250.	325.	450.	650.	1500.	2500.	6000.
1835	25.	30.	35.	60.	250.	325.	450.	650.	1500.	2500.	6000.
1836	25.	30.	35.	60.	250.	325.	450.	650.	1500.	2500.	6000.
1837	25.	30.	35.	60.	250.	325.	450.	650.	1500.	2500.	6000.

Seated Liberty dime

Date of authorization: April 2, 1792
Dates of issue: 1837-1891
Designer: (1837-1840)
Obverse: Thomas Sully-Christian Gobrecht
Reverse: Christian Gobrecht
(1840-1860)
Obverse: John Hughes-Gobrecht-Sully
Reverse: Christian Gobrecht
(1860-1891)
Obverse: James B. Longacre-Hughes-Gobrecht-Sully
Reverse: James B. Longacre
Engraver: (1837-1840): Christian Gobrecht
(1840-1860): Christian Gobrecht
(1860-1891): James B. Longacre
Diameter: 17.90 mm/0.71 inch
Weight: (1837-1853): 2.67 grams/0.09 ounce
(1853-1873): 2.49 grams/0.08 ounce
Metallic content:: 90% silver, 10% copper
Weight of pure silver: (1837-1853): 2.41 grams/0.08 ounce
(1853-1873): 2.24 grams/0.07 ounce
Edge: Reeded
Mint mark: Reverse within or below wreath

SEATED LIBERTY DIME (CONTINUED)

	G-4	VG-8	F-12	VF-20	EF-40	AU-50	AU-55	MS-60	MS-63	MS-64	MS-65	PF-63	PF-64	PF-65	PF-66
NO STARS															
1837	40.	50.	100.	300.	500.	700.	800.	1000.	2000.	4000.	—	15000.	22500.	30000.	—
1838-O	50.	85.	125.	400.	700.	1200.	1800.	3000.	7000.	9000.	—	*	*	*	*
NO DRAPERY															
1838 Small Stars	25.	40.	65.	100.	250.	500.	600.	900.	1500.	2500.	5000.	*	*	*	*
1838 Large Stars	20.	25.	30.	50.	125.	300.	400.	500.	1000.	1200.	3000.	*	*	*	*
1838 Partial Drapery	30.	40.	65.	150.	200.	400.	500.	700.	2000.	—	—	*	*	*	*
1839	20.	25.	30.	50.	125.	300.	400.	500.	1000.	1250.	3500.	16500.	—	—	—
1839-O Reverse of 1838	115.	200.	350.	475.	750.	—	—	—	—	—	—	*	*	*	*
1839-O	20.	25.	30.	50.	125.	300.	400.	600.	1350.	2250.	—	*	*	*	*
1840	20.	25.	30.	50.	125.	300.	400.	500.	1000.	1400.	—	12000.	24000.	—	—
1840-O	20.	25.	30.	60.	150.	350.	500.	1000.	2500.	6500.	—	*	*	*	*
DRAPERY															
1840	40.	60.	100.	200.	300.	600.	1000.	1800.	—	—	—	*	*	*	*
1841	20.	25.	30.	35.	55.	150.	250.	400.	800.	1400.	3000.	25000.	—	—	—
1841-O Open Bud Reverse	10.	12.	20.	38.	85.	215.	375.	900.	1950.	3000.	—	*	*	*	*
1842	20.	25.	30.	35.	50.	150.	250.	400.	800.	1400.	3000.	*	*	*	*
1842-O	20.	25.	30.	75.	250.	1200.	1500.	2500.	5000.	—	—	*	*	*	*
1843	20.	25.	30.	35.	50.	150.	200.	300.	1000.	1500.	3500.	—	15000.	—	*
1843/1843	11.	18.	27.	60.	115.	185.	250.	375.	—	2800.	—	*	*	*	*
1843-O	40.	65.	130.	250.	800.	1200.	1800.	3000.	—	—	—	*	*	*	*
1844	250.	400.	600.	800.	1200.	2000.	3000.	4000.	15000.	30000.	—	—	—	105000.	—
1845	20.	30.	35.	40.	50.	150.	200.	400.	1000.	1500.	5000.	—	—	25000.	—
1845/1845	12.	20.	37.	50.	150.	415.	—	—	—	—	—	*	*	*	*
1845-O	30.	40.	75.	250.	600.	1500.	2500.	4000.	3850.	—	—	*	*	*	*

—— = Insufficient pricing data   * = None issued

SEATED LIBERTY DIME (CONTINUED)

	G-4	VG-8	F-12	VF-20	EF-40	AU-50	AU-55	MS-60	MS-63	MS-64	MS-65	PF-63	PF-64	PF-65	PF-66
1846	100.	125.	200.	400.	1000.	2500.	4000.	—	—	—	—	12000.	15000.	25000.	—
1847	20.	30.	50.	80.	150.	400.	600.	1000.	2500.	—	—	—	—	30000.	—
1848	20.	25.	30.	65.	100.	200.	300.	700.	1500.	2500.	—	—	15000.	25000.	—
1849	20.	25.	30.	50.	65.	150.	250.	400.	1200.	2000.	4000.	—	—	20000.	—
1849-O	20.	30.	50.	150.	300.	800.	1500.	2500.	6000.	—	—	*	*	*	*
1850	20.	30.	35.	40.	65.	150.	200.	300.	800.	1500.	4000.	—	—	—	—
1850-O	20.	30.	40.	75.	175.	350.	600.	1500.	3000.	5000.	—	*	*	*	*
1851	20.	30.	35.	40.	50.	150.	200.	400.	1000.	2500.	—	*	*	*	*
1851-O	20.	25.	50.	75.	200.	500.	800.	2000.	3500.	—	—	*	*	*	*
1852	20.	25.	30.	35.	50.	150.	200.	300.	800.	1200.	2500.	7500.	10000.	—	—
1852-O	20.	30.	50.	150.	300.	500.	900.	1500.	3000.	4000.	—	*	*	*	*
1853	55.	80.	125.	200.	300.	500.	700.	1000.	1500.	2500.	3000.	*	*	*	*
ARROWS AT DATE															
1853	20.	25.	30.	35.	65.	200.	300.	400.	900.	1200.	3000.	3500.	—	—	—
1853-O	20.	25.	30.	50.	100.	350.	500.	1000.	3000.	6000.	—	*	*	*	*
1854	20.	25.	30.	35.	65.	200.	300.	400.	900.	1500.	—	10000.	20000.	30000.	—
1854-O	20.	25.	30.	35.	75.	250.	350.	450.	1200.	1800.	—	*	*	*	*
1855	20.	25.	30.	35.	65.	200.	300.	500.	1200.	2000.	—	10000.	20000.	35000.	—
DRAPERY															
1856 Small Date	20.	25.	30.	35.	65.	200.	300.	400.	800.	1500.	—	4000.	7500.	12000.	—
1856 Large Date	20.	25.	30.	40.	100.	400.	600.	800.	1500.	2500.	—	*	*	*	*
1856-O	20.	25.	30.	35.	75.	300.	500.	800.	1800.	3500.	7000.	*	*	*	*
1856-S	125.	200.	400.	600.	1200.	1800.	2500.	3500.	12000.	18000.	—	*	*	*	*
1857	20.	25.	30.	35.	50.	200.	300.	400.	800.	1200.	3000.	4000.	6000.	8500.	—
1857-O	20.	25.	30.	35.	75.	250.	350.	500.	1000.	2000.	3000.	*	*	*	*
1858	20.	25.	30.	35.	50.	150.	200.	400.	800.	1500.	3000.	2500.	3000.	5000.	—
1858-O	20.	30.	50.	100.	125.	350.	450.	800.	1500.	3500.	6000.	*	*	*	*

—— = Insufficient pricing data * = None issued

SEATED LIBERTY DIME (CONTINUED)

	G-4	VG-8	F-12	VF-20	EF-40	AU-50	AU-55	MS-60	MS-63	MS-64	MS-65	PF-63	PF-64	PF-65	PF-66
1858-S	100.	150.	250.	400.	900.	1500.	2000.	3000.	12000.	15000.	—	*	*	*	*
1859	20.	25.	30.	40.	65.	150.	200.	400.	800.	1200.	3000.	1500.	2500.	4000.	—
1859-O	20.	25.	30.	40.	100.	250.	350.	500.	800.	1400.	3000.	*	*	*	*
1859-S	100.	150.	250.	600.	1000.	2000.	3000.	—	—	—	—	*	*	*	*
1860-S	30.	40.	65.	150.	350.	700.	1000.	2500.	6000.	9000.	—	*	*	*	*
LEGEND OBVERSE															
1860	20.	25.	30.	40.	50.	100.	200.	300.	400.	800.	1500.	500.	700.	1500.	—
1860-O	400.	500.	900.	1800.	3500.	6000.	8000.	11000.	30000.	40000.	—	*	*	*	*
1861	20.	25.	30.	35.	40.	100.	150.	200.	350.	800.	1500.	600.	850.	1800.	—
1861-S	55.	90.	150.	300.	500.	850.	1100.	2000.	5000.	8000.	—	*	*	*	*
1862	20.	25.	30.	35.	40.	100.	150.	200.	350.	800.	—	600.	1000.	2000.	*
1862-S	50.	60.	100.	200.	400.	700.	1000.	1600.	3500.	7000.	—	*	*	*	*
1863	400.	500.	600.	700.	900.	1100.	1200.	1500.	2000.	3000.	5000.	600.	1000.	1800.	—
1863-S	50.	60.	75.	125.	200.	550.	800.	1500.	3000.	7500.	—	*	*	*	*
1864	250.	400.	500.	700.	900.	1000.	1100.	1200.	1500.	2500.	3500.	800.	1000.	1500.	—
1864-S	30.	40.	60.	100.	200.	400.	600.	1000.	1800.	3000.	—	*	*	*	*
1865	300.	400.	600.	800.	1000.	1200.	1300.	1500.	1800.	2000.	4500.	1000.	1200.	2500.	—
1865-S	30.	40.	60.	175.	300.	800.	1200.	2500.	7000.	—	—	*	*	*	*
1866	400.	500.	700.	900.	1100.	1400.	1500.	1700.	2000.	2500.	4000.	700.	900.	1500.	—
1866-S	50.	65.	100.	125.	250.	500.	800.	2000.	3000.	6000.	—	*	*	*	*
1867	500.	700.	900.	1100.	1500.	1800.	2000.	2500.	3000.	3500.	—	600.	800.	1800.	—
1867-S	35.	50.	75.	125.	250.	700.	1000.	2000.	4500.	—	—	*	*	*	*
1868	20.	25.	35.	50.	75.	200.	300.	400.	1000.	1500.	4500.	600.	800.	1500.	—
1868-S	20.	30.	40.	65.	125.	250.	350.	600.	1200.	2500.	—	*	*	*	*
1869	20.	30.	50.	85.	100.	200.	300.	600.	1200.	2500.	—	600.	800.	1500.	—
1869-S	20.	25.	30.	45.	85.	200.	300.	500.	1000.	1800.	4000.	*	*	*	*
1870	20.	25.	30.	35.	65.	125.	200.	300.	600.	1000.	2500.	600.	900.	1500.	—

—— = Insufficient pricing data * = None issued

SEATED LIBERTY DIME (CONTINUED)

	G-4	VG-8	F-12	VF-20	EF-40	AU-50	AU-55	MS-60	MS-63	MS-64	MS-65	PF-63	PF-64	PF-65	PF-66
1870-S	300.	400.	500.	600.	800.	1000.	1400	2000.	3000.	3500.	6000.	*	*	*	*
1871	20.	25.	30.	35.	65.	200.	300.	400.	700.	1200.	2500.	600.	900.	1500.	—
1871-CC	1400.	1800.	2500.	4000.	8000.	12500.	20000.	14500.	—	41000.	—	*	*	*	*
1871-S	25.	40.	65.	100.	175.	350.	500.	700.	1500.	3000.	—	*	*	*	*
1872	20.	25.	30.	35.	40.	100.	150.	200.	400.	800.	1500.	600.	800.	1600.	—
1872-CC	500.	750.	1200.	3000.	6000.	10000.	15000.	30000.	—	—	—	*	*	*	*
1872-S	20.	35.	100.	150.	250.	450.	700.	1400.	2500.	5000.	—	*	*	*	*
1873 Closed 3	20.	25.	30.	35.	40.	100.	150.	200.	400.	900.	1500.	600.	800.	1500.	—
1873 Open 3	20.	30.	65.	85.	125.	250.	350.	700.	1500.	—	—	*	*	*	*
1873-CC (unique) Eliasberg/Bolen specimen sold for $632,500.															
ARROWS AT DATE															
1873 Doubled Die (Shield)	—	350.	500.	775.	1000.	—	—	—	—	—	—	*	*	*	*
1873-CC	1000	2000.	3500.	6500.	10000.	12000.	15000.	25000.	50000.	80000.	—	*	*	*	*
1873-S	20.	25.	35.	75.	200.	400.	500.	1000.	2500	4000.	—	*	*	*	*
1873	20.	25.	30.	75.	150.	300.	400.	600.	1000	2000.	4000.	1200.	2500.	6000.	—
1874	20.	25.	30.	50.	150.	400.	500.	600.	1000	2000.	4000.	1200.	2500.	6000.	—
1874-CC	2500.	5000.	6500	12000.	20000.	25000.	30000.	40000.	—	—	—	*	*	*	*
1874-S	25.	50.	100	150.	300.	500.	600.	1000.	2500	5000.	8000.	*	*	*	*

—— = Insufficient pricing data * = None issued

Legend obverse

SEATED LIBERTY DIME (CONTINUED)

LEGEND OBVERSE	G-4	VG-8	F-12	VF-20	EF-40	AU-50	AU-55	MS-60	MS-63	MS-64	MS-65	PF-63	PF-64	PF-65	PF-66
1875	20.	25.	30.	35.	40.	100.	150.	200.	400.	600.	1000.	600.	800.	1500.	—
1875-CC	20.	25.	30.	45.	75.	125.	200.	300.	1000.	1500.	2500.	*	*	*	*
1875-CC in Wreath	20.	25.	30.	45.	60.	100.	150.	300.	900.	1500.	2500.	*	*	*	*
1875-S	20.	25.	30.	35.	40.	100.	150.	200.	400.	600.	1000.	*	*	*	*
1875-S S in Wreath	20.	25.	30.	35.	40.	100.	150.	200.	400.	600.	1000.	*	*	*	*
1876	20.	25.	30.	35.	40.	100.	150.	200.	400.	600.	1000.	600.	800.	1500.	—
1876-CC Doubled Die	25.	30.	50.	85.	225.	315.	390.	475.	1250.	—	—	*	*	*	*
1876-S	20.	25.	30.	35.	40.	100.	150.	200.	400.	600.	1000.	*	*	*	*
1876-CC	20.	25.	30.	35.	50.	100.	150.	250.	500.	600.	1500.	—	—	300000.	—
1877	20.	25.	30.	35.	40.	100.	150.	200.	400.	600.	1000.	600.	800.	1500.	—
1877-CC	20.	25.	30.	35.	50.	100.	150.	250.	500.	600.	1500.	*	*	*	*
1877-S	20.	25.	30.	35.	40.	100.	150.	200.	400.	600.	1000.	*	*	*	*
1878	20.	25.	30.	35.	40.	100.	150.	200.	400.	600.	1000.	600.	800.	1500.	—
1878-CC	50.	85.	125.	200.	400.	600.	700.	1200.	1800.	—	—	*	*	*	*
1879	200.	300.	400.	500.	600.	800.	900.	1000.	1200.	1500.	1800.	600.	800.	1500.	—
1880	200.	300.	400.	500.	600.	800.	900.	1000.	1200.	1500.	1800.	600.	800.	1500.	—
1881	200.	300.	400.	500.	600.	800.	900.	1000.	1200.	1500.	1800.	600.	800.	1500.	—
1882	20.	25.	30.	35.	40.	100.	150.	200.	400.	600.	1000.	600.	800.	1500.	—

—— = Insufficient pricing data   * = None issued

SEATED LIBERTY DIME (CONTINUED)

	G-4	VG-8	F-12	VF-20	EF-40	AU-50	AU-55	MS-60	MS-63	MS-64	MS-65	PF-63	PF-64	PF-65	PF-66
1883	20.	25.	30.	35.	40.	100.	150.	200.	400.	600.	1000.	600.	800.	1500.	—
1884	20.	25.	30.	35.	40.	100.	150.	200.	400.	600.	1000.	600.	800.	1500.	—
1884-S	20.	30.	40.	65.	100.	350.	500.	900.	1500.	2500.	—	*	*	*	*
1885	20.	25.	30.	35.	40.	100.	150.	200.	400.	600.	1000.	600.	800.	1500.	—
1885-S	500.	750.	1000.	1800.	2500.	3500.	4500.	6000.	9000.	15000.	—	*	*	*	*
1886	20.	25.	30.	35.	40.	100.	150.	200.	400.	600.	1000.	600.	800.	1500.	—
1886-S	35.	50.	65.	100.	150.	250.	350.	700.	1500.	—	—	*	*	*	*
1887	20.	25.	30.	35.	40.	100.	150.	200.	400.	600.	1000.	600.	800.	1500.	—
1887-S	20.	25.	30.	35.	40.	100.	150.	200.	400.	600.	1000.	*	*	*	*
1888	20.	25.	30.	35.	40.	100.	150.	200.	400.	600.	1000.	600.	800.	1500.	—
1888-S	20.	25.	30.	35.	50.	125.	200.	300.	700.	1200.	3000.	*	*	*	*
1889	20.	25.	30.	35.	40.	100.	150.	200.	400.	600.	1000.	600.	800.	1500.	—
1889-S	20.	25.	35.	50.	85.	200.	300.	400.	1200.	2000.	5000.	*	*	*	*
1890	20.	25.	30.	35.	40.	100.	150.	200.	400.	600.	1000.	600.	800.	1500.	—
1890-S	20.	25.	35.	60.	100.	200.	300.	400.	800.	1200.	2500.	*	*	*	*
1891	20.	25.	30.	35.	40.	100.	150.	200.	400.	600.	1000.	600.	800.	1500.	—
1891-O	20.	25.	30.	35.	40.	100.	150.	200.	400.	600.	1000.	*	*	*	*
1891-O/Horizontal O	50.	80.	115.	165.	225.	425.	—	—	—	—	—	*	*	*	*
1891-S	20.	25.	30.	35.	40.	100.	150.	200.	400.	600.	1000.	*	*	*	*

—— = Insufficient pricing data   * = None issued

Barber dime

Date of authorization:	April 2, 1792
Dates of issue:	1892-1916
Designer:	Obverse: Charles Barber Reverse: James B. Longacre
Engraver:	Charles Barber
Diameter:	17.91 mm/0.71 inch
Weight:	2.50 grams/0.08 ounce
Metallic content:	90% silver, 10% copper
Weight of pure silver:	2.25 grams/0.07 ounce
Edge:	Reeded
Mint mark:	Reverse within or below wreath

BARBER DIME (CONTINUED)

	G-4	VG-8	F-12	VF-20	EF-40	AU-50	MS-60	MS-63	MS-64	MS-65	MS-66	PF-63	PF-64	PF-65	PF-66
1892	4.00	6.00	17.	23.	26.	68.	95.	145.	235.	635.	—	330.	550.	1150.	—
1892-O	8.00	12.	27.	47.	55.	75.	140.	290.	515.	1250.	2150.	*	*	*	*
1892-S	55.	95.	175.	200.	245.	275.	375.	750.	1550.	2300.	3500.	*	*	*	*
1893/2	—	—	—	130.	275.	400.	550.	1350.	2200.	3550.	4500.	*	*	*	*
1893-O	26.	42.	115.	130.	160.	175.	265.	485.	1000.	2525.	5000.	*	*	*	*
1893-S	11.	19.	28.	39.	60.	125.	250.	525.	1500.	3875.	—	*	*	*	*
1893	6.50	12.	18.	25.	40.	68.	105.	170.	275.	950.	1450.	375.	550.	1150.	—
1894	17.	31.	110.	130.	155.	175.	275.	475.	750.	1300.	—	340.	525.	1125.	—
1894-O	54.	90.	195.	250.	325.	640.	1500.	2600.	4575.	10550.	—	*	*	*	*
1894-S (Proof only) PF-4 $40000, PF-60 $ 65000	*	*	*	*	*	*	*	*	*	*	*	125000.	—	450000.	—
1895	75.	140.	345.	460.	485.	540.	650.	1150.	1650.	2900.	—	425.	600.	1325.	—
1895-O	300	450.	700.	1000.	2000.	3000.	5000.	8000.	12000	15000.	—	*	*	*	*
1895-S	38	47.	130.	170.	210.	285.	475.	1000.	3050	7250.	—	*	*	*	*
1896	9.50	22.	52.	70.	88.	110.	175.	375.	750.	1450.	2200.	330.	525.	1100.	—
1896-O	60.	115.	265.	340.	400.	660.	1050.	2250.	4800.	8500.	21000.	*	*	*	*
1896-S	70.	135.	260.	285.	350.	475.	675.	1650.	3250.	3750.	6500.	*	*	*	*
1897	2.50	3.50	6.50	13.	25.	68.	100.	155.	275.	750.	1950.	330.	550.	1075.	—
1897-O	58.	110.	270.	340.	420.	540.	775.	1400.	2650.	4550.	—	*	*	*	*
1897-S	14.	30.	95.	100.	132.	225.	400.	1000.	2500.	4500.	9500.	*	*	*	*
1898	2.50	3.00	6.50	11.	23.	68.	90.	140.	275.	675.	1900.	330.	525.	1100.	—
1898-O	8.00	20.	85.	105.	155.	230.	450.	1150.	2250.	3500.	6850.	*	*	*	*
1898-S	5.50	12.	26.	37.	62.	115.	285.	950.	2625.	4550.	6000.	*	*	*	*
1899	2.75	3.50	6.50	10.	22.	68.	85.	140.	300.	775.	1700.	330.	525.	1100.	—
1899-O	6.00	16.	70.	55.	140.	235.	465.	1150.	2900.	5550.	7500.	*	*	*	*
1899-S	6.00	13.	20.	25.	42.	105.	290.	600.	1900.	3350.	5800.	*	*	*	*
1900	2.75	4.00	6.50	11.	22.	68.	85.	140.	275.	825.	2050.	330.	615.	1100.	—

—— = Insufficient pricing data * = None issued

BARBER DIME (CONTINUED)

	G-4	VG-8	F-12	VF-20	EF-40	AU-50	MS-60	MS-63	MS-64	MS-65	MS-66	PF-63	PF-64	PF-65	PF-66
1900-O	15.	34.	105.	132.	225.	425.	750.	1400.	2750.	5750.	9500.	*	*	*	*
1900-S	4.00	4.75	11.	14.	24.	75.	190.	450.	760.	1700.	3000.	*	*	*	*
1901	2.75	3.50	6.00	8.75	20.	60.	85.	140.	275.	750.	1850.	360.	500.	1150.	—
1901-O	3.50	5.25	12.	21.	45.	125.	370.	1050.	1850.	3300.	5250.	*	*	*	*
1901-S	75.	120.	335.	375.	435.	650.	1025.	2050.	2850.	4250.	6750.	*	*	*	*
1902	2.50	3.00	5.00	7.50	20.	60.	85.	140.	275.	675.	1950.	330.	500.	1150.	—
1902-O	3.00	7.00	14.	25.	46.	140.	425.	825.	1800.	3450.	5800.	*	*	*	*
1902-S	7.00	15.	53.	70.	110.	160.	350.	690.	1950.	3200.	7100.	*	*	*	*
1903	3.00	3.50	5.00	7.50	20.	60.	85.	150.	300.	950.	2300.	330.	500.	1150.	—
1903-O	3.00	5.50	11.	17.	30.	100.	250.	575.	1250.	4850.	—	*	*	*	*
1903-S	70.	125.	340.	475.	750.	850.	1250.	1750.	2175.	4000.	—	*	*	*	*
1904	2.50	3.00	6.00	10.	20.	60.	85.	200.	525.	1700.	3300.	325.	500.	1175.	—
1904-S	36.	62.	150.	195.	275.	460.	785.	1350.	2650.	4550.	11000.	*	*	*	*
1905	2.50	3.00	5.00	7.50	20.	60.	85.	140.	275.	675.	2200.	325.	500.	1125.	—
1905-O	3.00	7.50	32.	45.	65.	120.	225.	500.	900.	2125.	3000.	*	*	*	*
1905-O Micro O	25.	40.	75.	110.	175.	350.	850.	1650.	2850.	5300.	—	*	*	*	*
1905-S	3.00	5.00	8.00	14.	32.	80.	165.	315.	600.	1250.	—	*	*	*	*
1906	2.50	3.00	4.50	7.50	20.	60.	85.	140.	275.	650.	1500.	350.	550.	1150.	—
1906-D	3.00	4.75	10.	16.	31.	75.	160.	285.	925.	2150.	3250.	*	*	*	*
1906-O	5.00	10.	45.	65.	90.	130.	210.	325.	500.	1200.	—	*	*	*	*
1906-S	2.75	6.00	11.	19.	40.	90.	240.	365.	800.	1400.	2650.	*	*	*	*
1907	2.50	3.50	4.25	7.50	20.	60.	85.	155.	275.	650.	—	360.	525.	1150.	—
1907-D	3.00	5.00	9.00	16.	40.	95.	235.	775.	1700.	3800.	—	*	*	*	*
1907-O	2.75	6.00	32.	50.	55.	80.	190.	330.	675.	1325.	—	*	*	*	*
1907-S	2.75	6.00	12.	19.	43.	100.	300.	800.	1575.	2200.	4200.	*	*	*	*
1908	2.50	3.00	4.00	7.50	20.	60.	85.	140.	275.	650.	—	375.	575.	1200.	—
1908-D	2.50	3.00	7.50	12.	32.	60.	120.	200.	425.	1125.	—	*	*	*	*

—— = Insufficient pricing data   * = None issued

BARBER DIME (CONTINUED)

	G-4	VG-8	F-12	VF-20	EF-40	AU-50	MS-60	MS-63	MS-64	MS-65	MS-66	PF-63	PF-64	PF-65	PF-66
1903-O	4.00	12.	45.	60.	80.	160.	290.	475.	700.	1950.	2650.	*	*	*	*
1903-S	2.75	5.00	9.50	16.	35.	150.	265.	535.	1425.	2700.	3750.	*	*	*	*
1909	2.50	3.00	4.00	7.50	20.	30.	85.	150.	275.	650.	—	400.	575.	1200.	—
1909-D	6.00	16.	62.	95.	125.	235.	475.	1075.	1450.	3150.	5500.	*	*	*	*
1909-O	2.75	6.00	10.	18.	30.	95.	170.	460.	700.	1300.	—	*	*	*	*
1909-S	7.00	17.	85.	130.	170.	300.	575.	1350.	1900.	2700.	3300.	*	*	*	*
1910	2.50	3.00	7.00	10.	20.	60.	85.	140.	275.	650.	1350.	360.	525.	1200.	—
1910-D	2.50	5.00	8.00	17.	42.	95.	185.	490.	675.	1725.	2750.	*	*	*	*
1910-S	4.00	10.	52.	75.	105.	175.	275.	700.	1250.	2100.	—	*	*	*	*
1911	2.50	3.00	4.00	7.50	20.	60.	85.	140.	275.	625.	—	360.	500.	1225.	—
1911-D	2.50	3.00	4.50	8.00	21.	60.	95.	170.	275.	675.	1325.	*	*	*	*
1911-S	2.50	3.25	9.00	16.	35.	88.	135.	240.	600.	1050.	1650.	*	*	*	*
1912	2.50	3.00	4.00	7.75	21.	60.	85.	140.	275.	675.	1400.	330.	525.	1225.	—
1912-D	2.50	3.00	4.25	8.00	20.	60.	90.	150.	275.	700.	1400.	*	*	*	*
1912-S	2.50	3.00	8.00	13.	33.	88.	175.	315.	525.	1300.	—	*	*	*	*
1913	2.50	3.00	4.00	7.50	20.	60.	85.	140.	275.	650.	—	330.	500.	1250.	—
1913-S	10.	20.	30.	120.	210.	275.	400.	650.	[illegible]	1200.	2450.	*	*	*	*
1914	2.50	3.00	4.00	7.50	20.	60.	85.	140.	275.	650.	—	330.	575.	1250.	—
1914-D	2.50	3.00	4.00	7.75	21.	60.	90.	155.	[illegible]	650.	—	*	*	*	*
1914-S	2.50	3.00	5.00	16.	35.	75.	125.	350.	[illegible]	1350.	2800.	*	*	*	*
1915	2.50	3.00	4.00	8.25	20.	60.	85.	140.	[illegible]	675.	—	350.	575	1275.	—
1915-S	4.75	8.75	32.	43.	60.	130.	250.	475.	[illegible]	1600.	3200.	*	*	*	*
1916	2.50	3.00	4.00	7.75	20.	60.	85.	140.	[illegible]	625.	—	*	*	*	*
1916-S	2.50	3.00	5.75	8.00	21.	60.	90.	165.	[illegible]	825.	—	*	*	*	*

—— = Insufficient pricing data   * = None issued

Winged Liberty Head dime

"Mercury dime"

Date of authorization:	April 2, 1792
Dates of issue:	1916-1945
Designer:	Adolph Weinman
Engraver:	Charles Barber
Diameter:	17.91 mm/0.71 inch
Weight:	2.50 grams/0.08 ounce
Metallic content:	90% silver, 10% copper
Weight of pure silver:	2.25 grams/0.07 ounce
Edge:	Reeded
Mint mark:	Reverse left of base of fasces (bundle of rods)

NOTE: B refers to Full Split Bands on the fasces on the reverse.

WINGED LIBERTY HEAD DIME (CONTINUED)

	VG-8	F-12	VF-20	EF-40	AU-50	MS-60	MS-62	MS-63	MS-64	MS-64B	MS-65	MS-65B	MS-66	MS-66B	PF-63	PF-65	PF-66
1916	4.00	5.25	6.00	9.00	20.	26.	30.	40.	46.	55.	85.	115.	200.	350.	*	*	*
1916-D	1200.	2000.	3000.	4000	5500.	6500.	7000.	7500.	9000.	18000.	20000.	45000.	-	-	*	*	*
1916-S	4.00	6.75	8.00	16.	20.	35.	40.	60.	80.	150.	225.	575.	450.	1400.	*	*	*
1917	1.70	2.60	4.50	7.50	13.	23.	29.	55.	78.	95.	140.	390.	350.	800.	*	*	*
1917-D	5.00	9.00	18.	37.	80.	135.	245.	350.	475.	1150.	1350.	6000.	3000.	10000.	*	*	*
1917-S	2.25	3.25	5.00	9.00	26.	55.	75.	150.	210.	335.	465	1050.	500.	2000.	*	*	*
1918	2.50	5.25	9.50	26.	38.	68.	80.	95.	130.	225.	350.	1050.	1000.	2000.	*	*	*
1918-D	2.75	4.25	9.50	20.	39.	95.	130.	215.	365.	2800.	725.	42500.	1100.	-	*	*	*
1918-S	2.35	4.00	7.25	14.	30.	80.	140.	250.	375.	2300.	600.	7000.	2000.	11000.	*	*	*
1919	1.95	3.00	5.00	10.	21.	30.	38.	95.	125.	185.	300.	675.	600.	1200.	*	*	*
1919-D	5.00	9.25	18	32.	63.	190.	250.	400.	625.	2650.	1600.	-	3000.	-	*	*	*
1919-S	3.25	7.00	12	30.	65.	175.	225.	400.	700.	3500.	850.	11500.	1200.	-	*	*	*
1920	1.80	2.50	4.00	7.00	14.	24.	30.	70.	95.	120.	225.	500.	500.	850.	*	*	*
1920-D	2.40	3.50	6.75	15	40.	100.	165.	350.	390.	775.	750.	4500.	2000.	5000.	*	*	*
1920-S	2.25	4.00	7.00	15.	34.	100.	135.	315.	515.	2000	1350.	9250.	2500.	12000.	*	*	*
1921	60.	100.	250.	500.	800.	1000.	1200.	1400.	2000.	2500.	3000.	4000.	-	6000.	*	*	*
1921-D	100.	150.	350.	600.	1000.	1200.	1500.	1800.	2200.	2300.	3200.	5500.	4500.	7000.	*	*	*
1923	1.75	2.50	3.75	6.00	13.	27.	30.	38.	45.	65.	100.	275.	350.	450.	*	*	*
1923-S	2.35	6.00	10.	50.	85.	160.	225.	375.	775.	1550.	1500.	6500.	2500.	9000.	*	*	*
1924	1.60	2.50	5.00	12.	23.	35.	45.	80.	105.	150.	185.	545.	350.	650.	*	*	*
1924-D	3.50	5.00	11.	42.	90.	140.	185.	325.	565.	750	1050.	1400.	1500.	2500.	*	*	*
1924-S	2.25	3.25	9.00	40.	88.	140.	225.	450.	625.	2750	1025.	12500.	-	-	*	*	*
1925	1.60	2.50	5.00	7.00	18.	29.	34.	75.	110.	200	200.	850.	350.	2000.	*	*	*
1925-D	3.75	10.	30.	95.	130.	375.	450.	650.	900.	1350.	1600.	2950.	-	4000.	*	*	*
1925-S	2.25	4.50	10.	55.	85.	165.	240.	525.	800.	1200.	1700.	4500.	2300.	7000.	*	*	*
1926	1.50	2.00	3.50	4.75	12.	24.	30.	58.	105.	130.	265.	575.	400.	850.	*	*	*
1926-D	2.00	3.75	7.00	20.	39.	95.	125.	225.	300.	475.	550.	2750.	1200.	5000.	*	*	*

—— = Insufficient pricing data * = None issued

WINGED LIBERTY HEAD DIME (CONTINUED)

	VG-8	F-12	VF-20	EF-40	AU-50	MS-60	MS-62	MS-63	MS-64	MS-64B	MS-65	MS-65B	MS-66	MS-66B	PF-63	PF-65	PF-66
1926-S	7.00	18.	40.	180.	400.	775.	950.	1300.	1500.	2350.	2950.	6250.	4500.	14000.	*	*	*
1927	1.55	2.25	3.50	5.00	11.	22.	30.	45.	77.	105.	165.	400.	325.	600.	*	*	*
1927-D	4.00	5.50	18.	55.	95.	185.	250.	335.	475.	1500.	1375.	8000.	2300.	11000.	*	*	*
1927-S	2.75	4.00	7.00	21.	48.	235.	300.	485.	725.	1650.	1750.	7000.	2500.	8500.	*	*	*
1928	1.45	2.10	3.50	5.00	15.	25.	30.	45.	55.	90.	140.	350.	325.	500.	*	*	*
1928-D	3.65	7.00	18.	40.	80.	135.	160.	295.	400.	700.	800.	2800.	1200.	4000.	*	*	*
1928-S	2.00	2.75	5.25	15.	35.	90.	135.	225.	300.	600.	350.	1825.	400.	2500.	*	*	*
1929	1.45	2.25	3.30	4.25	10.	19.	22.	30.	36.	50.	60.	250.	125.	350.	*	*	*
1929-D	2.75	3.75	7.00	14.	21.	25.	30.	38.	42.	60.	80.	240.	125.	500.	*	*	*
1929-S	1.75	2.50	3.75	6.50	20.	38.	40.	50.	65.	125.	130.	525.	300.	850.	*	*	*
1930	1.70	2.25	3.50	6.00	13.	25.	30.	45.	50.	100.	145.	550.	200.	750.	*	*	*
1930-S	3.00	4.25	5.75	12.	38.	65.	72.	90.	95.	160.	155.	500.	300.	850.	*	*	*
1931	2.25	3.00	4.00	9.00	20.	35.	40.	55.	75.	150.	140.	800.	250.	1200.	*	*	*
1931-D	5.50	8.75	16.	30.	45.	80.	85.	95.	110.	160.	210.	325.	400.	500.	*	*	*
1931-S	2.35	3.50	6.00	12.	33.	70.	80.	100.	130.	600.	210.	1775.	500.	3000.	*	*	*
1934	0.80	1.25	2.25	4.00	7.00	14.	16.	18.	21.	35.	41.	145.	75.	200.	*	*	*
1934-D	1.30	2.75	6.00	11.	21.	33.	36.	40.	50.	90.	75.	350.	125.	750.	*	*	*
1935	0.80	1.00	1.35	2.50	5.00	8.00	10.	15.	24.	35.	40.	70.	60.	100.	*	*	*
1935-D	1.25	2.25	5.00	10.	20.	29.	32.	40.	42.	150.	65.	550.	175.	900.	*	*	*
1935-S	1.00	1.25	1.85	3.25	9.00	20.	22.	25.	28.	100.	38.	500.	60.	650.	*	*	*
1936	0.75	1.00	1.35	2.00	3.25	8.00	9.00	15.	20.	40.	28.	85.	50.	125.	1000.	2000.	3000.
1936-D	1.05	1.45	3.00	6.00	12.	20.	23.	25.	32.	75.	42.	325.	85.	400.	*	*	*
1936-S	0.95	1.10	1.80	3.50	9.00	15.	16.	18.	23.	35.	30.	75.	60.	125.	*	*	*
1937	0.75	1.00	1.35	1.95	4.00	8.00	9.00	12.	15.	25.	25.	38.	35.	60.	500.	1000.	1500.
1937-D	0.95	1.25	2.00	4.00	8.00	18.	19.	22.	27.	35.	45.	110.	80.	150.	*	*	*
1937-S	0.95	1.25	2.25	3.00	7.00	16.	17.	25.	29.	60.	35.	180.	60.	225.	*	*	*
1938	0.75	0.95	1.30	2.50	6.00	10.	11.	12.	16.	25.	24.	75.	50.	90.	250.	500.	800.

—— = Insufficient pricing data * = None issued

WINGED LIBERTY HEAD DIME (CONTINUED)

	VG-8	F-12	VF-20	EF-40	AU-50	MS-60	MS-62	MS-63	MS-64	MS-64B	MS-65	MS-65B	MS-66	MS-66B	PF-63	PF-65	PF-66
1938-D	1.50	1.75	2.25	4.50	9.00	12.	13.	16.	18.	25.	30.	60.	60.	85.	*	*	*
1938-S	1.00	1.20	1.75	3.00	6.00	14.	14.	18.	27.	35.	33.	135.	60.	200.	*	*	*
1939	0.75	1.00	1.30	1.95	3.00	8.00	9.75	12.	17.	40.	28.	170.	40.	200.	200.	400.	600.
1939-D	0.95	1.10	1.30	2.00	4.00	7.00	8.50	10.	17.	25.	25.	40.	40.	50.	*	*	*
1939-S	1.25	1.50	2.00	4.00	9.00	19.	22.	27.	35.	140.	40.	575.	60.	1000.	*	*	*
1940	0.75	0.85	1.00	1.95	2.75	5.50	7.00	10.	17.	25.	28.	50.	35.	60.	200.	400.	600.
1940-D	0.75	0.95	1.25	2.50	5.00	6.75	8.75	11.	20.	19.	23.	50.	35.	65.	*	*	*
1940-S	0.75	0.95	1.25	1.75	3.00	7.00	8.75	12.	16.	25.	25.	100.	30.	150.	*	*	*
1941	0.75	0.85	1.00	1.50	2.00	5.50	7.00	9.00	14.	20.	21.	40.	30.	50.	200.	400.	500.
1941-D	0.75	0.95	1.25	1.85	4.00	7.00	8.50	11.	15.	20.	25.	42.	30.	50.	*	*	*
1941-S	0.75	0.95	1.25	1.85	2.50	9.00	10.	12.	16.	20.	25.	45.	35.	65.	*	*	*
1942/1	600.	650.	8[illegible]0.	900.	1200.	2000.	3000.	4000.	5500.	10000.	4000.	35000.	-	-	*	*	*
1942/1-D	500.	550.	650.	800.	1100.	1800.	2500.	3500.	5000.	9000.	6000.	20000.	-	-	*	*	*
1942-D	0.75	0.95	1.25	1.85	2.75	7.00	8.50	12.	16.	20.	25.	35.	30.	45.	*	*	*
1942-S	0.75	0.95	1.35	2.00	2.50	9.00	10.	13.	20.	40.	28.	125.	40.	175.	*	*	*
1942	0.75	0.85	1.00	1.50	2.00	5.50	6.75	9.00	12.	20.	20.	45.	25.	60.	200.	400.	500.
1943	0.75	0.85	1.00	1.50	2.25	5.50	6.75	9.00	12.	20.	20.	50.	30.	60.	*	*	*
1943-D	0.75	0.95	1.25	1.85	2.50	7.00	8.25	10.	13.	20.	25.	38.	30.	45.	*	*	*
1943-S	0.75	0.95	1.25	1.85	2.75	9.00	10.	12.	17.	20.	24.	75.	30.	100.	*	*	*
1944	0.75	0.85	1.00	1.25	2.00	5.00	6.75	11.	13.	20.	20.	85.	25.	125.	*	*	*
1944-D	0.75	0.95	1.25	1.85	2.50	7.00	8.75	12.	14.	20.	24.	40.	30.	50.	*	*	*
1944-S	0.75	0.95	1.25	1.75	2.25	7.50	9.25	12.	20.	30.	25.	50.	30.	65.	*	*	*
1945	0.75	0.85	1.00	1.25	2.25	5.50	7.00	10.	15.	1400.	24.	7150.	35.	-	*	*	*
1945-D	0.75	0.95	1.25	2.00	3.50	7.00	8.75	10.	17.	20.	24.	40.	30.	50.	*	*	*
1945-S	0.75	0.95	1.25	1.90	2.50	7.00	9.00	13.	18.	28.	28.	125.	35.	175.	*	*	*
1945-S Micro S	1.25	1.50	2.50	5.00	15.	20.	21.	26.	30.	140.	57.	625.	100.	1000.	*	*	*

—— = Insufficient pricing data * = None issued

Roosevelt dime

Date of authorization:	April 2, 1792; July 23, 1965
Dates of issue:	1946-present
Designer/Engraver:	John R. Sinnock
Diameter:	17.91 mm/0.71 inch
Weight:	(1946-1964, 1992-present silver Proofs only): 2.50 grams/0.08 ounce (1965-present): 2.27 grams/0.07 ounce
Metallic content:	(1946-1964, 1992-present silver Proofs only): 90% silver, 10% copper (1965-present): 75% copper, 25% nickel clad to pure copper core
Weight of pure silver:	(1946-1964, 1992-present silver Proofs only): 2.25 grams/0.07 ounce
Edge:	Reeded
Mint mark:	(1946-1964): Reverse left of base of torch (1968-present): Obverse above date

Also, the letter C following a numerical grade for a Proof coin stands for "cameo," while the letters DC stand for "deep cameo." Cameo coins have contrasting surface finishes: mirror fields and frosted devices (raised areas). Deep cameo coins are the ultimate level of cameo, with deeply frosted devices. Cameo and deep cameo coins bring premiums.

	AU-50	MS-60	MS-63	MS-64	MS-65	MS-66	MS-67	MS-68	PF-63	PF-64	PF-65	PF-65C	PF-65DC	PF-66	PF-66C	PF-66DC	PF-67	PF-67C	PF-67DC	PF-68	PF-68C	PF-68DC	PF-69	PF-69DC	PF-70	PF-70DC
SILVER																										
1946	0.70	1.00	1.75	8.00	15.	30.	125.	—	*	*	*	*	*	*	*	*	*	*	*	*	*	*	*	*	*	—
1946-D	0.70	1.10	1.75	8.00	14.	30.	110.	—	*	*	*	*	*	*	*	*	*	*	*	*	*	*	*	*	*	—
1946-S	1.25	1.50	3.00	10.	18.	35.	100.	—	*	*	*	*	*	*	*	*	*	*	*	*	*	*	*	*	*	—
1947	0.90	1.40	1.75	7.00	12.	21.	65.	—	*	*	*	*	*	*	*	*	*	*	*	*	*	*	*	*	*	—
1947-D	1.75	2.20	4.00	7.00	12.	20.	37.	—	*	*	*	*	*	*	*	*	*	*	*	*	*	*	*	*	*	—
1947-S	1.25	1.75	3.00	8.00	15.	35.	125.	—	*	*	*	*	*	*	*	*	*	*	*	*	*	*	*	*	*	—
1948	1.55	4.00	5.50	8.00	14.	35.	100.	—	*	*	*	*	*	*	*	*	*	*	*	*	*	*	*	*	*	—
1948-D	2.00	2.50	4.00	7.00	12.	21.	100.	—	*	*	*	*	*	*	*	*	*	*	*	*	*	*	*	*	*	—
1948-S	1.25	1.90	5.00	7.00	10.	30.	120.	—	*	*	*	*	*	*	*	*	*	*	*	*	*	*	*	*	*	—
1949	4.00	9.00	15.	22.	30.	100.	135.	—	*	*	*	*	*	*	*	*	*	*	*	*	*	*	*	*	*	—
1949-D	3.25	3.75	7.00	11.	15.	25.	125.	—	*	*	*	*	*	*	*	*	*	*	*	*	*	*	*	*	*	—
1949-S	6.25	15.	25.	32.	40.	60.	200.	—	*	*	*	*	*	*	*	*	*	*	*	*	*	*	*	*	*	—
1950	1.40	1.90	6.00	9.00	12.	18.	145.	—	35.	40.	50.	60.	—	60.	135.	—	125.	350.	—	—	—	—	—	—	—	—
1950-D	1.00	3.00	5.00	7.00	10.	30.	105.	—	*	*	*	*	*	*	*	*	*	*	*	*	*	*	*	*	*	—
1950-S	6.00	9.50	18.	22.	30.	55	150.	—	*	*	*	*	*	*	*	*	*	*	*	*	*	*	*	*	*	—
1951	0.75	1.30	2.50	7.00	10.	40	105.	—	25.	50.	60.	70.	—	75.	175.	—	100.	200.	—	125.	3000.	—	—	—	—	—
1951-D	0.85	1.40	2.50	9.00	12.	20.	140.	—	*	*	*	*	*	*	*	*	*	*	*	*	*	*	*	*	*	—
1951-S	3.50	5.25	10.	15.	20.	50.	125.	—	*	*	*	*	*	*	*	*	*	*	*	*	*	*	*	*	*	—
1952	0.85	1.75	2.25	10.	24.	40.	100.	—	20.	35.	40.	50.	—	60.	—	—	30.	360.	—	75.	3500.	—	—	—	—	—
1952-D	0.80	1.00	2.00	7.00	10.	33.	40.	—	*	*	*	*	*	*	*	*	*	*	*	*	*	*	*	*	*	—
1952-S	1.50	3.75	6.00	8.00	12.	43.	80.	—	*	*	*	*	*	*	*	*	*	*	*	*	*	*	*	*	*	—
1953	0.95	1.10	2.00	8.00	13.	18.	90.	—	10.	40.	50.	60.	—	60.	75.	—	80.	250.	—	85.	4000.	—	—	—	—	—
1953-D	0.70	0.90	2.00	7.00	12.	47.	55.	—	*	*	*	*	*	*	*	*	*	*	*	*	*	*	*	*	*	—
1953-S	0.60	0.75	1.50	7.00	10.	35.	75.	—	*	*	*	*	*	*	*	*	*	*	*	*	*	*	*	*	*	—

—— = Insufficient pricing data   * = None issued

ROOSEVELT DIME (CONTINUED)

	AU-50	MS-60	MS-63	MS-64	MS-65	MS-66	MS-67	MS-68	PF-63	PF-64	PF-65	PF-65C	PF-65DC	PF-66	PF-66C	PF-66DC	PF-67	PF-67C	PF-67DC	PF-68	PF-68C	PF-68DC	PF-69	PF-69DC	PF-70	PF-70DC
1954	0.58	0.60	1.00	7.00	12.	25.	40.	—	4.00	15.	20.	80.	—	24.	150.	—	35.	350.	—	45.	800.	—	—	—	—	—
1954-D	0.58	0.60	1.00	7.00	12.	15.	40.	—	*	*	*	*	*	*	*	*	*	*	*	*	*	*	*	*	*	—
1954-S	0.65	0.70	1.50	7.00	10.	20.	58.	—	*	*	*	*	*	*	*	*	*	*	*	*	*	*	*	*	*	—
1955	0.75	0.80	1.00	7.00	12.	22.	35.	—	4.00	14.	20.	30.	—	25.	30.	—	30.	36.	235.	40.	90.	2000.	—	—	—	—
1955-D	0.68	0.70	1.00	7.00	10.	21.	38.	—	*	*	*	*	*	*	*	*	*	*	*	*	*	*	*	*	*	—
1955-S	0.68	0.70	1.00	8.00	10.	20.	75.	—	*	*	*	*	*	*	*	*	*	*	*	*	*	*	*	*	*	—
1956	0.60	0.63	1.00	7.00	8.50	18.	65.	—	2.00	3.00	5.00	20.	—	17.	20.	—	21.	24.	500.	25.	150.	—	—	—	—	—
1956-D	0.62	0.65	1.00	7.00	8.00	25.	50.	—	*	*	*	*	*	*	*	*	*	*	*	*	*	*	*	*	*	—
1957	0.60	0.63	1.00	7.00	9.00	20.	110.	—	2.00	3.00	4.00	20.	—	13.	30.	—	35.	50.	—	40.	90.	350.	—	—	—	—
1957-D	0.65	0.70	1.50	7.00	7.50	18.	25.	—	*	*	*	*	*	*	*	*	*	*	*	*	*	*	*	*	*	—
1958	0.62	0.65	1.00	7.00	12.	25.	70.	—	3.00	4.00	5.00	25.	—	10.	30.	—	12.	45.	—	15.	120.	475.	—	—	—	—
1958-D	0.58	0.60	1.00	7.00	10.	16.	70.	—	*	*	*	*	*	*	*	*	*	*	*	*	*	*	*	*	*	—
1959	0.58	0.60	1.00	7.00	8.50	27.	50.	—	2.00	3.00	4.00	35.	100.	10.	50.	160.	16.	90.	200.	20.	100.	1000.	—	—	—	—
1959-D	0.62	0.65	1.00	7.00	9.00	17.	30.	—	*	*	*	*	*	*	*	*	*	*	*	*	*	*	*	*	*	—
1960	0.58	0.60	1.00	6.50	9.00	16.	30.	—	2.00	3.00	4.00	20.	50.	20.	35.	75.	35.	50.	120.	60.	75.	150.	—	200.	—	—
1960-D	0.58	0.60	1.00	5.00	7.00	25.	130.	—	*	*	*	*	*	*	*	*	*	*	*	*	*	*	*	*	*	—
1961	0.58	0.60	1.00	6.00	8.50	28.	75.	—	2.00	3.00	4.00	15.	—	10.	—	—	15.	20.	35.	40.	50.	60.	—	150.	—	—
1961-D	0.58	0.60	1.00	5.00	7.00	21.	55.	—	*	*	*	*	*	*	*	*	*	*	*	*	*	*	*	*	*	—
1962	0.58	0.60	1.00	5.00	6.50	20.	115.	—	2.00	3.00	4.00	15.	—	10.	15.	35.	13.	35.	60.	16.	40.	100.	—	300.	—	—
1962-D	0.58	0.60	1.00	5.00	5.00	22.	65.	—	*	*	*	*	*	*	*	*	*	*	*	*	*	*	*	*	*	—
1963	0.58	0.60	1.00	6.00	8.50	20.	100.	—	2.00	3.00	4.00	15.	—	10.	15.	25.	13.	20.	35.	28.	30.	250.	—	100.	—	—
1963-D	0.58	0.60	1.00	6.00	8.50	23.	65.	—	*	*	*	*	*	*	*	*	*	*	*	*	*	*	*	*	*	—
1964	0.58	0.60	0.90	6.00	8.50	17.	85.	—	2.00	3.00	4.00	15.	—	10.	13.	—	14.	20.	—	20.	30.	50.	—	100.	—	—
1964-D	0.58	0.60	0.90	6.00	7.00	17.	150.	—	*	*	*	*	*	*	*	*	*	*	*	*	*	*	*	*	*	—

—— = Insufficient pricing data   * = None issued

	AU-50	MS-60	MS-63	MS-64	MS-65	MS-66	MS-67	MS-68	PF-63	PF-64	PF-65	PF-65C	PF-65DC	PF-66	PF-66C	PF-66DC	PF-67	PF-67C	PF-67DC	PF-68	PF-68C	PF-68DC	PF-69	PF-69DC	PF-70	PF-70DC
COPPER-NICKEL CLAD																										
1965	—	0.23	0.40	5.00	7.00	15.	50.	—	*	*	*	*	*	*	*	*	*	*	*	*	—	*	*	*	*	*
1966	—	0.25	0.40	5.00	7.50	12.	60.	—	*	*	*	*	*	*	*	*	*	*	*	*	—	*	*	*	*	*
1967	—	0.23	0.40	5.00	7.00	13.	50.	—	*	*	*	*	*	*	*	*	*	*	*	*	—	*	*	*	*	*
1968	—	0.23	0.40	5.50	7.00	13.	50.	60.	*	*	*	*	*	*	*	*	*	*	*	*	—	*	*	*	*	*
1968-D	—	0.23	0.40	5.00	7.00	12.	40.	—	*	*	*	*	*	*	*	*	*	*	*	*	—	*	*	*	*	*
1968-S	*	*	*	*	*	*	*	*	2.00	3.00	4.00	—	—	—	5.00	—	8.00	10.	25.	10.	—	35.	50.	125.	—	—
1968-S No S	*	*	*	*	*	*	*	*	7500.	8000.	8500.	—	—	—	—	—	—	—	—	—	22000.	—	—	—	—	—
1969	—	0.50	0.75	4.00	6.00	16.	75.	—	*	*	*	*	*	*	*	*	*	*	*	*	—	*	*	*	*	*
1969-D	—	0.25	0.40	4.00	6.00	15.	70.	—	*	*	*	*	*	*	*	*	*	*	*	*	—	*	*	*	*	*
1969-S	*	*	*	*	*	*	*	*	2.00	3.00	4.00	—	—	—	5.00	—	3.00	—	25.	10.	—	40.	15.	200.	—	—
1970	—	0.23	0.40	4.00	6.00	17.	75.	—	*	*	*	*	*	*	*	*	*	*	*	*	—	*	*	*	*	*
1970-D	—	0.23	0.40	4.00	6.00	12.	50.	—	*	*	*	*	*	*	*	*	*	*	*	*	—	*	*	*	*	*
1970-S	*	*	*	*	*	*	*	*	2.00	3.00	4.00	—	—	—	5.00	—	8.00	—	25.	10.	—	40.	15.	60.	—	—
1970-S No S	—	—	—	—	—	—	—	—	900.	950.	1000.	—	—	—	1100.	—	1200.	1300.	—	1400.	1500.	—	6000.	—	—	1300.
1971	—	0.27	0.45	7.00	10.	12.	65.	—	*	*	*	*	*	*	*	*	*	*	*	*	—	*	*	*	*	*
1971-D	—	0.23	0.40	4.00	9.00	16.	100.	—	*	*	*	*	*	*	*	*	*	*	*	*	—	*	*	*	*	*
1971-S	*	*	*	*	*	*	*	*	2.00	3.00	4.00	—	—	—	5.00	—	8.00	—	15.	10.	—	30.	18.	80.	—	—
1972	—	0.27	0.40	5.50	9.00	15.	200.	—	*	*	*	*	*	*	*	*	*	*	*	*	—	*	*	*	*	*
1972-D	—	0.25	0.40	5.50	10.	16.	85.	—	*	*	*	*	*	*	*	*	*	*	*	*	—	*	*	*	*	*
1972-S	*	*	*	*	*	*	*	*	2.00	3.00	4.00	—	—	—	5.00	—	8.00	—	12.	10.	—	15.	14.	60.	—	—
1973	—	0.23	0.40	4.00	7.00	11.	50.	—	*	*	*	*	*	*	*	*	*	*	*	*	—	*	*	*	*	*
1973-D	—	0.23	0.40	4.00	6.50	11.	170.	—	*	*	*	*	*	*	*	*	*	*	*	*	—	*	*	*	*	*
1973-S	*	*	*	*	*	*	*	*	2.00	3.00	4.00	—	—	—	5.00	—	8.00	—	12.	10.	—	17.	18.	80.	—	1700.
1974	—	0.23	0.40	4.00	6.50	11.	50.	—	*	*	*	*	*	*	*	*	*	*	*	*	—	*	*	*	*	*

—— = Insufficient pricing data   * = None issued

ROOSEVELT DIME (CONTINUED)

	AU-50	MS-60	MS-63	MS-64	MS-65	MS-66	MS-67	MS-68	PF-63	PF-64	PF-65	PF-65C	PF-65DC	PF-66	PF-66C	PF-66DC	PF-67	PF-67C	PF-67DC	PF-68	PF-68C	PF-68DC	PF-69	PF-69DC	PF-70	PF-70DC
1974-D	—	0.23	0.40	4.00	5.00	11.	50.	—	*	*	*	*	*	*	*	*	*	*	*	*	—	*	*	*	*	*
1974-S	*	*	*	*	*	*	*	*	2.00	3.00	4.00	—	—	—	5.00	—	8.00	—	12.	10.	—	16.	15.	35.	—	1700.
1975	—	0.25	0.45	4.00	5.00	10.	50.	—	*	*	*	*	*	*	*	*	*	*	*	*	—	*	*	*	*	*
1975-D	—	0.25	0.40	4.00	5.00	11.	75.	—	*	*	*	*	*	*	*	*	*	*	*	*	—	*	*	*	*	*
1975-S	*	*	*	*	*	*	*	*	2.00	3.00	4.00	—	—	—	5.00	—	8.00	—	12.	10.	—	14.	14.	30.	—	—
1975-S No S	*	*	*	*	*	*	*	*	35000.	40000.	45000.	—	—	—	—	—	—	—	—	—	—	—	—	—	—	—
1976	—	0.25	0.55	4.00	5.00	11.	50.	—	*	*	*	*	*	*	*	*	*	*	*	*	—	*	*	*	*	*
1976-D	—	0.25	0.55	4.00	5.50	11.	150.	—	*	*	*	*	*	*	*	*	*	*	*	*	—	*	*	*	*	*
1976-S	*	*	*	*	*	*	*	*	2.00	3.00	4.00	—	—	—	5.00	—	7.00	—	12.	8.00	—	14.	10.	30.	—	1000.
1977	—	0.20	0.35	4.00	5.50	10.	50.	—	*	*	*	*	*	*	*	*	*	*	*	*	—	*	*	*	*	*
1977-D	—	0.21	0.35	4.00	9.50	11.	50.	—	*	*	*	*	*	*	*	*	*	*	*	*	—	*	*	*	*	*
1977-S	*	*	*	*	*	*	*	*	2.00	3.00	4.00	—	—	—	5.00	—	8.00	—	10.	10.	—	12.	20.	15.	—	800.
1978	—	0.20	0.35	4.00	5.50	10.	80.	—	*	*	*	*	*	*	*	*	*	*	*	*	—	*	*	*	*	*
1978-D	—	0.21	0.35	4.00	5.00	6.25	65.	—	*	*	*	*	*	*	*	*	*	*	*	*	—	*	*	*	*	*
1978-S	*	*	*	*	*	*	*	*	2.00	3.00	4.00	—	—	—	5.00	—	8.00	—	10.	10.	—	12.	14.	15.	—	300.
1979	—	0.20	0.35	4.00	6.00	9.50	50.	—	*	*	*	*	*	*	*	*	*	*	*	*	—	*	*	*	*	*
1979-D	—	0.20	0.35	4.00	5.50	9.00	80.	—	*	*	*	*	*	*	*	*	*	*	*	*	—	*	*	*	*	*
1979-S Filled S	*	*	*	*	*	*	*	*	2.00	3.00	4.00	—	—	—	5.00	—	—	—	—	—	—	—	—	25.	—	350.
1979-S Clear S	*	*	*	*	*	*	*	*	2.00	3.00	4.00	—	—	—	5.00	—	—	—	—	—	—	—	—	30.	30.	300.
1980-P	—	0.20	0.35	5.00	10.	12.	50.	—	*	*	*	*	*	*	*	*	*	*	*	*	—	*	*	*	*	*
1980-D	—	0.20	0.35	3.00	4.75	13.	50.	—	*	*	*	*	*	*	*	*	*	*	*	*	—	*	*	*	*	*
1980-S	*	*	*	*	*	*	*	*	2.00	3.00	4.00	—	—	—	5.00	—	8.00	—	10.	10.	—	11.	14.	17.	20.	600.
1981-P	—	0.20	0.35	3.00	4.50	9.00	125.	—	*	*	*	*	*	*	*	*	*	*	*	*	—	*	*	*	*	*
1981-D	—	0.20	0.35	3.00	4.50	10.	30.	—	*	*	*	*	*	*	*	*	*	*	*	*	—	*	*	*	*	*
1981-S	*	*	*	*	*	*	*	*	2.00	3.00	4.00	—	—	—	5.00	—	8.00	—	10.	10.	—	11.	15.	18.	20.	350.

—— = Insufficient pricing data * = None issued

ROOSEVELT DIME (CONTINUED)

	AU-50	MS-60	MS-63	MS-64	MS-65	MS-66	MS-67	MS-68	PF-63	PF-64	PF-65	PF-65C	PF-65DC	PF-66	PF-66C	PF-66DC	PF-67	PF-67C	PF-67DC	PF-68	PF-68C	PF-68DC	PF-69	PF-69DC	PF-70	PF-70DC
1982 No Mint Mark, Strong Strike	—	85.	125.	165.	200.	300.	800.	1785.	*	*	*	*	*	*	*	*	*	*	*	*	—	*	*	*	*	*
1982-P	—	0.85	2.00	3.00	5.00	15.	65.	—	*	*	*	*	*	*	*	*	*	*	*	*	—	*	*	*	*	*
1982-D	—	0.30	0.55	3.00	4.00	14.	45.	—	*	*	*	*	*	*	*	*	*	*	*	*	—	*	*	*	*	*
1982-S	*	*	*	*	*	*	*	*	2.00	3.00	4.00	—	—	—	5.00	—	4.00	—	10.	7.00	—	14.	12.	35.	20.	300.
1983-P	—	0.30	1.25	3.00	4.00	14.	45.	—	*	*	*	*	*	*	*	*	*	*	*	*	—	*	*	*	*	*
1983-D	—	0.28	0.95	3.00	4.00	10.	45.	—	*	*	*	*	*	*	*	*	*	*	*	*	—	*	*	*	*	*
1983-S	*	*	*	*	*	*	*	*	2.00	3.00	4.00	—	—	—	5.00	—	4.00	—	10.	7.00	—	12.	12.	22.	20.	300.
1983-S No S	*	*	*	*	*	*	*	*	800.	900.	1000.	—	—	—	—	—	250.	—	—	—	—	550.	—	2000.	—	—
1984-P	—	0.20	0.50	3.00	4.00	10.	45.	—	*	*	*	*	*	*	*	*	*	*	*	*	—	*	*	*	*	*
1984-D	—	0.20	0.55	3.00	4.00	10.	45.	—	*	*	*	*	*	*	*	*	*	*	*	*	—	*	*	*	*	*
1984-S	*	*	*	*	*	*	*	*	2.00	3.00	4.00	—	—	—	5.00	—	4.00	—	10.	7.00	—	12.	12.	15.	20.	250.
1985-P	—	0.21	0.60	3.00	4.25	10.	57.	—	*	*	*	*	*	*	*	*	*	*	*	*	—	*	*	*	*	*
1985-D	—	0.20	0.50	3.00	4.00	10.	65.	—	*	*	*	*	*	*	*	*	*	*	*	*	—	*	*	*	*	*
1985-S	*	*	*	*	*	*	*	*	2.00	3.00	4.00	—	—	—	5.00	—	4.00	—	10.	7.00	—	12.	12.	13.	20.	300.
1986-P	—	0.20	0.75	3.00	4.00	9.50	45.	—	*	*	*	*	*	*	*	*	*	*	*	*	—	*	*	*	*	*
1986-D	—	0.20	0.75	3.00	4.00	10.	45.	—	*	*	*	*	*	*	*	*	*	*	*	*	—	*	*	*	*	*
1986-S	*	*	*	*	*	*	*	*	3.00	4.00	5.00	—	—	—	6.00	—	4.00	—	10.	7.00	—	12.	12.	16.	20.	200.
1987-P	—	0.20	0.35	3.00	4.00	10.	50.	180.	*	*	*	*	*	*	*	*	*	*	*	*	—	*	*	*	*	*
1987-D	—	0.20	0.35	3.00	4.00	10.	35.	—	*	*	*	*	*	*	*	*	*	*	*	*	—	*	*	*	*	*
1987-S	*	*	*	*	*	*	*	*	2.00	3.00	4.00	—	—	—	5.00	—	4.00	—	10.	7.00	—	12.	12.	15.	20.	300.
1988-P	—	0.20	0.40	3.00	4.00	10.	85.	—	*	*	*	*	*	*	*	*	*	*	*	*	—	*	*	*	*	*
1988-D	—	0.20	0.35	3.00	4.00	10.	100.	—	*	*	*	*	*	*	*	*	*	*	*	*	—	*	*	*	*	*
1988-S	*	*	*	*	*	*	*	*	3.00	4.00	5.00	—	—	—	6.00	—	4.00	—	10.	7.00	—	12.	12.	18.	20.	500.
1989-P	—	0.20	0.35	3.00	5.00	10.	35.	—	*	*	*	*	*	*	*	*	*	*	*	*	—	*	*	*	*	*

—— = Insufficient pricing data * = None issued

ROOSEVELT DIME (CONTINUED)

	AU-50	MS-60	MS-63	MS-64	MS-65	MS-66	MS-67	MS-68	PF-63	PF-64	PF-65	PF-65C	PF-65DC	PF-66	PF-66C	PF-66DC	PF-67	PF-67C	PF-67DC	PF-68	PF-68C	PF-68DC	PF-69	PF-69DC	PF-70	PF-70DC
1989-D	—	0.20	0.35	3.00	9.00	10.	35.	135.	*	*	*	*	*	*	*	*	*	*	*	*	—	*	*	*	*	*
1989-S	*	*	*	*	*	*	*	*	4.00	5.00	6.00	—	—	—	—	—	4.00	—	10.	7.00	—	11.	12.	16.	20.	350.
1990-P	—	0.20	0.35	3.00	5.00	10.	40.	—	*	*	*	*	*	*	*	*	*	*	*	*	—	*	*	*	*	*
1990-D	—	0.20	0.35	3.00	4.25	10.	50.	—	*	*	*	*	*	*	*	*	*	*	*	*	—	*	*	*	*	*
1990-S	*	*	*	*	*	*	*	*	2.00	3.00	4.00	—	—	—	5.00	—	4.00	—	10.	7.00	—	14.	12.	18.	20.	150.
1991-P	—	0.20	0.35	3.00	5.00	10.	45.	—	*	*	*	*	*	*	*	*	*	*	*	*	—	*	*	*	*	*
1991-D	—	0.20	0.35	3.00	5.00	10.	45.	—	*	*	*	*	*	*	*	*	*	*	*	*	—	*	*	*	*	*
1991-S	*	*	*	*	*	*	*	*	3.00	4.00	5.00	—	—	—	6.00	—	4.00	—	10.	7.00	—	12.	12.	15.	20.	200.
1992-P	—	0.20	0.35	3.00	5.00	11.	75.	—	*	*	*	*	*	*	*	*	*	*	*	*	—	*	*	*	*	*
1992-D	—	0.20	0.35	3.00	5.50	10.	65.	—	*	*	*	*	*	*	*	*	*	*	*	*	—	*	*	*	*	*
1992-S Clad	*	*	*	*	*	*	*	*	3.00	4.00	5.00	—	—	—	6.00	—	4.00	—	10.	7.00	—	11.	12.	18.	20.	175.
1992-S Silver	*	*	*	*	*	*	*	*	4.00	5.00	6.00	—	—	—	—	—	7.00	—	10.	7.00	—	14.	12.	20.	20.	500.
1993-P	—	0.20	0.35	3.00	5.00	10.	60.	—	*	*	*	*	*	*	*	*	*	*	*	*	—	*	*	*	*	*
1993-D	—	0.20	0.35	3.00	4.00	10.	50.	—	*	*	*	*	*	*	*	*	*	*	*	*	—	*	*	*	*	*
1993-S Clad	*	*	*	*	*	*	*	*	6.00	8.00	7.50	—	—	—	—	—	5.00	—	10.	7.00	—	11.	12.	18.	20.	250.
1993-S Silver	*	*	*	*	*	*	*	*	8.00	10.	8.00	—	—	—	—	—	6.00	—	10.	7.00	—	14.	12.	20.	20.	350.
1994-P	—	0.20	0.35	3.00	4.00	10.	50.	—	*	*	*	*	*	*	*	*	*	*	*	*	—	*	*	*	*	*
1994-D	—	0.20	0.35	3.00	4.00	10.	50.	—	*	*	*	*	*	*	*	*	*	*	*	*	—	*	*	*	*	*
1994-S Clad	*	*	*	*	*	*	*	*	5.00	7.00	5.00	—	—	—	—	—	4.00	—	10.	7.00	—	11.	12.	14.	20.	250.
1994-S Silver	*	*	*	*	*	*	*	*	8.00	10.	7.00	—	—	—	—	—	5.50	—	10.	7.00	—	14.	12.	21.	20.	300.
1995-P	—	0.20	0.35	3.00	5.00	8.00	75.	—	*	*	*	*	*	*	*	*	*	*	*	*	—	*	*	*	*	*
1995-D	—	0.20	0.35	3.00	5.00	10.	100.	—	*	*	*	*	*	*	*	*	*	*	*	*	—	*	*	*	*	*
1995-S Clad	*	*	*	*	*	*	*	*	20.	25.	10.	—	—	—	—	—	4.00	—	10.	7.00	—	11.	12.	13.	20.	300.
1995-S Silver	*	*	*	*	*	*	*	*	20.	25.	12.	—	—	—	—	—	5.00	—	10.	7.00	—	14.	12.	17.	20.	500.
1996-P	—	0.20	0.35	3.00	4.00	10.	55.	125.	*	*	*	*	*	*	*	*	*	*	*	*	—	*	*	*	*	*

—— = Insufficient pricing data * = None issued

ROOSEVELT DIME (CONTINUED)

	AU-50	MS-60	MS-63	MS-64	MS-65	MS-66	MS-67	MS-68	PF-63	PF-64	PF-65	PF-65C	PF-65DC	PF-66	PF-66C	PF-66DC	PF-67	PF-67C	PF-67DC	PF-68	PF-68C	PF-68DC	PF-69	PF-69DC	PF-70	PF-70DC
1996-W	—	7.50	10.	13.	20.	35.	75.	225.	*	*	*	*	*	*	*	*	*	*	*	*	—	*	*	*	*	*
1996-D	—	0.20	0.35	3.00	4.00	10.	20.	220.	*	*	*	*	*	*	*	*	*	*	*	*	—	*	*	*	*	*
1996-S Clad	*	*	*	*	*	*	*	*	3.00	4.00	5.00	—	—	—	6.00	—	4.00	—	10.	7.00	—	11.	12.	18.	20.	450.
1996-S Silver	*	*	*	*	*	*	*	*	8.00	10.	7.50	—	—	—	—	—	4.00	—	10.	7.00	—	14.	12.	20.	20.	300.
1997-P	—	0.20	0.35	3.00	5.00	13.	110.	—	*	*	*	*	*	*	*	*	*	*	*	*	—	*	*	*	*	*
1997-D	—	0.20	0.35	3.00	4.00	9.00	125.	—	*	*	*	*	*	*	*	*	*	*	*	*	—	*	*	*	*	*
1997-S Clad	*	*	*	*	*	*	*	*	12.	15.	4.00	—	—	—	—	—	4.00	—	10.	7.00	—	11.	12.	14.	20.	400.
1997-S Silver	*	*	*	*	*	*	*	*	20.	25.	7.50	—	—	—	—	—	4.00	—	10.	7.00	—	14.	12.	14.	20.	250.
1998-P	—	0.20	0.35	3.00	4.00	9.00	40.	—	*	*	*	*	*	*	*	*	*	*	*	*	—	*	*	*	*	*
1998-D	—	0.20	0.35	3.00	4.00	11.	35.	—	*	*	*	*	*	*	*	*	*	*	*	*	—	*	*	*	*	*
1998-S Clad	*	*	*	*	*	*	*	*	4.00	5.00	6.00	—	—	—	—	—	4.00	—	10.	7.00	—	11.	12.	14.	20.	550.
1998-S Silver	*	*	*	*	*	*	*	*	6.00	8.00	7.50	—	—	—	—	—	4.00	—	10.	7.00	—	14.	12.	24.	20.	400.
1999-P	—	0.20	0.35	3.00	4.00	9.00	25.	—	*	*	*	*	*	*	*	*	*	*	*	*	—	*	*	*	*	*
1999-D	—	0.20	0.35	3.00	4.00	9.00	25.	135.	*	*	*	*	*	*	*	*	*	*	*	*	—	*	*	*	*	*
1999-S Clad	*	*	*	*	*	*	*	*	3.00	4.00	5.00	—	—	—	6.00	—	4.00	—	10.	7.00	—	11.	12.	14.	20.	400.
1999-S Silver	*	*	*	*	*	*	*	*	6.00	8.00	6.00	—	—	—	—	—	4.00	—	10.	7.00	—	14.	12.	24.	20.	500.
2000-P	—	0.20	0.35	3.00	5.00	12.	25.	200.	*	*	*	*	*	*	*	*	*	*	*	*	—	*	*	*	*	*
2000-D	—	0.20	0.35	3.00	4.00	9.00	25.	—	*	*	*	*	*	*	*	*	*	*	*	*	—	*	*	*	*	*
2000-S Clad	*	*	*	*	*	*	*	*	2.00	3.00	4.00	—	—	—	5.00	—	4.00	—	10.	7.00	—	11.	12.	12.	20.	500.
2000-S Silver	*	*	*	*	*	*	*	*	4.00	5.00	6.00	—	—	—	—	—	4.00	—	10.	7.00	—	14.	12.	23.	20.	250.
2001-P	—	0.20	0.35	3.00	5.00	14.	25.	230.	*	*	*	*	*	*	*	*	*	*	*	*	—	*	*	*	*	*
2001-D	—	0.20	0.35	3.00	4.00	17.	25.	200.	*	*	*	*	*	*	*	*	*	*	*	*	—	*	*	*	*	*
2001-S Clad	*	*	*	*	*	*	*	*	2.00	3.00	4.00	—	—	—	5.00	—	4.00	—	10.	7.00	—	11.	12.	12.	20.	400.
2001-S Silver	*	*	*	*	*	*	*	*	4.00	5.00	6.00	—	—	—	—	—	4.00	—	10.	7.00	—	14.	12.	31.	20.	450.
2002-P	—	—	—	3.00	4.00	9.00	25.	—	*	*	*	*	*	*	*	*	*	*	*	*	—	*	*	*	*	*

—— = Insufficient pricing data * = None issued

ROOSEVELT DIME (CONTINUED)

	AU-50	MS-60	MS-63	MS-64	MS-65	MS-66	MS-67	MS-68	PF-63	PF-64	PF-65	PF-65C	PF-65DC	PF-66	PF-66C	PF-66DC	PF-67	PF-67C	PF-67DC	PF-68	PF-68C	PF-68DC	PF-69	PF-69DC	PF-70	PF-70DC
2002-D	—	—	—	3.00	4.00	9.00	25.	—	*	*	*	*	*	*	*	*	*	*	*	*	—	*	*	*	*	*
2002-S Clad	*	*	*	*	*	*	*	*	2.00	3.00	4.00	—	—	—	5.00	—	4.00	—	10.	7.00	—	11.	12.	12.	20.	500.
2002-S Silver	*	*	*	*	*	*	*	*	5.00	7.00	—	—	—	—	—	—	4.00	—	10.	7.00	—	14.	12.	30.	20.	400.
2003-P	—	—	—	3.00	4.00	9.00	25.	—	—	—	—	—	—	—	—	—	—	—	—	—	—	—	—	—	—	—
2003-D	—	—	—	3.00	4.00	9.00	25.	—	—	—	—	—	—	—	—	—	—	—	—	—	—	—	—	—	—	—
2003-S Clad	—	—	—	—	—	—	—	—	2.00	3.00	4.00	—	—	—	5.00	—	4.00	—	10.	7.00	—	11.	12.	12.	20.	400.
2003-S Silver	—	—	—	—	—	—	—	—	4.00	5.00	6.00	—	—	—	7.00	—	8.00	9.00	10.	9.00	—	14.	12.	30.	20.	125.
2004-P	—	—	—	3.00	4.00	9.00	25.	—	—	—	—	—	—	—	—	—	—	—	—	—	—	—	—	—	—	—
2004-D	—	—	—	3.00	4.00	9.00	25.	—	—	—	—	—	—	—	—	—	—	—	—	—	—	—	—	—	—	—
2004-S Clad	—	—	—	—	—	—	—	—	2.00	3.00	4.00	—	—	—	5.00	—	4.00	—	10.	7.00	—	11.	12.	12.	20.	400.
2004-S Silver	—	—	—	—	—	—	—	—	4.00	5.00	6.00	—	—	—	7.00	—	8.00	9.00	10.	9.00	—	14.	12.	30.	20.	125.

—— = Insufficient pricing data   * = None issued

Seated Liberty 20 cents

Date of authorization:	March 3, 1875
Dates of issue:	1875-1876
Designers:	Obverse: Thomas Sully-Christian Gobrecht-John Hughes-William Barber
	Reverse: William Barber
Engraver:	William Barber
Diameter:	22.50 mm/0.89 inch
Weight:	5.00 grams/0.16 ounce
Metallic content:	90% silver, 10% copper
Weight of pure silver:	4.50 grams/0.14 ounce
Edge:	Plain
Mint mark:	Reverse below eagle

SEATED LIBERTY 20 CENTS (CONTINUED)

	G-4	VG-8	F-12	VF-20	EF-40	AU-50	MS-60	MS-62	MS-63	MS-64	MS-65	MS-66
1875	110.	125.	200.	250.	300.	400.	700.	1000.	1500.	2500.	6000.	10000.
1875-CC	125.	200.	250.	300.	400.	600.	1000.	1200.	1800.	4000.	10000.	—
1875-S	110.	120.	135.	150.	200.	350.	700.	1000.	1300.	2000.	6000.	9000.
1876	150.	200.	300.	400.	500.	600.	1000.	1200.	1600.	2500.	6000.	12500.
1876-CC Eliasberg sale - April 1997, Cataloged as MS-65 $148,500												
1877 Proofs only	1800.	2000.	2400.	2700.	3000.	3500.	*	*	*	*	*	*
1878 Proofs only	1500.	1800.	2200.	2500.	2700.	3000.	*	*	*	*	*	*

—— = Insufficient pricing data   * = None issued

Draped Bust quarter dollar

Small Eagle

Heraldic Eagle

Date of authorization: April 2, 1792
Dates of issue: 1796, 1804-1807
Designers: Obverse: Gilbert Stuart-Robert Scot
Reverse:
(1796): Robert Scot-John Eckstein
(1804-1807): Robert Scot
Engraver: Robert Scot
Diameter: 27 mm/1.07 inches
Weight: 6.74 grams/0.22 ounce
Metallic content: 89.25% silver, 10.75% copper
Weight of pure silver: 6.02 grams/0.19 ounce
Edge: Reeded
Mint Mark: None

	G-4	VG-8	F-12	VF-20	EF-40	AU-50	AU-55	MS-60	MS-62	MS-63	MS-64
SMALL EAGLE											
1796	6000.	8000.	12000.	18000.	25000.	30000.	40000.	50000.	55000.	60000.	75000.

	G-4	VG-8	F-12	VF-20	EF-40	AU-50	AU-55	MS-60	MS-62	MS-63
HERALDIC EAGLE										
1804	2500.	3000.	4000.	6000.	9000.	18000.	25000.	40000.	60000.	85000.
1805	250.	350.	600.	1000.	1200.	2500.	3500.	7500.	12000.	18000.
1806/5	250.	400.	800.	1200.	1500.	3500.	5000.	9000.	18000.	25000.
1806	250.	350.	600.	1000.	1200.	2500.	3500.	7000.	10000.	12000.
1807	250.	350.	600.	1000.	1500.	3000.	4000.	7000.	10000.	12000.

Capped Bust quarter dollar

Date of authorization: April 2, 1792
Dates of issue: 1815-1838
Designer/Engraver: John Reich
Diameter: 1815-1828: 27.00 mm/1.07 inches
1831-1838: 24.26 mm/0.96 inch
Weight: 6.74 grams/0.22 ounce
Metallic content: 89.25% silver, 10.75% copper
Weight of pure silver: 6.02 grams/0.19 ounce
Edge: Reeded
Mint mark: None

	G-4	VG-8	F-12	VF-20	EF-40	AU-50	AU-55	MS-60	MS-62	MS-63
MOTTO, OPEN COLLAR STRIKE										
1815	60.	75.	125.	280.	850.	1200.	1600.	2300.	3000.	4000.
1818/5	60.	90.	125.	350.	900.	1200.	1600.	2300.	3000.	4500.
1818	60.	75.	125.	280.	850.	1200.	1600.	2300.	3000.	4000.
1819	60.	75.	125.	275.	850.	1200.	1600.	2300.	3000.	4800.
1820 Small O	60.	75.	125.	280.	850.	1200.	1600.	2300.	3000.	5000.
1820 Large O	60.	75.	125.	275.	850.	1200.	1600.	2300.	3000.	4800.
1821	60.	75.	125.	275.	850.	1200.	1600.	2300.	3000.	4000.
1822	60.	100.	150.	350.	900.	1700.	2300.	3000.	4000.	5500.
1822 25/50c	1650.	3250.	4100.	5500.	10000.	20000.	—	25000.	—	—
1823/2	12000.	18000.	25000.	35000.	50000.	65000.	85000.	—	—	—
1824/2	85.	125.	250.	550.	1700.	2500.	3500.	6000.	—	—
1825/2	145.	185.	300.	550.	1100.	1900.	2500.	3750.	5000.	6500.
1825/3	48.	60.	90.	250.	640.	950.	1325.	1950.	2300.	3775.
1825/4	65.	75.	125.	300.	900.	1200.	1700.	2400.	3000.	4000.
1827/3 Originals and Restrikes: Original VF-20/30 $40000; PF-60 $58500; PF-64 $120000; Restrike PF-62 $46000; PF-63 $47500; PF-65 $100000.										
1828	60.	75.	125.	350.	850.	1400.	1800.	2500.	3500.	5000.
1828 25/50c	140.	280.	450.	1000.	1600.	3600.	5000.	8500.	15000.	—
NO MOTTO, CLOSE COLLAR STRIKE										
1831	60.	70.	80.	100.	350.	600.	650.	800.	1500.	2500.
1832	60.	70.	80.	100.	350.	600.	700.	900.	1500.	3000.
1833	60.	70.	80.	150.	400.	800.	1000.	1400.	2000.	3500.
1834	60.	70.	80.	100.	350.	600.	650.	800.	1500.	2500.
1835	60.	70.	80.	100.	350.	600.	650.	800.	1500.	2500.

—— = Insufficient pricing data

	G-4	VG-8	F-12	VF-20	EF-40	AU-50	AU-55	MS-60	MS-62	MS-63
1836	60.	70.	80.	100.	350.	600.	750.	1200.	2000.	3500.
1837	60.	70.	80.	100.	350.	600.	650.	800.	1500.	2500.
1838	60.	70.	80.	100.	350.	600.	650.	850.	1500.	2500.

Seated Liberty quarter dollar

Date of authorization: April 2, 1792
Dates of issue: 1838-1891
Designers: (1838-1840):
Obverse: Thomas Sully-Christian Gobrecht
Reverse: John Reich-William Kneass-Gobrecht-Sully
(1840-1891):
Obverse: Robert B. Hughes-Gobrecht-Sully
Reverse: Hughes-Gobrecht-Sully
Engravers: Obverse: Christian Gobrecht
Reverse:
(1838-1853): Christian Gobrecht
(1853-1891): James B. Longacre
Diameter: 24.26 mm/0.96 inch
Weight: (1838-1873): 6.22 grams/0.20 ounce
(1873-1891): 6.25 grams/0.20 ounce
Metallic content: 90% silver, 10% copper
Weight of pure silver: (1838-1873): 5.60 grams/0.18 ounce
(1873-1891): 5.63 grams/0.18 ounce
Edge: Reeded
Mint mark: Reverse below eagle

Arrows at date,
Rays on reverse

SEATED LIBERTY QUARTER DOLLAR (CONTINUED)

	G-4	VG-8	F-12	VF-20	EF-40	AU-50	AU-55	MS-60	MS-62	MS-63	MS-64	MS-65	PF-63	PF-64	PF-65	PF-66
NO DRAPERY AT ELBOW																
1838	20.	30.	50.	100.	350.	600.	800.	1200.	2500.	4500.	8500.	—	*	*	*	*
1839	20.	30.	50.	100.	350.	600.	800.	1200.	2500.	4500.	10000.	—	*	*	*	*
1840-O	25.	35.	75.	125.	450.	750.	1000.	1500.	4000.	7500.	15000.	—	*	*	*	*
DRAPERY AT ELBOW																
1840	25.	35.	75.	125.	250.	400.	600.	1000.	3500.	5000.	12000.	—	25000.	35000.	45000.	—
1840-O Small O	35.	50.	100.	125.	300.	550.	800.	1200.	2000.	5000.	7500.	—	*	*	*	*
1840-O Large O	300.	360.	600.	1100.	—	—	—	—	—	—	—	—	*	*	*	*
1841	50.	100.	150.	200.	350.	450.	700.	1100.	3500.	5000.	8000.	—	*	*	*	*
1841-O	20.	30.	50.	100.	200.	350.	500.	800.	2000.	4500.	9000.	—	*	*	*	*
1842 Large Date	100.	125.	200.	300.	400.	900.	1500.	3000.	4500.	6500.	10000.	—	*	*	*	*
1842-O Small Date	400.	600.	1200.	2000.	4750.	7500.	9000.	16500.	—	—	—	—	*	*	*	*
1842-O Large Date	20.	30.	50.	75.	200.	600.	900.	2000.	4000.	6000.	10000.	—	*	*	*	*
1842 Small Date Proofs only	—	—	—	—	—	—	—	25000.	—	50000.	72500.	—	—	—	100000.	—
1843	20.	30.	50.	75.	100.	200.	300.	500.	700.	1200.	2500.	—	—	35000.	45000.	—
1843-O Small O	20.	30.	65.	125.	300.	900.	1500.	2500.	4000.	6000.	10000.	—	*	*	*	*
1843-O Large O	75.	110.	200.	400.	800.	—	—	—	—	—	18500.	—	*	*	*	*
1844	20.	30.	50.	75.	100.	200.	300.	500.	700.	1500.	4000.	—	*	*	*	*
1844-O	20.	30.	50.	100.	200.	400.	600.	1600.	2500.	4000.	6000.	—	*	*	*	*
1845	20.	30.	50.	75.	100.	200.	300.	500.	700.	1200.	3000.	—	—	—	32000.	—
1845/5	17.	22.	35.	55.	115.	265.	325.	725.	—	—	—	—	*	*	*	*
1846	20.	30.	50.	75.	100.	200.	300.	500.	800.	1500.	3500.	—	—	15000.	27500.	—
1846/1846	16.	20.	35.	58.	155.	325.	500.	—	—	—	—	—	*	*	*	*
1847	20.	30.	50.	75.	100.	200.	300.	500.	700.	1200.	3000.	—	*	*	*	*
1847/7	16.	25.	50.	62.	125.	285.	475.	—	—	—	—	—	*	*	*	*
1847-O	30.	50.	75.	150.	400.	800.	1500.	3500.	5000.	7500.	—	—	*	*	*	*

—— = Insufficient pricing data   * = None issued

SEATED LIBERTY QUARTER DOLLAR (CONTINUED)

	G-4	VG-8	F-12	VF-20	EF-40	AU-50	AU-55	MS-60	MS-62	MS-63	MS-64	MS-65	PF-63	PF-64	PF-65	PF-66
1848 (triple date)	25.	38.	82.	140.	210.	400.	550.	1050.	1550.	2350.	—	—	*	*	*	*
1848/1848	40.	55.	88.	170.	235.	590.	1150.	—	—	—	—	—	—	—	27500.	—
1849	20.	30.	50.	100.	200.	300.	500.	900.	1200.	1800.	3500.	—	15000.	—	—	—
1849-O	400.	600.	1000.	1800.	3500.	6000.	7000.	8000.	12000.	7000.	23000.	—	*	*	*	*
1850	30.	60.	100.	150.	250.	350.	550.	900.	1500	2500.	6000.	—	*	*	*	*
1850-O	25.	60.	100.	150.	200.	500.	850.	1400.	2000.	3500.	7500.	—	*	*	*	*
1851	50.	100.	150.	200.	300.	500.	650.	900.	1500.	2500.	3500.	—	*	*	*	*
1851-O	200.	300.	500.	800.	1500.	3000.	4000.	6000.	10000.	—	—	—	*	*	*	*
1852	60.	100.	125.	200.	300.	400.	600.	900.	1100.	1500.	3000.	—	*	*	*	*
1852-O	200.	300.	500.	1000.	2000.	4000.	5000.	8000.	12000.	19000.	—	—	*	*	*	*
1853/53 Recut Date	300.	400.	600.	900.	1500.	2500.	3000.	3500.	4500.	5500.	7000.	—	*	*	*	*
ARROWS AND RAYS																
1853	20.	30.	50.	75.	175.	350.	500.	1000.	1500.	2500.	5000.	—	62500.	92500.	—	—
1853/4	75.	100.	200.	300.	700.	1200.	2000.	3500.	5000.	12000.	25000.	—	*	*	*	*
1853-O	20.	30.	50.	100.	400.	1200.	1800.	3000.	3500.	10000.	15000.	—	*	*	*	*
1853-O/Horizontal O	28.	40.	75.	150.	400.	1800.	—	—	—	—	—	—	*	*	*	*
ARROWS, NO RAYS																
1854	20.	30.	50.	85.	125.	400.	500.	700.	1200.	2000.	4000.	—	8500.	14000.	24000.	—
1854-O Large O	20.	30.	50.	100.	150.	600.	800.	1200.	2000.	3000.	6000.	—	*	*	*	*
1854-O Huge O	600.	1200.	1800.	3000.	5000.	—	—	—	—	—	—	—	*	*	*	*
1855	20.	30.	50.	75.	100.	300.	400.	600.	1000.	2500.	5000.	—	12500.	18000.	28500.	—
1855-O	50.	75.	125.	350.	600.	1500.	2500.	3500.	5000.	9000.	20000.	—	*	*	*	*
1855-S	40.	65.	100.	200.	500.	1200.	2000.	2500.	4000.	6000.	12000.	—	*	*	*	*
DRAPERY AT ELBOW																
1856	20.	25.	35.	50.	100.	200.	250.	350.	500.	700.	1500.	—	3150.	7000.	11000.	—
1856-O	20.	30.	50.	75.	125.	400.	600.	1200.	1800.	2500.	5000.	—	*	*	*	*
1856-S	40.	75.	100.	200.	500.	1000.	2500.	3500.	5000.	9000.	—	—	*	*	*	*

—— = Insufficient pricing data   * = None issued

SEATED LIBERTY QUARTER DOLLAR (CONTINUED)

	G-4	VG-8	F-12	VF-20	EF-40	AU-50	AU-55	MS-60	MS-62	MS-63	MS-64	MS-65	PF-63	PF-64	PF-65	PF-66
1856-S/ Small S	75.	100.	200.	400.	1000.	2000.	—	—	—	—	—	—	*	*	*	*
1857	20.	25.	35.	50.	100.	200.	250.	350.	500.	700.	1500.	—	3000.	5650.	9500.	—
1857-O	20.	30.	40.	50.	125.	350.	600.	1200.	2000.	3000.	6000.	—	*	*	*	*
1857-S	60.	125.	250.	400.	600.	1200.	2000.	3000.	5000.	8000.	12000.	—	*	*	*	*
1858	20.	25.	35.	50.	100.	200.	250.	350.	500.	700.	1500.	—	1400.	2450.	5000.	—
1858-O	20.	30.	40.	75.	150.	500.	800.	1500.	3500.	6500.	8000.	—	*	*	*	*
1858-S	50.	100.	200.	300.	600.	1500.	3000.	6500.	—	—	—	—	*	*	*	*
1859	20.	25.	35.	50.	100.	200.	300.	400.	800.	1500.	3000.	—	1200.	1875.	5000.	—
1859-O	20.	30.	50.	100.	200.	500.	800.	1500.	3000.	6000.	10000.	—	*	*	*	*
1859-S	125.	200.	300.	500.	1500.	7500.	10000.	—	—	—	—	—	*	*	*	*
1860	20.	25.	35.	50.	100.	200.	300.	500.	650.	900.	1500.	—	1100.	1900.	5000.	—
1860-O	20.	30.	40.	75.	125.	350.	600.	1200.	1800.	2500.	4500.	—	*	*	*	*
1860-S	200.	350.	600.	1000.	4500.	10000.	—	—	—	—	—	—	*	*	*	*
1861	20.	25.	35.	50.	100.	200.	250.	350.	500.	700.	1500.	—	1225.	1900.	5500.	—
1861-S	60.	125.	250.	500.	1500.	6500.	—	—	—	—	—	—	*	*	*	*
1862	20.	25.	35.	50.	100.	200.	300.	400.	600.	900.	1500.	—	1175.	1925.	5000.	—
1862-S	75.	100.	200.	350.	750.	1200.	1800.	3000.	4500.	6000.	10000.	—	*	*	*	*
1863	30.	40.	60.	125.	200.	400.	500.	750.	1000.	1500.	2500.	—	950.	1850.	5500.	—
1864	75.	100.	125.	200.	300.	500.	650.	850.	1200.	1700.	2500.	—	975.	1825.	4850.	—
1864-S	350.	500.	800.	1200.	2500.	4000.	6000.	10000.	15000.	25000.	—	—	*	*	*	*
1865	75.	100.	150.	200.	300.	400.	500.	800.	1100.	1500.	3000.	—	950.	1900.	5250.	—
1865-S	100.	125.	200.	350.	800.	1200.	1800.	2500.	3000.	4000.	7500.	—	*	*	*	*
1866 Fantasy piece; DuPont specimen recovered, believed unique																
WITH MOTTO																
1866	400.	600.	800.	1000.	1200.	1500.	1700.	2000.	2400.	3000.	4000.	—	700.	1000.	2400.	—
1866-S	250.	350.	600.	1000.	1500.	2500.	3000.	4000.	5000.	6500.	8500.	—	*	*	*	*
1867	250.	350.	500.	700.	900.	1100.	1200.	1500.	1700.	2000.	4500.	—	650.	975.	2150.	—

—— = Insufficient pricing data   * = None issued

SEATED LIBERTY QUARTER DOLLAR (CONTINUED)

	G-4	VG-8	F-12	VF-20	EF-40	AU-50	AU-55	MS-60	MS-62	MS-63	MS-64	MS-65	PF-63	PF-64	PF-65	PF-66
1867-S	300.	500.	750.	1000.	1500.	2000.	3000.	5000.	7500.	—	—	—	*	*	*	*
1868	125.	200.	300.	400.	500.	600.	700.	900.	1400.	2000.	3000.	—	675.	1050.	2550.	—
1868-S	100.	150.	250.	500.	1000.	2000.	2500.	3000.	5500.	8000.	12000.	—	*	*	*	*
1869	300.	500.	600.	800.	1000.	1500.	1800.	2500.	3000.	3500.	—	—	625.	1100.	2450.	—
1869-S	100.	125.	250.	400.	800.	1500.	2000.	3000.	4000.	6000.	—	—	*	*	*	*
1870	75.	100.	125.	200.	350.	500.	700.	900.	1200.	2000.	3500.	—	625.	1150.	2500.	—
1870-CC	4000.	5000.	10000.	15000.	25000.	40000.	—	—	—	—	—	—	*	*	*	*
1871	40.	50.	75.	125.	250.	400.	500.	800.	1000.	1200.	2500.	—	675.	1125.	2200.	—
1871-CC	2000.	4000.	8000.	15000.	25000.	40000.	—	—	—	—	—	—	*	*	*	*
1871-S	300.	400.	600.	900.	1200.	2000.	2500.	3500.	4000.	5000.	7000.	—	*	*	*	*
1872	35.	50.	100.	125.	200.	300.	400.	900.	1500.	2500.	4000.	—	650.	925.	2150.	—
1872-CC	600.	1000.	2000.	3000.	6000.	10000.	15000.	25000.	50000.	—	—	—	*	*	*	*
1872-S	800.	1200.	1800.	2500.	4000.	6000.	7500.	10000.	15000.	25000.	—	—	*	*	*	*
1873 Closed 3	200.	300.	400.	600.	800.	1500.	2500.	4000.	—	—	—	—	675.	1075.	2300.	—
1873 Open 3	40.	50.	75.	125.	200.	300.	400.	600.	1000.	1500.	2500.	—	*	*	*	*
1873-CC R. Henry Norweb Specimen MS-64 (PCGS) sold for $209,000 on 2/9/98.																
ARROWS ADDED																
1873	20.	30.	50.	75.	250.	500.	600.	900.	1200.	2000.	2500.	—	1200.	2650.	6000.	—
1873-CC	2000.	3000.	6500.	10000.	15000.	—	35000.	—	—	100000.	140000.	—	*	*	*	*
1873-S	25.	40.	80.	200.	300.	600.	900.	1500.	2000.	3000.	5000.	—	*	*	*	*
1874	20.	30.	50.	75.	250.	500.	600.	900.	1200.	2000.	2500.	—	1150.	2200.	5250.	—
1874-S	25.	40.	80.	200.	300.	500.	600.	900.	1200.	2000.	2500.	—	*	*	*	*
WITH MOTTO																
1875	20.	30.	40.	50.	100.	200.	300.	400.	500.	700.	1000.	—	685.	1025.	2025.	—
1875-CC	85.	125.	200.	400.	600.	800.	1000.	2000.	2500.	3000.	5000.	—	*	*	*	*
1875-S	40.	75.	100.	125.	250.	400.	500.	800.	1200.	1800.	2500.	—	*	*	*	*
1876	20	30.	40	50.	100.	200.	300.	400.	500.	700.	1000.	—	675.	1000.	2000.	—

—— = Insufficient pricing data * = None issued

SEATED LIBERTY QUARTER DOLLAR (CONTINUED)

	G-4	VG-8	F-12	VF-20	EF-40	AU-50	AU-55	MS-60	MS-62	MS-63	MS-64	MS-65	PF-63	PF-64	PF-65	PF-66
1876-CC	30.	40.	50.	65.	100.	200.	300.	500.	800.	1500.	2000.	—	*	*	*	*
1876-S	20.	30.	40.	50.	100.	200.	300.	400.	500.	700.	1000.	—	*	*	*	*
1877	20.	30.	40.	50.	100.	200.	300.	400.	500.	700.	1000.	—	685.	1025.	2025.	—
1877-CC	30.	40.	50.	65.	100.	200.	300.	500.	700.	1000.	1500.	—	*	*	*	*
1877-S	20.	30.	40.	50.	100.	200.	300.	400.	500.	700.	1000.	—	*	*	*	*
1877-S/Horizontal S	35.	65.	100.	200.	350.	500.	700.	1000.	1500.	2500.	4500.	—	*	*	*	*
1878	20.	30.	40.	50.	100.	200.	300.	400.	500.	700.	1250.	—	625.	1000.	2000.	—
1878-CC	30.	40.	75.	125.	200.	300.	400.	600.	800.	1200.	2000.	—	*	*	*	*
1878-S	125.	200.	300.	400.	700.	900.	1100.	1500.	2000.	3000.	5000.	—	*	*	*	*
1879	200.	250.	300.	350.	450.	600.	700.	900.	1000.	1200.	1500.	—	625.	975.	2000.	—
1880	200.	250.	300.	350.	450.	600.	700.	900.	1000.	1200.	1500.	—	650.	950.	2000.	—
1881	250.	300.	350.	400.	500.	600.	700.	900.	1000.	1200.	1500.	—	625.	975.	2000.	—
1882	200.	250.	300.	400.	500.	600.	700.	1000.	1200.	1500.	2000.	—	650.	1035.	2000.	—
1883	200.	250.	300.	400.	500.	600.	700.	1000.	1200.	1500.	2000.	—	625.	1000.	2000.	—
1884	350.	450.	600.	750.	850.	1000.	1100.	1200.	1500.	2000.	2500.	—	650.	1000.	2000.	—
1885	200.	250.	300.	400.	500.	600.	700.	1000.	1200.	1500.	2500.	—	650.	1045.	2000.	—
1886	500.	600.	750.	850.	1000.	1200.	1500.	1800.	2000.	2500.	3000.	—	800.	1050.	2000.	—
1887	300.	400.	500.	600.	700.	1000.	1200.	1500.	1700.	2000.	2500.	—	650.	975.	2000.	—
1888	300.	400.	500.	600.	700.	1000.	1200.	1500.	1700.	2000.	2500.	—	625.	1000.	2000.	—
1888-S	20.	30.	40.	50.	100.	200.	300.	400.	700.	1200.	2000.	—	—	—	—	—
1889	250.	300.	350.	400.	500.	600.	700.	900.	1000.	1200.	1500.	—	775.	1025.	2000.	—
1890	65.	100.	125.	200.	300.	400.	500.	800.	1000.	1200.	1500.	—	800.	1000.	2000.	—
1891	20.	30.	40.	50.	100.	200.	300.	400.	500.	700.	1000.	—	750.	1025.	2000.	—
1891-O	150.	200.	400.	600.	1000.	1500.	2000.	3000.	4500.	7500.	—	—	*	*	*	*
1891-S	20.	30.	40.	50.	100.	200.	300.	400.	500.	700.	1200.	—	*	*	*	*

—— = Insufficient pricing data * = None issued

Barber quarter dollar

Date of authorization:	April 2, 1792
Dates of issue:	1892-1916
Designer/Engraver:	Charles Barber
Diameter:	24.26 mm/0.96 inch
Weight:	6.25 grams/0.20 ounce
Metallic content:	90% silver, 10% copper
Weight of pure silver:	5.63 grams/0.18 ounce
Edge:	Reeded
Mint mark:	Reverse below eagle's tail

BARBER QUARTER DOLLAR (CONTINUED)

	G-4	VG-8	F-12	VF-20	EF-40	AU-50	MS-60	MS-62	MS-63	MS-64	MS-65	PF-63	PF-64	PF-65	PF-66
1892	5.00	8.00	20.	30.	72.	125.	160.	210.	260.	450.	1200.	575.	825.	1900.	—
1892-O	7.00	12.	32.	42.	80.	150.	260.	310.	400.	700.	1750.	*	*	*	*
1892-S	17.	35.	60.	85.	125.	275.	400.	550.	750.	1550.	4500.	*	*	*	*
1892-S/S	25.	45.	75.	100.	195.	375.	500.	725.	1100.	2500.	—	*	*	*	*
1893	5.00	8.00	23.	35.	72.	125.	220.	260.	310.	600.	1500.	575.	825.	1900.	—
1893-O	6.00	10.	27.	45.	90.	155.	265.	380.	550.	825.	2000.	*	*	*	*
1893-S	10.	20.	50.	85.	130.	275.	420.	650.	950.	2350.	6500.	*	*	*	*
1894	6.00	10.	30.	40.	75.	135.	220.	270.	365.	575.	1650.	575.	825.	1900.	—
1894-O	7.00	12.	35.	55.	85.	195.	345.	525.	700.	1250.	2250.	*	*	*	*
1894-S	7.00	12.	35.	50.	85.	175.	325.	500.	750.	1400.	3000.	*	*	*	*
1895	6.00	10.	25.	35.	72.	135.	225.	360.	475.	650.	1575.	575.	875.	1900.	—
1895-O	8.00	12.	35.	50.	95.	220.	420.	650.	950.	1400.	2750.	*	*	*	*
1895-S	8.00	15.	45.	75.	100.	220.	375.	575.	1000.	2000.	3650.	*	*	*	*
1895-S/S	12.	25.	60.	90.	150.	300.	450.	750.	1500.	3750.	—	*	*	*	*
1896	6.00	10.	24.	35.	72.	135.	250.	325.	435.	600.	1750.	575.	825.	1900.	—
1896-O	10.	20.	80.	225.	335.	625.	875.	1275.	1850.	3950.	7250.	*	*	*	*
1896-S	500.	700.	1000.	1400.	2800.	4000.	5000.	7000.	9000.	14000.	25000.	*	*	*	*
1897	6.00	10.	20.	35.	72.	125.	175.	225.	300.	475.	1650.	575.	825.	1900.	—
1897-O	10.	25.	80.	190.	350.	625.	850.	1250.	1700.	2650.	3700.	*	*	*	*
1897-S	27.	65.	185.	245.	345.	650.	950.	1325.	1750.	3000.	6000.	*	*	*	*
1898	6.00	10.	25.	35.	70.	125.	175.	225.	300.	475.	1300.	600.	825.	1900.	—
1898-O	10.	20.	60.	115.	225.	415.	650.	950.	1500.	3300.	—	*	*	*	*
1898-S	8.00	14.	45.	55.	75.	180.	425.	800.	1200.	3500.	5500.	*	*	*	*
1899	6.00	10.	20.	35.	65.	125.	175.	215.	300.	475.	1750.	575.	825.	2025.	—
1899-O	6.00	12.	28.	45.	92.	260.	400.	600.	800.	1400.	4250.	*	*	*	*
1899-S	12.	25.	65.	80.	105.	230.	440.	650.	1200.	1850.	3500.	*	*	*	*
1900	6.00	10.	20.	35.	65.	125.	175.	215.	300.	475.	1750.	575.	825.	1900.	—

—— = Insufficient pricing data * = None issued

BARBER QUARTER DOLLAR (CONTINUED)

	G-4	VG-8	F-12	VF-20	EF-40	AU-50	MS-60	MS-62	MS-63	MS-64	MS-65	PF-63	PF-64	PF-65	PF-66
1900-O	8.00	22.	60.	100.	125.	325.	600.	750.	350	1650.	3300.	*	*	*	*
1900-S	8.00	12.	35.	48.	65.	125.	400.	650.	375	1800.	4500.	*	*	*	*
1901	8.00	12.	20.	30.	65.	125.	170.	215.	325	475.	2600.	575.	825.	1900.	—
1901-O	30.	45.	105.	200.	350.	615.	825.	1350.	2000	3750.	—	*	*	*	*
1901-S	4000.	6000.	9000.	12000.	17000.	20000.	25000.	27000.	30000	40000.	50000.	*	*	*	*
1902	5.00	8.00	19.	30.	65.	125.	175.	215.	235	475.	1200.	600.	875.	1900.	—
1902-O	6.00	12.	35.	55.	100.	200.	425.	675.	1250	2400.	4750.	*	*	*	*
1902-S	10.	15.	35.	60.	85.	200.	425.	575.	325	1575.	3500.	*	*	*	*
1903	5.00	8.00	19.	30.	65.	125.	175.	300.	475	725.	2100.	575.	825.	1900.	—
1903-O	8.00	12.	35.	48.	85.	225.	400.	775.	1200	2650.	5250.	*	*	*	*
1903-S	11.	20.	40.	70.	110.	250.	430.	575.	850	1385.	2450.	*	*	*	*
1904	5.00	8.00	19.	35.	65.	125.	175.	215.	300	575.	2100.	575.	825.	1900.	—
1904-O	8.00	13.	50.	85.	175.	375.	765.	1025.	1350	2200.	2850.	*	*	*	*
1905	5.00	8.00	25.	35.	65.	125.	175.	250.	375	575.	2250.	575.	825.	1900.	—
1905-O	12.	20.	75.	130.	200.	345.	475.	750.	1100	2100.	6000.	*	*	*	*
1905-S	10.	18.	35.	50.	90.	210.	350.	650.	1000	1400.	3600.	*	*	*	*
1906	5.00	8.00	20.	35.	65.	125.	165.	210.	275.	465.	1200.	575.	825.	1900.	—
1906-D	5.00	8.00	23.	40.	65.	145.	240.	315.	475.	775.	2500.	*	*	*	*
1906-O	5.00	8.00	38.	53.	85.	200.	300.	375.	50[illegible].	725.	1300.	*	*	*	*
1907	5.00	8.00	19.	30.	65.	125.	165.	210.	275.	465.	1200.	575.	825.	1900.	—
1907-D	5.00	8.00	25.	45.	80.	175.	250.	375.	775.	1275.	3050.	*	*	*	*
1907-O	5.00	8.00	19.	35.	65.	135.	185.	300.	40[illegible].	1000.	2950.	*	*	*	*
1907-S	5.00	12.	38.	60.	110.	250.	475.	700.	975.	2000.	3500.	*	*	*	*
1908	5.00	8.00	19.	30.	65.	125.	200.	235.	30[illegible].	465.	1500.	575.	825.	1900.	—
1908-D	5.00	8.00	19.	30.	65.	125.	225.	285.	39[illegible].	625.	1525.	*	*	*	*
1908-O	5.00	8.00	19.	30.	65.	125.	200.	250.	31[illegible].	500.	1625.	*	*	*	*
1908-S	12.	27.	75.	125.	250.	425.	700.	950.	40[illegible].	2250.	6000.	*	*	*	*

—— = Insufficient pricing data * = None issued

BARBER QUARTER DOLLAR (CONTINUED)

	G-4	VG-8	F-12	VF-20	EF-40	AU-50	MS-60	MS-62	MS-63	MS-64	MS-65	PF-63	PF-64	PF-65	PF-66
1909	5.00	8.00	19.	30.	65.	110.	165.	210.	275.	465.	1200.	575.	825.	1900.	—
1909-D	5.00	8.00	19.	30.	65.	150.	195.	250.	335.	525.	1800.	*	*	*	*
1909-O	15.	32.	85.	185.	285.	465.	750.	1025.	1475.	2600.	6750.	*	*	*	*
1909-S	5.00	8.00	30.	45.	65.	180.	325.	525.	800.	1400.	2400.	*	*	*	*
1910	5.00	8.00	25.	35.	65.	140.	190.	240.	300.	635.	1500.	575.	825.	1900.	—
1910-D	6.00	10.	36.	60.	100.	225.	335.	550.	1025.	1500.	2500.	*	*	*	*
1911	5.00	8.00	19.	35.	75.	130.	165.	210.	275.	465.	1200.	575.	825.	1900.	—
1911-D	10.	20.	80.	200.	285.	450.	650.	850.	1250.	2450.	5000.	*	*	*	*
1911-S	8.00	15.	45.	60.	135.	285.	400.	525.	725.	900.	1750.	*	*	*	*
1912	5.00	8.00	19.	35.	65.	125.	165.	210.	275.	465.	1200.	575.	825.	1900.	—
1912-S	8.00	12.	40.	60.	100.	220.	400.	675.	1050.	1500.	2900.	*	*	*	*
1913	10.	20.	65.	140.	375.	525.	950.	1025.	1200.	1700.	4350.	575.	825.	1900.	—
1913-D	7.50	12.	35.	45.	80.	160.	275.	325.	425.	675.	1600.	*	*	*	*
1913-S	800.	1500.	3000.	4000.	5000.	6000.	7000.	8000.	9000.	10000.	15000.	*	*	*	*
1914	5.00	8.00	19.	30.	65.	110.	165.	195.	275.	465.	1300.	600.	825.	2025.	—
1914-D	5.00	8.00	19.	30.	65.	110.	165.	215.	275.	475.	1650.	*	*	*	*
1914-S	75.	100.	175.	225.	450.	650.	950.	1200.	1500.	2500.	3500.	*	*	*	*
1915	5.00	8.00	19.	30.	65.	110.	165.	225.	285.	475.	1250.	575.	1000.	2300.	—
1915-D	5.00	8.00	19.	30.	65.	110.	165.	210.	285.	475.	1250.	*	*	*	*
1915-S	5.00	10.	27.	40.	80.	200.	240.	325.	450.	850.	1650.	*	*	*	*
1916	5.00	8.00	19.	30.	65.	110.	165.	210.	275.	465.	1200.	*	*	*	*
1916-D	5.00	8.00	19.	30.	65.	110.	165.	210.	275.	465.	1150.	*	*	*	*
1916-D Large D/Small D	10.	21.	40.	60.	110.	185.	300.	450.	700.	—	—	*	*	*	*

—— = Insufficient pricing data * = None issued

Standing Liberty quarter dollar

Bare breast, No stars below eagle

Date of authorization:	April 2, 1792
Dates of issue:	1916-1930
Designer:	Hermon MacNeil
Engravers:	Obverse: Hermon MacNeil Reverse: MacNeil, Charles Barber
Diameter:	24.26 mm/0.96 inch
Weight:	6.25 grams/0.20 ounce
Metallic content:	90% silver, 10% copper
Weight of pure silver:	5.63 grams/0.18 ounce
Edge:	Reeded
Mint mark:	Obverse left of date

NOTE: The H following the numerical grade, such as MS-65H, refers to head. Liberty's head should be well struck and fully defined.

Mailed breast, Stars below eagle

STANDING LIBERTY QUARTER DOLLAR (CONTINUED)

	G-4	VG-8	F-12	VF-20	EF-40	AU-50	MS-60	MS-63	MS-63H	MS-64	MS-64H	MS-65	MS-65H	MS-66	MS-66H
BARE BREAST															
1916	2500.	3500.	6000.	7500.	8500.	9500.	13000.	15000.	20000.	18000.	25000.	20000.	30000.	30000.	40000.
1917	25.	40.	50.	65.	85.	175.	250.	350.	400.	600.	800.	900.	1600.	1300.	2200.
1917-D	27.	40.	50.	65.	100.	175.	275.	375.	480.	650.	900.	1000.	2500.	2000.	2500.
1917-S	30.	40.	50.	75.	150.	200.	400.	500.	1000.	700.	1200.	1650.	3500.	2500.	5000.
MAILED BREAST, STARS BELOW EAGLE															
1917	20.	25.	30.	35.	50.	85.	150.	225.	550.	400.	700.	650.	1200.	1100.	3500.
1917-D	40.	50.	80.	90.	100.	150.	225.	300.	750.	600.	1400.	1400.	3500.	2000.	7000.
1917-S	40.	50.	75.	75.	85.	125.	200.	300.	800.	500.	2400.	1200.	4250.	2500.	9000.
1918	18.	20.	30.	35.	50.	90.	135.	250.	400.	350.	1000.	650.	1800.	1800.	3500.
1918-D	27.	37.	55.	65.	90.	150.	225.	325.	1200.	800.	3000.	1500.	5500.	3000.	12000.
1918-S	18.	25.	35.	45.	60.	125.	275.	300.	1800.	800.	8000.	1500.	14000.	2000.	35000.
1918/7-S	1500.	2000.	2500.	3000.	5000.	9000.	15000.	35000.	125000.	50000.	175000.	100000.	-	-	-
1919	35.	45.	55.	60.	70.	100.	150.	225.	350.	300.	750.	650.	1800.	1000.	2500.
1919-D	80.	125.	175.	275.	400.	500.	700.	1500.	5000.	2200.	15000.	2500.	25000.	4000.	30000.
1919-S	80.	150.	200.	300.	500.	650.	1000.	2000.	5000.	3000.	15000.	4500.	30000.	6000.	35000.
1920	15.	20.	28.	35.	45.	75.	125.	225.	350.	350.	800.	550.	2000.	1000.	5000.
1920-D	50.	55.	75.	100.	125.	180.	250.	800.	2000.	1400.	3500.	2500.	6500.	3500.	14000.
1920-S	20.	28.	35.	40.	60.	125.	250.	800.	8500.	1400.	15000.	2500.	25000.	6000.	70000.
1921	175.	200.	300.	400.	450.	500.	750.	1000.	1500.	1200.	2500.	1600.	4500.	2500.	7500.
1923	15.	20.	35.	40.	50.	75.	125.	225.	800.	400.	1500.	650.	4000.	1000.	4000.
1923-S	250.	375.	450.	600.	800.	1000.	1500.	1750.	2500.	2000.	3000.	2500.	4000.	3000.	6000.
1924	15.	20.	25.	28.	35.	75.	125.	225.	350.	350.	600.	500.	1800.	1000.	4000.
1924-D	55.	70.	85.	110.	175.	200.	250.	300.	1500.	400.	2500.	600.	4500.	1000.	12000.
1924-S	27.	35.	38.	45.	90.	200.	350.	1000.	2000.	1200.	3500.	2000.	5500.	2500.	9000.
1925	3.00	4.00	7.00	15.	35.	75.	125.	225.	350.	350.	600.	500.	1200.	900.	1700.
1926	3.00	4.00	7.00	15.	35.	75.	125.	225.	350.	350.	600.	500.	2000.	900.	5000.

—— = Insufficient pricing data   * = None issued

STANDING LIBERTY QUARTER DOLLAR (CONTINUED)

	G-4	VG-8	F-12	VF-20	EF-40	AU-50	MS-60	MS-63	MS-63H	MS-64	MS-64H	MS-65	MS-65H	MS-66	MS-66H
1926-D	6.50	8.00	15.	30.	50.	85.	125.	225.	8000.	350.	18000.	500.	25000.	2000.	30000.
1926-S	3.50	4.00	12.	25.	100.	250.	350.	850.	10000.	1300.	20000.	2100.	27000.	5000.	35000.
1927	3.00	4.00	6.00	15.	40.	80.	125.	225.	350.	350.	600.	500.	1200.	1500.	2500.
1927-D	14.	16.	20.	50.	125.	175.	225.	250.	1000.	400.	2000.	700.	3000.	1500.	5000.
1927-S	25.	30.	85.	300.	1200.	3000.	4000.	7000.	35000.	7500.	75000.	15000.	150000.	20000.	-
1928	3.00	4.00	5.00	15.	35.	75.	125.	225.	350.	350.	600.	500.	2500.	1000.	3000.
1928-D	4.50	5.00	7.00	20.	40.	100.	150.	225.	2000.	350.	4000.	500.	6000.	900.	7500.
1928-S	4.00	5.00	6.00	15.	35.	75.	150.	225.	350.	350.	750.	500.	1000.	900.	1700.
1929	3.00	4.00	5.00	12.	35.	75.	125.	225.	350.	350.	600.	500.	1200.	900.	2000.
1929-D	4.50	5.00	8.00	15.	35.	75.	150.	225.	1000.	350.	3000.	500.	6500.	1000.	11000.
1929-S	3.00	4.00	6.00	15.	35.	75.	150.	225.	350.	350.	600.	500.	900.	900.	1800.
1930	3.00	4.00	4.50	12.	35.	75.	125.	225.	350.	350.	600.	500.	900.	900.	1500.
1930-S	4.00	5.00	6.00	12.	35.	75.	125.	225.	400.	350.	600.	500.	900.	900.	2000.

—— = Insufficient pricing data   * = None issued

Washington quarter dollar

Date of authorization: April 2, 1792; July 23, 1965;
Oct. 18, 1973; Dec. 1, 1997
Dates of issue: 1932-present
Designers: John Flanagan
(Bicentennial Reverse): Jack L. Ahr
Engravers: John R. Sinnock (State Reverses): various
(Bicentennial Reverse): Frank
Gasparro (State Reverses): various
Diameter: 24.26 mm/0.96 inch
Weight: (1932-1964, 1992-present silver Proofs
only): 6.25 grams/0.20 ounce
(1965-present): 5.67 grams/0.18 ounce
1976 Bicentennial Proof and
Uncirculated: 5.75 grams/0.18
ounce
Metallic content: (1932-1964, 1992-present silver Proofs
only): 90% silver, 10% copper
(1976 Bicentennial Proof and
Uncirculated sets only): 80% silver,
20% copper bonded to a core of
21.5% silver, 78.5% copper
(1965-present): 75% copper, 25% nickel
clad to pure copper core
Weight of pure silver: (1932-1964, 1992-present silver Proofs
only): 5.63 grams/0.18 ounce
(1976 Bicentennial Proof and
Uncirculated sets only): 2.30
grams/0.07 ounce
Edge: Reeded
Mint mark: (1932-1964): Reverse below eagle
(1968-present): Obverse right of
Washington's ponytail

Also, the letter C following a numerical grade for a Proof coin stands for "cameo," while the letters DC stand for "deep cameo." Cameo coins have contrasting surface finishes: mirror fields and frosted devices (raised areas). Deep cameo coins are the ultimate level of cameo, with deeply frosted devices. Cameo and deep cameo coins bring premiums.

WASHINGTON QUARTER DOLLAR (CONTINUED)

	VF-20	EF-40	AU-50	MS-60	MS-63	MS-64	MS-65	MS-66	MS-67	PF-63	PF-64	PF-65	PF-66	PF-66DC	PF-67	PF-67C	PF-67DC	PF-68	PF-68C	PF-68DC	PF-69	PF-69DC
SILVER																						
1932	10.	12.	20.	30.	65.	125.	500.	2000.	—	*	*	*	*	*	*	*	*	*	*	*	*	*
1932-D	200.	300.	500.	1200.	3500.	7500.	25000.	100000.	—	*	*	*	*	*	*	*	*	*	*	*	*	*
1932-S	150.	200.	300.	500.	1500.	2500.	7000.	25000.	—	*	*	*	*	*	*	*	*	*	*	*	*	*
1934-D	20.	35.	100.	250.	350.	700.	1700.	5000.	—	*	*	*	*	*	*	*	*	*	*	*	*	*
1934	4.00	6.00	12.	30.	50.	75.	125.	300.	1000.	*	*	*	*	*	*	*	*	*	*	*	*	*
1934 Light Motto	10.	15.	20.	50.	100.	200.	500.	2000.	—	*	*	*	*	*	*	*	*	*	*	*	*	*
1934 Doubled Die	200.	300.	400.	750.	1500.	3500.	7500.	15000.	—	*	*	*	*	*	*	*	*	*	*	*	*	*
1935	4.00	8.00	13.	25.	40.	50.	150.	250.	1000.	*	*	*	*	*	*	*	*	*	*	*	*	*
1935-D	15.	35.	150.	300.	400.	600.	1200.	2000.	10000.	*	*	*	*	*	*	*	*	*	*	*	*	*
1935-S	8.00	18.	45.	125.	150.	200.	400.	1000.	7000.	*	*	*	*	*	*	*	*	*	*	*	*	*
1936	4.00	6.00	12.	25.	45.	65.	100.	250.	2000.	900.	1200.	1500.	4500.	—	9000.	—	—	—	—	—	—	—
1936-D	25.	80.	250.	500.	700.	1000.	1800.	4000.	17000.	*	*	*	*	*	*	*	*	*	*	*	*	*
1936-S	7.00	25.	60.	150.	200.	250.	500.	1500.	7500.	*	*	*	*	*	*	*	*	*	*	*	*	*
1937	5.00	12.	25.	30.	45.	65.	150.	400.	1800.	350.	500.	600.	900.	—	1800.	—	—	—	—	—	—	—
1937-D	7.00	15.	40.	75.	100.	125.	200.	600.	6500.	*	*	*	*	*	*	*	*	*	*	*	*	*
1937-S	20.	40.	125.	125.	175.	250.	350.	750.	2000.	*	*	*	*	*	*	*	*	*	*	*	*	*
1937 Doubled Die Obverse	—	—	—	—	—	—	—	—	—	—	—	—	—	—	—	—	—	—	—	—	—	—
1938	12.	18.	45.	85.	125.	150.	225.	500.	3500.	150.	250.	350.	500.	—	1200.	—	—	530.	—	—	—	—
1938-S	10.	25.	50.	100.	125.	150.	250.	500.	3000.	*	*	*	*	*	*	*	*	*	*	*	*	*
1939	3.00	4.00	10.	18.	40.	70.	100.	200.	400.	150.	250.	300.	400.	—	800.	—	—	—	—	—	—	—
1939-D	8.00	15.	20.	40.	60.	75.	125.	250.	1500.	*	*	*	*	*	*	*	*	*	*	*	*	*
1939-S	9.00	25.	60.	100.	125.	200.	300.	800.	8500.	*	*	*	*	*	*	*	*	*	*	*	*	*
1940	3.00	4.00	8.00	18.	35.	50.	125.	250.	1000.	125.	200.	300.	350.	—	600.	—	—	—	—	—	—	—
1940-D	15.	20.	65.	125.	175.	200.	300.	800.	3500.	*	*	*	*	*	*	*	*	*	*	*	*	*

—— = Insufficient pricing data * = None issued

WASHINGTON QUARTER DOLLAR (CONTINUED)

	VF-20	EF-40	AU-50	MS-60	MS-63	MS-64	MS-65	MS-66	MS-67	PF-63	PF-64	PF-65	PF-66	PF-66DC	PF-67	PF-67C	PF-67DC	PF-68	PF-68C	PF-68DC	PF-69	PF-69DC
1940-S	8.00	10.	18.	25.	40.	50.	125.	300.	1500.	*	*	*	*	*	*	*	*	*	*	*	*	*
1941	3.00	5.00	7.00	10.	20.	25.	75.	250.	1200.	100.	150.	250.	400.	—	500.	—	—	—	—	—	—	—
1941-D	5.00	10.	15.	30.	65.	100.	125.	400.	3000.	*	*	*	*	*	*	*	*	*	*	*	*	*
1941-S	3.00	5.00	9.00	25.	40.	65.	100.	300.	2500.	*	*	*	*	*	*	*	*	*	*	*	*	*
1942	3.00	4.00	5.00	10.	15.	25.	50.	400.	3500.	85.	125.	200.	300.	—	400.	—	—	—	—	—	—	—
1942-D	4.00	6.00	12.	17.	25.	35.	75.	250.	1300.	*	*	*	*	*	*	*	*	*	*	*	*	*
1942-S	4.00	8.00	20.	65.	100.	150.	200.	400.	2500.	*	*	*	*	*	*	*	*	*	*	*	*	*
1943	3.00	4.00	5.00	6.00	10.	25.	50.	150.	750.	*	*	*	*	*	*	*	*	*	*	*	*	*
1943-D	4.00	6.00	16.	25.	40.	60.	75.	250.	1400.	*	*	*	*	*	*	*	*	*	*	*	*	*
1943-S	5.00	8.00	15.	30.	45.	65.	75.	250.	1600.	*	*	*	*	*	*	*	*	*	*	*	*	*
1943-S Doubled Die	200.	250.	300.	500.	1500.	2000.	3500.	8000.	—	*	*	*	*	*	*	*	*	*	*	*	*	*
1944	2.75	3.00	3.50	5.00	11.	18.	45.	110.	750.	*	*	*	*	*	*	*	*	*	*	*	*	*
1944-D	2.25	5.50	8.50	14.	18.	25.	50.	100.	650.	*	*	*	*	*	*	*	*	*	*	*	*	*
1944-S	2.25	5.00	9.00	16.	22.	28.	55.	100.	750.	*	*	*	*	*	*	*	*	*	*	*	*	*
1945	2.25	2.35	3.00	4.00	10.	15.	50.	160.	2500.	*	*	*	*	*	*	*	*	*	*	*	*	*
1945-D	2.75	5.00	10.	15.	22.	35.	55.	125.	2000.	*	*	*	*	*	*	*	*	*	*	*	*	*
1945-S	3.50	5.00	8.00	12.	19.	30.	50.	125.	1700.	*	*	*	*	*	*	*	*	*	*	*	*	*
1946	2.25	2.50	3.25	5.50	9.00	15.	60.	225.	2000.	*	*	*	*	*	*	*	*	*	*	*	*	*
1946-D	2.35	2.75	5.50	9.00	10.	18.	45.	100.	1500.	*	*	*	*	*	*	*	*	*	*	*	*	*
1946-S	3.00	3.25	3.50	7.00	11.	20.	45.	100.	800.	*	*	*	*	*	*	*	*	*	*	*	*	*
1947	2.25	3.00	4.00	5.25	12.	20.	45.	75.	900.	*	*	*	*	*	*	*	*	*	*	*	*	*
1947-D	2.35	3.00	4.00	7.00	12.	20.	40.	75.	500.	*	*	*	*	*	*	*	*	*	*	*	*	*
1947-S	2.75	3.50	5.00	10.	12.	18.	40.	65.	300.	*	*	*	*	*	*	*	*	*	*	*	*	*
1948	2.25	2.65	3.00	5.00	10.	18.	50.	80.	550.	*	*	*	*	*	*	*	*	*	*	*	*	*
1948-D	2.35	2.80	5.00	7.00	10.	25.	45.	200.	2500.	*	*	*	*	*	*	*	*	*	*	*	*	*

—— = Insufficient pricing data   * = None issued

WASHINGTON QUARTER DOLLAR (CONTINUED)

	VF-20	EF-40	AU-50	MS-60	MS-63	MS-64	MS-65	MS-66	MS-67	PF-63	PF-64	PF-65	PF-66	PF-66DC	PF-67	PF-67C	PF-67DC	PF-68	PF-68C	PF-68DC	PF-69	PF-69DC
1948-S	3.25	4.00	5.00	7.50	11.	25.	45.	80.	1000.	*	*	*	*	*	*	*	*	*	*	*	*	*
1949	3.25	7.00	10.	25.	32.	45.	60.	140.	1400.	*	*	*	*	*	*	*	*	*	*	*	*	*
1949-D	3.75	4.50	11.	15.	20.	30.	55.	250.	1800.	*	*	*	*	*	*	*	*	*	*	*	*	*
1950	2.25	3.75	5.00	7.00	9.00	25.	40.	75.	1000.	55.	60.	75.	35.	—	100.	—	—	350.	—	—	—	—
1950-D	2.00	4.00	4.75	6.00	8.50	15.	40.	125.	1500.	*	*	*	*	*	*	*	*	*	*	*	*	*
1950-S	2.00	4.00	8.50	12.	18.	23.	75.	100.	800.	*	*	*	*	*	*	*	*	*	*	*	*	*
1950-D/S	55.	135.	200.	250.	400.	1000.	4500.	5000.	—	*	*	*	*	*	*	*	*	*	*	*	*	*
1950-S/D	60.	150.	200.	235.	300.	375.	1200.	3500.	—	*	*	*	*	*	*	*	*	*	*	*	*	*
1951	3.00	4.00	5.00	6.00	8.00	15.	35.	100.	750.	39.	45.	55.	70.	—	100.	315.	—	—	—	—	475.	—
1951-D	2.00	3.00	4.00	6.00	7.00	10.	40.	125.	2000.	*	*	*	*	*	*	*	*	*	*	*	*	*
1951-S	3.00	5.00	8.50	16.	27.	35.	50.	100.	600.	*	*	*	*	*	*	*	*	*	*	*	*	*
1952	2.50	3.00	7.75	10.	13.	15.	25.	100.	500.	28.	38.	50.	70.	—	100.	—	—	110.	500.	—	—	—
1952-D	2.00	2.50	3.00	6.00	10.	14.	50.	250.	5000.	*	*	*	*	*	*	*	*	*	*	*	*	*
1952-S	5.00	5.75	6.75	12.	25.	30.	45.	100.	400.	*	*	*	*	*	*	*	*	*	*	*	*	*
1953	2.00	3.25	5.00	7.00	9.50	14.	45.	100.	800.	20.	25.	30.	50.	—	90.	110.	—	—	450.	—	—	—
1953-D	2.00	2.25	2.50	3.00	5.00	13.	45.	250.	2000.	*	*	*	*	*	*	*	*	*	*	*	*	*
1953-S	2.00	2.75	4.00	5.50	7.00	12.	40.	80.	1200.	*	*	*	*	*	*	*	*	*	*	*	*	*
1954	2.00	2.50	3.00	3.75	13.	10.	35.	100.	1800.	10.	12.	20.	27.	—	35.	175.	—	130.	225.	—	175.	—
1954-D	2.00	2.50	3.25	6.00	9.50	12.	50.	350.	450.	*	*	*	*	*	*	*	*	*	*	*	*	*
1954-S	2.00	2.50	3.25	3.75	8.00	15.	40.	100.	300.	*	*	*	*	*	*	*	*	*	*	*	*	*
1955	2.00	3.00	4.00	4.75	5.50	11.	30.	50.	80.	9.00	10.	17.	25.	—	50.	200.	—	125.	375.	—	175.	—
1955-D	3.50	4.50	5.50	7.00	8.50	20.	68.	600.	750.	*	*	*	*	*	*	*	*	*	*	*	*	*
1956	2.00	3.00	4.00	6.50	10.	17.	25.	75.	200.	7.00	8.50	10.	25.	—	40.	95.	125.	100.	125.	200.	150.	—
1956-D	2.25	3.00	4.25	6.00	7.50	11.	35.	60.	110.	*	*	*	*	*	*	*	*	*	*	*	*	*
1957	3.00	3.50	4.25	6.00	8.00	10.	27.	60.	175.	2.75	7.00	10.	25.	—	40.	225.	320.	100.	—	—	150.	—

—— = Insufficient pricing data   * = None issued

WASHINGTON QUARTER DOLLAR (CONTINUED)

	VF-20	EF-40	AU-50	MS-60	MS-63	MS-64	MS-65	MS-66	MS-67	PF-63	PF-64	PF-65	PF-66	PF-66DC	PF-67	PF-67C	PF-67DC	PF-68	PF-68C	PF-68DC	PF-69	PF-69DC
1957-D	2.00	3.00	4.00	6.00	9.50	11.	25.	100.	250.	*	*	*	*	*	*	*	*	*	*	*	*	*
1958	2.00	2.50	3.00	3.50	4.00	10.	35.	50.	175.	5.00	7.00	10.	25.	—	40.	275.	—	100.	350.	—	150.	—
1958-D	2.00	2.50	3.00	4.75	6.25	9.00	30.	70.	200.	*	*	*	*	*	*	*	*	*	*	*	*	*
1959	2.50	3.00	3.50	4.00	5.50	15.	30.	100.	175.	2.75	7.00	10.	25.	—	40.	55.	235.	100.	325.	—	150.	—
1959-D	2.50	2.75	3.00	3.50	4.00	14.	42.	65.	100.	*	*	*	*	*	*	*	*	*	*	*	*	*
1960	2.00	2.50	3.00	3.50	4.00	16.	32.	100.	175.	1.75	7.00	10.	25.	—	40.	115.	240.	100.	135.	425.	150.	—
1960-D	2.00	2.50	3.00	3.50	4.00	5.50	27.	100.	285.	*	*	*	*	*	*	*	*	*	*	*	*	*
1961	2.00	2.50	3.00	3.50	4.00	5.00	27.	95.	180.	1.50	5.00	8.50	20.	—	30.	40.	35.	50.	125.	600.	100.	—
1961-D	2.00	2.50	3.00	3.50	4.00	8.50	28.	165.	275.	*	*	*	*	*	*	*	*	*	*	*	*	*
1962	2.00	2.50	3.00	3.50	4.00	6.50	30.	90.	125.	1.50	5.00	8.50	20.	—	30.	40.	—	40.	50.	100.	80.	—
1962-D	2.00	2.50	3.00	3.50	4.00	11.	24.	100.	175.	*	*	*	*	*	*	*	*	*	*	*	*	*
1963	2.00	2.50	3.00	3.50	4.00	10.	24.	65.	135.	1.50	5.00	8.50	20.	—	30.	80.	—	40.	125.	600.	80.	—
1963-D	2.00	2.50	3.00	3.50	4.00	9.00	22.	80.	200.	*	*	*	*	*	*	*	*	*	*	*	*	*
1964	2.00	2.50	3.00	3.50	4.00	8.75	25.	70.	125.	*	5.00	8.50	20.	—	30.	80.	—	50.	45.	90.	85.	—
1964-D	2.00	2.50	3.00	3.50	4.00	4.50	30.	75.	270.	*	*	*	*	*	*	*	*	*	*	*	*	*
COPPER-NICKEL CLAD																						
1965	—	—	—	—	0.70	2.75	14.	27.	—	*	*	*	*	*	*	*	*	*	*	*	*	*
1966	—	—	—	—	0.70	2.00	8.00	40.	—	*	*	*	*	*	*	*	*	*	*	*	*	*
1967	—	—	—	—	0.95	2.75	10.	50.	210.	*	*	*	*	*	*	*	*	*	*	*	*	*
1968	—	—	—	—	0.95	3.00	15.	35.	—	*	*	*	*	*	*	*	*	*	*	*	*	*
1968-D	—	—	—	—	0.95	4.25	7.00	20.	65.	*	*	*	*	*	*	*	*	*	*	*	*	*
1968-S	*	*	*	*	*	*	*	*	*	0.75	—	8.00	10.	—	12.	—	—	15.	—	—	20.	—
1969	—	—	—	—	1.25	10.	15.	50.	—	*	*	*	*	*	*	*	*	*	*	*	*	*
1969-D	—	—	—	—	1.25	3.50	10.	40.	300.	*	*	*	*	*	*	*	*	*	*	*	*	*
1969-S	*	*	*	*	*	*	*	*	*	0.75	—	8.00	10.	—	12.	—	—	15.	—	—	20.	—
1970	—	—	—	—	0.55	2.00	12.	60.	—	*	*	*	*	*	*	*	*	*	*	*	*	*

—— = Insufficient pricing data   * = None issued

WASHINGTON QUARTER DOLLAR (CONTINUED)

	VF-20	EF-40	AU-50	MS-60	MS-63	MS-64	MS-65	MS-66	MS-67	PF-63	PF-64	PF-65	PF-66	PF-66DC	PF-67	PF-67C	PF-67DC	PF-68	PF-68C	PF-68DC	PF-69	PF-69DC
1970-D	—	—	—	—	0.55	3.50	11.	20.	30.	*	*	*	*	*	*	*	*	*	*	*	*	*
1970-S	*	*	*	*	*	*	*	*	*	0.75	—	8.00	10.	—	12.	—	—	15.	—	—	20.	—
1971	—	—	—	—	0.95	3.25	9.00	35.	—	*	*	*	*	*	*	*	*	*	*	*	*	*
1971-D	—	—	—	—	0.95	2.00	2.25	25.	167.	*	*	*	*	*	*	*	*	*	*	*	*	*
1971-S	*	*	*	*	*	*	*	*	*	0.75	—	8.00	10.	—	12.	—	—	15.	—	—	20.	—
1972	—	—	—	—	0.65	2.00	7.00	35.	—	*	*	*	*	*	*	*	*	*	*	*	*	*
1972-D	—	—	—	—	0.65	3.50	9.75	25.	30.	*	*	*	*	*	*	*	*	*	*	*	*	*
1972-S	*	*	*	*	*	*	*	*	*	0.75	—	8.00	10.	—	12.	—	—	15.	—	—	20.	—
1973	—	—	—	—	0.65	3.50	10.	45.	—	*	*	*	*	*	*	*	*	*	*	*	*	*
1973-D	—	—	—	—	0.65	2.00	14.	20.	230.	*	*	*	*	*	*	*	*	*	*	*	*	*
1973-S	*	*	*	*	*	*	*	*	*	0.65	—	8.00	10.	—	12.	—	—	15.	—	—	20.	—
1974	—	—	—	—	0.65	3.50	10.	25.	—	*	*	*	*	*	*	*	*	*	*	*	*	*
1974-D	—	—	—	—	0.65	7.00	18.	30.	75.	*	*	*	*	*	*	*	*	*	*	*	*	*
1974-S	*	*	*	*	*	*	*	*	*	0.55	—	8.00	10.	—	12.	—	—	15.	—	—	20.	65.

Dual date

Bicentennial reverse

	VF-20	EF-40	AU-50	MS-60	MS-63	MS-64	MS-65	MS-66	MS-67	PF-63	PF-64	PF-65	PF-66	PF-66DC	PF-67	PF-67C	PF-67DC	PF-68	PF-68C	PF-68DC	PF-69	PF-69DC
DUAL DATE, BICENTENNIAL REVERSE																						
1776-1976	—	—	—	—	0.75	2.00	10.	25.	37.	*	*	*	*	*	*	*	*	*	*	*	*	*

—— = Insufficient pricing data   * = None issued

WASHINGTON QUARTER DOLLAR (CONTINUED)

	VF-20	EF-40	AU-50	MS-60	MS-63	MS-64	MS-65	MS-66	MS-67	PF-63	PF-64	PF-65	PF-66	PF-66DC	PF-67	PF-67C	PF-67DC	PF-68	PF-68C	PF-68DC	PF-69	PF-69DC
1776-1976-D	—	—	—	—	0.75	3.50	12.	32.	168.	*	*	*	*	*	*	*	*	*	*	*	*	*
1776-1976-S	*	*	*	*	*	*	*	*	*	—	—	8.00	10.	—	12.	—	—	15.	—	—	20.	80.
1776-1976-S 40% silver	—	—	—	—	2.50	—	3.75	—	—	—	—	10.	12.	—	15.	—	—	18.	—	—	25.	125.
EAGLE REVERSE RESUMED																						
1977	—	—	—	—	0.55	5.00	10.	25.	118.	*	*	*	*	*	*	*	*	*	*	*	*	*
1977-D	—	—	—	—	0.55	3.00	6.00	26.	—	*	*	*	*	*	*	*	*	*	*	*	*	*
1977-S	*	*	*	*	*	*	*	*	*	0.70	—	7.00	8.00	9.00	10.	—	12.	12.	—	15.	18.	25.
1978	—	—	—	—	0.55	3.00	10.	28.	144.	*	*	*	*	*	*	*	*	*	*	*	*	*
1978-D	—	—	—	—	0.55	5.00	12.	40.	—	*	*	*	*	*	*	*	*	*	*	*	*	*
1978-S	*	*	*	*	*	*	*	*	*	0.70	—	7.00	8.00	9.00	10.	—	12.	12.	—	15.	18.	25.
1979	—	—	—	—	0.65	5.00	10.	30.	—	*	*	*	*	*	*	*	*	*	*	*	*	*
1979-D	—	—	—	—	0.75	3.00	7.00	25.	—	*	*	*	*	*	*	*	*	*	*	*	*	*
1979-S Filled S	*	*	*	*	*	*	*	*	*	0.75	—	7.00	8.00	9.00	10.	—	12.	12.	—	15.	18.	25.
1979-S Clear S	*	*	*	*	*	*	*	*	*	0.95	—	8.00	9.00	11.	12.	—	14.	15.	—	18.	25.	35.
1980-P	—	—	—	—	0.55	3.00	9.00	20.	—	*	*	*	*	*	*	*	*	*	*	*	*	*
1980-D	—	—	—	—	0.55	3.00	8.75	30.	—	*	*	*	*	*	*	*	*	*	*	*	*	*
1980-S	*	*	*	*	*	*	*	*	*	0.75	—	7.00	8.00	9.00	10.	—	12.	12.	—	15.	18.	25.
1981-P	—	—	—	—	0.55	6.00	10.	35.	—	*	*	*	*	*	*	*	*	*	*	*	*	*
1981-D	—	—	—	—	0.55	7.50	6.50	18.	25.	*	*	*	*	*	*	*	*	*	*	*	*	*
1981-S	*	*	*	*	*	*	*	*	*	0.75	—	7.00	8.00	9.00	10.	—	12.	12.	—	15.	18.	25.
1982-P	—	—	—	—	4.00	15.	30.	75.	—	*	*	*	*	*	*	*	*	*	*	*	*	*
1982-D	—	—	—	—	1.50	10.	15.	70.	—	*	*	*	*	*	*	*	*	*	*	*	*	*
1982-S	*	*	*	*	*	*	*	*	*	0.85	—	7.00	8.00	9.00	10.	—	12.	12.	—	15.	18.	25.
1983-P	—	—	—	—	8.00	15.	63.	475.	—	*	*	*	*	*	*	*	*	*	*	*	*	*
1983-D	—	—	—	—	4.00	25.	45.	118.	—	*	*	*	*	*	*	*	*	*	*	*	*	*

—— = Insufficient pricing data * = None issued

WASHINGTON QUARTER DOLLAR (CONTINUED)

	VF-20	EF-40	AU-50	MS-60	MS-63	MS-64	MS-65	MS-66	MS-67	PF-63	PF-64	PF-65	PF-66	PF-66DC	PF-67	PF-67C	PF-67DC	PF-68	PF-68C	PF-68DC	PF-69	PF-69DC
1983-S	*	*	*	*	*	*	*	*	*	1.25	—	5.00	7.00	10.	10.	—	15.	15.	—	20.	18.	25.
1984-P	—	—	—	—	1.00	11.	15.	100.	—	*	*	*	*	*	*	*	*	*	*	*	*	*
1984-D	—	—	—	—	1.50	8.00	12.	57.	—	*	*	*	*	*	*	*	*	*	*	*	*	*
1984-S	*	*	*	*	*	*	*	*	*	0.75	—	5.00	7.00	10.	10.	—	15.	15.	—	20.	18.	25.
1985-P	—	—	—	—	1.50	10.	20.	50.	—	*	*	*	*	*	*	*	*	*	*	*	*	*
1985-D	—	—	—	—	1.50	4.00	10.	22.	—	*	*	*	*	*	*	*	*	*	*	*	*	*
1985-S	*	*	*	*	*	*	*	*	*	0.50	—	5.00	7.00	10.	10.	—	15.	15.	—	20.	18.	25.
1986-P	—	—	—	—	4.00	2.00	4.00	19.	—	*	*	*	*	*	*	*	*	*	*	*	*	*
1986-D	—	—	—	—	4.00	4.00	12.	53.	975.	*	*	*	*	*	*	*	*	*	*	*	*	*
1986-S	*	*	*	*	*	*	*	*	*	1.00	—	5.00	7.00	10.	10.	—	15.	15.	—	20.	18.	25.
1987-P	—	—	—	—	0.65	9.50	12.	—	—	*	*	*	*	*	*	*	*	*	*	*	*	*
1987-D	—	—	—	—	0.65	3.00	8.25	30.	350.	*	*	*	*	*	*	*	*	*	*	*	*	*
1987-S	*	*	*	*	*	*	*	*	*	0.65	—	5.00	7.00	10.	10.	—	15.	15.	—	20.	18.	25.
1988-P	—	—	—	—	1.65	3.00	20.	50.	—	*	*	*	*	*	*	*	*	*	*	*	*	*
1988-D	—	—	—	—	0.75	5.00	15.	20.	500.	*	*	*	*	*	*	*	*	*	*	*	*	*
1988-S	*	*	*	*	*	*	*	*	*	0.65	—	5.00	7.00	10.	10.	—	15.	15.	—	20.	18.	25.
1989-P	—	—	—	—	0.85	3.00	24.	100.	—	*	*	*	*	*	*	*	*	*	*	*	*	*
1989-D	—	—	—	—	0.85	2.00	4.25	50.	—	*	*	*	*	*	*	*	*	*	*	*	*	*
1989-S	*	*	*	*	*	*	*	*	*	0.65	—	5.00	7.00	10.	10.	—	15.	15.	—	20.	18.	25.
1990-P	—	—	—	—	0.75	3.00	18.	50.	—	*	*	*	*	*	*	*	*	*	*	*	*	*
1990-D	—	—	—	—	0.75	2.00	4.00	38.	—	*	*	*	*	*	*	*	*	*	*	*	*	*
1990-S	*	*	*	*	*	*	*	*	*	3.00	—	5.00	7.00	10.	10.	—	15.	15.	—	20.	18.	25.
1991-P	—	—	—	—	0.75	7.00	20.	150.	—	*	*	*	*	*	*	*	*	*	*	*	*	*
1991-D	—	—	—	—	0.75	5.00	15.	30.	—	*	*	*	*	*	*	*	*	*	*	*	*	*
1991-S	*	*	*	*	*	*	*	*	*	2.00	—	5.00	7.00	10.	10.	—	15.	15.	—	20.	18.	25.

—— = Insufficient pricing data * = None issued

WASHINGTON QUARTER DOLLAR (CONTINUED)

	VF-20	EF-40	AU-50	MS-60	MS-63	MS-64	MS-65	MS-66	MS-67	PF-63	PF-64	PF-65	PF-66	PF-66DC	PF-67	PF-67C	PF-67DC	PF-68	PF-68C	PF-68DC	PF-69	PF-69DC
1992-P	—	—	—	—	0.75	13.	22.	—	—	*	*	*	*	*	*	*	*	*	*	*	*	*
1992-D	—	—	—	—	0.75	6.50	30.	375.	—	*	*	*	*	*	*	*	*	*	*	*	*	*
1992-S Clad	*	*	*	*	*	*	*	*	*	2.70	—	5.00	7.00	10.	10.	—	15.	15.	—	15.	18.	25.
1992-S Silver	*	*	*	*	*	*	*	*	*	—	—	7.00	10.	15.	14.	—	20.	18.	—	18.	25.	35.
1993-P	—	—	—	—	0.75	4.00	10.	—	—	*	*	*	*	*	*	*	*	*	*	*	*	*
1993-D	—	—	—	—	0.75	8.00	12.	—	—	*	*	*	*	*	*	*	*	*	*	*	*	*
1993-S Clad	*	*	*	*	*	*	*	*	*	4.00	—	5.00	7.00	10.	10.	—	15.	15.	—	15.	18.	25.
1993-S Silver	*	*	*	*	*	*	*	*	*	—	—	7.00	10.	15.	14.	—	20.	18.	—	18.	25.	35.
1994-P	—	—	—	—	0.65	10.	25.	—	—	*	*	*	*	*	*	*	*	*	*	*	*	*
1994-D	—	—	—	—	0.65	5.00	12.	—	—	*	*	*	*	*	*	*	*	*	*	*	*	*
1994-S Clad	*	*	*	*	*	*	*	*	*	3.00	—	5.00	7.00	10.	10.	—	15.	15.	—	15.	18.	25.
1994-S Silver	*	*	*	*	*	*	*	*	*	—	—	7.00	10.	15.	14.	—	20.	18.	—	18.	25.	35.
1995-P	—	—	—	—	0.75	8.00	25.	60.	85.	*	*	*	*	*	*	*	*	*	*	*	*	*
1995-D	—	—	—	—	0.75	8.00	20.	50.	435.	*	*	*	*	*	*	*	*	*	*	*	*	*
1995-S Clad	*	*	*	*	*	*	*	*	*	15.	—	5.00	7.00	10.	10.	—	15.	15.	—	15.	18.	30.
1995-S Silver	*	*	*	*	*	*	*	*	*	—	—	7.00	10.	15.	14.	—	20.	18.	—	18.	25.	35.
1996-P	—	—	—	—	0.55	7.00	15.	20.	85.	*	*	*	*	*	*	*	*	*	*	*	*	*
1996-D	—	—	—	—	0.55	7.00	15.	20.	85.	*	*	*	*	*	*	*	*	*	*	*	*	*
1996-S Clad	*	*	*	*	*	*	*	*	*	3.00	—	5.00	7.00	10.	10.	—	15.	15.	—	15.	18.	25.
1996-S Silver	*	*	*	*	*	*	*	*	*	—	—	7.00	10.	15.	14.	—	20.	18.	—	18.	25.	35.
1997-P	—	—	—	—	0.55	7.00	10.	235.	495.	*	*	*	*	*	*	*	*	*	*	*	*	*
1997-D	—	—	—	—	0.55	10.	20.	50.	250.	*	*	*	*	*	*	*	*	*	*	*	*	*
1997-S Clad	*	*	*	*	*	*	*	*	*	7.00	—	5.00	7.00	10.	10.	—	15.	15.	—	15.	18.	30.
1997-S Silver	*	*	*	*	*	*	*	*	*	—	—	7.00	10.	15.	14.	—	20.	18.	—	18.	25.	45.
1998-P	—	—	—	—	0.40	7.25	13.	30.	200.	*	*	*	*	*	*	*	*	*	*	*	*	*

—— = Insufficient pricing data   * = None issued

	VF-20	EF-40	AU-50	MS-60	MS-63	MS-64	MS-65	MS-66	MS-67	PF-63	PF-64	PF-65	PF-66	PF-66DC	PF-67	PF-67C	PF-67DC	PF-68	PF-68C	PF-68DC	PF-69	PF-69DC
1998-D	—	—	—	—	0.40	9.50	12.	15.	—	*	*	*	*	*	*	*	*	*	*	*	*	*
1998-S Clad	*	*	*	*	*	*	*	*	*	7.00	—	5.00	7.00	10.	10.	—	15.	15.	—	15.	18.	25.
1998-S Silver	*	*	*	*	*	*	*	*	*	—	—	7.00	10.	15.	14.	—	20.	18.	—	18.	25.	35.
STATE REVERSE																						
1999-P DE	—	—	—	—	1.25	10.	15.	50.	300.	*	*	*	*	*	*	*	*	*	*	*	*	*
1999-D DE	—	—	—	—	1.25	15.	20.	75.	375.	*	*	*	*	*	*	*	*	*	*	*	*	*
1999-S Clad DE	*	*	*	*	*	*	*	*	*	—	—	6.00	7.00	8.00	8.00	—	10.	9.00	—	15.	10.	31.
1999-S Silver DE	*	*	*	*	*	*	*	*	*	—	—	8.00	9.00	10.	10.	—	15.	12.	—	25.	20.	31.
1999-P PA	—	—	—	—	1.40	15.	20.	60.	400.	*	*	*	*	*	*	*	*	*	*	*	*	*
1999-D PA	—	—	—	—	1.40	10.	15.	40.	470.	*	*	*	*	*	*	*	*	*	*	*	*	*
1999-S Clad PA	*	*	*	*	*	*	*	*	*	—	—	6.00	7.00	8.00	8.00	—	10.	9.00	—	15.	10.	34.
1999-S Silver PA	*	*	*	*	*	*	*	*	*	—	—	8.00	9.00	10.	10.	—	15.	12.	—	25.	20.	38.
1999-P NJ	—	—	—	—	0.75	14.	22.	65.	400.	*	*	*	*	*	*	*	*	*	*	*	*	*
1999-D NJ	—	—	—	—	1.25	12.	16.	65.	1000.	*	*	*	*	*	*	*	*	*	*	*	*	*
1999-S Clad NJ	*	*	*	*	*	*	*	*	*	—	—	6.00	7.00	8.00	8.00	—	10.	9.00	—	15.	10.	31.
1999-S Silver NJ	*	*	*	*	*	*	*	*	*	—	—	8.00	9.00	10.	10.	—	15.	12.	—	25.	20.	31.
1999-P GA	—	—	—	—	0.75	15.	35.	112.	1200.	*	*	*	*	*	*	*	*	*	*	*	*	*
1999-D GA	—	—	—	—	0.80	12.	35.	90.	860.	*	*	*	*	*	*	*	*	*	*	*	*	*
1999-S Clad GA	*	*	*	*	*	*	*	*	*	—	—	6.00	7.00	8.00	8.00	—	10.	9.00	—	15.	10.	52.
1999-S Silver GA	*	*	*	*	*	*	*	*	*	—	—	8.00	9.00	10.	10.	—	15.	12.	—	25.	20.	31.
1999-P CT	—	—	—	—	0.60	12.	15.	70.	275.	*	*	*	*	*	*	*	*	*	*	*	*	*
1999-D CT	—	—	—	—	0.60	10.	20.	35.	128.	*	*	*	*	*	*	*	*	*	*	*	*	*
1999-S Clad CT	*	*	*	*	*	*	*	*	*	—	—	6.00	7.00	8.00	8.00	—	10.	9.00	—	15.	10.	30.
1999-S Silver CT	*	*	*	*	*	*	*	*	*	—	—	8.00	9.00	10.	10.	—	15.	12.	—	25.	20.	31.
2000-P MA	—	—	—	—	0.55	3.00	10.	24.	55.	*	*	*	*	*	*	*	*	*	*	*	*	*

—— = Insufficient pricing data * = None issued

WASHINGTON QUARTER DOLLAR (CONTINUED)

	VF-20	EF-40	AU-50	MS-60	MS-63	MS-64	MS-65	MS-66	MS-67	PF-63	PF-64	PF-65	PF-66	PF-66DC	PF-67	PF-67C	PF-67DC	PF-68	PF-68C	PF-68DC	PF-69	PF-69DC
2000-D MA	—	—	—	—	0.55	6.50	10.	25.	82.	*	*	*	*	*	*	*	*	*	*	*	*	*
2000-S Clad MA	*	*	*	*	*	*	*	*	*	—	—	6.00	7.00	8.00	8.00	—	10.	9.00	—	15.	10.	26.
2000-S Silver MA	*	*	*	*	*	*	*	*	*	—	—	8.00	9.00	10.	10.	—	15.	12.	—	25.	20.	30.
2000-P MD	—	—	—	—	0.55	5.25	15.	40.	100.	*	*	*	*	*	*	*	*	*	*	*	*	*
2000-D MD	—	—	—	—	0.55	7.00	10.	29.	158.	*	*	*	*	*	*	*	*	*	*	*	*	*
2000-S Clad MD	*	*	*	*	*	*	*	*	*	—	—	6.00	7.00	8.00	8.00	—	10.	9.00	—	15.	10.	27.
2000-S Silver MD	*	*	*	*	*	*	*	*	*	—	—	8.00	9.00	10.	10.	—	15.	12.	—	25.	20.	38.
2000-P SC	—	—	—	—	0.55	7.00	10.	18.	50.	*	*	*	*	*	*	*	*	*	*	*	*	*
2000-D SC	—	—	—	—	0.55	10.	20.	30.	80.	*	*	*	*	*	*	*	*	*	*	*	*	*
2000-S Clad SC	*	*	*	*	*	*	*	*	*	—	—	6.00	7.00	8.00	8.00	—	10.	9.00	—	15.	10.	36.
2000-S Silver SC	*	*	*	*	*	*	*	*	*	—	—	8.00	9.00	10.	10.	—	15.	12.	—	25.	20.	40.
2000-P NH	—	—	—	—	0.55	10.	16.	47.	95.	*	*	*	*	*	*	*	*	*	*	*	*	*
2000-D NH	—	—	—	—	0.55	10.	20.	50.	128.	*	*	*	*	*	*	*	*	*	*	*	*	*
2000-S Clad NH	*	*	*	*	*	*	*	*	*	—	—	6.00	7.00	8.00	8.00	—	10.	9.00	—	15.	10.	36.
2000-S Silver NH	*	*	*	*	*	*	*	*	*	—	—	8.00	9.00	10.	10.	—	15.	12.	—	25.	20.	40.
2000-P VA	—	—	—	—	0.55	10.	15.	35.	75.	*	*	*	*	*	*	*	*	*	*	*	*	*
2000-D VA	—	—	—	—	0.55	10.	16.	40.	100.	*	*	*	*	*	*	*	*	*	*	*	*	*
2000-S Clad VA	*	*	*	*	*	*	*	*	*	—	—	6.00	7.00	8.00	8.00	—	10.	9.00	—	15.	10.	27.
2000-S Silver VA	*	*	*	*	*	*	*	*	*	—	—	8.00	9.00	10.	10.	—	15.	12.	—	25.	20.	34.
2001-P NY	—	—	—	—	0.50	10.	26.	35.	175.	*	*	*	*	*	*	*	*	*	*	*	*	*
2001-D NY	—	—	—	—	0.50	8.00	16.	25.	500.	*	*	*	*	*	*	*	*	*	*	*	*	*
2001-S Clad NY	*	*	*	*	*	*	*	*	*	—	—	6.00	7.00	8.00	8.00	—	10.	9.00	—	15.	10.	26.
2001-S Silver NY	*	*	*	*	*	*	*	*	*	—	—	8.00	9.00	10.	10.	—	15.	12.	—	25.	20.	53.
2001-P NC	—	—	—	—	0.50	7.00	15.	25.	50.	*	*	*	*	*	*	*	*	*	*	*	*	*
2001-D NC	—	—	—	—	0.50	10.	16.	25.	100.	*	*	*	*	*	*	*	*	*	*	*	*	*

—— = Insufficient pricing data * = None issued

	VF-20	EF-40	AU-50	MS-60	MS-63	MS-64	MS-65	MS-66	MS-67	PF-63	PF-64	PF-65	PF-66	PF-66DC	PF-67	PF-67C	PF-67DC	PF-68	PF-68C	PF-68DC	PF-69	PF-69DC
2001-S Clad NC	*	*	*	*	*	*	*	*	*	—	—	6.00	7.00	8.00	8.00	—	10.	9.00	—	15.	10.	35.
2001-S Silver NC	*	*	*	*	*	*	*	*	*	—	—	8.00	9.00	10.	10.	—	15.	12.	—	25.	20.	34.
2001-P RI	—	—	—	—	0.50	7.00	18.	25.	100.	*	*	*	*	*	*	*	*	*	*	*	*	*
2001-D RI	—	—	—	—	0.50	8.00	16.	26.	85.	*	*	*	*	*	*	*	*	*	*	*	*	*
2001-S Clad RI	*	*	*	*	*	*	*	*	*	—	—	6.00	7.00	8.00	8.00	—	10.	9.00	—	15.	10.	23.
2001-S Silver RI	*	*	*	*	*	*	*	*	*	—	—	8.00	9.00	10.	10.	—	15.	12.	—	25.	20.	34.
2001-P VT	—	—	—	—	0.50	8.00	10.	20.	100.	*	*	*	*	*	*	*	*	*	*	*	*	*
2001-D VT	—	—	—	—	0.50	9.00	12.	25.	150.	*	*	*	*	*	*	*	*	*	*	*	*	*
2001-S Clad VT	*	*	*	*	*	*	*	*	*	—	—	6.00	7.00	8.00	8.00	—	10.	9.00	—	15.	10.	22.
2001-S Silver VT	*	*	*	*	*	*	*	*	*	—	—	8.00	9.00	10.	10.	—	15.	12.	—	25.	20.	36.
2001-P KY	—	—	—	—	0.50	8.00	10.	20.	—	*	*	*	*	*	*	*	*	*	*	*	*	*
2001-D KY	—	—	—	—	0.50	9.00	12.	25.	—	*	*	*	*	*	*	*	*	*	*	*	*	*
2001-S Clad KY	*	*	*	*	*	*	*	*	*	—	—	6.00	7.00	8.00	8.00	—	10.	9.00	—	15.	10.	23.
2001-S Silver KY	*	*	*	*	*	*	*	*	*	—	—	8.00	9.00	10.	10.	—	15.	12.	—	25.	20.	33.
2002-P TN	—	—	—	—	0.45	8.00	10.	20.	—	*	*	*	*	*	*	*	*	*	*	*	*	*
2002-D TN	—	—	—	—	0.45	9.00	12.	25.	—		*	*	*	*	*	*	*	*	*	*	*	*
2002-S Clad TN	*	*	*	*	*	*	*	*	*	—	—	6.00	7.00	8.00	8.00	—	10.	9.00	—	15.	10.	20.
2002-S Silver TN	*	*	*	*	*	*	*	*	*	—	—	8.00	9.00	10.	10.	—	15.	12.	—	25.	20.	27.
2002-P OH	—	—	—	—	0.60	8.00	10.	20.	—	*	*	*	*	*	*	*	*	*	*	*	*	*
2002-D OH	—	—	—	—	0.50	9.00	12.	25.	—	*	*	*	*	*	*	*	*	*	*	*	*	*
2002-S Clad OH	*	*	*	*	*	*	*	*	*	—	—	6.00	7.00	8.00	8.00	—	10.	9.00	—	15.	10.	29.
2002-S Silver OH	*	*	*	*	*	*	*	*	*	—	—	8.00	9.00	10.	10.	—	15.	12.	—	25.	20.	32.
2002-P LA	—	—	—	—	0.45	8.00	10.	20.	—	*	*	*	*	*	*	*	*	*	*	*	*	*
2002-D LA	—	—	—	—	0.45	9.00	12.	25.	—	*	*	*	*	*	*	*	*	*	*	*	*	*
2002-S Clad LA	*	*	*	*	*	*	*	*	*	—	—	6.00	7.00	8.00	8.00	—	10.	9.00	—	15.	10.	25.

—— = Insufficient pricing data * = None issued

WASHINGTON QUARTER DOLLAR (CONTINUED)

	VF-20	EF-40	AU-50	MS-60	MS-63	MS-64	MS-65	MS-66	MS-67	PF-63	PF-64	PF-65	PF-66	PF-66DC	PF-67	PF-67C	PF-67DC	PF-68	PF-68C	PF-68DC	PF-69	PF-69DC
2002-S Silver LA	*	*	*	*	*	*	*	*	*	—	—	8.00	9.00	10.	10.	—	15.	12.	—	25.	20.	32.
2002-P IN	—	—	—	—	—	8.00	10.	20.	—	*	*	*	*	*	*	*	*	*	*	*	*	*
2002-D IN	—	—	—	—	—	9.00	12.	25.	—	*	*	*	*	*	*	*	*	*	*	*	*	*
2002-S Clad IN	*	*	*	*	*	*	*	*	*	—	—	6.00	7.00	8.00	8.00	—	10.	9.00	—	15.	10.	25.
2002-S Silver IN	*	*	*	*	*	*	*	*	*	—	—	8.00	9.00	10.	10.	—	15.	12.	—	25.	20.	32.
2002-P MS	—	—	—	—	—	8.00	10.	20.	—	*	*	*	*	*	*	*	*	*	*	*	*	*
2002-D MS	—	—	—	—	—	9.00	12.	25.	—	*	*	*	*	*	*	*	*	*	*	*	*	*
2002-S Clad MS	*	*	*	*	*	*	*	*	*	—	—	6.00	7.00	8.00	8.00	—	10.	9.00	—	15.	10.	18.
2002-S Silver MS	*	*	*	*	*	*	*	*	*	—	—	8.00	9.00	10.	10.	—	15.	12.	—	25.	20.	34.
2003-P IL	—	—	—	—	—	8.00	10.	20.	—	—	—	—	—	—	—	—	—	—	—	—	—	—
2003-D IL	—	—	—	—	—	9.00	12.	25.	—	—	—	—	—	—	—	—	—	—	—	—	—	—
2003-S Clad IL	—	—	—	—	—	—	—	—	—	—	—	6.00	7.00	8.00	8.00	—	10.	9.00	—	15.	10.	18.
2003-S Silver IL	—	—	—	—	—	—	—	—	—	—	—	8.00	9.00	10.	10.	—	15.	12.	—	25.	20.	34.
2003-P AL	—	—	—	—	—	8.00	10.	20.	—	—	—	—	—	—	—	—	—	—	—	—	—	—
2003-D AL	—	—	—	—	—	9.00	12.	25.	—	—	—	—	—	—	—	—	—	—	—	—	—	—
2003-S Clad AL	—	—	—	—	—	—	—	—	—	—	—	6.00	7.00	8.00	8.00	—	10.	9.00	—	15.	10.	18.
2003-S Silver AL	—	—	—	—	—	—	—	—	—	—	—	8.00	9.00	10.	10.	—	15.	12.	—	25.	20.	34.
2003-P ME	—	—	—	—	—	8.00	10.	20.	—	—	—	—	—	—	—	—	—	—	—	—	—	—
2003-D ME	—	—	—	—	—	9.00	12.	25.	—	—	—	—	—	—	—	—	—	—	—	—	—	—
2003-S Clad ME	—	—	—	—	—	—	—	—	—	—	—	6.00	7.00	8.00	8.00	—	10.	9.00	—	15.	10.	18.
2003-S Silver ME	—	—	—	—	—	—	—	—	—	—	—	8.00	9.00	10.	10.	—	15.	12.	—	25.	20.	34.
2003-P MO	—	—	—	—	—	8.00	10.	20.	—	—	—	—	—	—	—	—	—	—	—	—	—	—
2003-D MO	—	—	—	—	—	9.00	12.	25.	—	—	—	—	—	—	—	—	—	—	—	—	—	—
2003-S Clad MO	—	—	—	—	—	—	—	—	—	—	—	6.00	7.00	8.00	8.00	—	10.	9.00	—	15.	10.	18.
2003-S Silver MO	—	—	—	—	—	—	—	—	—	—	—	8.00	9.00	10.	10.	—	15.	12.	—	25.	20.	34.

—— = Insufficient pricing data * = None issued

	VF-20	EF-40	AU-50	MS-60	MS-63	MS-64	MS-65	MS-66	MS-67	PF-63	PF-64	PF-65	PF-66	PF-66DC	PF-67	PF-67C	PF-67DC	PF-68	PF-68C	PF-68DC	PF-69	PF-69DC
2003-P AR	—	—	—	—	—	8.00	10.	20.	—	—	—	—	—	—	—	—	—	—	—	—	—	—
2003-D AR	—	—	—	—	—	9.00	12.	25.	—	—	—	—	—	—	—	—	—	—	—	—	—	—
2003-S Clad AR	—	—	—	—	—	—	—	—	—	—	—	6.00	7.00	8.00	8.00	—	10.	9.00	—	15.	10.	18.
2003-S Silver AR	—	—	—	—	—	—	—	—	—	—	—	8.00	9.00	10.	10.	—	15.	12.	—	25.	20.	34.
2004-P Michigan	—	—	—	—	—	8.00	10.	20.	—	—	—	—	—	—	—	—	—	—	—	—	—	—
2004-D Michigan	—	—	—	—	—	9.00	12.	25.	—	—	—	—	—	—	—	—	—	—	—	—	—	—
2004-S Clad Michigan	—	—	—	—	—	—	—	—	—	—	—	6.00	7.00	8.00	8.00	—	10.	9.00	—	15.	10.	18.
2004-S Silver Michigan	—	—	—	—	—	—	—	—	—	—	—	8.00	9.00	10.	10.	—	15.	12.	—	25.	20.	34.
2004-P Florida	—	—	—	—	—	8.00	10.	20.	—	—	—	—	—	—	—	—	—	—	—	—	—	—
2004-D Florida	—	—	—	—	—	9.00	12.	25.	—	—	—	—	—	—	—	—	—	—	—	—	—	—
2004-S Clad Florida	—	—	—	—	—	—	—	—	—	—	—	6.00	7.00	8.00	8.00	—	10.	9.00	—	15.	10.	18.
2004-S Silver Florida	—	—	—	—	—	—	—	—	—	—	—	8.00	9.00	10.	10.	—	15.	12.	—	25.	20.	34.
2004-P Texas	—	—	—	—	—	8.00	10.	20.	—	—	—	—	—	—	—	—	—	—	—	—	—	—
2004-D Texas	—	—	—	—	—	9.00	12.	25.	—	—	—	—	—	—	—	—	—	—	—	—	—	—
2004-S Clad Texas	—	—	—	—	—	—	—	—	—	—	—	6.00	7.00	8.00	8.00	—	10.	9.00	—	15.	10.	18.
2004-S Silver Texas	—	—	—	—	—	—	—	—	—	—	—	8.00	9.00	10.	10.	—	15.	12.	—	25.	20.	34.
2004-P Iowa	—	—	—	—	—	8.00	10.	20.	—	—	—	—	—	—	—	—	—	—	—	—	—	—
2004-D Iowa	—	—	—	—	—	9.00	12.	25.	—	—	—	—	—	—	—	—	—	—	—	—	—	—
2004-S Clad Iowa	—	—	—	—	—	—	—	—	—	—	—	6.00	7.00	8.00	8.00	—	10.	9.00	—	15.	10.	18.
2004-S Silver Iowa	—	—	—	—	—	—	—	—	—	—	—	8.00	9.00	10.	10.	—	15.	12.	—	25.	20.	34.
2004-P Wisconsin	—	—	—	—	—	8.00	10.	20.	—	—	—	—	—	—	—	—	—	—	—	—	—	—
2004-D Wisconsin	—	—	—	—	—	9.00	12.	25.	—	—	—	—	—	—	—	—	—	—	—	—	—	—
2004-S Clad Wisconsin	—	—	—	—	—	—	—	—	—	—	—	6.00	7.00	8.00	8.00	—	10.	9.00	—	15.	10.	18.
2004-S Silver Wisconsin	—	—	—	—	—	—	—	—	—	—	—	8.00	9.00	10.	10.	—	15.	12.	—	25.	20.	34.

—— = Insufficient pricing data * = None issued

State Quarter designs

Common Obverse

1999

Delaware

Pennsylvania

New Jersey

Georgia

Connecticut

2000

Massachusetts

Maryland

South Carolina

New Hampshire

Virginia

2001

New York

North Carolina

Rhode Island

Vermont

Kentucky

2002

Tennessee

Ohio

Louisiana

Indiana

Mississippi

2003

Illinois

Alabama

Maine

Missouri

Arkansas

2004

Michigan

Florida

Texas

Iowa

Wisconsin

Flowing Hair half dollar

Date of authorization:	April 2, 1792
Dates of issue:	1794-1795
Designer:	Robert Scot
Engravers:	Robert Scot-John S. Gardner
Diameter:	32.50 mm/1.28 inches
Weight:	13.48 grams/0.43 ounce
Metallic content:	90% silver, 10% copper
Weight of pure silver:	12.13 grams/0.39 ounce
Edge:	Lettered (FIFTY CENTS OR HALF A DOLLAR)
Mint mark:	None

	AG-3	G-4	VG-8	F-12	VF-20	EF-40	EF-45	AU-50	MS-60
1794	1500.	2500.	4000.	6000.	10000.	20000.	30000.	45000.	100000.
1795 2 Leaves	350.	700.	1000.	1500.	3000.	8000.	10000.	12000.	25000.
1795 3 Leaves	600.	1000.	1800.	3500.	5500.	12000.	16500.	25000.	—

—— = Insufficient pricing data

Draped Bust half dollar

Small Eagle reverse

Heraldic Eagle reverse

Date of authorization: April 2, 1792
Dates of issue: 1796-1797, 1801-1807
Designers: Obverse: Gilbert Stuart-Robert Scot
Reverse:
(1796-1797): Scot-John Eckstein
(1801-1807): Robert Scot
Engraver: Robert Scot
Diameter: 32.50 mm/1.28 inches
Weight: 13.48 grams/0.43 ounce
Metallic content: 89.25% silver, 10.75% copper
Weight of pure silver: 12.03 grams/0.39 ounce
Edge: Lettered (FIFTY CENTS OR HALF A DOLLAR)
Mint mark: None

	AG-3	G-4	VG-8	F-12	VF-20	EF-40	EF-45	AU-50	MS-60
SMALL EAGLE									
1796 15 Stars	15000.	25000.	30000.	35000.	45000.	75000.	85000.	100000.	150000.
1796 16 Stars	16000.	30000.	35000.	40000.	50000.	85000.	90000.	100000.	175000.
1797 15 Stars	15000.	25000.	30000.	35000.	45000.	80000.	80000.	100000.	150000.
HERALDIC EAGLE									
1801	125.	250.	350.	600.	1000.	3000.	6000.	10000.	30000.
1802	125.	250.	350.	600.	1000.	3250.	6000.	12500.	35000.
1803 Small 3	100.	175.	225.	350.	600.	1500.	2000.	3500.	7500.
1803 Large 3	100.	175.	200.	300.	500.	1000.	1500.	2500.	6500.
1805/4	100.	200.	300.	500.	800.	1800.	3750.	6500.	28000.
1805	100.	175.	200.	250.	400.	1000.	1500.	2500.	6500.
1806/5	100.	175.	200.	300.	400.	1000.	1500.	2500.	6500.
1806/Inverted 6	100.	200.	300.	600.	1000.	2000.	2500.	4000.	9000.
1806 Knobbed 6, No Stem, VF-35 $57,500.	-	-	-	-	60000.	90000.	-	-	-
1806 Knobbed 6, Stems	100.	175.	200.	250.	400.	1000.	1500.	2500.	6000.
1806 Pointed 6, Stems	100.	175.	200.	250.	400.	1000.	1500.	2500.	6000.
1806 Pointed 6, No Stem	100.	175.	200.	250.	400.	1000.	1500.	2500.	6000.
1807	100.	175.	200.	250.	400.	1000.	1500.	2500.	6000.

—— = Insufficient pricing data * = None issued

Capped Bust half dollar

Date of authorization:	April 2, 1792
Dates of issue:	1807-1839
Designers:	Obverse: John Reich Reverse: (1807-1836): John Reich (1836-1839): Reich-Christian Gobrecht
Engraver:	John Reich
Diameter:	(1807-1836): 32.50 mm/1.28 inches (1836-1839): 30.61 mm/1.21 inches
Weight:	(1807-1836): 13.48 grams/0.43 ounce (1836-1839): 13.37 grams/0.43 ounce
Metallic Content:	(1807-1836): 89.25% silver, 10.75% copper (1836-1839): 90% silver, 10% copper
Weight of pure silver:	(1807-1836): 12.03 grams/0.39 ounce (1836-1839): 12.03 grams/0.39 ounce
Edge:	(1807-1836): Lettered (FIFTY CENTS OR HALF A DOLLAR) (1836-1839): Reeded
Mint mark:	1838-1839 only, obverse above date

	G-4	VG-8	F-12	VF-20	EF-40	AU-50	AU-58	MS-60	MS-62	MS-63	MS-64
1807 Small Stars	65.	100.	190.	345.	800.	2200.	2600.	3800.	5500.	10000.	—
1807 Large Stars	55.	90.	180.	300.	825.	2350.	2800.	4500.	7250.	12500.	25000.
1807 50/20C	50.	100.	155.	250.	475.	1750.	2150.	3750.	5000.	8500.	12500.
1807 Bearded Goddess	300.	465.	775.	1250.	2500.	7250.	—	—	—	—	—
1808/7	50.	60.	80.	160.	435.	975.	1400.	2250.	3750.	6250.	9500.
1808	50.	60.	75.	100.	245.	545.	825.	1450.	2600.	3900.	7000.
1809 Plain Edge	50.	60.	75.	100.	200.	525.	900.	1500.	2500.	3850.	9500.

—— = Insufficient pricing data * = None issued

CAPPED BUST HALF DOLLAR (CONTINUED)

	G-4	VG-8	F-12	VF-20	EF-40	AU-50	AU-58	MS-60	MS-62	MS-63	MS-64
1809 X Edge	50.	60.	75.	110.	230.	650.	1000.	1800.	2900.	—	—
1809 IIII Edge	50.	60.	75.	115.	245.	650.	1050.	2000.	3350.	6000.	—
1810	50.	60.	75.	100.	165.	400.	575.	1300.	2100.	3500.	6500.
1811 Small 8	50.	60.	75.	100.	160.	385.	460.	900.	1250.	1850.	3500.
1811 Large 8	50.	60.	75.	100.	170.	500.	585.	1000.	1350.	2450.	—
1811/0	50.	60.	80.	145.	300.	585.	675.	1250.	3500.	7000.	17500.
1812/1 Small 8	50.	65.	80.	165.	365.	675.	975.	2300.	3550.	5850.	10750.
1812/1 Large 8	1550.	2500.	3750.	6750.	11000.	17000.	—	—	—	—	—
1812	50.	60.	75.	100.	150.	375.	440.	750.	1100.	2150.	4250.
1813	50.	60.	75.	100.	175.	450.	550.	1000.	1600.	2850.	5250.
1813 50C/UNI	50.	60.	80.	135.	270.	600.	950.	1900.	3500.	6750.	8500.
1814	50.	60.	75.	100.	185.	475.	600.	1050.	1750.	3250.	4900.
1814 Single Leaf	50.	60.	80.	120.	325.	750.	1250.	2000.	—	—	—
1814/3	50	60.	92.	150.	375.	875.	1250.	2050.	3050.	5300.	—
1815/2	750.	1100.	1400.	1750.	3000.	4800.	6500.	9500.	14000.	24500.	48500.
1817/3	80.	125.	175	365.	775.	1600.	2500.	4750.	8000.	18500.	—
1817/4	—	—	52500.	110000.	—	—	—	—	—	—	—
1817	50.	60.	75.	100.	170.	390.	450.	950.	2050.	2900.	5250.
1817 Single Leaf	50.	60.	80.	120.	240.	750.	1250.	2150.	—	—	—
1818/7	50.	60.	75.	100	180.	750.	950.	1400.	3100.	6500.	—
1818	50.	60.	75.	100.	190	425.	550.	850.	1100.	2100.	3800.
1819/8 Small 9	50.	60.	75.	100.	190.	425.	575.	1300.	1400.	2050.	3950.
1819/8 Large 9	50.	60.	75.	100.	150.	425.	575.	1300.	1525.	2500.	4200.
1819	50.	60.	75.	100.	135.	275.	450.	875.	1500.	2750.	4350.
1820/19 Curl 2	50.	60.	75.	140.	275.	625.	975.	1400.	2500.	4000.	6750.
1820/19 Square 2	50.	60.	75.	150.	350.	800.	1050.	1600.	2500.	4350.	10500.
1820 Large Date	50.	60.	75.	115.	250.	525.	600.	1100.	1650.	3250.	6000.
1820 Small Date	50.	60.	75.	125.	275.	585.	700.	1250.	2250.	4100.	—
1821	50.	60.	75.	100.	145.	525.	700.	950.	1250.	2250.	3750.
1822	50.	60.	75.	100.	135.	285.	350.	675.	1200.	2000.	3000.
1822/1	50.	60.	75.	135.	275.	635.	800.	1200.	1750.	2900.	4400.
1823	50.	60.	75.	100.	125.	300.	400.	675.	1000.	1850.	3150.
1823 Broken 3	50.	60.	80.	125.	415.	725.	1250.	1650.	2250.	3500.	—
1823 Patched 3	50.	60.	80.	100.	175.	500.	800.	1400.	1900.	3000.	4500.
1823 Ugly 3	50.	60.	75.	100.	200.	575.	900.	1450.	1950.	3100.	—
1824/1	50.	60.	75.	100.	210.	400.	550.	950.	1400.	2850.	5750.
1824/2/0	50.	60.	75.	85.	150.	550.	900.	1100.	2250.	5000.	—
1824/4	50.	60.	75.	85.	145.	325.	550.	825.	1200.	1950.	3500.
1824	50.	60.	75.	85.	105.	275.	345.	575.	950.	1500.	3000.
1825	50.	60.	75.	85.	100.	250.	325.	525.	850.	1550.	3100.
1826	50.	60.	75.	85.	100.	250.	325.	525.	850.	1500.	3100.
1827/6	50.	60.	75.	85.	200.	375.	490.	950.	1300.	2325.	5500.

—— = Insufficient pricing data * = None issued

CAPPED BUST HALF DOLLAR (CONTINUED)

	G-4	VG-8	F-12	VF-20	EF-40	AU-50	AU-58	MS-60	MS-62	MS-63	MS-64
1827 Square 2	50.	60.	75.	85.	100.	250.	375.	600.	900.	1500.	3200.
1827 Curl 2	50.	60.	75.	85.	110.	250.	300.	525.	850.	1500.	3100.
1828	50.	60.	75.	85.	100.	200.	265.	500.	800.	1250.	2750.
1828 Small Letters	50.	60.	75.	100.	195.	625.	850.	1300.	1600.	2600.	3500.
1828 Large 8s	50.	60.	75.	85.	85.	235.	290.	500.	800.	1250.	2750.
1828 Small 8s	50.	60.	75.	85.	77.	230.	270.	500.	800.	1250.	2750.
1829/7	50.	60.	75.	85.	135.	350.	500.	1000.	1700.	3000.	6500.
1829	50.	60.	75.	85.	100.	250.	300.	500.	800.	1500.	3100.
1830 Large 0	50.	60.	75.	85.	100.	250.	300.	500.	800.	1500.	3100.
1830 Small 0	50.	60.	75.	85.	100.	250.	300.	500.	800.	1500.	3100.
1830 Large Letters	1500.	2100.	3000.	3850.	4500.	7750.	8500.	15000.	—	—	—
1831	50.	60.	75.	85.	100.	250.	300.	500.	800.	1500.	3100.
1832 Normal	50.	60.	75.	85.	100.	250.	300.	500.	800.	1500.	3100.
1832 Large Letters	50.	60.	75.	85.	135.	275.	325.	525.	950.	1750.	3100.
1833	50.	60.	75.	85.	100.	250.	300.	500.	800.	1500.	3100.
1834 All varieties	50.	60.	75.	85.	100.	250.	300.	500.	800.	1500.	3100.
1835	50.	60.	75.	85.	100.	250.	300.	500.	800.	1500.	3100.
1836	50.	60.	75.	85.	100.	250.	300.	500.	800.	1500.	3100.
1836/1336	50.	60.	75.	85.	100.	250.	300.	500.	825.	1500.	—
1836 50/00	50.	65.	75.	165.	250.	700.	825.	1600.	2250.	3950.	—

CAPPED BUST, REEDED EDGE HALF DOLLAR

50 CENTS reverse

HALF DOL. reverse

	G-4	VG-8	F-12	VF-20	EF-40	AU-50	AU-58	MS-60	MS-62	MS-63	MS-64
REEDED EDGE, 50 CENTS REVERSE											
1836	700.	900.	1200.	1500.	2500.	3500.	5000.	9000.	12000.	18000.	35000.
1837	50.	60.	75.	125.	175.	350.	500.	800.	1200.	2000.	5000.
HALF DOLLAR REVERSE											
1838	50.	60.	75.	125.	175.	350.	500.	800.	1200.	2000.	5000.
1838-O Proofs only	—	—	—	—	150000.	175000.	200000.	225000.	250000.	300000.	—
1839	60.	70.	85.	125.	200.	350.	500.	1000.	1500.	2500.	6000.
1839-O	135.	175.	250.	350.	700.	1200.	1500.	2800.	4000.	6000.	12000.

—— = Insufficient pricing data   * = None issued

Seated Liberty half dollar

Date of authorization:	April 2, 1792
Dates of issue:	1839-1891
Designers:	Obverse: Christian Gobrecht
	Reverse: John Reich-Gobrecht
Engraver:	Christian Gobrecht
Diameter:	30.61 mm/1.21 inches
Weight:	(1839-1853): 13.37 grams/0.43 ounce
	(1853-1873): 12.4 grams/0.40 ounce
	(1873-1891): 12.50 grams/0.40 ounce
Metallic Content:	90% silver, 10% copper
Weight of pure silver:	(1839-1853): 12.03 grams/0.39 ounce
	(1853-1873): 11.20 grams/0.36 ounce
	(1873-1891): 11.25 grams/0.36 ounce
Edge:	Reeded
Mint mark:	Reverse below eagle

Arrows at date, Rays on reverse

—— = Insufficient pricing data

SEATED LIBERTY HALF DOLLAR (CONTINUED)

	G-4	VG-8	F-12	VF-20	EF-40	AU-50	AU-58	MS-60	MS-62	MS-63	MS-64	MS-65	PF-63	PF-64	PF-65	PF-66
NO DRAPERY																
1839	50.	100.	150.	350.	800.	1800.	3000.	5000.	10000.	18000.	50000.	-	32000.	*	*	*
DRAPERY AT ELBOW																
1839	25.	35.	60.	100.	150.	300.	400.	600.	1100.	2500.	4000.	-	*	*	*	*
1840 Small Letters	30.	35.	55.	80.	125.	250.	400.	600.	1000.	1500.	3000.	-	*	*	*	*
1840 Medium Letters	125.	175.	250.	350.	700.	1200.	1500.	3500.	5000.	8000.	14000.	-	*	*	*	*
1840-O	30.	35.	60.	90.	125.	250.	400.	600.	1200.	2500.	-	-	*	*	*	*
1841	50.	65.	100.	150.	250.	450.	800.	1500.	2000.	3000.	5000.	-	-	25000.	-	-
1841-O	25.	35.	55.	100.	150.	250.	400.	800.	1500.	3000.	6000.	-	*	*	*	*
1842 Small Date	30.	45.	85.	100.	200.	400.	600.	1000.	1500.	3000.	-	-	-	22500.	-	-
1842 Medium Date	25.	35.	55.	75.	125.	250.	350.	700.	1000.	1500.	4000.	-	*	*	*	*
1842-O Medium Date	25.	35.	55.	75.	125.	300.	450.	1000.	2000.	4500.	11000.	-	*	*	*	*
1842-O Small Date	600.	900.	1400.	2000.	4500.	8500.	13000.	20000.	42500.	-	-	-	*	*	*	*
1843	25.	35.	50.	65.	100.	250.	350.	500.	800.	1200.	2800.	-	*	*	*	*
1843-O	25.	35.	50.	65.	100.	250.	400.	700.	1100.	2000.	5000.	-	*	*	*	*
1844	25.	35.	50.	65.	100.	250.	350.	500.	800.	1200.	4000.	-	*	*	*	*
1844-O	25.	35.	50.	65.	100.	250.	400.	750.	1200.	2500.	5000.	-	*	*	*	*
1844-O Doubled Date	500.	800.	1200.	1600.	2500.	6000.	8500.	12000.	-	-	-	-	*	*	*	*
1845	30.	50.	75.	125.	200.	350.	600.	900.	1500.	4000.	9000.	-	-	23000.	-	-
1845-O	25.	35.	60.	75.	125.	250.	400.	750.	1100.	2000.	6500.	-	*	*	*	*
1845-O No Drapery	30.	50.	85.	125.	200.	350.	600.	1400.	2500.	5000.	10000.	-	*	*	*	*
1846 Medium Date	25.	35.	50.	65.	125.	250.	400.	600.	1000.	1600.	3500.	-	14000.	-	-	-
1846 Tall Date	25.	35.	50.	75.	150.	300.	500.	900.	2000.	3500.	5000.	-	*	*	*	*
1846/Horizontal 6	150.	250.	300.	400.	600.	1200.	2000.	3500.	9000.	-	-	-	*	*	*	*
1846-O Medium Date	25.	35.	50.	65.	125.	250.	500.	1000.	1500.	2500.	4500.	-	*	*	*	*
1846-O Tall Date	150.	300.	400.	600.	1100.	2000.	3000.	6500.	8500.	12000.	-	-	*	*	*	*

—— = Insufficient pricing data * = None issued

SEATED LIBERTY HALF DOLLAR (CONTINUED)

	G-4	VG-8	F-12	VF-20	EF-40	AU-50	AU-58	MS-60	MS-62	MS-63	MS-64	MS-65	PF-63	PF-64	PF-65	PF-66
1847	25.	35.	50.	65.	125.	250.	400.	500.	800.	1200	2500.	8000.	15000.	-	-	-
1847-O	25.	35.	50.	65.	125.	300.	450.	800.	1500.	2500	-	-	*	*	*	*
1847/6	1800.	2500.	3500.	5000.	7500.	12000.	17500.	20000.	25000.	35000.	-	-	*	*	*	*
1848	40.	65.	100.	200.	300.	500.	700.	1000.	1400.	2000.	2800.	8000.	-	-	37500.	-
1848-O	25.	35.	50.	65.	130.	350.	500.	1000.	1500.	2500.	4000.	10000.	*	*	*	*
1849	35.	40.	60.	85.	150.	400.	600.	1000.	1500.	2500	4000.	-	-	26500.	-	-
1849 Doubled Date, bold 1800.	2500.	3500.	4500.	6500.	8500.	9500.	-	-	-	-	-	*	*	*	*	
1849-O	25.	35.	50.	65.	125.	300.	500.	900.	1500.	2500.	6000.	-	*	*	*	*
1850	250.	300.	450.	600.	800.	1000.	1300.	1800.	3000.	5500.	-	-	*	*	*	*
1850-O	25.	35.	50.	65.	125.	300.	400.	600.	900.	1600.	3000.	8000.	*	*	*	*
1851	300.	400.	500.	600.	800.	1100.	1400.	1800.	2500.	3000.	3500.	-	*	*	*	*
1851-O	25	50.	60.	100.	200.	400.	500.	700.	1000.	1500.	3000.	10000.	*	*	*	*
1852	400.	500.	650.	900.	1000.	1400.	1600.	2000.	2300.	2800.	4000.	10000.	12500.	-	-	-
1852-O	60.	125.	200.	350.	600.	1200.	2000.	4000.	5500.	9000.	14000.	25000.	40000.	-	-	-
1853-O (Beware Alterations)	125000.	160000.	-	175000.	-	-	-	-	-	-	-	-	*	*	*	*
ARROWS AND RAYS																
1853	30.	40.	60.	125	300.	600.	900.	1500.	3000	4000.	9000.	20000.	-	82500.	100000.	-
1853-O	30.	40.	60.	150.	300.	850.	1500.	3000.	4000	6000.	12500.	-	*	*	*	*
RAYS REMOVED																
1854	30.	40.	50.	80.	125.	350.	400.	750.	1250.	2000.	3500.	8500.	-	15000.	37500.	-
1854-O	30.	40.	50.	80.	125.	350.	400.	750.	1250.	2000.	4000.	8000.	*	*	*	*
1855/1854	75.	100.	200.	300.	400.	800.	1200.	2000.	2750.	4000.	7500.	18000.	-	26500.	-	-
1855	30.	40.	50.	80.	125.	350.	400.	750.	1250.	2000.	3500.	7500.	-	-	29000.	-
1855-O	30.	40.	50.	80.	125.	350.	400.	750.	1250.	2000.	3500.	7500.	*	*	*	*
1855-S	350.	600.	1000.	1500.	3500.	7500.	10000.	15000.	-	-	-	-	*	*	*	*

—— = Insufficient pricing data   * = None issued

SEATED LIBERTY HALF DOLLAR (CONTINUED)

DRAPERY AT ELBOW	G-4	VG-8	F-12	VF-20	EF-40	AU-50	AU-58	MS-60	MS-62	MS-63	MS-64	MS-65	PF-63	PF-64	PF-65	PF-66
1856	25.	35.	50.	65.	125.	300.	400.	600.	750.	1000.	2500.	6500.	8000.	12000.	20000.	-
1856-O	25.	35.	50.	65.	125.	300.	400.	600.	750.	1000.	3000.	7500.	*	*	*	*
1856-S	50.	75.	125.	300.	600.	1300.	2000.	4000.	-	-	-	-	*	*	*	*
1857	25.	35.	50.	65.	125.	300.	400.	600.	750.	1000.	2500.	6500.	5000.	8500.	-	-
1857-O	25.	35.	50.	65.	125.	300.	600.	1000.	2000.	3500.	-	-	*	*	*	*
1857-S	60.	100.	200.	300.	600.	1200.	1750.	4000.	5500.	8000.	12000.	-	*	*	*	*
1858	25.	35.	50.	65.	125.	300.	400.	600.	750.	1000.	2500.	6000.	3000.	6000.	15000.	-
1858-O	25.	35.	50.	65.	125.	300.	400.	600.	750.	1000.	2500.	8000.	*	*	*	*
1858-S	25.	35.	60.	125.	250.	400.	700.	1100.	2500.	4000.	7500.	-	*	*	*	*
1859	30.	50.	75.	100.	150.	300.	400.	600.	900.	1200.	2800.	6000.	1500.	4000.	6500.	-
1859-O	25.	35.	50.	65.	125.	300.	400.	600.	750.	1000.	3000.	-	*	*	*	*
1859-S	25.	35.	60.	125.	250.	400.	800.	1200.	2000.	3500.	5000.	-	*	*	*	*
1860	25.	35.	50.	65.	125.	350.	500.	750.	1000.	1400.	2500.	6000.	1000.	4000.	7000.	10000.
1860-O	25.	35.	50.	65.	125.	300.	400.	600.	750.	1000.	2500.	5500.	*	*	*	*
1860-S	25.	35.	50.	65.	125.	300.	500.	800.	1500.	3000.	-	-	*	*	*	*
1861	25.	35.	50.	65.	125.	300.	400.	600.	750.	1000.	2500.	5500.	1000.	4500.	7500.	-
1861-O	25.	35.	50.	65.	125.	300.	400.	600.	750.	1500.	2500.	6500.	*	*	*	*
1861-O struck by CSA, obverse die crack	75.	100.	200.	300.	400.	600.	800.	1200.	2000.	3500.	9000.	-	*	*	*	*
1861-S	25.	35.	50.	65.	125.	300.	700.	1200.	2000.	3500.	6000.	9000.	*	*	*	*
1862	30.	50.	75.	150.	250.	400.	500.	750.	900.	1100.	2500.	6500.	1000.	3000.	6000.	-
1862-S	25.	35.	50.	65.	125.	300.	400.	600.	1200.	2500.	5500.	-	*	*	*	*
1863	25.	35.	50.	65.	135.	300.	400.	600.	750.	1000.	2500.	6000.	1000.	3000.	6000.	-
1863-S	25.	35.	50.	65.	125.	300.	400.	600.	1200.	2500.	5000.	-	*	*	*	*
1864	30.	40.	60.	100.	175.	350.	450.	600.	750.	1000.	2500.	6000.	1000.	3000.	6000.	-
1864-S	25.	35.	50.	65.	125.	300.	450.	750.	1500.	3000.	6500.	15000.	*	*	*	*

—— = Insufficient pricing data   * = None issued

SEATED LIBERTY HALF DOLLAR (CONTINUED)

	G-4	VG-8	F-12	VF-20	EF-40	AU-50	AU-58	MS-60	MS-62	MS-63	MS-64	MS-65	PF-63	PF-64	PF-65	PF-66
1865 Doubled Date	60.	75.	125.	200.	300.	400.	500.	-	-	-	-	-	*	*	*	*
1865-S	25.	35.	50.	65.	125.	300.	550.	850.	1800.	3000.	6000.	-	*	*	*	*
1865	25.	40.	60.	85.	175.	350.	400.	600.	900.	1300.	2800.	5500.	1000.	3000.	6000.	15000.
1866-S	100.	125.	250.	400.	900.	2000.	3000.	5000.	7000.	12000.	-	-	*	*	*	*
1866 Fantasy Piece	Du Pont specimen recovered															
MOTTO ABOVE EAGLE																
1866	25.	35.	50.	65.	125.	300.	400.	500.	800.	1500.	2500.	6000.	1000.	1500.	4000.	8000.
1866-S	25.	35.	50.	65.	125.	275.	400.	600.	1200.	2500.	5000.	9000.	*	*	*	*
1867	30.	50.	75.	125.	200.	300.	400.	500.	800.	1400.	2500.	6500.	1000.	1500.	4000.	8000.
1867-S	25.	35.	50.	65.	150.	300.	400.	750.	1500.	3000.	7500.	-	*	*	*	*
1868	50.	65.	100.	200.	300.	400.	500.	650.	1000.	1500.	3000.	-	1000.	1500.	4000.	8000.
1868-S	25.	35.	50.	65.	125.	275.	400.	700.	1500.	2750.	-	-	*	*	*	*
1869	25.	35.	50.	65.	125.	250.	350.	500.	750.	1200.	2300.	5000.	1000.	1500.	4000.	8000.
1869-S	25.	35.	50.	65.	175.	400.	600.	1200.	2000.	3500.	-	-	*	*	*	*
1870	25.	35.	50.	65.	150.	275.	400.	500.	850.	1200.	3000.	-	1000.	1500.	4000.	8000.
1870-CC	1000.	2000.	3000.	7000.	15000.	25000.	-	-	-	16000.	-	-	*	*	*	*
1870-S	25.	35.	50	65.	150.	300.	500.	1000.	2000.	3500.	-	-	*	*	*	*
1871	25.	35.	50.	65.	125.	250.	300.	400.	650	1000.	2300.	5000.	1000.	1500.	4000.	10000.
1871-CC	200.	300.	500.	1000	2500.	6000.	8500.	15000.	25000	4500.	-	-	*	*	*	*
1871-S	25.	35.	50.	65.	125.	250.	400.	600.	1000	1750.	-	-	*	*	*	*
1872	25.	35.	50.	65.	125.	250.	400.	600.	1000.	1750.	2500.	5000.	1000.	1500.	4000.	9000.
1872-CC	75.	125.	250.	500.	1000.	2000.	4000.	7000.	-	-	-	-	*	*	*	*
1872-S	30.	50.	75.	125.	250.	400.	750.	1300.	2000.	3500.	7000.	-	*	*	*	*
1873 Closed 3	30.	50.	75.	125.	200.	300.	400.	600.	850.	1200.	2000.	-	1000.	1750.	4000.	8000.
1873 Open 3	3000.	3500.	4500.	6000.	8000.	12000.	16000.	25000.	32500.	57500.	-	-	*	*	*	*
1873-CC	200.	300.	400.	750.	1500.	5000.	7000.	10000.	25000.	50000.	60000.	75000.	*	*	*	*

—— = Insufficient pricing data   * = None issued

SEATED LIBERTY HALF DOLLAR (CONTINUED)

	G-4	VG-8	F-12	VF-20	EF-40	AU-50	AU-58	MS-60	MS-62	MS-63	MS-64	MS-65	PF-63	PF-64	PF-65	PF-66
ARROWS AT DATE																
1873	30.	50.	65.	125.	300.	500.	700.	1000.	1500.	2500.	5000.	17500.	2500.	3500.	15000.	25000.
1873-CC	150.	300.	400.	1000.	2000.	3000.	4500.	6500.	10000.	18000.	25000.	-	*	*	*	*
1873-S	75.	100.	150.	300.	500.	900.	1500.	2500.	4000.	6500.	15000.	-	*	*	*	*
1874	30.	50.	65.	125.	300.	500.	700.	1000.	1500.	2500.	4000.	14000.	2000.	3500.	12000.	25000.
1874-CC	400.	600.	1000.	1500.	2500.	4500.	6000.	12000.	18000.	25000.	-	-	*	*	*	*
1874-S	35.	50.	100.	250.	400.	800.	1200.	2000.	3000.	5000.	9000.	-	*	*	*	*
MOTTO ABOVE EAGLE																
1875	25.	40.	60.	75.	110.	200.	300.	500.	600.	750.	1500.	3500.	800.	1800.	4000.	-
1875-CC	25.	50.	75.	100.	200.	300.	400.	700.	1000.	1500.	3500.	-	*	*	*	*
1875-S	25.	40.	60.	75.	125.	250.	400.	500.	600.	750.	1400.	3500.	*	*	*	*
1876	25.	35.	50.	65.	110.	200.	300.	400.	500.	750.	1600.	3500.	800.	1800.	4500.	-
1876-CC	25.	40.	65.	85.	175.	300.	400.	700.	1000.	1800.	3000.	5000.	*	*	*	*
1876-S	25.	35.	50.	65.	110.	200.	300.	400.	600.	1000.	1500.	4000.	*	*	*	*
1877	25.	35.	50.	65.	110.	200.	300.	400.	600.	1000.	1500.	3500.	1000.	2500.	6500.	-
1877-CC	25.	35.	55.	75.	175.	300.	400.	750.	1000.	1400.	2500.	3500.	*	*	*	*
1877-S	25.	35.	50.	65.	110.	200.	300.	400.	500.	750.	2000.	3500.	*	*	*	*
1878	25.	40.	60.	100.	150.	250.	350.	500.	800.	1200.	2500.	4000.	800.	1500.	4000.	-
1878-CC	400.	600.	1000.	1800.	3500.	5000.	6500.	7500.	10000.	25000.	40000.	-	*	*	*	*
1878-S	15000.	18000.	25000.	30000.	35000.	40000.	45000.	50000.	60000.	100000.	175000.	-	*	*	*	*
1879	300.	350.	450.	500.	550.	600.	650.	800.	900.	1000.	1500.	3000.	700.	1500.	3500.	4500.
1880	300.	350.	400.	450.	500.	550.	600.	800.	900.	1000.	1500.	3500.	700.	1500.	3500.	4500.
1881	300.	350.	400.	450.	500.	550.	600.	800.	900.	1200.	1700.	4500.	700.	1500.	3500.	4500.
1882	350.	400.	450.	500.	550.	600.	650.	800.	900.	1200.	1700.	4000.	700.	1500.	3500.	4500.
1883	350.	400.	450.	500.	550.	600.	650.	800.	900.	1200.	1700.	4000.	700.	1500.	3500.	4500.
1884	400.	450.	500.	600.	650.	700.	750.	900.	1000.	1200.	1700.	3500.	700.	1500.	4000.	-
1885	400.	450.	500.	600.	650.	700.	750.	900.	1100.	1400.	2000.	3500.	700.	1500.	3500.	-

—— = Insufficient pricing data * = None issued

SEATED LIBERTY HALF DOLLAR (CONTINUED)

	G-4	VG-8	F-12	VF-20	EF-40	AU-50	AU-58	MS-60	MS-62	MS-63	MS-64	MS-65	PF-63	PF-64	PF-65	PF-66
1886	450.	600.	700.	800.	900.	1000.	1100.	1200.	1300.	1400.	1800.	3500.	700.	1500.	3500.	4500.
1887	500.	700.	800.	900.	1000.	1200.	1300.	1400.	1500.	1600.	1800.	3000.	700.	1500.	3500.	-
1888	300.	350.	400.	450.	500.	550.	600.	700.	850.	1100.	1500.	3000.	700.	1500.	3500.	4500.
1889	300.	350.	400.	450.	500.	550.	600.	700.	850.	1100.	1400.	3000.	700.	1500.	3500.	4500.
1890	300.	350.	400.	450.	500.	550.	600.	700.	850.	1100.	1500.	3000.	700.	1500.	3500.	4500.
1891	50.	75.	125.	150.	200.	250.	300.	400.	600.	850.	1400.	3000.	700.	1500.	3500.	4500.

—— = Insufficient pricing data * = None issued

Barber half dollar

Date of authorization:	April 2, 1792
Dates of issue:	1892-1915
Designer/Engraver:	Charles Barber
Diameter:	30.61 mm/1.21 inches
Weight:	12.50 grams/0.40 ounce
Metallic Content:	90% silver, 10% copper
Weight of pure silver:	11.25 grams/0.36 ounce
Edge:	Reeded
Mint mark:	Reverse below eagle

BARBER HALF DOLLAR (CONTINUED)

	G-4	VG-8	F-12	VF-20	EF-40	AU-50	AU-58	MS-60	MS-62	MS-63	MS-64	MS-65	PF-63	PF-64	PF-65	PF-66
1892	27.	37.	55.	90.	185.	280.	325.	380.	500.	675.	1175.	2800.	725.	1350.	3500.	-
1892-O	175.	230.	330.	350.	425.	450.	600.	875.	975.	1375.	2600.	4500.	*	*	*	*
1892-O Micro O	1750.	2500.	3250.	4000.	5500.	8000.	11500.	15000.	20000.	30000.	-	60000.	*	*	*	*
1892-S	150.	215.	265.	290.	400.	600.	700.	900.	1225.	1850.	2650.	5000.	*	*	*	*
1893	15.	23.	60.	85.	170.	320.	400.	515.	650.	1000.	1700.	3800.	725.	1350.	3500.	-
1893-O	25.	45.	80.	135.	285.	375.	475.	565.	625.	1000.	3900.	9150.	*	*	*	*
1893-S	120.	145.	215.	340.	425.	550.	850.	1175.	1550.	2550.	6000.	19750.	*	*	*	*
1894	20.	35.	80.	100.	225.	350.	400.	465.	575.	850.	1600.	3350.	725.	1350.	3500.	-
1894-O	15.	25.	65.	100.	235.	300.	400.	535.	600.	925.	2100.	5750.	*	*	*	*
1894-S	16.	23.	55.	75.	200.	350.	425.	475.	600.	1200.	3300.	6500.	*	*	*	*
1895	12.	17.	50.	85.	175.	310.	425.	570.	650.	975.	1900.	3150.	725.	1350.	3500.	-
1895-O	14.	25.	60.	100.	235.	375.	475.	600.	900.	1350.	3600.	6500.	*	*	*	*
1895-S	22.	40.	85.	125.	265.	400.	450.	535.	725.	1325.	2700.	6300.	*	*	*	*
1896	20.	25.	65.	100.	230.	325.	425.	550.	650.	950.	2900.	4000.	750.	1400.	3500.	-
1896-O	27.	38.	115.	150.	360.	665.	950.	1300.	1650.	3000.	7500.	10000.	*	*	*	*
1896-S	75.	105.	140.	215.	375.	575.	950.	1250.	1650.	2550.	7900.	11750.	*	*	*	*
1897	11.	12.	38.	75.	135.	310.	350.	445.	550.	780.	1250.	2800.	775.	1400.	3600.	-
1897-O	62.	125.	360.	725.	875.	1200.	1500.	1600.	2000.	2975.	4500.	6150.	*	*	*	*
1897-S	135.	165.	275.	425.	700.	1025.	1250.	1350.	1850.	3000.	4750.	7000.	*	*	*	*
1898	10.	12.	30.	72.	140.	315.	350.	410.	550.	780.	1400.	2750.	725.	1400.	3500.	-
1898-O	22.	45.	125.	190.	400.	500.	700.	975.	1250.	2500.	4650.	6750.	*	*	*	*
1898-S	12.	22.	45.	85.	205.	365.	575.	850.	1150.	2300.	5000.	8000.	*	*	*	*
1899	11.	12.	30.	72.	135.	305.	350.	410.	500.	780.	1400.	3350.	725.	1500.	3750.	-
1899-O	11.	15.	55.	90.	225.	355.	425.	550.	650.	1050.	2250.	4950.	*	*	*	*
1899-S	14.	23.	50.	85.	220.	350.	475.	635.	800.	1600.	3500.	5500.	*	*	*	*
1900	10.	12.	28.	72.	135.	315.	350.	410.	470.	775.	1450.	3300.	725.	1400.	3600.	-
1900-O	10.	14.	40.	90.	250.	315.	525.	800.	1250.	2900.	6250.	10650.	*	*	*	*

—— = Insufficient pricing data   * = None issued

BARBER HALF DOLLAR (CONTINUED)

	G-4	VG-8	F-12	VF-20	EF-40	AU-50	AU-58	MS-60	MS-62	MS-63	MS-64	MS-65	PF-63	PF-64	PF-65	PF-66
1900-S	10.	14.	40.	95.	195.	320.	450.	625.	850.	1900.	4750.	8500.	*	*	*	*
1901	10.	12.	28.	72.	135.	315.	350.	410.	500.	750.	1600.	3500.	775.	1400.	3500.	-
1901-O	11.	19.	55.	115.	290.	475.	825.	1350.	1750.	3200.	5750.	15750.	*	*	*	*
1901-S	21.	40.	125.	225.	550.	900.	1150.	1600.	2500.	4100.	6250.	16500.	*	*	*	*
1902	10.	12.	28.	65.	135.	265.	300.	385.	450.	675.	1400.	3750.	750.	1400.	3500.	-
1902-O	10.	14.	40.	80.	195.	360.	550.	725.	1250.	2350.	6400.	8500.	*	*	*	*
1902-S	10.	16.	50.	90.	200.	375.	500.	635.	925.	1800.	5300.	7000.	*	*	*	*
1903	10.	13.	40.	80.	200.	325.	375.	460.	625.	1375.	1950.	7250.	775.	1400.	3750.	-
1903-O	10.	14.	45.	85.	200.	350.	475.	700.	800.	1350.	3750.	8250.	*	*	*	*
1903-S	10.	14.	45.	78.	215.	365.	525.	600.	750.	1625.	2100.	5250.	*	*	*	*
1904	10.	12.	30.	72.	130.	300.	340.	410.	525.	1100.	1800.	4250.	750.	1350.	3500.	-
1904-O	12.	20.	55.	115.	310.	500.	750.	1100.	1500.	2800.	4750.	7250.	*	*	*	*
1904-S	20.	40.	165.	375.	700.	1250.	1500.	1950.	2500.	4250.	7250.	20000.	*	*	*	*
1905	14.	20.	65.	90.	225.	325.	425.	550.	650.	1200.	1800.	3750.	775.	1400.	3500.	-
1905-O	15.	30.	95.	155.	260.	425.	525.	725.	1050.	1700.	3500.	5500.	*	*	*	*
1905-S	10.	12.	40.	80.	200.	350.	450.	625.	900.	1900.	3300.	8500.	*	*	*	*
1906	10.	12.	30.	70.	140.	310.	350.	410.	470.	775.	1200.	2750.	750.	1350.	3500.	-
1906-D	10.	12.	30.	72.	140.	300.	340.	410.	470.	725.	1500.	3650.	*	*	*	*
1906-O	10.	12.	35.	75.	165.	325.	425.	600.	725.	1100.	2400.	3900.	*	*	*	*
1906-S	10.	15.	45.	80.	195.	325.	525.	600.	725.	1100.	2100.	3750.	*	*	*	*
1907	10.	12.	30.	80.	140.	275.	360.	410.	500.	675.	1200.	2750.	775.	1400.	3500.	-
1907-D	10.	12.	30.	80.	140.	310.	350.	425.	525.	725.	1350.	2750.	*	*	*	*
1907-O	10.	12.	30.	72.	150.	310.	390.	510.	600.	825.	1300.	3300.	*	*	*	*
1907-S	10.	15.	75.	110.	325.	525.	700.	925.	1400.	3100.	4750.	8500.	*	*	*	*
1907-S/S	13.	20.	100.	200.	425.	600.	775.	1025.	1500.	2850.	5250.	-	*	*	*	*
1908	10.	12.	30.	72.	155.	310.	350.	425.	525.	750.	1400.	4250.	750.	1400.	3500.	-
1908-D	10.	12.	30.	72.	145.	310.	350.	425.	535.	675.	1200.	2800.	*	*	*	*

—— = Insufficient pricing data   * = None issued

BARBER HALF DOLLAR (CONTINUED)

	G-4	VG-8	F-12	VF-20	EF-40	AU-50	AU-58	MS-60	MS-62	MS-63	MS-64	MS-65	PF-63	PF-64	PF-65	PF-66
1908-O	10.	12.	30.	72.	145.	310.	375.	500.	585.	850.	1200.	3000.	*	*	*	*
1908-S	10.	14.	50.	80.	200.	340.	500.	750.	1250	2100.	4000.	6500.	*	*	*	*
1909	10.	12.	30.	72.	140.	265.	315.	390.	475	675.	1200.	2750.	750.	1400.	3500.	-
1909-O	10.	12.	45.	88.	270.	500.	600.	750.	1000	1550.	2200.	4050.	*	*	*	*
1909-S	10.	12.	30.	72.	180.	340.	435.	575.	700	1200.	2350.	3900.	*	*	*	*
1910	12.	22.	75.	125.	280.	425.	500.	600.	725	1150.	1500.	3500.	750.	1350.	3500.	-
1910-S	10.	12.	30.	72.	180.	340.	450.	625.	925	1800.	2750.	4000.	*	*	*	*
1911	10.	12.	30.	70.	140.	310.	350.	425.	525	750.	1200.	2750.	750.	1350.	3500.	-
1911-D	10.	14.	40.	85.	195.	265.	375.	550.	650	850.	1200.	2800.	*	*	*	*
1911-S	10.	12.	33.	78.	165.	340.	450.	560.	700	1275.	2100.	4300.	*	*	*	*
1912	10.	12.	30.	70.	145.	310.	350.	410.	500	675	1200.	4000.	750.	1400.	3600.	-
1912-D	10.	12.	30.	72.	140.	310.	360.	435.	525	725	1275.	2750.	*	*	*	*
1912-S	10.	12.	30.	72.	165.	325.	400.	525.	650	1000	2350.	3750.	*	*	*	*
1913	23.	36.	120.	190.	365.	700.	800.	950.	1175.	1650	2100.	3250.	750.	1400.	3750.	-
1913-D	10.	12.	36.	72.	180.	300.	360.	455.	550.	875	1400.	5250.	*	*	*	*
1913-S	10.	12.	45.	85.	200.	350.	450.	500.	775.	1175	2100.	3450.	*	*	*	*
1914	35.	55.	190.	340.	500.	750.	850.	975.	1100.	1500	3500.	8750.	775.	1450.	3750.	-
1914-S	10.	12.	35.	72.	180.	350.	435.	560.	675.	1050	2150.	3800.	*	*	*	*
1915	25.	30.	100.	200.	375.	725.	850.	1025.	1250.	1875	3000.	4400.	800.	1450.	3750.	-
1915-D	10.	12.	30.	72.	140.	265.	315.	390.	475.	675	1175.	2750.	*	*	*	*
1915-S	10.	12.	30.	72.	145.	265.	315.	425.	500.	675	1200.	2750.	*	*	*	*

—— = Insufficient pricing data * = None issued

Walking Liberty half dollar

Date of authorization:	April 2, 1792
Dates of issue:	1916-1947
Designer:	Adolph Weinman
Engraver:	Charles Barber
Diameter:	30.61 mm/1.21 inches
Weight:	12.50 grams/0.40 ounce
Metallic Content:	90% silver, 10% copper
Weight of pure silver:	11.25 grams/0.36 ounce
Edge:	Reeded
Mint mark:	(1916): Obverse below IN GOD WE TRUST (1917): Obverse below IN GOD WE TRUST or reverse lower left

Obverse Mint mark

Reverse Mint mark

	VG-8	F-12	VF-20	EF-40	AU-50	MS-60	MS-62	MS-63	MS-64	MS-65	MS-66	PF-63	PF-64	PF-65	PF-66
1916	50.	75.	175.	225.	275.	350.	400	450.	800.	2000.	3500.	*	*	*	*
1916-D	40.	60.	125.	225.	275.	375.	500	650.	1000.	2300.	4500.	*	*	*	*
1916-S	150.	225.	400.	600.	800.	1200.	1500.	2000.	3500.	7500.	17000.	*	*	*	*
1917	7.00	10.	20.	45.	75.	140.	150.	200.	400.	1200.	2500.	*	*	*	*
1917-D Obverse Mint Mark	30.	60.	125.	225.	325.	600.	800.	1200.	3000.	8000.	18000.	*	*	*	*
1917-D Reverse Mint Mark	20.	40.	125.	275.	600.	1000.	1500.	2500.	7000.	30000.	50000.	*	*	*	*
1917-S Obverse Mint Mark	40.	90.	350.	800.	1400.	2500.	4000.	7500.	11000.	35000.	60000.	*	*	*	*
1917-S Reverse Mint Mark	10.	18.	40.	60.	175.	400.	1000.	2000.	4000.	18000.	30000.	*	*	*	*
1918	9.00	18.	60.	175.	275.	700.	900.	1200.	1800.	5000.	12000.	*	*	*	*
1918-D	15.	30.	75.	200.	500.	1200.	1800.	3000.	10000.	25000.	45000.	*	*	*	*
1918-S	8.00	18.	35.	60.	200.	600.	1000.	2500.	5000.	18000.	50000.	*	*	*	*
1919	30.	60.	250.	500.	900.	1300.	2000.	3500.	5000.	9000.	14000.	*	*	*	*
1919-D	30.	65.	250.	750.	1500.	6000.	12000.	20000.	35000.	10000.	—	*	*	*	*
1919-S	30.	50.	275.	900.	2000.	3500.	8000.	7500.	14000.	18000.	30000.	*	*	*	*
1920	8.00	15.	40.	75.	150.	350.	500.	700.	2000.	6000.	15000.	*	*	*	*
1920-D	15	45.	200.	450.	1000.	1500.	2500.	4500.	7000.	15000.	25000.	*	*	*	*
1920-S	9.00	20.	75.	275.	500.	1000.	1700.	3000.	6000.	15000.	25000.	*	*	*	*
1921	200	300.	800.	1800.	3000.	4000.	5500.	8000.	11000.	17000.	25000.	*	*	*	*
1921-D	300.	450.	900.	2500.	3500.	4500.	7500.	12000.	14000.	28000.	40000.	*	*	*	*
1921-S	75.	250.	1000.	5000.	9000.	14000.	20000.	30000.	60000.	10000.	150000.	*	*	*	*
1923-S	14.	25.	75.	275.	750.	1500.	2500.	4000.	7000.	18000.	40000.	*	*	*	*
1927-S	9.00	15.	45.	135.	375.	1100.	1400.	2000.	4000.	12000.	25000.	*	*	*	*
1928-S	9.00	18.	65.	175.	450.	1100.	1800.	3000.	4500.	12000.	25000.	*	*	*	*

—— = Insufficient pricing data * = None issued

WALKING LIBERTY HALF DOLLAR (CONTINUED)

	VG-8	F-12	VF-20	EF-40	AU-50	MS-60	MS-62	MS-63	MS-64	MS-65	MS-66	PF-63	PF-64	PF-65	PF-66
1929-D	11.	15.	30.	100.	225.	450.	600.	800.	1500.	4000.	6000.	*	*	*	*
1929-S	9.00	14.	30.	100.	250.	450.	650.	1000.	1500.	4000.	6000.	*	*	*	*
1933-S	12.	14.	20.	55.	250.	700.	1000.	1400.	2000.	4000.	6000.	*	*	*	*
1934	5.00	6.00	7.00	12.	30.	100.	90.	125.	150.	500.	750.	*	*	*	*
1934-D	7.00	8.00	12.	35.	100.	175.	200.	250.	400.	1200.	3000.	*	*	*	*
1934-S	5.00	6.00	8.00	35.	125.	400.	650.	1000.	1500.	5500.	6500.	*	*	*	*
1935	5.00	6.00	7.00	10.	25.	50.	60.	80.	125.	500.	750.	*	*	*	*
1935-D	7.00	8.00	10.	30.	60.	150.	200.	275.	400.	2500.	8500.	*	*	*	*
1935-S	5.00	6.00	8.00	30.	100.	350.	400.	500.	800.	3000.	5500.	*	*	*	*
1936	5.00	6.00	7.00	9.00	25.	40.	55.	75.	100.	250.	400.	2500.	4500.	6500.	9000.
1936-D	5.00	6.00	8.00	20.	50.	85.	100.	125.	200.	550.	1100.	*	*	*	*
1936-S	5.00	6.00	8.00	22.	65.	150.	200.	250.	300.	900.	1800.	*	*	*	*
1937	5.00	6.00	7.00	9.00	25.	45.	55.	70.	100.	275.	400.	800.	1000.	2500.	3500.
1937-D	7.00	8.00	13.	35.	125.	250.	300.	350.	400.	800.	1200.	*	*	*	*
1937-S	5.00	6.00	8.00	25.	65.	175.	200.	225.	300.	700.	1400.	*	*	*	*
1938	7.00	8.00	9.00	12.	45.	75.	110.	175.	200.	400.	750.	700.	900.	1200.	1800.
1938-D	70.	85.	100.	125.	275.	550.	600.	700.	800.	1400.	2000.	*	*	*	*
1939	5.00	6.00	7.00	9.00	25.	45.	60.	75.	85.	200.	400.	600.	800.	1000.	1500.
1939-D	5.00	6.00	7.00	10.	25.	45.	60.	85.	125.	225.	400.	*	*	*	*
1939-S	6.00	7.00	9.00	20.	75.	150.	175.	200.	225.	300.	750.	*	*	*	*
1940	5.00	6.00	7.00	9.00	15.	40.	50.	60.	75.	200.	400.	600.	800.	1000.	1400.
1940-S	5.00	6.00	7.00	9.00	25.	55.	60.	80.	150.	500.	2000.	*	*	*	*
1941	5.00	6.00	7.00	9.00	12.	40.	50.	60.	75.	225.	400.	600.	700.	900.	1200.
1941-D	5.00	6.00	7.00	9.00	18.	40.	50.	65.	100.	350.	500.	*	*	*	*
1941-S	5.00	6.00	7.00	9.00	30.	80.	100.	125.	300.	2000.	5500.	*	*	*	*
1942	5.00	6.00	7.00	9.00	12.	40.	50.	60.	75.	225.	500.	600.	700.	900.	1200.
1942-D	5.00	6.00	7.00	9.00	18.	40.	65.	85.	125.	450.	700.	*	*	*	*

—— = Insufficient pricing data * = None issued

WALKING LIBERTY HALF DOLLAR (CONTINUED)

	VG-8	F-12	VF-20	EF-40	AU-50	MS-60	MS-62	MS-63	MS-64	MS-65	MS-66	PF-63	PF-64	PF-65	PF-66
1942-S	5.00	6.00	7.00	9.00	18.	40.	50.	65.	125.	1400.	4000.	*	*	*	*
1943	5.00	6.00	7.00	9.00	12.	40.	50.	60.	75.	200.	400.	*	*	*	*
1943-D	5.00	6.00	7.00	9.00	20.	50.	60.	75.	150.	500.	750.	*	*	*	*
1943-S	5.00	6.00	7.00	9.00	20.	50.	55.	65.	100.	800.	2000.	*	*	*	*
1944	5.00	6.00	7.00	9.00	12.	40.	50.	60.	75.	275.	700.	*	*	*	*
1944-D	5.00	6.00	7.00	9.00	20.	40.	50.	65.	85.	250.	450.	*	*	*	*
1944-S	5.00	6.00	7.00	9.00	20.	40.	50.	60.	85.	1200.	4500.	*	*	*	*
1945	5.00	6.00	7.00	9.00	12.	40.	50.	60.	75.	250.	500.	*	*	*	*
1945-D	5.00	6.00	7.00	9.00	18.	40.	50.	60.	75.	250.	400.	*	*	*	*
1945-S	5.00	6.00	7.00	9.00	18.	40.	50.	60.	75.	300.	1500.	*	*	*	*
1946	5.00	6.00	7.00	9.00	12.	40.	50.	60.	75.	325.	1200.	*	*	*	*
1946-D	6.00	8.00	10.	13.	35.	55.	60.	70.	85.	175.	400.	*	*	*	*
1946-S	5.00	6.00	7.00	9.00	18.	45.	50.	60.	75.	250.	700.	*	*	*	*
1947	5.00	6.00	7.00	10.	20.	55.	60.	65.	75.	350.	900.	*	*	*	*
1947-D	5.00	6.00	7.00	12.	30.	55.	60.	65.	75.	250.	1100.	*	*	*	*

—— = Insufficient pricing data * = None issued

Franklin half dollar

Date of authorization:	April 2, 1792
Dates of issue:	1948-1963
Designer:	John Sinnock
Engraver:	Gilroy Roberts
Diameter:	30.61 mm/1.21 inches
Weight:	12.50 grams/0.40 ounce
Metallic Content:	90% silver, 10% copper
Weight of pure silver:	11.25 grams/0.36 ounce
Edge:	Reeded
Mint mark:	Reverse above bell beam

NOTE: MS-64F and MS-65F refer to Full Bell Lines.

Also, the letter C following a numerical grade for a Proof coin stands for "cameo," while the letters DC stand for "deep cameo." Cameo coins have contrasting surface finishes: mirror fields and frosted devices (raised areas). Deep cameo coins are the ultimate level of cameo, with deeply frosted devices. Cameo and deep cameo coins bring premiums.

FRANKLIN HALF DOLLAR (CONTINUED)

	EF-40	AU-50	MS-60	MS-63	MS-64	MS-64F	MS-65	MS-65F	MS-66	MS-66F	PF-63	PF-64	PF-64C	PF-65	PF-65C	PF-66	PF-66C	PF-66DC	PF-67	PF-67C	PF-67DC	PF-68	PF-68C	PF-68DC
1948	6.00	8.00	16.	25.	35.	60.	85.	200.	825.	350.	*	*	*	*	*	*	*	*	*	*	*	*	*	*
1948-D	6.00	9.00	16.	20	35.	60.	160.	275.	2100.	1200.	*	*	*	*	*	*	*	*	*	*	*	*	*	*
1949	9.00	15.	40.	55	60.	100.	175.	260.	950.	600.	*	*	*	*	*	*	*	*	*	*	*	*	*	*
1949-D	15.	25.	40.	30	100.	200.	1000.	1800.	—	—	*	*	*	*	*	*	*	*	*	*	*	*	*	*
1949-S	20.	35.	60.	75	100.	300.	175.	700.	250.	850.	*	*	*	*	*	*	*	*	*	*	*	*	*	*
1950	7.00	10.	25.	40	50.	100.	125.	300.	500.	800.	350.	400.	720.	550.	2000.	750.	6000.	—	1800.	—	—	—	—	—
1950-D	9.00	12.	25.	40	50.	125.	550.	1000.	—	4500.	*	*	*	*	*	*	*	*	*	*	*	*	*	*
1951	4.00	7.00	12.	20	25.	100.	75.	400.	800.	—	250.	350.	850.	400.	1500	500.	3500.	—	1000.	—	—	—	—	—
1951-D	12.	18.	25.	40	65.	100.	225.	550.	2100.	2500.	*	*	*	*	*	*	*	*	*	*	*	*	*	*
1951-S	10.	15.	25.	35	50.	225.	100.	800.	250.	2000.	*	*	*	*	*	*	*	*	*	*	*	*	*	*
1952	4.00	6.00	10.	20	40.	100.	90.	175.	200.	400.	125.	175.	310.	200	800	400.	1100.	—	1000.	1500.	—	—	—	—
1952-D	5.00	7.00	10.	20	40.	75.	200.	400.	800.	2000.	*	*	*	*	*	*	*	*	*	*	*	*	*	*
1952-S	17.	30.	45.	50	60.	400.	90.	1300.	350.	5300.	*	*	*	*	*	*	*	*	*	*	*	*	*	*
1953	7.00	13.	20.	25.	50.	200.	200.	1000.	1300.	3500.	75	150.	250.	200.	500	275.	1100.	—	350.	2500.	14375.	750.	—	—
1953-D	5.00	6.00	9.00	15.	25.	50.	200.	400.	2100.	2000.	*	*	*	*	*	*	*	*	*	*	*	*	*	*
1953-S	10.	15.	27.	30	40.	1250.	90.	15000.	550.	—	*	*	*	*	*	*	*	*	*	*	*	*	*	*
1954	4.00	6.00	8.00	15	35.	50.	85.	225.	400.	2500.	60.	85.	85.	120.	175	140.	250.	700.	200.	750.	4250.	360.	1800.	—
1954-D	4.00	6.00	8.00	15.	30.	40.	150.	225.	700.	2000.	*	*	*	*	*	*	*	*	*	*	*	*	*	*
1954-S	4.00	6.00	9.00	15.	25.	100.	60.	500.	350.	3500.	*	*	*	*	*	*	*	*	*	*	*	*	*	*
1955	10.	17.	20.	25.	30.	40.	55.	150.	450.	400.	40.	60.	60	75.	100	90.	260.	950.	150.	400.	1850.	300.	500.	—
1956	5.00	7.00	8.00	15.	25.	40.	50.	150.	70.	175.	18.	40.	40	50.	60	60.	70.	—	75.	100.	—	100.	400.	—
1957	3.50	6.00	7.00	12.	20.	50.	50.	110.	120.	175.	18.	20.	25.	30.	50.	35.	60.	750.	50.	225.	1000.	85.	300.	2500.
1957-D	3.50	5.00	6.00	12.	25.	35.	50.	110.	110.	175.	*	*	*	*	*	*	*	*	*	*	*	*	*	*
1958	3.50	5.00	6.00	15.	20.	50	60.	110.	70.	175.	20.	40.	30.	50.	55.	60.	85.	1250.	70.	200.	1800.	125.	800.	—

—— = Insufficient pricing data * = None issued

FRANKLIN HALF DOLLAR (CONTINUED)

	EF-40	AU-50	MS-60	MS-63	MS-64	MS-64F	MS-65	MS-65F	MS-66	MS-66F	PF-63	PF-64	PF-64C	PF-65	PF-65C	PF-66	PF-66C	PF-66DC	PF-67	PF-67C	PF-67DC	PF-68	PF-68C	PF-68DC
1958-D	3.50	5.00	6.00	12.	20.	35.	55.	100.	70.	175.	*	*	*	*	*	*	*	*	*	*	*	*	*	*
1959	3.50	5.00	6.00	12.	20.	40.	150.	300.	1250.	5000.	15.	20.	25.	25.	75.	100.	300.	—	50.	400.	—	110.	2500.	—
1959-D	3.50	5.00	6.00	12.	25.	40.	175.	250.	2650.	3000.	*	*	*	*	*	*	*	*	*	*	*	*	*	*
1960	3.50	5.00	6.00	13.	20.	40.	160.	350.	1000.	3500.	15.	18.	20.	25.	50.	30.	120.	175.	40.	150.	350.	75.	200.	800.
1960-D	3.50	5.00	6.00	13.	35.	40.	700.	1500.	—	—	*	*	*	*	*	*	*	*	*	*	*	*	*	*
1961	3.50	5.00	6.00	13.	30.	125.	175.	1400.	800.	—	15.	18.	20.	25.	45.	30.	100.	150.	45.	150.	300.	90.	275.	1000.
1961-D	3.50	5.00	6.00	13.	30.	50.	300.	900.	1500.	—	*	*	*	*	*	*	*	*	*	*	*	*	*	*
1962	3.50	5.00	6.00	13.	25.	150.	225.	1800.	900.	—	15.	18.	20.	25.	40.	30.	70.	250.	40.	100.	400.	65.	275.	800.
1962-D	3.50	5.00	6.00	12.	25.	50.	300.	600.	1000.	—	*	*	*	*	*	*	*	*	*	*	*	*	*	*
1963	3.50	5.00	6.00	12.	20.	125.	60.	1000.	500.	—	15.	18.	25.	30.	40.	40.	100.	200.	50.	150.	210.	125.	200.	750.
1963-D	3.50	5.00	6.00	12.	20.	35.	90.	250.	400.	2500.	*	*	*	*	*	*	*	*	*	*	*	*	*	*

—— = Insufficient pricing data   * = None issued

Kennedy half dollar

Date of authorization:	Dec. 30, 1963; July 23, 1965; Oct. 18, 1973
Dates of issue:	1964-present
Designer:	Obverse: Gilroy Roberts Reverse: Frank Gasparro Bicentennial Reverse: Seth G. Huntington
Engraver:	Gilroy Roberts
Bicentennial Obverse:	Frank Gasparro
Diameter:	30.61 mm/1.21 inches
Weight:	(1964, 1992-present silver Proof only): 12.50 grams/0.40 ounce (1965-1970): 11.50 grams/0.37 ounce (1971-present): 11.34 grams/0.36 ounce (1976 Bicentennial Proof and Uncirculated): 11.50 grams/ 0.37 ounce
Metallic Content:	(1964, 1992-present silver Proofs only): 90% silver, 10% copper (1965-1970): 80% silver, 20% copper bonded to a core of 21.5% silver, 78.5% copper (1971-present): 75% copper, 25% nickel bonded to pure copper core (1976 Bicentennial Proof and Uncirculated sets only): 80% silver, 20% copper bonded to a core of 21.5% silver, 78.5% copper
Weight of pure silver:	(1964, 1992-present silver Proofs only) 11.25 grams/0.36 ounce (1965-1970): 4.60 grams/0.15 ounce (1976 Bicentennial Proof and Uncirculated sets only): 4.60 grams/0.15 ounce
Edge:	Reeded

Mint mark: (1964): Reverse left near claw and laurel
(1968-present): Obverse below Kennedy

Bicentennial date, reverse

Also, the letter C following a numerical grade for a Proof coin stands for "cameo," while the letters DC stand for "deep cameo." Cameo coins have contrasting surface finishes: mirror fields and frosted devices (raised areas). Deep cameo coins are the ultimate level of cameo, with deeply frosted devices. Cameo and deep cameo coins bring premiums.

	MS-63	MS-64	MS-65	MS-66	MS-67	PF-63	PF-64	PF-65	PF-66	PF-67	PF-67C	PF-67DC	PF-68	PF-68C	PF-68DC	PF-69	PF-69C	PF-69DC	PF-70	PF-70C	PF-70DC
SILVER																					
1964	3.50	9.00	28.	50.	450.	—	—	12.	15.	20.	90.	155.	40.	100.	350.	70.	235.	1200.	1000.	—	—
1964-D	3.50	12.	25.	70.	750.	*	*	*	*	*	*	*	*	*	*	*	*	*	*	*	*
1964 Heavily accented hair	—	—	—	—	—	25.	35.	50.	65.	75.	150.	1500.	100.	300.	6000.	400.	—	—	—	—	—
40 PERCENT SILVER CLAD																					
1965	1.25	9.50	20.	50.	350.	*	*	*	*	*	*	*	*	*	*	*	*	*	*	*	*
1965 Special Mint Set	—	—	—	—	—	5.00	7.00	10.	15.	35.	175.	300.	200.	350.	—	—	—	—	—	—	—
1966	1.40	11.	15.	45.	225.	*	*	*	*	*	*	*	*	*	*	*	*	*	*	*	*
1966 Special Mint Set	—	—	—	—	—	5.00	7.00	10.	20.	35.	175.	300.	200.	350.	—	—	—	—	—	—	—
1967	1.50	9.50	25.	75.	150.	*	*	*	*	*	*	*	*	*	*	*	*	*	*	*	*
1967 Special Mint Set	—	—	—	—	—	5.00	7.00	10.	20.	35.	175.	300.	200.	350.	—	—	—	—	—	—	—
1968-D	1.50	9.00	25.	90.	325.	*	*	*	*	*	*	*	*	*	*	*	*	*	*	*	*
1968-S	*	*	*		*	—	—	7.00	10.	18.	25.	45.	25.	30.	110.	30.	55.	300.	—	—	—
1969-D	1.25	7.50	35.	170.	500.	*	*	*	*	*	*	*	*	*	*	*	*	*	*	*	*
1969-S	*	*	*		*	—	—	6.00	7.00	8.00	20.	50.	9.00	30.	100.	24.	40.	400.	—	90.	—
1970-D	10.	32.	45.	130.	750.	*	*	*	*	*	*	*	*	*	*	*	*	*	*	*	*
1970-S	*	*	*		*	—	—	8.00	12.	18.	25.	100.	20.	30.	200.	24.	90.	400.	—	—	—
COPPER-NICKEL CLAD																					
1971	1.50	12.	15.	50.	95.	*	*	*	*	*	*	*	*	*	*	*	*	*	*	*	*
1971-D	1.25	5.00	16.	35.	120.	*	*	*	*	*	*	*	*	*	*	*	*	*	*	*	*
1971-S	*	*	*		*	—	—	9.00	12.	15.	20.	175.	35.	25.	235.	45.	60.	300.	60.	—	—

—— = Insufficient pricing data   * = None issued

KENNEDY HALF DOLLAR (CONTINUED)

	MS-63	MS-64	MS-65	MS-66	MS-67	PF-63	PF-64	PF-65	PF-66	PF-67	PF-67C	PF-67DC	PF-68	PF-68C	PF-68DC	PF-69	PF-69C	PF-69DC	PF-70	PF-70C	PF-70DC
1972	1.50	9.00	25.	35.	170.	*	*	*	*	*	*	*	*	*	*	*	*	*	*	*	*
1972-D	1.50	6.00	15.	25.	85.	*	*	*	*	*	*	*	*	*	*	*	*	*	*	*	*
1972-S	*	*	*	*	*	—	—	10.	14.	18.	22.	30.	20.	25.	40.	50.	60.	80.	—	—	—
1973	1.50	6.00	15.	75.	140.	*	*	*	*	*	*	*	*	*	*	*	*	*	*	*	*
1973-D	1.25	5.50	15.	25.	80.	*	*	*	*	*	*	*	*	*	*	*	*	*	*	*	*
1973-S	*	*	*	*	*	—	—	10.	12.	15.	20.	25.	20.	25.	30.	30.	35.	90.	—	—	—
1974	1.00	4.75	22.	25.	85.	*	*	*	*	*	*	*	*	*	*	*	*	*	*	*	*
1974-D	1.00	6.00	20.	60.	100.	*	*	*	*	*	*	*	*	*	*	*	*	*	*	*	*
1974-S	*	*	*	*	*	—	—	12.	15.	20.	25.	30.	30.	35.	40.	35.	60.	60.	—	—	—
DUAL DATE, BICENTENNIAL REVERSE																					
1776-1976	1.00	10.	25.	45.	140.	*	*	*	*	*	*	*	*	*	*	*	*	*	*	*	*
1776-1976-D	1.00	6.00	7.00	21.	45.	*	*	*	*	*	*	*	*	*	*	*	*	*	*	*	*
1776-1976-S 40% silver	3.50	9.00	13.	35.	75.	—	—	8.00	10.	15.	20.	30.	25.	35.	45.	75.	95.	100.	—	—	—
1776-1976-S	*	*	*	*	*	—	—	7.00	9.00	12.	20.	30.	25.	35.	40.	70.	90.	90.	—	—	—
PRESIDENTIAL SEAL/EAGLE REVERSE RESUMED																					
1977	1.40	6.75	20.	35.	150.	*	*	*	*	*	*	*	*	*	*	*	*	*	*	*	*
1977-D	1.40	6.00	7.00	30.	130.	*	*	*	*	*	*	*	*	*	*	*	*	*	*	*	*
1977-S	*	*	*	*	*	—	—	8.00	10.	15.	18.	20.	18.	20.	25.	30.	35.	45.	35.	40.	—
1978	1.40	6.50	20.	35.	160.	*	*	*	*	*	*	*	*	*	*	*	*	*	*	*	*
1978-D	1.25	6.50	8.00	20.	95.	*	*	*	*	*	*	*	*	*	*	*	*	*	*	*	*
1978-S	*	*	*	*	*	—	—	8.00	10.	15.	18.	20.	18.	20.	25.	30.	35.	45.	—	—	—
1979	1.00	5.50	13.	40.	100.	*	*	*	*	*	*	*	*	*	*	*	*	*	*	*	*
1979-D	1.15	6.00	10.	30.	95.	*	*	*	*	*	*	*	*	*	*	*	*	*	*	*	*

—— = Insufficient pricing data   * = None issued

	MS-63	MS-64	MS-65	MS-66	MS-67	PF-63	PF-64	PF-65	PF-66	PF-67	PF-67C	PF-67DC	PF-68	PF-68C	PF-68DC	PF-69	PF-69C	PF-69DC	PF-70	PF-70C	PF-70DC
1979-S Filled S	*	*	*		*	—	—	8.00	10.	15.	18.	20.	18.	20.	25.	30.	35.	45.	—	—	105.
1979-S Clear S	*	*	*		*	—	—	15.	16.	17.	18.	20.	18.	20.	25.	30.	45.	70.	—	—	—
1980-P	1.00	5.00	11.	25	52.	*	*	*	*	*	*	*	*	*	*	*	*	*	*	*	*
1980-D	1.25	4.75	7.00	50	150.	*	*	*	*	*	*	*	*	*	*	*	*	*	*	*	*
1980-S	*	*	*		*	—	—	8.00	9.00	10	12.	15.	12.	15.	17.	20.	25.	35.	—	—	275.
1981-P	1.50	5.00	10.	35	50.	*	*	*	*	*	*	*	*	*	*	*	*	*	*	*	*
1981-D	1.50	4.50	11.	21	150.	*	*	*	*	*	*	*	*	*	*	*	*	*	*	*	*
1981-S	—	—	—	—	—	—	—	2.25	—	—	—	—	—	—	—	—	—	—	—	—	—
1981-S Filled S	*	*	*		*	—	—	8.00	9.00	10	12.	15.	12.	15.	17.	20.	25.	35.	—	—	245.
1982-P	1.65	5.00	7.00	20	40.	*	*	*	*	*	*	*	*	*	*	*	*	*	*	*	*
1982-P No FG	10.	14.	30.	60	—	*	*	*	*	*	*	*	*	*	*	*	*	*	*	*	*
1982-D	1.65	5.00	7.00	45	55.	*	*	*	*	*	*	*	*	*	*	*	*	*	*	*	*
1982-S	*	*	*		*	—	—	8.00	9.00	10	12.	15.	12.	15.	17.	20.	25.	35.	—	—	460.
1983-P	1.35	4.00	21.	40	200.	*	*	*	*	*	*	*	*	*	*	*	*	*	*	*	*
1983-D	1.35	5.00	7.00	50	130.	*	*	*	*	*	*	*	*	*	*	*	*	*	*	*	*
1983-S	*	*	*		*	—	—	8.00	9.00	10	12.	15.	12.	15.	17.	20.	25.	35.	—	—	520.
1984-P	1.45	5.00	10.	35	120.	*	*	*	*	*	*	*	*	*	*	*	*	*	*	*	*
1984-D	1.45	4.00	7.00	40	180.	*	*	*	*	*	*	*	*	*	*	*	*	*	*	*	*
1984-S	*	*	*		*	—	—	8.00	9.00	10	12.	15.	12.	15.	17.	20.	25.	40.	—	—	275.
1985-P	1.50	5.00	10.	50	65.	*	*	*	*	*	*	*	*	*	*	*	*	*	*	*	*
1985-D	1.50	5.00	12.	15	25.	*	*	*	*	*	*	*	*	*	*	*	*	*	*	*	*
1985-S	*	*	*		*	—	—	8.00	9.00	10	12.	15.	12.	15.	17.	20.	25.	35.	—	—	425.
1986-P	3.00	9.00	15.	50	60.	*	*	*	*	*	*	*	*	*	*	*	*	*	*	*	*
1986-D	3.35	7.00	10.	25	45.	*	*	*	*	*	*	*	*	*	*	*	*	*	*	*	*

—— = Insufficient pricing data * = None issued

KENNEDY HALF DOLLAR (CONTINUED)

	MS-63	MS-64	MS-65	MS-66	MS-67	PF-63	PF-64	PF-65	PF-66	PF-67	PF-67C	PF-67DC	PF-68	PF-68C	PF-68DC	PF-69	PF-69C	PF-69DC	PF-70	PF-70C	PF-70DC
1986-S	*	*	*	*	*	—	—	8.00	9.00	10.	12.	15.	12.	15.	17.	20.	25.	40.	—	—	275.
1987-P	4.00	9.00	15.	50.	75.	*	*	*	*	*	*	*	*	*	*	*	*	*	*	*	*
1987-D	4.00	9.00	10.	25.	75.	*	*	*	*	*	*	*	*	*	*	*	*	*	*	*	*
1987-S	*	*	*	*	*	—	—	8.00	9.00	10.	12.	15.	12.	15.	17.	20.	25.	35.	—	—	275.
1988-P	1.50	9.00	10.	36.	50.	*	*	*	*	*	*	*	*	*	*	*	*	*	*	*	*
1988-D	1.35	6.00	10.	25.	70.	*	*	*	*	*	*	*	*	*	*	*	*	*	*	*	*
1988-S	*	*	*	*	*	—	—	8.00	9.00	10.	12.	15.	12.	15.	17.	20.	25.	40.	—	—	—
1989-P	1.50	9.00	20.	45.	90.	*	*	*	*	*	*	*	*	*	*	*	*	*	*	*	*
1989-D	1.25	9.50	10.	32.	120.	*	*	*	*	*	*	*	*	*	*	*	*	*	*	*	*
1989-S	*	*	*	*	*	—	—	8.00	9.00	10.	12.	15.	12.	15.	17.	20.	25.	35.	—	—	350.
1990-P	1.25	15.	18.	20.	55.	*	*	*	*	*	*	*	*	*	*	*	*	*	*	*	*
1990-D	2.00	4.00	15.	23.	75.	*	*	*	*	*	*	*	*	*	*	*	*	*	*	*	*
1990-S	*	*	*	*	*	—	—	8.00	9.00	10.	12.	15.	12.	15.	17.	20.	25.	35.	—	—	300.
1991-P	1.75	7.00	18.	25.	50.	*	*	*	*	*	*	*	*	*	*	*	*	*	*	*	*
1991-D	2.00	11.	14.	16.	75.	*	*	*	*	*	*	*	*	*	*	*	*	*	*	*	*
1991-S	*	*	*	*	*	—	—	8.00	9.00	10.	12.	15.	12.	15.	17.	20.	25.	40.	—	—	290.
1992-P	1.25	6.00	20.	40.	100.	*	*	*	*	*	*	*	*	*	*	*	*	*	*	*	*
1992-D	2.00	6.00	8.00	26.	50.	*	*	*	*	*	*	*	*	*	*	*	*	*	*	*	*
1992-S Clad	*	*	*	*	*	—	—	8.00	9.00	10.	12.	15.	12.	15.	17.	20.	25.	35.	—	—	—
1992-S Silver	*	*	*	*	*	—	—	10.	12.	15.	18.	20.	20.	25.	30.	40.	45.	50.	—	—	500.
1993-P	1.25	10.	15.	40.	50.	*	*	*	*	*	*	*	*	*	*	*	*	*	*	*	*
1993-D	1.25	9.00	12.	28.	80.	*	*	*	*	*	*	*	*	*	*	*	*	*	*	*	*
1993-S Clad	*	*	*	*	*	—	—	8.00	9.00	10.	11.	12.	12.	13.	15.	20.	25.	40.	—	—	—
1993-S Silver	*	*	*	*	*	—	—	10.	12.	15.	18.	25.	18.	20.	40.	50.	60.	70.	—	—	—

—— = Insufficient pricing data * = None issued

	MS-63	MS-64	MS-65	MS-66	MS-67	PF-63	PF-64	PF-65	PF-66	PF-67	PF-67C	PF-67DC	PF-68	PF-68C	PF-68DC	PF-69	PF-69C	PF-69DC	PF-70	PF-70C	PF-70DC
1994-P	1.25	6.00	10.	4[illegible]	95.	*	*	*	*	*	*	*	*	*	*	*	*	*	*	*	*
1994-D	1.25	6.00	10.	5[illegible]	75.	*	*	*	*	*	*	*	*	*	*	*	*	*	*	*	*
1994-S Clad	*	*	*	*	*	—	—	8.00	9.00	10.	12.	15.	12.	15.	17.	20.	25.	35.	—	—	95.
1994-S Silver	*	*	*	*	*	—	—	30.	35.	40.	45.	50.	50.	55.	60.	60.	65.	75.	—	—	225.
1995-P	1.25	8.00	10.	2[illegible]	35.	*	*	*	*	*	*	*	*	*	*	*	*	*	*	*	*
1995-D	1.25	6.00	9.00	3[illegible]	50.	*	*	*	*	*	*	*	*	*	*	*	*	*	*	*	*
1995-S Clad	*	*	*	*	*	—	—	8.00	10.	12.	15.	25.	20.	25.	30.	35.	40.	90.	—	—	125.
1995-S Silver	*	*	*	*	*	—	—	70.	75.	80.	85.	90.	90.	95.	100.	100.	110.	150.	—	—	200.
1996-P	1.25	9.00	12.	2[illegible]	65.	*	*	*	*	*	*	*	*	*	*	*	*	*	*	*	*
1996-D	1.25	6.00	9.00	2[illegible]	36.	*	*	*	*	*	*	*	*	*	*	*	*	*	*	*	*
1996-S Clad	*	*	*	*	*	—	—	10.	12.	15.	18.	20.	18	20.	25.	30.	35.	40.	—	—	170.
1996-S Silver	*	*	*	*	*	—	—	40.	45.	50.	55.	60.	60	65.	70.	75.	85.	100.	—	—	200.
1997-P	1.25	9.00	15.	3[illegible]	55.	*	*	*	*	*	*	*	*	*	*	*	*	*	*	*	*
1997-D	1.25	6.00	10.	1[illegible]	26.	*	*	*	*	*	*	*	*	*	*	*	*	*	*	*	*
1997-S Clad	*	*	*	*	*	—	—	10.	12.	15.	20.	25.	25	30.	35.	40.	45.	75.	—	—	—
1997-S Silver	*	*	*	*	*	—	—	70.	80.	90.	30.	40.	100	45.	50.	75.	95.	150.	—	—	—
1998-P	1.50	4.00	12.	5[illegible]	125.	*	*	*	*	*	*	*	*	*	*	*	*	*	*	*	*
1998-D	1.25	4.00	12.	5[illegible]	65.	*	*	*	*	*	*	*	*	*	*	*	*	*	*	*	*
1998-S Clad	*	*	*	*	*	—	—	10.	12.	15.	18.	20.	18	20.	25.	25.	30.	35.	—	—	—
1998-S Silver	*	*	*	*	*	—	—	25.	30.	35.	40.	45.	40	45.	50.	50.	55.	50.	—	—	—
1998-S Silver Matte Finish	*	*	*	*	*	235.	240.	250.	275.	300.	—	—	325	—	—	350.	—	—	900.	—	—
1999-P	1.50	4.00	10.	4[illegible]	50.	*	*	*	*	*	*	*	*	*	*	*	*	*	*	*	*
1999-D	1.25	4.00	10.	2[illegible]	52.	*	*	*	*	*	*	*	*	*	*	*	*	*	*	*	*

—— = Insufficient pricing data * = None issued

KENNEDY HALF DOLLAR (CONTINUED)

	MS-63	MS-64	MS-65	MS-66	MS-67	PF-63	PF-64	PF-65	PF-66	PF-67	PF-67C	PF-67DC	PF-68	PF-68C	PF-68DC	PF-69	PF-69C	PF-69DC	PF-70	PF-70C	PF-70DC
1999-S Clad	*	*	*	*	*	—	—	8.00	10.	12.	15.	18.	15.	18.	20.	20.	25.	35.	—	—	110.
1999-S Silver	*	*	*	*	*	—	—	10.	12.	15.	18.	20.	18.	20.	25.	30.	35.	50.	—	—	130.
2000-P	1.50	4.00	10.	16.	75.	*	*	*	*	*	*	*	*	*	*	*	*	*	*	*	*
2000-D	1.25	4.00	6.00	30.	65.	*	*	*	*	*	*	*	*	*	*	*	*	*	*	*	*
2000-S Clad	*	*	*	*	*	—	—	8.00	9.00	10.	12.	15.	15.	18.	20.	25.	30.	35.	—	—	110.
2000-S Silver	*	*	*	*	*	—	—	10.	11.	12.	15.	18.	18.	20.	25.	30.	35.	60.	—	75.	130.
2001-P	1.50	4.00	10.	33.	80.	*	*	*	*	*	*	*	*	*	*	*	*	*	*	*	*
2001-D	1.25	4.00	10.	30.	200.	*	*	*	*	*	*	*	*	*	*	*	*	*	*	*	*
2001-S Clad	*	*	*	*	*	—	—	8.00	9.00	10.	12.	15.	15.	18.	20.	18.	20.	35.	—	—	110.
2001-S Silver	*	*	*	*	*	—	—	10.	11.	12.	15.	18.	18.	20.	25.	30.	35.	40.	—	—	130.
2002-P	1.50	4.00	10.	30.	50.	*	*	*	*	*	*	*	*	*	*	*	*	*	*	*	*
2002-D	1.25	4.00	10.	30.	75.	*	*	*	*	*	*	*	*	*	*	*	*	*	*	*	*
2002-S Clad	*	*	*	*	*	—	—	8.00	9.00	10.	12.	15.	15.	18.	20.	18.	20.	35.	—	—	130.
2002-S Silver	*	*	*	*	*	—	—	10.	11.	12.	15.	25.	18.	20.	30.	30.	35.	40.	—	—	130.
2003-P	—	—	—	—	—	*	*	*	*	*	*	*	*	*	*	*	*	*	*	*	*
2003-D	—	—	—	—	—	*	*	*	*	*	*	*	*	*	*	*	*	*	*	*	*
2003-S Clad	*	*	*	*	*	—	—	8.00	9.00	10.	12.	15.	15.	18.	20.	18.	20.	25.	—	—	130.
2003-S Silver	*	*	*	*	*	—	—	10.	11.	12.	15.	25.	18.	20.	30.	30.	35.	40.	—	—	130.
2004-P	—	—	—	—	—	*	*	*	*	*	*	*	*	*	*	*	*	*	*	*	*
2004-D	—	—	—	—	—	*	*	*	*	*	*	*	*	*	*	*	*	*	*	*	*
2004-S Clad	*	*	*	*	*	—	—	8.00	9.00	10.	12.	15.	15.	18.	20.	18.	20.	25.	—	—	130.
2004-S Silver	*	*	*	*	*	—	—	10.	11.	12.	15.	25.	18.	20.	30.	30.	35.	40.	—	—	130.

2002 to 2004 circulation-quality coins, collector sales only.

—— = Insufficient pricing data * = None issued

Flowing Hair dollar

Date of authorization:	April 2, 1792
Dates of issue:	1794-1795
Designer/Engraver:	Robert Scot
Diameter:	39.50 mm/1.56 inches
Weight:	26.96 grams/0.87 ounce
Metallic Content:	90% silver, 10% copper
Weight of pure silver:	24.26 grams/0.78 ounce
Edge:	Lettered (HUNDRED CENTS ONE DOLLAR OR UNIT)
Mint mark:	None

	AG-3	G-4	VG-8	F-12	VF-20	EF-40	EF-45	AU-50	AU-55	MS-60
1794	20000.	30000.	40000.	50000.	85000.	135000.	175000.	225000.	250000.	275000.
1795 2 leaves, Head of 1794	800.	1200.	2000.	3500.	6000.	12000.	15000.	18000.	25000.	40000.
1795 3 leaves, Head of 1795	750.	1200.	1800.	3500.	5500.	11000.	13000.	17000.	25000.	35000.

Draped Bust dollar

Small Eagle

Heraldic Eagle

Date of authorization:	April 2, 1792
Dates of issue:	1795-1803
Designers:	Obverse: Gilbert Stuart-Robert Scot Reverse: (1795-1798): Scot-John Eckstein (1798-1803): Robert Scot
Engraver:	Robert Scot
Diameter:	39.50 mm/1.56 inches
Weight:	26.96 grams/0.87 ounce
Metallic Content:	89.25% silver, 10.75% copper
Weight of pure silver:	24.06 grams/0.77 ounce
Edge:	Lettered (HUNDRED CENTS ONE DOLLAR OR UNIT)
Mint mark:	None

	AG-3	G-4	VG-8	F-12	VF-20	EF-40	EF-45	AU-50	AU-55	MS-60
SMALL EAGLE										
1795	600.	1100.	1400.	2500.	4000.	8500.	9500.	12000.	15000.	25000.
1796 Small Date, Small Letters	600.	1100.	1400.	2500.	4000.	8500.	9500.	12000.	15000.	—
1796 Large Date, Small Letters	600.	1100.	1400.	2500.	4000.	8500.	9500.	12000.	18000.	—
1796 Small Date, Large Letters	600.	1100.	1400.	2500.	4000.	8500.	9500.	12000.	15000.	16000.
1797 Stars 9x7, Small Letters	900.	1500.	2500.	3500.	6000.	12000.	20000.	30000.	45000.	—
1797 Stars 9x7, Large Letters	600.	1100.	1400.	2500.	4000.	8500.	9500.	12000.	15000.	—
1797 Stars 10x6	600.	1100.	1400.	2500.	4000.	8500.	9500.	12000.	17000.	—
1798 13 Stars	600.	1100.	1400.	2500.	4000.	8500.	9500.	12000.	20000.	—
1798 15 Stars	900.	1500.	2000.	3000.	4500.	10000.	10000.	20000.	—	—
HERALDIC EAGLE										
1798	500.	800.	1000.	1400.	2500.	4000.	5000.	6500.	8500.	15000.
1799	500.	800.	1000.	1400.	2500.	4000.	5000.	6500.	8500.	15000.
1799/8	600.	1000.	1200.	1700.	3000.	4500.	5500.	7500.	10000.	15000.
1799 Stars 8x5	600.	1000.	1400.	1800.	3500.	4800.	7000.	9000.	12000.	—
1800	500.	800.	1000.	1400.	2500.	4000.	5000.	6500.	85200.	15000.
1800 AMERICAI	600.	1200.	1400.	1800.	3500.	4700.	6000.	8000.	10000.	—
1800 Dotted Date	600.	1200.	1400.	1800.	3500.	4700.	6500.	8500.	10000.	—
1801	500.	1100.	1200.	1500.	2800.	4300.	5500.	7000.	9000.	—
1801 Proof restrike, die crack links base of digits to first two stars.										
1802/1	600.	1000.	1200.	1700.	3000.	4500.	5500.	8000.	12000.	9750.
1802	500.	1100.	1200.	1500.	2800.	4300.	5500.	7000.	9000.	15000.
1802 Proof restrike with old-style 180, 1820s style 2 in date PF-65 $175000.										
1803 Large 3	600.	900.	1200.	1500.	2700.	4500.	6000.	8500.	10000.	—
1803 Small 3	500.	800.	1100.	1400.	2500.	4300.	5500.	8000.	9000.	—
1803 Proof restrike with old-style digits PF-65 $135000.										
1804 Three varieties struck in 1834-5 and 1858 Class I Childs now PF-68 (PCGS) sold for $4.14 million; Class I Eliasberg now PF-65 (PCGS) sold for $1.815 million; Class III Flannagan now PF-58 (PCGS) sold for $874,000.										

—— = Insufficient pricing data

Seated Liberty dollar

Date of authorization: Jan. 18, 1837
Dates of issue: 1840-1873
Designers: Obverse: Robert Hughes-Christian Gobrecht-Thomas Sully
Reverse: John Reich-Christian Gobrecht
Engraver: Christian Gobrecht
Diameter: 38.10 mm/1.5 inches
Weight: 26.73 grams/0.86 ounce
Metallic Content: 90% silver, 10% copper
Weight of pure silver: 24.06 grams/0.77 ounce
Edge: Reeded
Mint mark: Reverse below eagle

SEATED LIBERTY DOLLAR (CONTINUED)

	G-4	VG-8	F-12	VF-20	EF-40	AU-50	AU-55	MS-60	MS-62	MS-63	MS-64	PF-63	PF-64	PF-65	PF-66
1840	175.	200.	250.	300.	500.	750.	1250.	4000.	10000.	20000.	—	30000.	50000.	—	—
1841	175.	200.	250.	300.	500.	700.	1100.	2000.	3000.	4500.	13000.	40000.	—	—	—
1842	175.	200.	250.	300.	400.	600.	1000.	2000.	3000.	5000.	7500.	50000.	—	—	—
1843	175.	200.	250.	300.	400.	600.	1000.	2000.	4000.	6000.	15000.	45000.	—	—	—
1844	175.	250.	300.	350.	500.	1000.	2000.	3500.	5000.	8000.	—	35000.	60000.	130000.	—
1845	200.	250.	300.	350.	500.	900.	3000.	12000.	26000.	35000.	—	30000.	35000.	60000.	—
1846	175.	200.	250.	300.	400.	700.	1200.	2000.	3000.	6000.	10000.	30000.	50000.	—	—
1846-O	200.	250.	300.	400.	600.	1500.	2000.	5000.	12000.	22500.	47500.	*	*	*	*
1847	175.	200.	250.	300.	400.	700.	1000.	1500.	2500.	4500.	9000.	25000.	35000.	60000.	—
1848	250.	300.	450.	600.	1000.	1500.	2500.	5000.	7000.	10500.	—	35000.	40000.	85000.	—
1849	175.	200.	250.	350.	500.	700.	1000.	2000.	3000.	5000.	11000.	35000.	60000.	100000.	—
1850	350.	500.	600.	900.	1500.	2000.	3000.	5500.	9500.	16500.	—	30000.	35000.	45000.	—
1850-O	250.	300.	400.	750.	1800.	3500.	6000.	15000.	20000.	30000.	—	*	*	*	*
1851 Original MS-60 $27500; MS-63 $40000; MS-65 $90000; Restrike PF-62 $21500; PF-63 $25000; PF-64 $35000.															
1852 AU-55 $15000; MS-60 $20000; MS-63 $32500; MS-65 $70000; Restrike PF-55 $20500; PF-63 $32500.															
1853	175.	200.	275.	400.	600.	1000.	1500.	2500.	4000.	7000.	10000.	—	—	—	—
1854	900.	1200.	1800.	2500.	4000.	5000.	6000.	7500.	8000.	10000.	14000.	20000.	30000.	50000.	—
1855	700.	1000.	1400.	2000.	4000.	4500.	6000.	8000.	15000.	27500.	—	20000.	25000.	45000.	—
1856	300.	350.	500.	800.	1500.	2000.	3000.	4000.	5000.	8000.	—	20000.	25000.	40000.	—
1857	300.	350.	500.	800.	1500.	2000.	2000.	3000.	4000.	5500.	11000.	12000.	18000.	40000.	—
1858 Proofs only	2500.	3000.	3500.	4000.	5000.	6000.	6500.	*	*	*	*	10000.	15000.	35000.	50000.
1859	250.	300.	350.	400.	600.	1200.	1800.	3000.	4000.	6000.	14000.	5000.	9000.	18000.	35000.
1859-O	175.	200.	250.	350.	500.	600.	750.	1200.	1300.	3500.	—	*	*	*	*
1859-S	250.	350.	500.	800.	2000.	3500.	5000.	9000.	20000.	50000.	—	*	*	*	*
1860	175.	200.	250.	400.	500.	700.	1000.	1500.	2500.	3500.	8000.	4000.	7000.	18000.	25000.
1860-O	175.	200.	250.	300.	400.	600.	800.	1500.	2500.	3500.	8000.	*	*	*	*
1861	500.	650.	800.	900.	1500.	2000.	2500.	3000.	4000.	5500.	9000.	4500.	9000.	20000.	25000.

—— = Insufficient pricing data   * = None issued

SEATED LIBERTY DOLLAR (CONTINUED)

	G-4	VG-8	F-12	VF-20	EF-40	AU-50	AU-55	MS-60	MS-62	MS-63	MS-64	PF-63	PF-64	PF-65	PF-66
1862	500.	650.	750.	900.	1500.	2000.	2500.	3200.	4500.	6500.	14000.	4000.	8500.	20000.	—
1863	200.	300.	400.	500.	800.	1500.	2000.	3000.	4000.	5000.	14000.	4000.	8000.	18000.	35000.
1864	200.	250.	350.	500.	800.	1500.	2000.	3000.	4500.	6000.	14000.	4000.	7500.	15000.	25000.
1865	200.	250.	300.	400.	800.	1500.	2000.	3000.	4500.	6000.	10000.	4000.	7500.	15000.	35000.
1866	—	—	—	—	—	—	—	—	—	—	—	—	—	—	—
MOTTO ABOVE EAGLE															
1866	175.	250.	300.	400.	500.	1000.	1500.	2000.	3000.	5000.	9000.	5000.	10000.	20000.	35000.
1867	175.	225.	300.	400.	650.	1000.	1400.	2000.	3000.	5000.	12000.	4000.	7500.	15000.	35000.
1868	175.	200.	250.	350.	600.	1000.	1400.	2000.	3500.	7500.	15000.	4000.	7500.	15000.	25000.
1869	175.	200.	250.	300.	400.	900.	1200.	1600.	2500.	4500.	10000.	4000.	7000.	15000.	25000.
1870	175.	200.	250.	300.	400.	800.	1000.	1500.	2500.	4000.	9000.	4000.	7000.	15000.	25000.
1870-CC	300.	400.	500.	800.	1500.	3500.	6000.	12000.	25000.	35000.	—	*	*	*	*
1870-S	—	—	60000.	82500.	125000.	200000.	—	300000.	—	600000.	—	*	*	*	*
1871	175.	200.	250.	300.	400.	600.	800.	1200.	2000.	3500.	7500.	4000.	7000.	15000.	25000.
1871-CC	1650.	2800.	4000.	5000.	9000.	20000.	30000.	90000.	—	125000.	—	*	*	*	*
1872	175.	200.	250.	300.	400.	600.	800.	1200.	2000.	3500.	7500.	4000.	7000.	15000.	25000.
1872-CC	800.	1200.	2000.	3000.	5000.	10000.	15000.	30000.	40000.	62500.	—	*	*	*	*
1872-S	225.	300.	400.	700.	2000.	4000.	6500.	10000.	15000.	30000.	50000.	*	*	*	*
1873	175.	200.	250.	300.	400.	700.	1000.	1500.	2000.	3500.	7500.	4000.	7000.	15000.	25000.
1873-CC	4000.	5000.	7000.	10000.	20000.	35000.	45000.	75000.	—	—	—	*	*	*	*
1873-S Unknown in any collection.															

—— = Insufficient pricing data   * = None issued

Trade dollar

Date of authorization:	Feb. 12, 1873
Dates of issue:	1873-1885
Designer/Engraver:	William Barber
Diameter:	38.10 mm/1.5 inches
Weight:	27.22 grams/0.88 ounce
Metallic Content:	90% silver, 10% copper
Weight of pure silver:	24.49 grams/0.79 ounce
Edge:	Reeded
Mint mark:	Reverse below eagle

—— = Insufficient pricing data * = None issued

TRADE DOLLAR (CONTINUED)

	G-4	VG-8	F-12	VF-20	EF-40	AU-50	AU-55	MS-60	MS-62	MS-63	MS-64	MS-65	PF-63	PF-64	PF-65	PF-66
1873	70.	85.	100.	150.	250.	350.	450.	1000.	1250.	1600.	4000.	9000.	3500.	6000.	11000.	18000.
1873-CC	75.	100.	175.	300.	600.	1500.	2000.	5000.	12000.	—	—	—	*	*	*	*
1873-S	70.	80.	125.	150.	200.	350.	500.	1000.	2000.	3000.	8000.	13000.	*	*	*	*
1874	70.	80.	125.	150.	250.	350.	450.	650.	1000.	1800.	4000.	12500.	3500.	6500.	11000.	18000.
1874-CC	75.	90.	110.	200.	300.	500.	700.	1500.	3000.	6000.	9000.	18000.	*	*	*	*
1874-S	70.	80.	100.	150.	200.	350.	450.	700.	1000.	2000.	5000.	15000.	*	*	*	*
1875	90.	135.	300.	400.	600.	750.	1000.	1500.	2500.	3000.	4500.	13000.	4000.	9000.	13000.	18000.
1875-CC	75.	100.	125.	175.	250.	350.	500.	1000.	2500.	3300.	10000.	—	*	*	*	*
1875-S	70.	100.	150.	175.	200.	300.	400.	700.	1200.	1800.	3500.	8500.	*	*	*	*
1875-S/CC	135.	200.	300.	400.	800.	1400.	1800.	2700.	4000.	10000.	20000.	50000.	*	*	*	*
1876	70.	80.	100.	135.	175.	250.	300.	500.	1500.	2000.	3500.	10000.	4000.	6000.	15000.	18000.
1876-CC	75.	90.	110.	175.	400.	1200.	1800.	5000.	12000.	20000.	35000.	—	*	*	*	*
1876-S	70.	80.	100.	125.	150.	300.	400.	700.	1000.	1400.	4000.	9000.	*	*	*	*
1877	70.	90.	120.	150.	200.	300.	350.	700.	900.	1700.	6000.	15000.	4000.	6500.	15000.	18000.
1877-CC	85.	125.	200.	275.	500.	700.	1000.	1800.	5000.	7500.	25000.	—	*	*	*	*
1877-S	70.	90.	100.	125.	200.	350.	450.	800.	900.	1400.	3000.	8500.	*	*	*	*
1878 Proof	550.	700.	800.	900.	1000.	1200.	1500.	*	*	*	*	*	3500.	6500.	14000.	17000.
1878-CC	250.	350.	600.	1200.	2500.	3500.	5000.	8500.	12000.	20000.	35000.	—	*	*	*	*
1878-S	70.	80.	100.	125.	200.	300.	400.	500.	1200.	2000.	3000.	8000.	*	*	*	*
1879	550.	600.	700.	800.	1000.	1100.	1400.	*	*	*	*	*	3500.	5000.	11000.	15000.
1880	550.	600.	700.	800.	1000.	1100.	1400.	*	*	*	*	*	3500.	5000.	11000.	15000.
1881	550.	600.	700.	900.	1100.	1200.	1500.	*	*	*	*	*	3500.	5000.	12000.	15000.
1882	550.	600.	700.	900.	1100.	1200.	1500.	*	*	*	*	*	3500.	5000.	11000.	14000.
1883	550.	600.	700.	900.	1100.	1200.	1500.	*	*	*	*	*	3500.	6000.	11000.	15000.
1884	*	*	*	*	*	*	*	*	*	*	*	*	125000.	265000.	400000.	—
1885	*	*	*	*	*	*	*	*	*	*	*	*	325000.	450000.	900000.	1500000.

—— = Insufficient pricing data * = None issued

Morgan dollar

Date of authorization:	Feb. 28, 1878
Dates of issue:	1878-1921
Designer/Engraver:	George T. Morgan
Diameter:	38.10 mm/1.5 inches
Weight:	26.73 grams/0.86 ounce
Metallic Content:	90% silver, 10% copper
Weight of pure silver:	24.06 grams/0.77 ounce
Edge:	Reeded
Mint mark:	Reverse below eagle

Note: MS-63D, MS-64D, MS-65D refer to Deep Mirror Prooflike

MORGAN DOLLAR (CONTINUED)

	G-4	VG-8	F-12	VF-20	EF-40	AU-50	AU-58	MS-60	MS-62	MS-63	MS-63D	MS-64	MS-64D	MS-65	MS-65D	MS-66	PF-63	PF-64	PF-65	PF-66
1878 8 Tail Feathers	20.	23.	25.	28.	32.	45.	65.	125.	150.	200.	375.	450.	2500.	1400.	7000.	14000.	2000.	3500.	5500.	20000.
1878 7 Tail Feathers, Reverse of 1878	14.	18.	20.	22.	25.	35.	40.	60.	75.	125.	200.	300.	600.	1600.	6500.	10000.	3500.	5000.	15000.	25000.
1878 7 Tail Feathers, Reverse of 1879	14.	18.	20.	22.	25.	35.	40.	75.	125.	200.	800.	600.	3000.	3200.	8500.	—	—	—	—	—
1878 Strongly Doubled Tail Feathers	15.	20.	22.	30.	35.	55.	75.	150.	225.	400.	550.	550.	4000.	3500.	15000.	20000.	*	*	*	*
1878-CC	70.	90.	100.	110.	125.	135.	175.	250.	300.	450.	500.	650.	1000.	2200.	5000.	5000.	*	*	*	*
1878-S	15.	18.	20.	22.	25.	35.	40.	50.	60.	75.	175.	125.	700.	300.	4000.	1100.	*	*	*	*
1878-S Long Nock	75.	100.	125.	250.	450.	750.	1000.	1500.	—	—	—	—	—	—	—	—	*	*	*	*
1879	12.	15.	16.	18.	20.	22.	25.	35.	50.	75.	275.	150.	1700.	1300.	8000.	5500.	2000.	3000.	8000.	11000.
1879-CC	75.	100.	110.	200.	650.	1300.	1800.	2800.	4000.	7500.	8000.	11000.	15000.	25000.	—	—	*	*	*	*
1879-CC Large CC/Small CC	75.	100.	110.	175.	450.	1100.	1700.	2700.	3500.	6500.	8500.	9000.	18000.	45000.	—	—	*	*	*	*
1879-O	12.	15.	18.	20.	22.	25.	45.	85.	125.	225.	1200.	550.	3000.	4000.	18000.	—	*	*	*	*
1879-S Reverse of 1878	12.	15.	18.	20.	22.	35.	45.	90.	175.	400.	4000.	1500.	8500.	8000.	25000.	—	*	*	*	*
1879-S	12.	15.	16.	18.	20.	25.	30.	40.	45.	50.	100.	65.	275.	175.	750.	450.	*	*	*	*
1880	12.	15.	16.	18.	20.	22.	25.	35.	45.	60.	275.	140.	1200.	900.	4000.	7000.	2000.	3000.	5000.	15000.
1880/79-CC Reverse of 1878	75.	100.	125.	150.	200.	275.	350.	500.	600.	700.	1200.	1200.	5000.	3000.	13000.	8000.	*	*	*	*
1880-CC	85.	125.	175.	200.	250.	350.	400.	500.	525.	575.	600.	900.	1200.	1800.	5000.	4000.	*	*	*	*
1880-O	12.	15.	16.	17.	18.	20.	30.	75.	150.	375.	1600.	2000.	6500.	25000.	65000.	—	*	*	*	*
1880-S	12.	15.	16.	17.	18.	20.	24.	35.	40.	50.	90.	65.	275.	200.	600.	450.	*	*	*	*
1881	12.	15.	16.	17.	18.	20.	24.	35.	45.	60.	550.	175.	1700.	1000.	14000.	4500.	2000.	5500.	6500.	10000.
1881-CC	225.	300.	325.	350.	375.	400.	450.	500.	525.	550.	600.	600.	1000.	900.	2500.	1500.	*	*	*	*
1881-O	12.	15.	16.	17.	18.	20.	24.	35.	40.	50.	200.	175.	1100.	1800.	16000.	—	*	*	*	*

—— = Insufficient pricing data   * = None issued

	G-4	VG-8	F-12	VF-20	EF-40	AU-50	AU-58	MS-60	MS-62	MS-63	MS-63D	MS-64	MS-64D	MS-65	MS-65D	MS-66	PF-63	PF-64	PF-65	PF-66
1881-S	12.	15.	16.	17.	18.	20.	21.	35.	40.	50.	90.	65.	275.	175.	600.	450.	*	*	*	*
1882	12.	15.	16.	17.	18.	20.	23.	35.	40.	50.	300.	65.	600.	475.	5000.	2000.	2000.	3000.	5000.	9000.
1882-CC	65.	90.	100.	110.	125.	135.	175.	225.	250.	275.	400.	300.	500.	550	1400.	1800.	*	*	*	*
1882-O	12.	15.	16.	17.	18.	20.	24.	35.	40.	50.	200.	75.	1000.	900	4500.	7000.	*	*	*	*
1882-O/S	12.	15.	16.	17.	20.	50.	90.	250.	500.	1400.	—	4500.	—	—	—	—	*	*	*	*
1882-S	12.	15.	16.	17.	18.	20.	23.	35.	40.	50.	200.	65.	400.	175.	1500.	450.	*	*	*	*
1883	12.	15.	16.	17.	18.	20.	22.	35.	40.	50.	125.	65.	275.	200.	1000.	450.	2000.	3000.	5000.	8000.
1883-CC	65.	85.	100.	110.	125.	135.	165.	210.	225.	250.	300.	300.	400.	425.	1100.	1000.	*	*	*	*
1883-O	12.	15.	16.	17.	18.	20.	21.	35.	40.	50.	90.	65.	275.	175.	700.	450.	—	35000.	—	—
1883-S	12.	16.	20.	25.	50.	200.	425.	600.	1500.	3000.	15000.	5000.	—	23000.	—	—	*	*	*	*
1884	12.	15.	16.	17.	18.	20.	22.	30.	35.	50.	200.	55.	900.	325.	3000.	1100.	2000.	3000.	5000.	9000.
1884-CC	65.	85.	100.	110.	125.	135.	165.	210.	225.	250.	300.	275.	400.	425.	1100.	1000.	*	*	*	*
1884-O	12.	15.	16.	17.	18.	20.	25.	35.	40.	50.	90.	55.	275.	175.	800.	450.	*	*	*	*
1884-S	12.	15.	17.	20.	50.	350.	1500.	5000.	10000.	25000.	—	—	—	—	—	—	*	*	*	*
1885	12.	15.	16.	17.	18.	20.	22.	35.	40.	50.	100.	65.	275.	175.	800.	450.	2000.	3000.	6500.	10000.
1885-CC	300.	375.	400.	425.	450.	475.	500.	525.	550.	575.	600.	800.	900.	1400.	2300.	2500.	*	*	*	*
1885-O	12.	15.	16.	17.	18.	20.	25.	35.	40.	50.	90.	65.	275.	175.	750.	450.	*	*	*	*
1885-S	15.	18.	20.	25.	35.	75.	100.	200.	225.	275.	2000.	700.	5500.	2200.	—	5500.	*	*	*	*
1886	12.	15.	15.	17.	18.	20.	25.	35.	40.	50.	90.	65.	275.	175.	700.	500.	2000.	3000.	5000.	12000.
1886-O	12.	15.	13.	20.	25.	85.	150.	600.	1500.	4500.	12000.	9000.	50000.	—	—	—	*	*	*	*
1886-S	20.	30.	40.	50.	60.	85.	125.	300.	350.	450.	1400.	750.	4500.	3500.	—	7500.	*	*	*	*
1887/6	15.	20.	25.	30.	50.	110.	135.	300.	450.	750.	4000.	1200.	6000.	4500.	20000.	—	*	*	*	*
1887/6-O	15.	20.	25.	35.	60.	135.	200.	400.	1000.	3000.	15000	12500.	—	30000.	—	—	*	*	*	*
1887-O	12.	15.	18.	20.	23.	25.	35.	65.	85.	125.	400	450.	2500.	5000.	9000.	—	*	*	*	*
1887-S	13.	17.	18.	20.	25.	45.	65.	100.	175.	300.	1200	800.	3500.	4500.	—	11500.	*	*	*	*

—— = Insufficient pricing data * = None issued

MORGAN DOLLAR (CONTINUED)

	G-4	VG-8	F-12	VF-20	EF-40	AU-50	AU-58	MS-60	MS-62	MS-63	MS-63D	MS-64	MS-64D	MS-65	MS-65D	MS-66	PF-63	PF-64	PF-65	PF-66
1887	12.	15.	16.	17.	20.	22.	25.	35.	40.	50.	90.	65.	275.	175.	700.	450.	2400.	3000.	5000.	8500.
1888	12.	15.	16.	17.	18.	20.	25.	35.	40.	50.	225.	65.	400.	275.	2300.	800.	2000.	3000.	5000.	9000.
1888-O	12.	15.	16.	17.	20.	22.	25.	35.	40.	50.	200.	65.	400.	500.	2000.	3500.	*	*	*	*
1888-O "Hot Lips," VAM-4	—	—	40.	50.	115.	525.	—	—	—	—	—	—	—	—	—	—	*	*	*	*
1888-S	35.	50.	80.	90.	100.	110.	150.	275.	325.	450.	600.	900.	2500.	4000.	10000.	12500.	*	*	*	*
1889	12.	15.	16.	17.	18.	20.	25.	35.	40.	50.	250.	65.	800.	375.	3500.	2800.	2000.	3000.	6500.	8000.
1889-CC	400.	650.	1200.	2000.	3500.	6000.	7500.	18000.	23000.	30000.	30000.	50000.	65000.	—	300000.	—	*	*	*	*
1889-O	12.	15.	16.	17.	20.	35.	50.	175.	250.	500.	1200.	1000.	4500.	6000.	15000.	18000.	*	*	*	*
1889-S	25.	35.	45.	50.	60.	70.	125.	225.	275.	450.	1200.	600.	3500.	2100.	9000.	5500.	*	*	*	*
1890	12.	15.	16.	17.	18.	20.	25.	35.	40.	50.	400.	135.	2500.	3000.	13000.	13000.	2000.	3000.	5000.	8000.
1890-CC	75.	100.	110.	120.	160.	200.	250.	375.	500.	900.	1000.	2500.	3000.	7000.	13000.	25000.	*	*	*	*
1890-O	12.	15.	16.	17.	20.	25.	35.	60.	85.	125.	250.	350.	1700.	2100.	8500.	9000.	*	*	*	*
1890-S	12.	15.	16.	17.	18.	21.	25.	60.	85.	125.	500.	325.	1400.	1200.	9000.	3500.	*	*	*	*
1891	12.	15.	16.	17.	18.	23.	30.	60.	100.	175.	1500.	600.	6000.	7500.	—	16000.	2000.	3500.	5000.	9000.
1891-CC	75.	100.	110.	120.	160.	200.	250.	375.	500.	900.	1000.	1400.	4000.	5000.	25000.	9500.	*	*	*	*
1891-O	12.	15.	16.	18.	20.	35.	50.	175.	250.	350.	2800.	750.	6000.	10000.	25000.	—	*	*	*	*
1891-S	12.	15.	16.	18.	20.	25.	30.	65.	90.	140.	450.	275.	1400.	1500.	9500.	4500.	*	*	*	*
1892	14.	18.	20.	25.	35.	80.	100.	200.	300.	450.	1400.	1100.	3500.	4000.	18000.	—	2000.	3000.	6500.	20000.
1892-CC	85.	110.	125.	125.	375.	500.	600.	900.	1400.	2200.	2000.	3000.	6000.	11000.	30000.	28000.	*	*	*	*
1892-O	12.	15.	20.	22.	35.	65.	90.	200.	250.	350.	6500.	800.	7500.	6300.	—	—	*	*	*	*
1892-S	15.	20.	25.	50.	250.	2000.	6000.	35000.	40000.	55000.	75000.	90000.	100000.	165000.	185000.	200000.	*	*	*	*
1893	75.	125.	150.	160.	200.	250.	400.	700.	900.	1300.	13000.	2000.	—	7500.	—	—	2000.	3000.	6000.	18000.
1893-CC	175.	200.	275.	400.	1600.	2000.	2700.	3200.	3500.	7500.	17000.	14000.	35000.	50000.	90000.	—	*	*	*	*
1893-O	85.	175.	140.	175.	275.	650.	900.	2000.	3500.	6500.	12000.	22000.	50000.	—	—	—	*	*	*	*

—— = Insufficient pricing data * = None issued

MORGAN DOLLAR (CONTINUED)

	G-4	VG-8	F-12	VF-20	EF-40	AU-50	AU-58	MS-60	MS-62	MS-63	MS-63D	MS-64	MS-64D	MS-65	MS-65D	MS-66	PF-63	PF-64	PF-65	PF-66
1893-S	1500.	2500.	3500.	5000.	8500.	22000.	30000.	70000.	80000.	100000.	—	225000.	—	375000.	—	—	*	*	*	*
1894	700.	1100.	1200.	1400.	1800.	2500.	2700.	3500.	4500.	6000.	13000.	7500.	—	25000.	—	45000.	2500.	3000.	5000.	10000.
1894-O	25.	40.	45.	60.	100.	275.	400.	750.	1500.	3500.	12000.	8000.	—	50000.	—	—	*	*	*	*
1894-S	25.	35.	50.	75.	125.	500.	550.	600.	700.	1200.	4000.	2000.	11000.	5500.	22000.	13000.	*	*	*	*
1895 Proof only	15000.	22000.	28000.	30000.	33000.	38000.	42000.	*	*	*	*	*	*	*	*	*	50000.	55000.	65000.	70000.
1895-O	125.	250.	275.	350.	425.	1500.	5000.	15000.	20000.	40000.	—	90000.	—	200000.	—	—	*	*	*	*
1895-S	150.	200.	300.	350.	500.	1700.	2000.	2400.	3500.	5000.	7000.	7000.	12000.	20000.	45000.	—	*	*	*	*
1896	12.	15.	16.	17.	18.	20.	25.	35.	40.	50.	100.	75.	275.	225.	1400.	800.	2000.	3500.	5000.	11000.
1896-O	12.	15.	16.	17.	25.	200.	350.	1200.	3000.	7500.	15000.	50000.	—	175000.	—	—	*	*	*	*
1896-S	16.	20.	30.	50.	175.	550.	800.	1300.	1500.	2500.	17000.	3500.	11500.	17000.	20000.	—	*	*	*	*
1897	12.	15.	16.	17.	18.	20.	23.	35.	40.	50.	135.	65.	400.	275.	3000.	1500.	2000.	3000.	5000.	11000.
1897-O	12.	15.	18.	20.	25.	125.	200.	750.	2500.	5500.	20000.	16000.	35000.	50000.	60000.	70000.	*	*	*	*
1897-S	12.	15.	18.	20.	23.	25.	32.	60.	85.	125.	275.	200.	350.	800.	2300.	1800.	*	*	*	*
1898	12.	15.	16.	18.	20.	22.	25.	35.	40.	50.	175.	65.	300.	275.	1300.	1650.	2000.	3000.	5000.	10000.
1898-O	12.	15.	16.	17.	18.	20.	23.	35.	40.	50.	100.	65.	275.	175.	700.	450.	*	*	*	*
1898-S	12.	15.	18.	20.	30.	75.	125.	300.	350.	500.	800.	1000.	3000.	2500.	13000.	—	*	*	*	*
1899	20.	30.	45.	50.	60.	85.	100.	125.	175.	275.	350.	400.	800.	1000.	2800.	2200.	2000.	3500.	5000.	10000.
1899-O	12.	15.	16.	17.	18.	20.	23.	35.	40.	50.	135.	65.	350.	175.	1100.	450.	*	*	*	*
1899-S	15.	18.	20.	25.	40.	100.	150.	350.	400.	500.	800.	900.	3000.	2400.	9000.	3300.	*	*	*	*
1900	12.	15.	16.	17.	18.	20.	23.	35.	40.	50.	1800.	65.	5000.	225.	12000.	900.	2000.	3000.	5000.	9000.
1900-O	12.	15.	16.	17.	20.	25.	28.	40.	45.	50.	500.	55.	800.	175.	3500.	750.	*	*	*	*
1900-O/CC	17.	25.	30.	40.	60.	135.	200.	300.	400.	800.	6500.	1200.	10000.	2700.	—	6500.	*	*	*	*
1900-S	14.	18.	20.	23.	40.	100.	125.	275.	300.	425.	3000.	550.	6000.	1800.	10000.	4500.	*	*	*	*
1901	16.	20.	25.	35.	85.	400.	1000.	2500.	5000.	17000.	—	60000.	—	—	—	—	2500.	3500.	5500.	10000.

—— = Insufficient pricing data   * = None issued

MORGAN DOLLAR (CONTINUED)

	G-4	VG-8	F-12	VF-20	EF-40	AU-50	AU-58	MS-60	MS-62	MS-63	MS-63D	MS-64	MS-64D	MS-65	MS-65D	MS-66	PF-63	PF-64	PF-65	PF-66
1901 "Shifted Eagle," VAM-3	—	—	60.	140.	300.	600.	1500.	2500.	—	—	—	—	—	—	—	—	*	*	*	*
1901-O	12.	15.	16.	17.	20.	23.	25.	35.	40.	50.	300.	70.	800.	250.	6500.	1500.	*	*	*	*
1901-S	12.	17.	25.	35.	50.	200.	250.	350.	450.	750.	5000.	1000.	9000.	4000.	—	13000.	*	*	*	*
1902	12.	16.	18.	20.	22.	25.	30.	50.	65.	120.	2200.	150.	10000.	550.	18000.	1500.	2000.	3000.	6500.	10000.
1902-O	12.	15.	18.	20.	23.	25.	27.	35.	40.	50.	400.	65.	550.	175.	8500.	800.	*	*	*	*
1902-S	20.	35.	50.	100.	125.	275.	300.	375.	500.	700.	3500.	1100.	—	3500.	—	8500.	*	*	*	*
1903	35.	45.	50.	55.	60.	65.	70.	75.	80.	85.	1400.	100.	2500.	325.	9500.	750.	2000.	3000.	5000.	9000.
1903-O	175.	225.	250.	300.	350.	375.	400.	425.	450.	475.	550.	550.	1300.	750.	5000.	1100.	*	*	*	*
1903-S	35.	45.	50.	125.	300.	1800.	2300.	3700.	4200.	5500.	12000.	7000.	—	8000.	—	16000.	*	*	*	*
1904	12.	16.	18.	20.	25.	35.	40.	100.	150.	275.	7500.	700.	—	4500.	—	9000.	2000.	3000.	5500.	15000.
1904-O	12.	15.	18.	20.	23.	30.	32.	35.	40.	50.	100.	75.	275.	175.	750.	450.	*	*	*	*
1904-S	15.	20.	30.	80.	250.	600.	700.	1400.	1800.	2800.	5500.	3500.	7000.	7500.	20000.	23000.	*	*	*	*
1921	10.	12.	13.	14.	15.	16.	18.	25.	30.	40.	2200.	50.	6500.	150.	13000.	1200.	3500.	5000.	10000.	30000.
1921-D	10.	12.	13.	14.	15.	16.	25.	45.	55.	70.	1700.	150.	4500.	350.	—	1400.	*	*	*	*
1921-S	10.	12.	13.	14.	15.	16.	20.	35.	50.	75.	4000.	200.	13000.	1700.	—	13000.	*	*	*	*

—— = Insufficient pricing data   * = None issued

Peace dollar

Date of authorization:	Feb. 28, 1878
Dates of issue:	1921-1935
Designer:	Anthony deFrancisci
Engraver:	George T. Morgan
Diameter:	38.10 mm/1.5 Inches
Weight:	26.73 grams/0.86 ounce
Metallic Content:	90% silver, 10% copper
Weight of pure silver:	24.06grams/0.77 ounce
Edge:	Reeded
Mint mark:	Reverse at lower tip of eagle's wing

PEACE DOLLAR (CONTINUED)

	VG-8	F-12	VF-20	EF-40	AU-50	AU-58	MS-60	MS-62	MS-63	MS-64	MS-65	MS-66
1921	70.	80.	90.	110.	125.	150.	225.	300.	400.	750.	2500.	8000.
1922	12.	14.	16.	18.	20.	22.	25.	27.	30.	50.	200.	800.
1922-D	12.	14.	16.	18.	20.	22.	28.	35.	50.	125.	450.	2300.
1922-S	12.	14.	16.	18.	20.	22.	25.	50.	85.	350.	2500.	12000.
1923	12.	14.	16.	18.	20.	22.	25.	27.	30.	50.	200.	8000.
1923-D	12.	14.	16.	18.	25.	35.	60.	90.	140.	300.	1400.	7000.
1923-S	12.	14.	16.	18.	20.	24.	30.	50.	75.	300.	7500.	17000.
1924	12.	14.	16.	18.	20.	22.	25.	30.	35.	60.	200.	800.
1924-S	15.	20.	25.	30.	60.	100.	225.	350.	500.	1200.	9000.	45000.
1925	12.	14.	16.	18.	20.	22.	25.	30.	35.	60.	200.	800.
1925-S	15.	17.	20.	23.	40.	55.	75.	100.	175.	750.	20000.	30000.
1926	15.	17.	20.	23.	25.	30.	40.	50.	70.	100.	450.	2300.
1926-D	15.	17.	20.	23.	35.	45.	70.	100.	150.	300.	800.	2500.
1926-S	15.	17.	20.	23.	25.	30.	45.	65.	100.	300.	1200.	6000.
1927	20.	25.	30.	35.	50.	60.	85.	110.	175.	350.	2500.	20000.
1927-D	20.	25.	28.	35.	85.	125.	175.	250.	350.	750.	6500.	22000.
1927-S	20.	25.	28.	35.	75.	125.	175.	250.	350.	1000.	14000.	45000.
1928	350.	400.	425.	450.	475.	500.	525.	550.	650.	1000.	5000.	15000.
1928-S	22.	28.	30.	35.	55.	85.	175.	300.	600.	2000.	23000.	30000.
1934	20.	25.	28.	30.	45.	75.	110.	135.	200.	350.	1200.	4500.
1934-D	20.	25.	28.	30.	45.	60.	100.	175.	350.	600.	2000.	6000.
1934-S	20.	25.	65.	200.	600.	1000.	2000.	2500.	3500.	5000.	7500.	20000.
1935	18.	20.	22.	25.	35.	50.	70.	80.	110.	250.	750.	2200.
1935-S	18.	20.	22.	30.	100.	150.	250.	300.	400.	600.	1400.	3500.

—— = Insufficient pricing data   * = None issued

Eisenhower dollar

Date of authorization:	Dec. 31, 1970; Oct. 18, 1973
Dates of issue:	1971-1978
Designers:	Frank Gasparro (Bicentennial Reverse): Dennis R. Williams
Engraver:	Frank Gasparro
Diameter:	38.10 mm/1.5 inches
Weight:	(1971-1978): 22.68 grams/0.73 ounce (1971-1976 Bicentennial Proof and Uncirculated sets only): 24.59 grams/0.79 ounce
Metallic Content:	(1971-1978): 75% copper, 25% nickel bonded to a core of pure copper (1971-1976 Bicentennial Proof and Uncirculated sets only): 80% silver, 20% copper, bonded to a core of 21.5% silver, 78.5% copper
Weight of pure silver:	(1971-1976 Bicentennial Proof and Uncirculated sets only): 9.84 grams/0.32 ounce
Edge:	Reeded
Mint mark:	Obverse above date

EISENHOWER DOLLAR (CONTINUED)

	MS-63	MS-64	MS-65	MS-66	MS-67	PF-64	PF-65	PF-65C	PF-65DC	PF-66	PF-66C	PF-66DC	PF-67	PF-67C	PF-67DC	PF-68	PF-68C	PF-68DC	PF-69DC
MOON LANDING REVERSE																			
1971	14.	60.	300.	650.	—	*	*	*	*	*	*	*	*	*	*	*	*	*	*
1971-D	8.00	17.	75.	170.	350.	*	*	*	*	*	*	*	*	*	*	*	*	*	*
1971-S 40% silver	8.50	20.	30.	60.	525.	12.	20.	22.	25.	30.	35.	40.	40.	45.	50.	45.	50.	55.	75.
1972	10.	20.	150.	—	—	*	*	*	*	*	*	*	*	*	*	*	*	*	*
1972 High Relief Earth	20.	45.	385.	—	—	*	*	*	*	*	*	*	*	*	*	*	*	*	*
1972-D	8.00	17.	75.	435.	650.	*	*	*	*	*	*	*	*	*	*	*	*	*	*
1972-S 40% silver	6.00	8.00	28.	45.	65.	15.	25.	30.	35.	45.	50.	55.	55.	60.	65.	60.	65.	70.	85.
1973	10.	28.	120.	735.	—	*	*	*	*	*	*	*	*	*	*	*	*	*	*
1973-D	10.	17.	80.	275.	—	*	*	*	*	*	*	*	*	*	*	*	*	*	*
1973-S copper-nickel clad (Proof Only)	*	*	*	*	*	10.	14.	17.	25.	20.	25.	30.	35.	40.	45.	45.	47.	50.	165.
1973-S 40% silver	10.	12.	27.	45.	80.	22.	25.	27.	30.	27.	30.	35.	30.	32.	38.	32.	35.	40.	100.
1974	8.00	28.	100.	200.	350.	*	*	*	*	*	*	*	*	*	*	*	*	*	*
1974-D	10.	18.	60.	250.	400.	*	*	*	*	*	*	*	*	*	*	*	*	*	*
1974-S copper-nickel clad (Proof Only)	*	*	*	*	*	8.00	9.00	10.	12.	10.	12.	15.	20.	22.	25.	30.	35.	50.	155.
1974-S 40% silver	8.00	10.	17.	40.	80.	7.00	8.00	9.00	10.	10.	12.	15.	20.	22.	25.	25.	30.	35.	85.
DUAL DATE, BICENTENNIAL REVERSE																			
1776-1976 Bold Reverse Letters	10.	30.	245.	—	—	*	*	*	*	*	*	*	*	*	*	*	*	*	*
1776-1976 Thin Reverse Letters	6.00	25.	85.	240.	—	*	*	*	*	*	*	*	*	*	*	*	*	*	*
1776-1976-D Bold Reverse Letters	9.00	20.	150.	475.	—	*	*	*	*	*	*	*	*	*	*	*	*	*	*
1776-1976-D Thin Reverse Letters	7.00	25.	35.	125.	1525.	*	*	*	*	*	*	*	*	*	*	*	*	*	*

—— = Insufficient pricing data * = None issued

EISENHOWER DOLLAR (CONTINUED)

	MS-63	MS-64	MS-65	MS-66	MS-67	PF-64	PF-65	PF-65C	PF-65DC	PF-66	PF-66C	PF-66DC	PF-67	PF-67C	PF-67DC	PF-68	PF-68C	PF-68DC	PF-69DC
1776-1976-S Bold Reverse Letters, copper-nickel clad (Proof Only)	*	*	*	*	*	9.00	12.	15.	20.	15.	20	25.	25.	30.	35.	30.	35.	40.	300.
1776-1976-S Thin Reverse Letters, copper-nickel clad (Proof Only) *	*	*	*	*	7.00	8.00	9.00	10.	10.	12.	15	20.	22.	25.	25.	30.	35.	200.	
1776-1976-S 40% silver	10.	20.	25.	40.	85.	15.	17.	20.	27.	21.	25	35.	25.	30.	40.	30.	35.	50.	200.
MOON LANDING REVERSE																			
1977	9.50	20.	70.	300.	—	*	*	*	*	*	*	*	*	*	*	*	*	*	*
1977-D	10.	16.	50.	230.	—	*	*	*	*	*	*	*	*	*	*	*	*	*	*
1977-S copper-nickel clad (Proof Only)	*	*	*	*	*	8.00	10.	12.	15.	15.	17	20.	15.	18.	25.	22.	25.	30.	75.
1978	6.00	25.	60.	290.	4350.	*	*	*	*	*	*	*	*	*	*	*	*	*	*
1978-D	6.00	15.	90.	320.	—	*	*	*	*	*	*	*	*	*	*	*	*	*	*
1978-S copper-nickel clad (Proof Only)	*	*	*	*	*	9.00	10.	12.	15.	15.	17	20.	15.	18.	25.	22.	25.	30.	70.

Bicentennial date, reverse

—— = Insufficient pricing data   * = None issued

Anthony dollar

Date of authorization:	Oct. 10, 1978
Dates of issue:	1979-1981, 1999
Designer/Engraver:	Frank Gasparro
Diameter:	26.50 mm/1.05 inches
Weight:	8.10 grams/0.26 ounce
Metallic Content:	75% copper, 25% nickel bonded to a core of pure copper
Edge:	Reeded
Mint mark:	Obverse left of bust

	MS-65	MS-66	MS-67	PF-65DC	PF-66DC	PF-67DC	PF-68DC	PF-69DC	PF-70DC
1979-P Near Date	100.	190.	—	*	*	*	*	*	*
1979-P	12.	27.	35.	*	*	*	*	*	*
1979-D	16.	30.	50.	*	*	*	*	*	*
1979-S	8.00	38.	—	10.	15.	20.	25.	85.	325.
1979-S Clear S	*	*	*	90.	110.	160.	170.	225.	835.
1980-P	12.	60.	—	*	*	*	*	*	*
1980-D	12.	43.	70.	*	*	*	*	*	*
1980-S	25.	60.	265.	10.	15.	20.	25.	35.	350.
1981-P	75.	140.	—	*	*	*	*	*	*
1981-D	30.	55.	475.	*	*	*	*	*	*
1981-S Filled S	42.	225.	525.	10.	15.	20.	25.	40.	425.
1981-S Clear S	*	*	*	125.	150.	175.	200.	325.	1700.
1999-P	5.00	7.00	16.	10.	20.	30.	40.	50.	175.
1999-D	5.00	11.	18.	*	*	*	*	*	*

—— = Insufficient pricing data * = None issued

Sacagawea dollar

Date of authorization:	Dec. 1, 1997
Dates of issue:	2000-present
Designer/Engraver:	Obverse: Glenna Goodacre Reverse: Thomas Rogers
Diameter:	26.50 mm/1.05 inches
Weight:	8.1 grams/0.20 ounce
Metallic Content:	77% copper, 12% zinc, 7% manganese, 4% nickel, bonded to a core of pure copper
Edge:	Plain
Mint mark:	Obverse below date

	MS-64	MS-65	MS-66	MS-67	MS-68	PF-66DC	PF-67DC	PF-68DC	PF-69DC
2000-P	2.00	5.00	10.	20.	75.	*	*	*	*
2000-D	3.00	12.	15.	25.	235.	*	*	*	*
2000-S	*	*	*	*	*	10.	15.	20.	40.
2001-P	2.00	4.00	6.00	17.	60.	*	*	*	*
2001-D	2.00	7.00	15.	170.	—	*	*	*	*
2001-S	*	*	*	*	*	10.	15.	20.	40.
2002-P	2.00	5.00	8.00	36.	100.	*	*	*	*
2002-D	2.00	5.00	9.00	60.	—	*	*	*	*
2002-S	*	*	*	*	*	10.	15.	20.	40.
2003-P	2.00	5.00	8.00	36.	100.	*	*	*	*
2003-D	2.00	5.00	9.00	60.	*	*	*	*	*
2003-S	*	*	*	*	*	10.	15.	20.	40.
2004-P	2.00	5.00	8.00	36.	100.	*	*	*	*
2004-D	2.00	5.00	9.00	60.	*	*	*	*	*
2004-S	*	*	*	*	*	10.	15.	20.	40.

2002 to 2004 circulation-quality coins, collector sales only.

—— = Insufficient pricing data * = None issued

Coronet gold dollars

Enlarged to show detail

Date of authorization: Jan. 18, 1837
Dates of issue: 1849-1954
Designer/Engraver: James B. Longacre
Diameter: 13.00 mm/0.51 inch
Weight: 1.67 grams/0.05
Metallic Content: 90% gold, 10% copper and silver
Weight of pure gold: 1.50 grams/0.05 ounce
Edge: Reeded
Mint mark: Reverse below wreath

	VF-20	EF-40	AU-50	AU-55	AU-58	MS-60	MS-62	MS-63	MS-64	MS-65
1849 Open Wreath, L, Small Head	150.	200.	225.	250.	300.	375.	775.	1800.	3000.	6750.
1849 Open Wreath, No L, Small Head	150.	225.	300.	375.	500.	600.	1000.	2500.	3150.	7000.
1849 Open Wreath, Large Head	150.	200.	225.	250.	300.	375.	600.	1700.	2500.	6000.
1849 Closed Wreath	150.	200.	225.	250.	300.	375.	600.	1700.	2500.	6000.
1849-C Closed Wreath	1200.	1500.	2500.	4500.	6000.	10000.	15000.	20000.	—	—
1849-C Open Wreath	—	—	—	—	—	—	—	—	—	—
1849-D	1200.	1500.	2000.	3000.	4000.	5000.	10000.	15000.	25000.	50000.
1849-O	175.	250.	350.	550.	700.	1100.	2000.	3500.	6500.	16000.
1850	155.	200.	225.	250.	300.	375.	550.	1400.	3000.	8000.
1850-C	1200.	1500.	2500.	5500.	7500.	10000.	18000.	30000.	—	—
1850-D	1200.	1500.	3000.	6000.	8000.	11000.	20000.	30000.	—	—
1850-O	300.	400.	900.	1500.	2000.	3750.	4500.	7000.	16000.	30000.
1851	150.	200.	225.	250.	275.	350.	500.	1300.	2000.	5500.
1851-C	1200.	1500.	1800.	2200.	2500.	3000.	5000.	7000.	15000.	30000.
1851-D	1200.	1500.	2000.	2700.	3500.	6000.	10000.	15000.	20000.	41000.
1851-O	175.	250.	300.	400.	500.	800.	1500.	2500.	6000.	16000.
1852	150.	200.	225.	250.	275.	350.	500.	1300.	2000.	5500.
1852-C	1200.	1500.	1800.	2500.	3000.	5000.	8000.	12000.	25000.	35000.
1852-D	1200.	1500.	2500.	4000.	5000.	9000.	18000.	—	—	—
1852-O	175.	250.	450.	850.	1100.	1500.	2500.	6000.	12000.	26500.

—— = Insufficient pricing data   * = None issued

CORONET GOLD DOLLAR (CONTINUED)

	VF-20	EF-40	AU-50	AU-55	AU-58	MS-60	MS-62	MS-63	MS-64	MS-65
1853	150.	200.	225.	250.	275.	350.	500.	1300.	1700.	5500.
1853-C	1200.	1500.	2000.	2500.	3500.	6000.	10000.	15000.	30000.	—
1853-D	1200.	1500.	2500.	4500.	6000.	10000.	20000.	35000.	—	—
1853-O	160.	250.	300.	400.	500.	700.	1300.	3000.	6500.	14000.
1854	150.	200.	225.	250.	275.	350.	500.	1300.	2000.	6750.
1854-D	1500.	2500.	6000.	8500.	10000.	12000.	20000.	—	—	—
1854-S	350.	500.	750.	1100.	1500.	2300.	3350.	6750.	15000.	25000.

—— = Insufficient pricing data * = None issued

Indian Head gold dollar

Date of authorization: Jan. 18, 1837
Dates of issue: 1854-1889
Designer/Engraver: James B. Longacre
Diameter: 14.06 mm/0.59 inch
Weight: 1.67 grams/0.05 ounce
Metallic Content: 90% gold, 10% copper and silver
Weight of pure gold: 1.50 grams/0.95 ounce
Edge: Reeded
Mint mark: Reverse below wreath

Small Head

Large Head

	VF-20	EF-40	AU-50	AU-55	AU-58	MS-60	MS-62	MS-63	MS-64	MS-65
SMALL HEAD										
1854	325.	450.	700.	1100.	1500.	3500.	6500.	15000.	20000.	42500.
1855	325.	450.	700.	1100.	1500.	3500.	6500.	15000.	20000.	42500.
1855-C	1600.	3500.	7000.	12500.	15000.	25000.	—	—	—	—
1855-D	5000.	8500.	22000.	26000.	30000.	50000.	60000.	—	—	—
1855-O	500.	750.	1500.	2500.	4500.	7000.	15000.	30000.	40000.	—
1856-S	1000.	1500.	2500.	3000.	5000.	7500.	15000.	30000.	45000.	—
LARGE HEAD										
1856 Upright 5	175.	200.	300.	350.	400.	650.	800.	1400.	1800.	5000.
1856 Slant 5	160.	175.	250.	275.	300.	400.	500.	1200.	1500.	4000.
1856-D	4000.	6000.	8500.	12000.	20000.	35000.	50000.	—	—	—
1857	150.	200.	225.	250.	275.	300.	500.	1200.	1500.	4000.
1857-C	1200.	1800.	4000.	7000.	10000.	15000.	—	—	—	—
1857-D	1500.	2500.	4500.	6500.	8000.	12000.	18000.	—	—	—
1857-S	500.	650.	1400.	2000.	2500.	6000.	10000.	22000.	—	—
1858	150.	200.	225.	250.	275.	350.	600.	1200.	2000.	5000.

—— = Insufficient pricing data * = None issued

	VF-20	EF-40	AU-50	AU-55	AU-58	MS-60	MS-62	MS-63	MS-64	MS-65
1858-D	1100.	1500.	3000.	5000.	7000.	10000.	20000.	30000.	45000.	75000.
1858-S	400.	600.	1400.	1700.	2000.	6000.	9000.	17000.	—	—
1859	150.	200.	225.	250.	275.	350.	600.	1200.	1600.	4000.
1859-C	1100.	1800.	4000.	8500.	12000.	17000.	30000.	40000.	60000.	125000.
1859-D	1100.	1800.	3000.	5500.	8000.	12000.	20000.	30000.	—	—
1859-S	250.	600.	1350.	2100.	3000.	5850.	9750.	19000.	—	—
1860	175.	200.	250.	275.	300.	450.	600.	1500.	3000.	6000.
1860-D	3000.	4000.	7500.	12000.	18000.	25000.	35000.	—	—	—
1860-S	400.	500.	800.	1200.	1500.	2500.	4000.	7500.	15000.	30000.
1861	150.	200.	225.	250.	275.	350.	600.	1200.	1500.	3500.
1861-D	7000.	10000.	20000.	25000.	30000.	35000.	50000.	75000.	100000.	125000.
1862	150.	200.	250.	275.	300.	350.	500.	1200.	1500.	3000.
1863	500.	1000.	2200.	3000.	3500.	4000.	5000.	8000.	12000.	20000.
1864	350.	450.	800.	900.	1000.	1200.	1600.	2700.	4000.	8000.
1865	350.	600.	800.	1000.	1200.	1700.	2500.	3500.	5000.	9000.
1866	350.	500.	700.	750.	800.	1000.	1400.	2000.	3000.	5500.
1867	400.	550.	700.	750.	800.	1200.	1500.	2000.	3000.	6000.
1868	300.	400.	500.	550.	700.	1000.	1200.	2000.	3300.	6000.
1869	350.	500.	700.	800.	900.	1200.	1400.	2300.	3000.	6000.
1870	300.	400.	500.	550.	600.	800.	1200.	1800.	2500.	5000.
1870-S	500.	800.	1200.	1500.	1800.	2750.	4250.	7750.	14500.	30000.
1871	300.	400.	500.	550.	600.	800.	1200.	1800.	2500.	4500.
1872	300.	400.	500.	550.	600.	1000.	1500.	2500.	4000.	6000.
1873 Closed 3	450.	850.	1000.	1250.	1400.	1750.	2750.	5000.	10000.	22500.
1873 Open 3	150.	200.	250.	275.	300.	350.	550.	1200.	1500.	2500.
1874	150.	200.	250.	275.	300.	350.	550.	1200.	1500.	2500.
1875	2500.	4000.	5000.	5500.	6000.	6500.	7500.	9000.	15000.	28000.
1876	300.	350.	500.	550.	600.	700.	800.	1300.	2000.	4500.
1877	200.	350.	450.	500.	550.	700.	800.	1300.	2000.	4500.
1878	250.	350.	500.	550.	600.	700.	800.	1300.	2000.	4000.
1879	225.	325.	350.	375.	400.	550.	800.	1300.	1800.	3000.
1880	175.	200.	250.	275.	300.	450.	600.	1300.	1500.	2100.
1881	175.	200.	250.	275.	300.	450.	600.	1300.	1500.	2400.
1882	175.	200.	250.	275.	300.	450.	600.	1300.	1500.	2100.
1883	175.	200.	250.	275.	300.	450.	600.	1300.	1500.	2100.
1884	175.	200.	250.	275.	300.	450.	600.	1300.	1800.	2400.
1885	175.	200.	250.	275.	300.	450.	600.	1300.	1800.	2400.
1886	175.	200.	250.	275.	300.	450.	600.	1300.	1800.	2600.
1887	175.	200.	250.	275.	300.	450.	600.	1300.	1500.	2100.
1888	175.	200.	250.	275.	300.	450.	600.	1300.	1500.	2000.
1889	175.	200.	250.	275.	300.	425.	600.	1300.	1500.	1800.

—— = Insufficient pricing data   * = None issued

Capped Bust $2.50 quarter eagle

No Stars obverse

With Stars obverse

Date of authorization:	April 2, 1792
Dates of issue:	1796-1807
Designer/Engraver:	Robert Scot
Diameter:	20.00 mm/0.79 inch
Weight:	4.37 grams/0.14 ounce
Metallic Content:	91.67% gold, 8.33% copper and silver
Weight of pure gold:	4.01 grams/0.13 ounce
Edge:	Reeded
Mint mark:	None

	F-12	VF-20	EF-40	EF-45	AU-50	AU-55	AU-58	MS-60
1796 No Stars	30000.	40000.	70000.	80000.	90000.	100000.	125000.	175000.
1796 Stars	27000	35000	65000	75000	80000	90000.	100000.	135000.
1797	17000.	20000.	30000.	40000.	50000.	60000.	85000.	125000.
1798	7000.	10000.	13000.	20000.	30000.	35000.	40000	60000
1802/1	6000.	8000.	10000.	12000.	14000.	16000.	20000.	30000.
1804 13 Stars	30000.	40000.	75000.	100000.	135000.	175000.	225000.	—
1804 14 Stars	6000	8000	10000	12000	14000	16000.	18000.	30000.
1805	6000.	8000.	10000.	12000.	14000.	16000.	18000.	30000.
1806/4	6000.	8000.	10000.	12000.	14000.	16000.	20000.	30000.
1806/5	10000.	16000.	20000.	30000.	40000.	55000.	75000.	100000.
1807	6000.	8000.	10000.	12000.	14000.	16000.	18000.	30000.

—— = Insufficient pricing data

Capped Draped Bust
$2.50 quarter eagle

Date of authorization: April 2, 1792
Dates of issue: 1808
Designer/Engraver: John Reich
Diameter: 20.00 mm/0.79 inch
Weight: 4.37 grams/0.14 ounce
Metallic Content: 91.67% gold, 8.33% copper and silver
Weight of pure gold: 4.01 grams/0.13 ounce
Edge: Reeded
Mint mark: None

	F-12	VF-20	EF-40	EF-45	AU-50	AU-55	AU-58	MS-60
1808	25000.	35000.	45000.	55000.	65000.	75000.	85000.	100000.

Capped Head $2.50 quarter eagle

Date of authorization: April 2, 1792
Dates of issue: 1821-1834
Designers: Obverse: John Reich-Robert Scot
Reverse: John Reich
Engravers: Obverse: Robert Scot
Reverse: John Reich
Diameter: (1821-1827): 18.50 mm/0.73 inch
(1829-1834): 18.20 mm/0.72 inch
Weight: 4.37 grams/0.14 ounce
Metallic Content: 91.67% gold, 8.33% copper and silver
Weight of pure gold: 4.01 grams/0.13 ounce
Edge: Reeded
Mint mark: None

	F-12	VF-20	EF-40	EF-45	AU-50	AU-55	AU-58	MS-60	MS-62	MS-63
1821	6000.	7500.	9000.	10000.	12000.	14000.	16000.	25000.	35000.	45000.
1824/1	6000.	7500.	9000.	10000.	12000.	14000.	16000.	20000.	27000.	35000.
1825	6000.	7500.	9000.	10000.	12000.	14000.	16000.	20000.	25000.	35000.
1826	6000.	7500.	9500.	11000.	13000.	18500.	25000.	37500.	—	—
1827	6500.	8000.	10000.	12000.	14000.	14000.	16000.	20000.	30000.	40000.
REDUCED DIAMETER										
1829	5000.	6500.	7500.	8500.	10000.	11000.	12000.	14000.	20000.	25000.
1830	5000.	6500.	7500.	8500.	10000.	11000.	12000.	14000.	20000.	25000.
1831	5000.	6500.	7500.	8500.	10000.	11000.	12000.	14000.	20000.	25000.
1832	5000.	6500.	7500.	8500.	10000.	11000.	12000.	14000.	25000.	30000.
1833	5000.	6500.	7500.	8500.	10000.	11000.	12000.	15000.	25000.	35000.
1834 Motto	10000.	14000.	18000.	25000.	30000.	33000.	35000.	40000.	—	—

—— = Insufficient pricing data

Classic Head $2.50 quarter eagle

Date of authorization: June 28, 1834, Jan. 18, 1837
Dates of issue: 1834-1839
Designers: Obverse: William Kneass
Reverse: John Reich-William Kneass
Engraver: William Kneass
Diameter: 18.20 mm/0.72 inch
Weight: 4.18 grams/0.13 ounce
Metallic Content: (1834-1836): 89.92% gold, 10.08% copper and silver
(1837-1839): 90% gold, 10% copper and silver
Weight of pure gold: (1834-1836): 3.758 grams/0.12 ounce
(1837-1839): 3.762 grams/0.12 ounce
Edge: Reeded
Mint mark: 1838-1839 only, obverse above

	F-12	VF-20	EF-40	EF-45	AU-50	AU-55	AU-58	MS-60	MS-62	MS-63
1834 No Motto	275.	375.	500.	600.	800.	1200.	1700.	2500.	3500.	5500.
1835	275.	375.	500.	600.	800.	1200.	1700.	2500.	4500.	8500.
1836	275.	375.	500.	600.	800.	1200.	1700.	2500.	3500.	6000.
1837	350.	450.	600.	900.	1300.	1700.	2500.	3500.	4500.	12000.
1838	275.	400.	500.	650.	900.	1200.	1800.	2500.	4000.	7000.
1838-C	1000.	1500.	2500.	4000.	6500.	10000.	15000.	25000.	30000.	40000.
1839/8	275.	400.	700.	1000.	2000.	3500.	4500.	6000.	—	—
1839-C	1000.	1500.	2500.	3000.	4000.	7500.	12000.	25000.	35000.	55000.
1839-D	1000.	1500.	3000.	4000.	6000.	10000.	14000.	25000.	35000.	50000.
1839-O	400.	500.	1000.	1300.	1700.	3000.	4000.	6000.	14000.	25000.

—— = Insufficient pricing data

Coronet $2.50 quarter eagle

Date of authorization: Jan. 18, 1837
Dates of issue: 1840-1907
Designers: Obverse: Christian Gobrecht
Reverse: Christian Gobrecht-John Reich-William Kneass
Engraver: Christian Gobrecht
Diameter: 18.20 mm/0.72 inch
Weight: 4.18 grams/0.13 ounce
Metallic Content: 90% gold, 10% copper
Weight of pure gold: 3.76 grams/0.12 ounce
Edge: Reeded
Mint mark: Reverse below eagle

	F-12	VF-20	EF-40	EF-45	AU-50	AU-55	AU-58	MS-60	MS-62	MS-63
1840	160.	290.	775.	1500.	3350.	4150.	4850.	7000.	—	—
1840-C	1200.	1200.	1800.	2500.	4500.	7500.	10000.	13500.	27500.	—
1840-D	2000.	3000.	9000.	12000.	15000.	25000.	35000.	—	—	—
1840-O	190.	330.	725.	1150.	1900.	3000.	5750.	9500.	17000.	—
1841 Proof only	—	—	50000.	—	75000.	—	—	100000.	—	175000.
1841-C	900.	1200.	1800.	2500.	3500.	6500.	12000.	18000.	45000.	—
1841-D	1500.	2000.	3500.	5000.	10000.	15000.	18500.	28000.	60000.	—
1842	330.	800.	3100.	3800.	7000.	15000.	—	—	—	—
1842-C	1000.	1500.	3200.	4500.	8500.	12500.	16500.	25000.	—	—
1842-D	1000.	1800.	3500.	6500.	10500.	17500.	25000.	—	—	—
1842-O	250.	525.	1250.	1750.	2950.	6000.	9500.	15000.	—	—
1843	175.	250.	500.	600.	1000.	1400.	2200.	3000.	4500.	7000.
1843-C Large Date	800.	1200.	1800.	2500.	3500.	6000.	7000.	9000.	17500.	22500.
1843-C Small Date	1800.	2500.	5000.	6000.	9000.	12500.	17000.	25000.	50000.	—
1843-D	800.	1200.	1800.	2500.	3000.	4500.	6500.	10000.	25000.	—
1843-O Large Date	225.	325.	500.	1050.	2300.	4600.	6250.	9000.	13500.	28500.
1843-O Small Date	155.	190.	265.	325.	425.	800.	1200.	2400.	3000.	6000.
1844	275.	490.	900.	1225.	2250.	3950.	—	—	—	—
1844-C	900.	1200.	2000.	3000.	6500.	10000.	13500.	21500.	—	—
1844-D	900.	1200.	1800.	2500.	3000.	4000.	5500.	9000.	16000.	30000.
1845	150.	220.	300.	330.	475.	750.	825.	1500.	2600.	4150.
1845-D	900.	1200.	1800.	2500.	3000.	5500.	8500.	15000.	—	—

—— = Insufficient pricing data

CORONET $2.50 QUARTER EAGLE (CONTINUED)

	F-12	VF-20	EF-40	EF-45	AU-50	AU-55	AU-58	MS-60	MS-62	MS-63
1845-O	550.	1150.	2400.	3050.	5750.	9000.	12500.	18000.	—	—
1846	215.	365.	525.	600.	1150.	2100.	2950.	6250.	—	—
1846-C	1000.	1500.	2500.	4500.	10000.	12500.	15000.	20000.	30000.	45000.
1846-D	900.	1200.	1800.	2500.	3000.	5500.	7500.	12000.	—	—
1846-O	160.	280.	480.	575.	1050.	1950.	3750.	5850.	17500.	—
1847	140.	235.	420.	525.	975.	1600.	2500.	4250.	6500.	11000.
1847-C	900.	1200.	1800.	2500.	3000.	4000.	5000.	7500.	11000.	18500.
1847-D	900.	1200.	1800.	2500.	3000.	5000.	8000.	12000.	20000.	—
1847-O	150.	275.	445.	590.	1050.	2200.	3000.	4650.	11500.	—
1848	300.	525.	950.	1200.	1750.	2750.	3850.	6250.	9000.	17250.
1848 CAL.	9000.	12000.	24000.	27000.	30000.	35000.	40000.	50000.	55000.	60000.
1848-C	900.	1200.	1800.	2500.	3000.	6000.	9000.	15000.	30000.	—
1848-D	900.	1200.	1800.	2500.	3000.	5000.	8000.	12000.	20000.	—
1849	145.	255.	450.	565.	1000.	1600.	2500.	3100.	4950.	—
1849-C	900.	1200.	2000.	3000.	5000.	10000.	15000.	25000.	60000.	—
1849-D	900.	1200.	1800.	2500.	3500.	7500.	10000.	17500.	35000.	—
1850	135.	160.	195.	225.	305.	600.	850.	1250.	2200.	3350.
1850-C	900.	1200.	1800.	2500.	3500.	7500.	12000.	18500.	—	—
1850-D	900.	1200.	1800.	2500.	3500.	7000.	11000.	15000.	—	—
1850-O	160.	250.	350.	475.	1500.	2250.	3000.	4750.	7000.	14000.
1851	135.	150.	180.	190.	215.	265.	315.	370.	775.	1850.
1851-C	900.	1200.	1800.	2500.	5000.	7500.	11000.	14000.	30000.	—
1851-D	900.	1200.	1800.	2500.	3500.	7000.	9000.	14000.	—	—
1851-O	145.	165.	400.	675.	1000.	2500.	3500.	5500.	9750.	15500.
1852	135.	160.	190.	200.	240.	275.	325.	375.	750.	1850.
1852-C	900.	1200.	2000.	2500.	5000.	9000.	12500.	20000.	—	—
1852-D	1000.	1500.	3000.	4000.	8000.	12000.	15000.	25000.	45000.	—
1852-O	145.	185.	300.	400.	975.	1400.	2600.	5250.	10500.	15000.
1853	135.	150.	170.	180.	205.	255.	305.	365.	775.	1800.
1853-D	1200.	2000.	3000.	4000.	6000.	9000.	12000.	20000.	—	—
1854	135.	150.	170.	180.	205.	255.	305.	380.	750.	2100.
1854-C	900.	1200.	2500.	4000.	6000.	9000.	12000.	20000.	40000.	—
1854-D	2500.	3500.	7000.	8000.	15000.	20000.	25000.	40000.	70000.	—
1854-O	150.	200.	250.	285.	425.	735.	1025.	1650.	2650.	—
1854-S	—	—	—	—	—	—	—	—	—	—
1855	135.	150.	180.	190.	215.	265.	325.	385.	850.	2450.
1855-C	1500.	2000.	3500.	4500.	7500.	15000.	20000.	35000.	—	—
1855-D	2500.	4000.	8000.	12000.	20000.	30000.	—	—	—	—
1856	125.	150.	180.	190.	205.	250.	305.	355.	750.	2250.
1856-C	900.	1200.	2500.	3500.	5000.	9000.	12000.	15000.	25000.	—
1856-D	5000.	6500.	11000.	15000.	25000.	35000.	42500.	55000.	—	—
1856-O	175.	350.	675.	875.	1350.	2950.	4250.	7500.	—	—
1856-S	150.	205.	415.	650.	1275.	2000.	3250.	5850.	8250.	12500.
1857	135.	150.	185.	195.	205.	255.	305.	360.	900.	2500.
1857-D	900.	1500.	2500.	3500.	4000.	7500.	14000.	17500.	27500.	—
1857-O	155.	180.	350.	525.	1175.	2150.	3250.	5400.	7950.	16000.
1857-S	150.	180.	375.	500.	1000.	2500.	4750.	8250.	10500.	—

—— = Insufficient pricing data

CORONET $2.50 QUARTER EAGLE (CONTINUED)

	F-12	VF-20	EF-40	EF-45	AU-50	AU-55	AU-58	MS-60	MS-62	MS-63
1858	135.	155.	220.	260.	350.	575.	800.	1400.	2400.	3250.
1858-C	900.	1200.	1800.	2500.	3500.	4500.	6500.	10000.	25000.	—
1859 Reverse of 1858	185.	225.	400.	475.	875.	1250.	2000.	3700.	6250.	12500.
1859 Reverse of 1859-1907	135.	155.	270.	350.	500.	625.	800.	1250.	2300.	3400.
1859-D	1500.	2000.	3500.	4500.	6000.	9000.	12500.	25500.	—	—
1859-S	225.	500.	825.	1200.	2700.	3675.	4500.	8500.	11000.	16500.
1860 Reverse of 1858	1600.	1900.	2375.	2950.	3850.	4750.	6500.	10500.	—	—
1860 Small Letters & Arrowhead, Reverse of 1859-1907	135.	155.	255.	345.	475.	575.	775.	1100.	1850.	3050.
1860-C	900.	1200.	2000.	3000.	4000.	8000.	14000.	25000.	—	60000.
1860-S	195.	300.	700.	875.	1225.	2150.	2850.	4200.	7500.	15000.
1861 Reverse of 1858	600.	1000.	1450.	1650.	2250.	2750.	3250.	5000.	8000.	12750.
1861 Reverse of 1859-1907	135.	150.	185.	195.	205.	240.	290.	345.	625.	975.
1861-S	210.	425.	950.	1750.	3500.	5250.	—	—	—	—
1862	140.	170.	255.	350.	500.	600.	900.	1500.	2750.	4200.
1862/1	600.	1000.	2200.	2750.	3500.	4500.	7250.	12000.	—	—
1862-S	485.	950.	2000.	2850.	4250.	8500.	9750.	19500.	—	—
1863-S	400.	650.	1700.	2900.	4450.	9500.	12500.	19000.	—	—
1863 Proofs Only PF-60 $17000 PF-63(PCGS) $30800 PF-64 $47500.										
1864	2750.	5500.	14000.	21000.	27500.	—	—	—	—	—
1865	2200.	4500.	9250.	15500.	22000.	—	35000.	—	—	—
1865-S	180.	285.	625.	1250.	1600.	2350.	3250.	5750.	—	—
1866	650.	1350.	3500.	4400.	7000.	9750.	11500.	16500.	27500.	—
1866-S	195.	325.	950.	1350.	1950.	3600.	4500.	9750.	—	25500.
1867	200.	385.	575.	825.	1400.	1800.	2650.	3600.	4850.	8750.
1867-S	190.	270.	600.	850.	1650.	2250.	3150.	4950.	—	14000.
1868	160.	205.	345.	425.	615.	925.	1500.	2800.	—	10000.
1868-S	160.	190.	475.	650.	1100.	1850.	3250.	5750.	7500.	13500.
1869	165.	210.	375.	515.	700.	1400.	2100.	3500.	6400.	10500.
1869-S	175.	235.	450.	575.	1350.	1850.	3000.	5500.	—	14000.
1870	155.	195.	350.	475.	650.	1150.	2250.	3250.	5250.	10250.
1870-S	160.	200.	425.	500.	1000.	1650.	2750.	5150.	9000.	—
1871	160.	200.	300.	390.	500.	1000.	1250.	2250.	2700.	4250.
1871-S	155.	175.	340.	400.	525.	925.	1200.	2350.	2850.	4650.
1872	250.	425.	650.	800.	1250.	2600.	3500.	6000.	—	—
1872-S	165.	225.	490.	550.	1225.	1750.	2850.	5000.	7250.	12000.
1873 Closed 3	140.	165.	185.	200.	250.	350.	450.	625.	1100.	2200.
1873	135.	150.	175.	180.	190.	240.	290.	345.	675.	925.
1873-S	170.	220.	475.	525.	1100.	1400.	1750.	2500.	4250.	9000.
1874	180.	230.	365.	405.	725.	1150.	1300.	2650.	4200.	7850.
1875	2500.	3500.	4650.	5500.	7500.	9650.	14500.	19000.	—	—
1875-S	145.	190.	350.	400.	625.	1000.	1900.	4050.	5900.	10500.
1876	170.	320.	535.	650.	1100.	1950.	2750.	3550.	4250.	10500.

—— = Insufficient pricing data

CORONET $2.50 QUARTER EAGLE (CONTINUED)

	F-12	VF-20	EF-40	EF-45	AU-50	AU-55	AU-58	MS-60	MS-62	MS-63
1876-S	145.	215.	525.	650.	1075.	2025.	2350.	3900.	5100.	11500.
1877	305.	385.	540.	625.	875.	1275.	2200.	2750.	3650.	7750.
1877-S	140.	155.	175.	185.	220.	280.	325.	750.	1850.	2600.
1878	135.	150.	165.	170.	180.	210.	255.	325.	550.	800.
1878-S	135.	150.	170.	180.	200.	235.	280.	385.	900.	2400.
1879	135.	150.	165.	170.	185.	220.	270.	345.	550.	1475.
1879-S	140.	170.	225.	425.	850.	1200.	1600.	2200.	2700.	5800.
1880	155.	225.	290.	350.	475.	675.	1150.	1300.	1800.	3500.
1881	725.	1650.	2450.	2900.	4250.	5250.	6500.	10500.	22500.	—
1882	180.	220.	255.	280.	390.	425.	575.	725.	1500.	2750.
1883	180.	245.	475.	550.	800.	1100.	1600.	1900.	3250.	6250.
1884	180.	230.	385.	410.	525.	725.	1200.	1700.	2000.	3100.
1885	400.	750.	1500.	1750.	2250.	2650.	3250.	4200.	5750.	7250.
1886	165.	210.	275.	315.	450.	625.	850.	1275.	1650.	3000.
1887	165.	190.	220.	245.	350.	400.	600.	1050.	1500.	2850.
1888	165.	180.	195.	210.	255.	280.	350.	500.	575.	875.
1889	165.	180.	195.	205.	220.	250.	325.	435.	550.	875.
1890	165.	180.	195.	205.	230.	265.	350.	530.	750.	900.
1891	165.	180.	190.	200.	210.	240.	300.	425.	625.	1000.
1892	165.	205.	275.	310.	485.	560.	700.	950.	1250.	2600.
1893	145.	160.	185.	195.	205.	230.	290.	400.	565.	850.
1894	155.	180.	270.	295.	375.	425.	500.	635.	1100.	1750.
1895	135.	145.	190.	200.	230.	255.	350.	450.	525.	1000.
1896	135.	145.	165.	170.	180.	190.	230.	325.	450.	800.
1897	135.	150.	170.	175.	185.	200.	230.	310.	450.	735.
1898	135.	145.	165.	170.	180.	190.	230.	300.	450.	735.
1899	135.	145.	165.	175.	190.	205.	235.	320.	450.	735.
1900	135.	160.	225.	265.	300.	325.	350.	400.	500.	700.
1901	130.	140.	165.	170.	180.	190.	225.	290.	425.	700.
1902	130.	140.	165.	170.	180.	190.	225.	290.	425.	700.
1903	130.	140.	165.	170.	180.	190.	225.	290.	400.	650.
1904	130.	140.	165.	170.	180.	190.	225.	290.	400.	675.
1905	130.	140.	165.	170.	180.	190.	225.	290.	400.	650.
1906	130.	140.	165.	170.	180.	190.	225.	290.	400.	650.
1907	130.	140.	165.	170.	180.	190.	225.	290.	400.	650.

—— = Insufficient pricing data

Indian Head $2.50 quarter eagle

Date of authorization: Jan. 18, 1837
Dates of issue: 1908-1929
Designer: Bela Lyon Pratt
Engraver: Charles Barber
Diameter: 17.78 mm/0.70 inch
Weight: 4.18 grams/0.13 ounce
Metallic Content: 90% gold, 10% copper
Weight of pure gold: 3.76 grams/0.12 ounce
Edge: Reeded
Mint mark: Reverse lower left

	EF-40	AU-50	AU-55	MS-60	MS-62	MS-63	MS-64	MS-65	MS-66
1908	185.	200.	225.	300.	600.	1500.	2000.	5500.	7000.
1909	185.	200.	225.	300.	700.	2200.	3000.	7500.	8500.
1910	185.	200.	225.	275.	700.	2000.	3500.	8500.	10000.
1911	185.	200.	225.	275.	600.	1500.	2500.	8000.	—
1911-D	1800.	2500.	3000.	6000.	13000.	25000.	35000.	80000.	—
1912	185.	200.	225.	300.	750.	2500.	3500.	12000.	13000.
1913	185.	200.	225.	300.	600.	1500.	3000.	9000.	10000.
1914	200.	225.	275.	500.	2000.	6000.	10000.	19000.	—
1914-D	200.	210.	235.	300.	800.	2500.	5500.	22000.	—
1915	185.	200.	225.	275.	600.	1500.	2500.	8000.	—
1925-D	185.	200.	225.	275.	600.	1400.	1800.	5000.	7500.
1926	185.	200.	225.	275.	600.	1400.	1800.	5000.	7500.
1927	185.	200.	225.	275.	600.	1400.	1800.	5000.	8000.
1928	185.	200.	225.	275.	600.	1400.	1800.	5000.	8000.
1929	185.	200.	225.	275.	600.	1400.	2000.	7000.	—

Indian Head $3 gold

Date of authorization: Feb. 21, 1853
Dates of issue: 1854-1889
Designer/Engraver: James B. Longacre
Diameter: 20.63 mm/0.81 inch
Weight: 5.02 grams/0.16 ounce
Metallic Content: (1854-1873): 90% gold, 10% copper and silver
(1873-1889): 90% gold, 10% copper
Weight of pure gold: 4.51 grams/0.15 ounce
Edge: Reeded
Mint mark: Reverse below wreath

	F-12	VF-20	EF-40	AU-50	AU-55	MS-60	MS-62	MS-63	MS-64	MS-65
1854	600.	750.	1100.	1400.	1800.	3000.	4000.	6500.	9000.	18000.
1854-D	7000.	10000.	18000.	35000.	50000.	90000.	135000.	—	—	—
1854-O	750.	1500.	2500.	4500.	10000.	25000.	—	—	—	—
1855	600.	750.	1100.	2000.	2500.	3500.	5000.	7000.	13000.	35000.
1855-S	800.	1200.	3000.	7000.	9000.	25000.	—	—	—	—
1856	600.	750.	1100.	1500.	1800.	3000.	5000.	7500.	12000.	30000.
1856-S	650.	800.	1400.	2500.	4500.	10000.	18000.	25000.	45000.	—
1857	600.	750.	1100.	1500.	2000.	3500.	6000.	11000.	20000.	35000.
1857-S	800.	1200.	3500.	6500.	8000.	17000.	—	—	—	—
1858	700.	1000.	1600.	3500.	4500.	8000.	12000.	20000.	—	—
1859	600.	750.	1300.	1600.	1800.	2800.	5000.	6500.	11000.	22000.
1860	650.	800.	1300.	1800.	2000.	3500.	5000.	7000.	11000.	25000.
1860-S	700.	1000.	2000.	6500.	10000.	—	—	—	—	—
1861	650.	850.	1300.	1800.	2000.	3500.	6000.	10000.	16000.	30000.
1862	650.	850.	1300.	1800.	2000.	3500.	6000.	10000.	17000.	32000.
1863	650.	850.	1300.	1800.	2000.	3500.	6000.	10000.	18000.	25000.
1864	700.	1000.	1200.	1800.	2200.	3500.	6500.	10000.	18000.	32000.
1865	1000.	1400.	2500.	5000.	6000.	11000.	16500.	20000.	30000.	45000.
1866	700.	950.	1100.	1800.	2000.	3500.	6500.	10000.	16000.	35000.
1867	700.	950.	1100.	2000.	2200.	3500.	6000.	11000.	16000.	35000.
1868	650.	800.	1100.	1700.	2000.	3300.	5500.	9000.	15500.	25000.
1869	700.	1000.	1100.	1800.	2000.	4000.	7000.	11000.	22000.	37000.
1870	700.	1000.	1500.	2200.	2500.	4500.	6500.	12000.	23000.	40000.
1870-S unique.										
1871	700.	1000.	1300.	2000.	2200.	4000.	6500.	10000.	17000.	35000.
1872	700.	900.	1200.	1800.	2200.	4000.	6500.	10000.	17000.	35000.

—— = Insufficient pricing data

INDIAN HEAD $3 GOLD (CONTINUED)

	F-12	VF-20	EF-40	AU-50	AU-55	MS-60	MS-62	MS-63	MS-64	MS-65
1873 Open 3 Proof Only	3000.	3500.	4500.	11000.	15000.	17000.	20000.	25000.	40000.	90000.
1873 Closed 3 originals	2500.	3500.	4500.	9000.	14000.	25000.	30000.	40000.	55000.	—
1874	600.	750.	1100.	1400.	1800.	2800.	3500.	6000.	7500.	15000.
1875 Proof Only	15000.	22000.	30000.	45000.	50000.	40000.	50000.	67500.	100000.	215000.
1876 Proof Only	4000.	6000.	11000.	14000.	17000.	17500.	20000.	24500.	39000.	67500.
1877	900.	1400.	3000.	7500.	9000.	16000.	25000.	40000.	—	—
1878	600.	750.	1100.	1400.	1800.	2800.	4000.	6000.	7500.	13000.
1879	600.	750.	1100.	1600.	1900.	2800.	4500.	6500.	8000.	15000.
1880	650.	800.	1700.	2400.	2700.	3200.	5000.	7000.	10000.	17000.
1881	800.	1400.	2400.	4500.	5000.	6500.	9000.	13000.	20000.	40000.
1882	700.	1000.	1200.	1800.	2200.	3500.	5000.	7000.	10000.	23000.
1883	650.	900.	1300.	2500.	2800.	3600.	6000.	7000.	10000.	23000.
1884	900.	1400.	1600.	2500.	2800.	3600.	5500.	7000.	10000.	25000.
1885	900.	1400.	1600.	2500.	3000.	4000.	5500.	7500.	11000.	25000.
1886	850.	1300.	1800.	2500.	3000.	4500.	6000.	8500.	17000.	35000.
1887	650.	800.	1100.	2000.	2300.	3500.	4000.	6000.	7500.	15000.
1888	650.	800.	1100.	2000.	2200.	2800.	4000.	6000.	7500.	15000.
1889	650.	800.	1100.	1600.	2200.	2800.	4000.	6000.	7500.	15000.

—— = Insufficient pricing data

Capped Bust $5 half eagle

Small Eagle

Heraldic Eagle

Date of authorization: April 2, 1792
Dates of issue: 1795-1807
Designer/Engraver: Robert Scot
Diameter: 25.00 mm/0.99 inch
Weight: 8.75 grams/0.28 ounce
Metallic Content: 91.67% gold, 8.33% copper and silver
Weight of pure gold: 8.02 grams/0.26 ounce
Edge: Reeded
Mint mark: None

SMALL EAGLE

	F-12	VF-20	EF-40	AU-50	AU-58	MS-60	MS-62	MS-63
1795	10000.	15000.	20000.	30000.	40000.	50000.	85000.	165000.
1796/5	12000.	16000.	24000.	35000.	40000.	65000.	—	—
1797 15 Stars	15000.	18000.	35000.	65000.	100000.	—	—	—
1797 16 Stars	14000.	17000.	30000.	50000.	85000.	135000.	175000.	225000.
1798	—	—	300000.	—	—	—	—	—

HERALDIC EAGLE

	F-12	VF-20	EF-40	AU-50	AU-58	MS-60	MS-62	MS-63	MS-64
1795	8000.	14000.	20000.	40000.	70000.	100000.	125000.	—	—
1797/5	8000.	14000.	20000.	60000.	—	—	—	—	—
1797 16 Stars	—	—	—	—	—	—	—	—	—
1798 Small 8	2700.	3500.	5500.	12000.	20000.	25000.	—	—	—
1798 Large 8, 13 Stars	2700.	3500.	5000.	8000.	15000.	18000.	25000.	60000.	100000.
1798 Large 8, 14 Stars	3000.	4000.	7500.	18500.	—	—	—	—	—
1799 Small Stars	2700.	3500.	4000.	8000.	15000.	20000.	35000.	—	—
1799 Large Stars	3000.	4000.	5000.	10000.	20000.	25000.	50000.	—	—
1800	2700.	3500.	4000.	5500.	6500.	8000.	12000.	20000.	45000.
1802/1	2700.	3500.	4000.	5500.	6500.	8000.	9000.	14250.	27500.
1803/2	2700.	3500.	4000.	5500.	6500.	8000.	10500.	14750.	32500.
1804 Small 8	2700.	3500.	4000.	5500.	6500.	8000.	10000.	18250.	40500.
1804 Small 8/Large 8	2700.	3500.	4000.	5500.	6500.	8500.	12000.	24000.	55000.
1805	2700.	3500.	4000.	5500.	6500.	8000.	10000.	14750.	32500.
1806 Pointed 6, 8X5 Stars	2700.	3500.	4000.	5500.	8000.	10000.	15000.	25500.	37500.
1806 Round 6, 7X6 Stars	2700.	3500.	4000.	5500.	6500.	8000.	9000.	13500.	25000.
1807	2700.	3500.	4000.	5500.	6500.	8000.	10000.	16000.	35000.

—— = Insufficient pricing data

Capped Draped Bust $5 half eagle

Date of authorization:	April 2, 1792
Dates of issue:	1807-1812
Designer/Engraver:	John Reich
Diameter:	25.00 mm/0.99 inch
Weight:	8.75 grams/0.28 ounce
Metallic Content:	91.67% gold, 8.33% copper and silver
Weight of pure gold:	8.02 grams/0.26 ounce
Edge:	Reeded
Mint mark:	None

	F-12	VF-20	EF-40	AU-50	AU-58	MS-60	MS-62	MS-63	MS-64
1807	2000.	2500.	3500.	5000.	6500.	7500.	10000.	15000.	25000.
1808/7	2000.	3500.	4000.	6500.	10000.	14000.	15000.	30000.	50000.
1808	2000.	2500.	3500.	5000.	6500.	7500.	10000.	20000.	35000.
1809/8	2000.	2500.	3500.	5000.	6500.	7500.	10000.	20000.	30000.
1810 Small Date, Small 5	10000.	25000.	35000.	50000.	—	—	—	—	—
1810 Small Date, Tall 5	2000.	2500.	3500.	5000.	6500.	7500.	10000.	21000.	40000.
1810 Large Date, Small 5	—	—	—	—	—	—	—	—	—
1810 Large Date, Large 5	2000.	2500.	3500.	5000.	6500.	7500.	10000.	18000.	25000.
1811 Small 5	2000.	2500.	3500.	5000.	6500.	7500.	10000.	20000.	30000.
1811 Tall 5	2000.	2500.	3500.	5000.	6500.	7500.	15000.	25000.	50000.
1812	2000.	2500.	3500.	5000.	6500.	7500.	10000.	18000.	25000.

—— = Insufficient pricing data

Capped Head $5 half eagle

Date of authorization: April 2, 1792
Dates of issue: 1813-1834
Designer/Engraver: John Reich
Diameter: (1813-1829): 25.00 mm/0.99 inch
(1829-1834): 22.50 mm/0.89 inch
Weight: 8.75 grams/0.28 ounce
Metallic Content: 91.67% gold, 8.33% copper and silver
Weight of pure gold: 8.02 grams/0.26 ounce
Edge: Reeded
Mint mark: None

	F-12	VF-20	EF-40	AU-50	AU-58	MS-60	MS-62	MS-63	MS-64
1813	2500.	3000.	4000.	5000.	6500.	8000.	12000.	17500.	26000.
1814/3	2500.	3000.	4000.	5000.	8000.	10000.	20000.	30000.	60000.
1815	—	—	75000.	100000.	150000.	155000.	—	—	—
1818	2500.	3000.	4000.	5000.	7500.	8500.	18000.	27500.	—
1818 STATESOF	3000.	3500.	4500.	8500.	12000.	15000.	25000.	50000.	—
1818 5D/50	—	—	—	12000.	18000.	25000.	35000.	50000.	75000.
1819 Wide Date	—	—	25000.	55000.	—	—	—	—	—
1819 Close Date	—	15000.	22500.	50000.	—	—	—	—	—
1819 5D/50	—	18000.	25000.	40000.	—	—	—	100000.	—
1820 Curved Base 2, Small Letters	2500.	3000.	5000.	7000.	—	—	—	—	—
1820 Curved Base 2, Large Letters	2500.	3000.	5000.	7500.	—	—	—	35000.	—
1820 Square Base 2, Large Letters	2500.	3000.	4000.	6000.	9000.	10000.	18000.	25000.	40000.
1821	10000.	18000.	25000.	30000.	50000.	65000.	85000.	125000.	—
1822 3 known, 2 in Smithsonian Institution, Last sale 1982, $687,500, VF-30.									
1823	2500.	3500.	5000.	7500.	14000.	18000.	25000.	30000.	—
1824	5000.	11000.	15000.	25000.	30000.	35000.	45000.	60000.	75000.
1825/1	5000.	10000.	12000.	20000.	30000.	35000.	45000.	60000.	110000.
1825/4	—	—	265000.	—	—	—	—	—	—
1826	4000.	8000.	10000.	15000.	25000.	30000.	—	—	—
1827	—	—	—	—	30000.	35000.	45000.	60000.	90000.
1828/7	—	—	—	40000.	85000.	125000.	200000.	—	—
1828	—	—	—	35000.	60000.	75000.	—	—	—
1829 Large Planchet	—	—	—	—	—	—	—	—	300000.
SMALL PLANCHET									
1829	—	—	85000.	175000.	—	—	—	—	475000.

—— = Insufficient pricing data

	F-12	VF-20	EF-40	AU-50	AU-58	MS-60	MS-62	MS-63	MS-64
1830 Small 5D	14000.	18000.	22000.	25000.	35000.	40000.	45000.	55000.	90000.
1830 Large 5D	14000.	18000.	22000.	25000.	35000.	40000.	45000.	60000.	100000.
1831 Small 5D	14000.	18000.	22000.	25000.	35000.	40000.	—	—	—
1831 Large 5D	14000.	18000.	22000.	25000.	35000.	40000.	45000.	55000.	90000.
1832 Curl Base 2, 12 Stars	—	100000.	150000.	—	—	—	—	400000.	—
1832 Square Base 2, 13 Stars	14000.	18000.	22000.	25000.	35000.	40000.	45000.	55000.	—
1833 Large Date	14000.	18000.	22000.	25000.	35000.	40000.	45000.	55000.	85000.
1833 Small Date	14000.	18000.	22000.	25000.	35000.	40000.	45000.	60000.	90000.
1834 Plain 4	14000.	18000.	22000.	25000.	35000.	40000.	45000.	55000.	90000.
1834 Crosslet 4	14000.	18000.	22000.	25000.	35000.	40000.	50000.	80000.	—

Classic Head $5 half eagle

Date of authorization: April 2, 1792
Dates of issue: 1834-1838
Designer: Obverse: William Kneass
Reverse: John Reich-William Kneass
Engraver: William Kneass
Diameter: 22.50 mm/0.89 inch
Weight: 8.36 grams/0.27 ounce
Metallic Content: (1834-1836): 89.92% gold, 10.8% copper and silver
(1837-1838): 90% gold, 10% copper and silver
Weight of pure gold: (1834-1836): 7.516 grams/0.24 ounce
(1837-1838): 7.523 grams/0.24 ounce
Edge: Reeded
Mint mark: 1838 only, obverse above date

	F-12	VF-20	EF-40	EF-45	AU-50	AU-55	AU-58	MS-60	MS-62	MS-63
1834 Plain 4	240.	300.	450.	525.	750.	1250.	1800.	2700.	3800.	7250.
1834 Crosslet 4	850.	1500.	3100.	4250.	5750.	8250.	11250.	16500.	31500.	45000.
1835	240.	295.	475.	550.	675.	1350.	1850.	2650.	4750.	9750.
1836	240.	295.	450.	525.	675.	1300.	1800.	2600.	3900.	7500.
1837	260.	310.	470.	585.	775.	1500.	2300.	3600.	—	15000.
1838	250.	305.	435.	525.	700.	1290.	2100.	3450.	4750.	10750.
1838-C	1500.	2500.	4000.	7000.	14000.	20000.	26000.	40000.	75000.	—
1838-D	1200.	2000.	4000.	5000.	7000.	12500.	17500.	25000.	35000.	45000.

—— = Insufficient pricing data

Coronet $5 half eagle

Date of authorization: Jan. 18, 1837
Dates of issue: 1839-1908
Designer: Obverse: Christian Gobrecht
Reverse: John Reich-William Kneass-Christian Gobrecht
Engraver: Christian Gobrecht
Diameter: (1839-1840): 22.50 mm/0.89 inch
(1840-1908): 21.54 mm/0.85 inch
Weight: 8.36 grams/0.27 ounce
Metallic Content: (1839-1849): 89.92% gold, 10.8% copper and silver
(1849-1908): 90% gold, 10% copper
Weight of pure gold: 7.52 grams/0.24 ounce
Edge: Reeded
Mint mark: Reverse below eagle

	F-12	VF-20	EF-40	EF-45	AU-50	AU-55	AU-58	MS-60	MS-62	MS-63	MS-64
NO MOTTO											
1839	210.	270.	460.	775.	1150.	1600.	2200.	3600.	9500.	20000.	—
1839-C	1400.	2500.	3000.	4500.	7000.	12000.	16000.	25000.	35000.	—	—
1839-D	1400.	2000.	2500.	4000.	6000.	10000.	14000.	20000.	30000.	—	—
1840 Broad Mill	215.	245.	850.	1200.	2300.	3750.	5450.	8250.	—	25000.	—
1840 Narrow Mill	190.	210.	375.	585.	1350.	2200.	2800.	3850.	6250.	13000.	—
1840-C	1400.	2500.	3000.	4500.	8000.	14000.	20000.	30000.	—	—	—
1840-D	1400.	1800.	2000.	4000.	7000.	10000.	12000.	18000.	30000.	—	—
1840-O Broad Mill	325.	600.	1300.	1750.	2900.	—	—	—	—	—	—
1840-O Narrow Mill	235.	425.	975.	1275.	1700.	3000.	4400.	6750.	—	—	—
1841	245.	415.	975.	1250.	1600.	2350.	3725.	5750.	8000.	12500.	—
1841-C	1400.	1600.	1800.	2500.	3500.	7500.	14000.	22000.	34000.	—	—
1841-D	1400.	1600.	2000.	3000.	5000.	7500.	10000.	14000.	20000.	34000.	—
1842 Small Letters	180.	350.	1050.	1950.	3750.	6750.	—	—	—	—	—
1842 Large Letters	400.	825.	2000.	2800.	4250.	7850.	8750.	10000.	—	—	—

—— = Insufficient pricing data

	F-12	VF-20	EF-40	EF-45	AU-50	AU-55	AU-58	MS-60	MS-62	MS-63	MS-64
1842-C Large Date	1400.	1600.	1800.	2500.	3500.	6500.	12000.	20000.	28000.	40000.	—
1842-C Small Date	5000.	10000.	25000.	40000.	55000.	80000.	105000.	140000.	230000.	—	—
1842-D Large Date, Large Letters	2000.	2500.	6000.	9000.	15000.	25000.	35000.	50000.	—	—	—
1842-D Small Date, Small Letters	1400.	1600.	1800.	2500.	3000.	5000.	8500.	16000.	26000.	—	—
1842-O	375.	900.	3500.	5750.	12500.	—	—	—	—	42500.	—
1843	165.	185.	200.	235.	300.	525.	900.	1500.	3750.	9500.	19000.
1843-C	1400.	1600.	1800.	2500.	5000.	7500.	12000.	18000.	28000.	40000.	65000.
1843-D	1400.	1600.	1800.	2500.	3000.	5000.	6500.	12000.	20000.	30000.	—
1843-O Small Letters	365.	725.	1800.	2100.	3000.	6000.	12000.	30000.	40000.	—	—
1843-O Large Letters	180.	260.	1200.	1550.	2350.	4550.	8000.	12000.	17500.	—	—
1844	165.	190.	235.	275.	365.	500.	875.	1800.	4250.	8750.	26000.
1844-C	1400.	1600.	3000.	5000.	7500.	12000.	15000.	25000.	30000.	40000.	—
1844-D	1400.	1600.	1800.	2500.	3000.	5500.	8000.	12000.	20000.	35000.	—
1844-O	165.	255.	375.	500.	775.	1500.	2650.	5000.	7250.	14500.	35000.
1845	165.	195.	220.	255.	300.	545.	1000.	1800.	5750.	12000.	—
1845-D	1400.	1600.	1800.	2200.	2800.	4750.	7000.	12250.	19000.	26000.	—
1845-O	255.	400.	825.	1600.	3500.	6750.	9750.	14500.	19000.	27500.	—
1846 Small Date	165.	200.	230.	315.	700.	1600.	2200.	3250.	—	—	—
1846	165.	195.	225.	300.	350.	575.	1000.	2300.	4800.	12250.	—
1846-C	1400.	1600.	3000.	5000.	7500.	12000.	16000.	25000.	40000.	80000.	—
1846-D	1400.	1600.	1800.	2500.	4000.	5000.	7500.	14000.	25000.	—	—
1846-D/D	1400.	1600.	1800.	2500.	3500.	4500.	6000.	12000.	20000.	30000.	50000.
1846-O	235.	375.	1000.	1500.	4000.	6750.	8625.	12000.	17500.	25000.	—
1847	165.	215.	245.	265.	325.	400.	775.	1400.	3900.	8500.	24000.
1847/7	190.	220.	265.	350.	550.	1200.	1650.	2400.	4750.	10000.	—
1847-C	1400.	1600.	1800.	2500.	3500.	6000.	10000.	15000.	23000.	32500.	—
1847-D	1400.	1600.	1800.	2500.	3000.	4500.	6000.	8000.	14000.	18000.	—
1847-O	600.	2500.	7000.	8750.	12500.	—	—	—	—	—	—
1848	165.	225.	270.	300.	425.	675.	900.	1450.	2500.	11000.	—
1848-C	1400.	1600.	1800.	2500.	3000.	7500.	12000.	20000.	40000.	65000.	—
1848-D	1400.	1600.	1800.	2500.	3000.	6000.	9000.	15000.	25000.	—	—
1849	165.	190.	225.	365.	745.	1275.	1900.	2900.	6250.	16000.	—
1849-C	1400.	1600.	1800.	2500.	3000.	6000.	9000.	15000.	25000.	35000.	—
1849-D	1400.	1600.	1800.	2500.	3500.	7000.	10000.	18000.	30000.	—	—
1850	210.	275.	675.	800.	1050.	1700.	2450.	3750.	7500.	17000.	—
1850-C	1400.	1600.	1800.	2500.	3000.	6000.	9000.	15000.	25000.	30000.	55000.
1850-D	1400.	1600.	1800.	2500.	5000.	9000.	15000.	30000.	40000.	—	—
1851	165.	215.	235.	265.	360.	500.	1000.	2600.	4500.	10500.	—
1851-C	1400.	1600.	1800.	2500.	3500.	7000.	10000.	18000.	30000.	70000.	85000.
1851-D	1400.	1600.	1800.	2500.	4000.	7500.	10000.	15000.	25000.	35000.	—
1851-O	290.	575.	1250.	2500.	3800.	6750.	9500.	14000.	—	—	—
1852	165.	215.	245.	275.	325.	440.	675.	1250.	3500.	10000.	25000.

—— = Insufficient pricing data

CORONET $5 HALF EAGLE (CONTINUED)

	F-12	VF-20	EF-40	EF-45	AU-50	AU-55	AU-58	MS-60	MS-62	MS-63	MS-64
1852-C	1400.	1600.	1800.	2500.	3000.	4500.	6000.	8000.	18000.	30000.	40000.
1852-D	1400.	1600.	1800.	2500.	3500.	5000.	8000.	15000.	25000.	35000.	—
1853	165.	215.	245.	275.	360.	450.	725.	1350.	3050.	9000.	18500.
1853-C	1400.	1600.	1800.	2500.	3000.	4500.	6000.	8000.	20000.	35000.	—
1853-D	1400.	1600.	1800.	2500.	3000.	4000.	5000.	7000.	18000.	25000.	—
1854	165.	215.	255.	355.	600.	1125.	1400.	2100.	4000.	11000.	25000.
1854-C	1400.	1600.	1800.	2500.	4000.	7000.	10000.	15000.	30000.	45000.	60000.
1854-D	1400.	1600.	1800.	2500.	3000.	5000.	7000.	10000.	20000.	30000.	—
1854-O	240.	300.	525.	825.	1450.	2200.	4000.	8000.	16000.	25000.	—
1854-S AU-55 $210000.											
1855	165.	215.	250.	275.	365.	625.	950.	1650.	4200.	8250.	—
1855-C	1400.	1600.	2000.	3000.	4000.	6000.	12000.	18000.	25000.	40000.	—
1855-D	1400.	1600.	1800.	2500.	3500.	6000.	12000.	20000.	30000.	45000.	—
1855-O	380.	700.	2000.	3000.	4750.	6000.	11625.	21000.	—	—	—
1855-S	215.	385.	1200.	1800.	3050.	5500.	7250.	14500.	—	—	—
1856	165.	215.	245.	275.	325.	575.	950.	2200.	5250.	13500.	22500.
1856-C	1400.	1600.	1800.	2500.	3500.	7000.	12000.	20000.	—	—	—
1856-D	1400.	1600.	1800.	2500.	3500.	6000.	9000.	15000.	25000.	45000.	—
1856-O	400.	650.	1650.	2250.	5250.	7350.	11750.	15000.	—	—	—
1856-S	200.	300.	725.	875.	1200.	2250.	3250.	6250.	—	36500.	—
1857	165.	215.	245.	260.	400.	450.	800.	1500.	4600.	9000.	—
1857-C	1400.	1600.	1800.	2500.	3500.	5000.	8000.	12000.	25000.	35000.	79000.
1857-D	1400.	1600.	1800.	2500.	3500.	7000.	11000.	15000.	25000.	—	—
1857-O	355.	675.	1400.	1850.	4250.	7500.	10500.	15000.	—	50000.	—
1857-S	205.	300.	700.	850.	1350.	2600.	4000.	12000.	—	—	—
1858	195.	245.	550.	600.	700.	1650.	2450.	3750.	6000.	13400.	24000.
1858-C	1400.	1600.	1800.	2500.	3500.	6000.	10000.	15000.	25000.	50000.	—
1858-D	1400.	1600.	1800.	2500.	3500.	6000.	10000.	15000.	25000.	—	—
1858-S	475.	875.	2500.	3300.	7250.	—	—	—	—	—	—
1859	200.	320.	600.	675.	800.	1700.	2850.	6500.	8000.	—	—
1859-C	1400.	1600.	1800.	2500.	4000.	7000.	10000.	20000.	35000.	55000.	—
1859-D	1400.	1600.	1800.	2500.	3500.	6000.	8000.	15000.	30000.	50000.	—
1859-S	600.	1650.	4000.	4750.	6000.	11500.	15000.	—	—	—	—
1860	190.	250.	575.	700.	1100.	1750.	2500.	3750.	7000.	15000.	—
1860-C	1400.	1600.	2500.	3000.	4000.	8500.	11000.	15000.	25000.	35000.	—
1860-D	1400.	1600.	2500.	3000.	4000.	9000.	14000.	20000.	30000.	50000.	—
1860-S	550.	1100.	2000.	2900.	6500.	10000.	16500.	—	—	—	—
1861	165.	215.	250.	275.	360.	435.	750.	1250.	3600.	7500.	12500.
1861-C	1200.	2000.	5000.	7000.	9000.	15000.	22500.	37500.	75000.	115000.	—
1861-D	3000.	5000.	8000.	12000.	20000.	27500.	35000.	50000.	—	—	—
1861-S	525.	1200.	4100.	5000.	8000.	—	17500.	—	—	—	—
1862	455.	850.	1600.	1850.	3500.	—	—	—	—	—	—
1862-S	1300.	3000.	5600.	10000.	15000.	—	—	—	—	—	—
1863	450.	1175.	3500.	4750.	7750.	—	—	—	—	—	—
1863-S	625.	1450.	4250.	6500.	13500.	—	—	—	—	—	—
1864	360.	675.	1750.	2000.	3750.	7000.	10250.	15500.	—	—	—
1864-S	2900.	8000.	14250.	—	45000.	—	—	—	—	—	—
1865	500.	1400.	3750.	6000.	12500.	—	—	—	—	—	—

—— = Insufficient pricing data

CORONET $5 HALF EAGLE (CONTINUED)

	F-12	VF-20	EF-40	EF-45	AU-50	AU-55	AU-58	MS-60	MS-62	MS-63	MS-64
1865-S	525.	1475.	2500.	3500.	5850.	9000.	12500.	21000.	—	—	—
1866-S	775.	1600.	3750.	6500.	13750.	—	—	—	—	—	—
MOTTO ON REVERSE											
1866	375.	850.	1450.	1950.	3400.	5500.	—	—	—	—	—
1866-S	600.	900.	2850.	5250.	9250.	—	—	—	—	—	—
1867	275.	400.	1375.	1850.	3150.	4900.	—	—	—	—	—
1867-S	750.	1425.	2950.	5750.	14250.	—	—	—	—	—	—
1868	265.	500.	925.	2100.	3250.	5750.	8000.	12000.	—	—	—
1868-S	280.	375.	1475.	1600.	3600.	6250.	11000.	18000.	—	—	—
1869	425.	900.	1650.	2000.	4150.	—	—	—	—	—	36000.
1869-S	365.	525.	1800.	2900.	—	8250.	—	—	—	—	—
1870	350.	700.	1750.	2000.	3350.	5650.	—	—	—	—	—
1870-CC	1850.	4500.	14500.	19500.	27500.	32000.	—	75000.	—	—	—
1870-S	500.	1050.	2500.	4750.	9000.	14000.	—	—	—	—	—
1871	385.	725.	1500.	2000.	3375.	6250.	8500.	12000.	—	—	—
1871-CC	650.	1200.	3500.	8850.	15000.	—				—	—
1871-S	270.	355.	1150.	1800.	4150.	8500.	11500.	17000.	—	—	—
1872	400.	675.	1150.	1800.	2850.	4500.	7500.	12250.	15000.	21500.	—
1872-CC	575.	1100.	5250.	11500.	25000.	—	—	—	—	—	—
1872-S	275.	500.	775.	1000.	3250.	7000.	12250.	21000.	—	—	—
1873 Closed 3	150.	165.	190.	260.	500.	600.	875.	1275.	4500.	9250.	—
1873 Open 3	150.	165.	185.	225.	300.	350.	450	665	1800.	6250.	—
1873-CC	1250.	2750.	11500.	19500.	32500.	—	—	—	60000.	—	—
1873-S	340.	675.	975.	1600.	4000.	6500.	12000.	21000.	—	—	—
1874	315.	500.	1125.	1300.	2500.	4200.	5500.	—	—	—	—
1874-CC	500.	800.	2450.	4350.	11500.	16500.	23500.	34000.	—	—	—
1874-S	425.	800.	1725.	3600.	5000.	—	—	—	—	—	—
1875-CC	800.	1600.	3600.	5500.	12250.	22500.	—	—	—	—	—
1875-S	500.	775.	2400.	3900.	6800.	9500.	16250.	27500.	—	—	—
1875 EF-40 $47500 EF-45 $57500 AU-50 $75000 PF 63 $50000 PF 64 $100000.											
1876	445.	825.	1950.	2350.	3550.	6250.	8750.	12500.	16000.	22500.	30000.
1876-CC	550.	1350.	4350.	5200.	12500.	16000.	—	—	—	—	
1876-S	800.	1350.	3850.	7500.	—	—	—	—	—	—	—
1877	420.	825.	1750.	2250.	3500.	5000.	—	—	—	—	—
1877-CC	465.	1000.	3600.	4250.	8250.	11000.	—	—	—	—	—
1877-S	175.	275.	575.	975.	1850.	5100.	—	—	—	—	—
1878	150.	165.	170.	180.	230.	250.	325.	450.	750.	2250.	5000.
1878-CC	2000.	4000.	12000.	14000.	22000.	—	—	—	—	—	—
1878-S	150.	165.	175.	190.	240.	535.	750.	1075.	2000.	5000.	8500.
1879	150.	165.	170.	175.	200.	240.	300.	400.	600.	1700.	3600.
1879-CC	350.	500.	1600.	2000.	3200.	6000.	—	—	—	—	—
1879-S	150.	165.	170.	180.	210.	270.	550.	1050.	1850.	4250.	7500.
1880	150.	165.	170.	175.	200.	215.	225.	245.	350.	1300.	2300.
1880-CC	270.	375.	725.	775.	1450.	4500.	7125.	11500.	—	—	—
1880-S	150.	165.	170.	175.	200.	215.	235.	260.	340.	1100.	2150.
1881	150.	165.	170.	175.	200.	215.	225.	240.	335.	825.	2000.
1881/0	250.	315.	600.	675.	800.	1000.	1150.	1350.	3100.	7000.	13000.

—— = Insufficient pricing data

CORONET $5 HALF EAGLE (CONTINUED)

	F-12	VF-20	EF-40	EF-45	AU-50	AU-55	AU-58	MS-60	MS-62	MS-63	MS-64
1881-CC	330.	450.	1600.	3750.	6500.	9250.	13250.	20000.	—	—	—
1881-S	150.	165.	170.	175.	200.	215.	230.	255.	395.	1175.	2400.
1882	150.	165.	170.	175.	200.	215.	225.	240.	345.	925.	2000.
1882-CC	250.	300.	450.	550.	725.	1850.	3750.	6750.	—	—	—
1882-S	150.	165.	170.	175.	200.	215.	235.	265.	350.	1025.	2050.
1883	150.	165.	170.	175.	200.	215.	250.	300.	575.	1700.	4850.
1883-CC	290.	385.	900.	1550.	3150.	7000.	11250.	18500.	—	—	—
1883-S	150.	165.	200.	210.	235.	330.	550.	925.	1550.	3750.	—
1884	150.	165.	175.	185.	220.	325.	575.	950.	1600.	3900.	—
1884-CC	315.	500.	950.	1800.	2550.	4500.	9500.	17500.	—	—	—
1884-S	150.	170.	180.	190.	220.	240.	275.	325.	650.	1950.	6000.
1885	150.	165.	170.	175.	200.	215.	225.	245.	500.	1200.	2100.
1885-S	150.	165.	170.	175.	200.	215.	225.	240.	335.	775.	2000.
1886	150.	165.	170.	175.	200.	225.	240.	270.	575.	1200.	3750.
1886-S	150.	165.	170.	175.	200.	225.	235.	250.	345.	775.	2050.
1887-S	150.	165.	170.	175.	200.	215.	225.	240.	400.	925.	—

1887 Proof Only PF-50 $17000;PF-58 $18000; PF-60 $25000; PF-62 $32500; PF-63(PCGS) $58000; PF-64 $72500; PF-65 $150000.

	F-12	VF-20	EF-40	EF-45	AU-50	AU-55	AU-58	MS-60	MS-62	MS-63	MS-64
1888	150.	165.	200.	225.	280.	350.	425.	550.	1400.	2750.	—
1888-S	155.	175.	230.	240.	330.	750.	875.	1100.	2500.	—	—
1889	165.	250.	330.	415.	525.	675.	775.	950.	2400.	5000.	—
1890	215.	325.	485.	565.	675.	900.	1150.	1600.	4200.	11500.	—
1890-CC	185.	245.	320.	350.	450.	600.	750.	1000.	2200.	4500.	12000.
1891	150.	165.	190.	200.	225.	275.	350.	500.	900.	1900.	5250.
1891-CC	175.	240.	290.	330.	380.	435.	525.	700.	1325.	3350.	8750.
1892	150.	165.	170.	175.	200.	215.	225.	240.	350.	1275.	3500.
1892-CC	180.	240.	315.	375.	450.	875.	1150.	1550.	3250.	7750.	—
1892-O	360.	460.	750.	825.	1200.	1700.	2100.	2800.	6300.	12500.	—
1892-S	150.	165.	180.	190.	230.	430.	525.	675.	1200.	3750.	—
1893	150.	165.	170.	175.	200.	215.	225.	245.	335.	650.	1950.
1893-CC	185.	245.	325.	385.	550.	775.	1075.	1575.	3800.	8000.	13500.
1893-O	150.	185.	215.	240.	275.	450.	675.	1075.	2300.	6100.	—
1893-S	150.	165.	175.	185.	200.	275.	300.	350.	525.	1250.	4650.
1894	150.	165.	170.	175.	200.	215.	225.	240.	335.	700.	3500.
1894-O	150.	175.	260.	280.	350.	750.	1000.	1450.	2650.	5500.	—
1894-S	165.	200.	325.	360.	600.	1000.	1525.	2400.	3250.	9750.	—
1895	150.	165.	170.	175.	200.	215.	225.	240.	335.	700.	1300.
1895-S	150.	195.	280.	290.	500.	1000.	1750.	3000.	4000.	—	—
1896	150.	165.	175.	185.	200.	225.	275.	350.	515.	1650.	3750.
1896-S	150.	190.	285.	315.	400.	700.	975.	1450.	2950.	—	—
1897	150.	165.	170.	175.	200.	215.	225.	240.	335.	775.	1650.
1897-S	150.	170.	225.	240.	275.	360.	550.	875.	1500.	6900.	11500.
1898	150.	165.	170.	175.	200.	215.	225.	240.	345.	750.	2100.
1898-S	150.	165.	170.	175.	200.	215.	230.	250.	390.	1175.	5750.
1899	150.	165.	170.	175.	200.	215.	225.	240.	335.	575.	1200.
1899-S	150.	170.	170.	170.	200.	215.	225.	240.	350.	800.	2800.
1900	150.	165.	170.	175.	200.	215.	225.	240.	335.	550.	1250.
1900-S	150.	170.	190.	200.	230.	250.	300.	375.	500.	1150.	2300.

—— = Insufficient pricing data

CORONET $5 HALF EAGLE (CONTINUED)

	F-12	VF-20	EF-40	EF-45	AU-50	AU-55	AU-58	MS-60	MS-62	MS-63	MS-64
1901	150.	165.	170.	175.	200.	215.	225.	240.	335.	650.	1700.
1901-S	150.	165.	170.	175.	200.	215.	225.	240.	335.	550.	900.
1901/0-S	150.	170.	210.	220.	265.	310.	330.	360.	475.	775.	2550.
1902	150.	165.	170.	175.	200.	215.	225.	240.	350.	775.	1875.
1902-S	150.	165.	170.	175.	200.	215.	225.	240.	340.	675.	1000.
1903	150.	165.	170.	175.	200.	215.	225.	240.	350.	800.	1750.
1903-S	150.	165.	170.	175.	200.	215.	225.	240.	340.	575.	1000.
1904	150.	165.	170.	175.	200.	215.	225.	240.	335.	675.	1700.
1904-S	150.	165.	185.	195.	270.	475.	700.	1050.	1850.	3500.	15000.
1905	150.	165.	170.	175.	200.	215.	230.	250.	345.	1050.	2000.
1905-S	150.	165.	170.	180.	225.	325.	425.	600.	1150.	2600.	5500.
1906	150.	165.	170.	175.	200.	215.	225.	240.	350.	1100.	1700.
1906-D	150.	165.	170.	175.	200.	215.	225.	240.	335.	650.	1600.
1906-S	150.	165.	170.	170.	200.	215.	255.	320.	490.	1500.	2600.
1907	150.	165.	170.	175.	200.	215.	225.	240.	335.	575.	1300.
1907-D	150.	165.	170.	175.	200.	215.	225.	240.	335.	600.	1400.
1908	150.	165.	170.	175.	200.	215.	225.	240.	325.	575.	950.

Indian Head $5 half eagle

Date of authorization: Jan. 18, 1837
Dates of issue: 1908-1929
Designer: Bela Lyon Pratt
Engraver: Charles Barber
Diameter: 21.54 mm/0.85 inch
Weight: 8.36 grams/0.27 ounce
Metallic Content: 90% gold, 10% copper
Weight of pure gold: 7.52 grams/0.24 ounce
Edge: Reeded
Mint mark: Reverse lower left

	EF-40	AU-50	AU-55	MS-60	MS-62	MS-63	MS-64	MS-65
1908	225.	250.	275.	350.	700.	1800.	3700.	13000.
1908-D	225.	250.	275.	350.	700.	1800.	3700.	25000.
1908-S	425.	500.	700.	1300.	1800.	3000.	6000.	16000.
1909	225.	250.	275.	350.	700.	1800.	3700.	14000.
1909-D	225.	250.	275.	350.	700.	1800.	3700.	14000.
1909-O	2500.	3500.	5000.	12000.	22000.	60000.	—	—
1909-S	275.	350.	450.	1500.	3700.	12000.	30000.	41500.
1910	225.	250.	275.	350.	700.	1800.	4000.	20000.
1910-D	225.	300.	325.	425.	700.	2200.	10000.	—
1910-S	275.	350.	600.	1200.	4000.	6500.	25000.	—
1911	225.	250.	275.	350.	700.	1800.	3700.	16000.
1911-D	500.	650.	1200.	3800.	12000.	35000.	50000.	—
1911-S	275.	300.	350.	600.	1000.	2800.	30000.	—
1912	225.	250.	275.	350.	700.	1800.	3700.	16000.
1912-S	350.	400.	550.	1700.	4500.	14000.	30000.	—
1913	225.	250.	275.	350.	700.	1800.	3700.	15000.
1913-S	300.	400.	600.	1400.	3500.	14000.	35000.	—
1914	225.	250.	275.	365.	700.	1800.	3700.	16000.
1914-D	225.	250.	275.	550.	800.	3000.	5000.	28000.
1914-S	300.	350.	550.	1500.	3500.	14000.	35000.	—
1915	225.	250.	275.	350.	700.	1800.	3700.	16000.
1915-S	400.	500.	700.	2000.	5000.	18000.	35000.	—
1916-S	300.	350.	400.	600.	1200.	3000.	7500.	25000.
1929	6500.	7500.	8000.	9500.	10000.	11000.	15000.	45000.

—— = Insufficient pricing data

Capped Bust $10 eagle

Small Eagle reverse

Heraldic Eagle reverse

Date of authorization: April 2, 1792
Dates of issue: 1795-1804
Designer/Engraver: Robert Scot
Diameter: 33.00 mm/1.30 inches
Weight: 17.50 grams/0.56 ounce
Metallic Content: 91.67% gold, 8.33% copper and silver
Weight of pure gold: 16.04 grams/0.52 ounce
Edge: Reeded
Mint mark: None

	F-12	VF-20	EF-40	EF-45	AU-50	AU-55	MS-60	MS-62	MS-63	MS-64
SMALL EAGLE										
1795 13 Leaves	16000.	20000.	30000.	32000.	35000.	40000.	60000.	85000.	140000.	225000.
1795 9 Leaves	30000.	45000.	60000.	70000.	90000.	115000.	200000.	—	—	—
1796	18000.	25000.	35000.	40000.	45000.	50000.	75000.	125000.	200000.	—
1797	25000.	30000.	35000.	45000.	70000.	85000.	—	—	—	—
HERALDIC EAGLE										
1797	7500.	9000.	13000.	15000.	18000.	20000.	35000.	50000.	—	—
1798/7 9 X 4 Stars	12000.	20000.	30000.	35000.	45000.	60000.	100000.	150000.	—	—

—— = Insufficient pricing data

CAPPED BUST $10 EAGLE (CONTINUED)

	F-12	VF-20	EF-40	EF-45	AU-50	AU-55	MS-60	MS-62	MS-63	MS-64
1798/7 7 X 6 Stars	25000.	40000.	65000.	85000.	125000.	150000.	225000.	—	—	—
1799	7500.	8500.	12000.	13000.	15000.	18000.	22000.	30000.	35000.	55000.
1800	7000.	8000.	11000.	12000.	14000.	17000.	25000.	40000.	60000.	—
1801	7000.	8000.	11000.	12000.	14000.	16000.	20000.	25000.	35000.	55000.
1803 Small Stars	7000.	8000.	11000.	12000.	14000.	17000.	25000.	35000.	50000.	65000.
1803 Large Stars	7000.	8500.	10000.	15000.	18000.	20000.	30000.	50000.	75000.	90000.
1803 14 Reverse Stars	9000.	12000.	15000.	20000.	25000.	30000.	40000.	60000.	—	—
1804	6500.	9000.	14000.	17000.	20000.	25000.	35000.	60000.	—	—

Coronet $10 eagle

Date of authorization: Jan. 18, 1837
Dates of issue: 1838-1907
Designers: Obverse: Christian Gobrecht
Reverse: John Reich-William Kneass-Christian Gobrecht
Engraver: Christian Gobrecht
Diameter: 27.00 mm/1.07 inches
Weight: 16.72 grams/.54 ounce
Metallic Content: (1838-1873)90% gold,10% copper and silver
(1873-1907): 90% gold, 10% copper
Weight of pure gold: 15.05 grams/0.48 ounce
Edge: Reeded
Mint mark: Reverse below eagle

	F-12	VF-20	EF-40	EF-45	AU-50	AU-55	AU-58	MS-60	MS-62	MS-63
NO MOTTO										
1838	600.	1150.	2900.	4025.	6250.	11000.	16000.	27500.	55000.	—
1839 Old Portrait	535.	900.	1850.	3000.	4950.	9250.	12750.	25000.	—	47500.
1839 New Portrait	850.	1750.	3200.	4500.	6750.	11500.	20000.	—	—	—
1840	305.	360.	575.	850.	1600.	3000.	5250.	10500.	—	—

—— = Insufficient pricing data

CORONET $10 EAGLE (CONTINUED)

	F-12	VF-20	EF-40	EF-45	AU-50	AU-55	AU-58	MS-60	MS-62	MS-63
1841	300.	325.	550.	700.	1375.	2450.	4000.	8500.	20000.	—
1841-O	1250.	2200.	4500.	5750.	11500.	19500.	—	—	—	—
1842 Small Date	270.	330.	400.	700.	2050.	3150.	4675.	9750.	—	—
1842 Large Date	280.	340.	450.	700.	1250.	3000.	4500.	8750.	12750.	20000.
1842-O	285.	375.	625	1000	2450.	6250.	11500.	26500.	—	—
1843 Doubled Date	295.	425.	575.	750.	3050.	—	—	—	—	—
1843	280.	330.	400.	625.	1700.	5450.	—	—	—	—
1843-O	275.	320.	375.	600.	1375.	3500.	6750.	12500.	18000.	—
1844	575.	1500.	2700.	3400.	6000.	—	12000.	18000.	—	—
1844-O	265.	330.	440.	775.	1650.	3250.	6500.	17000.	38500.	—
1845	400	525.	750.	1300.	2000.	3150.	5500.	12500.	21500.	—
1845-O	280.	360.	700.	1250.	2250.	7500.	10500.	19000.	40000.	70000.
1846	450.	575.	1025.	2500.	5250.	10500.	—	—	—	—
1846-O	290.	425.	700.	2400.	4800.	—	—	—	27500.	—
1846/5-O	320.	625.	1050.	1550.	3100.	7000.	12500.	—	—	50000.
1847	245.	290.	340.	390.	525.	825.	1500.	3500.	7000.	17500.
1847-O	265.	300.	375.	450.	575.	1100.	2000.	4500.	9000.	18250.
1848	270.	320.	400.	500.	775.	1300.	2300.	5300.	10000.	27500.
1848-O	320.	500.	1100.	1750.	3500.	8000.	10750.	15000.	23500.	37500.
1849	255.	290.	350.	450.	600.	900.	1600.	3550.	5900.	13250.
1849/1848	450	700.	975.	1300.	1800.	3500.	—	—	—	—
1849-O	385.	750.	1700.	2900.	5500.	7500.	—	20000.	—	
1850 Large Date	255.	290.	370.	435.	650.	950.	1700.	3950.	7500.	15000.
1850 Small Date	320.	375.	925.	1450.	2350.	4050.	5500.	9500.	—	—
1850-O	295.	425.	1000.	1600.	2550.	6000.	—	—	—	—
1851	255.	290.	395.	525.	925.	1400.	2250.	4650.	—	25500.
1851-O	250.	290.	500.	700.	1150.	2950.	3775.	6250.	—	30000.
1852	255.	290.	335.	440.	600.	1100.	1850.	4050.	7000.	—
1852-O	370.	685.	1125.	2250.	3500.	8500.	11250.	18000.	37500.	—
1853	255.	290.	335.	415.	560.	850.	1450.	3750.	6250.	—
1853/2	420.	600.	800.	950.	1650.	3650.	—	—	—	—
1853-O	290.	320.	415.	575.	1000.	2500.	5250.	—	—	—
1854	295.	315.	385.	515.	775.	1400.	2475.	5700.	16500.	—
1854-O Small Date	270.	350.	675.	900.	1400.	3000.	—	—	—	—
1854-O Large Date	365.	500.	800.	1100.	1800.	3700.	4900.	8500.	19500.	41500.
1854-S	275.	305.	425.	560.	1275.	1900.	4100.	10750.	—	—
1855	260.	290.	360.	430.	575.	1100.	1950.	4500.	9500.	24000.
1855-O	315.	575.	1300.	2450.	5250.	8250.	12500.	—	—	—
1855-S	750.	1150.	2350.	3000.	6000.	8250.	—	—	—	—
1856	270.	290.	350.	430.	575.	1100.	2000.	4650.	6150.	13500.
1856-O	415.	625.	975.	2150.	3750.	6750.	10500.	—	—	—
1856-S	250.	290.	525.	675.	1100.	2600.	4150.	8750.	—	—
1857	290.	525.	925.	1250.	2200.	3500.	5500.	—	—	—
1857 overdate	600.	1400.	2850.	3750.	7500.	—	—	—	—	—
1857-O	600.	1100.	1850.	2300.	3200.	5750.	9500.	20000.	—	—

—— = Insufficient pricing data

	F-12	VF-20	EF-40	EF-45	AU-50	AU-55	AU-58	MS-60	MS-62	MS-63
1857-S	315.	415.	1100.	1400.	2200.	4500.	8750.	—	—	—
1858	—	4750.	8000.	10250.	13500.	—	—	—	—	—
1858-O	270.	330.	625.	775.	1650.	3250.	4825.	9500.	19000.	—
1858-S	800.	1600.	3250.	3500.	5750.	15000.	30000.	—	—	—
1859	285.	365.	700.	900.	1250.	2750.	4500.	10000.	—	—
1859-O	1800.	3750.	7700.	12500.	17000.	—	—	—	—	—
1859-S	1100.	1650.	4100.	8000.	14750.	—	—	—	—	—
1860	260.	415.	650.	1050.	1500.	2800.	3550.	8000.	—	30000.
1860-O	375.	550.	1050.	1300.	1950.	4000.	7500.	—	32500.	—
1860-S	1850.	3400.	5500.	8250.	15750.	—	—	—	—	—
1861	250.	300.	355.	440.	525.	875.	1625.	3900.	7000.	15500.
1861-S	625.	1650.	2600.	3925.	7000.	10500.	—	—	—	—
1862	255.	600.	975.	1450.	2100.	2750.	—	—	20000.	—
1862-S	650.	1750.	2800.	3500.	6500.	—	—	—	—	—
1863	—	3650.	7500.	11000.	17000.	23000.	30500.	40000.	55000.	75000.
1863-S	675.	1725.	3600.	5000.	9750.	—	17500.	27500.	—	—
1864	725.	1600.	2750.	3800.	6250.	—	12000.	19000.	—	—
1864-S	2750.	5250.	12500.	17000.	26000.	—	—	—	—	—
1865	700.	1750.	3450.	4000.	6350.	—	—	—	—	—
1865-S	2250.	6750.	12000.	—	—	—	—	—	—	—
1865-S Inverted 865/186	1100.	2300.	6250.	8750.	14000.	—	—	—	—	75000.
1866-S	1350.	2400.	3400.	4100.	10250.	16500.	27500.	—	—	—
MOTTO ON REVERSE										
1866	515.	850.	1700.	2550.	3950.	8250.	16500.	—	—	—
1866-S	575.	1550.	3375.	4100.	7250.	—	—	—	—	—
1867	600.	1475.	2550.	3450.	5000.	7250.	14500.	—	—	—
1867-S	1100.	2150.	4750.	6950.	10250.	16500.	30000.	—	—	—
1868	440.	475.	725.	1200.	1900.	3400.	6220.	17500.	—	—
1868-S	600.	1300.	2250.	2800.	4250.	—	—	—	—	—
1869	750.	1300.	2600.	3200.	6750.	12500.	15000.	24500.	—	—
1869-S	825.	1700.	2650.	3350.	7000.	14000.	16750.	27500.	—	—
1870	435.	725.	1100.	1375.	2675.	6250.	12500.	—	—	—
1870-CC	5000.	12000.	27000.	35000.	50000.	—	—	—	—	—
1870-S	675.	1250.	2650.	3500.	7250.	14500.	25000.	—	—	—
1871	—	1200.	1925.	2750.	4500.	10000.	15000.	22500.	—	—
1871-CC	1350.	2100.	4950.	8500.	19000.	—	—	—	—	—
1871-S	625.	1100.	1800.	2150.	5500.	12500.	20000.	—	—	—
1872	1300.	2100.	3450.	5500.	10500.	—	—	17500.	22500.	—
1872-CC	1600.	3450.	10750.	12000.	—	—	—	—	—	—
1872-S	400.	585.	950.	1125.	1750.	5000.	10000.	—	—	—
1873	—	4500.	9500.	11250.	15000.	17500.	22500.	—	—	—
1873-CC	2000.	6750.	12750.	18500.	29000.	—	—	—	—	—
1873-S	585.	950.	2300.	3250.	4750.	6000.	10000.	—	—	—
1874	240.	265.	280.	290.	350.	425.	725.	1850.	5200.	10000.
1874-CC	560.	875.	2400.	5000.	8750.	—	—	—	—	—
1874-S	600.	1200.	3500.	4250.	7350.	11750.	20000.	—	—	—
1875	—	42000.	60000.	80000.	90000.	—	—	—	—	—

—— = Insufficient pricing data

CORONET $10 EAGLE (CONTINUED)

	F-12	VF-20	EF-40	EF-45	AU-50	AU-55	AU-58	MS-60	MS-62	MS-63
1875-CC	2000.	4500.	10000.	15000.	—	—	—	—	—	—
1876	—	3100.	6000.	12000.	17500.	—	—	—	—	—
1876-CC	1650.	3150.	6250.	9500.	22500.	29000.	40000.	—	—	—
1876-S	625.	1100.	1950.	2750.	5600.	—	—	—	—	—
1877	—	1950.	3400.	5500.	9000.	10750.	14500.	—	—	—
1877-CC	1550.	2500.	5000.	7000.	12000.	—	—	—	—	—
1877-S	325.	475.	700.	1200.	2200.	3200.	5500.	—	—	—
1878	230.	250.	290.	300.	325.	450.	600.	1050.	2350.	4750.
1878-CC	2550.	4300.	9000.	14000.	20000.	—	—	—	—	—
1878-S	300.	400.	600.	1150.	1975.	3150.	5500.	12500.	—	—
1879	210.	225.	250.	260.	340.	425.	495.	775.	1450.	3250.
1879/8	290.	350.	400.	500.	750.	850.	925.	1200.	1900.	—
1879-CC	5000.	10000.	15000.	20000.	25000.	30000.	35000.	—	—	—
1879-O	2050.	2400.	3800.	5500.	9000.	14750.	25000.	—	—	—
1879-S	210.	225.	250.	260.	275.	650.	800.	1200.	3500.	—
1880	210.	225.	250.	260.	275.	280.	285.	300.	700.	2250.
1880-CC	340.	450.	725.	1000.	1600.	3900.	5750.	12500.	—	—
1880-O	265.	385.	750.	900.	1300.	2100.	3500.	9000.	—	—
1880-S	210.	230.	250.	300.	350.	375.	400.	465.	1300.	3500.
1881	210.	225.	250.	260.	275.	280.	285.	300.	490.	900.
1881-CC	315.	360.	475.	625.	900.	1200.	2500.	7000.	12000.	—
1881-O	250.	375.	650.	825.	1225.	2050.	3200.	7750.	—	—
1881-S	210.	225.	250.	260.	275.	280.	285.	400.	825.	6000.
1882	210.	225.	250.	260.	275.	280.	285.	300.	485.	900.
1882-CC	475.	650.	1100.	1850.	2800.	6750.	12500.	—	—	—
1882-O	260.	350.	525.	750.	1025.	2000.	3250.	8250.	—	—
1882-S	210.	225.	250.	260.	275.	280.	350.	450.	1550.	5000.
1883	210.	225.	250.	260.	275.	280.	285.	310.	650.	1750.
1883-CC	340.	425.	650.	1150.	2250.	4500.	6000.	11500.	—	—
1883-O	1350.	3550.	7000.	—	10250.	13000.	22500.	—	—	—
1883-S	210.	230.	350.	365.	400.	550.	710.	1350.	4500.	15000.
1884	210.	225.	250.	260.	275.	375.	460.	800.	1750.	4250.
1884-CC	395.	600.	900.	1350.	2200.	4100.	5300.	10000.	—	—
1884-S	210.	225.	250.	260.	275.	375.	430.	650.	1650.	—
1885	210.	225.	250.	260.	275.	280.	290.	410.	675.	3750.
1885-S	210.	225.	250.	260.	275.	280.	285.	375.	1500.	4200.
1886	210.	225.	250.	260.	275.	280.	200.	400.	600.	2500.
1886-S	210.	225.	250.	260.	275.	280.	285.	315.	455.	1000.
1887	210.	275.	250.	260.	330.	475.	545.	825.	2050.	4250.
1887-S	210.	225.	250.	260.	275.	280.	285.	305.	625.	2500.
1888	210.	275.	250.	260.	325.	515.	585.	825.	4850.	—
1888-O	210.	225.	250.	260.	275.	400.	430.	550.	1850.	6000.
1888-S	210.	225.	250.	260.	275.	280.	285.	300.	1100.	2950.
1889	275.	355.	500.	580.	900.	1750.	2100.	3150.	—	—
1889-S	210.	225.	250.	260.	275.	280.	285.	300.	460.	1750.
1890	210.	225.	250.	260.	330.	500.	575.	875.	2650.	4650.
1890-CC	310.	350.	475.	510.	725.	950.	1250.	2400.	6000.	15000.
1891	210.	225.	250.	260.	275.	280.	285.	300.	650.	2700.

—— = Insufficient pricing data

CORONET $10 EAGLE (CONTINUED)

	F-12	VF-20	EF-40	EF-45	AU-50	AU-55	AU-58	MS-60	MS-62	MS-63
1891-CC	275.	335.	385.	415.	475.	525.	565.	725.	1400.	5000.
1892	210.	225.	250.	260.	275.	280.	285.	300.	430.	1400.
1892-CC	295.	325.	400.	475.	625.	1200.	2000.	3500.	5000.	9500.
1892-O	210.	225.	250.	260.	275.	290.	350.	400.	2350.	—
1892-S	210.	225.	250.	260.	275.	280.	285.	385.	825.	2350.
1893	210.	225.	250.	260.	275.	280.	285.	300.	395.	775.
1893-CC	325.	400.	600.	800.	1450.	2600.	4000.	7800.	—	—
1893-O	210.	225.	290.	300.	325.	410.	450.	600.	2450.	5250.
1893-S	210.	225.	250.	260.	275.	325.	385.	525.	1400.	3975.
1894	210.	225.	250.	260.	275.	280.	285.	300.	420.	800.
1894-O	210.	225.	250.	310.	375.	550.	640.	1000.	2350.	5000.
1894-S	250.	295.	415.	500.	875.	—	—	3250.	—	—
1895	210.	225.	250.	260.	275.	280.	285.	300.	425.	875.
1895-O	210.	225.	250.	260.	275.	360.	385.	485.	1300.	3650.
1895-S	255.	305.	365.	400.	775.	1250.	1500.	2500.	5000.	—
1896	210.	225.	250.	260.	275.	280.	285.	300.	525.	1750.
1896-S	210.	225.	325.	350.	500.	600.	1025.	2750.	—	10000.
1897	210.	225.	250.	260.	275.	280.	285.	300.	420.	750.
1897-O	210.	225.	295.	305.	355.	375.	455.	775.	1300.	2150.
1897-S	210.	230.	300.	315.	370.	400.	490.	850.	1800.	3400.
1898	210.	225.	250.	260.	275.	280.	285.	300.	430.	900.
1898-S	210.	225.	250.	260.	275.	280.	285.	400.	635.	2750.
1899	210.	225.	250.	260.	275.	280.	285.	300.	415.	700.
1899-O	210.	230.	250.	260.	275.	385.	410.	500.	1150.	3600.
1899-S	210.	225.	250.	260.	275.	280.	285.	300.	600.	2250.
1900	210.	225.	250.	260.	275.	280.	285.	300.	415.	750.
1900-S	210.	230.	295.	325.	375.	525.	615.	975.	2100.	3900.
1901	210.	225.	250.	260.	275.	280.	285.	300.	415.	675.
1901-O	210.	225.	250.	260.	275.	350.	365.	410.	900.	2400.
1901-S	210.	225.	250.	260.	275.	280.	285.	300.	410.	675.
1902	210.	225.	250.	260.	275.	280.	285.	300.	575.	1500.
1902-S	210.	225.	250.	260.	275.	280.	285.	300.	415.	675.
1903	210.	225.	250.	260.	275.	280.	285.	300.	445.	1600.
1903-O	210.	225.	250.	260.	275.	280.	285.	375.	650.	2350.
1903-S	210.	225.	250.	260.	275.	280.	285.	300.	455.	1000.
1904	210.	225.	250.	260.	275.	280.	285.	300.	420.	1600.
1904-O	210.	225.	250.	260.	275.	280.	285.	385.	800.	2300.
1905	210.	225.	250.	260.	275.	280.	285.	300.	415.	1200.
1905-S	210.	225.	250.	260.	330.	450.	625.	1250.	3900.	4750.
1906	210.	225.	250.	260.	275.	280.	285.	300.	420.	950.
1906-D	210.	225.	250.	260.	275.	280.	285.	300.	470.	1000.
1906-O	210.	230.	250.	260.	350.	390.	425.	575.	950.	2500.
1906-S	210.	225.	250.	260.	275.	295.	375.	485.	1100.	3500.
1907	210.	225.	250.	260.	275.	280.	285.	300.	410.	800.
1907-D	210.	225.	250.	260.	275.	280.	285.	300.	455.	1200.
1907-S	210.	225.	250.	260.	275.	280.	400.	675.	1175.	2650.

—— = Insufficient pricing data

Indian Head $10 eagle

Date of authorization: Jan. 18, 1837
Dates of issue: 1907-1933
Designer: Augustus Saint-Gaudens
Engraver: Charles Barber
Diameter: 27.00 mm/1.07 inches
Weight: 16.72 grams/0.54 ounce
Metallic Content: 90% gold, 10% copper
Weight of pure gold: 15.05 grams/0.48 ounce
Edge: Starred
Mint mark: Reverse left of TEN DOLLARS

	EF-40	AU-50	AU-55	MS-60	MS-62	MS-63	MS-64	MS-65
NO MOTTO ON REVERSE								
1907 Wire Rim, Periods	5000.	8000.	14000.	18000.	20000.	25000.	35000.	50000.
1907 Rolled Rim, Periods	22000.	27000.	30000.	35000.	45000.	60000.	85000.	110000.
1907 No Periods	400.	450.	500.	600.	1100.	2700.	3800.	7500.
1908	425.	500.	600.	1000.	1600.	4500.	6500.	15000.
1908-D	400.	450.	500.	800.	2000.	7000.	18000.	45000.
MOTTO ON REVERSE								
1908	400.	450.	500.	600.	800.	2000.	3500.	6500.
1908-D	400.	450.	500.	800.	2000.	6500.	14000.	30000.
1908-S	450.	600.	800.	2000.	3500.	9000.	14000.	25000.
1909	400.	450.	500.	600.	800.	2500.	3500.	9000.
1909-D	400.	450.	600.	700.	1400.	4000.	11000.	45000.
1909-S	400.	450.	500.	700.	1500.	4500.	7000.	14000.
1910	400.	450.	500.	600.	800.	1400.	2500.	6500.
1910-D	400.	450.	500.	600.	700.	1200.	2000.	6000.
1910-S	400.	450.	500.	800.	1500.	6500.	17000.	50000.
1911	400.	450.	500.	600.	800.	1400.	2500.	6500.
1911-D	700.	1000.	1500.	4000.	8000.	18000.	55000.	100000.
1911-S	550.	650.	750.	1200.	2500.	8500.	11000.	13000.
1912	400.	450.	500.	600.	800.	1400.	3500.	8000.
1912-S	400.	450	600	900.	1800.	5500.	9000.	50000.
1913	400.	450.	500.	600.	800.	1200.	2500.	5500.
1913-S	700.	900.	1800.	4000.	10000.	30000.	55000.	—
1914	400	450	500.	600.	900.	2000.	3000.	8500.
1914-D	400.	450.	500.	600.	900.	2000.	4000.	13000.

—— = Insufficient pricing data

	EF-40	AU-50	AU-55	MS-60	MS-62	MS-63	MS-64	MS-65
1914-S	400.	450.	500.	800.	2500.	6500.	14000.	45000.
1915	400.	450.	500.	600.	800.	1500.	2500.	6500.
1915-S	700.	900.	1400.	3500.	6000.	11000.	32000.	65000.
1916-S	450.	500.	550.	900.	1500.	4000.	10000.	20000.
1920-S	7000.	9000.	11000.	18000.	35000.	55000.	75000.	—
1926	400.	450.	500.	600.	750.	1000.	1800.	4500.
1930-S	6000.	7000.	8000.	11000.	15000.	20000.	30000.	40000.
1932	400.	450.	500.	600.	750.	1000.	1800.	4500.
1933	—	—	—	80000.	110000.	135000.	200000.	575000.

Coronet $20 double eagle

Date of authorization: March 3, 1849
Dates of issue: 1850-1907
Designer/Engraver: James B. Longacre
Diameter: 34.29 mm/1.35 inches
Weight: 33.44 grams/1.07 ounce
Metallic Content: (1850-1873): 90% gold, 10% copper and silver
(1873-1907): 90% gold, 10% copper
Weight of pure gold: 30.09 grams/0.97 ounce
Edge: Reeded
Mint mark: Reverse below eagle

	VF-20	EF-40	EF-45	AU-50	AU-55	AU-58	MS-60	MS-62	MS-63
NO MOTTO ON REVERSE									
1849 One Specimen, Smithsonian collection.									
1850	700.	1100.	1400.	2500.	3500.	4500.	6500.	20000.	40000.
1850-O	1000.	1500.	3000.	7500.	18000.	25000.	40000.	—	—
1851	700.	750.	800.	900.	1500.	2300.	3750.	8250.	18000.
1851-O	1000.	1200.	1800.	2500.	9000.	15000.	25000.	40000.	60000.
1852	625.	700.	800.	1000.	1400.	2500.	3500.	7500.	14000.
1852-O	1000.	1300.	1800.	2500.	7500.	12000.	20000.	35000.	50000.

—— = Insufficient pricing data

CORONET $20 DOUBLE EAGLE (CONTINUED)

	VF-20	EF-40	EF-45	AU-50	AU-55	AU-58	MS-60	MS-62	MS-63
1853	700.	800.	900.	1000.	1500.	2500.	5000.	14000.	26000.
1853/2	750.	1300.	2000.	4000.	6000.	15000.	35000.	—	—
1853-O	1000.	1500.	2500.	3500.	10000.	20000.	35000.	—	—
1854	625.	675.	750.	925.	1500.	2500.	6000.	14000.	—
1854-O	40000.	60000.	90000.	125000.	175000.	285000.	—	—	—
1854-S	700.	900.	1200.	1550.	2250.	3250.	5000.	8000.	12500.
1855	650.	700.	900.	1500.	2500.	4000.	10000.	20000.	45000.
1855-O	3500.	6500.	14000.	25000.	35000.	60000.	85000.	—	—
1855-S	750.	900.	1200.	1500.	2500.	4000.	7000.	—	20000.
1856	650.	750.	900.	1200.	2500.	4500.	9000.	15000.	31500.
1856-O	50000.	75000.	100000.	125000.	200000.	225000.	250000.	300000.	400000.
1856-S	700.	800.	1100.	1400.	2600.	3500.	5000.	7500.	10000.
1857	650.	700.	800.	1000.	1600.	2500.	3500.	10000.	27500.
1857-O	1200.	2500.	3500.	5000.	12000.	20000.	30000.	—	—
1857-S	700.	925.	950.	1200.	2000.	2500.	3500.	5000.	6500.
1858	750.	900.	1100.	1500.	3000.	3500.	6000.	20000.	35000.
1858-O	1800.	2500.	3500.	6500.	12000.	20000.	—	—	—
1858-S	700.	1100.	1400.	1850.	2750.	5500.	10000.	15000.	—
1859	1000.	2500.	3500.	4500.	8000.	12000.	—	—	—
1859-O	5000.	10000.	18000.	25000.	40000.	60000.	90000.	—	—
1859-S	700.	800.	1250.	1700.	3000.	4500.	6000.	12000.	—
1860	700.	800.	900.	1000.	1500.	2500.	4000.	10000.	20000.
1860-O	5000.	10000.	18000.	25000.	40000.	60000.	90000.	—	—
1860-S	1000.	1600.	1800.	2000.	4000.	5000.	7500.	14000.	—
1861	700.	750.	800.	900.	1400.	2500.	3000.	6000.	10000.
1861-O	3500.	7000.	14000.	18000.	30000.	45000.	75000.	—	—
1861-S	750.	1000.	1575.	2500.	4000.	6000.	10000.	—	30000.
1861-S Paquet Reverse	8000.	20000.	25000.	50000.	65000.	110000.	—	—	—
1861 Paquet Reverse MS-67 (NGC—Norweb specimen) sold for $660,000.									
1862	1000.	1500.	2500.	3500.	6000.	10000.	15000.	25000.	35000.
1862-S	750.	1450.	1825.	2200.	4000.	7250.	12500.	—	—
1863	700.	1000.	1500.	2500.	5000.	8000.	18000.	28000.	40000.
1863-S	700.	1200.	1500.	2000.	3000.	5000.	9000.	20000.	35000.
1864	700.	1000.	1500.	2500.	4000.	7000.	14000.	—	—
1864-S	700.	1000.	1500.	2000.	3500.	5000.	8000.	18000.	35000.
1865	700.	750.	850.	1000.	2000.	3000.	7000.	18000.	30000.
1865-S	700.	750.	850.	1200.	2000.	2750.	4000.	5500.	8000.
1866-S	3000.	5000.	7500.	30000.	40000.	—	—	—	—
MOTTO ON REVERSE									
1866	520.	620.	920.	1300.	2250.	3500.	6500.	20000.	32000.
1866-S	500.	620.	750.	2100.	5250.	10000.	16500.	—	—
1867	495.	565.	590.	705.	1200.	1450.	2150.	6000.	19000.
1867-S	495.	630.	750.	1500.	3600.	8000.	16000.	—	—
1868	565.	950.	1150.	1625.	3250.	5000.	9000.	—	32500.
1868-S	495.	610.	660.	1250.	2500.	5000.	11000.	30000.	—
1869	545.	660.	775.	1000.	2500.	3250.	5500.	12500.	20000.
1869-S	495.	530.	700.	950.	2000.	3000.	5000.	15000.	28000.

—— = Insufficient pricing data

CORONET $20 DOUBLE EAGLE (CONTINUED)

	VF-20	EF-40	EF-45	AU-50	AU-55	AU-58	MS-60	MS-62	MS-63
1870	565.	700.	1100.	1500.	2250.	4500.	9000.	—	—
1870-CC	80000.	110000.	150000.	—	—	—	—	—	—
1870-S	495.	545.	580.	705.	1150.	2500.	5500.	—	25000.
1871	565.	670.	825.	1400.	2250.	3000.	4500.	10000.	21000.
1871-CC	5500.	9000.	12000.	18000.	25000.	35000.	50000.	—	—
1871-S	495.	530.	545.	645.	1100.	2000.	4500.	12000.	20000.
1872	505.	520.	545.	635.	1150.	1850.	3250.	12000.	21000.
1872-CC	1800.	2500.	3500.	6000.	10000.	17000.	27000.	—	—
1872-S	485.	520.	525.	600.	1100.	1600.	3000.	12000.	24000.
1873 Closed 3	545.	635.	685.	800.	1200.	1700.	3000.	9000.	—
1873 Open 3	485.	520.	525.	550.	600.	700.	1000.	3500.	10500.
1873-CC	2000.	3500.	4500.	6000.	12000.	17000.	32000.	50000.	—
1873-S Closed 3	485.	535.	540.	560.	800.	1150.	1600.	6500.	21500.
1873-S Open 3	535.	580.	660.	950.	2250.	3500.	6000.	—	—
1874	495.	535.	540.	560.	670.	925.	1500.	9000.	18500.
1874-CC	1200.	1500.	1800.	2500.	3500.	5000.	8500.	—	—
1874-S	485.	520.	525.	550.	670.	950.	1600.	9000.	22000.
1875	495.	520.	525.	550.	620.	700.	1000.	4500.	11500.
1875-CC	1200.	1400.	1500.	1800.	2000.	2200.	2800.	9000.	20000.
1875-S	485.	520.	525.	550.	625.	750.	1000.	5000.	17500.
1876	485.	520.	525.	550.	600.	700.	1000.	4250.	11500.
1876-CC	1100.	1300.	1400.	1500.	2400.	3000.	5500.	14000.	35000.
1876-S	485.	520.	525.	550.	620.	700.	1000.	4000.	11500.
TWENTY DOLLARS REVERSE									
1877	480.	500.	525.	560.	605.	640.	700.	2000.	4750.
1877-CC	1200.	1500.	2000.	2500.	4000.	8000.	17000.	30000.	46500.
1877-S	470.	485.	515.	555.	605.	630.	675.	1825.	10250.
1878	485.	495.	515.	545.	575.	600.	645.	1600.	5000.
1878-CC	2000.	2800.	3500.	5000.	10000.	13000.	25000.	—	—
1878-S	485.	505.	555.	570.	640.	750.	935.	3650.	20000.
1879	490.	510.	535.	555.	625.	750.	1000.	5000.	14000.
1879-CC	2000.	3000.	4000.	5500.	10000.	16000.	30000.	—	—
1879-O	3100.	4150.	5600.	9000.	15000.	25000.	40000.	—	90000.
1879-S	485.	505.	540.	560.	620.	800.	1100.	11875.	19500.
1880	500.	545.	580.	665.	900.	1650.	2900.	5500.	18500.
1880-S	490.	515.	545.	570.	615.	740.	950.	2975.	14375.
1881	3600.	7000.	8500.	11500.	16000.	—	—	—	—
1881-S	485.	505.	525.	540.	565.	700.	925.	2200.	13750.
1882	8500.	16000.	24000.	29500.	42500.	—	—	—	—
1882-CC	1200.	1400.	1700.	2000.	3000.	4000.	7000.	12000.	25000.
1882-S	480.	495.	515.	535.	555.	630.	750.	1700.	11875.
1883-CC	1100.	1300.	1500.	1700.	2000.	2500.	5000.	8500.	22000.
1883-S	475.	485.	505.	535.	550.	590.	650.	1200.	5625.
1883 Proofs Only—PF-60 $30000 PF-63 $44000 PF-64 $75000 PF-65 $195000.									
1884-CC	1100.	1300.	1400.	1600.	2000.	2500.	3000.	6500.	20000.
1884-S	470.	480.	495.	535.	550.	575.	610.	1300.	4750.
1884 Proofs Only—PF-60 $35000 PF-63 $48500 PF-64 $85000.									

—— = Insufficient pricing data

	VF-20	EF-40	EF-45	AU-50	AU-55	AU-58	MS-60	MS-62	MS-63
1885	—	6250.	7250.	10500.	15000.	21250.	34000.	40000.	—
1885-CC	2000.	3000.	4000.	5500.	6500.	8000.	11000.	28000.	45000.
1885-S	475.	485.	505.	535.	550.	595.	665.	1125.	4750.
1886	5750.	12000.	15500.	19250.	25000.	30000.	40000.	47500.	67500.
1887-S	490.	500.	520.	555.	570.	600.	650.	2200.	9000.
1887 Proofs Only—PF-60 $25000 PF-63 $40000 PF-64 $80000.									
1888	485.	510.	530.	550.	620.	650.	700.	1100.	4900.
1888-S	475.	490.	500.	505.	535.	575.	650.	975.	3750.
1889	460.	505.	525.	575.	630.	675.	725.	1200.	8750.
1889-CC	1300.	1500.	1700.	2000.	2200.	2500.	4000.	8500.	16000.
1889-S	460.	500.	515.	530.	545.	585.	650.	1075.	4250.
1890	460.	505.	525.	550.	580.	600.	635.	1400.	4500.
1890-CC	1100.	1200.	1300.	1400.	1700.	2000.	3000.	8500.	25000.
1890-S	460.	505.	520.	535.	550.	580.	625.	800.	6000.
1891	2060.	4000.	5000.	7750	11750	—	—	—	—
1891-CC	3500.	5000.	6000.	7500.	9000.	11000.	15000.	30000.	—
1891-S	435.	450.	465.	500.	520.	550.	600.	750	2700.
1892	900.	1350.	1550.	2000.	3050.	3750.	4900.	9500	19000
1892-CC	1200.	1400.	1700.	2000.	2200.	2500.	3500.	8500	25000.
1892-S	435.	450.	465.	520.	535.	550.	580.	650.	2700.
1893	450.	480.	500.	530.	545.	560.	590.	775.	2000.
1893-CC	1400.	1700.	1800.	2000.	2200.	2500	3500	8500.	14000.
1893-S	435.	450.	465.	510.	525.	545.	575.	725.	2700.
1894	435.	450.	465.	505.	520.	540.	565.	595.	1375.
1894-S	435.	450.	465.	525.	540.	555.	580.	700.	1750.
1895	435.	450.	465.	495.	510.	525.	550.	560.	1100.
1895-S	435.	450.	465.	510.	525.	540.	570.	675.	1700.
1896	435.	450.	465.	505.	515.	530.	550.	585.	1200.
1896-S	435.	450.	465.	510.	535.	560.	600.	800.	1725.
1897	435.	450.	465.	500.	515.	530.	550.	600.	1100.
1897-S	435.	450.	465.	510.	525.	540.	565.	640.	1200.
1898	450.	475.	500.	525.	555.	610.	700.	1650.	5850.
1898-S	435.	450.	465.	495.	500.	515.	540.	625.	1100.
1899	435.	450.	465.	495.	500.	515.	540.	585.	1000.
1899-S	435.	450.	465.	505.	520.	540.	575.	625.	1475.
1900	435.	450.	465	490	500.	515.	540.	550.	675.
1900-S	435.	450.	465.	505.	535.	555.	590.	625.	1975.
1901	450.	470.	480.	490.	520.	540.	570.	595.	725.
1901-S	435.	450.	465.	515.	530.	550.	575.	800.	2700.
1902	460.	505.	540.	665.	735.	800.	900.	1400.	7500.
1902-S	435.	450.	465.	510.	525.	535.	555.	600.	2625.
1903	450.	480.	485.	490.	500.	515.	540.	550.	675.
1903-S	435.	450.	465.	510	525.	540.	565.	595.	1250.
1904	435.	450.	465.	490.	510.	515.	540.	550.	675.
1904-S	435.	450.	465.	490.	510.	515.	540.	565.	675.
1905	460.	535.	560.	615.	825	925.	1100.	5000.	15000.
1905-S	435.	450.	465.	525.	540.	555.	585.	645.	2625.

—— = Insufficient pricing data

	VF-20	EF-40	EF-45	AU-50	AU-55	AU-58	MS-60	MS-62	MS-63
1906	460.	520.	525.	560.	600.	655.	800.	1200.	6000.
1906-D	435.	450.	465.	505.	545.	580.	630.	645.	2000.
1906-S	435.	450.	465.	495.	510.	525.	550.	700.	1650.
1907	435.	450.	465.	490.	500.	515.	540.	555.	750.
1907-D	435.	450.	465.	500.	515.	530.	550.	670.	1250.
1907-S	435.	450.	465.	490.	510.	530.	555.	610.	1600.

Saint-Gaudens $20 double eagle

Date of authorization: March 3, 1849
Dates of issue: 1907-1933
Designer: Augustus Saint-Gaudens
Engraver: Charles Barber
Diameter: 34.29 mm/1.35 inches
Weight: 33.47 grams/1.07 ounce
Metallic Content: 90% gold, 10% copper
Weight of pure gold: 30.09 grams/0.97 ounce
Edge: Lettered (E PLURIBUS UNUM, with stars dividing words)
Mint mark: Obverse above date

	EF-40	AU-50	AU-55	AU-58	MS-60	MS-61	MS-62	MS-63	MS-64	MS-65	MS-66
NO MOTTO ON REVERSE											
1907 High Relief, Roman Numerals, Wire Rim	7000.	8000.	8500.	9500.	12000.	13000.	15000.	25000.	28000.	40000.	50000.
1907 High Relief, Roman Numerals, Flat Rim	7000.	8000.	8500.	9500.	12000.	13000.	15000.	25000.	28000.	40000.	50000.
1907	525.	550.	575.	600.	650.	700.	800.	1100.	2000.	4000.	7500.
1907 Extremely High Relief, Proofs Only, Norweb Specimen sold for $1.21 million.											
1908	525.	550.	575.	600.	650.	700.	750.	800.	850.	1500.	2500.
1908-D	525.	575.	600.	650.	750.	800.	900.	1200.	3000.	12000.	—
MOTTO ON REVERSE											
1908	525.	550.	575.	600.	650.	800.	1000.	2000.	6000.	25000.	—
1908-D	525.	550.	575.	600.	650.	700.	800.	1300.	2000.	6500.	12000.
1908-S	1500.	2000.	3000.	4500.	5500.	7000.	9000.	14000.	25000.	45000.	60000.

—— = Insufficient pricing data * = None issued

SAINT-GAUDENS $20 DOUBLE EAGLE (CONTINUED)

	EF-40	AU-50	AU-55	AU-58	MS-60	MS-61	MS-62	MS-63	MS-64	MS-65	MS-66
1909/8	600.	700.	850.	1100.	1500.	2500.	3500.	7000.	16000.	35000.	60000.
1909	525.	550.	575.	600.	700.	1000.	1500.	4000.	12000.	40000.	50000.
1909-D	750.	800.	1000.	1200.	1500.	2300.	3500.	8500.	16000.	40000.	50000.
1909-S	525.	550.	575.	600.	650.	700.	750.	900.	1800.	6500.	—
1910	525.	550.	575.	600.	650.	700.	750.	800.	1600.	9000.	18000.
1910-D	525.	550.	575.	600.	650.	700.	750.	800.	1000.	4000.	6500.
1910-S	525.	550.	575.	600.	650.	700.	900.	1200.	3000.	10000.	20000.
1911	525.	550.	575.	600.	650.	700.	900.	2500.	4500.	17000.	25000.
1911-D	525.	550.	575.	600.	650.	700.	750.	800.	900.	1800.	3500.
1911-S	525.	550.	575.	600.	650.	700.	750.	800.	1500.	6500.	12000.
1912	525.	550.	575.	600.	650.	700.	900.	1600.	5000.	20000.	—
1913	525.	550.	575.	600.	650.	700.	1200.	3500.	10000.	35000.	—
1913-D	525.	550.	575.	600.	650.	700.	750.	1000.	2000.	6500.	—
1913-S	800.	900.	1000.	1200.	1500.	2000.	2500.	4500.	8500.	45000.	—
1914	525.	550.	575.	600.	650.	750.	1000.	2000.	4000.	17000.	—
1914-D	525.	550.	575.	600.	650.	700.	750.	800.	1200.	3500.	6500.
1914-S	525.	550.	575.	600.	650.	700.	750.	800.	1000.	2700.	6500.
1915	525.	550.	575.	600.	750.	800.	1000.	2500.	6000.	25000.	—
1915-S	525.	550.	575.	600.	650.	700.	750.	800.	1000.	2500.	6500.
1916-S	525.	550.	575.	600.	650.	700.	750.	1100.	1700.	3000.	5500.
1920	525.	550.	575.	600.	650.	700.	750.	1100.	5000.	40000.	—
1920-S	15000.	17000.	20000.	25000.	35000.	40000.	45000.	60000.	80000.	—	—
1921	20000.	25000.	30000.	35000.	45000.	60000.	85000.	135000.	150000.	300000.	—
1922	525.	550.	575.	600.	650.	700.	750.	800.	1000.	4500.	12000.
1922-S	800.	850.	900.	950.	1000.	1400.	1800.	3000.	7500.	40000.	—
1923	525.	550.	575.	600.	650.	700.	750.	800.	1000.	7500.	—
1923-D	525.	550.	575.	600.	650.	700.	750.	800.	900.	1600.	3500.
1924	525.	550.	575.	600.	650.	700.	750.	800.	900.	1500.	2500.
1924-D	1500.	1600.	1700.	2000.	2500.	3000.	4000.	8000.	15000.	60000.	—
1924-S	1600.	1700.	1900.	2300.	3000.	3500.	4500.	8000.	20000.	45000.	—
1925	525.	550.	575.	600.	650.	700.	750.	800.	900.	1500.	3000.
1925-D	2200.	2500.	2800.	3200.	3500.	4200.	5500.	10000.	30000.	60000.	—
1925-S	1800.	2300.	3000.	4500.	6500.	8000.	10000.	22000.	50000.	90000.	—
1926	525.	550.	575.	600.	650.	700.	750.	800.	900.	1500.	3000.
1926-D	3500.	4000.	5000.	6000.	9500.	12000.	15000.	25000.	55000.	110000.	—
1926-S	1600.	1800.	1900.	2000.	2200.	2600.	3500.	5000.	7500.	40000.	—
1927	525.	550.	575.	600.	650.	700.	750.	800.	900.	1500.	2500.
1927-D	—	—	—	—	—	—	—	300000.	400000.	650000.	1000000.
1927-S	7000.	7500.	8500.	10000.	14000.	20000.	40000.	55000.	65000.	110000.	—
1928	525.	550.	575.	600.	650.	700.	750.	800.	900.	1500.	2500.
1929	8000.	9000.	10000.	12000.	13000.	14000.	17000.	25000.	30000.	40000.	—
1930-S	20000.	24000.	26000.	28000.	30000.	35000.	40000.	50000.	65000.	100000.	—
1931	12000.	13000.	15000.	18000.	20000.	25000.	30000.	35000.	40000.	60000.	75000.
1931-D	12000.	16000.	18000.	22000.	30000.	32000.	35000.	40000.	50000.	75000.	—
1932	15000.	17000.	18000.	20000.	22000.	25000.	30000.	35000.	40000.	60000.	75000.

1933 Farouk/Fenton speciman sold for $7.59 million on July 30, 2002.

—— = Insufficient pricing data

Commemorative coins 1892-1954

	EF-40	AU-50	MS-60	MS-63	MS-64	MS-65	MS-66
WORLD'S COLUMBIAN EXPOSITION							
1893 Isabella quarter dollar	400.	500.	600.	700.	1200.	3000.	4500.
1892 silver half dollar	18.	20.	30.	85.	200.	800.	2000.
1893 silver half dollar	15.	18.	30.	85.	225.	900.	2300.
LAFAYETTE MONUMENT							
1900 silver dollar	250.	400.	650.	1500.	3500.	10000.	18000.
LOUISIANA PURCHASE							
1903 Jefferson gold dollar	325.	400.	500.	800.	2000.	3500.	4800.
1903 McKinley gold dollar	300.	350.	450.	750.	1900.	3600.	5000.
LEWIS & CLARK EXPEDITION							
1904 gold dollar	450.	600.	900.	2000.	5000.	10000.	15000.
1905 gold dollar	450.	600.	1000.	2800.	7000.	20000.	30000.
PANAMA-PACIFIC EXPOSITION							
1915-S silver half dollar	175.	350.	400.	700.	1300.	2500.	4000.
1915-S gold dollar	300.	375.	450.	750.	1400.	3500.	5000.
1915-S gold $2.50	1100.	1300.	1700.	3500.	5000.	6500.	8000.
1915-S gold $50 Round	24000.	26000.	30000.	45000.	60000.	125000.	185000.
1915-S gold $50 Octagonal	22000.	24000.	27000.	40000.	55000.	110000.	175000.
MCKINLEY MEMORIAL							
1916 gold dollar	275.	300.	400.	750.	1250.	3000.	5000.
1917 gold dollar	310.	400.	550.	1200.	2500.	4500.	6000.
ILLINOIS CENTENNIAL							
1918 silver half dollar	75.	85.	110.	135.	200.	500.	1000.
MAINE CENTENNIAL							
1920 silver half dollar	75.	100.	125.	175.	300.	550.	1200.
PILGRIM TERCENTENARY							
1920 silver half dollar	50.	60.	75.	100.	175.	600.	1600.
1921 silver half dollar	100.	125.	150.	200.	300.	700.	2000.
MISSOURI CENTENNIAL							
1921 silver half dollar, No 2*4	225.	275.	500.	900.	1700.	6000.	11000.
1921 silver half dollar, 2*4	300.	450.	600.	1000.	2000.	6500.	15000.
ALABAMA CENTENNIAL							
1921 silver half dollar, 2x2	125.	200.	300.	550.	1000.	2800.	6000.
1921 silver half dollar, No 2x2	75.	125.	220.	475.	750.	2200.	7500.
GRANT MEMORIAL							
1922 silver half dollar, No Star	65.	85.	100.	175.	300.	1000.	2000.
1922 silver half dollar, Star	500.	700.	1500.	1700.	2500.	8000.	18000.
1922 gold dollar, Star	1200.	1400.	1600.	2100.	3500.	4000.	5000.
1922 gold dollar, No Star	1100.	1300.	1500.	2000.	3500.	4000.	5000.
MONROE DOCTRINE CENTENNIAL							
1923-S silver half dollar	30.	40.	50.	200.	500.	3500.	6500.
HUGUENOT-WALLOON TERCENTENARY							
1924 silver half dollar	85.	100.	125.	200.	250.	550.	1500.
LEXINGTON-CONCORD SESQUICENTENNIAL							
1925 silver half dollar	50.	75.	100.	125.	200.	700.	2000.
STONE MOUNTAIN MEMORIAL							
1925 silver half dollar	40.	50.	65.	75.	100.	250.	700.
CALIFORNIA DIAMOND JUBILEE							
1925-S silver half dollar	90.	125.	150.	200.	350.	1200.	2000.
FORT VANCOUVER CENTENNIAL							
1925 silver half dollar	200.	250.	300.	400.	650.	1700.	2500.
AMERICAN INDEPENDENCE SESQUICENTENNIAL							
1926 silver half dollar	50.	65.	85.	175.	600.	6000.	20000.
1926 gold $2.50	275.	300.	350.	650.	1200.	4500.	21000.

	EF-40	AU-50	MS-60	MS-63	MS-64	MS-65	MS-66
OREGON TRAIL MEMORIAL							
1926 silver half dollar	80.	100.	110.	125.	175.	300.	500.
1926-S silver half dollar	80.	100.	110.	125.	175.	250.	500.
1928 silver half dollar	150.	175.	200.	225.	250.	325.	450.
1933-D silver half dollar	225.	250.	275.	300.	350.	550.	900.
1934-D silver half dollar	125.	150.	175.	200.	225.	350.	900.
1936 silver half dollar	110.	125.	150.	175.	200.	250.	350.
1936-S silver half dollar	125.	150.	175.	200.	225.	325.	400.
1937-D silver half dollar	125.	150.	175.	200.	225.	275.	350.
1938 silver half dollar PDS set	500.	550.	600.	700.	750.	850.	1000.
1939 silver half dollar PDS set	1000.	1200.	1300.	1400.	1500.	2100.	2600.
VERMONT-BENNINGTON SESQUICENTENNIAL							
1927 silver half dollar	150.	175.	200.	225.	300.	1000.	2300.
HAWAII DISCOVERY SESQUICENTENNIAL							
1928 silver half dollar	1000.	1300.	1600.	2100.	3000.	5500.	10000.
MARYLAND TERCENTENARY							
1934 silver half dollar	110.	125.	150.	175.	200.	375.	1000.
TEXAS INDEPENDENCE CENTENNIAL							
1934 silver half dollar	80.	100.	120.	135.	150.	200.	250.
1935 silver half dollar PDS set	250.	300.	350.	375.	450.	600.	800.
1936 silver half dollar PDS set	250.	300.	350.	375.	450.	600.	800.
1937 silver half dollar PDS set	250.	300.	350.	375.	450.	600.	800.
1938 silver half dollar PDS set	300.	600.	700.	850.	1000.	1500.	2000.
DANIEL BOONE BICENTENNIAL							
1934 silver half dollar	70.	85.	100.	125.	150.	200.	400.
1935 silver half dollar PDS set, Small 1934	500.	600.	700.	900.	1200.	2000.	4000.
1935 silver half dollar PDS set	200.	225.	275.	300.	350.	600.	1400.
1936 silver half dollar PDS set	200.	225.	275.	300.	350.	600.	1400.
1937 silver half dollar PDS set	250.	600.	650.	750.	900.	1200.	2100.
1938 silver half dollar PDS set	650.	800.	900.	1100.	1300.	1700.	3500.
CONNECTICUT TERCENTENARY							
1935 silver half dollar	175.	200.	250.	300.	400.	600.	1100.
ARKANSAS CENTENNIAL							
1935 silver half dollar PDS set	200.	225.	250.	300.	350.	850.	4000.
1936 silver half dollar PDS set	200.	225.	250.	300.	350.	1000.	3500.
1936 silver half dollar single	60.	75.	100.	125.	150.	250.	1000.
1937 silver half dollar PDS set	200.	225.	250.	325.	350.	1100.	7000.
1938 silver half dollar PDS set	225.	275.	400.	450.	550.	2000.	8500.
1939 silver half dollar PDS set	300.	600.	700.	1000.	1200.	3500.	11000.
ARKANSAS-ROBINSON							
1936 silver half dollar	100.	120.	125.	150.	200.	400.	1200.
HUDSON, NY, SESQUICENTENNIAL							
1935 silver half dollar	400.	450.	550.	600.	800.	1500.	3000.
CALIFORNIA-PACIFIC EXPOSITION (SAN DIEGO)							
1935-S silver half dollar	55.	65.	100.	110.	100.	125.	200.
1936-D silver half dollar	55.	65.	120.	130.	140.	175.	250.
OLD SPANISH TRAIL							
1935 silver half dollar	750.	800.	850.	900.	1000.	1200.	1500.
PROVIDENCE, RI, TERCENTENARY							
1936 silver half dollar single	75.	85.	100.	110.	125.	250.	700.
1936 silver half dollar PDS set	200.	225.	250.	300.	350.	800.	3500.
CLEVELAND CENTENNIAL AND GREAT LAKES EXPOSITION							
1936 silver half dollar	60.	70.	80.	90.	110.	225.	750.
WISCONSIN TERRITORIAL CENTENNIAL							
1936 silver half dollar	150.	160.	175.	200.	250.	300.	400.

	EF-40	AU-50	MS-60	MS-63	MS-64	MS-65	MS-66
CINCINNATI MUSIC CENTER							
1936 silver half dollar PDS set	650.	700.	750.	800.	1000.	3000.	7500.
1936 silver half dollar single	200.	225.	250.	275.	350.	700.	2000.
LONG ISLAND TERCENTENARY							
1936 silver half dollar	65.	70.	80.	100.	150.	450.	1300.
YORK COUNTY, MAINE, TERCENTENARY							
1936 silver half dollar	150.	160.	175.	200.	225.	250.	300.
BRIDGEPORT, CT, CENTENNIAL							
1936 silver half dollar	100.	110.	125.	150.	200.	300.	700.
LYNCHBURG, VA, SESQUICENTENNIAL							
1936 silver half dollar	150.	160.	175.	200.	250.	325.	900.
ALBANY, NY, CHARTER 250TH ANNIVERSARY							
1936 silver half dollar	200.	225.	250.	275.	300.	400.	800.
ELGIN, IL, PIONEER MEMORIAL							
1936 silver half dollar	160.	170.	180.	200.	225.	250.	600.
SAN FRANCISCO - OAKLAND BAY BRIDGE							
1936-S silver half dollar	90.	110.	125.	150.	200.	300.	600.
COLUMBIA, SC, SESQUICENTENNIAL							
1936 silver half dollar 150th PDS set	500.	525.	550.	600.	650.	850.	1200.
1936 silver half dollar 150th single	165.	175.	200.	225.	250.	300.	400.
DELAWARE TERCENTENARY							
1936 silver half dollar	185.	225.	250.	275.	300.	400.	750.
BATTLE OF GETTYSBURG 75TH ANNIVERSARY							
1936 silver half dollar	250.	300.	325.	400.	450.	700.	1100.
NORFOLK, VA, BICENTENNIAL & TERCENTENARY							
1936 silver half dollar	300.	375.	400.	425.	450.	500.	600.
ROANOKE COLONIZATION 350TH ANNIVERSARY							
1937 silver half dollar	160.	200.	225.	250.	300.	350.	450.
BATTLE OF ANTIETAM 75TH ANNIVERSARY							
1937 silver half dollar	400.	425.	450.	500.	600.	750.	1000.
NEW ROCHELLE, NY, 250TH ANNIVERSARY							
1938 silver half dollar	250.	275.	300.	325.	350.	400.	700.
IOWA STATEHOOD CENTENNIAL							
1946 silver half dollar	70.	80.	100.	110.	125.	150.	200.
BOOKER T. WASHINGTON MEMORIAL							
1946 silver half dollar PDS set	35.	45.	50.	85.	100.	150.	650.
1946 silver half dollar single	14.	17.	20.	30.	50.	75.	250.
1947 silver half dollar PDS set	35.	55.	80.	100.	125.	300.	2000.
1948 silver half dollar PDS set	50.	90.	150.	150.	175.	200.	1300.
1949 silver half dollar PDS set	125.	175.	250.	275.	300.	375.	850.
1950 silver half dollar PDS set	50.	80.	125.	150.	175.	225.	1600.
1951 silver half dollar PDS set	55.	85.	120.	150.	175.	225.	1000.
BOOKER T. WASHINGTON - GEORGE WASHINGTON CARVER							
1951 silver half dollar PDS set	40.	60.	90.	125.	150.	600.	2400.
1951 silver half dollar single	15.	20.	35.	50.	75.	100.	800.
1952 silver half dollar PDS set	40.	60.	90.	125.	185.	425.	1800.
1953 silver half dollar PDS set	40.	60.	90.	125.	185.	600.	2400.
1954 silver half dollar PDS set	40.	60.	90.	110.	150.	500.	2400.

Commemorative coins 1982-2004

	MS-65	MS-69	MS-70	PF-65	PF-69DC
WASHINGTON'S BIRTH 250TH ANNIVERSARY					
1982-D silver half dollar	8.00	—	—	*	*
1982-S silver half dollar	*	*	*	8.00	30.
GAMES OF THE XXIII OLYMPIAD, LOS ANGELES					
1983-P silver dollar	13.	35.	—	*	*
1983-D silver dollar	14.	35.	—	*	*
1983-S silver dollar	13.	35.	—	14.	35.
1984-P silver dollar	15.	35.	—	*	*
1984-D silver dollar	20.	45.	—	*	*
1984-S silver dollar	22.	45.	—	14.	35.
1984-P gold $10 eagle	*	*	*	260.	300.
1984-D gold $10 eagle	*	*	*	275.	325.
1984-S gold $10 eagle	*	*	*	235.	260.
1984-W gold $10 eagle	225.	250.	—	235.	250.
STATUE OF LIBERTY—ELLIS ISLAND CENTENNIAL					
1986-D clad half dollar	8.00	30.	—	*	*
1986-S clad half dollar	*	*	*	8.00	30.
1986-P silver dollar	18.	40.	—	*	*
1986-S silver dollar	*	*	*	18.	40.
1986-W gold half eagle	125.	135.	600.	125.	135.
CONSTITUTION BICENTENNIAL					
1987-P silver dollar	14.	35.	215.	*	*
1987-S silver dollar	*	*	*	14.	35.
1987-W gold half eagle	125.	135.	350.	125.	135.
GAMES OF THE XXIV OLYMPIAD, CALGARY, SEOUL					
1988-D silver dollar	15.	35.	—	*	*
1988-S silver dollar	*	*	*	15.	35.
1988-W gold half eagle	125.	135.	—	125.	135.
BICENTENNIAL OF CONGRESS					
1989-D clad half dollar	9.00	30.	—	*	*
1989-S clad half dollar	*	*	*	9.00	30.
1989-D silver dollar	18.	40.	—	*	*
1989-S silver dollar	*	*	*	25.	45.
1989-W gold half eagle	135.	150.	250.	135.	150.
EISENHOWER BIRTH CENTENNIAL					
1990-W silver dollar	20.	45.	300.	*	*
1990-P silver dollar	*	*	*	25.	50.
MOUNT RUSHMORE 50TH ANNIVERSARY					
1991-D clad half dollar	18.	40.	—	*	*
1991-S clad half dollar	*	*	*	20.	40.
1991-P silver dollar	35.	60.	300.	*	*
1991-S silver dollar	*	*	*	45.	65.
1991-W gold half eagle	170.	200.	650.	165.	180.
KOREAN WAR 38TH ANNIVERSARY					
1991-D silver dollar	17.	40.	300.	*	*
1991-P silver dollar	*	*	*	18.	45.
UNITED SERVICE ORGANIZATIONS 50TH ANNIVERSARY					
1991-D silver dollar	17.	40.	300.	*	*
1991-S silver dollar	*	*	*	18.	45.
GAMES OF THE XXV OLYMPIAD, ALBERTVILLE, BARCELONA					
1992-P clad half dollar	9.00	35.	300.	*	*
1992-S clad half dollar	*	*	*	9.00	35.
1992-D silver dollar	27.	45.	—	*	*
1992-S silver dollar	*	*	*	30.	50.

—— = Insufficient pricing data * = None issued

	MS-65	MS-69	MS-70	PF-65	PF-69DC
1992-W gold half eagle	160.	200.	300.	140.	160.
WHITE HOUSE BICENTENNIAL					
1992-D silver dollar	42.	65.	350.	*	*
1992-W silver dollar	*	*	*	42.	65.
COLUMBUS DISCOVERY QUINCENTENNIAL					
1992-D clad half dollar	13.	35.	—	*	*
1992-S clad half dollar	*	*	*	14.	35.
1992-P silver dollar	*	*	*	45.	70.
1992-D silver dollar	35.	55.	300.	*	*
1992-W gold half eagle	190.	230.	600.	165.	190.
BILL OF RIGHTS—JAMES MADISON					
1993-W silver half dollar	20.	40.	—	*	*
1993-S silver half dollar	*	*	*	18.	40.
1993-D silver dollar	21.	40.	—	*	*
1993-S silver dollar	*	*	*	23.	40.
1993-W gold half eagle	200.	225.	—	175.	200.
WORLD WAR II 50TH ANNIVERSARY, DUAL DATES 1991-1995					
(1993)-P WWII clad half dollar	30.	45.	—	30.	40.
(1993)-D silver dollar	30.	45.	—	*	*
(1993)-W silver dollar	*	*	*	36.	60.
(1993)-W WWII gold half eagle	200.	235.	—	180.	200.
SOCCER WORLD CUP					
1994-D clad half dollar	12.	35.	300.	*	*
1994-P clad half dollar	*	*	*	12.	35.
1994-D silver dollar	30.	50.	—	*	*
1994-S silver dollar	*	*	*	35.	60.
1994-W gold half eagle	185.	230.	—	155.	175.
THOMAS JEFFERSON 250TH ANNIVERSARY 1743-1993					
(1994)-P silver dollar	30.	50.	300.	*	*
(1994)-S silver dollar	*	*	*	33.	60.
WOMEN IN MILITARY SERVICE MEMORIAL					
1994-W silver dollar	40.	65.	300.	*	*
1994-P silver dollar	*	*	*	35.	60.
VIETNAM VETERANS' MEMORIAL					
1994-W silver dollar	70.	110.	—	*	*
1994-P silver dollar	*	*	*	85.	120.
PRISONER OF WAR MUSEUM					
1994-W silver dollar	80.	110.	650.	*	*
1994-P silver dollar	*	*	*	60.	90.
UNITED STATES CAPITOL BICENTENNIAL					
1994-D silver dollar	25.	40.	325.	*	*
1994-S silver dollar	*	*	*	30.	50.
CIVIL WAR BATTLEFIELDS					
1995-S clad half dollar	40.	65.	200.	40.	65.
1995-P silver dollar	50.	80.	—	*	*
1995-S silver dollar	*	*	*	65.	100.
1995-W gold half eagle	400.	500.	2400.	325.	375.
SPECIAL OLYMPICS WORLD GAMES					
1995-W silver dollar	25.	40.	—	*	*
1995-P silver dollar	*	*	*	25.	40.
GAMES OF THE XXVI OLYMPIAD, ATLANTA					
1995-S Basketball clad half dollar	24.	40.	200.	18.	38.
1995-S Baseball clad half dollar	24.	45.	200.	18.	38.
1996-S Swimming clad half dollar	125.	175.	—	30.	55.

—— = Insufficient pricing data   * = None issued

	MS-65	MS-69	MS-70	PF-65	PF-69DC
1996-S Soccer clad half dollar	60.	100.	—	90.	125.
1995-D Gymnastics silver dollar	60.	85.	400.	*	*
1995-P Gymnastics silver dollar	*	*	*	35.	50.
1995-D Cycling silver dollar	100.	140.	—	*	*
1995-P Cycling silver dollar	*	*	*	40.	65.
1995-D Track & Field silver dollar	65.	120.	—	*	*
1995-P Track & Field silver dollar	*	*	*	35.	60.
1995-D Paralympic, blind runner silver dollar	85.	110.	—	*	*
1995-P Paralympic, blind runner silver dollar	*	*	*	38.	60.
1996-D Tennis silver dollar	200.	275.	—	*	*
1996-P Tennis silver dollar	*	*	*	65.	100.
1996-D Rowing silver dollar	225.	325.	—	*	*
1996-P Rowing silver dollar	*	*	*	55.	85.
1996-D High Jump silver dollar	275.	350.	—	*	*
1996-P High Jump silver dollar	*	*	*	45.	70.
1996-D Paralympic, wheelchair athlete silver dollar	275.	375.	485.	*	*
1996-P Paralympic, wheelchair athlete silver dollar	*	*	*	65.	90.
1995-W Torch Runner gold half eagle	250.	375.	2000.	180.	225.
1996-W Atlanta Stadium gold half eagle	315.	450.	—	265.	300.
1996-W Olympic Flame brazier gold half eagle	350.	500.	—	300.	350.
1996-W Flagbearer gold half eagle	350.	500.	—	325.	350.
NATIONAL COMMUNITY SERVICE					
1996-S silver dollar	225.	275.	2000.	80.	110.
SMITHSONIAN INSTITUTION 150TH ANNIVERSARY					
1996-D silver dollar	100.	150.	—	*	*
1996-P silver dollar	*	*	*	55.	110.
1996-W gold half eagle	450.	675.	—	300.	400.
U.S. BOTANIC GARDEN					
1997-P silver dollar	40.	60.	—	45.	65.
FRANKLIN DELANO ROOSEVELT					
1997-W gold half eagle	275.	350.	—	265.	325.
U.S. BOTANIC GARDEN COINAGE AND CURRENCY SET					
1997-P Unc. dollar, 1997-P Matte Finish Jefferson 5-cent coin & Series 1995 $1 FRN	230.	—	—	*	*
NATIONAL LAW ENFORCEMENT OFFICERS MEMORIAL					
1997-P silver dollar	140.	200.	—	125.	175.
JACKIE ROBINSON					
1997-S silver dollar	65.	100.	—	60.	90.
1997-W gold half eagle	1400.	1800.	—	425.	525.
BLACK REVOLUTIONARY WAR PATRIOTS					
1998-S silver dollar	100.	150.	—	100.	140.
ROBERT F. KENNEDY					
1998-S silver dollar	35.	55.		45.	70.
GEORGE WASHINGTON					
1999-W gold half eagle	275.	310.	3500.	275.	300.
YELLOWSTONE NATIONAL PARK					
1999-P silver dollar	50.	75.	—	50.	75.
DOLLEY MADISON					
1999-P silver dollar	45.	65.	350.	50.	70.
LIBRARY OF CONGRESS BICENTENNIAL					
2000-P silver dollar	40.	60.	300.	45.	65.
2000-W bimetallic $10 eagle	1000.	1200.	3500.	550.	600.
LEIF ERICSON MILLENNIUM SILVER DOLLAR					
2000-P silver dollar	70.	110.	350.	55.	100.

—— = Insufficient pricing data   * = None issued

	MS-65	MS-69	MS-70	PF-65	PF-69DC
AMERICAN BUFFALO					
2001-D silver dollar	150.	200.	335.	*	*
2001-P silver dollar	*	*	*	150.	200.
CAPITOL VISITOR CENTER					
2001-P half dollar	15.	35.	50.	20.	40.
2001-P silver dollar	50.	70.	—	50.	75.
2001-W $5 half eagle	575.	650.	1400.	300.	325.
U.S. MILITARY ACADEMY BICENTENNIAL					
2002-W silver dollar	40.	65.	175.	45.	65.
SALT LAKE CITY OLYMPIC GAMES					
2002-P silver dollar	40.	65.	300.	45.	65.
2002-W $5 half eagle	275.	325.	—	250.	275.
FIRST FLIGHT CENTENNIAL					
2003-P clad half dollar	11.	—	—	14.	—
2003-P silver dollar	33.	—	—	37.	—
2003-W gold $10 eagle	365.	—	—	375.	—
LEWIS & CLARK BICENTENNIAL					
2004-P silver dollar	—	—	—	—	—
THOMAS ALVA EDISON					
2004-P silver dollar	—	—	—	—	—

—— = Insufficient pricing data   * = None issued

Proof Sets

Year	Price Range	
1936	5500.	8000.
1937	3000.	3500.
1938	1500.	2000.
1939	1400.	1800.
1940	1100.	1500.
1941	1200.	1600.
1942 5-piece	1000.	1400.
1942 6-piece	1100.	1500.
1950	550.	700.
1951	500.	650.
1952	275.	350.
1953	275.	350.
1954	160.	200.
1955 Flat	160.	200.
1956	65.	90.
1957	30.	45.
1958	70.	90.
1959	30.	45.
1960	20.	30.
1960 Small Date cent	50.	70.
1961	10.	15.
1962	10.	15.
1963	15.	20.

Year	Price Range	
1964	12.	18.
1968-S	8.00	12.
1969-S	8.00	12.
1970-S	14.	18.
1970-S Level 7 (Small Date)	100.	125.
1971-S	7.00	10.
1972-S	6.00	9.00
1973-S	12.	15.
1974-S	11.	14.
1975-S	15.	20.
1976-S	9.00	13.
1976-S Bicentennial 3-piece	18.	25.
1977-S	9.00	13.
1978-S	10.	14.
1979-S Filled S	12.	15.
1979-S Clear S	115.	150.
1980-S	12.	15.
1981-S Filled S	10.	14.
1981-S Clear S	300.	375.
1982-S	6.00	9.00
1983-S	8.00	12.
1983-S Prestige	80.	100.
1984-S	12.	15.

Proof Sets

Year	Price Range	
1984-S Prestige	20.	30.
1985-S	7.00	11.
1986-S	18.	25.
1986-S Prestige	30.	40.
1987-S	6.00	9.00
1987-S Prestige	20.	30.
1988-S	12.	15.
1988-S Prestige	30.	40.
1989-S	10.	14.
1989-S Prestige	35.	50.
1990-S	10.	14.
1990-S No S Lincoln cent	5500.	7000.
1990-S Prestige	28.	35.
1991-S	18.	25.
1991-S Prestige	75.	100.
1992-S	8.00	12.
1992-S Prestige	80.	100.
1992-S Silver	15.	20.
1992-S Silver Premier	15.	20.
1993-S	15.	20.
1993-S Prestige	45.	60.
1993-S Silver	35.	50.
1993-S Silver Premier	35.	50.
1994-S	23.	30.
1994-S Prestige	50.	70.
1994-S Silver	40.	50.
1994-S Silver Premier	40.	50.
1995-S	75.	100.
1995-S Prestige	250.	300.
1995-S Silver	90.	110.
1995-S Silver Premier	90.	110.

Year	Price Range	
1996-S	15.	20.
1996-S Prestige	425.	500.
1996-S Silver	50.	65.
1996-S Silver Premier	50.	65.
1997-S	55.	70.
1997-S Prestige	180.	225.
1997-S Silver	80.	100.
1997-S Silver Premier	80.	100.
1998-S	33.	45.
1998-S Silver	35.	45.
1998-S Silver Premier	35.	45.
1999-S (9 coin set)	80.	100.
1999-S Quarters (5 coin set)	45.	60.
1999-S Silver	235.	275.
2000-S (10 coin set)	20.	25.
2000-S Silver	32.	40.
2000-S Quarters	18.	25.
2001-S	65.	80.
2001-S Silver	100.	125.
2001-S Quarters	30.	40.
2002-S	45.	60.
2002-S Silver	65.	85.
2002-S Quarters	25.	35.
2003-S	30.	40.
2003-S Silver	35.	45.
2003-S Quarters	18.	25.
2004-S	30.	40.
2004-S Silver	35.	45.
2004-S Quarters	18.	25.
2004-S Silver Quarters	35.	45.

—— = Insufficient pricing data   * = None issued

Uncirculated Mint sets

Year	Price Range	
1947 Double set	1000.	1250.
1948 Double set	450.	600.
1949 Double set	700.	900.
1950 No Sets Issued	*	*
1951 Double set	625.	750.
1952 Double set	575.	750.
1953 Double set	425.	475.
1954 Double set	250.	300.
1955 Double set	140.	200.
1956 Double set	125.	160.
1957 Double set	200.	250.
1958 Double set	135.	165.
1959 Single set	30.	40.
1960	20.	25.
1961	35.	40.
1962	15.	20.
1963	12.	15.
1964	10.	15.
1965 Special Mint Sets	10.	13.
1966 Special Mint Sets	11.	14.
1967 Special Mint Sets	15.	18.
1968 (PD&S)	5.00	7.00
1969 (PD&S)	7.00	9.00
1970 (PD&S)	18.	25.
1971 (PD&S)	5.00	7.00
1972 (PD&S)	5.00	7.00
1973 (PD&S)	24.	29.
1974 (PD&S)	9.00	12.
1975	11.	15.

Year	Price Range	
1976-S 3-piece 40% silver	17.	20.
1976	12.	17.
1977	9.00	11.
1978	10.	12.
1979	7.00	10.
1980	7.00	10.
1981	17.	23.
1984	7.00	10.
1985	8.00	11.
1986	25.	35.
1987	8.00	12.
1988	9.00	14.
1989	9.00	14.
1990	8.00	12.
1991	13.	18.
1992	7.00	11.
1993	11.	14.
1994	12.	15.
1995	20.	27.
1996	22.	28.
1997	23.	30.
1998	19.	33.
1999	28.	32.
2000	15.	20.
2001	20.	30.
2002	15.	20.
2003	15.	20.
2004	15.	20.

—— = Insufficient pricing data   * = None issued

American Eagle silver bullion

Date of authorization: Dec. 17, 1985
Dates of issue: 1986-present
Designers: Obverse: Adolph A. Weinman
Reverse: John Mercanti
Engravers: Obverse: Edgar Steever
Reverse: John Mercanti
Diameter: 40.10 mm/1.58 inches
Weight: 31.10 grams/1.00 ounce
Metallic Content: 100% silver (.999 fine)
Weight of pure silver: 31.10 grams/1.00 ounce
Edge: Reeded
Mint mark: Proofs only, reverse left of eagle's tail

	MS-65	PF-65
1986	20.	35.
1987	12.	35.
1988	12.	60.
1989	12.	35.
1990	12.	35.
1991	12.	50.
1992	12.	40.
1993	12.	125.
1994	12.	120.
1995	12.	90.
1995-W	*	2400.
1996	30.	50.
1997	12.	80.
1998	12.	35.
1999	12.	60.
2000	12.	35.
2001	12.	30.
2002	10.	30.
2003	10.	30.
2004	10.	30.

* = None issued

American Eagle platinum bullion

Date of authorization: Sept. 30, 1996
Dates of issue: 1997-present
Designers/Engravers: Obverse: John Mercanti
Reverse: Thomas D. Rogers Sr. (Unc. and 1997 Proof only)
Diameter: $100: 32.70 mm/1.29 inches
$50: 27.00 mm/1.07 inches
$25: 22.00 mm/0.87 inch
$10: 16.50 mm/0.65 inch
Weight: $100: 31.10 grams/1.00 ounce
$50: 15.55 grams/0.50 ounce
$25: 7.78 grams/0.25 ounce
$10: 3.11 grams/0.10 ounce
Metallic Content: 100% platinum (.9995 fine)
Weight of pure platinum: $100: 1.00 ounce; $50: 0.50 ounce
$25: 0.25 ounce; $10: 0.10 ounce
Edge: Reeded
Mint mark: Proofs only, left, between rays

NOTE: Prices are for MS-65 and Proof 65

	$10 platinum	$25 platinum	$50 platinum	$100 platinum	platinum set
1997 Unc.	110.	260.	435.	850.	1600.
1997 Proof	100.	250.	475.	850.	1600.
1998 Unc.	110.	240.	435.	850.	1600.
1998 Proof	100.	250.	475.	850.	1600.
1999 Unc.	110.	240.	435.	850.	1600.
1999 Proof	110.	250.	475.	850.	1600.
2000 Unc.	110.	260.	435.	850.	1600.
2000 Proof	125.	275.	475.	850.	1600.
2001 Unc.	110.	260.	435.	850.	1600.
2001 Proof	175.	300.	500.	850.	1600.
2002 Unc.	160.	240.	435.	850.	1600.
2002 Proof	135.	325.	500.	850.	1600.
2003 Unc.	110.	240.	450.	850.	1600.
2003 Proof	135.	325.	500.	850.	1600.

* = None issued

AMERICAN EAGLE PLATINUM BULLION (CONTINUED)

	$10 platinum	$25 platinum	$50 platinum	$100 platinum	platinum set
2004 Unc.	110.	240.	450.	850.	1600.
2004 Proof	135.	325.	500.	850.	1600.

American Eagle gold bullion

Date of authorization: Dec. 17, 1985
Dates of issue: 1986-present
Designers: Obverse: Augustus Saint-Gaudens
Reverse: Miley Busiek
Engravers: Obverse: Matthew Peloso
Reverse: Sheri Winter
Diameter: $50: 32.70 mm/1.29 inches
$25: 27.00 mm/1.07 inches
$10: 22.00 mm/0.87 inch
$5: 16.50 mm/0.65 inch
Weight: $50: 33.93 grams/1.09 ounce
$25: 16.97 grams/0.55 ounce
$10: 8.48 grams/0.27 ounce
$5: 3.39 grams/0.11 ounce
Metallic Content: 91.67% gold, 5.33% copper, 3% silver
Weight of pure gold: $50: 1.00 ounce
$25: 0.50 ounce
$10: 0.25 ounce
$5: 0.10 ounce
Edge: Reeded
Mint mark: Proofs only, obverse below date

NOTE: Prices are for MS-65 and Proof 65.

	$5 gold	$10 gold	$25 gold	$50 gold	gold set
1986 Unc.	50.00	125.	250.	385.	810.
1986 Proof ($50 gold - W)	*	*	*	600.	*
1987 Unc.	50.00	125.	275.	385.	835.

* = None issued

	$5 gold	$10 gold	$25 gold	$50 gold	gold set
1987 Proof (gold $25 - P, $50 - W)	*	*	325.	600.	925.
1988 Unc.	50.00	125.	325.	385.	885.
1988 Proof (gold $5, $10, $25 - P, $50 - W)	75.00	165.	325.	600.	1165.
1989 Unc.	200.	125.	425.	385.	1135.
1989 Proof (gold $5, $10, $25 - P, $50 - W)	75.00	165.	325.	600.	1165.
1990 Unc.	80.00	135.	275.	385.	875.
1990 Proof (gold $5, $10, $25 - P, $50 - W)	80.00	165.	325.	600.	1170.
1991 Unc.	60.00	135.	325.	385.	905.
1991 Proof (gold $5, $10, $25 - P, $50 - W)	70.00	165.	325.	600.	1160.
1992 Unc.	110.	125.	425.	385.	1045.
1992 Proof (gold $5, $10, $25 - P, $50 - W)	75.00	165.	325.	600.	1165.
1993 Unc.	60.00	250.	350.	385.	1045.
1993 Proof (gold $5, $10, $25 - P, $50 - W)	90.00	165.	325.	600.	1180.
1994 Unc.	60.00	125.	650.	385.	1220.
1994 Proof (gold $5, $10, $25 - P, $50 - W)	75.00	165.	325.	600.	1165.
1995 Unc.	60.00	125.	250.	385.	820.
1995 Proof (gold $5, $10, $25, $50 - W, 10th Anniversary set)	75.00	165.	325.	600.	1165.
1996 Unc.	60.00	125.	250.	385.	820.
1996 Proof (gold $5, $10, $25, $50 - W)	70.00	165.	325.	600.	1160.
1997 Unc.	60.00	125.	250.	385.	820.
1997 Proof (gold $5, $10, $25, $50 - W)	90.00	165.	325.	600.	1180.
1998 Unc.	55.00	125.	250.	385.	815.
1998 Proof (gold $5, $10, $25, $50 - W)	110.	165.	325.	600.	1200.
1999 Unc.	55.00	125.	250.	385.	815.
1999 Proof (gold $5, $10, $25, $50 - W)	70.00	165.	325.	600.	1160.
2000 Unc.	55.00	125.	250.	385.	815.
2000 Proof (gold $5, $10, $25, $50 - W)	70.00	165.	325.	600.	1160.
2001 Unc.	55.00	125.	250.	385.	815.
2001 Proof (gold $5, $10, $25, $50 - W)	90.00	165.	325.	600.	1180.
2002 Unc.	55.00	125.	250.	450.	880.
2002 Proof (gold $5, $10, $25, $50 - W)	90.00	165.	325.	600.	1180.
2003 Unc.	55.00	125.	250.	450.	880.
2003 Proof (gold $5, $10, $25, $50 - W)	75.00	165.	325.	600.	1165.
2004 Unc.	55.00	125.	250.	450.	800.
2004 Proof (gold $5, $10, $25, $50 - W)	75.00	165.	325.	600.	1165.

* = None issued

U.S Type Coin Trend Values

	G-4	VG-8	F-12	VF-20	EF-40	AU-50	MS-60	MS-63	MS-64	MS-65
HALF CENTS										
Flowing Hair 1793	2000.	3000.	4500.	6000.	18500.	24000.	35000.	55000.	115000.	——
Liberty Cap 1794-1797	300.	450.	700.	1100.	2750.	5000.	8500.	16500.	37500.	82500.
Draped Bust 1800-1808	50.00	60.00	80.00	125.	250.	400.	1000.	2650.	4000.	20000.
Classic Head 1809-1835	35.00	40.00	55.00	70.00	80.00	160.	300.	450.	725.	7500.
Coronet 1849-1857	35.00	45.00	60.00	75.00	100.	150.	300.	400.	1000.	4000.
CENTS - (LARGE)										
Flowing Hair, Chain 1793	5000.	7500.	10000.	16000.	25000.	45000.	100000.	110000.	160000.	——
Flowing Hair, Wreath 1793	2000.	2500.	4000.	6000.	10000.	16000.	20000.	42500.	77500.	185000.
Liberty Cap 1793-1796	400.	500.	700.	1400.	3000.	5000.	7500.	6500.	12500.	62500.
Draped Bust 1796-1807	75.00	100.	200.	300.	1000.	2000.	2100.	5750.	11500.	60000.
Classic Head 1808-1814	60.00	125.	300.	600.	1100.	2000.	3800.	10000.	15000.	55000.
Coronet 1816-1839	16.00	22.00	30.00	70.00	150.	225.	350.	600.	1000.	7500.
Coronet 1839-1857	15.00	20.00	25.00	35.00	75.00	150.	250.	350.	500.	2500.
CENTS - (SMALL)										
Flying Eagle 1856-1858	25.00	30.00	35.00	50.00	135.	200.	300.	1000.	1650.	4000.
Indian copper-nickel 1859	14.00	16.00	20.00	50.00	125.	200.	250.	500.	1500.	3500.
Indian copper-nickel, Shield 1860-64	9.00	10.00	12.00	18.00	30.00	60.00	100.	175.	350.	1000.
Indian Bronze 1864-1909	2.00	2.50	2.75	3.50	8.00	17.00	25.00	40.00	85.00	500.
TWO CENTS										
1864-1873	10.00	12.00	25.00	30.00	40.00	75.00	100.	165.	275.	1500.
THREE CENT NICKEL										
1865-1889	10.00	12.00	18.00	23.00	30.00	50.00	100.	175.	300.	700.
THREE CENT SILVER										
1851-1853 One Outline of Star	17.50	30.00	35.00	40.00	65.00	150.	200.	300.	500.	1000.
1854-1858 Three Outlines of Star	17.50	30.00	35.00	50.00	100	225.	350.	800.	1800.	3500.
1859-1873 Two Outlines of Star	15.00	30.00	35.00	40.00	75.00	150.	200.	300.	500.	1000.

U.S Type Coin Trend Values (continued)

	G-4	VG-8	F-12	VF-20	EF-40	AU-50	MS-60	MS-63	MS-64	MS-65
NICKEL FIVE CENT										
Shield, With Rays 1866-1867	25.00	35.00	45.00	60.00	175.	225.	250.	400.	800.	2500.
Shield, No Rays 1867-1883	18.00	20.00	25.00	30.00	40.00	75.00	100.	200.	300.	750.
Liberty Head, No CENTS 1883	4.00	6.00	7.00	8.00	10.00	14.00	30.00	50.00	75.00	250.
Liberty Head, With CENTS 1883-1912	1.05	3.00	5.00	12.00	25.00	50.00	65.00	125.	250.	700.
Indian Head, Bison on Mound 1913	8.00	11.00	13.00	15.00	20.00	25.00	35.00	50.00	75.00	150.
Indian Head, Bison on Plain 1913-38	1.00	1.50	2.00	2.50	3.00	9.00	18.00	30.00	40.00	50.00
HALF DIMES										
Flowing Hair 1794-1795	1000.	1200.	1700.	2500.	4000.	6500.	10000.	15000.	10750.	27000.
Draped Bust, Small Eagle 1796-1797	1000.	1400.	2000.	3500.	6000.	9000.	15000.	25000.	32500.	75000.
Draped Bust, Heraldic Eagle 1800-05	700.	1000.	1800.	2500.	4000.	7500.	12000.	25000.	13000.	26500.
Capped Bust 1829-1837	20.00	27.50	32.50	60.00	100.	200.	275.	800.	1600.	2500.
Seated Liberty, No Stars 1837-1838	40.00	50.00	85.00	150.	300.	500.	900.	1200.	1800.	3500.
Seated Liberty, No Drapery 1838-1840	20.00	25.00	30.00	40.00	80.00	150.	400.	600.	1000.	2500.
Seated Liberty, Drapery 1840-1859	20.00	25.00	30.00	40.00	65.00	150.	250.	400.	800.	1500.
Seated Liberty, Arrows 1853-1855	20.00	25.00	30.00	40.00	65.00	150.	250.	400.	700.	2000.
Seated Liberty, Legend 1860-1873	20.00	25.00	30.00	35.00	65.00	100.	200.	300.	500.	1200.
DIMES										
Draped Bust, Small Eagle 1796-1797	1500.	2000.	2500.	3500.	5000.	7500.	15000.	25000.	22500.	45000.
Draped Bust, Heraldic Eagle 1798-1807	500.	750.	1000.	1400.	2000.	3000.	5000.	10000.	12000.	24000.
Capped Bust, Large Planchet 1809-27	25.00	30.00	45.00	110.	375.	550.	900.	2000.	4000.	8500.
Capped Bust, Small Planchet 1828-37	25.00	30.00	35.00	60.00	250.	325.	650.	1500.	2500.	6000.
Seated Liberty, No Stars 1837-1838	40.00	50.00	100.	300.	500.	700.	1000.	2000.	4000.	5750.
Seated Liberty, No Drapery 1838-1840	20.00	25.00	30.00	50.00	125.	300.	500.	1000.	1200.	3400.
Seated Liberty, Drapery 1840-1860	10.00	12.50	20.00	35.00	50.00	150.	300.	800.	1200.	2250.
Seated Liberty, Arrows 1853-1855	20.00	25.00	30.00	35.00	65.00	200.	400.	900.	1200.	2500.
Seated Liberty, Legend 1860-1891	20.00	25.00	30.00	35.00	40.00	100.	200.	350.	600.	1050.
Seated Liberty, Arrows 1873-1874	20.00	25.00	30.00	50.00	150.	300.	600.	1000.	2000.	4000.

U.S Type Coin Trend Values (continued)

	G-4	VG-8	F-12	VF-20	EF-40	AU-50	MS-60	MS-63	MS-64	MS-65
Barber 1892-1916	2.50	3.00	4.00	7.50	20.00	60.00	85.00	140.	235.	625.
Winged Liberty Head 1916-1945	0.60	0.75	0.85	1.00	1.25	2.00	5.00	9.00	12.50	20.00
TWENTY CENT PIECE										
Seated Liberty 1875-1878	42.00	48.00	135.	150.	200.	350.	700.	1300.	2000.	6000.
QUARTERS										
Draped Bust, Small Eagle 1796	6000.	8000.	12000.	18000.	25000.	30000.	50000.	60000.	75000.	125000.
Draped Bust, Heraldic Eagle 1804-07	250.	350.	600.	1000.	1200.	2500.	7000.	12000.	25000.	50000.
Capped Bust, Open Collar Strike 1815-28	60.00	75.00	125.	275.	850.	1200.	2300.	4000.	5500.	16000.
Capped Bust, Closed Collar Strike 1831-38	50.00	70.00	80.00	100.	350.	600.	800.	2500.	5000.	14000.
Seated Liberty, No Motto 1840-65	15.75	20.00	35.00	50.00	100.	200.	350.	700.	1500.	3500.
Seated Liberty, Arrows & Rays 1853	20.00	30.00	50.00	75.00	175.	350.	1000.	2500.	5000.	14750.
Seated Liberty, Arrows 1854-55	20.00	30.00	50.00	75.00	100.	300.	600.	2000.	4000.	7000.
Seated Liberty, Motto 1866-91	20.00	30.00	40.00	50.00	100.	200.	400.	700.	700.	1525.
Seated Liberty, Arrows 1873-74	20.00	30.00	50.00	75.00	250.	500.	900.	2000.	2500.	3250.
Barber 1892-1916	5.00	8.00	19.00	30.00	65.00	110.	160.	260.	450.	1150.
Standing Liberty, Bared Breast 1916-17	25.00	18.00	27.00	65.00	85.00	175.	250.	350.	600.	900.
Standing Liberty, Mailed Breast 1917-30	3.00	3.75	4.50	12.50	35.00	75.00	125.	225.	300.	500.
HALF DOLLARS										
Flowing Hair 1794-1795	700.	1000.	1500.	3000.	8000	12000.	25000.	47500.	90000.	——
Draped Bust, Small Eagle 1796-1797	25000.	30000.	35000.	45000.	75000	100000.	150000.	175000.	175000.	——
Draped Bust, Heraldic Eagle 1801-07	175.	200.	250.	400.	1000.	2500.	6000.	14000.	19500.	42500.
Capped Bust, Lettered Edge 1807-36	50.00	60.00	75.00	35.00	77.00	200.	500.	1250.	2750.	6250.
Capped Bust, Reeded Edge 1836-39	50.00	60.00	75.00	125.	175.	350.	800.	2000.	5000.	15000.
Seated Liberty, No Motto 1839-66	25.00	35.00	50.00	65.00	100.	250.	500.	1000.	2500.	4500.
Seated Liberty, Arrows & Rays 1853	30.00	40.00	60.00	125.	300.	600.	1500.	4000.	9000.	21000.
Seated Liberty, Arrows 1854-55	30.00	40.00	50.00	80.00	125.	350.	750.	2000.	3500.	7600.

—— = Insufficient pricing data

U.S Type Coin Trend Values (continued)

	G-4	VG-8	F-12	VF-20	EF-40	AU-50	MS-60	MS-63	MS-64	MS-65
Seated Liberty, Motto 1866-91	25.00	35.00	50.00	65.00	110.	200.	400.	750.	1400.	3000.
Seated Liberty, Arrows 1873-74	30.00	50.00	65.00	125.	300.	500.	1000.	2500.	4000.	14500.
Barber 1892-1915	10.00	12.00	28.00	65.00	130.	265.	380.	675.	1175.	2750.
Walking Liberty 1916-1947	4.50	5.00	6.00	7.00	9.00	12.00	40.00	60.00	75.00	175.
DOLLARS										
Flowing Hair 1794-1795	1200.	1800.	3500.	5500.	11000.	17000.	35000.	65000.	100000.	225000.
Draped Bust, Small Eagle 1795-1798	1100.	1400.	2500.	4000.	8500.	12000.	25000.	60000.	90000.	150000.
Draped Bust, Heraldic Eagle 1798-1803	800.	1000.	1200.	2500.	4000.	6500.	15000.	40000.	37500.	80000.
Gobrecht 1836	4500.	5500.	6500.	7500.	9000.	12000.	——	——	——	60000.
Seated Liberty, No Motto 1840-66	175.	200.	250.	300.	400.	600.	1200.	3500.	7500.	16000.
Seated Liberty, Motto 1866-73	175.	200.	250.	300.	400.	600.	1200.	3500.	7500.	24500.
Morgan 1878-1921	10.00	12.00	13.00	14.00	15.00	16.00	25.00	40.00	50.00	50.00
Peace 1921-1935	8.00	8.50	14.00	16.00	18.00	20.00	25.00	30.00	50.00	200.
Trade 1873-1885	40.00	55.00	100.	125.	150.	250.	500.	1400.	3000.	8000.

U.S Gold Type Coin Trend Values

	F-12	VF-20	EF-40	AU-50	MS-60	MS-63	MS-64	MS-65
GOLD DOLLARS								
Coronet 1849-1854	120.	150.	200.	225.	350.	1300.	1700.	5500.
Indian Head Small Head 1854-1856	225.	325.	450.	700.	3500.	15000.	20000.	42500.
Indian Head Large Head 1856-1889	125.	150.	175.	225.	300.	1200.	1500.	1800.
QUARTER EAGLES								
Capped Bust, No Stars 1796	30000.	40000.	70000.	90000.	175000.	275000.	——	——
Capped Bust 1796-1807	6000.	8000.	10000.	14000.	30000.	50000.	——	——

—— = Insufficient pricing data

U.S Gold Type Coin Trend Values (continued)

	F-12	VF-20	EF-40	AU-50	MS-60	MS-63	MS-64	MS-65
Capped Draped Bust 1808	25000.	35000.	45000.	65000.	100000.	——	——	——
Capped Head 1821-1834	5000.	6500.	7500.	10000.	14000.	25000.	40000.	57500.
Classic Head 1834-1839	275.	375.	500.	800.	2500.	5500.	11000.	28500.
Coronet 1840-1907	125.	140.	165.	180.	290.	650.	775.	1350.
Indian Head 1908-1929	140.	160.	185.	200.	275.	1400.	1800.	5000.
THREE DOLLARS								
Indian Head 1854-1889	600.	750.	1100.	1400.	2800.	6000.	7500.	13000.
FOUR DOLLAR (STELLA)								
Flowing Hair - 1879-1880 (Proof Only)	16000.	18000.	20000.	30000.	47500.	65000.	87500.	110000.
Coiled Hair - 1879-1880 (Proof Only)	——	——	——	——	100000.	150000.	250000.	400000.
HALF EAGLES								
Capped Bust, Small Eagle 1795-1798	10000.	15000.	20000.	30000.	50000.	165000.	——	——
Capped Bust, Heraldic Eagle 1795-1807	2700.	3500.	4000.	5500.	8000.	13500.	25000.	90000.
Capped Draped Bust 1807-1812	2000.	2500.	3500.	5000.	7500.	15000.	25000.	85000.
Capped Head 1813-1834	2500.	3000.	4000.	5000.	8000.	17500.	26000.	80000.
Classic Head 1834-1838	240.	295.	435.	675.	2600.	7250.	17500.	62500.
Coronet, No Motto 1839-1866	165.	185.	200.	300.	1250.	7500.	12500.	42000.
Coronet, Motto 1866-1908	150.	165.	170.	200.	240.	550.	900.	2750.
Indian Head 1908-1929	175.	190.	225.	250.	350.	1800.	3700.	13000.
EAGLES								
Capped Bust, Small Eagle 1795-1797	16000.	20000.	30000.	35000.	60000.	140000.	225000.	——
Capped Bust, Heraldic Eagle 1797-1804	6500.	8000.	10000.	14000.	20000.	35000.	55000.	150000.
Coronet, No Motto 1838-1866	245.	290.	335.	325.	3500.	13250.	28000.	75000.
Coronet, Motto 1866-1907	210.	225.	250.	275.	300.	675.	1150.	4500.
Indian Head, No Motto 1907-1908	350.	370.	400.	450.	600.	2700.	3800.	7500.
Indian Head, 1908-1933	325.	350.	400.	450.	600.	1000.	1800.	4500.

—— = Insufficient pricing data

U.S Gold Type Coin Trend Values (continued)

	F-12	VF-20	EF-40	AU-50	MS-60	MS-63	MS-64	MS-65
DOUBLE EAGLES								
Coronet, No Motto 1849-1866	490.	625.	675.	900.	3000.	6500.	9250.	22500.
Coronet, TWENTY D. 1866-1876	450.	485.	520.	550.	1000.	10500.	21000.	65000.
Coronet, TWENTY DOLLARS 1877-1907	400.	435.	450.	490.	540.	675.	1150.	4500.
Saint-Gaudens, Roman Numerals, High Relief 1907	4000.	5000.	7000.	8000.	12000.	25000.	28000.	40000.
Saint-Gaudens, Arabic Numerals, No Motto 1907-08	460.	480.	525.	550.	650.	800.	850.	1500.
Saint-Gaudens, Motto 1908-1933	425.	450.	525.	550.	650.	800.	900.	1500.

—— = Insufficient pricing data

Mintage figures

6

The mintage figures that follow are based on years of study by various numismatists, including *Coin World* staff members. The figures were compiled from official Mint Reports, data from the National Archives, conversations with other experts and in some cases, an educated guess. In many instances, the figures given are based on the best information available to researchers today. Before 1950, the generally accepted source of mintage figures was the *Annual Report of the Director of the Mint.* Since the Mint Report for many years was simply a bookkeeper's record of how many coins were issued in a given year, the figures given often had no relation to the actual number of coins struck with each date. Particularly for many 18th century and early 19th century coins, mintage figures here reflect the number of coins struck during the year, no matter the date on the coin.

Mintage figures should not be mistaken for survival figures. For example, 12,000 1895 Morgan dollars were recorded as having been struck, but none are known today. It is likely that all were melted before any entered circulation, if any were struck at all (some researchers doubt the coins were dated 1895). Similarly, some coins' survival rates may suggest higher mintages than are recorded.

The mintage figures in this book differ from those in other works, particularly for coins struck since 1965. A coinage shortage in the mid-1960s led Mint officials to suspend the use of Mint marks from 1965 to 1967. Three facilities—the Philadelphia and Denver Mints and the San Francisco Assay Office—struck coins but their separate products are indistinguishable from each other.

This book also clarifies mintage figures, particularly for coins struck at the former San Francisco Assay Office and West Point Bullion Depository (both received Mint status in 1988) since the mid-1970s. Like most Philadelphia coins struck until 1979 to 1980, none have Mint marks. For various reasons, in most price guides and other numismatic works, mintages for coins struck at the West Point and San Francisco facilities have been added to the Philadelphia mintages, since no Mint marks were used on any of the coins.

This book differs. Separate mintage figures are given for all coins by striking facility; we have not combined mintage figures just because the coins have no Mint marks. To indicate those coins that do not have Mint marks, the Mint mark letter is enclosed in parentheses. To illustrate: A coin indicated by a P has a P Mint mark, as in 2001-P; one indicated by (P) does not have a Mint mark but was struck at the Philadelphia Mint, as in 2001(P).

Since the Mint has changed its bookkeeping practices several times, some mintage figures for circulation coins include the pieces struck for assay purposes and those business strikes struck for Uncirculated Mint sets, while other figures may not include those pieces.

In years before 1860, when Proof mintages were small and were not recorded, a delta (Δ) marks those issues that are known or are thought to exist. In many instances from 1860 to 1922 the figures shown are approximate, the result of incomplete records, restrikes and the melting of unsold Proofs. Where a delta is followed by an R in parentheses [Δ(R)], the original Proof mintage is unknown, but original specimens are believed to exist, and restrikes are known.

Since 1950, Proof coins have been available from the Mint in sets only (designated by ‹§› in the Notes column). Therefore, Proof mintages since 1950 listed here represent the official tally of Proof sets sold, distributed across the coins included in the set. Proof coins sold as part of a special set, such as a Prestige Proof set, are also included.

Where [——] appears under a mintage column, no coins of that date/Mint were issued.

Some final comments about "mintages" for commemorative coins struck since 1982, recent Proof coins (2003, for example), various sets issued by the U.S. Mint and Proof American Eagles: The figures presented here and in other chapters are sales figures, not mintages. More importantly, these figures are subject to change even years after a program has officially closed. "Final" sales figures can change when buyers return coins or sets to the Mint after a program has closed. When sales figures for programs reported as "sold out" are tabulated, the total figure may be less than the maximum mintage (for example, sales for the sold-out 2001 American Buffalo silver dollar total 499,865, out of a maximum of 500,000 coins). Collectors should understand that these figures, as reported here, represent figures at a specific point in time, and may change in the future. Figures presented here may differ slightly from figures presented in other sources, due to these factors.

Liberty Cap, Left half cent

DATE	NOTE	BUSINESS	PROOF
1793		35,334	—

Liberty Cap, Right half cent

DATE	NOTE	BUSINESS	PROOF
1794		81,600	—
1795		139,690	—
1796		1,390	—
1797		127,840	—

Draped Bust half cent

DATE	NOTE	BUSINESS	PROOF
1800		202,908	—
1802		20,266	—
1803		92,000	—
1804		1,055,312	—
1805		814,464	—
1806		356,000	—
1807		476,000	—
1808		400,000	—

Classic Head half cent

DATE	NOTE	BUSINESS	PROOF
1809		1,154,572	—
1810		215,000	—
1811	‹1›	63,140	—
1825		63,000	Δ
1826		234,000	Δ
1828		606,000	Δ
1829		487,000	Δ
1831		2,200	Δ (R)
1832	‹2›	154,000	Δ
1833	‹2›	120,000	Δ
1834	‹2›	141,000	Δ
1835	‹2›	398,000	Δ
1836		—	Δ (R)

Coronet half cent

DATE	NOTE	BUSINESS	PROOF
1840 (P)		—	Δ (R)
1841 (P)		—	Δ (R)
1842 (P)		—	Δ (R)
1843 (P)		—	Δ (R)
1844 (P)		—	Δ (R)
1845 (P)		—	Δ (R)
1846 (P)		—	Δ (R)
1847 (P)		—	Δ (R)
1848 (P)		—	Δ (R)
1849 (P)		43,364	Δ (R)
1850 (P)		39,812	Δ
1851 (P)		147,672	Δ
1852 (P)		—	Δ (R)
1853 (P)		129,694	—
1854 (P)		55,358	Δ
1855 (P)		56,500	Δ
1856 (P)		40,430	Δ (R)
1857 (P)		35,180	Δ (R)

Flowing Hair, Chain cent

DATE	NOTE	BUSINESS	PROOF
1793		36,103	—

Flowing Hair, Wreath cent

DATE	NOTE	BUSINESS	PROOF
1793		63,353	—

Liberty Cap cent

DATE	NOTE	BUSINESS	PROOF
1793		11,056	—
1794		918,521	—
1795		538,500	—
1796		109,825	—

Draped Bust cent

DATE	NOTE	BUSINESS	PROOF
1796		363,375	—
1797		897,510	—
1798		1,841,745	—
1799		42,540	—
1800		2,822,175	—
1801		1,362,837	—
1802		3,435,100	—
1803		3,131,691	—
1804	‹1›	96,500	—
1805		941,116	—
1806		348,000	—
1807		829,221	—

Classic Head cent

DATE	NOTE	BUSINESS	PROOF
1808		1,007,000	—
1809		222,867	—
1810		1,458,500	—
1811		218,025	—
1812		1,075,500	—
1813		418,000	—
1814		357,830	—

Coronet cent

DATE	NOTE	BUSINESS	PROOF
1816		2,820,982	—
1817		3,948,400	Δ
1818		3,167,000	Δ
1819		2,671,000	Δ
1820		4,407,550	Δ
1821		389,000	Δ
1822		2,072,339	Δ
1823	‹1, 3›	68,061	Δ
1824		1,193,939	—
1825		1,461,100	Δ
1826		1,517,425	Δ
1827		2,357,732	Δ
1828		2,260,624	Δ
1829		1,414,500	Δ
1830		1,711,500	Δ
1831		3,539,260	Δ
1832		2,362,000	Δ
1833		2,739,000	Δ
1834		1,855,100	Δ
1835		3,878,400	Δ
1836		2,111,000	Δ
1837		5,558,300	Δ
1838 (P)		6,370,200	Δ
1839 (P)		3,128,661	Δ
1840 (P)		2,462,700	Δ
1841 (P)		1,597,367	Δ
1842 (P)		2,383,390	Δ
1843 (P)		2,425,342	Δ
1844 (P)		2,398,752	Δ
1845 (P)		3,894,804	Δ
1846 (P)		4,120,800	Δ
1847 (P)		6,183,669	Δ
1848 (P)		6,415,799	Δ
1849 (P)		4,178,500	Δ

DATE	NOTE	BUSINESS	PROOF
1850 (P)		4,426,844	Δ
1851 (P)		9,889,707	—
1852 (P)		5,063,094	Δ
1853 (P)		6,641,131	—
1854 (P)		4,236,156	Δ
1855 (P)		1,574,829	Δ
1856 (P)	‹4›	2,690,463	Δ
1857 (P)		333,456	Δ

Flying Eagle cent

DATE	NOTE	BUSINESS	PROOF
1857 (P)		17,450,000	Δ
1858 (P)		24,600,000	Δ

Indian Head cent

DATE	NOTE	BUSINESS	PROOF
1859 (P)		36,400,000	Δ
1860 (P)		20,566,000	1,000
1861 (P)		10,100,000	1,000
1862 (P)		28,075,000	550
1863 (P)		49,840,000	460
1864 (P)			
C-N	‹5›	13,740,000	300
bronze	‹5›	39,233,714	170
1865 (P)		35,429,286	500
1866 (P)		9,826,500	725
1867 (P)		9,821,000	625
1868 (P)		10,266,500	600
1869 (P)		6,420,000	600
1870 (P)		5,275,000	1,000
1871 (P)		3,929,500	960
1872 (P)		4,042,000	950
1873 (P)	‹6›	11,676,500	1,100
1874 (P)		14,187,500	700
1875 (P)		13,528,000	700
1876 (P)		7,944,000	1,150
1877 (P)	‹7›	852,500	510
1878 (P)		5,797,500	2,350
1879 (P)		16,228,000	3,200
1880 (P)		38,961,000	3,955
1881 (P)		39,208,000	3,575
1882 (P)		38,578,000	3,100
1883 (P)		45,591,500	6,609
1884 (P)		23,257,800	3,942
1885 (P)		11,761,594	3,790
1886 (P)		17,650,000	4,290
1887 (P)		45,223,523	2,960
1888 (P)		37,489,832	4,582
1889 (P)		48,866,025	3,336
1890 (P)		—	2,740
1891 (P)		—	2,350
1892 (P)		37,647,087	2,745
1893 (P)		46,640,000	2,195
1894 (P)		16,749,500	2,632
1895 (P)		38,341,574	2,062
1896 (P)		39,055,431	1,862
1897 (P)		50,464,392	1,938
1898 (P)		49,821,284	1,795
1899 (P)		53,598,000	2,031
1900 (P)		66,821,284	2,262
1901 (P)		79,609,158	1,985
1902 (P)		87,374,704	2,018
1903 (P)		85,092,703	1,790

DATE	NOTE	BUSINESS	PROOF
1904 (P)		61,326,198	1,817
1905 (P)		80,717,011	2,152
1906 (P)		96,020,530	1,725
1907 (P)		108,137,143	1,475
1908 (P)		32,326,367	1,620
1908-S		1,115,000	—
1909 (P)		14,368,470	2,175
1909-S		309,000	—

Lincoln cent

DATE	NOTE	BUSINESS	PROOF
1909 (P)			
VDB		27,994,580	420
No VDB		72,700,420	2,198
1909-S			
VDB		484,000	—
No VDB		1,825,000	—
1910 (P)		146,798,813	2,405
1910-S		6,045,000	—
1911 (P)		101,176,054	1,733
1911-D		12,672,000	—
1911-S		4,026,000	—
1912 (P)		68,150,915	2,145
1912-D		10,411,000	—
1912-S		4,431,000	—
1913 (P)		76,529,504	2,848
1913-D		15,804,000	—
1913-S		6,101,000	—
1914 (P)		75,237,067	1,365
1914-D		1,193,000	—
1914-S		4,137,000	—
1915 (P)		29,090,970	1,150
1915-D		22,050,000	—
1915-S		4,833,000	—
1916 (P)		131,832,627	1,050
1916-D		35,956,000	—
1916-S		22,510,000	—
1917 (P)		196,429,785	Δ
1917-D		55,120,000	—
1917-S		32,620,000	—
1918 (P)		288,104,634	—
1918-D		47,830,000	—
1918-S		34,680,000	—
1919 (P)		392,021,000	—
1919-D		57,154,000	—
1919-S		139,760,000	—
1920 (P)		310,165,000	—
1920-D		49,280,000	—
1920-S		46,220,000	—
1921 (P)		39,157,000	—
1921-S		15,274,000	—
1922-D	‹8›	7,160,000	—
1923 (P)		74,723,000	—
1923-S		8,700,000	—
1924 (P)		75,178,000	—
1924-D		2,520,000	—
1924-S		11,696,000	—
1925 (P)		139,949,000	—
1925-D		22,580,000	—
1925-S		26,380,000	—
1926 (P)		157,088,000	—

DATE	NOTE	BUSINESS	PROOF
1926-D		28,020,000	—
1926-S		4,550,000	—
1927 (P)		144,440,000	—
1927-D		27,170,000	—
1927-S		14,276,000	—
1928 (P)		134,116,000	—
1928-D		31,170,000	—
1928-S		17,266,000	—
1929 (P)		185,262,000	—
1929-D		41,730,000	—
1929-S		50,148,000	—
1930 (P)		157,415,000	—
1930-D		40,100,000	—
1930-S		24,286,000	—
1931 (P)		19,396,000	—
1931-D		4,480,000	—
1931-S		866,000	—
1932 (P)		9,062,000	—
1932-D		10,500,000	—
1933 (P)		14,360,000	—
1933-D		6,200,000	—
1934 (P)		219,080,000	—
1934-D		28,446,000	—
1935 (P)		245,388,000	—
1935-D		47,000,000	—
1935-S		38,702,000	—
1936 (P)		309,632,000	5,569
1936-D		40,620,000	—
1936-S		29,130,000	—
1937 (P)		309,170,000	9,320
1937-D		50,430,000	—
1937-S		34,500,000	—
1938 (P)		156,682,000	14,734
1938-D		20,010,000	—
1938-S		15,180,000	—
1939 (P)		316,466,000	13,520
1939-D		15,160,000	—
1939-S		52,070,000	—
1940 (P)		586,810,000	15,872
1940-D		81,390,000	—
1940-S		112,940,000	—
1941 (P)		887,018,000	21,100
1941-D		128,700,000	—
1941-S		92,360,000	—
1942 (P)		657,796,000	32,600
1942-D		206,698,000	—
1942-S		85,590,000	—
1943 (P)	‹9›	684,628,670	—
1943-D	‹9›	217,660,000	—
1943-S	‹9›	191,550,000	—
1944 (P)		1,435,400,000	—
1944-D		430,578,000	—
1944-S		282,760,000	—
1945 (P)		1,040,515,000	—
1945-D		226,268,000	—
1945-S		181,770,000	—
1946 (P)		991,655,000	—
1946-D		315,690,000	—
1946-S		198,100,000	—
1947 (P)		190,555,000	—
1947-D		194,750,000	—
1947-S		99,000,000	—
1948 (P)		317,570,000	—
1948-D		172,637,500	—
1948-S		81,735,000	—
1949 (P)		217,775,000	—
1949-D		153,132,500	—
1949-S		64,290,000	—
1950 (P)	‹§›	272,635,000	51,386
1950-D		334,950,000	—
1950-S		118,505,000	—
1951 (P)	‹§›	294,576,000	57,500
1951-D		625,355,000	—
1951-S		136,010,000	—
1952 (P)	‹§›	186,765,000	81,980
1952-D		746,130,000	—
1952-S		137,800,004	—
1953 (P)	‹§›	256,755,000	128,800
1953-D		700,515,000	—
1953-S		181,835,000	—
1954 (P)	‹§›	71,640,050	233,300
1954-D		251,552,500	—
1954-S		96,190,000	—
1955 (P)	‹§›	330,580,000	378,200
1955-D		563,257,500	—
1955-S		44,610,000	—
1956 (P)	‹§›	420,745,000	669,384
1956-D		1,098,210,100	—
1957 (P)	‹§›	282,540,000	1,247,952
1957-D		1,051,342,000	—
1958 (P)	‹§›	252,525,000	875,652
1958-D		800,953,300	—
1959 (P)	‹§›	609,715,000	1,149,291
1959-D		1,279,760,000	—
1960 (P)	‹§, 10›	586,405,000	1,691,602
1960-D		1,580,884,000	—
1961 (P)	‹§›	753,345,000	3,028,244
1961-D		1,753,266,700	—
1962 (P)	‹§›	606,045,000	3,218,019
1962-D		1,793,148,400	—
1963 (P)	‹§›	754,110,000	3,075,645
1963-D		1,774,020,400	—
1964 (P)	‹§, 11›	2,648,575,000	3,950,762
1964-D	‹11›	3,799,071,500	—
1965 (P)	‹11›	301,470,000	—
1965 (D)	‹11›	973,364,000	—
1965 (S)	‹11›	220,030,000	—
1966 (P)	‹11›	811,100,000	—
1966 (D)	‹11›	991,431,200	—
1966 (S)	‹11›	383,355,000	—
1967 (P)	‹11›	907,575,000	—
1967 (D)	‹11›	1,327,377,100	—
1967 (S)	‹11›	813,715,000	—
1968 (P)		1,707,880,970	—
1968-D		2,886,269,600	—
1968-S	‹§›	258,270,001	3,041,506
1969 (P)		1,136,910,000	—
1969-D		4,002,832,200	—
1969-S	‹§›	544,375,000	2,934,631
1970 (P)		1,898,315,000	—

DATE	NOTE	BUSINESS	PROOF
1970-D		2,891,438,900	——
1970-S	‹§›	690,560,004	2,632,810
1971 (P)		1,919,490,000	——
1971-D		2,911,045,600	——
1971-S	‹§›	525,130,054	3,220,733
1972 (P)		2,933,255,000	——
1972-D		2,655,071,400	——
1972-S	‹§›	380,200,104	3,260,996
1973 (P)		3,728,245,000	——
1973-D		3,549,576,588	——
1973-S	‹§›	319,937,634	2,760,339
1974 (P)		4,232,140,523	——
1974-D		4,235,098,000	——
1974-S	‹§›	409,421,878	2,612,568
1975 (P)		3,874,182,000	——
1975-D		4,505,275,300	——
1975-S	‹§›	——	2,845,450
1975 (W)		1,577,294,142	——
1976 (P)		3,133,580,000	——
1976-D		4,221,592,455	——
1976-S		——	4,123,056
1976 (W)		1,540,695,000	——
1977 (P)		3,074,575,000	——
1977-D		4,194,062,300	——
1977-S	‹§›	——	3,236,798
1977 (W)		1,395,355,000	——
1978 (P)		3,735,655,000	——
1978-D		4,280,233,400	——
1978 (S)		291,700,000	——
1978-S	‹§›	——	3,120,285
1978 (W)		1,531,250,000	——
1979 (P)		3,560,940,000	——
1979-D		4,139,357,254	——
1979 (S)		751,725,000	——
1979-S	‹§›	——	3,677,175
1979 (W)		1,705,850,000	——
1980 (P)		6,230,115,000	——
1980-D		5,140,098,660	——
1980 (S)		1,184,590,000	——
1980-S	‹§›	——	3,554,806
1980 (W)		1,576,200,000	——
1981 (P)		6,611,305,000	——
1981-D		5,373,235,677	——
1981 (S)		880,440,000	——
1981-S	‹§›	——	4,063,083
1981 (W)		1,882,400,000	——
1982 (P)	‹12›	7,135,275,000	——
1982-D	‹12›	6,012,979,368	——
1982 (S)	‹12›	1,587,245,000	——
1982-S	‹§›	——	3,857,479
1982 (W)	‹12›	1,990,005,000	——
1983 (P)		5,567,190,000	——
1983-D		6,467,199,428	——
1983 (S)		180,765,000	——
1983-S	‹§›	——	3,279,126
1983 (W)		2,004,400,000	——
1984 (P)		6,114,864,000	——
1984-D		5,569,238,906	——
1984-S	‹§›	——	3,065,110
1984 (W)		2,036,215,000	——
1985 (P)		4,951,904,887	——
1985-D		5,287,399,926	——
1985-S	‹§›	——	3,362,821
1985 (W)		696,585,000	——
1986 (P)		4,490,995,493	——
1986-D		4,442,866,698	——
1986-S	‹§›	——	3,010,497
1986 (W)		400,000	——
1987 (P)		4,682,466,931	——
1987-D		4,879,389,514	——
1987-S	‹§›	——	3,792,233
1988 (P)		6,092,810,000	——
1988-D		5,253,740,443	——
1988-S	‹§›	——	3,262,948
1989 (P)		7,261,535,000	——
1989-D		5,345,467,711	——
1989-S	‹§›	——	3,220,914
1990 (P)		6,851,765,000	——
1990-D		4,922,894,553	——
1990-S	‹§›	——	3,299,559
1991 (P)		5,165,940,000	——
1991-D		4,158,442,076	——
1991-S	‹§›	——	2,867,787
1992 (P)		4,648,905,000	——
1992-D		4,448,673,300	——
1992-S	‹§›	——	4,176,544
1993 (P)		5,684,705,000	——
1993-D		6,426,650,571	——
1993-S	‹§›	——	3,360,876
1994 (P)		6,500,850,000	——
1994-D		7,131,765,000	——
1994-S	‹§›	——	3,222,140
1995 (P)		6,411,440,000	——
1995-D		7,128,560,000	——
1995-S	‹§›	——	2,791,067
1996 (P)		6,612,465,000	——
1996-D		6,510,795,000	——
1996-S	‹§›	——	2,920,158
1997 (P)		4,622,800,000	——
1997-D		4,576,555,000	——
1997-S	‹§›	——	2,796,194
1998 (P)		5,032,200,000	——
1998-D		5,225,200,000	——
1998-S	‹§›	——	2,965,503
1999 (P)		5,237,600,000	——
1999-D		6,360,065,000	——
1999-S	‹§, 121›	——	3,362,464
2000 (P)		5,503,200,000	——
2000-D		8,774,220,000	——
2000-S	‹§, 121›	——	4,062,402
2001 (P)		4,959,600,000	——
2001-D		5,374,990,000	——
2001-S	‹§, 121›	——	2,618,086
2002 (P)		3,260,800,000	——
2002-D		4,028,055,000	——
2002-S	‹§›	——	3,210,674
2003 (P)		3,300,000,000	——
2003-D		3,548,000,000	——
2003-S		——	3,293,934

DATE	NOTE	BUSINESS	PROOF
Two cents			
1864 (P)	‹13›	19,847,500	100
1865 (P)		13,640,000	500
1866 (P)		3,177,000	725
1867 (P)		2,938,750	625
1868 (P)		2,803,750	600
1869 (P)		1,546,500	600
1870 (P)		861,250	1,000
1871 (P)		721,250	960
1872 (P)		65,000	950
1873 (P)	‹6, 14›	——	1,100
Copper-nickel 3 cents			
1865 (P)		11,382,000	400
1866 (P)		4,801,000	725
1867 (P)		3,915,000	625
1868 (P)		3,252,000	600
1869 (P)		1,604,000	600
1870 (P)		1,335,000	1,000
1871 (P)		604,000	960
1872 (P)		862,000	950
1873 (P)	‹6›	1,173,000	1,100
1874 (P)		790,000	700
1875 (P)		228,000	700
1876 (P)		162,000	1,150
1877 (P)	‹7›	——	510
1878 (P)		——	2,350
1879 (P)		38,000	3,200
1880 (P)		21,000	3,955
1881 (P)		1,077,000	3,575
1882 (P)		22,200	3,100
1883 (P)		4,000	6,609
1884 (P)		1,700	3,942
1885 (P)		1,000	3,790
1886 (P)		——	4,290
1887 (P)	‹15›	5,001	2,960
1888 (P)		36,501	4,582
1889 (P)		18,125	3,336
Silver 3 cents			
1851 (P)		5,447,400	Δ
1851-O		720,000	Δ
1852 (P)		18,663,500	——
1853 (P)	‹16›	11,400,000	——
1854 (P)		671,000	Δ
1855 (P)		139,000	Δ
1856 (P)		1,458,000	Δ
1857 (P)		1,042,000	Δ
1858 (P)		1,604,000	Δ
1859 (P)		365,000	Δ
1860 (P)		286,000	1,000
1861 (P)		497,000	1,000
1862 (P)		343,000	550
1863 (P)	‹17›	21,000	460
1864 (P)	‹18›	12,000	470
1865 (P)		8,000	500
1866 (P)		22,000	725
1867 (P)		4,000	625
1868 (P)		3,500	600
1869 (P)		4,500	600
1870 (P)		3,000	1,000

DATE	NOTE	BUSINESS	PROOF
1871 (P)		3,400	960
1872 (P)		1,000	950
1873 (P)	‹6›	——	600
Shield 5 cents			
1866 (P)		14,742,500	125
1867 (P)	‹19›	30,909,500	625
1868 (P)		28,817,000	600
1869 (P)		16,395,000	600
1870 (P)		4,806,000	1,000
1871 (P)		561,000	960
1872 (P)		6,036,000	950
1873 (P)	‹6›	4,550,000	1,100
1874 (P)		3,538,000	700
1875 (P)		2,097,000	700
1876 (P)		2,530,000	1,150
1877 (P)	‹7›	——	510
1878 (P)		——	2,350
1879 (P)		25,900	3,200
1880 (P)		16,000	3,955
1881 (P)		68,800	3,575
1882 (P)		11,473,500	3,100
1883 (P)		1,451,500	5,419
Liberty Head 5 cents			
1883 (P)			
No CENTS		5,474,300	5,219
CENTS		16,026,200	6,783
1884 (P)		11,270,000	3,942
1885 (P)		1,472,700	3,790
1886 (P)		3,326,000	4,290
1887 (P)		15,260,692	2,960
1888 (P)		10,715,901	4,582
1889 (P)		15,878,025	3,336
1890 (P)		16,256,532	2,740
1891 (P)		16,832,000	2,350
1892 (P)		11,696,897	2,745
1893 (P)		13,368,000	2,195
1894 (P)		5,410,500	2,632
1895 (P)		9,977,822	2,062
1896 (P)		8,841,058	1,862
1897 (P)		20,426,797	1,938
1898 (P)		12,530,292	1,795
1899 (P)		26,027,000	2,031
1900 (P)		27,253,733	2,262
1901 (P)		26,478,228	1,985
1902 (P)		31,487,561	2,018
1903 (P)		28,004,935	1,790
1904 (P)		21,401,350	1,817
1905 (P)		29,825,124	2,152
1906 (P)		38,612,000	1,725
1907 (P)		39,213,325	1,475
1908 (P)		22,684,557	1,620
1909 (P)		11,585,763	4,763
1910 (P)		30,166,948	2,405
1911 (P)		39,557,639	1,733
1912 (P)		26,234,569	2,145
1912-D		8,474,000	——
1912-S		238,000	——
1913 (P)	‹20›	——	——

DATE	NOTE	BUSINESS	PROOF
Indian Head 5 cents			
1913 (P)			
Mound		30,992,000	1,520
Plain		29,857,186	1,514
1913-D			
Mound		5,337,000	—
Plain		4,156,000	—
1913-S			
Mound		2,105,000	—
Plain		1,209,000	—
1914 (P)		20,664,463	1,275
1914-D		3,912,000	—
1914-S		3,470,000	—
1915 (P)		20,986,220	1,050
1915-D		7,569,500	—
1915-S		1,505,000	—
1916 (P)		63,497,466	600
1916-D		13,333,000	—
1916-S		11,860,000	—
1917 (P)		51,424,029	Δ
1917-D		9,910,800	—
1917-S		4,193,000	—
1918 (P)		32,086,314	—
1918-D		8,362,000	—
1918-S		4,882,000	—
1919 (P)		60,868,000	—
1919-D		8,006,000	—
1919-S		7,521,000	—
1920 (P)		63,093,000	—
1920-D		9,418,000	—
1920-S		9,689,000	—
1921 (P)		10,663,000	—
1921-S		1,557,000	—
1923 (P)		35,715,000	—
1923-S		6,142,000	—
1924 (P)		21,620,000	—
1924-D		5,258,000	—
1924-S		1,437,000	—
1925 (P)		35,565,100	—
1925-D		4,450,000	—
1925-S		6,256,000	—
1926 (P)		44,693,000	—
1926-D		5,638,000	—
1926-S		970,000	—
1927 (P)		37,981,000	—
1927-D		5,730,000	—
1927-S		3,430,000	—
1928 (P)		23,411,000	—
1928-D		6,436,000	—
1928-S		6,936,000	—
1929 (P)		36,446,000	—
1929-D		8,370,000	—
1929-S		7,754,000	—
1930 (P)		22,849,000	—
1930-S		5,435,000	—
1931-S		1,200,000	—
1934 (P)		20,213,003	—
1934-D		7,480,000	—
1935 (P)		58,264,000	—
1935-D		12,092,000	—
1935-S		10,300,000	—
1936 (P)		118,997,000	4,420
1936-D		24,814,000	—
1936-S		14,930,000	—
1937 (P)		79,480,000	5,769
1937-D		17,826,000	—
1937-S		5,635,000	—
1938-D		7,020,000	—
Jefferson 5 cents			
1938 (P)		19,496,000	19,365
1938-D		5,376,000	—
1938-S		4,105,000	—
1939 (P)		120,615,000	12,535
1939-D		3,514,000	—
1939-S		6,630,000	—
1940 (P)		176,485,000	14,158
1940-D		43,540,000	—
1940-S		39,690,000	—
1941 (P)		203,265,000	18,720
1941-D		53,432,000	—
1941-S		43,445,000	—
1942 (P)	‹21›	49,789,000	29,600
1942-P	‹21›	57,873,000	27,600
1942-D	‹21›	13,938,000	—
1942-S	‹21›	32,900,000	—
1943-P	‹21›	271,165,000	—
1943-D	‹21›	15,294,000	—
1943-S	‹21›	104,060,000	—
1944-P	‹21, 22›	119,150,000	—
1944-D	‹21›	32,309,000	—
1944-S	‹21›	21,640,000	—
1945-P	‹21›	119,408,100	—
1945-D	‹21›	37,158,000	—
1945-S	‹21›	58,939,000	—
1946 (P)		161,116,000	—
1946-D		45,292,200	—
1946-S		13,560,000	—
1947 (P)		95,000,000	—
1947-D		37,822,000	—
1947-S		24,720,000	—
1948 (P)		89,348,000	—
1948-D		44,734,000	—
1948-S		11,300,000	—
1949 (P)		60,652,000	—
1949-D		36,498,000	—
1949-S		9,716,000	—
1950 (P)	‹§›	9,796,000	51,386
1950-D		2,630,030	—
1951 (P)	‹§›	28,552,000	57,500
1951-D		20,460,000	—
1951-S		7,776,000	—
1952 (P)	‹§›	63,988,000	81,980
1952-D		30,638,000	—
1952-S		20,572,000	—
1953 (P)	‹§›	46,644,[illegible]	128,800
1953-D		59,878,600	—
1953-S		19,210,900	—
1954 (P)	‹§›	47,684,050	233,300
1954-D		117,136,560	—

DATE	NOTE	BUSINESS	PROOF
1954-S		29,384,000	——
1955 (P)	‹§›	7,888,000	378,200
1955-D		74,464,100	——
1956 (P)	‹§›	35,216,000	669,384
1956-D		67,222,640	——
1957 (P)	‹§›	38,408,000	1,247,952
1957-D		136,828,900	——
1958 (P)	‹§›	17,088,000	875,652
1958-D		168,249,120	——
1959 (P)	‹§›	27,248,000	1,149,291
1959-D		160,738,240	——
1960 (P)	‹§›	55,416,000	1,691,602
1960-D		192,582,180	——
1961 (P)	‹§›	73,640,000	3,028,244
1961-D		229,342,760	——
1962 (P)	‹§›	97,384,000	3,218,019
1962-D		280,195,720	——
1963 (P)	‹§›	175,776,000	3,075,645
1963-D		276,829,460	——
1964 (P)	‹§, 11›	1,024,672,000	3,950,762
1964-D	‹11›	1,787,297,100	——
1965 (P)	‹11›	12,440,000	——
1965 (D)	‹11›	82,291,380	——
1965 (S)	‹11›	39,040,000	——
1966 (P)	‹11, 23›	——	Δ
1966 (D)	‹11›	103,546,700	——
1966 (S)	‹11›	50,400,000	——
1967 (P)	‹11›	——	——
1967 (D)	‹11›	75,993,800	——
1967 (S)	‹11›	31,332,000	——
1968 (P)		——	——
1968-D		91,227,880	——
1968-S	‹§›	100,396,004	3,041,506
1969 (P)		——	——
1969-D		202,807,500	——
1969-S	‹§›	120,165,000	2,934,631
1970-D		515,485,380	——
1970-S	‹§›	238,832,004	2,632,810
1971 (P)		106,884,000	——
1971-D		316,144,800	——
1971-S	‹24›	——	3,220,733
1972 (P)		202,036,000	——
1972-D		351,694,600	——
1972-S	‹§›	——	3,260,996
1973 (P)		384,396,000	——
1973-D		261,405,400	——
1973-S	‹§›	——	2,760,339
1974 (P)		601,752,000	——
1974-D		277,373,000	——
1974-S	‹§›	——	2,612,568
1975 (P)		181,772,000	——
1975-D		401,875,300	——
1975-S	‹§›	——	2,845,450
1976 (P)		367,124,000	——
1976-D		563,964,147	——
1976-S		——	——
1977 (P)		585,376,000	——
1977-D		297,313,422	——
1977-S	‹§›	——	3,236,798
1978 (P)		391,308,000	——
1978-D		313,092,780	——
1978-S	‹§›	——	3,120,285
1979 (P)		463,188,000	——
1979-D		325,867,672	——
1979-S	‹§›	——	3,677,175
1980-P	‹25›	593,004,000	——
1980-D		502,323,448	——
1980-S	‹§›	——	3,554,806
1981-P		657,504,000	——
1981-D		364,801,843	——
1981-S	‹§›	——	4,063,083
1982-P		292,355,000	——
1982-D		373,726,544	——
1982-S	‹§›	——	3,857,479
1983-P		561,615,000	——
1983-D		536,726,276	——
1983-S	‹§›	——	3,279,126
1984-P		746,769,000	——
1984-D		517,675,146	——
1984-S	‹§›	——	3,065,110
1985-P		647,114,962	——
1985-D		459,747,446	——
1985-S	‹§›	——	3,362,821
1986-P		536,883,493	——
1986-D		361,819,144	——
1986-S	‹§›	——	3,010,497
1987-P		371,499,481	——
1987-D		410,590,604	——
1987-S	‹§›	——	3,792,233
1988-P		771,360,000	——
1988-D		663,771,652	——
1988-S	‹§›	——	3,262,948
1989-P		898,812,000	——
1989-D		570,842,474	——
1989-S	‹§›	——	3,220,914
1990-P		661,636,000	——
1990-D		663,938,503	——
1990-S	‹§›	——	3,299,559
1991-P		614,104,000	——
1991-D		436,496,678	——
1991-S	‹§›	——	2,867,787
1992-P		399,552,000	——
1992-D		450,565,113	——
1992-S	‹§›	——	4,176,544
1993-P		412,070,000	——
1993-D		406,084,135	——
1993-S	‹§›	——	3,360,876
1994-P	‹116›	722,160,000	——
1994-D		715,762,110	——
1994-S	‹§›	——	3,222,140
1995-P		774,156,000	——
1995-D		888,112,000	——
1995-S	‹§›	——	2,791,067
1996-P		829,332,000	——
1996-D		817,736,000	——
1996-S	‹§›	——	2,920,158
1997-P		470,972,000	——
1997-D		466,640,000	——
1997-S	‹§›	——	2,796,194
1998-P		688,292,000	——

DATE	NOTE	BUSINESS	PROOF
1998-D		635,380,000	——
1998-S	‹§›	——	2,965,503
1999-P		1,212,000,000	——
1999-D		1,066,720,000	——
1999-S	‹§, 121›	——	3,362,464
2000-P		846,240,000	——
2000-D		1,509,520,000	——
2000-S	‹§, 121›	——	4,062,402
2001-P		675,704,000	——
2001-D		627,680,000	——
2001-S	‹§, 121›	——	2,618,086
2002-P		539,280,000	——
2002-D		691,200,000	——
2002-S	‹§›	——	3,210,674
2003-P		441,840,000	——
2003-D		383,040,000	——
2003-S		——	3,293,934
Flowing Hair half dime			
1794		7,756	——
1795		78,660	——
Draped Bust half dime			
1796		10,230	——
1797		44,527	——
1800		40,000	——
1801		33,910	——
1802		13,010	——
1803		37,850	——
1805		15,600	——
Capped Bust half dime			
1829		1,230,000	Δ
1830		1,240,000	Δ
1831		1,242,700	Δ
1832		965,000	Δ
1833		1,370,000	Δ
1834		1,480,000	Δ
1835		2,760,000	Δ
1836		1,900,000	Δ
1837		871,000	Δ
Seated Liberty half dime			
1837		1,405,000	——
1838 (P)		2,255,000	Δ
1838-O	‹26›	115,000	——
1839 (P)		1,069,150	Δ
1839-O		981,550	——
1840 (P)		1,344,085	Δ
1840-O		935,000	——
1841 (P)		1,150,000	Δ
1841-O		815,000	——
1842 (P)		815,000	Δ
1842-O		350,000	——
1843 (P)		1,165,000	Δ
1844 (P)		430,000	Δ
1844-O		220,000	——
1845 (P)		1,564,000	Δ
1846 (P)		27,000	Δ
1847 (P)		1,274,000	Δ
1848 (P)		668,000	Δ
1848-O		600,000	——

DATE	NOTE	BUSINESS	PROOF
1849 (P)		1,309,000	Δ
1849-O		140,000	——
1850 (P)		955,000	Δ
1850-O		690,000	——
1851 (P)		781,000	Δ
1851-O		860,000	——
1852 (P)		1,000,500	Δ
1852-O		260,000	——
1853 (P)			
No Arrows	‹16›	135,000	——
Arrows	‹16›	13,210,020	Δ
1853-O			
No Arrows	‹16›	160,000	——
Arrows	‹16›	2,200,000	——
1854 (P)		5,740,000	Δ
1854-O		1,560,000	——
1855 (P)		1,750,000	Δ
1855-O		600,000	——
1856 (P)		4,880,000	Δ
1856-O		1,100,000	——
1857 (P)		7,280,000	Δ
1857-O		1,380,000	——
1858 (P)		3,500,000	Δ
1858-O		1,660,000	——
1859 (P)		340,000	Δ
1859-O		560,000	——
1860 (P)	‹28›	798,000	1,000
1860-O	‹28, 29›	1,060,000	Δ
1861 (P)		3,360,000	1,000
1862 (P)		1,492,000	550
1863 (P)		18,000	460
1863-S		100,000	——
1864 (P)	‹18›	48,000	470
1864-S		90,000	——
1865 (P)		13,000	500
1865-S		120,000	——
1866 (P)		10,000	725
1866-S		120,000	——
1867 (P)		8,000	625
1867-S		120,000	——
1868 (P)		88,600	600
1868-S		280,000	——
1869 (P)		208,000	600
1869-S		230,000	——
1870 (P)		535,600	1,000
1871 (P)		1,873,000	960
1871-S		161,000	——
1872 (P)		2,947,000	950
1872-S		837,000	——
1873 (P)	‹6›	712,000	600
1873-S	‹6›	324,000	——
Draped Bust dime			
1796		22,135	——
1797		25,261	——
1798		27,550	——
1800		21,760	——
1801		34,640	——
1802		10,975	——
1803		33,040	——

DATE	NOTE	BUSINESS	PROOF
1804		8,265	—
1805		120,780	—
1807		165,000	—
Capped Bust dime			
1809		51,065	—
1811		65,180	—
1814		421,500	—
1820		942,587	Δ
1821		1,186,512	Δ
1822		100,000	Δ
1823	‹3›	440,000	Δ
1824		100,000	Δ
1825		410,000	Δ
1827		1,215,000	Δ
1828		125,000	Δ
1829		770,000	Δ
1830		510,000	Δ
1831		771,350	Δ
1832		522,500	Δ
1833		485,000	Δ
1834		635,000	Δ
1835		1,410,000	Δ
1836		1,190,000	Δ
1837		359,500	Δ
Seated Liberty dime			
1837		682,500	—
1838 (P)		1,992,500	Δ
1838-O	‹26›	406,034	—
1839 (P)		1,0,115	Δ
1839-O		1,323,000	—
1840 (P)		1,358,580	Δ
1840-O		1,175,000	—
1841 (P)		1,622,500	Δ
1841-O		2,007,500	—
1842 (P)		1,887,500	Δ
1842-O		2,020,000	—
1843 (P)		1,370,000	Δ
1843-O		50,000	—
1844 (P)		72,500	Δ
1845 (P)		1,755,000	Δ
1845-O		230,000	—
1846 (P)		31,300	Δ
1847 (P)		245,000	Δ
1848 (P)		451,500	Δ
1849 (P)		839,000	Δ
1849-O		300,000	—
1850 (P)		1,931,500	Δ
1850-O		510,000	—
1851 (P)		1,026,500	Δ
1851-O		400,000	—
1852 (P)		1,535,500	Δ
1852-O		430,000	—
1853 (P)			
No Arrows	‹16›	95,000	—
With Arrows	‹16›	12,078,010	Δ
1853-O		1,100,000	—
1854 (P)		4,470,000	Δ
1854-O		1,770,000	—
1855 (P)		2,075,000	Δ

DATE	NOTE	BUSINESS	PROOF
1856 (P)		5,780,000	Δ
1856-O		1,180,000	—
1856-S		70,000	—
1857 (P)		5,580,000	Δ
1857-O		1,540,000	—
1858 (P)		1,540,000	—
1858-O		290,000	Δ
1858-S		60,000	—
1859 (P)		430,000	Δ
1859-O		480,000	—
1859-S		60,000	—
1860 (P)	‹28›	606,000	1,000
1860-O	‹28›	40,000	—
1860-S	‹28›	140,000	—
1861 (P)		1,883,000	1,000
1861-S		172,500	—
1862 (P)		847,000	550
1862-S		180,750	—
1863 (P)		14,000	460
1863-S		157,500	—
1864 (P)	‹18›	11,000	470
1864-S		230,000	—
1865 (P)		10,000	500
1865-S		175,000	—
1866 (P)		8,000	725
1866-S		135,000	—
1867 (P)		6,000	625
1867-S		140,000	—
1868 (P)		464,000	600
1868-S		260,000	—
1869 (P)		256,000	600
1869-S		450,000	—
1870 (P)		470,500	1,000
1870-S		50,000	—
1871 (P)		906,750	960
1871-CC		20,100	—
1871-S		320,000	—
1872 (P)		2,395,500	950
1872-CC		35,480	—
1872-S		190,000	—
1873 (P)			
No Arrows	‹6›	1,568,000	600
With Arrows	‹6›	2,377,700	800
1873-CC			
No Arrows	‹6, 30›	12,400	
With Arrows	‹6›	18,791	—
1873-S			
With Arrows	‹6›	455,000	—
1874 (P)		2,940,000	700
1874-CC		10,817	—
1874-S		240,000	—
1875 (P)		10,350,000	700
1875-CC		4,645,000	—
1875-S		9,070,000	—
1876 (P)		11,460,000	1,150
1876-CC		8,270,000	—
1876-S		10,420,000	—
1877 (P)		7,310,000	510
1877-CC		7,700,000	—
1877-S		2,340,000	—

DATE	NOTE	BUSINESS	PROOF
1878 (P)		1,678,000	800
1878-CC		200,000	—
1879 (P)		14,000	1,100
1880 (P)		36,000	1,355
1881 (P)		24,000	975
1882 (P)		3,910,000	1,100
1883 (P)		7,674,673	1,039
1884 (P)		3,365,505	875
1884-S		564,969	—
1885 (P)		2,532,497	930
1885-S		43,690	—
1886 (P)		6,376,684	886
1886-S		206,524	—
1887 (P)		11,283,229	710
1887-S		4,454,450	—
1888 (P)		5,495,655	832
1888-S		1,720,000	—
1889 (P)		7,380,000	711
1889-S		972,678	—
1890 (P)		9,910,951	590
1890-S		1,423,076	—
1891 (P)		15,310,000	600
1891-O		4,540,000	—
1891-S		3,196,116	—

Barber dime

DATE	NOTE	BUSINESS	PROOF
1892 (P)		12,120,000	1,245
1892-O		3,841,700	—
1892-S		990,710	—
1893 (P)		3,340,000	792
1893-O		1,760,000	—
1893-S		2,491,401	—
1894 (P)		1,330,000	972
1894-O		720,000	—
1894-S	‹31›	—	—
1895 (P)		690,000	880
1895-O		440,000	—
1895-S		1,120,000	—
1896 (P)		2,000,000	762
1896-O		610,000	—
1896-S		575,056	—
1897 (P)		10,868,533	731
1897-O		666,000	—
1897-S		1,342,844	—
1898 (P)		16,320,000	735
1898-O		2,130,000	—
1898-S		1,702,507	—
1899 (P)		19,580,000	846
1899-O		2,650,000	—
1899-S		1,867,493	—
1900 (P)		17,600,000	912
1900-O		2,010,000	—
1900-S		5,168,270	—
1901 (P)		18,859,665	813
1901-O		5,620,000	—
1901-S		593,022	—
1902 (P)		21,380,000	777
1902-O		4,500,000	—
1902-S		2,070,000	—
1903 (P)		19,500,000	755
1903-O		8,180,000	—
1903-S		613,300	—
1904 (P)		14,600,357	670
1904-S		800,000	—
1905 (P)		14,551,623	727
1905-O		3,400,000	—
1905-S		6,855,199	—
1906 (P)		19,957,731	675
1906-D	‹32›	4,060,000	Δ
1906-O		2,610,000	—
1906-S		3,136,640	—
1907 (P)		22,220,000	575
1907-D		4,080,000	—
1907-O		5,058,000	—
1907-S		3,178,470	—
1908 (P)		10,600,000	545
1908-D		7,490,000	—
1908-O		1,789,000	—
1908-S		3,220,000	—
1909 (P)		10,240,000	650
1909-D		954,000	—
1909-O		2,287,000	—
1909-S		1,000,000	—
1910 (P)		11,520,000	551
1910-D		3,490,000	—
1910-S		1,240,000	—
1911 (P)		18,870,000	543
1911-D		11,209,000	—
1911-S		3,520,000	—
1912 (P)		19,350,000	700
1912-D		11,760,000	—
1912-S		3,420,000	—
1913 (P)		19,760,000	622
1913-S		510,000	—
1914 (P)		17,360,230	—
1914-D		11,908,000	425
1914-S		2,100,000	—
1915 (P)		5,620,000	450
1915-S		960,000	—
1916 (P)		18,490,000	Δ
1916-S		5,820,000	—

Winged Liberty Head dime

DATE	NOTE	BUSINESS	PROOF
1916 (P)		22,180,080	—
1916-D		264,000	—
1916-S		10,450,000	—
1917 (P)		55,230,000	—
1917-D		9,402,000	—
1917-S		27,330,000	—
1918 (P)		26,680,000	—
1918-D		22,674,800	—
1918-S		19,300,000	—
1919 (P)		35,740,000	—
1919-D		9,939,000	—
1919-S		8,850,000	—
1920 (P)		59,030,000	—
1920-D		19,171,000	—
1920-S		13,820,000	—
1921 (P)		1,230,000	—
1921-D		1,080,000	—

DATE	NOTE	BUSINESS	PROOF
1923 (P)	‹22›	50,130,000	—
1923-S		6,440,000	—
1924 (P)		24,010,000	—
1924-D		6,810,000	—
1924-S		7,120,000	—
1925 (P)		25,610,000	—
1925-D		5,117,000	—
1925-S		5,850,000	—
1926 (P)		32,160,000	—
1926-D		6,828,000	—
1926-S		1,520,000	—
1927 (P)		28,080,000	—
1927-D		4,812,000	—
1927-S		4,770,000	—
1928 (P)		19,480,000	—
1928-D		4,161,000	—
1928-S		7,400,000	—
1929 (P)		25,970,000	—
1929-D		5,034,000	—
1929-S		4,730,000	—
1930 (P)	‹22›	6,770,000	—
1930-S		1,843,000	—
1931 (P)		3,150,000	—
1931-D		1,260,000	—
1931-S		1,800,000	—
1934 (P)		24,080,000	—
1934-D		6,772,000	—
1935 (P)		58,830,000	—
1935-D		10,477,000	—
1935-S		15,840,000	—
1936 (P)		87,500,000	4,130
1936-D		16,132,000	—
1936-S		9,210,000	—
1937 (P)		56,860,000	5,756
1937-D		14,146,000	—
1937-S		9,740,000	—
1938 (P)		22,190,000	8,728
1938-D		5,537,000	—
1938-S		8,090,000	—
1939 (P)		67,740,000	9,321
1939-D		24,394,000	—
1939 S		10,540,000	—
1940 (P)		65,350,000	11,827
1940-D		21,198,000	—
1940-S		21,560,000	—
1941 (P)		175,090,000	16,557
1941-D		45,634,000	—
1941-S		43,090,000	—
1942 (P)		205,410,000	22,329
1942-D		60,740,000	—
1942-S		49,300,000	—
1943 (P)		191,710,000	—
1943-D		71,949,000	—
1943-S		60,400,000	—
1944 (P)		231,410,000	—
1944-D		62,224,000	—
1944-S		49,490,000	—
1945 (P)		159,130,000	—
1945-D		40,245,000	—
1945-S		41,920,000	—

DATE	NOTE	BUSINESS	PROOF
Roosevelt dime			
1946 (P)		255,250,000	—
1946-D		61,043,500	—
1946-S		27,900,000	—
1947 (P)		121,520,000	—
1947-D		46,835,000	—
1947-S		34,840,000	—
1948 (P)		74,950,000	—
1948-D		52,841,000	—
1948-S		35,520,000	—
1949 (P)		30,940,000	—
1949-D		26,034,000	—
1949-S		13,510,000	—
1950 (P)	‹§›	50,130,114	51,386
1950-D		46,803,000	—
1950-S		20,440,000	—
1951 (P)	‹§›	102,880,102	57,500
1951 D		56,529,000	—
1951-S		31,630,000	—
1952 (P)	‹§›	99,040,093	81,980
1952-D		122,100,000	—
1952-S		44,419,500	—
1953 (P)	‹§›	53,490,120	128,800
1953-D		136,433,000	—
1953-S		39,180,000	—
1954 (P)	‹§›	114,010,203	233,300
1954-D		106,397,000	—
1954-S		22,860,000	—
1955 (P)	‹§›	12,450,181	378,200
1955-D		13,959,000	—
1955-S		18,510,000	—
1956 (P)	‹§›	108,640,000	669,384
1956-D		108,015,100	—
1957 (P)	‹§›	160,160,000	1,247,952
1957-D		113,354,330	—
1958 (P)	‹§›	31,910,000	875,652
1958-D		136,564,600	—
1959 (P)	‹§›	85,780,000	1,149,291
1959-D		164,919,790	—
1960 (P)	‹§›	70,390,000	1,691,602
1960-D		200,160,400	—
1961 (P)	‹§›	93,730,000	3,028,244
1961-D		209,146,550	—
1962 (P)	‹§›	72,450,000	3,218,019
1962-D		334,948,380	—
1963 (P)	‹§›	123,650,000	3,075,645
1963-D		421,476,530	—
1964 (P)	‹§, 11›	929,360,000	3,950,762
1964-D	‹11›	1,357,517,180	—
1965 (P)	‹11›	845,130,000	—
1965 (D)	‹11›	757,472,820	—
1965 (S)	‹11›	47,177,750	—
1966 (P)	‹11›	622,550,000	—
1966 (D)	‹11›	683,771,010	—
1966 (S)	‹11›	74,151,947	—
1967 (P)	‹11›	1,030,110,000	—
1967 (D)	‹11›	1,156,277,320	—
1967 (S)	‹11›	57,620,000	—
1968 (P)		424,470,400	—
1968 D		480,748,280	—

DATE	NOTE	BUSINESS	PROOF
1968-S	‹§, 33›	——	3,041,506
1969 (P)		145,790,000	——
1969-D		563,323,870	——
1969-S	‹§›	——	2,934,631
1970 (P)		345,570,000	——
1970-D		754,942,100	——
1970-S	‹§, 34›	——	2,632,810
1971 (P)		162,690,000	——
1971-D		377,914,240	——
1971-S	‹§›	——	3,220,733
1972 (P)		431,540,000	——
1972-D		330,290,000	——
1972-S	‹§›	——	3,260,996
1973 (P)		315,670 ,000	——
1973-D		455,032,426	——
1973-S	‹§›	——	2,760,339
1974 (P)		470,248,000	——
1974-D		571,083,000	——
1974-S	‹§›	——	2,612,568
1975 (P)		513,682,000	——
1975-D		313,705,300	——
1975 (S)		71,991,900	——
1976 (P)		568,760,000	——
1976-D		695,222,774	——
1976-S		——	——
1977 (P)		796,930,000	——
1977-D		376,607,228	——
1977-S	‹§›	——	3,236,798
1978 (P)		663,980,000	——
1978-D		282,847,540	——
1978-S	‹§›	——	3,120,285
1979 (P)		315,440,000	——
1979-D		390,921,184	——
1979-S	‹§›	——	3,677,175
1980-P	‹25›	735,170,000	——
1980-D		719,354,321	——
1980-S	‹§›	——	3,554,806
1981-P		676,650,000	——
1981-D		712,284,143	——
1981-S	‹§›	——	4,063,083
1982-P	‹35›	519,475,000	——
1982-D		542,713,584	——
1982-S	‹§›	——	3,857,479
1983-P		647,025,000	——
1983-D		730,129,224	——
1983-S	‹§›	——	3,279,126
1984-P		856,669,000	——
1984-D		704,803,976	——
1984-S	‹§›	——	3,065,110
1985-P		705,200,962	——
1985-D		587,979,970	——
1985-S	‹§›	——	3,362,821
1986-P		682,649,693	——
1986-D		473,326,974	——
1986-S	‹§›	——	3,010,497
1987-P		762,709,481	——
1987-D		653,203,402	——
1987-S	‹§›	——	3,792,233
1988-P		1,030,550,000	——
1988-D		962,385,488	——
1988-S	‹§›	——	3,262,948
1989-P		1,298,400,000	——
1989-D		896,535,597	——
1989-S	‹§›	——	3,220,914
1990-P		1,034,340,000	——
1990-D		839,995,824	——
1990-S	‹§›	——	3,299,559
1991-P		927,220,000	——
1991-D		601,241,114	——
1991-S	‹§›	——	2,867,787
1992-P		593,500,000	——
1992-D		616,273,932	——
1992-S	‹§›		
Clad		——	2,858,903
90% silver		——	1,317,641
1993-P		766,180,000	——
1993-D		750,110,166	——
1993-S	‹§›		
Clad		——	2,569,882
90% silver		——	790,994
1994-P		1,189,000,000	——
1994-D		1,303,268,110	——
1994-S	‹§›		
Clad		——	2,443,590
90% silver		——	778,550
1995-P		1,125,500,000	——
1995-D		1,274,890,000	——
1995-S	‹§›		
Clad		——	2,124,790
90% silver		——	666,277
1996-P		1,421,630,000	——
1996-D		1,400,300,000	——
1996-S	‹§›		
Clad		——	2,145,077
90% silver		——	775,081
1996-W	‹118›	U	——
1996-W	‹118›	1,450,440	——
1997-P		991,640,000	——
1997-D		979,810,000	——
1997-S	‹§›		
Clad		——	2,055,000
90% silver		——	741,194
1998-P		1,163,000,000	——
1998-D		1,172,300,000	——
1998-S	‹§›		
Clad		——	2,086,507
90% silver		——	878,996
1999-P		2,164,000,000	——
1999-D		1,397,750,000	——
1999-S	‹§›		
Clad	‹121›	——	2,557,899
90% silver		——	804,565
2000-P		1,842,500,000	——
2000-D		1,818,700,000	——
2000-S	‹§›		
Clad	‹121›	——	3,096,981
90% silver		——	965,421
2001-P		1,369,590,000	——
2001-D		1,412,800,000	——

DATE	NOTE	BUSINESS	PROOF
2001-S	‹§›		
Clad	‹121›	——	2,300,944
90% silver		——	317,142
2002-P		1,187,500,000	——
2002-D		1,379,500,000	——
2002-S	‹§›		
Clad		——	2,321,848
90% silver		——	888,826
2003-P		1,085,500,000	——
2003-D		986,500,000	——
2003-S	‹§›		
Clad		——	2,206,190
90% silver		——	1,087,744

Twenty cents

DATE	NOTE	BUSINESS	PROOF
1875 (P)		38,500	1,200
1875-CC		133,290	——
1875-S	‹36›	1,155,000	Δ
1876 (P)		14,750	1,150
1876-CC	‹37›	10,000	——
1877 (P)		——	510
1878 (P)		——	600

Draped Bust quarter dollar

DATE	NOTE	BUSINESS	PROOF
1796		6,146	——
1804		6,738	——
1805		121,394	——
1806		286,424	——
1807		140,343	——

Capped Bust quarter dollar

DATE	NOTE	BUSINESS	PROOF
1815		89,235	——
1818		361,174	Δ
1819		144,000	——
1820		127,444	Δ
1821		216,851	Δ
1822		64,080	Δ
1823	‹3›	1,800	Δ
1824		16,000	Δ
1825		168,000	Δ
1827	‹38›	——	Δ (R)
1828		102,000	Δ
1831		398,000	Δ
1832		320,000	Δ
1833		156,000	Δ
1834		286,000	Δ
1835		1,952,000	Δ
1836		472,000	Δ
1837		252,400	Δ
1838 (P)		366,000	Δ

Seated Liberty quarter dollar

DATE	NOTE	BUSINESS	PROOF
1838 (P)		466,000	——
1839 (P)		491,146	Δ
1840 (P)		188,127	Δ
1840-O		425,200	——
1841 (P)		120,000	Δ
1841-O		452,000	——
1842 (P)		88,000	Δ
1842-O		769,000	——
1843 (P)		645,600	Δ
1843-O		968,000	——
1844 (P)		421,200	Δ
1844-O		740,000	——
1845 (P)		922,000	Δ
1846 (P)		510,000	Δ
1847 (P)		734,000	Δ
1847-O		368,000	——
1848 (P)		146,000	Δ
1849 (P)		340,000	Δ
1849-O		16,000	——
1850 (P)		190,800	Δ
1850-O		396,000	——
1851 (P)		160,000	Δ
1851-O		88,000	——
1852 (P)		177,060	Δ
1852-O		96,000	——
1853 (P)			
No Arr. & Rays	‹16›	44,200	——
Arrows & Rays	‹16›	15,210,020	Δ
1853-O		1,332,000	——
1854 (P)		12,380,000	Δ
1854-O		1,404,000	——
1855 (P)		2,857,000	Δ
1855-O		176,000	——
1855-S	‹39›	396,400	Δ
1856 (P)		7,264,000	Δ
1856-O		968,000	——
1856-S		286,000	——
1857 (P)		9,644,000	Δ
1857-O		1,180,000	——
1857-S		82,000	——
1858 (P)		7,368,000	Δ
1858-O		520,000	——
1858-S		121,000	——
1859 (P)		1,344,000	Δ
1859-O		260,000	——
1859-S		80,000	——
1860 (P)		804,400	1,000
1860-O		388,000	——
1860-S		56,000	——
1861 (P)		4,853,600	1,000
1861-S		96,000	——
1862 (P)		932,000	550
1862-S		67,000	——
1863 (P)		191,600	460
1864 (P)		93,600	470
1864-S		20,000	——
1865 (P)		58,800	500
1865-S		41,000	——
1866 (P)	‹40›	16,800	725
1866-S	‹40›	28,000	——
1867 (P)		20,000	625
1867-S		48,000	——
1868 (P)		29,400	600
1868-S		96,000	——
1869 (P)		16,000	600
1869-S		76,000	——
1870 (P)		86,400	1,000
1870-CC		8,340	——
1871 (P)		118,200	960
1871-CC		10,890	——

DATE	NOTE	BUSINESS	PROOF
1871-S		30,900	——
1872 (P)		182,000	950
1872-CC		22,850	——
1872-S		83,000	——
1873 (P)			
No Arrows	‹6›	212,000	600
With Arrows	‹6›	1,271,160	540
1873-CC			
No Arrows	‹6›	4,000	——
With Arrows	‹6›	12,462	——
1873-S			
With Arrows	‹6›	156,000	——
1874 (P)		471,200	700
1874-S		392,000	——
1875 (P)		4,292,800	700
1875-CC		140,000	——
1875-S		680,000	——
1876 (P)		17,816,000	1,150
1876-CC		4,944,000	——
1876-S		8,596,000	——
1877 (P)		10,911,200	510
1877-CC		4,192,000	——
1877-S		8,996,000	——
1878 (P)		2,260,000	800
1878-CC		996,000	——
1878-S		140,000	——
1879 (P)	‹41›	14,450	250
1880 (P)		13,600	1,355
1881 (P)		12,000	975
1882 (P)		15,200	1,100
1883 (P)		14,400	1,039
1884 (P)		8,000	875
1885 (P)		13,600	930
1886 (P)		5,000	886
1887 (P)		10,000	710
1888 (P)		10,001	832
1888-S		1,216,000	——
1889 (P)		12,000	711
1890 (P)		80,000	590
1891 (P)		3,920,000	600
1891-O	‹42›	68,000	Δ
1891-S		2,216,000	——
Barber quarter dollar			
1892 (P)		8,236,000	1,245
1892-O		2,640,000	——
1892-S		964,079	——
1893 (P)		5,444,023	792
1893-O		3,396,000	——
1893-S		1,454,535	——
1894 (P)		3,432,000	972
1894-O		2,852,000	——
1894-S		2,648,821	——
1895 (P)		4,440,000	880
1895-O		2,816,000	——
1895-S		1,764,681	——
1896 (P)		3,874,000	762
1896-O		1,484,000	——
1896-S		188,039	——
1897 (P)		8,140,000	731

DATE	NOTE	BUSINESS	PROOF
1897-O		1,414,800	——
1897-S		542,229	——
1898 (P)		11,100,000	735
1898-O		1,868,000	——
1898-S		1,020,592	——
1899 (P)		12,624,000	846
1899-O		2,644,000	——
1899-S		708,000	——
1900 (P)		10,016,000	912
1900-O		3,416,000	——
1900-S		1,858,585	——
1901 (P)		8,892,000	813
1901-O		1,612,000	——
1901-S		72,664	——
1902 (P)		12,196,967	777
1902-O		4,748,000	——
1902-S		1,524,612	——
1903 (P)		9,669,309	755
1903-O		3,500,000	——
1903-S		1,036,000	——
1904 (P)		9,588,143	670
1904-O		2,456,000	——
1905 (P)		4,967,523	727
1905-O		1,230,000	——
1905-S		1,884,000	——
1906 (P)		3,655,760	675
1906-D		3,280,000	——
1906-O		2,056,000	——
1907 (P)		7,192,000	575
1907-D		2,484,000	——
1907-O		4,560,000	——
1907-S		1,360,000	——
1908 (P)		4,232,000	545
1908-D		5,788,000	——
1908-O		6,244,000	——
1908-S		784,000	——
1909 (P)		9,268,000	650
1909-D		5,114,000	——
1909-O		712,000	——
1909-S		1,348,000	——
1910 (P)		2,244,000	551
1910-D		1,500,000	——
1911 (P)		3,720,000	543
1911-D		933,600	——
1911-S		988,000	——
1912 (P)		4,400,000	700
1912-S		708,000	——
1913 (P)		484,000	613
1913-D		1,450,800	——
1913-S		40,000	——
1914 (P)		6,244,230	380
1914-D		3,046,000	——
1914-S		264,000	——
1915 (P)		3,480,000	450
1915-D		3,694,000	——
1915-S		704,000	——
1916 (P)		1,788,000	——
1916-D		6,540,800	——

DATE	NOTE	BUSINESS	PROOF
Standing Liberty quarter dollar			
1916 (P)		52,000	—
1917 (P)			
Bare Breast		8,740,000	Δ
Mailed Breast		13,880,000	—
1917-D			
Bare Breast		1,509,200	—
Mailed Breast		6,224,400	—
1917-S			
Bare Breast		1,952,000	—
Mailed Breast		5,552,000	—
1918 (P)		14,240,000	—
1918-D		7,380,000	—
1918-S		11,072,000	—
1919 (P)		11,324,000	—
1919-D		1,944,000	—
1919-S		1,836,000	—
1920 (P)		27,860,000	—
1920-D		3,586,400	—
1920-S		6,380,000	—
1921 (P)		1,916,000	—
1923 (P)		9,716,000	—
1923-S		1,360,000	—
1924 (P)		10,920,000	—
1924-D		3,112,000	—
1924-S		2,860,000	—
1925 (P)		12,280,000	—
1926 (P)		11,316,000	—
1926-D		1,716,000	—
1926-S		2,700,000	—
1927 (P)		11,912,000	—
1927-D		976,400	—
1927-S		396,000	—
1928 (P)		6,336,000	—
1928-D		1,627,600	—
1928-S		2,644,000	—
1929 (P)		11,140,000	—
1929-D		1,358,000	—
1929-S		1,764,000	—
1930 (P)		5,632,000	—
1930-S		1,556,000	—
Washington quarter dollar			
1932 (P)		5,404,000	—
1932-D		436,800	—
1932-S		408,000	—
1934 (P)		31,912,052	—
1934-D		3,527,200	—
1935 (P)		32,484,000	—
1935-D		5,780,000	—
1935-S		5,660,000	—
1936 (P)		41,300,000	3,837
1936-D		5,374,000	—
1936-S		3,828,000	—
1937 (P)		19,696,000	5,542
1937-D		7,189,600	—
1937-S		1,652,000	—
1938 (P)		9,472,000	8,045
1938-S		2,832,000	—
1939 (P)		33,540,000	8,795
1939-D		7,092,000	—
1939-S		2,628,000	—
1940 (P)		35,704,000	11,246
1940-D		2,797,600	—
1940-S		8,244,000	—
1941 (P)		79,032,000	15,287
1941-D		16,714,800	—
1941-S		16,080,000	—
1942 (P)		102,096,000	21,123
1942-D		17,487,200	—
1942-S		19,384,000	—
1943 (P)		99,700,000	—
1943-D		16,095,600	—
1943-S		21,700,000	—
1944 (P)		104,956,000	—
1944-D		14,600,800	—
1944-S		12,560,000	—
1945 (P)		74,372,000	—
1945-D		12,341,600	—
1945-S		17,004,001	—
1946 (P)		53,436,000	—
1946-D		9,072,800	—
1946-S		4,204,000	—
1947 (P)		22,556,000	—
1947-D		15,338,400	—
1947-S		5,532,000	—
1948 (P)		35,196,000	—
1948-D		16,766,800	—
1948-S		15,960,000	—
1949 (P)		9,312,000	—
1949-D		10,068,400	—
1950 (P)	‹§›	24,920,126	51,386
1950-D		21,075,600	—
1950-S		10,284,004	—
1951 (P)	‹§›	43,448,102	57,500
1951-D		35,354,800	—
1951-S		9,048,000	—
1952 (P)	‹§›	38,780,093	81,980
1952-D		49,795,200	—
1952-S		13,707,800	—
1953 (P)	‹§›	18,536,120	128,800
1953-D		56,112,400	—
1953-S		14,016,000	—
1954 (P)	‹§›	54,412,203	233,300
1954-D		42,305,500	—
1954-S		11,834,722	—
1955 (P)	‹§›	18,180,181	378,200
1955-D		3,182,400	—
1956 (P)	‹§›	44,144,000	669,384
1956-D		32,334,500	—
1957 (P)	‹§›	46,532,000	1,247,952
1957-D		77,924,160	—
1958 (P)	‹§›	6,360,000	875,652
1958-D		78,124,900	—
1959 (P)	‹§›	24,384,000	1,149,291
1959-D		62,054,232	—
1960 (P)	‹§›	29,164,000	1,691,602
1960-D		63,000,324	—
1961 (P)	‹§›	37,036,000	3,028,244
1961-D		83,656,928	—

DATE	NOTE	BUSINESS	PROOF
1962 (P)	‹§›	36,156,000	3,218,019
1962-D		127,554,756	——
1963 (P)	‹§›	74,316,000	3,075,645
1963-D		135,288,184	——
1964 (P)	‹§, 11›	560,390,585	3,950,762
1964-D	‹11›	704,135,528	——
1965 (P)	‹11›	1,082,216,000	——
1965 (D)	‹11›	673,305,540	——
1965 (S)	‹11›	61,836,000	——
1966 (P)	‹11›	404,416,000	——
1966 (D)	‹11›	367,490,400	——
1966 (S)	‹11›	46,933,517	——
1967 (P)	‹11›	873,524,000	——
1967 (D)	‹11›	632,767,848	——
1967 (S)	‹11›	17,740,000	——
1968 (P)		220,731,500	——
1968-D		101,534,000	——
1968-S	‹§›	——	3,041,506
1969 (P)		176,212,000	——
1969-D		114,372,000	——
1969-S	‹§›	——	2,934,631
1970 (P)		136,420,000	——
1970-D		417,341,364	——
1970-S	‹§›	——	2,632,810
1971 (P)		109,284,000	——
1971-D		258,634,428	——
1971-S	‹§›	——	3,220,733
1972 (P)		215,048,000	——
1972-D		311,067,732	——
1972-S	‹§›	——	3,260,996
1973 (P)		346,924,000	——
1973-D		232,977,400	——
1973-S	‹§›	——	2,760,339
1974 (P)	‹43›	801,456,000	——
1974-D	‹43›	353,160,300	——
1974-S	‹§, 43›	——	2,612,568
1976 (P)	‹43›	809,408,016	——
1976-D	‹43›	860,118,839	——
1976-S	‹43›	——	——
1976 (W)	‹43›	376,000	——
1977 (P)		461,204,000	——
1977-D		256,524,978	——
1977-S	‹§›	——	3,236,798
1977 (W)		7,352,000	——
1978 (P)		500,652,000	——
1978-D		287,373,152	——
1978-S	‹§›	——	3,120,285
1978 (W)		20,800,000	——
1979 (P)		493,036,000	——
1979-D		489,789,780	——
1979-S	‹§›	——	3,677,175
1979 (W)		22,672,000	——
1980-P	‹25›	635,832,000	——
1980-D		518,327,487	——
1980-S	‹§›	——	3,554,806
1981-P		601,716,000	——
1981-D		575,722,833	——
1981-S	‹§›	——	4,063,083
1982-P		500,931,000	——
1982-D		480,042,788	——

DATE	NOTE	BUSINESS	PROOF
1982-S	‹§›	——	3,857,479
1983-P		673,535,000	——
1983-D		617,806,446	——
1983-S	‹§›	——	3,279,126
1984-P		676,545,000	——
1984-D		546,483,064	——
1984-S	‹§›	——	3,065,110
1985-P		775,818,962	——
1985-D		519,962,888	——
1985-S	‹§›	——	3,362,821
1986-P		551,199,333	——
1986-D		504,298,660	——
1986-S	‹§›	——	3,010,497
1987-P		582,499,481	——
1987-D		655,595,696	——
1987-S	‹§›	——	3,792,233
1988-P		562,052,000	——
1988-D		596,810,688	——
1988-S	‹§›	——	3,262,948
1989-P		512,868,000	——
1989-D		896,733,858	——
1989-S	‹§›	——	3,220,914
1990-P		613,792,000	——
1990-D		927,638,181	——
1990-S	‹§›	——	3,299,559
1991-P		570,960,000	——
1991-D		630,966,693	——
1991-S	‹§›	——	2,867,787
1992-P		384,764,000	——
1992-D		389,777,107	——
1992-S	‹§›		
Clad		——	2,858,903
90% silver		——	1,317,641
1993-P		639,276,000	——
1993-D		645,476,128	——
1993-S	‹§›		
Clad		——	2,569,882
90% silver		——	790,994
1994-P		825,600,000	——
1994-D		880,034,110	——
1994-S	‹§›		
Clad		——	2,443,590
90% silver		——	778,550
1995-P		1,004,336,000	——
1995-D		1,103,216,000	——
1995-S	‹§›		
Clad		——	2,124,790
90% silver		——	666,277
1996-P		925,040,000	——
1996-D		906,868,000	——
1996-S	‹§›		
Clad		——	2,145,077
90% silver		——	775,081
1997-P		595,740,000	——
1997-D		599,680,000	——
1997-S	‹§›		
Clad		——	2,055,000
90% silver		——	741,194
1998-P		960,400,000	——
1998-D		907,000,000	——

DATE	NOTE	BUSINESS	PROOF
1998-S	‹§›		
Clad		——	2,086,507
90% silver		——	878,996
1999-P DE		373,400,000	——
1999-D DE		401,424,000	——
1999-S DE	‹§›		
Clad	‹121›	——	3,727,857
90% silver		——	804,565
1999-P PA		349,000,000	——
1999-D PA		358,332,000	——
1999-S PA	‹§›		
Clad	‹121›	——	3,727,857
90% silver		——	804,565
1999-P NJ		363,200,000	——
1999-D NJ		299,028,000	——
1999-S NJ	‹§›		
Clad	‹121›	——	3,727,857
90% silver		——	804,565
1999-P GA		451,188,000	——
1999-D GA		488,744,000	——
1999-S GA	‹§›		
Clad	‹121›	——	3,727,857
90% silver		——	804,565
1999-P CT		688,744,000	——
1999-D CT		657,880,000	——
1999-S CT	‹§›		
Clad	‹121›	——	3,727,857
90% silver		——	804,565
2000-P MA		628,600,000	——
2000-D MA		535,184,000	——
2000-S MA	‹§›		
Clad	‹121›	——	4,092,784
90% silver		——	965,421
2000-P MD		678,200,000	——
2000-D MD		556,532,000	——
2000-S MD	‹§›		
Clad	‹121›	——	4,092,784
90% silver		——	965,421
2000-P SC		742,576,000	——
2000-D SC		566,208,000	——
2000-S SC	‹§›		
Clad	‹121›	——	4,092,784
90% silver		——	965,421
2000-P NH		673,040,000	——
2000-D NH		495,976,000	——
2000-S NH	‹§›		
Clad	‹121›	——	4,092,784
90% silver		——	965,421
2000-P VA		943,000,000	——
2000-D VA		651,616,000	——
2000-S VA	‹§›		
Clad	‹121›	——	4,092,784
90% silver		——	965,421
2001-P NY		655,400,000	——
2001-D NY		619,640,000	——
2001-S NY	‹§›		
Clad	‹121›	——	3,100,680
90% silver		——	317,142
2001-P NC		627,600,000	——
2001-D NC		427,876,000	——
2001-S NC	‹§›		
Clad	‹121›	——	3,100,680
90% silver		——	317,142
2001-P RI		423,000,000	——
2001-D RI		447,100,000	——
2001-S RI	‹§›		
Clad	‹121›	——	3,100,680
90% silver		——	317,142
2001-P VT		423,400,000	——
2001-D VT		459,404,000	——
2001-S VT	‹§›		
Clad	‹121›	——	3,100,680
90% silver		——	317,142
2001-P KY		353,000,000	——
2001-D KY		370,564,000	——
2001-S KY	‹§›		
Clad	‹121›	——	3,100,680
90% silver		——	317,142
2002-P TN		361,600,000	——
2002-D TN		286,468,000	——
2002-S TN	‹§›		
Clad		——	3,085,940
90% silver		——	888,826
2002-P OH		217,200,000	——
2002-D OH		414,832,000	——
2002-S OH	‹§›		
Clad		——	3,085,940
90% silver			888,826
2002-P LA		362,000,000	——
2002-D LA		402,204,000	——
2002-S LA	‹§›		
Clad		——	3,085,940
90% silver		——	888,826
2002-P IN		362,600,000	——
2002-D IN		327,200,000	——
2002-S IN	‹§›		
Clad		——	3,085,940
90% silver		——	888,826
2002-P MS		290,000,000	——
2002-D MS		289,600,000	——
2002-S MS	‹§›		
Clad		——	3,085,940
90% silver		——	888,826
2003-P IL		225,800,000	——
2003-D IL		237,400,000	——
2003-S IL	‹§›		
Clad		——	3,438,295
90% silver		——	1,087,744
2003-P AL		225,000,000	——
2003-D AL		232,400,000	——
2003-S AL	‹§›		
Clad		——	3,438,295
90% silver		——	1,087,744
2003-P ME		217,400,000	——
2003-D ME		231,400,000	——
2003-S ME	‹§›		
Clad		——	3,438,295
90% silver		——	1,087,744
2003-P MO		225,000,000	——
2003-D MO		228,200,000	——

DATE	NOTE	BUSINESS	PROOF
2003-S MO	‹§›		
Clad		——	3,438,295
90% silver		——	1,087,744
2003-P AR		228,000,000	——
2003-D AR		229,800,000	——
2003-S AR	‹§›		
Clad		——	3,438,295
90% silver		——	1,087,744
2004-P MI		233,800,000	——
2004-D MI		225,800,000	——
2004-S MI	‹§›		
Clad		——	Pending
90% silver		——	Pending
2004-P FL		240,200,000	——
2004-D FL		241,600,000	——
2004-S FL	‹§›		
Clad		——	Pending
90% silver		——	Pending
2004-P TX		278,800,000	——
2004-D TX		263,000,000	——
2004-S TX	‹§›		
Clad		——	Pending
90% silver		——	Pending
Flowing Hair half dollar			
1794		23,464	——
1795		299,680	——
Draped Bust, Small Eagle half dollar			
1796		934	——
1797		2,984	——
Draped Bust, Heraldic Eagle half dollar			
1801		30,289	——
1802		29,890	——
1803		188,234	——
1805		211,722	——
1806		839,576	——
1807		301,076	——
Capped Bust half dollar			
1807		750,500	——
1808		1,368,600	——
1809		1,405,810	——
1810		1,276,276	——
1811		1,203,644	——
1812		1,628,059	——
1813		1,241,903	——
1814		1,039,075	——
1815		47,150	——
1817	‹44›	1,215,567	Δ
1818		1,960,322	Δ
1819		2,208,000	Δ
1820		751,122	Δ
1821		1,305,797	Δ
1822		1,559,573	Δ
1823		1,694,200	Δ
1824		3,504,954	Δ
1825		2,943,166	Δ
1826		4,004,180	Δ
1827		5,493,400	Δ
1828		3,075,200	Δ

DATE	NOTE	BUSINESS	PROOF
1829		3,712,156	Δ
1830		4,764,800	Δ
1831		5,873,660	Δ
1832		4,797,000	Δ
1833		5,206,000	Δ (R)
1834		6,412,004	Δ (R)
1835		5,352,006	Δ (R)
1836			
Lettered Edge		6,545,000	Δ
Reeded Edge	‹45›	1,200	Δ
1837		3,629,820	Δ
1838 (P)		3,546,000	Δ
1838-O	‹46›	——	Δ
1839 (P)		1,362,160	Δ
1839-O	‹47›	178,976	Δ
Seated Liberty half dollar			
1839 (P)	‹48›	1,972,400	Δ
1840 (P)		1,435,008	Δ
1840-O		855,100	——
1841 (P)		310,000	Δ
1841-O		401,000	——
1842 (P)		2,012,764	Δ
1842-O		957,000	——
1843 (P)		3,844,000	Δ
1843-O		2,268,000	——
1844 (P)		1,766,000	Δ
1844-O		2,005,000	——
1845 (P)		589,000	Δ
1845-O		2,094,000	——
1846 (P)		2,210,000	Δ
1846-O		2,304,000	——
1847 (P)		1,156,000	Δ
1847-O		2,584,000	——
1848 (P)		580,000	Δ
1848-O		3,180,000	——
1849 (P)		1,252,000	Δ
1849-O		2,310,000	——
1850 (P)		227,000	Δ
1850-O		2,456,000	——
1851 (P)		200,750	——
1851-O		402,000	——
1852 (P)		77,130	Δ
1852-O		144,000	——
1853 (P)	‹16, 49›	3,532,708	Δ
1853-O	‹49›	1,328,000	——
1854 (P)		2,982,000	Δ
1854-O		5,240,000	——
1855 (P)		759,500	Δ
1855-O		3,688,000	——
1855-S	‹50›	129,950	Δ
1856 (P)		938,000	Δ
1856-O		2,658,000	——
1856-S		211,000	——
1857 (P)		1,988,000	Δ
1857-O		818,000	——
1857-S		158,000	——
1858 (P)		4,226,000	Δ
1858-O		7,294,000	——
1858-S		476,000	——

DATE	NOTE	BUSINESS	PROOF
1859 (P)		748,000	Δ
1859-O		2,834,000	——
1859-S		566,000	——
1860 (P)		302,700	1,000
1860-O		1,290,000	——
1860-S		472,000	——
1861 (P)		2,887,400	1,000
1861-O	‹51›	2,532,633	Δ
1861-S		939,500	——
1862 (P)		253,000	550
1862-S		1,352,000	——
1863 (P)		503,200	460
1863-S		916,000	——
1864 (P)		379,100	470
1864-S		658,000	——
1865 (P)		511,400	500
1865-S		675,000	——
1866 (P)	‹40›	744,900	725
1866-S			
No Motto	‹40›	60,000	——
Motto	‹40›	994,000	——
1867 (P)		449,300	625
1867-S		1,196,000	——
1868 (P)		417,600	600
1868-S		1,160,000	——
1869 (P)		795,300	600
1869-S		656,000	——
1870 (P)		633,900	1,000
1870-CC		54,617	——
1870-S		1,004,000	——
1871 (P)		1,203,600	960
1871-CC		153,950	——
1871-S		2,178,000	——
1872 (P)		880,600	950
1872-CC		257,000	——
1872-S		580,000	——
1873 (P)			
No Arrows	‹6›	801,200	600
With Arrows	‹6›	1,815,150	550
1873-CC			
No Arrows	‹6, 52›	122,500	——
With Arrows	‹6›	214,560	——
1873-S			
No Arrows	‹6›	5,000	——
With Arrows	‹6›	228,000	——
1874 (P)		2,359,600	700
1874-CC		59,000	——
1874-S		394,000	——
1875 (P)		6,026,800	700
1875-CC		1,008,000	——
1875-S		3,200,000	——
1876 (P)		8,418,000	1,150
1876-CC		1,956,000	——
1876-S		4,528,000	——
1877 (P)		8,304,000	510
1877-CC		1,420,000	——
1877-S		5,356,000	——
1878 (P)		1,377,600	800
1878-CC		62,000	——
1878-S		12,000	——

DATE	NOTE	BUSINESS	PROOF
1879 (P)		4,800	1,100
1880 (P)		8,400	1,355
1881 (P)		10,000	975
1882 (P)		4,400	1,100
1883 (P)		8,000	1,039
1884 (P)		4,400	875
1885 (P)		5,200	930
1886 (P)		5,000	886
1887 (P)		5,000	710
1888 (P)		12,001	832
1889 (P)		12,000	711
1890 (P)		12,000	590
1891 (P)		200,000	600
Barber half dollar			
1892 (P)		934,245	1,245
1892-O		390,000	——
1892-S		1,029,028	——
1893 (P)		1,826,000	792
1893-O		1,389,000	——
1893-S		740,000	——
1894 (P)		1,148,000	972
1894-O		2,138,000	——
1894-S		4,048,690	——
1895 (P)		1,834,338	880
1895-O	‹53›	1,766,000	Δ
1895-S		1,108,086	——
1896 (P)		950,000	762
1896-O		924,000	——
1896-S		1,140,948	——
1897 (P)		2,480,000	731
1897-O		632,000	——
1897-S		933,900	——
1898 (P)		2,956,000	735
1898-O		874,000	——
1898-S		2,358,550	——
1899 (P)		5,538,000	846
1899-O		1,724,000	——
1899-S		1,686,411	——
1900 (P)		4,762,000	912
1900-O		2,744,000	——
1900-S		2,560,322	——
1901 (P)		4,268,000	813
1901-O		1,124,000	——
1901-S		847,044	——
1902 (P)		4,922,000	777
1902-O		2,526,000	——
1902-S		1,460,670	——
1903 (P)		2,278,000	755
1903-O		2,100,000	——
1903-S		1,920,772	——
1904 (P)		2,992,000	670
1904-O		1,117,600	——
1904-S		553,038	——
1905 (P)		662,000	727
1905-O		505,000	——
1905-S		2,494,000	——
1906 (P)		2,638,000	675
1906-D		4,028,000	——
1906-O		2,446,000	——

DATE	NOTE	BUSINESS	PROOF
1906-S		1,740,154	——
1907 (P)		2,598,000	575
1907-D		3,856,000	——
1907-O		3,946,600	——
1907-S		1,250,000	——
1908 (P)		1,354,000	545
1908-D		3,280,000	——
1908-O		5,360,000	——
1908-S		1,644,828	——
1909 (P)		2,368,000	650
1909-O		925,400	——
1909-S		1,764,000	——
1910 (P)		418,000	551
1910-S		1,948,000	——
1911 (P)		1,406,000	543
1911-D		695,080	——
1911-S		1,272,000	——
1912 (P)		1,550,000	700
1912-D		2,300,800	——
1912-S		1,370,000	——
1913 (P)		188,000	627
1913-D		534,000	——
1913-S		604,000	——
1914 (P)		124,230	380
1914-S		992,000	——
1915 (P)		138,000	450
1915-D		1,170,400	——
1915-S		1,604,000	——

Walking Liberty half dollar

DATE	NOTE	BUSINESS	PROOF
1916 (P)		608,000	Δ
1916-D		1,014,400	——
1916-S		508,000	——
1917 (P)		12,292,000	——
1917-D			
Obv. Mint Mark		765,400	——
Rev. Mint Mark		1,940,000	——
1917-S			
Obv. Mint Mark		952,000	——
Rev. Mint Mark		5,554,000	——
1918 (P)		6,634,000	——
1918-D		3,853,040	——
1918-S		10,282,000	——
1919 (P)		962,000	——
1919-D		1,165,000	——
1919-S		1,552,000	——
1920 (P)		6,372,000	——
1920-D		1,551,000	——
1920-S		4,624,000	——
1921 (P)		246,000	——
1921-D		208,000	——
1921-S		548,000	——
1923-S		2,178,000	——
1927-S		2,392,000	——
1928-S		1,940,000	——
1929-D		1,001,200	——
1929-S		1,902,000	——
1933-S		1,786,000	——
1934 (P)		6,964,000	——
1934-D		2,361,400	——
1934-S		3,652,000	——
1935 (P)		9,162,000	——
1935-D		3,003,800	——
1935-S		3,854,000	——
1936 (P)		12,614,000	3,901
1936-D		4,252,400	——
1936-S		3,884,000	——
1937 (P)		9,522,000	5,728
1937-D		1,676,000	——
1937-S		2,090,000	——
1938 (P)		4,110,000	8,152
1938-D		491,600	——
1939 (P)		6,812,000	8,808
1939-D		4,267,800	——
1939-S		2,552,000	——
1940 (P)		9,156,000	11,279
1940-S		4,550,000	——
1941 (P)		24,192,000	15,412
1941-D		11,248,400	——
1941-S		8,098,000	——
1942 (P)		47,818,000	21,120
1942-D		10,973,800	——
1942-S		12,708,000	——
1943 (P)		53,190,000	——
1943-D		11,346,000	——
1943-S		13,450,000	——
1944 (P)		28,206,000	——
1944-D		9,769,000	——
1944-S		8,904,000	——
1945 (P)		31,502,000	——
1945-D		9,996,800	——
1945-S		10,156,000	——
1946 (P)		12,118,000	——
1946-D		2,151,000	——
1946-S		3,724,000	——
1947 (P)		4,094,000	——
1947-D		3,900,600	——

Franklin half dollar

DATE	NOTE	BUSINESS	PROOF
1948 (P)		3,006,814	——
1948-D		4,028,600	——
1949 (P)		5,614,000	——
1949-D		4,120,600	——
1949-S		3,744,000	——
1950 (P)	‹§›	7,742,123	51,386
1950-D		8,031,600	——
1951 (P)	‹§›	16,802,102	57,500
1951-D		9,475,200	——
1951-S		13,696,000	——
1952 (P)	‹§›	21,192,093	81,980
1952-D		25,395,600	——
1952-S		5,526,000	——
1953 (P)	‹§›	2,668,120	128,800
1953-D		20,900,400	——
1953-S		4,148,000	——
1954 (P)	‹§›	13,188,203	233,300
1954-D		25,445,580	——
1954-S		4,993,400	——
1955 (P)	‹§›	2,498,181	378,200
1956 (P)	‹§›	4,032,000	669,384

DATE	NOTE	BUSINESS	PROOF
1957 (P)	‹§›	5,114,000	1,247,952
1957-D		19,966,850	——
1958 (P)	‹§›	4,042,000	875,652
1958-D		23,962,412	——
1959 (P)	‹§›	6,200,000	1,149,291
1959-D		13,0,750	——
1960 (P)	‹§›	6,024,000	1,691,602
1960-D		18,215,812	——
1961 (P)	‹§›	8,290,000	3,028,244
1961-D		20,276,442	——
1962 (P)	‹§›	9,714,000	3,218,019
1962-D		35,473,281	——
1963 (P)	‹§›	22,164,000	3,075,645
1963-D		67,069,292	——

Kennedy half dollar

DATE	NOTE	BUSINESS	PROOF
1964 (P)	‹§, 11›	273,304,004	3,950,762
1964-D	‹11›	156,205,446	——
1965 (P)	‹11›	——	——
1965 (D)	‹11›	63,049,366	——
1965 (S)	‹11, 54›	470,000	——
1966 (P)	‹11›	——	——
1966 (D)	‹11›	106,439,312	——
1966 (S)	‹11, 54›	284,037	——
1967 (P)	‹11›	——	——
1967 (D)	‹11›	293,183,634	——
1967 (S)	‹11, 54›	——	——
1968-D		246,951,930	——
1968-S	‹§›	——	3,041,506
1969-D		129,881,800	——
1969-S	‹§›	——	2,934,631
1970-D	‹55›	2,150,000	——
1970-S	‹§›	——	2,632,810
1971 (P)		155,164,000	——
1971-D		302,097,424	——
1971-S	‹§›	——	3,220,733
1972 (P)		153,180,000	——
1972-D		141,890,000	——
1972-S	‹§›	——	3,260,996
1973 (P)		64,964,000	——
1973-D		83,171,400	——
1973-S	‹§›	——	2,760,339
1974 (P)	‹43›	201,596,000	——
1974-D	‹43›	79,066,300	——
1974-S	‹§, 43›	——	2,612,568
1976 (P)	‹43›	234,308,000	——
1976-D	‹43›	287,565,248	——
1976-S	‹43›	——	——
1977 (P)		43,598,000	——
1977-D		31,449,106	——
1977-S	‹§›	——	3,236,798
1978 (P)		14,350,000	——
1978-D		13,765,799	——
1978-S	‹§›	——	3,120,285
1979 (P)		68,312,000	——
1979-D		15,815,422	——
1979-S	‹§›	——	3,677,175
1980-P	‹25›	44,134,000	——
1980-D		33,456,449	——
1980-S	‹§›	——	3,554,806

DATE	NOTE	BUSINESS	PROOF
1981-P		29,544,000	——
1981-D		27,839,533	——
1981-S	‹§›	——	4,063,083
1982-P		10,819,000	——
1982-D		13,140,102	——
1982-S	‹§›	——	3,857,479
1983-P		34,139,000	——
1983-D		32,472,244	——
1983-S	‹§›	——	3,279,126
1984-P		26,029,000	——
1984-D		26,262,158	——
1984-S	‹§›	——	3,065,110
1985-P		18,706,962	——
1985-D		19,814,034	——
1985-S	‹§›	——	3,362,821
1986-P		13,107,633	——
1986-D		15,366,145	——
1986-S	‹§›	——	3,010,497
1987-P	‹55›	——	——
1987-D	‹55›		
1987-S	‹§›	——	3,792,233
1988-P		13,626,000	——
1988-D		12,000,096	——
1988-S	‹§›	——	3,262,948
1989-P		24,542,000	——
1989-D		23,000,216	——
1989-S	‹§›	——	3,220,914
1990-P		22,278,000	——
1990-D		20,096,242	——
1990-S	‹§›	——	3,299,559
1991-P		14,874,000	——
1991-D		15,054,678	——
1991-S	‹§›	——	2,867,787
1992-P		17,628,000	——
1992-D		17,000,106	——
1992-S	‹§›		
Clad		——	2,858,903
90% Silver		——	1,317,641
1993-P		15,510,000	——
1993-D		15,000,006	——
1993-S	‹§›		
Clad		——	2,569,882
90% Silver		——	790,994
1994-P		23,718,000	——
1994-D		23,828,110	——
1994-S	‹§›		
Clad		——	2,443,590
90% Silver		——	778,550
1995-P		26,496,000	——
1995-D		26,288,000	——
1995-S	‹§›		
Clad		——	2,124,790
90% Silver		——	666,277
1996-P		24,442,000	——
1996-D		24,744,000	——
1996-S	‹§›		
Clad		——	2,145,077
90% silver		——	775,081
1997-P		20,882,000	——
1997-D		19,876,000	——

DATE	NOTE	BUSINESS	PROOF
1997-S	‹§›		
Clad		——	2,055,000
90% silver		——	741,194
1998-P		15,646,000	——
1998-D		15,064,000	——
1998-S	‹§›		
Clad		——	2,086,507
90% silver		——	878,996
1999-P		8,900,000	——
1999-D		10,682,000	——
1999-S	‹§›		
Clad	‹121›	——	2,557,899
90% silver		——	804,077
2000-P		22,600,000	——
2000-D		19,466,000	——
2000-S	‹§›		
Clad	‹121›	——	3,096,981
90% silver		——	965,421
2001-P		21,200,000	——
2001-D		19,504,000	——
2001-S	‹§›		
Clad	‹121›	——	2,300,944
90% silver		——	317,142
2002-P	‹120›	3,100,000	——
2002-D	‹120›	2,500,000	——
2002-S	‹§›		
Clad		——	2,321,848
90% silver		——	888,826
2003-P	‹120›	2,500,000	——
2003-D	‹120›	2,500,000	——
2003-S	‹§›		
Clad		——	2,206,190
90% silver		——	1,087,744
Flowing Hair silver dollar			
1794		1,758	——
1795		160,295	——
Draped Bust silver dollar			
1795		42,738	——
1796		72,920	——
1797		7,776	——
1798	‹56›	327,536	——
1799		423,515	——
1800		220,920	——
1801	‹57›	54,454	——
1802	‹57›	41,650	——
1803	‹57›	85,634	——
1804	‹58›	——	——
1805	‹59›	——	——
Gobrecht silver dollar			
1836	‹60›	1,600	Δ
1838	‹60›	——	Δ
1839 (P)	‹60›	300	Δ
Seated Liberty silver dollar			
1840 (P)		61,005	Δ (R)
1841 (P)		173,000	Δ (R)
1842 (P)		184,618	Δ (R)
1843 (P)		165,100	Δ (R)
1844 (P)		20,000	Δ (R)

DATE	NOTE	BUSINESS	PROOF
1845 (P)		24,500	Δ (R)
1846 (P)		110,600	Δ (R)
1846-O		59,000	—— (R)
1847 (P)		140,750	Δ (R)
1848 (P)		15,000	Δ (R)
1849 (P)		62,600	Δ (R)
1850 (P)		7,500	Δ (R)
1850-O		40,000	—— (R)
1851 (P)		1,300	Δ (R)
1852 (P)		1,100	Δ (R)
1853 (P)	‹16, 61›	46,110	—— (R)
1854 (P)		33,140	Δ
1855 (P)		26,000	Δ
1856 (P)		63,500	Δ
1857 (P)		94,000	Δ
1858 (P)	‹62›	——	Δ
1859 (P)		256,500	Δ
1859-O		360,000	——
1859-S		20,000	——
1860 (P)		217,600	1,330
1860-O		515,000	——
1861 (P)		77,500	1,000
1862 (P)		11,540	550
1863 (P)		27,200	460
1864 (P)		30,700	470
1865 (P)		46,500	500
1866 (P)	‹40›	48,900	725
1867 (P)		46,900	625
1868 (P)		162,100	600
1869 (P)		423,700	600
1870 (P)		415,000	1,000
1870-CC	‹63›	12,462	Δ
1870-S	‹64›	——	——
1871 (P)		1,073,800	960
1871-CC		1,376	——
1872 (P)		1,105,500	950
1872-CC		3,150	——
1872-S		9,000	——
1873 (P)	‹6›	293,000	600
1873-CC	‹6›	2,300	——
1873-S	‹6, 65›	700	——
Morgan silver dollar			
1878 (P)	‹66›	10,508,550	1,000
1878-CC		2,212,000	——
1878-S		9,774,000	——
1879 (P)		14,806,000	1,100
1879-CC		756,000	——
1879-O	‹67›	2,887,000	Δ
1879-S		9,110,000	——
1880 (P)		12,600,000	1,355
1880-CC		591,000	——
1880-O		5,305,000	——
1880-S		8,900,000	——
1881 (P)		9,163,000	975
1881-CC		296,000	——
1881-O		5,708,000	——
1881-S		12,760,000	——
1882 (P)		11,100,000	1,100
1882-CC	‹68›	1,133,000	Δ

DATE	NOTE	BUSINESS	PROOF
1882-O		6,090,000	—
1882-S		9,250,000	—
1883 (P)		12,290,000	1,039
1883-CC	‹69›	1,204,000	Δ
1883-O	‹70›	8,725,000	Δ
1883-S		6,250,000	—
1884 (P)		14,070,000	875
1884-CC	‹71›	1,136,000	Δ
1884-O		9,730,000	—
1884-S		3,200,000	—
1885 (P)		17,786,837	930
1885-CC		228,000	—
1885-O		9,185,000	—
1885-S		1,497,000	—
1886 (P)		19,963,000	886
1886-O		10,710,000	—
1886-S		750,000	—
1887 (P)		20,290,000	710
1887-O		11,550,000	—
1887-S		1,771,000	—
1888 (P)		19,183,000	832
1888-O		12,150,000	—
1888-S		657,000	—
1889 (P)		21,726,000	811
1889-CC		350,000	—
1889-O		11,875,000	—
1889-S		700,000	—
1890 (P)		16,802,000	590
1890-CC		2,309,041	—
1890-O		10,701,000	—
1890-S		8,230,373	—
1891 (P)		8,693,556	650
1891-CC		1,618,000	—
1891-O		7,954,529	—
1891-S		5,296,000	—
1892 (P)		1,036,000	1,245
1892-CC		1,352,000	—
1892-O		2,744,000	—
1892-S		1,200,000	—
1893 (P)		389,000	792
1893-CC	‹72›	677,000	Δ
1893-O		300,000	—
1893-S		100,000	—
1894 (P)		110,000	972
1894-O		1,723,000	—
1894-S		1,260,000	—
1895 (P)	‹73›	12,000	880
1895-O		450,000	—
1895-S		400,000	—
1896 (P)		9,976,000	762
1896-O		4,900,000	—
1896-S		5,000,000	—
1897 (P)		2,822,000	731
1897-O		4,004,000	—
1897-S		5,825,000	—
1898 (P)		5,884,000	735
1898-O		4,440,000	—
1898-S		4,102,000	—
1899 (P)		330,000	846
1899-O		12,290,000	—
1899-S		2,562,000	—
1900 (P)		8,830,000	912
1900-O		12,590,000	—
1900-S		3,540,000	—
1901 (P)		6,962,000	813
1901-O		13,320,000	—
1901-S		2,284,000	—
1902 (P)		7,994,000	777
1902-O		8,636,000	—
1902-S		1,530,000	—
1903 (P)		4,652,000	755
1903-O		4,450,000	—
1903-S		1,241,000	—
1904 (P)		2,788,000	650
1904-O		3,720,000	—
1904-S		2,304,000	—
1921 (P)		44,690,000	Δ
1921-D		20,345,000	—
1921-S		21,695,000	—

Peace silver dollar

DATE	NOTE	BUSINESS	PROOF
1921 (P)	‹74›	1,006,473	—
1922 (P)		51,737,000	Δ
1922-D		15,063,000	—
1922-S		17,475,000	—
1923 (P)		30,800,000	—
1923-D		6,811,000	—
1923-S		19,020,000	—
1924 (P)		11,811,000	—
1924-S		1,728,000	—
1925 (P)		10,198,000	—
1925-S		1,610,000	—
1926 (P)		1,939,000	—
1926-D		2,348,700	—
1926-S		6,980,000	—
1927 (P)		848,000	—
1927-D		1,268,900	—
1927-S		866,000	—
1928 (P)		360,649	—
1928-S		1,632,000	—
1934 (P)		954,057	—
1934-D		1,569,500	—
1934-S		1,011,000	—
1935 (P)		1,576,000	—
1935-S		1,964,000	—

Trade dollar

DATE	NOTE	BUSINESS	PROOF
1873 (P)	‹6, 75›	396,635	865
1873-CC	‹6›	124,500	—
1873-S	‹6›	703,000	—
1874 (P)		987,100	700
1874-CC		1,373,200	—
1874-S		2,549,000	—
1875 (P)		218,200	700
1875-CC		1,573,700	—
1875-S		4,487,000	—
1876 (P)		455,000	1,150
1876-CC		509,000	—
1876-S		5,227,000	—
1877 (P)		3,039,200	510
1877-CC		534,000	—

DATE	NOTE	BUSINESS	PROOF
1877-S		9,519,000	——
1878 (P)		——	900
1878-CC		97,000	——
1878-S		4,162,000	——
1879 (P)		——	1,541
1880 (P)		——	1,987
1881 (P)		——	960
1882 (P)		——	1,097
1883 (P)		——	979
1884 (P)	‹76›	——	10
1885 (P)	‹76›	——	5

Eisenhower dollar

DATE	NOTE	BUSINESS	PROOF
1971 (P)		47,799,000	——
1971-D		68,587,424	——
1971-S			
40% silver	‹§, 77›	6,868,530	4,265,234
1972 (P)		75,890,000	——
1972-D		92,548,511	——
1972-S			
40% silver	‹77›	2,193,056	1,811,631
1973 (P)	‹78›	2,000,056	——
1973-D	‹78›	2,000,000	——
1973-S			
copper-nickel	‹§›	——	2,760,339
40% silver	‹77›	1,883,140	1,013,646
1974 (P)	‹43›	27,366,000	——
1974-D	‹43›	45,517,000	——
1974-S			
copper-nickel	‹§, 43›	——	2,612,568
40% silver	‹43, 77›	1,900,156	1,306,579
1976 (P)	‹43›	117,337,000	——
1976-D	‹43›	103,228,274	——
1976-S	‹43, 77›	——	——
1977 (P)		12,596,000	——
1977-D		32,983,006	——
1977-S	‹§›	——	3,236,798
1978 (P)		25,702,000	——
1978-D		33,012,890	——
1978-S	‹§›	——	3,120,285

Anthony dollar

DATE	NOTE	BUSINESS	PROOF
1979-P	‹25›	360,222,000	——
1979-D		288,015,744	——
1979-S	‹§›	109,576,000	3,677,175
1980-P		27,610,000	——
1980-D		41,628,708	——
1980-S	‹§›	20,422,000	3,554,806
1981-P	‹79›	3,000,000	——
1981-D	‹79›	3,250,000	——
1981-S	‹§, 79›	3,492,000	4,063,083
1999-P		29,592,000	——
1999-D		11,776,000	——
1999-P		——	749,090

Sacagawea golden dollar

DATE	NOTE	BUSINESS	PROOF
2000-P		767,140,000	——
2000-D		518,916,000	——
2000-S	‹§›	——	4,062,402
2001-P		62,468,000	——
2001-D		70,939,500	——
2001-S	‹§›	——	2,618,086
2002-P	‹120›	3,865,610	——
2002-D	‹120›	3,732,000	——
2002-S	‹§›	——	3,210,674
2003-P	‹120›	3,080,000	——
2003-D	‹120›	3,080,000	——
2003-S	‹§›	——	3,293,934

Coronet gold dollar

DATE	NOTE	BUSINESS	PROOF
1849 (P)		688,567	Δ
1849-C		11,634	——
1849-D		21,588	——
1849-O		215,000	——
1850 (P)		481,953	——
1850-C		6,966	——
1850-D		8,382	——
1850-O		14,000	——
1851 (P)		3,317,671	——
1851-C		41,267	——
1851-D		9,882	——
1851-O		290,000	——
1852 (P)		2,045,351	——
1852-C		9,434	——
1852-D		6,360	——
1852-O		140,000	——
1853 (P)		4,076,051	——
1853-C		11,515	——
1853-D		6,583	——
1853-O		290,000	——
1854 (P)		736,709	Δ
1854-D		2,935	——
1854-S		14,632	——

Indian Head gold dollar

DATE	NOTE	BUSINESS	PROOF
1854 (P)		902,736	Δ
1855 (P)		758,269	Δ
1855-C		9,803	——
1855-D		1,811	——
1855-O		55,000	——
1856 (P)			
Large Head		1,762,936	Δ
1856-D			
Large Head		1,460	——
1856-S			
Small Head		24,600	——
1857 (P)		774,789	Δ
1857-C		13,280	——
1857-D		3,533	——
1857-S		10,000	——
1858 (P)		117,995	Δ
1858-D		3,477	——
1858-S		10,000	——
1859 (P)		168,244	Δ
1859-C		5,235	——
1859-D		4,952	——
1859-S		15,000	——
1860 (P)		36,514	154
1860-D		1,566	——
1860-S		13,000	——
1861 (P)		527,150	349
1861-D	‹80›	——	——

DATE	NOTE	BUSINESS	PROOF
1862 (P)		1,361,365	35
1863 (P)		6,200	50
1864 (P)		5,900	50
1865 (P)		3,700	25
1866 (P)		7,100	30
1867 (P)		5,200	50
1868 (P)		10,500	25
1869 (P)		5,900	25
1870 (P)		6,300	35
1870-S	‹81›	3,000	—
1871 (P)		3,900	30
1872 (P)		3,500	30
1873 (P)	‹6›	125,100	25
1874 (P)		198,800	20
1875 (P)		400	20
1876 (P)		3,200	45
1877 (P)		3,900	20
1878 (P)		3,000	20
1879 (P)		3,000	30
1880 (P)		1,600	36
1881 (P)		7,620	87
1882 (P)		5,000	125
1883 (P)		10,800	207
1884 (P)		5,230	1,006
1885 (P)		11,156	1,105
1886 (P)		5,000	1,016
1887 (P)		7,500	1,043
1888 (P)		15,501	1,079
1889 (P)		28,950	1,779
Capped Bust $2.50 quarter eagle			
1796		1,395	—
1797		427	—
1798		1,094	—
1802		3,035	—
1804		3,327	—
1805		1,781	—
1806		1,616	—
1807		6,812	—
Capped Draped Bust quarter eagle			
1808		2,710	—
Capped Head $2.50 quarter eagle			
1821		6,448	Δ
1824		2,600	Δ
1825		4,434	Δ
1826		760	Δ
1827		2,800	Δ
1829		3,403	Δ
1830		4,540	Δ
1831		4,520	Δ
1832		4,400	Δ
1833		4,160	Δ
1834	‹82›	4,000	Δ
Classic Head $2.50 quarter eagle			
1834		113,370	Δ
1835		131,402	Δ
1836		547,986	Δ
1837		45,080	Δ
1838 (P)		47,030	—

DATE	NOTE	BUSINESS	PROOF
1838-C		7,908	—
1839 (P)		27,021	—
1839-C		18,173	—
1839-D		13,674	—
1839-O		17,781	—
Coronet $2.50 quarter eagle			
1840 (P)		18,859	Δ
1840-C		12,838	—
1840-D		3,532	—
1840-O		33,580	—
1841 (P)	‹83›	—	Δ
1841-C		10,297	—
1841-D		4,164	—
1842 (P)		2,823	Δ
1842-C		6,737	—
1842-D		4,643	—
1842-O		19,800	—
1843 (P)		100,546	Δ
1843-C		26,096	—
1843-D		36,209	—
1843-O		368,002	—
1844 (P)		6,784	Δ
1844-C		11,622	—
1844-D		17,332	—
1845 (P)		91,051	Δ
1845-D		19,460	—
1845-O		4,000	—
1846 (P)		21,598	Δ
1846-C		4,808	—
1846-D		19,303	—
1846-O		62,000	—
1847 (P)		29,814	Δ
1847-C		23,226	—
1847-D		15,784	—
1847-O		124,000	—
1848 (P)		7,497	Δ
CAL.	‹84›	1,389	—
1848-C		16,788	—
1848-D		13,771	—
1849 (P)		23,294	Δ
1849-C		10,220	—
1849-D		10,945	—
1850 (P)		252,923	—
1850-C		9,148	—
1850-D		12,148	—
1850-O		84,000	—
1851 (P)		1,372,748	—
1851-C		14,923	—
1851-D		11,264	—
1851-O		148,000	—
1852 (P)		1,159,681	—
1852-C		9,772	—
1852-D		4,078	—
1852-O		140,000	—
1853 (P)		1,404,668	—
1853-D		3,178	—
1854 (P)		596,258	Δ
1854-C		7,295	—
1854-D		1,760	—

DATE	NOTE	BUSINESS	PROOF
1854-O		153,000	—
1854-S		246	—
1855 (P)		235,480	Δ
1855-C		3,677	—
1855-D		1,123	—
1856 (P)		384,240	Δ
1856-C		7,913	—
1856-D		874	—
1856-O		21,100	—
1856-S		71,120	—
1857 (P)		214,130	Δ
1857-D		2,364	—
1857-O		34,000	—
1857-S		69,200	—
1858 (P)		47,377	Δ
1858-C		9,056	—
1859 (P)		39,444	Δ
1859-D		2,244	—
1859-S		15,200	—
1860 (P)		22,563	112
1860-C		7,469	—
1860-S		35,600	—
1861 (P)		1,272,428	90
1861-S		24,000	—
1862 (P)		98,508	35
1862-S		8,000	—
1863 (P)		—	30
1863-S		10,800	—
1864 (P)		2,824	50
1865 (P)		1,520	25
1865-S		23,376	—
1866 (P)		3,080	30
1866-S		38,960	—
1867 (P)		3,200	50
1867-S		28,000	—
1868 (P)		3,600	25
1868-S		34,000	—
1869 (P)		4,320	25
1869-S		29,500	—
1870 (P)		4,520	35
1870-S		16,000	—
1871 (P)		5,320	30
1871-S		22,000	—
1872 (P)		3,000	30
1872-S		18,000	—
1873 (P)	‹6›	178,000	25
1873-S	‹6›	27,000	—
1874 (P)		3,920	20
1875 (P)		400	20
1875-S		11,600	—
1876 (P)		4,176	45
1876-S		5,000	—
1877 (P)		1,632	20
1877-S		35,400	—
1878 (P)		286,240	20
1878-S		178,000	—
1879 (P)		88,960	30
1879-S		43,500	—
1880 (P)		2,960	36
1881 (P)		640	51
1882 (P)		4,000	67
1883 (P)		1,920	82
1884 (P)		1,950	73
1885 (P)		800	87
1886 (P)		4,000	88
1887 (P)		6,160	122
1888 (P)		16,006	92
1889 (P)		17,600	48
1890 (P)		8,720	93
1891 (P)		10,960	80
1892 (P)		2,440	105
1893 (P)		30,000	106
1894 (P)		4,000	122
1895 (P)		6,000	119
1896 (P)		19,070	132
1897 (P)		29,768	136
1898 (P)		24,000	165
1899 (P)		27,200	150
1900 (P)		67,000	205
1901 (P)		91,100	223
1902 (P)		133,540	193
1903 (P)		201,060	197
1904 (P)		160,790	170
1905 (P)		217,800	144
1906 (P)		176,330	160
1907 (P)		336,294	154

Indian Head $2.50 quarter eagle

DATE	NOTE	BUSINESS	PROOF
1908 (P)		564,821	236
1909 (P)		441,760	139
1910 (P)		492,000	682
1911 (P)		704,000	191
1911-D		55,680	—
1912 (P)		616,000	197
1913 (P)		722,000	165
1914 (P)		240,000	117
1914-D		448,000	—
1915 (P)		606,000	100
1925-D		578,000	—
1926 (P)		446,000	—
1927 (P)		388,000	—
1928 (P)		416,000	—
1929 (P)		532,000	—

Three dollar gold

DATE	NOTE	BUSINESS	PROOF
1854 (P)		138,618	Δ
1854-D		1,120	—
1854-O		24,000	—
1855 (P)		50,555	Δ
1855-S		6,600	—
1856 (P)		26,010	Δ
1856-S		34,500	—
1857 (P)		20,891	Δ
1857-S		14,000	—
1858 (P)		2,133	Δ
1859 (P)		15,638	Δ
1860 (P)		7,036	119
1860-S	‹85›	4,408	—
1861 (P)		5,959	113
1862 (P)		5,750	35
1863 (P)		5,000	39

DATE	NOTE	BUSINESS	PROOF
1864 (P)		2,630	50
1865 (P)		1,140	25
1866 (P)		4,000	30
1867 (P)		2,600	50
1868 (P)		4,850	25
1869 (P)		2,500	25
1870 (P)		3,500	35
1870-S	‹86›	——	——
1871 (P)		1,300	30
1872 (P)		2,000	30
1873 (P)	‹6, 87›	——	25 (R)
1874 (P)		41,800	20
1875 (P)		——	20 (R)
1876 (P)		——	45
1877 (P)		1,468	20
1878 (P)		82,304	20
1879 (P)		3,000	30
1880 (P)		1,000	36
1881 (P)		500	54
1882 (P)		1,500	76
1883 (P)		900	89
1884 (P)		1,000	106
1885 (P)		800	110
1886 (P)		1,000	142
1887 (P)		6,000	160
1888 (P)		5,000	291
1889 (P)		2,300	120

Capped Bust $5 half eagle

DATE	NOTE	BUSINESS	PROOF
1795		8,707	——
1796		6,196	——
1797		3,609	——
1798	‹88›	24,867	——
1799		7,451	——
1800		37,628	——
1802		53,176	——
1803		33,506	——
1804		30,475	——
1805		33,183	——
1806		64,093	——
1807		32,488	——

Capped Draped Bust $5 half eagle

DATE	NOTE	BUSINESS	PROOF
1807		51,605	——
1808		55,578	——
1809		33,875	——
1810		100,287	——
1811		99,581	——
1812		58,087	——

Capped Head $5 half eagle

DATE	NOTE	BUSINESS	PROOF
1813		95,428	——
1814		15,454	——
1815		635	——
1818		48,588	——
1819		51,723	——
1820		263,806	Δ
1821		34,641	Δ
1822	‹89›	17,796	——
1823		14,485	Δ
1824		17,340	Δ
1825	‹90›	29,060	Δ
1826		18,069	Δ
1827		24,913	Δ
1828	‹91›	28,029	Δ
1829		57,442	Δ
1830		126,351	Δ
1831		140,594	Δ
1832		157,487	Δ
1833		193,630	Δ
1834		50,141	Δ

Classic Head $5 half eagle

DATE	NOTE	BUSINESS	PROOF
1834		657,460	Δ
1835		371,534	Δ
1836		553,147	Δ
1837		207,121	Δ
1838 (P)		286,588	Δ
1838-C		19,145	——
1838-D		20,583	——

Coronet $5 half eagle

DATE	NOTE	BUSINESS	PROOF
1839 (P)		118,143	Δ
1839-C		17,235	——
1839-D		18,939	——
1840 (P)		137,382	Δ
1840-C		19,028	——
1840-D		22,896	——
1840-O		38,700	——
1841 (P)		15,833	Δ
1841-C		21,511	——
1841-D		30,495	——
1841-O		50	——
1842 (P)		27,578	Δ
1842-C		27,480	——
1842-D		59,608	——
1842-O		16,400	——
1843 (P)		611,205	Δ
1843-C		44,353	——
1843-D		98,452	——
1843-O		101,075	——
1844 (P)		340,330	Δ
1844-C		23,631	——
1844-D		88,982	——
1844-O	‹92›	364,600	Δ
1845 (P)		417,099	Δ
1845-D		90,629	——
1845-O		41,000	——
1846 (P)		395,942	Δ
1846-C		12,995	——
1846-D		80,294	——
1846-O		58,000	——
1847 (P)		915,981	Δ
1847-C		84,151	——
1847-D		64,405	——
1847-O		12,000	——
1848 (P)		260,775	Δ
1848-C		64,472	——
1848-D		47,465	——
1849 (P)		133,070	——
1849-C		64,823	——
1849-D		39,036	——

DATE	NOTE	BUSINESS	PROOF
1850 (P)		64,491	——
1850-C		63,591	——
1850-D		43,984	——
1851 (P)		377,505	——
1851-C		49,176	——
1851-D		62,710	——
1851-O		41,000	——
1852 (P)		573,901	——
1852-C		72,574	——
1852-D		91,584	——
1853 (P)		305,770	——
1853-C		65,571	——
1853-D		89,678	——
1854 (P)		160,675	——
1854-C		39,283	——
1854-D		56,413	——
1854-O		46,000	——
1854-S		268	——
1855 (P)		117,098	Δ
1855-C		39,788	——
1855-D		22,432	——
1855-O		11,100	——
1855-S		61,000	——
1856 (P)		197,990	Δ
1856-C		28,457	——
1856-D		19,786	——
1856-O		10,000	——
1856-S		105,100	——
1857 (P)		98,188	Δ
1857-C		31,360	——
1857-D		17,046	——
1857-O		13,000	——
1857-S		87,000	——
1858 (P)		15,136	Δ
1858-C		38,856	——
1858-D		15,362	——
1858-S		18,600	——
1859 (P)		16,814	Δ
1859-C		31,847	——
1859-D		10,366	——
1859-S		13,220	——
1860 (P)		19,763	62
1860-C		14,813	——
1860-D		14,635	——
1860-S		21,200	——
1861 (P)		688,084	66
1861-C	‹93›	6,879	——
1861-D		1,597	——
1861-S		18,000	——
1862 (P)		4,430	35
1862-S		9,500	——
1863 (P)		2,442	30
1863-S		17,000	——
1864 (P)		4,220	50
1864-S		3,888	——
1865 (P)		1,270	25
1865-S		27,612	——
1866 (P)	‹40›	6,700	30
1866-S			
No Motto	‹40›	9,000	——
Motto	‹40›	34,920	——
1867 (P)		6,870	50
1867-S		29,000	——
1868 (P)		5,700	25
1868-S		52,000	——
1869 (P)		1,760	25
1869-S		31,000	——
1870 (P)		4,000	35
1870-CC		7,675	——
1870-S		17,000	——
1871 (P)		3,200	30
1871-CC		20,770	——
1871-S		25,000	——
1872 (P)		1,660	30
1872-CC		16,980	——
1872-S		36,400	——
1873 (P)	‹6›	112,480	25
1873-CC	‹6›	7,416	——
1873-S	‹6›	31,000	——
1874 (P)		3,488	20
1874-CC		21,198	——
1874-S		16,000	——
1875 (P)		200	20
1875-CC		11,828	——
1875-S		9,000	——
1876 (P)		1,432	45
1876-CC		6,887	——
1876-S		4,000	——
1877 (P)		1,132	20
1877-CC		8,680	——
1877-S		26,700	——
1878 (P)		131,720	20
1878-CC		9,054	——
1878-S		144,700	——
1879 (P)		301,920	30
1879-CC		17,281	——
1879-S		426,200	——
1880 (P)		3,166,400	36
1880-CC		51,017	——
1880-S		1,348,900	——
1881 (P)		5,708,760	42
1881-CC		13,886	——
1881-S		969,000	——
1882 (P)		2,514,520	48
1882-CC		82,817	——
1882-S		969,000	——
1883 (P)		233,400	61
1883-CC		12,958	——
1883-S		83,200	——
1884 (P)		191,030	48
1884-CC		16,402	——
1884-S		177,000	——
1885 (P)		601,440	66
1885-S		1,211,500	——
1886 (P)		388,360	72
1886-S		3,268,000	——
1887 (P)		——	87
1887-S		1,912,000	——

DATE	NOTE	BUSINESS	PROOF
1888 (P)		18,202	94
1888-S		293,900	—
1889 (P)		7,520	45
1890 (P)		4,240	88
1890-CC		53,800	—
1891 (P)		61,360	53
1891-CC		208,000	—
1892 (P)		753,480	92
1892-CC		82,968	—
1892-O		10,000	—
1892-S		298,400	—
1893 (P)		1,528,120	77
1893-CC		60,000	—
1893-O		110,000	—
1893-S		224,000	—
1894 (P)		957,880	75
1894-O		16,600	—
1894-S		55,900	—
1895 (P)		1,345,855	81
1895-S		112,000	—
1896 (P)		58,960	103
1896-S		155,400	—
1897 (P)		867,800	83
1897-S		354,000	—
1898 (P)		633,420	75
1898-S		1,397,400	—
1899 (P)		1,710,630	99
1899-S	‹94›	1,545,000	Δ
1900 (P)		1,405,500	230
1900-S		329,000	—
1901 (P)		615,900	140
1901-S		3,648,000	—
1902 (P)		172,400	162
1902-S		939,000	—
1903 (P)		226,870	154
1903-S		1,855,000	—
1904 (P)		392,000	136
1904-S		97,000	—
1905 (P)		302,200	108
1905-S		880,700	—
1906 (P)		348,735	85
1906-D	‹95›	320,000	—
1906-S		598,000	—
1907 (P)		626,100	92
1907-D	‹95›	888,000	—
1908 (P)		421,874	—

Indian Head $5 half eagle

DATE	NOTE	BUSINESS	PROOF
1908 (P)		577,845	167
1908-D		148,000	—
1908-S		82,000	—
1909 (P)		627,060	78
1909-D		3,423,560	—
1909-O		34,200	—
1909-S		297,200	—
1910 (P)		604,000	250
1910-D		193,600	—
1910-S		770,200	—
1911 (P)		915,000	139
1911-D		72,500	—
1911-S		1,416,000	—
1912 (P)		790,000	144
1912-S		392,000	—
1913 (P)		916,000	99
1913-S		408,000	—
1914 (P)		247,000	125
1914-D		247,000	—
1914-S		263,000	—
1915 (P)		588,000	75
1915-S		164,000	—
1916-S		240,000	—
1929 (P)		662,000	—

Capped Bust $10 eagle

DATE	NOTE	BUSINESS	PROOF
1795		5,583	—
1796		4,146	—
1797	‹96›	14,555	—
1798		1,742	—
1799		37,449	—
1800		5,999	—
1801		44,344	—
1803		15,017	—
1804		3,757	—

Coronet $10 eagle

DATE	NOTE	BUSINESS	PROOF
1838 (P)		7,200	Δ
1839 (P)	‹97›	38,248	Δ
1840 (P)		47,338	Δ
1841 (P)		63,131	Δ
1841-O		2,500	—
1842 (P)		81,507	Δ
1842-O		27,400	—
1843 (P)		75,462	Δ
1843-O		175,162	—
1844 (P)		6,361	Δ
1844-O	‹98›	118,700	Δ
1845 (P)		26,153	Δ
1845-O		47,500	—
1846 (P)		20,095	Δ
1846-O		81,780	—
1847 (P)		862,258	Δ
1847-O		571,500	—
1848 (P)		145,484	Δ
1848-O		35,850	—
1849 (P)		653,618	—
1849-O		23,900	—
1850 (P)		291,451	—
1850-O		57,500	—
1851 (P)		176,328	—
1851-O		263,000	—
1852 (P)		263,106	—
1852-O	‹99›	18,000	Δ
1853 (P)		201,253	—
1853-O	‹100›	51,000	Δ
1854 (P)		54,250	—
1854-O		52,500	—
1854-S		123,826	—
1855 (P)		121,701	Δ
1855-O		18,000	—
1855-S		9,000	—
1856 (P)		60,490	Δ

DATE	NOTE	BUSINESS	PROOF
1856-O		14,500	—
1856-S		68,000	—
1857 (P)		16,606	Δ
1857-O		5,500	—
1857-S		26,000	—
1858 (P)		2,521	Δ
1858-O		20,000	—
1858-S		11,800	—
1859 (P)		16,093	Δ
1859-O		2,300	—
1859-S		7,000	—
1860 (P)		15,055	50
1860-O		11,100	—
1860-S		5,000	—
1861 (P)		113,164	69
1861-S		15,500	—
1862 (P)		10,960	35
1862-S		12,500	—
1863 (P)		1,218	30
1863-S		10,000	—
1864 (P)		3,530	50
1864-S		2,500	—
1865 (P)		3,980	25
1865-S		16,700	—
1866 (P)	‹40›	3,750	30
1866-S			
No Motto	‹40›	8,500	—
Motto	‹40›	11,500	—
1867 (P)		3,090	50
1867-S		9,000	—
1868 (P)		10,630	25
1868-S		13,500	—
1869 (P)		1,830	25
1869-S		6,430	—
1870 (P)		3,990	35
1870-CC		5,908	—
1870-S		8,000	—
1871 (P)		1,790	30
1871-CC		8,085	—
1871-S		16,500	—
1872 (P)		1,620	30
1872-CC		4,600	—
1872-S		17,300	—
1873 (P)	‹6›	800	25
1873-CC	‹6›	4,543	—
1873-S	‹6›	12,000	—
1874 (P)		53,140	20
1874-CC		16,767	—
1874-S		10,000	—
1875 (P)		100	20
1875-CC		7,715	—
1876 (P)		687	45
1876-CC		4,696	—
1876-S		5,000	—
1877 (P)		797	20
1877-CC		3,332	—
1877-S		17,000	—
1878 (P)		73,780	20
1878-CC		3,244	—
1878-S		26,100	—

DATE	NOTE	BUSINESS	PROOF
1879 (P)		384,740	30
1879-CC		1,762	—
1879-O		1,500	—
1879-S		224,000	—
1880 (P)		1,644,840	36
1880-CC		11,190	—
1880-O		9,200	—
1880-S		506,250	—
1881 (P)		3,877,220	42
1881-CC		24,015	—
1881-O		8,350	—
1881-S		970,000	—
1882 (P)		2,324,440	44
1882-CC		6,764	—
1882-O		10,820	—
1882-S		132,000	—
1883 (P)		208,700	49
1883-CC		12,000	—
1883-O		800	—
1883-S		38,000	—
1884 (P)		76,890	45
1884-CC		9,925	—
1884-S		124,250	—
1885 (P)		253,462	67
1885-S		228,000	—
1886 (P)		236,100	60
1886-S		826,000	—
1887 (P)		53,600	80
1887-S		817,000	—
1888 (P)		132,924	72
1888-O		21,335	—
1888-S		648,700	—
1889 (P)		4,440	45
1889-S		425,400	—
1890 (P)		57,980	63
1890-CC		17,500	—
1891 (P)		91,820	48
1891-CC		103,732	—
1892 (P)		797,480	72
1892-CC		40,000	—
1892-O		28,688	—
1892-S		115,500	—
1893 (P)		1,840,840	55
1893-CC		14,000	—
1893-O		17,000	—
1893-S		141,350	—
1894 (P)		2,470,735	43
1894-O		107,500	—
1894-S		25,000	—
1895 (P)		567,770	56
1895-O		98,000	—
1895-S		49,000	—
1896 (P)		76,270	78
1896-S		123,750	—
1897 (P)		1,000,090	69
1897-O		42,500	—
1897-S		234,750	—
1898 (P)		812,130	67
1898-S		473,600	—
1899 (P)		1,262,219	86

DATE	NOTE	BUSINESS	PROOF
1899-O		37,047	—
1899-S		841,000	—
1900 (P)		293,840	120
1900-S		81,000	—
1901 (P)		1,718,740	85
1901-O		72,041	—
1901-S		2,812,750	—
1902 (P)		82,400	113
1902-S		469,500	—
1903 (P)		125,830	96
1903-O		112,771	—
1903-S		538,000	—
1904 (P)		161,930	108
1904-O		108,950	—
1905 (P)		200,992	86
1905-S		369,250	—
1906 (P)		165,420	77
1906-D	‹101›	981,000	Δ
1906-O		86,895	—
1906-S		457,000	—
1907 (P)		1,203,899	74
1907-D		1,030,000	—
1907-S		210,500	—
Indian Head $10 eagle			
1907 (P)	‹102›	239,406	—
1908 (P)			
Without Motto		33,500	—
With Motto		341,370	116
1908-D			
Without Motto		210,000	—
With Motto		836,500	—
1908-S			
With Motto		59,850	—
1909 (P)		184,789	74
1909-D		121,540	—
1909-S		292,350	—
1910 (P)		318,500	204
1910-D		2,356,640	—
1910-S		811,000	—
1911 (P)		505,500	95
1911-D		30,100	—
1911-S		51,000	—
1912 (P)		405,000	83
1912-S		300,000	—
1913 (P)		442,000	71
1913-S		66,000	—
1914 (P)		151,000	50
1914-D		343,500	—
1914-S		208,000	—
1915 (P)		351,000	75
1915-S		59,000	—
1916-S		138,500	—
1920-S		126,500	—
1926 (P)		1,014,000	—
1930-S		96,000	—
1932 (P)		4,463,000	—
1933 (P)	‹103›	312,500	—
Coronet $20 double eagle			
1849 (P)	‹104›	—	Δ

DATE	NOTE	BUSINESS	PROOF
1850 (P)	‹105›	1,170,261	Δ
1850-O		141,000	—
1851 (P)		2,087,155	—
1851-O		315,000	—
1852 (P)		2,053,026	—
1852-O		190,000	—
1853 (P)		1,261,326	—
1853-O		71,000	—
1854 (P)		757,899	—
1854-O		3,250	—
1854-S	‹106›	141,468	Δ
1855 (P)		364,666	—
1855-O		8,000	—
1855-S		879,675	—
1856 (P)		329,878	Δ
1856-O		2,250	—
1856-S		1,189,780	—
1857 (P)		439,375	—
1857-O		30,000	—
1857-S		970,500	—
1858 (P)		211,714	Δ
1858-O		35,250	—
1858-S		846,710	—
1859 (P)		43,597	Δ
1859-O		9,100	—
1859-S		636,445	—
1860 (P)		577,611	59
1860-O		6,600	—
1860-S		544,950	—
1861 (P)	‹107›	2,976,387	66
1861-O	‹108›	17,741	—
1861-S	‹109›	768,000	—
1862 (P)		92,098	35
1862-S		854,173	—
1863 (P)		142,760	30
1863-S		966,570	—
1864 (P)		204,235	50
1864-S		793,660	—
1865 (P)		351,175	25
1865-S		1,042,500	—
1866 (P)	‹40, 110›	698,745	30
1866-S			
No Motto	‹40, 110›	120,000	—
With Motto	‹40, 110›	722,250	—
1867 (P)		251,015	50
1867-S		920,750	—
1868 (P)		98,575	25
1868-S		837,500	—
1869 (P)		175,130	25
1869-S		686,750	—
1870 (P)		155,150	35
1870-CC		3,789	—
1870-S		982,000	—
1871 (P)		80,120	30
1871-CC		17,387	—
1871-S		928,000	—
1872 (P)		251,850	30
1872-CC		26,900	—
1872-S		780,000	—
1873 (P)	‹6›	1,709,800	25

DATE	NOTE	BUSINESS	PROOF
1873-CC	‹6›	22,410	—
1873-S	‹6›	1,040,600	—
1874 (P)		366,780	20
1874-CC		115,000	—
1874-S		1,214,000	—
1875 (P)		295,720	20
1875-CC		111,151	—
1875-S		1,230,000	—
1876 (P)		583,860	45
1876-CC		138,441	—
1876-S		1,597,000	—
1877 (P)	‹111›	397,650	20
1877-CC		42,565	—
1877-S		1,735,000	—
1878 (P)		543,625	20
1878-CC		13,180	—
1878-S		1,739,000	—
1879 (P)		207,600	30
1879-CC		10,708	—
1879-O		2,325	—
1879-S		1,223,800	—
1880 (P)		51,420	36
1880-S		836,000	—
1881 (P)		2,220	61
1881-S		727,000	—
1882 (P)		590	59
1882-CC		39,140	—
1882-S		1,125,000	—
1883 (P)		—	92
1883-CC		59,962	—
1883-S		1,189,000	—
1884 (P)		—	71
1884-CC		81,139	—
1884-S		916,000	—
1885 (P)		751	77
1885-CC		9,450	—
1885-S		683,500	—
1886 (P)		1,000	106
1887 (P)		—	121
1887-S		283,000	—
1888 (P)		226,164	102
1888-S		859,600	—
1889 (P)		44,070	41
1889-CC		30,945	—
1889-S		774,700	—
1890 (P)		75,940	55
1890-CC		91,209	—
1890-S		802,750	—
1891 (P)		1,390	52
1891-CC		5,000	—
1891-S		1,288,125	—
1892 (P)		4,430	93
1892-CC		27,265	—
1892-S		930,150	—
1893 (P)		344,280	59
1893-CC		18,402	—
1893-S		996,175	—
1894 (P)		1,368,940	50
1894-S		1,048,550	—
1895 (P)		1,114,605	51

DATE	NOTE	BUSINESS	PROOF
1895-S		1,143,500	—
1896 (P)		792,535	128
1896-S		1,403,925	—
1897 (P)		1,383,175	86
1897-S		1,470,250	—
1898 (P)		170,395	75
1898-S		2,575,175	—
1899 (P)		1,669,300	84
1899-S		2,010,300	—
1900 (P)		1,874,460	124
1900-S		2,459,500	—
1901 (P)		111,430	96
1901-S		1,596,000	—
1902 (P)		31,140	114
1902-S		1,753,625	—
1903 (P)		287,270	158
1903-S		954,000	—
1904 (P)		6,256,699	98
1904-S		5,134,175	—
1905 (P)		58,919	90
1905-S		1,813,000	—
1906 (P)		69,596	94
1906-D	‹112›	620,250	Δ
1906-S		2,065,750	—
1907 (P)		1,451,786	78
1907-D	‹113›	842,250	Δ
1907-S		2,165,800	—

Saint-Gaudens $20 double eagle

DATE	NOTE	BUSINESS	PROOF
1907 (P)			
Roman Numerals	‹114›	11,250	—
Arabic Numerals		361,667	—
1908 (P)			
No Motto		4,271,551	—
With Motto		156,258	101
1908-D			
No Motto		663,750	—
With Motto		349,500	—
1908-S			
With Motto		22,000	—
1909 (P)		161,215	67
1909-D		52,500	—
1909-S		2,774,925	—
1910 (P)		482,000	167
1910-D		429,000	—
1910-S		2,128,250	—
1911 (P)		197,250	100
1911-D		846,500	—
1911-S		775,750	—
1912 (P)		149,750	74
1913 (P)		168,780	58
1913-D		393,500	—
1913-S		34,000	—
1914 (P)		95,250	70
1914-D		453,000	—
1914-S		1,498,000	—
1915 (P)		152,000	50
1915-S		567,500	—
1916-S		796,000	—
1920 (P)		228,250	—

DATE	NOTE	BUSINESS	PROOF
1920-S		558,000	——
1921 (P)		528,500	——
1922 (P)		1,375,500	——
1922-S		2,658,000	——
1923 (P)		566,000	——
1923-D		1,702,250	——
1924 (P)		4,323,500	——
1924-D		3,049,500	——
1924-S		2,927,500	——
1925 (P)		2,831,750	——
1925-D		2,938,500	——
1925-S		3,776,500	——
1926 (P)		816,750	——
1926-D		481,000	——
1926-S		2,041,500	——
1927 (P)		2,946,750	——
1927-D		180,000	——
1927-S		3,107,000	——
1928 (P)		8,816,000	——
1929 (P)		1,779,750	——
1930-S		74,000	——
1931 (P)		2,938,250	——
1931-D		106,500	——
1932 (P)		1,101,750	——
1933 (P)	‹115›	445,000	——

American Eagle 1-oz silver $1

DATE	NOTE	BUSINESS	PROOF
1986 (S)		5,393,005	——
1986-S		——	1,446,778
1987 (S)		11,442,335	——
1987-S		——	904,732
1988 (S)		5,004,646	——
1988-S		——	557,370
1989 (S or W)		5,203,327	——
1989-S		——	617,694
1990 (S or W)		5,840,110	——
1990-S		——	695,510
1991 (S or W)		7,191,066	——
1991-S		——	511,924
1992 (S or W)		5,540,068	——
1992-S		——	498,543
1993 (S or W)		6,763,762	——
1993-P		——	405,913
1994 (S or W)		4,227,319	——
1994-P		——	372,168
1995 (S or W)		4,672,051	——
1995-P		——	438,511
1995-W	‹119›	——	30,125
1996 (S or W)		3,603,386	——
1996-P		——	500,000
1997 (S or W)		4,295,004	——
1997-P		——	435,368
1998 (S or W)		4,847,549	——
1998-P		——	450,000
1999 (S or W)		7,408,640	——
1999-P		——	549,769
2000 (S or W)		9,239,132	——
2000-P		——	600,000
2001 (S or W)		9,001,711	——
2001-W		——	746,154
2002 (S or W)		10,539,026	——
2002-W		——	647,342
2003 (S or W)		8,495,008	——
2003-W		——	750,000

American Eagle 1/10-oz gold $5

DATE	NOTE	BUSINESS	PROOF
1986 (W)	‹117›	912,609	
1987 (W)	‹117›	580,266	——
1988 (W)	‹117›	159,500	——
1988-P	‹117›	——	143,881
1989 (W)	‹117›	264,790	——
1989-P	‹117›	——	84,647
1990 (W)	‹117›	210,210	——
1990-P	‹117›	——	99,349
1991 (W)	‹117›	165,200	——
1991-P	‹117›	——	70,334
1992 (W)		209,300	——
1992-P		——	64,874
1993 (W)		210,709	——
1993-P		——	58,649
1994 (W)		206,380	——
1994-P		——	62,849
1995 (W)		223,025	——
1995-W		——	62,673
1996 (W)		401,964	——
1996-W		——	56,700
1997 (S or W)		528,515	——
1997-W		——	34,984
1998 (S or W)		1,344,520	——
1998-W		——	20,000
1999 (S or W)		2,750,338	——
1999-W		——	48,426
2000 (S or W)		569,153	——
2000-W		——	49,970
2001 (S or W)		269,147	——
2001-W		——	37,547
2002 (S or W)		230,027	——
2002-W		——	40,864
2003 (S or W)		245,029	——
2003-W		——	46,000

American Eagle 1/4-oz gold $10

DATE	NOTE	BUSINESS	PROOF
1986 (W)	‹117›	726,031	——
1987 (W)	‹117›	269,255	——
1988 (W)	‹117›	49,000	——
1988-P	‹117›	——	98,028
1989 (W)	‹117›	81,789	——
1989-P	‹117›	——	54,170
1990 (W)	‹117›	41,000	——
1990-P	‹117›	——	62,674
1991 (W)	‹117›	36,100	——
1991-P	‹117›	——	50,839
1992 (W)		59,546	——
1992-P		——	46,269
1993 (W)		71,864	——
1993-P		——	46,464
1994 (W)		72,650	——
1994-P		——	48,172
1995 (W)		83,752	——
1995-W		——	47,484
1996 (W)		60,318	——

DATE	NOTE	BUSINESS	PROOF
1996-W		——	37,900
1997 (S or W)		108,805	——
1997-W		——	29,808
1998 (S or W)		309,829	——
1998-W		——	29,733
1999 (S or W)		564,232	——
1999-W		——	34,416
2000 (S or W)		128,964	——
2000-W		——	36,033
2001 (S or W)		71,280	——
2001-W		——	25,630
2002 (S or W)		62,027	——
2002-W		——	29,242
2003 (S or W)		74,029	——
2003-W		——	31,000

American Eagle 1/2-oz gold $25

1986 (W)	‹117›	599,566	——
1987 (W)	‹117›	131,255	——
1987-P	‹117›	——	143,398
1988 (W)	‹117›	45,000	——
1988-P	‹117›	——	76,528
1989 (W)	‹117›	44,829	——
1989-P	‹117›	——	44,798
1990 (W)	‹117›	31,000	——
1990-P	‹117›	——	51,636
1991 (W)	‹117›	24,100	——
1991-P	‹117›	——	53,125
1992 (W)		54,404	——
1992-P		——	40,976
1993 (W)		73,324	——
1993-P		——	43,319
1994 (W)		62,400	——
1994-P		——	44,584
1995 (W)		53,474	——
1995-W		——	45,442
1996 (W)		39,287	——
1996-W		——	34,700
1997 (S or W)		79,605	——
1997-W		——	26,340
1998 (S or W)		169,029	——
1998-W		——	25,549
1999 (S or W)		263,013	——
1999-W		——	30,452
2000 (S or W)		79,287	——
2000-W		——	32,027
2001 (S or W)		48,047	——
2001-W		——	23,261
2002 (S or W)		70,027	——
2002-W		——	26,646
2003 (S or W)		79,029	——
2003-W		——	33,000

American Eagle 1-oz gold $50

DATE	NOTE	BUSINESS	PROOF
1986 (W)	‹117›	1,362,650	——
1986-W	‹117›	——	446,290
1987 (W)	‹117›	1,045,500	——
1987-W	‹117›	——	147,498
1988 (W)	‹117›	465,500	——
1988-W	‹117›	——	87,133
1989 (W)	‹117›	415,790	——
1989-W	‹117›	——	54,570
1990 (W)	‹117›	373,210	——
1990-W	‹117›	——	62,401
1991 (W)	‹117›	243,100	——
1991-W	‹117›	——	50,411
1992 (W)		275,000	——
1992-W		——	44,826
1993 (W)		480,192	——
1993-W		——	34,389
1994 (W)		221,663	——
1994-W		——	46,674
1995 (W)		200,636	——
1995-W		——	46,484
1996 (W)		189,148	——
1996-W		——	36,000
1997 (S or W)		664,508	——
1997-W		——	27,554
1998 (S or W)		1,468,530	——
1998-W		——	26,060
1999 (S or W)		1,505,026	——
1999-W		——	31,446
2000 (S or W)		433,319	——
2000-W		——	33,006
2001 (S or W)		143,605	——
2001-W		——	24,580
2002 (S or W)		222,029	——
2002-W		——	27,499
2003 (S or W)		416,032	——
2003-W		——	33,000

American Eagle 1/10-oz platinum $10

1997 (W)		70,250	——
1997-W		——	37,025
1998 (W)		39,525	——
1998-W		——	19,832
1999 (W)		55,955	——
1999-W		——	19,123
2000 (W)		34,027	——
2000-W		——	15,651
2001 (W)		52,017	——
2001-W		——	12,193
2002 (W)		23,005	——
2002-W		——	12,365
2003 (W)		22,007	——
2003-W		——	9,249

American Eagle 1/4-oz platinum $25

1997 (W)		27,100	——
1997-W		——	18,661
1998 (W)		38,887	——
1998-W		——	14,860
1999 (W)		39,734	——
1999-W		——	13,514
2000 (W)		20,054	——
2000-W		——	11,995
2001 (W)		21,815	——
2001-W		——	8,858
2002 (W)		27,405	——
2002-W		——	9,282
2003 (W)		25,207	——
2003-W		——	6,829

DATE	NOTE	BUSINESS	PROOF
American Eagle 1/2-oz platinum $50			
1997 (W)		20,500	——
1997-W		——	15,463
1998 (W)		32,419	——
1998-W		——	13,821
1999 (W)		32,309	——
1999-W		——	11,098
2000 (W)		18,892	——
2000-W		——	11,049
2001 (W)		12,815	——
2001-W		——	8,268
2002 (W)		24,005	——
2002-W		——	8,772
2003 (W)		17,409	——
2003-W		——	6,963
American Eagle 1-oz platinum $100			
1997 (W)		56,000	——
1997-W		——	18,000
1998 (W)		133,002	——
1998-W		——	14,203
1999 (W)		56,707	——
1999-W		——	12,351
2000 (W)		10,003	——
2000-W		——	12,453
2001 (W)		14,070	——
2001-W		——	8,990
2002 (W)		11,502	——
2002-W		——	9,834
2003 (W)		8,007	——
2003-W		——	8,106

MINTAGE NOTES

Many different Proof issues before 1880 were restruck in Proof one or more times. In some instances, as with the 1873 $3 gold piece, there are more coins of this date known than were "officially" struck.

KEY

(R): Known to have been restruck at least once.
(§): Proofs originally sold in sets only.
——: None issued.
Δ: Specimens known or believed to exist; no official mintage reported.
U: Final, official mintages unreported by the U.S. Mint.

NOTES

1. 1804, 1823 cent, and 1811 half cent: Counterfeits, called restrikes, exist, which were made outside the Mint, using old, genuine but mismatched Mint dies.
2. 1832-35 half cent: The figures shown are listed in the Mint Report for 1833-36 instead, but are assumed to be misplaced.
3. 1823 cent, dime, quarter dollar: Proofs exist with overdate, 1823/2.
4. 1856 cent: More than 1,000 1856 Flying Eagle cents were struck in Proof and Uncirculated, in this and later years. As they were patterns they are not included in the Mint Report or this figure.

MINTAGE NOTES

5. 1864 cent: Proof breakdown by varieties thought to be about 300 to 350 copper-nickel and about 100 to 150 bronze coins without the designer's initial L. Perhaps 20 or fewer Proofs with initial L were struck. Business strike bronze coins with designer's initial L are also rarer.
6. 1873 coinage: Early in the year a relatively closed style of 3 was used in the date on all denominations. In response to complaints that the 3 looked like an 8, a new, more open 3 was introduced. Most types were struck with both styles, except for those that were created or discontinued by the Coinage Act of Feb. 12, 1873. This law created the Trade dollar and eliminated the standard silver dollar, the silver 5-cent piece, the 3-cent piece and the 2-cent piece. The weight of the dime, quarter dollar and half dollar were slightly increased, and the heavier coins were marked by arrows for the remainder of 1873 and all of 1874. All Proofs are of the relatively Closed 3 variety.
7. 1877 minor coinages: Proof estimates for this year vary considerably, usually upwards. For lack of any records, the number shown is that of the silver Proofs of this year, conforming with the method used in the preceding years. These figures may be considerably low.
8. 1922 "Plain" cent: No cents were struck in Philadelphia in 1922. Some 1922-D cents are found with the Mint mark missing due to obstructed dies. Beware of altered coins.
9. 1943-(P), D, S cent: All 1943 cents were made of zinc-plated steel. A few 1943 bronze and 1944 steel cents were made by accident. Many fakes of these have been produced. Test any suspected off-metal 1943 or 1944 cent with a magnet to see if it has been plated, and check the date for alterations. Cents struck on steel planchets produced in 1942 weigh 41.5 grains, while those struck on planchets produced later in 1943 weigh 42.5 grains.
10. 1960 cent: Includes Large Date and Small Date varieties. The Small Date is the scarcer for both Proof and business strikes.
11. 1964-67 coinage: All coins dated 1965-67 were made without Mint marks. Many coins dated 1964-66 were struck in later years.
12. 1982 cent: The composition of the cent changed from 95 percent copper, 5 percent zinc to 97.5 percent zinc, 2.5 percent copper (composed of a planchet of 99.2 percent zinc, 0.8 percent copper, plated with pure copper). Some 1982 cents were struck in late 1981.
13. 1864 2 cents: Struck with Large and Small Motto IN GOD WE TRUST. The Small Motto in Proof is rare.
14. 1873 2 cents: Originally struck in Proof only early in 1873 with a Closed 3. An estimated 500 restrikes in Proof with an Open 3.
15. 1887 copper-nickel 3 cents: Many Proofs struck from an overdated die, 1887/6.
16. 1853 silver coinage: In early 1853 the weight of all fractional silver coins was reduced by about 7 percent, to prevent hoarding and melting. To distinguish between the old and new weights, arrows were placed on either side of the date on the half dime through

half dollar, and rays were put around the eagle on the quarter and half dollar. The rays were removed after 1853, and the arrows after 1855. Much of the old silver was withdrawn from circulation and melted. The exception to all this was the silver 3-cent piece, which was decreased in weight but increased in fineness, making it intrinsically worth more than before and proportionate with the other fractional silver coins. No coins of the new weight were struck until 1854, at which time an olive branch and a cluster of arrows was added to the reverse.

17. 1863 silver 3 cents: It is possible that all of these non-Proofs were dated 1862. Proof coins dated 1863/2 were struck in 1864. Obviously these were hard times at the Mint.

18. 1864-(P) silver 3 cents, half dime, and dime: These figures, like many others in the years 1861-1871, are highly controversial due to extraordinary bookkeeping methods used in the Mint in this era.

19. 1867 copper-nickel 5 cents: Struck with rays on reverse (type of 1866) and without rays (type of 1868-83). Approximately 25 Proofs struck With Rays on reverse (type of 1866), and 600 Without Rays (type of 1868-83).

20. 1913 Liberty Head copper-nickel 5 cents: Five unauthorized pieces were struck by person or persons unknown, using Mint machinery and dies. All five accounted for by some sources, although numismatic researcher Walter Breen states that one piece is missing. Beware of forgeries.

21. 1942-1945-(P), P, D, S 5 cents: To conserve nickel during the war, the composition of the 5-cent piece was changed to a 56 percent copper, 35 percent silver, and 9 percent manganese alloy. Coins of this alloy were marked with a large Mint mark over the dome of Monticello, including those from Philadelphia. They consist of some 1942-P, all 1942-S, and all 1943-45 coins. The 1942 Philadelphia coins were made either way. Many wartime alloy 5-cent coins have been melted for their silver content.

22. 1944 copper-nickel 5 cents, 1923-D and 1930-D dimes: All are counterfeits made for circulation. Not all counterfeits are of rare dates, meant to sell at high prices. Some were meant to circulate.

23. 1966 5-cent piece: Two Proof Jefferson 5-cent pieces were struck to mark the addition of designer Felix Schlag's initials, F.S., to the obverse design. At least one coin was presented to Schlag; the other may have been retained by the Mint.

24. 1971 5 cents: Some Proof sets contain 5-cent coins which were struck from a Proof die without a Mint mark. This was an engraver's oversight and is not a filled die. Official estimate of 1,655 sets released.

25. P Mint mark: The P Mint mark, placed on the 1979 Anthony dollar, was added to all 1980 denominations from the Philadelphia Mint except for the cent.

26. 1838-O half dime and dime: Both are of Seated Liberty, Without Stars design (type of 1837). 1838 Philadelphia coins have stars, as do all others through 1859.

27. 1856-O half dime: One Proof known, reason for issue unknown.

28. 1860-(P), O, S half dime and dime: Beginning in 1860 (with the exception of the 1860-S dime), the half dime and dime were redesigned by eliminating the stars, moving the legend UNITED STATES OF AMERICA to the obverse, and using a larger, more elaborate wreath on the reverse. A number of fabrications with the obverse of 1859 and the reverse of 1860 (thereby omitting the legend UNITED STATES OF AMERICA), were struck by order of the Director of the Mint. These consist of half dimes dated 1859 or 1860, and dimes dated 1859. Although they are considered by some to be patterns, that designation is doubtful as the intentions of the Director were highly questionable.

29. 1860-O half dime: Three Proofs known, reason for issue unknown.

30. 1873-CC dime: One known, all others presumably were melted.

31. 1894-S dime: Twenty-four Proof or specimen strikings were made for private distribution by the Superintendent of the San Francisco Mint. Twelve can be traced today, including two circulated pieces.

32. 1906-D dime: Proofs struck in honor of the opening of the Denver Mint.

33. 1968 dime: Some Proof sets contain dimes that were struck from a Proof die without a Mint mark. This was an engraver's oversight and is not a filled die. It has been unofficially estimated that only 20 specimens from this die are known. Beware of sets opened and reclosed with "processed" P-Mint coins inserted. Check the edge of the case for signs of tampering.

34. 1970 dime: Some Proof sets contain dimes that were struck from a Proof die without a Mint mark. This was an engraver's oversight and is not a filled die. Official estimate is that 2,200 sets were released with this error.

35. 1982 No-P dimes: Some 1982 dimes were released without a Mint mark, although dimes have been Mint marked since 1980. Distribution of the coins, many found in the Sandusky, Ohio, area, indicates they were from the Philadelphia Mint.

36. 1875-S 20 cents: Six to seven Proofs known, probably struck to celebrate the first (or last) year of this denomination at this Mint.

37. 1876-CC 20 cents: Virtually all remelted at the Mint. A few escaped, possibly as souvenirs given to visitors. Fewer than 20 are known today.

38. 1827 quarter dollar: Although the Mint Report lists a mintage of 4,000 pieces for this year, it is likely that all of these coins were dated 1825 except for a few Proofs. Later this date was unofficially (but intentionally) restruck at the Mint using an obverse die dated 1827 and a reverse die that had been used in 1819, and that had a Square Base 2 in quarter dollar, rather than the Curled Base 2 of the original 1827.

39. 1855-S quarter dollar: One Proof known, presumably struck to celebrate the beginning of silver coinage at the San Francisco Mint.

40. 1866 coinage: It was decided to add the motto IN

GOD WE TRUST to the reverse of all double eagles, eagles, half eagles, silver dollars, half dollars and quarter dollars beginning in 1866. Early in the year, before the new reverse dies had arrived, the San Francisco Mint produced $20, $10, $5, and half dollar coins without the motto. These are regular issue coins and are not patterns or errors. They are not to be confused with a peculiar set of Philadelphia Mint silver coins without motto, consisting of two dollars, one half dollar and one quarter dollar, which was clandestinely struck inside (but not by) the Mint for sale to a collector. A three-piece set containing the unique quarter dollar and half dollar and one of the two known silver dollars was stolen from the Willis H. DuPont collection in 1967 and never recovered. Beware of regular coins with motto or Mint mark removed.

41. 1879 quarter dollar: The Proof figure is official, but may be wrong. The true number might be near or equal to 1,100.

42. 1891-O quarter dollar: Two Proofs known, probably struck to celebrate the resumption of fractional silver coinage at this Mint.

43. 1974-1976 quarter dollars, half dollars and dollars: The circulating commemorative coinage dated 1776-1976 in celebration of the nation's Bicentennial wreaked havoc on mintage bookkeeping. In anticipation of the program, 1974-dated coins of these denominations were struck in calendar years 1974 and 1975. No 1975-dated quarter dollars, half dollars or dollars were struck; 1975 Proof and Mint sets contain Bicentennial dates. 1776-1976-dated dollars, half dollars and quarter dollars were struck in calendar years 1975 and 1976. The 1976-S mintages for these denominations includes copper-nickel clad Proofs sold in 1975 and 1976 in six-piece Proof sets, and 40 percent silver clad Proofs and Uncirculateds, of which 15 million pieces of each denomination were struck.

44. 1817 half dollar: Only one Proof known, with overdate 1817/3.

45. 1836 Reeded Edge half dollar: Actually a pattern of the design adopted the following year, but much of the mintage was placed into circulation.

46. 1838-O half dollar: It is thought that 20 Proof specimens were struck as souvenirs in honor of the opening of the New Orleans Mint. No regular issue coins of this date and Mint were struck, and it is possible that these were struck in 1839.

47. 1839-O half dollar: Three or four Proofs known.

48. 1839-(P) half dollar: Although Christian Gobrecht's half dollar design was slightly modified during 1839 by the addition of a small drapery fold beneath the elbow, the design was never as fully modified as the other Seated Liberty denominations were in 1840. In subsequent years individual dies would occasionally be over-polished, thus removing this small drapery fold. Coins struck from these inferior dies are sometimes referred to as having a "No-Drapery design," when in fact no design change was intended or made.

49. 1853-(P), O half dollar: All 1853-(P) and virtually all 1853-O half dollars are of the new weight. Two or three 1853-O are known without the arrows and rays. Beware of alterations from 1858-O.

50. 1855-S half dollar: Three Proofs known, presumably struck to celebrate the beginning of silver coinage at the San Francisco Mint.

51. 1861-O half dollar: Mintage includes 330,000 struck by the USA; 1,240,000 by the State of Louisiana; and 962,633 by the Confederate States of America. It is impossible to tell them apart. One obverse die is identifiable as having been used with the CSA reverse to strike four pattern coins, but there is no way of telling when that die was used with a regular reverse die or who issued the coins struck from it. Three to six Proofs known, probably struck under the authority of either the state of Louisiana or the CSA.

52. 1873-S half dollar: The 1873-S Seated Liberty, Without Arrows half dollar is unknown in any condition in any collection. Presumably they were all melted with the 1873-S silver dollars. Beware of any regular 1873-S with the arrows removed. The difference in weight between the two issues is insignificant, and useless in checking a suspected altered coin.

53. 1895-O half dollar: Proofs issued to mark reopening of New Orleans Mint.

54. Proof set sales suspended 1965-67.

55. 1970-D and 1987 half dollar: Struck only for inclusion in Mint sets. Not a regular issue coin. 1987 coins were struck for Uncirculated sets, Proof sets and Souvenir Mint sets only, forcing a change in the Mint's accounting procedures. Previously, business strikes intended for Uncirculated Mint sets and Souvenir sets had been reported with coins intended for circulation. However, upon seeing "circulation" mintages where none should be, the Mint began separating the mintages of coins intended for sale to collectors from those intended for commerce.

56. 1798 silver dollar: Mintage includes both reverse designs.

57. 1801, 1802, and 1803 silver dollar: All three dates were restruck in Proof in 1858 with a plain edge, using obverse dies made in 1834-5 and the reverse die from the Class I 1804 dollar, which was also made in 1834. Due to the scandal caused by the private issue of 1804 dollars in 1858, these coins were not offered for sale to collectors until 1875, by which time their edges had been lettered.

58. 1804 silver dollar: Although the Mint Report lists 19,570 dollars for this year, it is assumed that they were all dated 1803. The 1804 dollars were first struck in 1834-35 for inclusion in diplomatic presentation sets. A few pieces, possibly flawed Proofs or production overruns, reached collectors via trades with the Mint or in circulation and the coin was popularized as a rarity. In 1858 the son of a Mint employee used the obverse die prepared in 1834 and a newly prepared reverse die plus a plain collar to secretly strike 1804 dollars, a few of which were sold to collectors. While the Mint had intended to do exactly the same thing with dollars dated 1801-04, Mint officials were forced to cancel the project due to the public scandal over the privately issued 1804s. The privately struck coins were recalled, and all but one (which went to the Mint Cabinet collection) were allegedly melted. Instead, they and the plain edged 1801-03s were put in storage and offered for sale in 1875, by which time their edges had been mechanically lettered.

59. 1805 silver dollar: The 321 dollars listed in the Mint Report for 1805 were older dollars that were found in deposits of Spanish-American silver and that were re-issued through the Treasury. On the basis of this misinformation, a few coins have been altered to this date in the past.

60. 1836, 1838, and 1839 silver dollar: Gobrecht dollars, some patterns and some intended for circulation, were struck in these years. Also, some varieties were restruck in later years, making mintage figures questionable. Varieties exist with or without stars and/or the designer's name, some of them exceedingly scarce. The 1,600 mintage figure for 1836 represents 1,000 struck for circulation on the 1836 standard of 416 grains, and 600 pieces struck in 1837 (dated 1836) on the new standard of 412.5 grains.

61. 1853 silver dollar: All Proofs are restrikes, made 1864-5.

62. 1858 silver dollar: It is estimated that 80 Proofs were struck, some of them possibly at a later date.

63. 1870-CC silver dollar: Proofs mintage unknown, possibly struck to mark first Carson City dollar coinage.

64. 1870-S silver dollar: Not listed in the Mint Report, but a few pieces may have been struck as souvenirs of the opening of the new Mint.

65. 1873-S silver dollar: Presumably all or most were melted at the Mint after production of standard silver dollars was suspended.

66. 1878-(P) silver dollar: Three slightly different designs were used for both the obverse and reverse of this date, including some dies with the second designs impressed over the first. All 1878-CC and 1878-S are from the second designs. Most 1879-1904 dollars are of the third design, except for some second design reverses on 1879-S and 1880-CC coins. New, slightly different master hubs were prepared for 1921. Proof mintage includes 700 of the 8 Tail Feathers variety and 300 of the 7 Tail Feathers, flat eagle breast variety. Beware of any early strike, prooflike surface Morgan dollar being sold as a Proof.

67. 1879-O silver dollar: Two Proofs now known of 12 struck to celebrate the re-opening of the New Orleans Mint.

68. 1882-CC silver dollar: Proof mintage unknown, reason for issue unknown.

69. 1883-CC silver dollar: Proof mintage unknown, reason for issue unknown.

70. 1883-O silver dollar: One Proof now known of 12 struck for presentation to various local dignitaries. Occasion uncertain.

71. 1884-CC silver dollar: One Proof reported, reason for issue unknown.

72. 1893-CC silver dollar: 12 Proofs struck for presentation to Mint officials to mark the closing of the Carson City Mint.

73. 1895 silver dollar: Apparently virtually all business strike coins were never issued and were probably melted in the great silver melt of 1918. One circulated business strike coin has reportedly been authenticated. Beware of altered dates and removed Mint marks.

74. 1921-(P) Peace silver dollar: The 1921 Peace dollars, (and a very few Proof 1922s), are of a higher relief than the 1922-35s.

75. 1873 Trade silver dollar: All Proofs are of the Open 3 variety.

76. 1884-85 Trade dollar: Struck in Proof in the Mint for private distribution by person or persons unknown. Not listed in the Mint Report.

77. S-Mint clad dollars: Struck only for sale to collectors. In 1971-72 struck in 40 percent clad silver in Proof and Uncirculated for individual sale. Beginning in 1973 a copper-nickel clad dollar was added to the Proof sets.

78. 1973-(P), D copper-nickel dollar: Struck only for inclusion in Mint sets. Not a regular issue coin. 1,769,258 Mint sets were sold. 439,899 excess dollars melted, presumably of near-equal distribution. 21,641 coins were kept for possible replacement of defective sets and may have been melted.

79. Anthony dollars: Anthony dollars were sold in three-coin sets only in 1981. None were released into circulation.

80. 1861-D gold dollar: A small number were struck by the CSA.

81. 1870-S gold dollar: 2,000 coins were struck without a Mint mark. It is unknown if they were melted and recoined or released as is and included in the Mint Report figure of 3,000 coins.

82. 1834 $2.50: Most or all were melted. It may be that all survivors are Proofs and circulated Proofs.

83. 1841-(P) $2.50: Struck in Proof only, possibly at a later date. Unlisted in Mint Report. Nine known, several of them circulated or otherwise impaired.

84. 1848-(P) $2.50: Approximately 1,389 coins were counterstamped CAL. above the eagle to show that they were made from California gold. This was done while the coins were resting on an inverted obverse die on a worktable. This virtually eliminated distortion of the obverse, which will probably show on a genuine coin with a fake counterstamp.

85. 1860-S $3: Out of 7,000 coins struck, 2,592 pieces were not released because of short weight. They were melted in 1869 for use in other denominations.

86. 1870-S $3: Not included in the Mint Report, supposedly one piece was struck for inclusion in the cornerstone of the new San Francisco Mint. One piece is known in a private collection, and the present whereabouts of the cornerstone piece is unknown. It is possible there is only one piece.

87. 1873 $3: All original Proofs are of the more Open 3 variety. There were two restrikes with the Closed 3 and one with the Open 3.

88. 1798 $5: Mint Report of 24,867 coins includes Small Eagle reverse coins dated 1798, as well as Heraldic Eagle coins dated 1795, 1797 and 1798. This mixture of mulings is the result of an emergency coinage late in 1798 after the Mint had been closed for a while due to yellow fever. Quantities struck of each are unknown and can only be a guess.

89. 1822 $5: Although the Mint Report says 17,796 coins were struck, only three pieces are known, and it is likely that most of this mintage was from dies dated 1821.

90. 1825 $5: Struck from the regular overdated dies. 1825/4, one known, and 1825/1, two known.

91. 1828 $5: Includes at least one overdate, 1828/7.

92. 1844-O half eagle: One Proof known, reason for issue unknown.

93. 1861-C $5: Mintage includes 5,992 pieces coined by USA and 887 by CSA. It is impossible to prove the issuer.

94. 1899-S half eagle: One or two Proofs known, reason for issue unknown.

95. 1906-D and 1907-D $5: These were, of course, struck at the Denver Mint. This is the only design that was struck at both Dahlonega and Denver.

96. 1797 $10: Mintage includes both reverse types.

97. 1839 $10: Includes first design head (type of 1838) and modified head (type of 1840-1907). Proofs are of the type of 1838, with large letters and different hair style.

98. 1844-O eagle: One Proof known, reason for issue unknown.

99. 1852-O eagle: Three Proofs known, reason for issue unknown.

100. 1853-O eagle: Proof mintage unknown, reason for issue unknown.

101. 1906-D eagle: Proofs struck in honor of the opening of the Denver Mint.

102. 1907 $10: An unknown number of Indian Head patterns were also struck in Proof.

103. 1933 $10: Very few of these were issued, perhaps several dozens known. Beware of counterfeits.

104. 1849 $20: One specimen in gold survives of a small number of trial strikes produced in December 1849. The dies were rejected, allegedly because of improper high relief, but in actuality to discredit Longacre in an attempt to force his removal. The attempt failed and Longacre eventually produced a second set of dies, but they were not completed until the following month and so they were dated 1850. The one known Proof gold specimen is in the National Numismatic Collection at the Smithsonian Institution and all others were melted.

105. 1850 $20: One Proof was once owned by the engraver, James B. Longacre. Whereabouts presently unknown.

106. 1854-S double eagle: One Proof known, in the Smithsonian Institution. Struck in honor of the opening of the San Francisco Mint.

107. 1861-(P) $20: A few trial pieces are known with a reverse as engraved by Paquet, with taller, thinner letters and a narrow rim. The design was judged unacceptable because the narrow reverse rim would not stack easily.

108. 1861-O $20: Mintage includes 5,000 coins struck by the USA; 9,750 by the State of Louisiana; and 2,991 by the Confederate States of America. It is impossible to prove the issuer of any given coin.

109. 1861-S $20: Mintage includes 19,250 pieces struck with the Paquet reverse and released into circulation. Most of these were recalled and melted during the next few years, but specie hoarding during the Civil War probably preserved a number of them until later years when the problem was forgotten.

110. 1866-(P), S $20: When the reverse of the double eagle was altered to include the motto, there were also a few minor changes made in the scrollwork, the most prominent being the change in the shield from flat-sided to curved. Check any alleged 1866-S No Motto $20 for this feature.

111. 1877 $20: In this year the master hubs were redesigned slightly, raising the head and changing TWENTY D. to TWENTY DOLLARS.

112. 1906-D double eagle: Two Proofs now known of 12 struck in honor of the opening of the Denver Mint.

113. 1907-D double eagle: One Proof known, possibly struck as a specimen of the last year of this design.

114. 1907 $20: An unknown number of Saint-Gaudens type coins of pattern or near-pattern status were also struck in extremely high relief Proof.

115. 1933 $20: This issue was officially never released, so all but one of the coins are considered illegal to own. The specimen once owned by Egypt's King Farouk, brought back into the United States in the 1990s, was declared legal for private ownership in 2000. It was sold at auction July 30, 2002, for $7.59 million, a world record price for a coin. Two are held in the National Numismatic Collection at the Smithsonian Institution. Most late-date gold never filtered down through the banks and so it was returned to the Mint for melting.

116. 1994-P 5¢: The Mint double-struck 167,703 "Uncirculated" pieces from specially prepared, sandblast dies, essentially creating a Matte Proof, for inclusion in a special packaging set with the 1993 Jefferson commemorative silver dollar.

117. American Eagle gold bullion: Roman numerals used in date.

118. 1996-W Roosevelt dime: Produced with a West Point Mint mark for inclusion in 1996 Uncirculated Mint sets on the occasion of the 50th anniversary of the Roosevelt dime.

119. 1995-W American Eagle silver bullion dollar: Produced for sale only in special "10th Anniversary" sets.

120. Circulation-quality, but not released into circulation. Sold to collectors in bags and rolls.

121. Mint officials reopened sales of 1999, 2000 and 2001 Proof sets on May 29, 2002, in an unprecedented and controversial offering. The 1999 and 2000 Proof set programs long had been closed, and sales of the 2001 sets had ended as 2002 sets went on sale. Officials halted sales June 25, 2002, citing damage to some of the coins in some of the 1999 sets. Sales figures for the three sets quoted here are preliminary (as of July 23, 2003) and subject to change.

7

Grading coins

Probably no other subject has been more hotly debated in American numismatics by collectors, dealers and investors than grading. There has been controversy since a dealer first charged a higher price for one specimen of a coin than for another of the same type, date and Mint mark simply because one had less wear than the other.

The grade of a coin (or note, medal or token) represents what professional numismatist and researcher Dr. Richard Bagg aptly called its "level of preservation." The grading controversy arises both from disagreements over the grade of a coin and often the enormous differences in price between two specimens of the same type and date of a U.S. coin, even when the only difference lies in the placement of one or two marks or surface abrasions from contact with other coins, commonly referred to as "contact marks" or "bag marks." Prices can also differ for coins bearing the "same" grade, but assigned by different private grading services that use different grading standards.

The grade measures both the amount of wear, natural mishaps and other surface degradation a coin has received after leaving the coining press and its "eye appeal," a subjective determination that may differ from observer to observer. The more wear and surface marks a coin has received, the less it is worth compared to other specimens of the same coin with less surface degradation.

However, not all coins have received circulation wear since they were struck. These coins are called Uncirculated or Mint State. Rather than being easier to grade because there are no points of wear to determine, Uncirculated coins are much harder to grade.

In fact, hobbyists identify graduated levels of Mint State, at least 11 (from Mint State 60 to Mint State 70), determined by such factors as contact marks, luster and—depending on the grading standard being used—the strength of the strike and eye appeal of toning. Therein lies the heart of the controversy.

For decades, the controversy lay mainly in the differences between the dealer's opinion about the grade for a specific coin and that of the collector, and thus their disagreement over a coin's value. As grading became more complex and values increased in greater increments between coins of different grades, third-party grading services began operation. Third-party grading has become a lucrative business, with many dealers and collectors willing to pay fees for someone else's opinion about the grade of their coins.

The first third-party grading service, the International Numismatic Society Authentication Bureau, began grading coins in December 1976, several months after it began authenticating coins. It laid the groundwork for third-party grading services, all of which provide an opinion about a coin's grade for a fee. INSAB was followed March 1, 1979, when the American Numismatic Association Certification Service began grading coins for a fee.

Another major step in third-party grading services was taken by the Professional Coin Grading Service, a private business founded in February 1986. PCGS is responsible for two firsts. It was the first grading service to encapsulate the coins it graded into hard plastic holders, nicknamed "slabs," and it was the first grading service to use 11 levels of Mint State, from MS-60 to MS-70. It rapidly overtook ANACS, until then the most active of grading services in terms of numbers of coins graded.

Numismatic Guaranty Corporation of America opened for business in 1987 and immediately challenged PCGS for market share. As encapsulated coins became more popular with dealers and collectors, existing grading firms expanded their services. INSAB offered a "slab" service beginning in 1989, as did the ANA with its ANACS Cache.

In 1990, the American Numismatic Association sold ANACS—its grading and certification service—to Amos Press Inc., publisher of *Coin World* and other hobby publications, including this book. Amos Press Inc. retained the ANACS name, but the acronym no longer refers to the American Numismatic Association. Amos Press moved ANACS from ANA headquarters in Colorado Springs, Colo., to Dublin, Ohio.

Over the years, other grading services have entered the market, some specializing in paper money and world coins. Not all of the companies have succeeded; several have closed over the years.

The firms that grade coins charge fees for their services. Fees differ from company to company; a company may have different fees based on the level of service expected.

Services differ

Fees are not the only things that differ between companies. Coins graded by some companies often bring higher prices than do coins assigned the same grades by other companies. Those higher prices generally indicate greater market confidence in the firm grading the coin. Lower prices for coins graded by other companies often indicate a lower level of market confidence in the ability of the firm's graders to grade accurately to market standards, or even a distrust of the firm's adherence to market standards or ability to detect altered or counterfeit coins.

The differing levels of dealer and collector confidence in various grading services have long been the subject of heated debate at coin club meetings, coin shows and online at coin collector forums and bulletin boards. In recent years, the debate seems to have intensified as more and more coins are sold online through dealer sites and eBay. The debate has resulted in at least one lawsuit, filed by the owners of a grading service against collectors and dealers who are critical of the service.

The growth in online sales has made possible for collectors who never go to coin shows or auctions to compete with other collectors in online auctions. Many of the coins sold online are graded and encapsulated ("slabbed") by the various grading services, but because *new* collectors may be unaware that the market distinguishes between the services, some pay prices that would not be sustained in the more established market because of lower confidence in the grading service that graded the coins.

The debate over grading services got even hotter in October 2002 with the publication of the results of a grading service survey conducted by Professional Numismatists Guild (a coin dealer's organization) and the Industry Council for Tangible Assets (a trade/lobbying organization), and in May 2003 with the publication of the results of a grading test conducted by *Coin World.*

PNG and ICTA surveyed "more than 300" dealer members (no collectors were surveyed) in August 2002 and asked them to rate seven private grading services in specific categories. The survey results were based on the 151 surveys that were returned and tabulated in September. The PNG-ICTA survey was not a scientific survey.

Proponents of high-rated services and critics of the low-rated firms championed the survey as an important milestone in informing the public about the differences between the grading services. Representatives of the services that were rated as "poor" or "unacceptable" protested the methodology of the survey and called its results biased and inaccurate.

The PNG-ICTA survey results are posted online at **www.pngdealers.com/public/SurveyResults2002_detail.cfm.**

Coin World conducted a different kind of grading test; it arranged for the president and chief executive officer of the Chicago Better Business Bureau, who is also a coin collector, to send the same 15 coins in turn to eight grading services. *Coin World* embarked upon the test in May 2002. To test all eight services took 11 months: time for the coins to be graded and returned to the submitter, who in turn sent the coins to *Coin World* where the grades were recorded, the coins were photographed in the various services' "slabs," removed from their slabs and finally sent to the next service. None of services were told of the testing (including ANACS, the grading firm owned by Amos Press).

Coin World published the results of its test in its May 26 and June 2, 2003, issues.

Of the 15 coins used in the test, not one was graded the same by all eight services. Some firms refused to grade certain coins, citing that they had been cleaned or otherwise altered; other firms graded the cleaned and altered coins, but noted the cleaning or alteration on the holders; and some firms graded, without notation, coins other services would not grade.

Coin World also published details about the cost per firm and amount of time each firm took to evaluate and/or grade the 15 coins and return them.

Coin World also published details about each firm: who owned the service, how many years it has been in business, how many graders it employs, how many graders grade each coin, the grading system/standard used, whether it offers authenticity and grading guarantees, whether it grades problem coins and notes the problems on the holders, and whether the firm accepts direct submissions from collectors.

Another danger threatens new collectors: coins promoted in online sales as third-party graded but in actuality graded by the seller and housed within a generic holder mimicking those used by the grading services. Third-party grading is supposed to offer an independent opinion of a coin's grade; the grader has no financial interests in the coin other than the fee charged for grading it. However, some online sellers promote coins as having been graded by an independent service that is nothing more than a made-up name designed to lend a degree of legitimacy to the auction.

These self-graded "slabbed" coins may be housed in holders similar to those used by grading services. The sales division of Amos Press Inc. markets, under the *Coin World* label, two different sizes of holders compatible with the slabs used by PCGS and ANACS (collectors can buy these holders to house their coins that do not warrant the expense of third-party grading and store them in the same boxes as their slabbed coins). These Amos Press holders bear the *Coin World* name and globe, but bear black or dark green inserts (the similarly sized holders ANACS and PCGS use for slabbing bear white inserts) and, unlike coins certified and slabbed by grading services, are not sonically sealed. Although *Coin World* does not grade or authenticate coins, some online sellers have identified coins (through ignorance or malice) placed into these commercially available holders as being "certified" by *Coin World.* Collectors seeing such auction descriptions should understand that *Coin World* has not certified or graded such pieces. Beware of bidding on the coins.

Which grading service should you choose? Ask other collectors and dealers for their recommendations, at a coin club meeting, at a coin show or convention or at any of the several coin-related newsgroups or message forums. View the results of the PNG-ICTA survey online. *Coin World's* articles on its own grading test are archived at **www.coinworldonline.com**.

Grading: What's involved?

Dr. Richard Bagg, in *Grading Coins: A Collection of Readings* that he co-edited in 1977 with James J. Jelinski, described the grade of a coin as its "level of preservation." It is not entirely accurate to call grading the charting of wear on a coin. The very definition of an Uncirculated coin (also called Mint State) is "a coin which has seen no circulation" (in *Official American Numismatic Association Grading Standards for United States Coins*) and a coin with "no wear" (in *New Photograde: A Photographic Grading Guide for United States Coins*). However, Uncirculated coins are subject to forms of surface degradation other than circulation wear.

A coin struck for circulation becomes subject to external factors affecting its surface from the second it leaves the press. The moment a coin is struck, it is pushed from the surface of the anvil die. The coin then falls into a bin of other coins. When the coin hits the previously struck coins lying in the bin, the portion of its surface coming into contact with the other coins will probably be marred. Then, as the coins are bundled into bags or other bins for shipment to commercial counting rooms and banks, the coins will incur additional damage.

Contact marks

The collisions of coins create a variety of surface marks called "contact marks" or "bag marks." A contact mark may range in severity from a light, minor disruption of the coin's surface to a large, heavy scrape. Generally, the bigger and heavier the coin, the larger and more unsightly the contact marks, due both to its own weight and that of other coins of the same dimension jostling against it.

The location of contact marks plays a major role in determining at what level of Mint State a coin may be categorized. For example, marks that are clearly visible in the field of a coin, or on the cheeks, chin or forehead of a Liberty Head device are more distracting than marks of equal severity hidden in curls of Liberty's hair.

The size of contact marks also plays a role in determining the particular Mint State level. Larger marks, of course, are more distracting than smaller marks. Remember, however, that a contact mark 1 millimeter long is less distracting on a large coin such as a silver dollar (diameter of 38.1 millimeters) than it is on a smaller coin such as a silver half dime (diameter of 15.5 millimeters).

The number of contact marks also plays a significant role in determining the particular level of a Mint State coin. A coin with numerous contact marks is less appealing to the eye than a coin with one or two distracting marks. The diameter of the coin plays a role too. A silver dollar with five contact marks scattered across its surfaces may be judged appealing; a much smaller half dime with five contact marks may be judged less appealing, since the half dime is smaller.

Luster

Another factor involved in determining the level of Mint State and high-level circulated grades is luster. "Luster is simply the way light reflects from the microscopic flow lines of a coin," according to ANACS grader-authenticator Michael Fahey in *Basic Grading,* a reprint from his series of articles in the ANA's *The Numismatist.* James L. Halperin, author of the Numismatic Certification Institute's (a former grading service) *Grading U.S. Coins,* defines luster as, "The brightness of a coin which results from the way in which it reflects light."

Luster is imparted to the surfaces of a coin at the moment of striking. The immense pressures used in the coining process create flow lines, the microscopic lines that trace the paths the metal took while filling the crevices of the die that compose the designs.

A coin with full luster is generally one that has a bright, shiny surface (although toning, to be discussed later, may obscure full luster), caused by the light reflecting off the surface of the coin. If the luster has been disturbed, the light reflects from the surface of the coin differently; the coin may appear dull.

Circulation wear erases the microscopic flow lines that cause the luster. Heavy cleaning or cleaning with a substance that removes a microscopic layer of the surface metal will also damage the flow lines and disrupt or eliminate the luster of a coin.

A Mint State coin cannot be lackluster. At best, an Uncirculated coin without full luster can be no higher than Mint State 63 under the American Numismatic Association grading standards. High-level circulated coins may show patches of luster in protected areas.

Wear vs. friction

Once a coin enters commerce, it begins to receive wear. The amount of wear a coin receives determines its grade among the circulated grade levels. The high points of a design are usually the first to depict wear, since they are the most exposed. Then the raised inscriptions and date exhibit wear, and finally, the flat fields.

Circulation wear erases design details, ultimately to the point where the design features are only slightly visible to the naked eye. The separate curls of hair tend to merge, the eagle's feathers are rubbed away and the inscriptions begin to disappear into the fields.

Coins with only the slightest hint of wear are called About Uncirculated. Then, in descending order, are Extremely Fine, Very Fine, Fine, Very Good, Good, About Good, Fair (and many years ago, Poor). Graders use several levels for some of the higher circulated grades to denote, for example, an Extremely Fine coin of higher quality than another legitimate Extremely Fine coin (EF-45 vs. EF-40).

Many hobbyists differentiate between circulation wear and another form of wear labeled "friction." According to Halperin, friction is "A disturbance which appears either on the high points of a coin or in the fields, as a result of that coin rubbing against other projections." It is often referred to as cabinet friction, a term applied to the minute wear a coin received when sliding back and forth in the drawer of a cabinet used for storage by earlier collectors.

According to some grading services, friction does disturb the luster of the coin, but it should not disturb the metal underneath. If it does, the disturbance falls into the category of wear, they believe.

Strike

Strike is "The sharpness of detail which the coin had when it was Mint State," according to Halperin. Fahey defines it as "the evenness and fullness of metal-flow into all the crevices of a die."

The amount of pressure used to strike a coin controls the sharpness of a strike. Design elements may also affect the strike; if two large design features are centered on both sides of the same coin, there may not be enough metal to flow into every little crevice of the design, thus leaving some details weak and ill-defined.

A coin with a sharp strike has sharp design details. For example, the curls of hair on Liberty's head are strong and distinct. The feathers on the eagle's wings and breast are clearly visible. All of the other design details, legends and other elements are sharp and well defined.

A coin with a weak strike has weak and ill-defined design details. It may look worn, since design details are missing from the high points of a coin. However, luster is unimpaired. Lower striking pressures may not force the metal into the deepest crevices on the die (the highest point on the coin); thus, the weaker design details.

Grading services, dealers and collectors consider strike an important part of a coin's grade. An Uncirculated coin relatively free of marks and with full luster may still be placed at the lower end of the Mint State scale if it has a weak strike.

Strike affects the value of a coin. A coin with a sharp strike will generally have a higher value than a coin with a weak strike, all other factors being equal.

Toning and color

As a coin ages, the original color changes through chemical reaction to the environment. The original red of copper coins becomes brown (or green). Silver coins may tone into any color of the rainbow, depending on environmental factors. Gold is a more stable metal and generally shows little change in tone and color, although the silver or copper many gold coin coins contain in their alloys will tone.

Many years ago, toned coins, particularly silver coins, were judged unattractive. Silver coins were "dipped" or placed into a chemical solution that removed the toning and restored the shiny surface by stripping away the outer surface of the silver or the dirt. Dipping continues today, and while many in the market generally accept it, some hobbyists consider "dipping" unacceptable.

Attractively toned coins have become more appreciated from an aesthetic viewpoint by some. A silver dollar or other coin with original rainbow toning may bring a considerable premium because of its coloration. However, a coin with patchy, hazy or mottled toning (sometimes referred to as tarnish) generally will be considered less desirable than a nicely toned coin or an original untoned specimen.

Coins that exhibit bright white, original surfaces are prized.

Because attractively toned coins often bring higher prices, some unscrupulous individuals (called "coin doctors") have devised ways of artificially toning coins.

Novices will find it difficult to distinguish between natural toning and artificial toning. Experience is important here. An individual who has looked at a large number of coins will find that he can determine at a glance whether the toning is natural or whether it has been artificially generated. Collectors should not pay a premium for an artificially toned coin.

Coin doctoring is universally condemned, although not everyone agrees on what classifies as "doctoring" (for example, some consider dipping a coin to remove tarnish a form of doctoring; others consider it an acceptable practice that need not be noted in a coin's description).

Other factors

Other factors under some grading standards do not affect the grade but may affect the value. Under other standards, those same factors affect both the grade and the value of the coin.

Among these factors are die scratches, not to be confused with "hairline" scratches. Die scratches are thin raised lines on a coin, resulting from minute scratches in the surface of the die. A hairline is a thin scratch scraped into the surface of a coin inflicted after the coin is struck.

A close examination of a coin's surface through a magnifying glass should indicate whether a line on a coin is raised, and thus a die scratch, or incused, making it a hairline scratch.

Hairlines tend to affect the value more than die scratches. Most grading services, however, will lower the grade of a coin for more extensive, distracting die scratches.

Adjustment marks are often found on older U.S. silver and gold coins. Planchets (unstruck coins) were individually weighed before striking. If the coin was found to be a little overweight, the excess gold or silver was filed away. The striking pressures often did not obliterate the adjustment marks, which may resemble a series of parallel grooves. Adjustment marks may affect both the grade and the value.

Eye appeal

All of the factors mentioned earlier are ultimately considered when graders, dealers and collectors decide on the "eye appeal" of a coin. Eye appeal relates to the overall attractiveness of a coin and ultimately determines its value. A potential buyer, whether he is a dealer, collector or investor, decides just how attractive he believes the coin to be.

Judging eye appeal is a purely subjective action. For example, a coin could have a strong strike and full details, possess full luster and have few large, distracting contact marks and still not have eye appeal if it has toned to an unattractive color.

When examining a coin, a buyer must decide for himself just how attractive and appealing the coin is and whether its attractiveness warrants the price being asked. Only the buyer can decide the eye appeal.

'Raw' coins vs. 'slabbed' coins

When the Professional Coin Grading Service began grading coins in early 1986, it introduced a new product onto the market: the "slabbed" coin. A "slab" is the hard plastic holder into which a coin graded by a third-party grading service is encapsulated. The grading information is contained in the slab as well. The slab permits both obverse and reverse of the coin to be viewed.

Proponents of the "slab" cite several benefits:

1. A coin encased within a slab is protected somewhat from environmental factors that could cause a deterioration in the coin's surfaces, and a lowering of its grade. However, in recent years, testing has shown that coins encapsulated in grading services' slabs *can* continue to tone. That's because the plastic is permeable; the chemicals that cause a coin to tone can permeate the plastic. Slabbed coins should be inspected routinely to ensure that the environment in which they are stored is not causing the coins to tone unattractively.

2. By encapsulating a coin into the same holder that contains the grading information, a buyer is "assured" that a coin meets the grading requirements of a specific grading service, if graded accurately.

An encapsulated, or slabbed, coin

3. It permits the "sight unseen" trading of a coin (in other words, various dealers have agreed to purchase coins graded by a particular grading service at the grade indicated on the slab, even without seeing the coin first).

Individuals who do not like slabbed coins cite detracting factors:

1. A collector cannot handle the coin directly.

2. Most slabs do not permit the edge of the coin to be viewed.

3. It may be difficult to form one's own opinion about a coin's grade if it has already been encapsulated, since many like to grade a coin without having to examine it through a holder.

4. Grading standards change over time. Grading services may loosen or tighten their standards in reaction to market conditions.

Another term is the "raw" coin. A "raw" coin is the nickname some use for a coin that has not been graded and encapsulated by a third-party grading service.

Differences in value

Several times in this chapter, we have stressed that coins of different grades will sell for different prices. Sometimes, those differences in grade can be minute yet represent thousands of dollars. Take, as an example, the 1881 Morgan dollar. In Mint State 64, it is worth about $140. In Mint State 64 deep mirror prooflike (the same grade, but with a particularly reflective surface), the coin is worth about $1,700. In MS-65, one level up from an MS-64 coin, the 1881 Morgan dollar is worth $900, and in MS-65 deep mirror prooflike, the coin is worth $14,000! The same coin jumps in value from $140 to $14,000 for a one-point increase in grade and an increase in reflectivity! In such cases, accurate grading is essential. No one wants to pay $14,000 for a coin graded at one level that most collectors or dealers would grade one level lower and would say does not meet the higher reflectivity standards, thus being worth $140.

Ultimately, collectors should learn how to grade coins. It is not an easy task, nor one that can be learned in a few days. Individuals the market considers expert graders have taken years to hone their craft. They have looked at hundreds of thousands of coins, maybe more. Collectors should not feel intimidated at this, however. Most collectors can learn to grade coins fairly accurately, if they are willing to devote time to this educational process. There are even classes they can take (some conducted for free, some for a fee) that teach the fundamentals of grading. The time and effort are well worth the expense if one plans to collect coins as a hobby.

Coins for collectors

In recent years, the U.S. Mint has been producing quantities of high-quality coins for collectors. Coins struck for inclusion in Proof sets, Silver Proof sets and State Quarters Proof sets often are of extreme high quality, as are Uncirculated and Proof commemorative coins and American Eagle bullion coins. Grading services often grade these coins Proof 68, Proof 69 or Proof 70, or MS-68, MS-69 or MS-70, depending on whether a coin is a Proof or Uncirculated strike.

Coin collector publications such as *Coin World* are filled with ads from dealers seeking to sell examples of these super high grades.

Grading guidelines

The following guidelines are not presented as grading standards, but as introductions to the terminology of grading and its usage.

A few words regarding grading usage. When two grades are linked together by a virgule—as in Mint State 64/65—it may mean that the coin has two grades (the first grade represents the obverse and the second, the reverse) or that the coin falls into a range between the two grades. When two grades are linked by a hyphen—as in Mint State 64-65—it means that the grade for both sides lies somewhere between the two grades given. Collectors might want to exercise caution about buying a coin graded AU-BU. A coin is either circulated or Uncirculated—it cannot fall somewhere in between.

Plus signs are used by many to indicate a coin slightly better than the numerical grade indicated, but not as good as the next numerical grade. A coin graded MS-60+ is better than a typical MS-60 coin, but not as good as an MS-61 coin. The term "Premium Quality" means pretty much the same thing as a plus sign: that a coin is in the upper range for that grade and is very close to the next grade level.

Many dealers and collectors use adjectives instead of numerals, or combine adjectives and numerals when speaking about Mint State coins. A superb or superb gem coin is generally MS-67. A gem coin is usually MS-65. Some dealers use choice to describe an MS-63 coin, and others use choice for an MS-65 coin. Mint State 60 coins are generally referred to as Uncirculated or Brilliant Uncirculated; sometimes an MS-60 coin is called typical Uncirculated. Because of the disagreement over what the adjectives represent numerically, collectors should determine what adjectival "system" the dealer uses when no numerals are present.

Buyers should remember that different dealers, different collectors and investors use different grading systems. Although various grading services use an 11-point Mint State system, this does not necessarily mean they use the same criteria for assigning grades. In fact, there is no universally accepted standard for determining grades for U.S. coins.

Collectors should also know that grading standards can change over time. Standards sometimes tighten up, with a coin once considered Mint State 65 now considered MS-64. Standards can also loosen, with an MS-64 coin grading MS-65 under the looser standards. This can be troublesome, especially if a novice collector buys a slabbed coin graded during a period of loose standards; even if the slab is marked as MS-65, current standards might consider the coin no higher than MS-64. That's why it is vital that collectors learn how to grade coins, in order to protect themselves when buying coins.

A coin that is "market graded" bears a numerical grade that generally matches the grade at which it would be traded on the rare coin market. As market standards change, so do the standards used by grading services that "market grade."

Proof: Traditionally, Proof describes a method of manufacture, not a grade. However, since numerals are often assigned to Proof coins, there are different qualities of Proof coins; in effect, different grades. A circulated Proof is often called an "impaired Proof." Proof is rarely abbreviated (if so, it often appears abbreviated as PF or PRF).

Proof coins are struck on highly polished planchets, using slower, high-pressure presses. Proof coins are struck two or more times to bring up greater detail in the design.

Mint State and Uncirculated: The two terms are interchangeable and describe a coin that has no wear. To qualify as Mint State, a coin must not have any level of wear. Even the slightest amount of wear will drop the coin into the About Uncirculated level. (Coins described by some dealers as "Borderline Uncirculated" have wear and are actually About Uncirculated.)

Mint State is most often used with numerals. The numerical Mint State system so widely used in the current rare coin market is based on a system created by Dr. William H. Sheldon for the U.S. large cents of 1793 to 1814. When the numerical system began to spread to other series, three levels of Mint State were used: Mint State 60, for an Uncirculated coin of average luster, strike and marks; MS-65, an

Uncirculated coin of above average quality; and MS-70, a perfect coin as regards luster, strike and marks. All 11 numbers are now used from MS-60 to MS-70.

Uncirculated is usually abbreviated as Unc. It often appears as Brilliant Uncirculated, abbreviated as BU. Sometimes the term is used with numerals, generally as Unc. 60, Unc. 61 and so on. Some dealers use a plus sign to indicate a coin better than one level of Mint State, but not as good as the next level.

About Uncirculated: This is a coin with only the barest traces of wear on the highest points of the design. It is abbreviated AU and often appears with numerals as AU-50, AU-55 and AU-58. The term has gained acceptance despite seeming inconsistency. Some people in the hobby still say that no coin can be About Uncirculated—it is either Uncirculated or it is not. Some use "Almost" Uncirculated, although all major U.S. grading guides use "About." The AU-58 grade has been described as an MS-63 coin with just the slightest hint of wear. It should have fewer contact marks than lower level Mint State coins: MS-60, MS-61 and MS-62. It may be more attractive and more valuable than these lower Mint State coins.

Extremely Fine: Light overall wear on highest points, but with all design elements sharp and clear, distinguishes this grade. Most hobbyists abbreviate it as EF, although a few use XF. It appears as EF-40 and EF-45.

Very Fine: The coin has light to moderate even wear on surface and high points of design. Abbreviated VF, it appears with numerals as VF-20 and VF-30. The abbreviations VF-25 and VF-35 are infrequently used.

Fine: The wear is considerable, although the entire design is still strong and visible. It is abbreviated as F-12 and F-15.

Very Good: The design and fields are well worn, and main features are clear but flat. Abbreviated as VG, it is used with numerals as VG-8 and VG-10.

Good: Design and surface are heavily worn, with some details weak and many details flat. It is often abbreviated when used with numerals, G-4; G-6 is infrequently used. Ironically, a coin in Good condition is not a "good" coin to collect except for the rarer and scarcer pieces; a Good coin is generally the lowest collectible grade.

About Good: The design is heavily worn with fields fading into rim and many details are weak or missing. Abbreviated as AG, it is used with a numeral as AG-3. Few coins are collectible in About Good condition. Dealers also use the terms Fair and Fair 3 to describe a coin in this state of preservation.

Mint marks and Mints

8

Coin collectors, whether novice or advanced, need to know how to identify which Mint facility struck a particular coin. This information is vital because value can vary between coins of the same denomination, type and date, but different Mints.

For example, consider an 1893 Morgan dollar. Four Mints struck 1893 Morgan dollars: Philadelphia, Carson City, New Orleans and San Francisco. In the lowest level of Mint State (MS-60), a Philadelphia-struck 1893 Morgan dollar is worth $700, one struck at the Carson City Mint is worth $3,200, one struck at the New Orleans Mint is worth $2,000 and one struck at San Francisco—an 1893-S Morgan dollar—is worth $70,000. In the higher grade of MS-65, the difference in value between the Philadelphia and San Francisco Mint specimens is even greater: $7,500 for the Philadelphia Mint dollar and $375,000 for the San Francisco coin!

While often the difference in value between similar coins from different Mints is not as extreme as the example given, knowing the issuing Mint is essential information for any collector. Fortunately, the U.S. Mint has made it easy to identify which Mints struck which coins (most of the time): Many coins bear a small letter that collectors call a "Mint mark."

Mint marks have been used almost as long as coins have been produced. The ancient Greeks and Romans identified the Mints that issued their coins. When the United States began striking its own coinage in 1792, Mint marks were unnecessary because just one striking facility was in use, in Philadelphia. However, the introduction in 1838 of secondary Mint facilities—Branch Mints—made Mint marks a necessity in the United States.

Why is it important to identify which Mint struck a particular coin? When coins still had intrinsic value, when many were composed of silver and gold, any coin containing less than the intended amount of metal was underweight and thus undervalued. A Mint mark allowed officials to identify which Mint was issuing the undervalued coins and make it easier to take corrective actions to restore full value to the coins.

Mint marks appear in different locations on coins. Sometimes they appear on the obverse, and other times, on the reverse. This price guide includes information about the placement of the Mint mark on every major design type. That information can be found at the beginning of each coinage type section.

D Mint mark on Walking Liberty half reverse.

When looking at a list of coins—for example, a price list of coins available for purchase—one can easily determine the issuing Mint for a particular coin because most hobbyists have adopted a similar style for identifying them: The Mint mark appears after the date, generally linked to the date by a hyphen, as in 1893-S, 1998-D and 2002-S.

Sometimes, however, some hobbyists dispense with the hyphen and type a date and Mint mark as follows: 1983S or 1983 S. Beware, however, when someone makes a reference to the 1983s; they may be using the "s" to make the date plural (*Coin World* publications avoid this confusing plural usage).

The following Mint marks have been used on U.S. coins:
C for Charlotte, N.C., (gold coins only), 1838 to 1861
CC for Carson City, Nev., 1870 to 1893
D for Dahlonega, Ga. (gold coins only), 1838 to 1861
D for Denver, Colo., 1906 to present
O for New Orleans, La., 1838 to 1861; 1879 to 1909
P for Philadelphia, Pa., 1793 to present
S for San Francisco, Calif., 1854 to 1955; 1968 to present
W for West Point, N.Y., 1984 to present

Confusion sometimes reigns

Collectors sometimes get confused over Mint marks (or the lack thereof). Sometimes they cannot find a Mint mark and wonder whether they have found a valuable error coin. Other times, they identify what they believe to be a Mint mark that was not used on that date and denomination and wonder whether they have bought a counterfeit coin. While sometimes they are right—the coin proves to be an error (though not always a valuable one) or a worthless counterfeit—more often than not they are just confused through lack of knowledge.

First, what about a coin lacking a Mint mark? The coin in all likelihood is normal even without a Mint mark, since not all U.S. coins bear Mint marks.

P Mint mark on Kennedy half dollar obverse.

From 1792, when the Philadelphia Mint was founded, until 1979, the only coins struck there to bear the P Mint mark were the silver alloy, Jefferson, Wartime 5-cent coins of 1942 to 1945 (the P Mint mark was used to make it easy to distinguish the silver-alloy coins from the traditional copper-nickel alloy pieces). In 1979, the Mint added the P Mint mark to the new Anthony dollar, and in 1980, to all other denominations except for the Lincoln cent. However, to this day, Lincoln cents struck at the Philadelphia Mint bear no Mint marks (and *Coin World* frequently gets letters, telephone calls and e-mails from collectors who find a cent without a Mint mark and think it is an error coin).

Even coins struck at Branch Mints, which normally bear Mint marks, sometimes lack any identification of the issuing Mint. From 1965 to 1967, a period of a significant coinage shortage in the United States, the U.S. Mint stopped using Mint marks so coin collectors would not be tempted to save large numbers of coins from each Mint. Mint officials blamed the coin shortage in part on coin collectors, who often want an example of each Mint's coins. (In reality, other causes were chiefly responsible for the shortage.) And from the mid-1970s to the mid-1980s, some coins struck at the San Francisco and West Point facilities do not bear Mint marks and thus are indistinguishable from their Philadelphia counterparts.

The mintage chapter in this book is a good guide to which Mints struck coins lacking Mint marks. Be sure to pay close attention to how the coins are listed.

Second, what should a collector do if he has found a coin with a Mint mark it should not have? Often collectors contact *Coin World*.

In one case, a collector contacted *Coin World* to complain that a recent news story in the weekly *Coin World* magazine had been in error. Within a couple of days of the first collector, another collector stopped by our offices to report he had been sold a 1923-S Saint-Gaudens $20 double eagle (he knew none had been struck, but the holder was marked "1923-S" and the collector thought he detected an S Mint mark beneath the date).

In both of these examples, the collectors had mistaken a designer's initial or monogram for a Mint mark. In the first example, the collector interpreted the designer's initial D on the coin as a D Mint mark. In the second example, the "S Mint mark" on the double eagle was actually designer Augustus Saint-Gaudens' monogram; in reality, the coin had been struck at the Philadelphia Mint and thus had no Mint mark.

U.S. Mint history

The first U.S. Mint was established in Philadelphia because that city was then the national capital. Later, when the capital was moved to the muddy patch of land and swamp eventually named for the nation's first president, the Mint stayed in place in Philadelphia.

The first Philadelphia Mint was primitive by modern standards. The presses were hand-operated, with the other equipment powered by human or horse. The typical coining press in use at the Mint was the screw press, powered by human muscle. A planchet was placed on the bottom die by an early feed system and two men grasped ropes tied to the two arms of the press and pulled quickly, causing the upper die to descend and strike the coin. The first steam-powered equipment was installed June 24, 1816. Steam powered the machines that rolled the coinage metal to the proper thickness and the punch press used to produce planchets. Further mechanization came in 1833, when the second Philadelphia Mint was opened. The man-powered screw presses were replaced with steam-powered coining presses within a few years. Other equipment was also mechanized.

O Mint mark on Morgan dollar reverse.

The growth of the United States Mint was linked to the westward expansion of the nation. Despite the improved output of the second Philadelphia Mint, by the mid-1830s additional coining facilities were needed. Gold discoveries in the Appalachian Mountains triggered America's first gold rush.

To meet the growing coinage needs of an ever-expanding country and population, Congress authorized the first Branch Mints in 1835, in Dahlonega, Ga.; Charlotte, N.C.; and New Orleans. All of the Southern Branch Mints opened for coining in 1838. The Dahlonega and Charlotte Mints were never prolific; they struck gold coins only, generally in smaller numbers than struck at Philadelphia. The New Orleans Mint was a better match for the Philadelphia Mint, striking both silver and gold coins.

When William Marshall discovered gold in California on the American River in 1848, the find triggered the biggest gold rush in U.S.

history. Ever larger numbers of men with visions of unlimited wealth undertook the hazardous journey from the East to the gold fields. California became a state in 1850; the population grew, as did the need for coinage. However, the closest Mint was in New Orleans. A number of private mints sprang up in California, striking pioneer gold coins out of native gold and fulfilling a need for coinage the U.S. Mint was unable to fill until Congress authorized the San Francisco Mint in 1852. The government Mint began operations in 1854, striking both silver and gold coins.

S Mint mark on Washington quarter obverse.

Even as thousands moved west to seek their fortune, the nation moved ever closer to war. California had entered the Union a free state, without slavery, the result of the Compromise of 1850. However, the Compromise only postponed the inevitable. The sectional troubles that had been tearing the country apart for decades burst into full, horrible bloom following the election of Abraham Lincoln as president in 1860. One by one, the Southern states seceded from the Union. As Louisiana, Georgia and North Carolina left the Union, the federal Mints in those states changed hands. There was no need for Southern troops to use force to capture the facilities; the majority of Mint officials and employees at the three facilities were sympathetic to the Confederate cause. All three facilities struck small quantities of coins in early 1861, the New Orleans facility even striking four half dollars with a special Confederate design on one side. However, coinage at all three Mints ended in 1861 due to dwindling Confederate resources. The Dahlonega and Charlotte Mints never reopened following the war; New Orleans resumed coining activities from 1879 to 1909.

Other gold and silver discoveries in the West, particularly in Nevada and Colorado, triggered the need for additional Mints.

The federal government in 1863 purchased the private Clark, Gruber & Co. mint in Denver and extensively remodeled the building. Although officially designated a Branch Mint, it served instead as an Assay Office (a place where precious metals ores are refined and tested). A new Mint was built in Denver at the turn of the century, opening for coining in 1906. The Denver Mint has struck coins of copper, copper-nickel, silver and gold.

CC Mint mark on Coronet $10 eagle reverse.

The Carson City Mint in Nevada opened

in 1870 and closed in 1893. The Carson City Mint struck silver and gold coins only.

The San Francisco Mint closed after striking 1955 coinage, its presses no longer needed to keep up with the national demand for coinage. Congress revised its status in 1962, naming it the San Francisco Assay Office. However, as noted, a coin shortage struck the country, and in 1965, the Assay Office resumed striking coins. The facility regained Mint status in 1988.

The U.S. Mint facility at West Point has been striking coins since 1974, although none of the coins struck for circulation there have borne the W Mint mark. The West Point Mint is the newest Branch Mint, having gained Mint status in early 1988; previously, it had been the West Point Bullion Depository (opening in 1938).

Currently, four federal Mints operate in the United States. The Philadelphia Mint strikes all denominations of coins for circulation and some collectors' coins; the engraving staff works there; and the Philadelphia Mint produces coining dies. The Denver Mint is in its original 1906 building, although there have been recent additions; it, too, strikes a combination of circulation issues and collectors' coins, and has had a die production shop since 1996. The San Francisco Mint is in its third building, opened in 1937; today, it strikes coins for collectors only, although it struck coins for circulation as recently as 1980. The West Point Mint is currently used only for collectors' programs and bullion coins, although it has struck coins for circulation in the recent past. All platinum and most gold bullion and gold commemorative coins are struck at West Point. A special 1996-W Roosevelt dime was struck at West Point to commemorate the 50th anniversary of the coin's introduction. It was included at no extra charge in 1996 Uncirculated Mint sets.

W Mint mark on Roosevelt dime obverse

How to buy and sell coins

9

New collectors often ask two questions: "How do I buy coins?" and "How do I sell coins?"

There have long been traditional methods of buying and selling coins—a local coin dealer, mail-order dealers, at auction and from government Mints. Now, even more buying and selling venues exist with the advent of the Internet and easy access to online auctions at such Web sites as eBay.

All collectors, but especially new ones, need to be aware of the benefits and pitfalls of each method of buying and selling coins. This chapter will offer some advice based on years of experience by *Coin World* staff members, both as collectors and as journalists observing the coin collecting market.

How to buy coins

"How do you buy coins?"

"What's the best way to buy coins?"

"Where do I find coins for my collection?"

Such questions are frequently asked by beginning collectors. They're being asked more and more by those who once collected and are now re-entering the hobby, encountering a marketplace somewhat different from what they remember or experienced years ago.

One fundamental hasn't changed: Know what coin or coins you want to buy. "Knowing" necessarily today includes understanding how to grade coins and being cognizant of how the grade relates to the coin's value (see the chapter on grading for more information about the topic).

Additionally, the firmer grasp one has of the history of the coin or the series, its characteristics, mintage, survivability rates (rarity) and current value, the more one's chances improve for making good purchases. Therein rests the wisdom of the often-quoted adage: "Buy the book before the coin."

For our discussion, we'll assume Joe Collector has at least covered the basics of acquiring knowledge, whether from books, educational seminars, videos, coin shows or coin club attendance. He has a reliable and up-to-date price guide. And he's now ready to venture into buying.

Where does one start?

The most likely place, especially for a true beginner, is nearby: a local bank, a nearby coin shop or the comfort of one's own home, using mail order or the Internet.

One of the easiest and most nonthreatening ways to ease into the hobby is to "buy" coins at the bank: That is, exchange paper dollars for rolls of coins—any of the circulating denominations—to search for dates and Mint marks at one's leisure. The out-of-pocket costs can be limited, and the fun builds.

To find coins not readily available in circulation, other nearby sources can be tapped.

In *Coin World's* most recent readership survey, 59 percent of those polled said their numismatic purchases in the previous 12 months were made from dealers/retail coin shops.

Although local retail coin shops and hobby stores with a good selection of collectible coins are not as prevalent as they once were, they do exist in most large metropolitan areas and some are still to be found in small towns and cities throughout the country. A check in the Yellow Pages of the local telephone directory or the classified ad section of the local newspaper often will reveal whether a local dealer or retail shop exists.

Most coin dealers start out as collectors. Many continue to collect although they may also have elected to become professional numismatists. Coin dealers often have expertise in more than one collecting specialty and may be willing to provide collecting tips, especially to new collectors. They usually have numismatic reference books and may be willing to assist collectors in research.

Absent dealer referral, finding a local or regional coin club may be a matter of checking the community calendar or meeting announcements in the local newspaper, contacting the local library or the local Chamber of Commerce, or contacting the American Numismatic Association (**www.money.org**), which maintains an online roster of coin clubs.

Coin clubs generally provide members opportunities for buying, selling and trading coins and other numismatic collectibles during or after meetings. Many sponsor periodic coin shows, affording local collectors the opportunity to purchase from dealers and collectors on a regional or state basis. Large clubs sometimes attract dealers from across the country to their shows. In addition, commercial entities sponsor both small and large coin shows.

The big advantage of finding coins at a local coin shop, a local club meeting or during a coin show is the ability to inspect coins firsthand, without major travel expense. Because some of the large regional and national coin shows alternate show sites, many collectors have an opportunity to attend a show offering several hundred dealers under one roof on a fairly frequent basis. A good source of upcoming coin shows and locations is the Event and Show Calendar in publications such as *Coin World* (online at **www.coinworld.com**).

Many collectors like the convenience of buying coins by mail order. It is especially handy for collectors unable or too busy to travel frequently to shows or attend coin club meetings.

Today the mail-order marketplace offers the most extensive purchasing opportunities. *Coin World*, as the largest weekly numismatic publication, through its advertising pages is the largest mail-order market by virtue of the number of advertisers and the wide variety of numismatic items available for purchase.

As with any buying experience, it pays to comparison shop. Another time-proven adage is especially important to bear in mind: "There are no Santa Clauses in numismatics." A variation on this theme is: "If it looks too good to be true, it probably is." As in any community or marketplace, there are dealers (in coins) who conduct business honestly and there are those who conduct business dishonestly. Collectors need to learn the differences between an honest dealer and dishonest one.

Collectors who expect to purchase coins from advertisements in *Coin World* or any other periodical should seek out and acquaint themselves with the publication's basic mail-order policy. This policy is an attempt to ensure equity for both buyers and sellers. A key component of the basic mail-order policy is inspection and return privileges. (Publications differ on the standards and requirements, so check before ordering.)

A cardinal rule of successful buying by mail order is upon receipt to immediately inspect the ordered coin or other numismatic material to verify that it is what was ordered. Do not remove the coin from the holder in which it was shipped; to do so voids any return privileges. If the coin does not meet expectations, it is incumbent upon the collector to return the coin to the seller within the time allowed.

Another popular way of acquiring coins is from auctions. Auction lot previewing is generally accorded potential buyers a day or two in advance of public auctions, generally at the auction site.

Veteran collectors and dealers who buy coins at auction caution to "never bid blind." That is, they suggest any coin being considered for purchase at auction should be examined. They also suggest if you don't know how to grade coins that you seek the assistance of a professional coin dealer. Often the professional, for a modest fee, will buy coins for you or act as your agent at an auction.

Another important tip veteran collectors offer is to establish a bidding limit before the sale begins, whether you are personally bidding or you have contracted an agent to bid for you. Do price research on the desired coin before the sale begins. Set a maximum price you are willing to pay and stick with it. One should also factor in the buyer's fee. Most U.S. auction firms charge a 15 percent or higher buyer's fee—15 percent of the hammer price is added onto the hammer bid to arrive at the total price.

The largest and most direct sources of new coin issues are the government Mints and sometimes private mints that produce the coins. The U.S. Mint advertises its products in coin periodicals, but it also sells directly to the public via mail order and over its Web site (**www.usmint.gov**). Some Mint products are available only through its Web site.

To obtain information and pre-issue offers from the U.S. Mint, a collector may sign up for the Mint's mailing list at the Mint Web site or telephone (800) 872-6468. Many foreign Mints also sell by mail order or through business agents established within the United States.

For the truly adventurous, occasional sources to find coins are estate auctions and flea markets. Since the auctioneers selling this material often have no specialized coin knowledge, bidders should carefully inspect each lot before bidding, in order to confirm description, grade and authenticity. Depending on the material offered and the knowledge level of the competing bidders, such sales either may offer bargains, or bids may reach levels well above the coins' market values.

Whatever the source, the key to successful coin buying is to know what you are looking for and what you are willing to pay for it.

How to sell coins

"Where can I sell my coins?"

Such a seemingly simple question is not so simply answered, although it is a question frequently asked by beginning collectors, those who have been away from the hobby for a number of years, and by family members who have recently inherited a coin collection.

Let's begin at the beginning.

The first rule of thumb is know what you have to sell. Knowing entails identifying the coin or coins in the collection by type, date, Mint mark and variety, if appropriate. Equally important is knowing the state of preservation or grade. Grade is particularly important if one intends to sell United States coins because a coin's "condition" or grade is a primary determinant of value.

Also important to value is the coin's rarity.

Even rarity does not automatically mean that a coin is of great value. There are some rare coins that can be purchased for modest sums simply because few people are interested in collecting them or purchasing them.

Ultimately a coin's market value is determined by demand. Demand is determined by the number of buyers desirous of acquiring the coin. Collectors are the ultimate buyers for most coins. Collectors primarily buy a coin because it is "needed" or "fits" in their collections.

Virtually all of the basic information needed to identify and grade coins is available in print, online or video form. Current retail values can be found in price guides and regular updates such as the monthly *Coin Values* published as a supplement in *Coin World* and sold on newsstands and the weekly edition at Coin World Online (**www.coinvaluesonline.com**).

Additional ways of acquiring information include talking with coin collectors and coin dealers and attending coin shows, coin club meetings and educational presentations. However, if one is unable or unwilling to spend the time necessary to acquire basic knowledge about coins and their values, he or she may wish to engage the services of a professional numismatist or professional coin appraiser. Professionals, whether dealers or appraisers, usually charge an hourly rate and will provide a preliminary estimate of cost of the appraisal based on the number of coins to be evaluated and the time needed to perform the service. If a dealer is providing an estimate with intent to purchase, he or she may waive the appraisal fee. Under such circumstances, the seller may wish to have more than one prospective buyer provide an estimate of value and submit a proposal to purchase.

If the seller is the person who acquired the coins, he or she likely will have some ideas about prospective buyers. The most logical candidates are other collectors or dealers specializing in the coins one has for sale. Often collectors make acquaintances with others in their collecting fields through local coin clubs or regional or national organizations. Many local coin clubs hold "club auctions" in which members buy and sell coins. Some clubs hold member auctions as often as they meet. Others sponsor "bid-boards" on which members can list coins for sale or allow members to advertise items for sale in the club's newsletter. Regional and national specialty organizations offer similar venues for members to buy, sell or trade their numismatic collectibles.

Clubs and organizations also sponsor shows, inviting members, local coin dealers and dealers from out of state or from various collecting specialties to buy and sell on the coin show's bourse.

"Bourse" is the French word for "exchange." Thus, a coin bourse is literally a place to buy and sell coins and other numismatic collectibles. Dealers pay a fee to the show promoter to have a presence on the bourse. Usually this means the show promoter provides a display case, lights, and a table and chairs at an assigned space on the floor where the dealer may transact business.

If selling coins is your prime objective at a coin show, the best use of time would be to first identify those dealers who are selling the various types and grades of coins that you may have for sale. The best way to determine this is to spend time going from table to table and looking at what is on display in the dealer's case. After identifying the most likely candidates, the next step is to inquire as to whether the dealer is interested in buying. You will be expected to be able to generally describe your coins by type and grade and have them available for inspection in a reasonably organized and efficient manner. The dealer may not be interested at all. He may already be overstocked and have a large inventory of coins just like yours. If he expresses no interest, thank him politely and move on to the next dealer that you have reason to believe may be interested.

If the dealer looks at your coin or coins and offers a price, you will be expected to respond as to whether the price quoted is agreeable. Sometimes rather than quoting a price, the dealer may ask: "What do you want for this?" or "What's your price?" When asked, be prepared to give a serious and reasonable answer. It is your responsibility as the seller to know the value of what you are selling and to be able to make a decision as to what price is acceptable.

In general, dealers expect to buy at wholesale. The wholesale market has a rather wide range, from 30 to 40 percent of the retail price up to 80 percent and sometimes higher. The price a dealer quotes depends on his individual needs. It is not unusual to obtain different bids on the same coin from different dealers. It is up to the seller to determine when his price has been met and whether he desires to sell the coin.

Although some dealers will bargain, others are not so inclined, especially if they are only marginally interested in purchasing. You may have a price in mind for the initial response and a "fall-back" or bottom line in case bargaining is a possibility. However, have those numbers in mind before approaching any prospective buyer.

Sometimes buyers will be interested only in certain dates or certain grades. If you are attempting to sell a collection, determine whether your strategy is to sell it intact or to sell some or all of the coins individually. Often other collectors or dealers may be interested in key dates or semi-key dates and have little or no interest in purchasing the entire collection.

Also, some dealers today only buy and sell coins that have been graded by a third-party grading service and sonically sealed in plastic holders known as "slabs." Upon your initial inquiry, the dealer may ask whether your coin is "raw" or "slabbed." The term "raw" as used in the coin marketplace refers to a coin that is not encapsulated and graded by a third-party grading service. It may benefit you to have the rarer and more valuable coins in your collection graded by a major grading service; having them slabbed may make them easier to sell. However, low-value coins generally should not be slabbed; the cost of the slabbing may exceed the value of the coin.

Many collectors who are ready to sell coins do not have the time or the inclination to travel to coin shows or club meetings. Thus, mail order becomes an option. Seasoned collectors sometimes sell their coins via "fixed-price" lists that they advertise in the classified sections of publications such as *Coin World* or to individuals whom they have identified as having an interest in purchasing coins they may have. Classified ads also are a vehicle for selling specific coins.

Many dealers who advertise in publications such as *Coin World* buy as well as sell coins. Often they will list coins that they are interested in obtaining. In most cases, the transaction is contingent upon the dealer being able to inspect the coin, to confirm grade. Whenever sending coins via mail, a cover letter stating terms of sale and an inventory list of what is being offered should be included in the package. In addition, coins should be sent by registered mail and insured.

Transactions can be conducted entirely by mail. Before sending any coins, the seller should inquire as to whether the dealer or potential collector-buyer is interested. Again, terms of sale should be stated in a forthright manner and an inventory list presented, listing coin type, date, Mint mark, variety, grade and any other important information about the coin. The seller should list a price at which he desires to sell. If he does not list a price, he may ask the dealer to quote a price.

Coins should never be sent on a "blind" inquiry. They should be forwarded only after a prospective buyer has expressed interest in purchasing. If possible, the seller should maintain a photographic record of any coins sent to a prospective buyer. Absent good photographs, detailed inventory records, including grade, should be kept by the seller in order to be certain that any coins returned are the same ones he sent for possible purchase (coin switching should not be a problem as long as you deal with an established dealer with a good reputation).

Sometimes dealers or other collectors will take groups of coins or collections on consignment. Consignment agreements should be made in writing and should detail the coins, terms of consignment (percentage the consignment agent will receive for selling the coins) and the length of time covered by the agreement.

Public auction is a popular method of selling collectible coins, especially extensive collections and highly collectible coins. Most auction firms that advertise in *Coin World* specialize in numismatic collectibles. They have extensive lists of identified customers who have purchased coins in the past, thus providing greater exposure to potential buyers.

Most of the numismatic auction firms have full-time staff that research and prepare descriptions of the coins that they publish in an auction catalog provided to prospective buyers. Most auction houses also extensively advertise forthcoming auctions to the widest possible audiences. Often auction preview days are designated just prior to the sale so that prospective buyers or their agents can inspect the coins. Auction firms charge the seller a fee, usually based on a percentage of the price the coin achieves at auction. Reputable auction firms require consignors to sign contracts, which state the terms and conditions of the sale. In selecting an auction firm to sell your coins, it would be important to read and compare consignment contracts.

You should contact more than one auction house and seek to gain the best deal possible. When the coin market is hot, auction houses will compete with each other to obtain desirable consignments.

Depending on the number of coins to be sold in an auction and whether specialized material is being offered, the number of days between consignment and the actual sale date can vary. There could also be a delay of from 30 to 60 days from the date of sale until the consignor receives payment in traditional auctions.

The impact of the Internet on buyers mentioned earlier also holds true for sellers. Sellers may wish to register with an online auction site and offer their coins directly to collectors worldwide. As with buying coins over the Internet, sellers should also take precautions. A seller may not want to ship coins to a successful bidder until payment has been received. Sellers also should be sure they describe their coins accurately in order to avoid deceiving potential bidders.

Some collectors buy coins with the avowed intent never to sell any. Other collectors buy and sell on a regular basis. Whether the collector sells his coins or they will be passed on to future generations, good records and inventory lists will assist when it does come time to sell.

As we have shown, there are many ways to sell coins. Each seller must determine the best method, depending on the time and energy that can be devoted to the activity.

Internet transactions

Although the majority of transactions that take place on the Internet benefit both the seller and buyer, it's important not to gaze on your computer screen with rose-colored glasses. Some online transactions turn out badly for the buyer—the item sold is either inaccurately (whether intentionally or not) described or the seller never intends to provide the item once the fee is collected.

The buyer must always be wary, but particularly wary online. It is best to shop with a trusted dealer or company that is known for its exemplary service either online or in the "real" world. It is also best to shop with a company that is more than just *familiar* with numismatic items. Remember that part of the price of every coin in a dealer's inventory is the value of his or her expertise.

Before you buy, be aware of the return policy and the amount of time you have to examine an item to see if it is satisfactory to you (if no return privileges are offered, it is probably a good idea to not purchase or bid on the item).

Never give your credit card number unless using a "secured site," one that encrypts your personal and credit card information for its trip through the information highway. It is not advisable to e-mail that information, since e-mail is not encrypted.

While most sites that accept credit card numbers have taken adequate measures to ensure security, it is best to refer to the padlock icon that appears within the browser (on Netscape, find it in the toolbar; on Internet Explorer, find it in the icons at the bottom of the window) before submitting that type of information. Although there are no 100 percent guarantees, as long as the padlock appears closed, it is at least as secure as, say, handing your credit card to a waiter at a restaurant.

Regardless of how you submit your order, if possible know a company's physical address and telephone number before you order.

Online auctions

Before you bid on any online auction site, you have to register. Always read the user's agreement carefully to know what kind of obligations and recourse you will have. Before you bid on an item, pay close attention to the return policies of the seller. Be sure to contact that person if you have any questions.

Often online auctions will provide rating information about buyers and sellers. People who have done business with these sellers in the past will rate their attitude, promptness, honesty and so on. Keep this information in mind when buying or selling. Keep also in mind that rating systems are not foolproof; some sellers may solicit positive feedback from friends rather than from actual buyers.

Don't be too quick to trust a photograph of the lot. Photo quality is often poor and inconsistent. Digital images can be enhanced. The item offered may not be the item delivered. Of course, a photo might also be very telling; you may be able to determine the authenticity of a questionable item by looking at the photo.

This brings up another important point: There is a certain amount of risk in not purchasing or selling through a dealer or numismatic auctioneer. You don't get the benefit of their expertise and staff or return policies.

While a vast number of individuals selling coins on the Internet are honest people, there are some who either accidentally (due to their limited knowledge) or intentionally take advantage of or defraud a customer. Because the Internet affords all users a certain amount of anonymity, criminals find they can use this to their advantage and disappear.

There are three broad categories of auctioneers on the Internet: auction venues (middlemen), live auctioneers on the Internet (a company that incorporates online bidding into its live auctions) and Internet auction companies (companies that catalog and auction consigned coins).

Storage and preservation

10

Coins and paper money change over time, and not necessarily for the better. Collectors, dealers and investors too often neglect this simple maxim. Deterioration is at odds with the long-accepted belief that the better the condition of a numismatic collectible, the more it is worth.

The greater awareness of coin and paper money storage and preservation in recent decades has resulted in safer storage materials being offered. However, some coins and paper money sold, bought and stored are probably being housed in holders that do not offer much protection or may even cause harm.

Everyday hazards

Metals vary in their resistance to corrosion; however, all coinage metals can be affected by everyday hazards. Gold is probably the most resistant coinage metal, being unaffected by most corrosive agents. A problem arises with some gold coins because they contain copper or silver, and a poor mix can result in areas of high concentration of copper or silver that can corrode, causing streaks, spotting and other surface blemishes.

Fortunately, this does not often occur. Gold coins are remarkably resistant to damage from storage in dangerous coin holders, polluted atmospheres and under other adverse conditions.

Silver is also quite resistant, but subject to tarnish, especially in the presence of sulfur compounds and nitrates. Since sulfur and nitrate compounds are frequent components of air pollution, modern times are especially hard on silver coins.

As with gold, most silver U.S. coins contain copper. Since the percentage of copper is about 10 percent, it is possible to oxidize copper at the coin's surface, resulting in green to blue corrosion. Some collectors consider attractive, iridescent patina desirable on silver coins. This patina results from complex chemical processes over a long period, thus the rainbow hues seen on some 19th century silver coins.

Collectors should remember that toning and tarnishing represent the same thing: a chemical change to the metal on the surface of the coin. The "difference" between toning and tarnish is the degree of chemical change and how collectors and dealers perceive the change.

Essentially, "toning" is used to describe attractive, desirable color; "tarnish" is used to describe unattractive, undesirable color. If unchecked, desirable toning can progress to undesirable tarnish.

There have been modern-day attempts to duplicate natural toning when it was discovered that toned coins sometimes bring premium prices. By experimenting with various chemicals and techniques, some found that they could produce artificial toning. "Midnight labs" operated by "coin doctors" in various parts of the country turn out these coins. The "doctors" have developed many different techniques to enhance a coin's appearance. Most forms of rapid artificial toning are considered unacceptable, although disagreement exists over the appropriateness of certain procedures.

Beware when toning is used to cover up signs of light wear or "rub" on an Uncirculated coin or hairlines on a Proof coin.

The copper-nickel alloy used in U.S. coins is even more susceptible to chemical attack because of the 75 percent copper present. Not only is it affected by atmospheric contaminants, but it is also more subject to electrochemical action (battery action) than silver and gold. Small black spots, called "carbon spots," are sometimes seen. These may be the result of a contaminant imbedded in the coin's surface, which later corrodes or oxidizes, or causes the surrounding metal to corrode or oxidize, or the presence of an impurity in the metal that corrodes faster than the alloy of the coin.

Copper is one of the most fragile commonly used U.S. coinage materials. Upon oxidation, it forms green to blue copper oxide. Copper alloy coins are very susceptible to carbon spots. The zinc cents, first produced for 1982, are plated with a thin layer of copper and are especially fragile. If the copper plating is broken, the coin can corrode rapidly.

The atmosphere

It should be obvious that airborne gases can adversely affect a coin. Normal pollutants found in the air can cause long-term problems. They can combine with oxygen at the coin's surface. Gases produced while a coin is in a plastic holder, coming from the plastic itself, can also have an adverse effect.

The atmosphere also contains moisture and dust, both dangerous to a coin's surface. Both are carriers of oxygen and other compounds, bringing them into intimate contact with the coin's surface. Since we don't have much direct control over the air around us, the only way to protect a coin from the atmospheric pollutants is to isolate it in a container that is airtight and inert, so the container itself won't contaminate the coin.

Contaminants

Coins are dirty, even when coming off the coinage press! Since the metal is rolled, punched, annealed, struck by dies and handled by various mechanical devices, even a Mint State coin may be contaminated with metallic particles, oil and grease, rag dust, and other foreign material.

Once the coins leave the Mint, they are further contaminated by counting machines, rolling machines and handling by the collector himself.

Coin holders themselves can contaminate the coin. They may contain dust particles picked up by static electricity from the air or surfaces. Many also contain paper or cardboard dust, highly dangerous to pristine coins. Some plastic holders give off dangerous gases due to their volatility, including acetic, hydrochloric and other acids. Some "sweat," and the liquid coming out of the plastic is deposited on the coin, causing corrosion.

Dust particles on the coins are dangerous because they themselves may be corrosive. When a particle rests on a coin, it can cause a localized chemical reaction with the coinage metal. A spot may form as a result, and the surface of the coin pits directly under the dust particle. Experience indicates that paper and cardboard dust particles are especially prone to forming this kind of corrosion.

Handling

Improper handling causes abrasion, decreasing the value of the coin itself, and exposes fresh metal that can oxidize and corrode. Although every collector should be aware of these facts, some can be seen carelessly handling coins. Don't allow coins to contact each other or other surfaces if you value their long-term life.

When you lay a coin down, be aware of the surface. Is it clean? If not, the coin may pick up contaminants. Coins stored in slide-type albums may develop "slide mark" abrasion on the high points from sliding the windows past the coins.

Don't eat or speak over a coin, for you may inadvertently spray spittle on the coin. Human saliva can be quite corrosive to a coin over time.

Storage materials

The factors described will have an adverse effect on coins over time, but can be reduced and perhaps eliminated by careful selection of materials for storage or display. It is foolish not to take the steps necessary to protect one's coins.

The following statement may shock you, but it is a fact: Many of the coin holders on the market are not suitable for long-term storage. The following first discusses some general subjects and then the most common coin holders and their suitability.

Basic criteria

Susan L. Maltby is a Toronto-based conservation expert and author of a monthly column in *Coin World*, "Preserving Collectibles." Over the years that she has written her column, she frequently has addressed safe and unsafe storage materials.

She recommends coin holders that are see-through (allowing the owner to view the coin within the holder), made of a safe material (more on this in the next section), easy to use (a holder or album that permits one to remove the coin without risking damage to it) and that hold the coin securely (a coin that slides or rolls in its holder may be subject to wear).

Maltby identifies the following plastics as safe and therefore suitable to coin holders and albums: polyethylene, polypropylene, Mylar D (polyethylene terephthalate), Kodar (similar in composition to Mylar D), and polymethyl methacrylate (Plexiglas is a brand name for this plastic).

She cautions against using holders or albums made of cellulose acetate.

Maltby warns that collectors should never use holders made of the following: glassine, polyvinyl chloride (PVC), polyvinylidene chloride (Saran) and paper (the commonly used paper envelopes are not see-through and the purity of the paper can be a concern, she says).

Coin albums

Traditional cardboard albums with plastic slides are potentially bad because of the cardboard and paper, the abrasion possible with the plastic slides, and the fact that a large number of coins are exposed at the same time when the slides are pulled.

These albums also don't protect against the atmosphere or moisture since the cardboard is porous. Some newer albums are made of plastic, and though they eliminate the slides, they are unsuitable because the plastic itself may not be inert. Some of them "sweat" over time, causing tarnish or green corrosion. Coin boards without any covering should obviously never be used for high-grade, valuable coins.

Two-by-twos

Probably the most common coin holder is the cardboard 2-by-2-inch or 1.5-by-1.5-inch square container. They come as one piece usually, with a Mylar window, and are stapled or glued together with the coin placed in between. They are inexpensive, one can view both obverse and reverse, and the cardboard provides space for identifying the coin.

Maltby notes that while the cardboard is potentially dangerous, the Mylar separates the coin from the cardboard, affording the coin protection. She said she has examined coins that have been housed in these holders for decades and most of the coins have held up well.

One potential problem involves the rusting of the staples in high-humidity climates. Regular monitoring should keep this problem to a minimum. Use silica gel to help with the humidity and replace holders with rusting staples with new holders.

Another potential: The Mylar plastic is thin and can tear somewhat easily, so a collector should use care in placing the coins into the holders.

Flips

This is the name given to the 2-by-2-inch plastic holders. They usually have two sections hinged at the top, and one section contains a paper insert for labeling.

Some are made of polyvinyl chloride, a dangerous plastic because it can combine with oxygen to form compounds that will attack the coin. Do not use these holders.

Some are made of Mylar, a polyethylene derivative, and these are basically inert, but are moisture permeable. The Mylar holders are reasonably safe for short-term storage though. There is a possibility of contaminating the interiors of the flips with paper dust from the inserts. In addition, the flips do not seal at the top; thus, the coins are exposed to the atmosphere.

Plexiglas

Three-layer Plexiglas holders are available for single coins or sets. They are much better than most holders, but have the disadvantage of high cost. However, Plexiglas contains polymethacrylic acid, which can attack the coin's surface. The coins usually are loose in the holes and can rattle around, abrading the plastic and picking up dust from the plastic; thus, the acid can contact the coin. Plexiglas can also absorb moisture.

Polystyrene holders

Single coin or Proof and Mint holders, as well as roll tubes, are available. Made of clear brittle plastic, the holders usually snap together. Polystyrene is one of the few inert plastics and therefore can be considered safe. The edges of these holders, however, do not seal airtight.

Slabs

The sonically sealed plastic encapsulations used by third-party grading services, euphemistically known as "slabs," offer some protection but are not a panacea for all storage problems. Contaminants trapped on a coin when it is being slabbed can continue to cause damage after slabbing. Over time, corrosive chemicals can permeate the plastic and attack the coin housed within the slab. Coins can tone inside a slab that is kept in a corrosive atmosphere.

Intercept Shield

A new product was introduced in a variety of coin storage systems during the summer of 1999 that holds the potential for protecting coins for decades, according to the developers. The technology was developed and patented by Lucent Technologies Bell Labs to protect sensitive electrical components from atmospheric contamination and corrosion. The technology, which is being incorporated into the lining of coin albums and folders, 2-by-2-inch and slab-sized storage boxes, individual slab storage boxes and inserts placed inside slabs and envelopes, absorbs harmful chemicals and keeps them away from coins stored within the devices. Under proper conditions, the Intercept Shield could protect coins from toning for decades, according to testing by Lucent.

Collectors should base their holder choices on the quality and value of the coins in their collections. Not many experienced collectors would choose to house a $5,000 coin in a 5-cent holder, nor would many send a coin worth $1 to a grading service that charges $15 to grade and encapsulate the coin in a slab. Choose the safe holder that best suits your needs and budget.

Following these suggestions will not guarantee that a coin will not deteriorate, but the methods are the best known to ensure that coins that are the pride and joy of a collector will survive for the lifetime of this and future generations of collectors.

U.S. coinage history

11

United States coinage history is a fascinating subject involving economics, politics, artistic expression, personal rivalry, technological breakthroughs, gold and silver discoveries and more. In short, the history of the country's coinage is the history of the United States.

Denominations

Since coinage began at the Philadelphia Mint in 1793, more than 20 denominations have been used as circulating, commemorative and bullion coins of the United States. In platinum, the denominations have been $100, $50, $25 and $10. In gold, the denominations have been $50 (commemorative and bullion coins only), $25 (the American Eagle bullion coin), $20, $10, $5, $3, $2.50 and $1. The U.S. Mint has issued one platinum-gold ringed bimetallic coin, with a denomination of $10. Among silver coins (many later changed to copper-nickel clad by the Coinage Act of 1965), the Mint has issued the silver dollar, the Trade dollar, the half dollar (50 cents), the quarter dollar (25 cents), 20-cent coin, dime (10 cents), half dime (5 cents) and 3-cent coin. The Mint has also struck copper-nickel 5-cent, 3-cent and 1-cent coins; a bronze 2-cent coin; cents in copper, copper-nickel, bronze, brass, zinc-coated steel and copper-plated zinc; and a copper half cent.

Production of U.S. coinage began in earnest in 1793 with the production of copper half cents and cents. The Mint began striking silver half dimes, half dollars and dollars in 1794, and silver dimes and quarter dollars in 1796. Gold coinage began in 1795 with the $5 half eagle and the $10 eagle, followed by the $2.50 quarter eagle in 1796.

During the earlier years of the U.S. Mint, not all denominations were struck in all years. In 1804, coinage of the silver dollar ceased with the striking of 1803-dated coins; dollar coinage was not resumed until 1836. A few gold eagles were struck in 1804, but coinage of the $10 coin then ceased until 1838. No quarter eagles were struck from 1809 through 1820. Production of the other denominations was sporadic except for the cent. Planchet shortages prevented any 1815-dated cents from being produced; otherwise, the cent series has been issued without interruption since 1793.

Meanwhile, as the country's borders and population grew, the monetary system grew with them. The denominations authorized in

1792 were no longer sufficient to meet the country's monetary needs at the midpoint of the 19th century, and new denominations were authorized. Congress authorized a gold dollar and a gold $20 double eagle, both under the Act of March 3, 1849. Two years later, a silver 3-cent coin was authorized to facilitate the purchase of 3-cent postage stamps. A gold $3 coin was introduced in 1854, again to help in the purchase of 3-cent stamps (in sheets of 100). A smaller, copper-nickel cent was approved in 1857, replacing the pure copper large cent. The half cent was eliminated, also in 1857.

The American Civil War erupted in 1861, causing massive hoarding of coinage and the necessity of coinage substitutes like encased postage stamps, privately produced copper-alloy cent-like tokens and finally, the first federal paper money (including denominations of less than a dollar). More changes to U.S. coins began in 1864, when the composition of the cent was changed to 95 percent copper and 5 percent tin and zinc (bronze), and when a bronze 2-cent coin was introduced.

A copper-nickel 3-cent coin was issued beginning in 1865 to circulate alongside the silver 3-cent coin (the latter was eliminated after 1873). A copper-nickel 5-cent coin was introduced in 1866; the silver half dime was eliminated after 1873.

In a bit of numismatic trivia that might be surprising to most noncollectors, the first coin to be called a "nickel" was the copper-nickel cent, issued from 1857 to 1864 in two design types (Flying Eagle and Indian Head). The copper-nickel 3-cent coin was also called a "nickel" by 19th century users of the coin, with the copper-nickel 5-cent coin, introduced in 1866, finally appropriating the nickname. The nickname persists to this day, although the term "nickel" as a denomination appears in none of the legislation authorizing the 5-cent coin. The nickname is based on the copper-nickel alloy that composes the coin, although ironically, the alloy is 75% copper and just 25% nickel.

The year 1873 brought significant, unprecedented changes to the U.S. coinage system, under the Act of Feb. 12, 1873. Four denominations were abolished by the act: the 2-cent coin, the silver 3-cent coin, the half dime and the standard silver dollar. It authorized a Trade silver dollar for use by merchants in Asia (Congress revoked the Trade dollar's legal tender status in the United States in 1876; it has since been restored). The weights of the silver dime, quarter dollar and half dollar were increased. In addition, the act, in effect, demonetized silver and placed the United States on a gold standard.

Another new denomination was authorized in 1875—the silver 20-cent coin. The coin was struck for circulation in 1875 and 1876, setting the record for the shortest-lived silver denomination in U.S. coinage history. Coinage of Proof 20-cent coins continued in 1877 and 1878.

Congress reauthorized the standard silver dollar in 1878 after lobbying efforts on behalf of the silver mine owners. The denomination would be struck through 1904, when production was halted (millions of the coins rested in vaults unneeded and unused in circulation).

The gold dollar and gold $3 denominations were struck for the last time in 1889.

The circulating silver dollar was resurrected twice for circulation: in 1921, to continue through 1935; and in 1964. Although 1964-D Peace silver dollars were struck, the government withdrew support for them and ordered the coins destroyed, in part to ensure that none inadvertently entered circulation or collector circles. There is no credible evidence (though plenty of rumors) that any of the coins survive.

The copper-nickel dollar was introduced in 1971, and a smaller dollar (the Anthony dollar) was issued briefly from 1979 to 1981 and in 1999. A new golden-colored, Anthony-dollar sized dollar coin depicting Sacagawea entered circulation in 2000, but has not circulated widely. None of the 2002, 2003 or 2004 circulation-quality coins struck were released for circulation.

The standard silver dollar lives on in commemorative coinage, with nearly 50 different commemorative dollars struck from 1983 through 2004. In addition, there is a 1-ounce silver bullion coin that bears a $1 denomination (the American Eagle silver bullion coin).

Since the Mint Act of 1875, only three new denominations have been authorized, none for circulation. A gold $50 coin was approved to commemorate the 1915 Panama-Pacific International Exposition, held in San Francisco. More than 70 years later, in 1986, the $50 denomination was revived and a new denomination ($25) was authorized, both for the American Eagle gold bullion coin program. A $100 denomination was given to the 1-ounce platinum American Eagle bullion coin.

The last gold denominations struck for circulation occurred in 1933, when coinage of the eagle and double eagle ceased under President Franklin Roosevelt's anti-gold executive orders. The gold quarter eagles and half eagles were last struck in 1929. All gold coins struck since 1984 have been commemorative or bullion coins.

Designs

The story behind the designs of U.S. coinage is one of artistic experimentation and drone-like uniformity; of political necessity and political favoritism; of beauty tempered by the realities of the coining process.

The members of Congress who approved the original U.S. monetary system created design parameters that affect new U.S. coin designs even today. The Mint Act of April 2, 1792, specified that certain design features and legends appear on the coins that were authorized. On one side of all coins was to be an impression symbolic of Liberty, plus the word LIBERTY and the year of coinage. For the silver and gold coins, an eagle and UNITED STATES OF AMERICA were to appear on the reverse. The denomination was to appear on the reverses of the half cents and cents.

For more than 115 years in the history of U.S. coinage, Liberty was portrayed by allegorical female figures.

The 1793 half cents and cents introduced the allegorical themes used on U.S. coins: The half cent depicts a bust of Liberty with her hair flowing free. A Liberty Cap on a pole, a familiar symbol of Liberty in the American and French revolutions of the latter 18th century, rests on her right shoulder, giving the design its name: the Liberty Cap.

Since the Mint Act of 1792 required only the denomination to appear on the reverses of the copper coins, the Mint engravers had a free rein. The first half cents have a wreath on the reverse, a device used as late as 1958 on the Lincoln cent as two heads of wheat.

On the first cents of 1793, another Flowing Hair Liberty appears, though with no cap; the design was not popularly received: Liberty was said to look frightened. The public also panned the reverse design: a 15-link chain meant to represent the unity of the 15 states. The public believed the chain was a symbol of enslavement perceived to represent "a bad omen for Liberty." Changes in the design of both sides of the cent came rapidly; neither lasted more than a few weeks. A Wreath reverse replaced the Chain reverse, and a slightly different Flowing Hair Liberty was used on the obverse. Shortly after those designs were introduced, the unpopular obverse design was replaced with a Liberty Cap design similar to that on the half cent, and a revised version of the Wreath reverse replaced the original Wreath reverse. Thus, three distinct cents were struck with the 1793 date (Flowing Hair, Chain; Flowing Hair, Wreath; Liberty Cap, Wreath).

Additional design changes were instituted for the cent in 1796, when a Draped Bust design was introduced and used through 1807. Liberty appears without a cap, her hair falling over bare shoulders. Loose drapery covers Liberty's bust.

Another Liberty Head design called the Classic Head design was used on the cent from 1808 to 1814. It differs considerably from the earlier allegorical motifs, with Liberty wearing a ribbon inscribed with LIBERTY around her hair. Throughout the period from 1796 to 1814, different Wreath reverse designs were used. The wreath used with the Draped Bust designs consists of two branches tied together at the bottom by a ribbon with a bow. The wreath on the Classic Head cent consists of a single branch bent into a circle and secured at the bottom by a ribbon.

The design type introduced in 1816 on the large cent and used through 1857 is known broadly as the Coronet; it was paired with the one-branch Wreath reverse design. The Coronet Liberty design underwent many changes on the cent, with the distinctive versions known by various names, depending on the reference book. The cents of 1816 to 1835 (or to 1839) are called the Matron Head by some. The design went through a series of transitions from 1836 to 1839, with several distinctive types: Head of 1836, Head of 1838, Silly Head and Booby Head; the 1839 cents are found with all four types. The final version, the Braided Hair Coronet, was introduced in 1839 (making five versions of the design with that date) and used for the remainder of the series.

The Coronet Liberty design concept would prove one of the most versatile of the 19th century. A variation of the Coronet design would appear both on copper coins until 1857 and on most of the gold denominations from the 1830s to the first decade of the 20th century. The design is similar on all of the coins, depicting Liberty wearing a coronet inscribed with LIBERTY.

Designs for the half cent were generally similar to the cent's designs, although the timetable for introduction was often different. The half cent used a Liberty Cap design until 1797, and from 1800 to 1808 a Draped Bust design was used. The Classic Head design was used on the half cent from 1809 to 1836 and the Coronet design was introduced in 1840.

The silver coins of the 18th century feature designs similar to those on the copper coins. The silver coins used a Flowing Hair design in 1794 and 1795, and in 1795 and 1796, a Draped Bust design was introduced on all silver coins. The Capped Bust design was used first for the half dollar in 1807, with the dime following in 1809, the quarter dollar in 1815 and the half dime in 1829. The eagles appearing on the reverse of the silver coins appeared in several forms, first in a Small Eagle design that some critics likened to a pigeon. A Heraldic Eagle was used on the dollar beginning in 1798, the half dollar in 1801 and the quarter dollar in 1804.

Allegorical Liberty figures with similar themes but somewhat different details were used on the early gold coins. A Capped Bust, Heraldic Eagle design was used from 1796 to 1807 for the quarter eagle, then replaced in 1808 with the one-year-only Capped Draped Bust type. The Capped Head quarter eagle was struck between 1821 and 1834. On the half eagle, the Capped Bust design was used from 1796 to 1807; the Small Eagle reverse was used from 1796 to 1798, and a Heraldic Eagle design was used from 1795 to 1807, concurrently with the Small Eagle at first. The Capped Draped Bust was used on the half eagle from 1807 to 1812, and the Capped Head, from 1813 to 1829. The Classic Head design was used briefly, from 1834 to 1838. For the $10 eagle, the Capped Bust design was used from 1795 to 1804, when production of the denomination ceased. On the reverse of the $10 coin, the Small Eagle was used from 1795 to 1797, and the Heraldic Eagle design was used from 1797 to 1804.

Production of the silver dollar resumed in 1836 with the Gobrecht dollar, named after the engraver credited with the design (sketches by several artists were used during the design process, but Gobrecht gets credit for the coin). The obverse depicts a Seated Liberty figure on a rock, her body draped in robes. The reverse depicts a Flying Eagle. This dollar was the first of several coins that would use a similar theme.

With the creation of the Seated Liberty design, a new age of uniformity ensued on U.S. coins. A modification of the Seated Liberty obverse design from the dollar was introduced on the half dime and dime in 1837, the quarter dollar in 1838 and the half dollar in 1839. An 1837 act dropped the requirement that an eagle appear on the reverses of the half dime and dime, permitting placement of a wreath on the half dime and dime that year. Eagles appeared on the new quarter dollar and half dollar, and the dollar received a new eagle design in 1840, with the Flying Eagle replaced by an eagle similar to those on the quarter dollar and half dollar.

Gold coins, too, entered the uniform age of coin designs when the Coronet (sometimes called Liberty Head) design was introduced in 1838 for the eagle, in 1839 for the half eagle and in 1840 for the quarter eagle. When the gold dollar and $20 double eagle were introduced in 1849 and 1850, respectively, the Coronet design was used for both. Like the silver coins, with the exception of the dollar, the gold coins would not break out of uniformity until the early 20th century.

A new theme was introduced in 1854 on the gold $3 coin, which depicts Liberty as an Indian Head portrait. The portrait, by James B. Longacre, was the first in a series of coinage tributes to the first native Americans. However, the portrait does not depict a true Indian; Longacre simply placed an Indian headdress on the same Liberty figure he would use in many different versions of the design. The reverse depicts a wreath. Later in 1854, Longacre created an imperfect copy of his Indian Head portrait for the gold dollar, replacing the Coronet figure.

However, this design did not strike well, and Longacre copied his $3 portrait more faithfully in creating an Indian Head portrait for the gold dollar beginning in 1856.

When the large cent was abandoned in 1857 for a smaller cent, a Flying Eagle design was placed on the obverse (the 1856 Flying Eagle cents are patterns). The obverse design was changed to an Indian Head design in 1859. Wreaths of various types appear on the reverses of both (two distinctly different on the Indian cent).

Several nonallegorical designs began to appear on U.S. coins in the 1850s. On the silver 3-cent coin, a six-point star appears as the central obverse design; the reverse depicts the Roman numeral III inside what resembles a large letter "C." Shields appear on the obverses of the 2-cent coin and the first copper-nickel 5-cent coin.

A Liberty Head design replaced the Shield design on the 5-cent coin in 1883. The standard silver dollar, abandoned in 1873 and reinstated in 1878, depicts a Liberty Head and an eagle (the coin is called the Morgan dollar in reference to the sculptor-engraver who designed it). A version of the Seated Liberty coinage design was placed on the short-lived 20-cent coin of 1875 to 1878.

Coinage designs came under stricter congressional control with passage of a new law in 1890. Previously, design changes could occur at whatever frequency Mint officials determined to be appropriate. Designs sometimes changed after being used only a few weeks or months.

The new law prohibited design changes unless the designs had been used for at least 25 years. Congress had to authorize changes to designs in use for less than the required period. This brought an end to frequent design changes and, in the 20th century, would lead to design stagnation as Mint officials began viewing design changes as undesirable.

The Seated Liberty design, used on most of the silver coins since 1836, was finally abandoned at the end of 1891. By that time, it was in use only on the dime, quarter dollar and half dollar, the other denominations having been repealed or redesigned. Chief Mint Sculptor-Engraver Charles Barber's Liberty Head design replaced it in 1892. Barber also created a Heraldic Eagle for use on the reverse of the quarter dollar and half dollar; the reverse wreath appearing on the Seated Liberty dime was maintained on the reverse of the "Barber" dime. The Barber designs were used through mid-1916 for the dime and quarter dollar, and through 1915 for the half dollar.

The first two decades of the 20th century resulted in two major design trends for U.S. coins. One, beginning in 1907, resulted in what many cite as the "Golden Age of U.S. Coin Designs." The other, beginning in 1909, was the first step away from allegorical depictions in favor of medallic tributes to prominent political figures from American history.

The "Golden Age" began with the elevation of Theodore Roosevelt to president of the United States. Roosevelt did more to improve the aesthetics of U.S. coins than any other politician since Washington. He invited Augustus Saint-Gaudens, the premier U.S. sculptor of the day, to create coin designs Roosevelt hoped would equal the artistic beauty found on ancient Greek coins. Saint-Gaudens submitted designs for the cent, eagle and double eagle, but, seriously ill, died before the designs could be finalized for regular production. Roosevelt chose from the submissions the designs for the two gold coins. The $10 coin depicts an allegorical Liberty Head wearing an Indian headdress on the obverse, and a standing eagle on the reverse. The double eagle depicts a Standing Liberty facing the viewer on the obverse, and a Flying Eagle design for the reverse.

Saint-Gaudens' double eagle designs are considered by many collectors to be the finest ever portrayed on a U.S. coin. However, the first $20 coins struck in 1907 contain extremely high relief features, a wonderfully artistic feature that was impractical for production. The coins required too many strikings for efficient production, so the relief was lowered later in 1907.

The "Golden Age" continued in 1908, with new designs for the $2.50 and $5 coins by Bela Lyon Pratt: an American Indian on the obverse, and a Standing Eagle on the reverse. These were the first true Indians to appear on U.S. coins. What made the designs so unusual, however, was their placement on the coin. The designs were created in the oxymoronic "incused relief." Often incorrectly referred to as incused, the designs are raised, but sunken into the fields so the highest points are level with the flat fields.

In 1913, the designs for the 5-cent coin were changed. An American Indian was placed on the obverse, and an American bison was placed on the reverse. The coin, known variously as the Indian Head, Bison or Buffalo 5-cent coin (also nicknamed the Buffalo nickel), is considered the most American of U.S. coin designs because of the two themes portrayed on the coin. The Indian design appearing on the obverse is probably the finest to be placed on a U.S. coin. Three Indians—often identified as Iron Tail, Two Moons and Chief John Tree—reportedly posed for designer James Earle Fraser, who created a composite portrait. The model for the bison was Black Diamond, a resident of the New York Zoological Gardens. Variations of Fraser's designs were used in 2001 to strike the American Buffalo commemorative silver dollar.

More design changes were made in 1916, when the Barber designs for the dime and quarter dollar were replaced in mid-year. The dime features a Winged Liberty Head on the obverse. The design is often called the "Mercury" dime, although the artist never intended the female figure to represent the male god Mercury. The reverse depicts a fasces.

The quarter dollar design introduced in 1916 proved short-lived. The Standing Liberty figure had an exposed right breast. Liberty's bare breast was covered with a coat of mail in 1917 (both varieties of the 1917 coin exist). Although many numismatic books claim there was a hue and cry over Liberty's bare breast, no contemporary evidence exists that backs that theory (in fact, the coat of chain mail more likely indicates the nation's preparation to enter the war in Europe, a common allegorical theme). The reverse depicts a Flying Eagle; its position was modified slightly in 1917 at the same time that changes were made to the obverse. The obverse change may have been illegal, since Congress did not authorize it as required by the 1890 law; Congress did approve the reverse changes.

The Walking Liberty half dollar, designed by Adolph A. Weinman, was also introduced in 1916. The obverse depicts a Walking Liberty figure. The reverse depicts one of the most attractive eagles on a regular issue of U.S. coins.

The Peace dollar replaced the Morgan dollar in 1921. The Morgan dollar, which had last been struck in 1904, was briefly resurrected in 1921 before it was replaced by the Peace dollar. The Peace dollar commemorates the peace that followed the end of World War I. Coinage of the dollar for circulation ceased at the end of 1935.

The second coinage trend to begin in the early 20th century occurred in 1909 when a portrait of Abraham Lincoln replaced the Indian Head on the cent, to celebrate Lincoln's 100th birthday. Lincoln's portrait was the first of an actual person to appear on a circulating U.S. coin, although portraits of actual persons had appeared on noncirculating commemorative coins since 1892. Presidential portraits had been considered off limits for the first 100 years or so of U.S. coinage history, due to George Washington's opposition to the concept.

Lincoln's 150th birthday in 1959 resulted in the Lincoln Memorial replacing the wheat heads found on the Lincoln cents of 1909 to 1958.

The portrait trend continued in 1932, when the Standing Liberty quarter dollar was replaced with the George Washington portrait on the bicentennial of Washington's birth; congressional approval was necessary for the change since the designs being replaced had not been in use for the required 25 years. A portrait of Thomas Jefferson replaced the American Indian in 1938 on the 5-cent coin. Franklin Roosevelt's portrait was placed on the dime in 1946, a year after his death (the first time an American president was portrayed on a coin so soon after his death). A portrait of Benjamin Franklin was placed on the half dollar in 1948, replacing the Walking Liberty designs. Franklin was replaced in turn in 1964 by a portrait of John F. Kennedy in a numismatic tribute to the assassinated president. In 1971, a copper-nickel dollar coin was introduced bearing President Dwight D. Eisenhower's portrait on the obverse (two years after his death) and an allegorical figure of an eagle landing on Earth's moon, commemorating the Apollo 11 moon landing.

The Bicentennial of the Declaration of Independence in 1976 brought changes to the reverses of the quarter dollar, half dollar and dollar. The reverse of the 1976 quarter dollar depicts a Revolutionary War drummer; the half dollar depicts Independence Hall in Philadelphia; and the dollar depicts the Liberty Bell superimposed over the moon. The designs reverted to their original versions in 1977.

In 1979, a new copper-nickel dollar sized between the quarter dollar and half dollar was introduced, replacing the Eisenhower dollar, as suggested by a study of the U.S. coinage system. The new design depicts feminist Susan B. Anthony and a reduced version of the moon-landing design, an odd choice since it has nothing in common with the obverse theme. The Anthony portrait and moon-landing eagle designs were not popular with collectors, since many had hoped the coin would depict the Flowing Hair Liberty and Flying Eagle designs created by Chief Sculptor-Engraver Frank Gasparro for the smaller dollar when the denomination was first proposed, and some objected to Anthony's political, feminist and nonreligious views. The coin did not circulate well, mainly because of its similarity in size to the quarter dollar (many found the two coins too close to each other in diameter) and because the dollar bill remained in production. The 1979 and 1980 coins were struck for circulation, and the 1981 coins were struck for collectors only. Millions of the coins clogged Treasury and Federal Reserve vaults for two decades before being depleted in 1999. With new dollar coins needed, the Anthony dollar was struck in 1999 for a few months only, both for circulation and in collector versions.

In the 1980s, older designs were reused on the American Eagle bullion coins.

The obverse of the American Eagle silver dollar depicts Weinman's Walking Liberty half dollar obverse, enlarged for placement on the larger coin. A new Heraldic Eagle appears on the reverse.

For the gold bullion coins, Saint-Gaudens' obverse Liberty for the double eagle was chosen, but not until Treasury Secretary James A.

Baker III ordered Liberty on a diet in 1986. The Mint engraver assigned to the project was ordered to reduce Liberty's apparent weight by giving her slimmer arms and legs. Members of the Commission of Fine Arts decried the changes to what many consider the most beautiful U.S. coinage design. The Commission of Fine Arts was also critical of Miley Busiek's reverse, a Family of Eagles design. The legislation authorizing the gold coins mandated the design, which shows two adult eagles and two younger birds.

The newest members of the bullion coin family, the platinum American Eagles, stay near the tried-and-true designs of the past. On the obverse, John Mercanti rendered a medium close-up view of the Statue of Liberty, but deliberately thinned Liberty's lips and made other cosmetic changes. The reverse depicts a fairly realistic rendering of an eagle in flight with the sun in the background.

While the original reverse design remains in use on the Uncirculated versions of the coins, Mint officials decided that beginning in 1998, the Proof versions of the platinum coin would depict a new reverse design every year for five years in a Vistas of Liberty series. Each coin depicts an eagle flying over a scene representative of a region of the United States. Since that series ended with the Proof 2002 coins, the Mint has used a unique reverse design every year on the Proof pieces.

As the 1990s ended, the most exciting news for collectors was a decision to introduce new designs into circulation. For decades, hobbyists and others had called for new designs on circulating coins while Mint officials had publicly opposed changes, stating that new designs would cause hoarding and coin shortages.

Administration and congressional officials debated coinage redesign for years in the 1980s and 1990s, but took little action. At one point in early 1992, it appeared as though the Senate and House had reached agreement on coinage redesign. A redesign measure was added to an omnibus coin bill seeking a variety of commemorative coins for 1992 and beyond. However, on the day the vote was scheduled, someone began spreading the false rumor that the legislation would eliminate "In God We Trust" from U.S. coinage. The House defeated the bill because of the rumor and remained hostile to coinage redesign for several years.

Finally, however, Congress changed its mind and authorized limited coinage redesign through the 50 States circulating commemorative quarter dollar program. Fifty new reverse designs will be introduced over a 10-year period beginning in 1999 at a rate of five per year, approximately every 10 weeks.

New designs were used on the new dollar coin introduced in

January 2000. An unusual mixture of allegorical and historical themes was considered, with the coin depicting an allegorical image of the teenaged interpreter for the Lewis and Clark Expedition, Sacagawea, and her baby. This design concept was selected after unprecedented public discourse on the subject on June 8 to 9, 1998, in Philadelphia. Members of the public were invited to speak before a panel empowered to recommend coinage designs for the dollar coin. Artists, coin collectors and others recommended such subjects as Eleanor Roosevelt, allegorical portraits of Liberty and other themes, with the Sacagawea-inspired theme selected by the panel. The obverse depicts Sacagawea carrying her infant son, Jean-Baptiste, in a cradle on her back—the first mother and child depicted on a circulating U.S. coin. The reverse depicts an eagle.

Mint officials, having embraced coinage redesign with the State quarter dollars program and the Sacagawea dollar, began considering changes to other circulating coins, ending decades of official opposition to design changes. In 2002, U.S. Mint Director Henrietta Holsman Fore began publicly discussing possible, temporary design changes to the Jefferson 5-cent coin in 2003 in commemoration of the bicentennial of the Lewis and Clark expedition, which Jefferson ordered. The first hints came during meetings Fore conducted with collectors at coin shows and State quarter dollar launch ceremonies.

In June 2002, details of the planned design began to emerge. A new portrait of a younger Jefferson (based on the portrait used in 1994 on a silver dollar commemorating the 1993 bicentennial celebration of Jefferson's birth) was planned, with Monticello to be replaced by a scene of an American Indian and an eagle. However, Virginia legislators reacted angrily to the proposal that Monticello (in Virginia) be removed. One legislator from Virginia introduced legislation that became law in 2003 approving commemorative designs from 2003 to 2005, but mandating Monticello's return to the reverse in 2006.

Mint officials were unable to introduce new designs for the 5-cent coin in 2003, but in 2004, two new reverses were introduced (the coin retained its 1938 obverse). The first design introduced, called the Peace Medal design, is based on the reverse design of the medal depicting Thomas Jefferson that Lewis and Clark distributed to Indian leaders on their expedition. The second 2004 coin, the Keelboat design, illustrates a keelboat used early in the expedition, before the waters grew too shallow for the vessel.

Two more reverse designs and a new portrait of Jefferson for the 2005 5-cent coins were in the final stages of preparation as this edition was being edited.

Beginning in 2006, however, the Jefferson and Monticello themes become mandatory, although new renditions will replace those by Felix Schlag, introduced in 1938.

Future design changes for circulating coinage may include a Presidential dollar series as a temporary replacement for the Sacagawea design and another presidential portrait in commemoration of the "Great Communicator," Ronald Reagan

If legislation before Congress becomes law in 2004, the Presidential dollar series would comprise four coins every year, depicting each president in the order he (or she, in any future election) served in the office. Most obverse and reverse legends, the date and the Mint mark would be moved to the edge to make space for larger images (the reverse would depict the Statue of Liberty).

The other possible change could result in a portrait of President Ronald Reagan on the dime or half dollar, or one of the current Federal Reserve notes. Even before President Reagan's death, Republican lawmakers had introduced legislation seeking Reagan's portrait on the dime in place of that of Franklin Roosevelt. However, Democrats in Congress sought a resolution to prevent the act from becoming law, and Nancy Reagan publicly stated that she did not want Roosevelt replaced on the coin by her husband. With Reagan's death, many Republicans called for his depiction on coinage or paper money, although the current designs for the suggested denominations all have their supporters. The Bush administration does not need congressional authorization to change the design of the dime, half dollar or any of the FRN denominations because Secretary of the Treasury John Snow has the authority to order change after coin designs have been in circulation for 25 years. Except for the dollar, all of the denominations under consideration qualify, and there is no time limitation on paper currency.

Specifications

The physical specifications of U.S. coins—metallic content, weights, diameters—have been ever changing. Changes were in response to increases and decreases in metal prices, public rejection of large-diameter or small-diameter coins, and other factors.

Even before the first copper coins were struck in 1793, their weights were reduced from what Congress had originally authorized in 1792. Weights for both copper coins were again reduced in 1795.

The 1794 and 1795 silver coinage was struck in a composition of 90 percent silver and 10 percent copper, according to some sources. When additional silver denominations were added in 1796, the composition for all five coins was changed to 89.2427 percent silver and 10.7572 percent copper, as required in the 1792 law (meaning the composition violated the law for several years).

Composition of the first gold coins is 91.6667 percent gold and 8.3333 percent copper and silver.

In 1834, the weight of gold coins was reduced and the alloy changed for two years to 89.9225 percent gold and 10.0775 percent copper and silver. In 1836, the gold alloy was changed again, to 90 percent gold and 10 percent copper and silver, an alloy unchanged until 1873. Changes were made to silver coins in 1836 as well, when the silver content was changed to 90 percent silver and 10 percent copper, an alloy used until the mid-1960s.

The rising price of silver resulted in a reduction in weights for the silver coins during 1853 (except for the silver dollar). Arrows were added to both sides of the dates on the reduced weight half dimes, dimes, quarter dollars and dollars to distinguish them from the older, heavier coins; the arrows were used for the 1853 and 1854 coins. The arrows were removed in 1855 although the weights of the silver coins remained the same.

The first gold dollars, introduced in 1849, are about 13 millimeters in diameter, or about half an inch. This was by far the smallest size coin issued by the United States government to that time. Citizens easily lost the coins or paid them out for lower-denomination coins in error. The Mint increased the diameter to 14.86 millimeters in 1854 while retaining the legally mandated weight (the coin was made thinner to compensate for the larger diameter).

Dissatisfaction with the size of the large cent helped drive its replacement by a smaller version. A smaller cent composed of 88 percent copper and 12 percent nickel replaced the pure copper cent in 1857. Diameter of the large cent is approximately 29 millimeters; the new cent has a diameter of 19 millimeters.

The weights of the Seated Liberty silver coinage increased in 1873, and again arrows were placed at either side of the date to signify the increased weight. Silver was dropped from the gold-coin alloy, which changed to 90 percent gold and 10 percent copper.

The next major compositional changes in U.S. coins were made during World War II. Several metals used in coinage became strategically important to the war effort. The first to be affected was the 5-cent coin, which had nickel removed in mid-1942 after some copper-nickel specimens were struck, creating a nickel-less "nickel." The new composition was 56 percent copper, 35 percent silver and

9 percent manganese. The old alloy was resumed in 1946.

In addition, during the war, the composition of the cent changed. First, tin was removed late in 1942. Then, in 1943, a zinc-coated steel cent was introduced to conserve copper (the decision was a mistake; the cents quickly corroded and rusted). The brass alloy of 95 percent copper and 5 percent zinc used late in 1942 was resumed from 1944 through 1946. The 95 percent copper, 5 percent tin and zinc composition resumed in 1947 and continued until late 1962. Once again, tin was removed from the bronze alloy, turning the alloy into the same composition, called brass, used in 1944 through 1946.

The 175-year-old history of United States coinage was changed with the stroke of a pen on July 23, 1965. On that day, President Lyndon Johnson signed into law the Coinage Act of 1965, the most sweeping changes to the U.S. coinage system since the Mint Act of 1873. The 1965 act eliminated silver in dimes and quarter dollars and reduced the silver content of the half dollars to 40 percent.

Special congressional hearings relative to the nationwide coin shortage were first held in 1964. Coin shortages had continually worsened in the decade prior to 1965 as a result of the population growth, expanding vending machine businesses, the popularity of Kennedy half dollars and the worldwide silver shortage.

In the face of the escalating silver price, it was essential that dependence on silver for coinage be reduced. Otherwise, the country would be faced with a chronic coin shortage.

A clad metal composed of three bonded layers of metal was selected for the new composition. The dimes and quarter dollars were composed of two layers of 75 percent copper and 25 percent nickel bonded to a core of pure copper. The half dollars were composed of two layers of 80 percent silver and 20 percent copper bonded to a core of approximately 20 percent silver and 80 percent copper; the entire coin is composed of 40 percent silver.

The combination of copper-nickel and copper gave the new dimes and quarter dollars the required electrical conductivity, a necessary property for vending machines. The copper-nickel surfaces also continued the traditional silvery color of the coins and made counterfeiting more difficult.

The legal weights of the coins were affected by the change in alloy. The clad dime weight is 2.27 grams, the quarter dollar weighs 5.67 grams and the half dollar weighs 11.5 grams. With the elimination of silver from half dollars in 1971 and the introduction of a copper-nickel clad version, the weight was changed to 11.34 grams.

In an effort to maximize coin production, 1964-dated silver coins were struck into 1965. The Coinage Act of 1965 also made it mandatory that clad coins be dated not earlier than 1965. All clad coins actually made in 1965 bear that date. The first clad dimes were struck in late December 1965 and were released March 8, 1966. The first clad quarter dollars were struck Aug. 23, 1965, and released Nov. 1, 1965. The first silver-clad half dollars were released March 8, 1966, but were struck starting Dec. 30, 1965. The 1965 date was retained until July 31, 1966, when the date was changed to 1966. Normal dating resumed Jan. 1, 1967.

Another great compositional change to U.S. circulating coinage came in mid-1982, when the brass cent was replaced with a cent of nearly pure zinc, plated with a thin layer of pure copper to retain its copper appearance, in reaction to rising copper prices. The switch to the copper-plated zinc cent was made with few noting the difference.

When the American Eagle bullion coins were introduced in 1986, some collectors were critical of the .9167 gold content, a composition they deemed "nontraditional"; there was some preference for a .900 gold content. However, the chosen composition is virtually identical to the alloy first used for U.S. gold coins, from 1795 to 1834. A new silver composition was introduced with the production of the .999 fine silver American Eagle dollar.

The Treasury secretary now has authority under a change in the law in 1992 to produce a .9999 gold bullion coin, but to date has not done so. This is envisioned as a separate product, not a change in bullion content for the gold American Eagle.

The platinum American Eagle bullion coins, introduced in 1997, are .9995 fine.

Mint officials struck the United States' first ringed bimetallic coins in 2000 (the Library of Congress gold-platinum $10 commemorative coin), after experimenting with test pieces in early 1993. The Library of Congress coins consist of an outer ring of gold bonded to an inner ring of platinum.

The introduction of the 2000 "golden" dollar depicting Sacagawea resulted in another new alloy. U.S. Mint officials selected a composition that has two outer layers composed of manganese-bronze (77 percent copper, 12 percent zinc, 7 manganese and 4 percent nickel) bonded to an inner core of pure copper. Overall, the total composition is 88.5 percent copper, 6 percent zinc, 3.5 percent manganese and 2 percent nickel.

Commemorative coins

12

America's commemorative coins are graphic reminders of the United States' past, honoring its history, its heroes and its accomplishments.

They are special coinage issues, authorized by acts of Congress to recognize the people and events that have shaped the United States. They occasionally honor an individual, like Ulysses S. Grant. They may honor a historical event such as the Battle of Gettysburg or a current event such as the 1996 Olympic Games in Atlanta (commemorated with coins in 1995 and 1996).

They are rarely issued for circulation, although that changed in 1999. The United States Mint began a 10-year program that, when completed, will have resulted in 50 different circulating quarter dollars, each commemorating one of the 50 states in the Union. The Mint also is issuing circulating Jefferson 5-cent coins commemorating the Bicentennials of the Louisiana Purchase and Lewis and Clark Expedition (two each in 2004 and 2005).

The first series of U.S. commemorative coins dates from 1892 until 1954, when Department of Treasury support for commemorative coins ended after decades of abuse. The abuses were many, with numerous coins issued for events of purely local interest or even to commemorate nonevents. Administrations from the Eisenhower presidency to the Carter presidency opposed all commemorative coinage. There was so much opposition that when the 1976 Bicentennial of the Declaration of Independence quarter dollars, half dollars and dollars were issued in 1975 and 1976, Treasury officials carefully avoided any use of the word "commemorative," although clearly the coins are commemorative in nature.

It came as a surprise, then, when in 1981 United States Treasurer Angela M. Buchanan announced Treasury Department support for a commemorative half dollar honoring George Washington's 250th birthday in 1982. Buchanan said that the Treasury Department "has not objected to special coinage authorized by Congress for the government's own account," referring specifically to the 40 percent silver versions of the Bicentennial coinage. Buchanan said that the Treasury Department had always objected to "the issuance of commemorative coins for the benefit of private sponsors and organizations." With the Treasury Department supportive of the measure, Congress passed the Washington half dollar bill and President Reagan signed it into law. Thus, the commemorative coin program in the United States was reborn.

Since 1982, commemorative coins have been issued in every year except 1985, often with more than one program in each year. In fact, many of the abuses of the past have resurfaced. Some recent years have witnessed multiple programs, making acquiring one of every coin an expensive proposition. Congress has also authorized programs of extremely limited interest (as shown by shrinking sales figures), many to raise funds for various congressional projects, such as the 2001 Capitol Visitor Center program. Special-interest groups have come to consider coin collectors a "cash cow," since surcharges added to the cost of modern commemorative coins are given to various special-interest groups to fund a variety of memorials and projects. In one case, $1 million in surcharges originally intended for funding scholarships for disadvantaged youth (from the sales of the Jackie Robinson commemoratives) was diverted to the Botanic Garden, even though the Botanic Garden had already received money from the sales of its own commemorative coin program. The diversion of funds occurred because the wife of the member of Congress sponsoring the diversion of funds was closely connected to the Botanic Garden.

In this section, commemorative issues are presented by year of their first issuance. For early commemoratives, those produced from 1892 to 1954, original mintage, number melted and final mintage are listed. For commemorative coins produced since 1982, the final net mintage only (reflecting sales figures) is listed. The U.S. Mint no longer makes public the original mintage, number of coins melted, or whether coins have been held in inventory or stored in Treasury vaults. Each coin is listed with the designers, and original issue prices are given, so that the collector may determine the coin's performance against its original cost.

For a complete history of the commemorative coin story, complete with politics and intrigue, consult *Commemorative Coins of the United States* by Anthony Swiatek, published by *Coin World.*

Commemorative				Designer
Date	Original Mintage	Melted	Final Mintage	Original Price

Commemoratives 1892-1954

Date	Original Mintage	Melted	Final Mintage	Original Price
Columbian Exposition half dollar				**Charles E. Barber/George Morgan**
1892	950,000	None	950,000	$1.00
1893	4,052,105	2,501,700	1,550,405	$1.00
Isabella quarter dollar				**Charles E. Barber**
1893	40,023	15,809	24,124	$1.00
Lafayette-Washington silver dollar				**Charles E. Barber**
1900	50,026	14,000	36,026	$2.00
Louisiana Purchase Exposition gold dollar				**Charles E. Barber**
1903	250,258	215,250	each type 17,375	$3.00
Lewis and Clark Exposition gold dollar				**Charles E. Barber**
1904	25,028	15,003	10,025	$2.00
1905	35,041	25,000	10,041	$2.00
Panama-Pacific Exposition half dollar				**Charles E. Barber**
1915-S	60,030	32,896	27,134	$1.00
Panama-Pacific Exposition gold dollar				**Charles Keck**
1915-S	25,034	10,034	15,000	$2.00
Panama-Pacific Exposition quarter eagle				**Charles E. Barber**
1915-S	10,017	3,278	6,749	$4.00
Panama-Pacific Exposition $50				**Robert Aitken**
1915-S Round	1,510	1,027	483	$100
1915-S Octag.	1,509	864	645	$100
McKinley Memorial gold dollar				**Charles E. Barber/George T. Morgan**
1916	20,026	10,049	9,977	$3.00
1917	10,014	14	10,000	$3.00
Illinois Centennial half dollar				**George T. Morgan/John R. Sinnock**
1918	100,058	None	100,058	$1.00
Maine Centennial half dollar				**Harry Hayman Cochrane**
1920	50,028	None	50,028	$1.00
Pilgrim Tercentenary half dollar				**Cyrus E. Dallin**
1920	200,112	48,000	152,112	$1.00
1921	100,053	80,000	20,053	$1.00
Missouri Centennial half dollar				**Robert Aitken**
1921 2*4	5,000	None	5,000	$1.00
1921 No 2*4	45,028	29,600	15,428	$1.00
Alabama Centennial half dollar				**Laura Gardin Fraser**
1921 2X2	6,006	None	6,006	$1.00
1921 No 2X2	64,038	5,000	59,038	$1.00
Grant Memorial half dollar				**Laura Gardin Fraser**
1922 Star	5,006	750	4,256	$1.00
1922 No Star	95,055	27,650	67,405	$1.00
Grant Memorial gold dollar				**Laura Gardin Fraser**
1922 Star	5,016	None	5,016	$3.50
1922 No Star	5,000	None	5,000	$3.00
Monroe Doctrine Centennial half dollar				**Chester Beach**
1923-S	274,077	None	274,077	$1.00
Huguenot-Walloon Tercentenary half dollar				**George T. Morgan**
1924	142,080	None	142,080	$1.00

Commemorative Date	Original Mintage	Melted	Final Mintage	Designer Original Price
Lexington-Concord Sesquicentennial half dollar				**Chester Beach**
1925	162,099	86	162,013	$1.00
Stone Mountain half dollar				**Gutzon Borglum**
1925	2,314,709	1,000,000	1,314,709	$1.00
California Diamond Jubilee half dollar				**Jo Mora**
1925-S	150,200	63,606	86,594	$1.00
Fort Vancouver Centennial half dollar				**Laura Gardin Fraser**
1925	50,028	35,034	14,994	$1.00
American Independence Sesquicentennial half dollar				**John R. Sinnock**
1926	1,000,528	859,408	141,120	$1.00
American Independence Sesquicentennial quarter eagle				**John R. Sinnock**
1926	200,226	154,207	46,019	$4.00
Oregon Trail Memorial half dollar				**James E. and Laura G. Fraser**
1926	48,030	75	47,955	$1.00
1926-S	100,055	17,000	83,055	$1.00
1928	50,028	44,000	6,028	$2.00
1933-D	5,250	242	5,008	$2.00
1934-D	7,006	None	7,006	$2.00
1936	10,006	None	10,006	$1.60
1936-S	5,006	None	5,006	$1.60
1937-D	12,008	None	12,008	$1.60
1938	6,006	None	6,006	$6.25
1938-D	6,005	None	6,005	for
1938-S	6,006	None	6,006	three
1939	3,004	None	3,004	$7.50
1939-D	3,004	None	3,004	for
1939-S	3,005	None	3,005	three
Vermont Sesquicentennial half dollar				**Charles Keck**
1927	40,034	11,872	28,162	$1.00
Hawaiian Sesquicentennial half dollar				**Juliette Mae Fraser/Chester Beach**
1928	10,000	None	10,000	$2.00
Maryland Tercentenary half dollar				**Hans Schuler**
1934	25,015	None	25,015	$1.00
Texas Independence Centennial				**Pompeo Coppini**
1934	205,113	143,650	61,463	$1.00
1935	10,008	12	9,996	$1.50
1935-D	10,007	None	10,007	$1.50
1935-S	10,008	None	10,008	$1.50
1936	10,008	1,097	8,911	$1.50
1936-D	10,007	968	9,039	$1.50
1936-S	10,008	943	9,055	$1.50
1937	8,005	1,434	6,571	$1.50
1937-D	8,006	1,401	6,605	$1.50
1937-S	8,007	1,370	6,637	$1.50
1938	5,005	1,225	3,780	$2.00
1938-D	5,005	1,230	3,775	$2.00
1938-S	5,006	1,192	3,814	$2.00
Daniel Boone Bicentennial half dollar				**Augustus Lukeman**
1934	10,007	None	10,007	$1.60
1935	10,010	None	10,010	$1.10
1935-D	5,005	None	5,005	$1.60
1935-S	5,005	None	5,005	$1.60
1935 w/1934	10,008	None	10,008	$1.10

Commemorative				Designer
Date	Original Mintage	Melted	Final Mintage	Original Price
1935-D w/1934	2,003	None	2,003	$3.70
1935-S w/1934	2,004	None	2,004	for two
1936	12,012	None	12,012	$1.10
1936-D	5,005	None	5,005	$1.60
1936-S	5,006	None	5,006	$1.60
1937	15,010	5,200	9,810	$1.60, $7.25 set
1937-D	7,506	5,000	2,506	$7.25 in set
1937-S	5,006	2,500	2,506	$5.15
1938	5,005	2,905	2,100	$6.50
1938-D	5,005	2,905	2,100	for
1938-S	5,006	2,906	2,100	three
Connecticut Tercentenary half dollar				**Henry G. Kreiss**
1935	25,018	None	25,018	$1.00
Arkansas Centennial half dollar				**Edward E. Burr**
1935	13,012	None	13,012	$1.00
1935-D	5,005	None	5,005	$1.00
1935-S	5,506	None	5,006	$1.00
1936	10,010	350	9,660	$1.50
1936-D	10,010	350	9,660	$1.50
1936-S	10,012	350	9,662	$1.50
1937	5,505	None	5,505	$8.75
1937-D	5,505	None	5,505	for
1937-S	5,506	None	5,506	three
1938	6,006	2,850	3,156	$8.75
1938-D	6,005	2,850	3,155	for
1938-S	6,006	2,850	3,156	three
1939	2,104	None	2,104	$10
1939-D	2,104	None	2,104	for
1939-S	2,105	None	2,105	three
Arkansas-Robinson half dollar				**Edward E. Burr/Henry G. Kreiss**
1936	25,265	None	25,265	$1.85
Hudson, N.Y., Sesquicentennial half dollar				**Chester Beach**
1935	10,008	None	10,008	$1.00
California-Pacific International Expo				**Robert Aitken**
1935-S	250,132	180,000	70,132	$1.00
1936-D	180,092	150,000	30,092	$1.50
Old Spanish Trail half dollar				**L.W. Hoffecker**
1935	10,008	None	10,000	$2.00
Providence, R.I., Tercentenary				**John H. Benson/Abraham G. Carey**
1936	20,013	None	20,013	$1.00
1936-D	15,010	None	15,010	$1.00
1936-S	15,011	None	15,011	$1.00
Cleveland, Great Lakes Exposition half dollar				**Brenda Putnam**
1936	50,030	None	50,030	$1.50
Wisconsin Territorial Centennial half dollar				**David Parsons/Benjamin Hawkins**
1936	25,015	None	25,015	$1.50
Cincinnati Music Center half dollar				**Constance Ortmayer**
1936	5,005	None	5,005	$7.75
1936-D	5,005	None	5,005	for
1936-S	5,006	None	5,006	three
Long Island Tercentenary half dollar				**Howard K. Weinmann**
1936	100,053	18,227	81,826	$1.00

Commemorative Date	Original Mintage	Melted	Final Mintage	Designer Original Price
York County, Maine, Tercentenary half dollar				**Walter H. Rich**
1936	25,015	None	25,015	$1.50
Bridgeport, Conn., Centennial half dollar				**Henry G. Kreiss**
1936	25,015	None	25,015	$2.00
Lynchburg, Va., Sesquicentennial half dollar				**Charles Keck**
1936	20,013	None	20,013	$1.00
Elgin, Ill., Centennial half dollar				**Trygve Rovelstad**
1936	25,015	5,000	20,015	$1.50
Albany, N.Y., half dollar				**Gertrude K. Lathrop**
1936	25,013	7,342	17,671	$2.00
San Francisco-Oakland Bay Bridge half dollar				**Jacques Schnier**
1936-S	100,055	28,631	71,424	$1.50
Columbia, S.C., Sesquicentennial half dollar				**A. Wolfe Davidson**
1936	9,007	None	9,007	$6.45
1936-D	8,009	None	8,009	for
1936-S	8,007	None	8,007	three
Delaware Tercentenary half dollar				**Carl L. Schmitz**
1936	25,015	4,022	20,993	$1.75
Battle of Gettysburg half dollar				**Frank Vittor**
1936	50,028	23,100	26,928	$1.65
Norfolk, Va., Bicentennial half dollar				**William M. Simpson/Marjorie E. Simpson**
1936	25,013	8,077	16,936	$1.50
Roanoke Island, N.C., half dollar				**William M. Simpson**
1937	50,030	21,000	29,030	$1.65
Battle of Antietam half dollar				**William M. Simpson**
1937	50,028	32,000	18,028	$1.65
New Rochelle, N.Y., half dollar				**Gertrude K. Lathrop**
1938	25,015	9,749	15,266	$2.00
Iowa Statehood Centennial half dollar				**Adam Pietz**
1946	100,057	None	100,057	$2.50/$3.00
Booker T. Washington half dollar				**Isaac S. Hathaway**
1946	1,000,546	?	?	$1.00
1946-D	200,113	?	?	$1.50
1946-S	500,279	?	?	$1.00
1947	100,017	?	?	$6.00
1947-D	100,017	?	?	for
1947-S	100,017	?	?	three
1948	20,005	12,000	8,005	$7.50
1948-D	20,005	12,000	8,005	for
1948-S	20,005	12,000	8,005	three
1949	12,004	6,000	6,004	$8.50
1949-D	12,004	6,000	6,004	for
1949-S	12,004	6,000	6,004	three
1950	12,004	6,000	6,004	$8.50
1950-D	12,004	6,000	6,004	for
1950-S	512,091	?	?	three
1951	510,082	?	?	$3 or $10
1951-D	12,004	5,000	7,004	for
1951-S	12,004	5,000	7,004	three
Booker T. Washington/George Washington Carver				**Isaac S. Hathaway**
1951	?	?	110,018	$10
1951-D	?	?	10,004	for
1951-S	?	?	10,004	three

Commemorative Date	Original Mintage	Melted	Final Mintage	Designer Original Price
1952	?	?	2,006,292	$10
1952-D	?	?	8,006	for
1952-S	?	?	8,006	three
1953	?	?	8,003	$10
1953-D	?	?	8,003	for
1953-S	?	?	108,020	three
1954	?	?	12,006	$10
1954-D	?	?	12,006	for
1954-S	?	?	122,024	three

Commemorative coins 1982-2004

Commemorative Date	Final Mintage	Designer Pre-Issue/ Regular Price
George Washington half dollar		**Elizabeth Jones**
1982-D	2,210,458	$8.50/$10[1]
1982-S	4,894,044	$10/$12[1]
Los Angeles Olympic Games silver dollar		**Elizabeth Jones**
1983-P Unc.	294,543	$28 or $89[2]
1983-D Unc.	174,014	for
1983-S Unc.	174,014	three
1983-S Proof	1,577,025	$24.95[2]
Los Angeles Olympic Games silver dollar		**Robert Graham**
1984-P Unc.	217,954	$28 or $89[2]
1984-D Unc.	116,675	for
1984-S Unc.	116,675	three
1984-S Proof	1,801,210	$32[2]
Los Angeles Olympic Games gold eagle		**James Peed/John Mercanti**
1984-P Proof	33,309	$352[2]
1984-D Proof	34,533	$352[2]
1984-S Proof	48,551	$352[2]
1984-W Proof	381,085	$352[2]
1984-W Unc.	75,886	$339[2]
Statue of Liberty, Immigrant half dollar		**Edgar Z. Steever IV/Sherl J. Winter**
1986-D Unc.	928,008	$5/$6[3]
1986-S Proof	6,925,627	$6.50/$7.50[3]
Statue of Liberty, Ellis Island dollar		**John Mercanti/Matthew Peloso**
1986-P Unc.	723,635	$20.50/$22[3]
1986-S Proof	6,414,638	$22.50/$24[3]
Statue of Liberty half eagle		**Elizabeth Jones**
1986-W Unc.	95,248	$160/$165[3]
1986-W Proof	404,013	$170/$175[3]
Constitution Bicentennial silver dollar		**Patricia L. Verani**
1987-P Unc.	451,629	$22.50/$26[3]
1987-S Proof	2,747,116	$24/$28[3]
Constitution Bicentennial half eagle		**Marcel Jovine**
1987-W Unc.	214,225	$195/$215[3]
1987-W Proof	651,659	$200/$225[3]
1988 Olympic Games silver dollar		**Patricia L. Verani/Sherl J. Winter**
1988-D Unc.	191,368	$22/$27[3]
1988-S Proof	1,359,366	$23/$29[3]

Commemorative Date	Final Mintage	Designer Pre-Issue/ Regular Price
1988 Olympic Games gold half eagle		**Elizabeth Jones/Marcel Jovine**
1988-W Unc.	62,913	$200/$225[3]
1988-W Proof	281,465	$205/$235[3]
Congress Bicentennial half dollar		**Patricia L. Verani/William Woodward**
1989-D Unc.	163,753	$5/$6[3]
1989-S Proof	767,897	$7/$8[3]
Congress Bicentennial silver dollar		**William Woodward**
1989-D Unc.	135,203	$23/$26[3]
1989-S Proof	762,198	$25/$29[3]
Congress Bicentennial half eagle		**John Mercanti**
1989-W Unc.	46,899	$185/$200[3]
1989-W Proof	164,690	$195/$215[3]
Eisenhower Birth Centennial silver dollar		**John Mercanti/Marcel Jovine**
1990-W Unc.	241,669	$23/$26[3]
1990-P Proof	1,144,461	$25/$29[3]
Mount Rushmore 50th Anniversary half dollar		**Marcel Jovine/T. James Ferrell**
1991-D Unc.	172,754	$6/$7[3]
1991-S Proof	753,257	$8.50/$9.50[3]
Mount Rushmore 50th Anniversary silver dollar		**Marika Somogyi/Frank Gasparro**
1991-P Unc.	133,139	$23/$26[3]
1991-S Proof	738,419	$28/$31[3]
Mount Rushmore 50th Anniversary half eagle		**John Mercanti/Robert Lamb**
1991-W Unc.	31,959	$185/$210[3]
1991-W Proof	111,991	$195/$225[3]
Korean War Memorial silver dollar		**John Mercanti/T. James Ferrell**
1991-D Unc.	213,049	$23/$26[3]
1991-P Proof	618,488	$28/$31[3]
USO 50th Anniversary silver dollar		**Robert Lamb/John Mercanti**
1991-D Unc.	124,958	$23/$26[3]
1991-S Proof	321,275	$28/$31[3]
1992 Olympics clad half dollar		**William Cousins/Steven Bieda**
1992-P Unc.	161,607	$6/$7.50[3]
1992-S Proof	519,645	$8.50/$9.50[3]
1992 Olympics silver dollar		**John R. Deecken/Marcel Jovine**
1992-D Unc.	187,552	$24/$29[3]
1992-S Proof	504,505	$28/$32[3]
1992 Olympic gold half eagle		**Jim Sharpe/Jim Peed**
1992-W Unc.	27,732	$185/$215[3]
1992-W Proof	77,313	$195/$230[3]
White House Bicentennial silver dollar		**Edgar Z. Steever IV/Chester Y. Martin**
1992-D Unc.	123,803	$23/$28[3]
1992-W Proof	375,851	$28/$32[3]
Columbus Quincentenary clad half dollar		**T. James Ferrell**
1992-D Unc.	135,702	$6.50/$7.50[3]
1992-S Proof	390,154	$8.50/$9.50[3]
Columbus Quincentenary silver dollar		**John M. Mercanti/Thomas D. Rogers Sr.**
1992-D Unc.	106,949	$23/$28[3]
1992-P Proof	385,241	$27/$31[3]
Columbus Quincentenary half eagle		**T. James Ferrell/Thomas D. Rogers Sr.**
1992-W Unc.	24,329	$180/$210[3]
1992-W Proof	79,730	$190/$225[3]

Commemorative Date	Final Mintage	Designer Pre-Issue/ Regular Price
Bill of Rights/Madison silver half dollar		**T. James Ferrell/Dean E. McMullen**
1993-W Unc.	193,346	$9.75/$11.50[3]
1993-S Proof	586,315	$12.50/$13.50[3]
Bill of Rights/Madison silver dollar		**William J. Krawczewicz/Dean E. McMullen**
1993-D Unc.	98,383	$22/$27[3]
1993-S Proof	534,001	$25/$29[3]
Bill of Rights/Madison gold $5 half eagle		**Scott R. Blazek/Joseph D. Pena**
1993-W Unc.	23,266	$175/$205[3]
1993-W Proof	78,651	$185/$220[3]
World War II 50th Anniversary clad half dollar		**George Klauba/Bill J. Leftwich**
1991-1995-P Unc. (1993[4])	197,072	$8/$9[3]
1991-1995-S Proof (1993[4])	317,396	$9/$10[3]
World War II 50th Anniversary silver dollar		**Thomas D. Rogers Sr.**
1991-1995-D Unc. (1993[4])	107,240	$23/$28[3]
1991-1995-W Proof (1993[4])	342,041	$27/$31[3]
World War II 50th Anniversary gold $5 half eagle		**Charles J. Madsen/ Edward Southworth Fisher**
1991-1995-W Unc. (1993[4])	23,672	$170/$200[3]
1991-1995-W Proof (1993[4])	67,026	$185/$220[3]
Thomas Jefferson 250th Anniversary silver dollar		**James Ferrell**
1743-1993-P Unc. (1994[5])	266,927	$27/$32[3]
1743-1993-S Proof (1994[5])	332,891	$31/$35[3]
World Cup Soccer clad half dollar		**Richard T. LaRoche/Dean E. McMullen**
1994-D Unc.	168,208	$8.75/$9.50[3]
1994-P Proof	609,354	$9.75/$10.50[3]
World Cup Soccer silver dollar		**Dean E. McMullen**
1994-D Unc.	81,524	$23/$28[3]
1994-S Proof	577,090	$27/$31[3]
World Cup Soccer gold $5 half eagle		**William J. Krawczewicz/Dean E. McMullen**
1994-W Unc.	22,447	$170/$200[3]
1994-W Proof	89,614	$185/$220[3]
Prisoner of War silver dollar		**Tom Nielsen and Alfred Maletsky/Edgar Z. Steever IV**
1994-W Unc.	54,790	$27/$32[3]
1994-P Proof	220,100	$31/$35[3]
Vietnam Veterans Memorial silver dollar		**John Mercanti/Thomas D. Rogers Sr.**
1994-W Unc.	57,317	$27/$32[3]
1994-P Proof	226,262	$31/$35[3]
Women in Military Service silver dollar		**T. James Ferrell/Thomas D. Rogers Sr.**
1994-W Unc.	53,054	$27/$32[3]
1994-P Proof	213,201	$31/$35[3]
U.S. Capitol Bicentennial silver dollar		**William C. Cousins/John Mercanti**
1994-D Unc.	68,332	$32/$37[3]
1994-S Proof	279,579	$36/$40[3]
Civil War Battlefields clad half dollar		**Don Troiani/T. James Ferrell**
1995-S Unc	113,045	$9.50/$10.25[3]
1995-S Proof	326,801	$10.75/$11.75[3]
Civil War Battlefields silver dollar		**Don Troiani/John Mercanti**
1995-P Unc	51,612	$27/$29[3]
1995-S Proof	327,686	$30/$34[3]
Civil War Battlefields gold half eagle		**Don Troiani/Alfred Maletsky**
1995-W Unc.	12,623	$180/$190[3]
1995-W Proof	54,915	$195/$225[3]

Commemorative		Designer
Date	Final Mintage	Pre-Issue/ Regular Price
Special Olympics World Games silver dollar		**Jamie Wyeth & T. James Ferrell/ Thomas D. Rogers Sr.**
1995-W Unc.	89,298	$29/$31[3,6]
1995-P Proof	352,449	$31/$35[3,6]
Games of the XXVI Olympiad, Atlanta clad half dollar		**Clint Hansen/T. James Ferrell**
1995-S Basketball Unc.	169,527	$10.50/$11.50[7]
1995-S Basketball Proof	170,733	$11.50/$12.50[7]
Games of the XXVI Olympiad, Atlanta clad half dollar		**Edgar Z. Steever IV/ T. James Ferrell**
1995-S Baseball Unc.	164,759	$10.50/$11.50[7]
1995-S Baseball Proof	119,396	$11.50/$12.50[7]
Games of the XXVI Olympiad, Atlanta silver dollar		**Jim Sharpe/William Krawczewicz**
1995-D Gymnastics Unc.	43,003	$27.95/$31.95[7]
1995-S Gymnastics Proof	185,158	$30.95/$34.95[7]
Games of the XXVI Olympiad, Atlanta silver dollar		**John Mercanti/William Krawczewicz**
1995-D Cycling Unc.	20,122	$27.95/$31.95[7]
1995-S Cycling Proof	127,465	$30.95/$34.95[7]
Games of the XXVI Olympiad, Atlanta silver dollar		**John Mercanti/ William Krawczewicz**
1995-D Track & Field Unc.	25,425	$27.95/$31.95[7]
1995-S Track & Field Proof	143,304	$30.95/$34.95[7]
Games of the XXVI Olympiad, Atlanta silver dollar		**Jim Sharpe/William Krawczewicz**
1995-D Paralympic, blind runner Unc.	29,015	$27.95/$31.95[7]
1995-S Paralympic, blind runner Proof	139,831	$30.95/$34.95[7]
Games of the XXVI Olympiad, Atlanta gold half eagle		**Frank Gasparro**
1995-W Torch Runner gold Unc.	14,817	$229/$249[7]
1995-W Torch Runner gold Proof	57,870	$239/$259[7]
Games of the XXVI Olympiad, Atlanta gold half eagle		**Marcel Jovine/Frank Gasparro**
1995-W Atlanta Stadium gold Unc.	10,710	$229/$249[7]
1995-W Atlanta Stadium gold Proof	43,399	$239/$259[7]
Games of the XXVI Olympiad, Atlanta clad half dollar		**William Krawczewicz/ Malcolm Farley**
1996-S Swimming clad Unc.	50,077	$10.50/$11.50[7]
1996-S Swimming clad Proof	114,890	$11.50/$12.50[7]
Games of the XXVI Olympiad, Atlanta clad half dollar		**Clint Hansen/Malcolm Farley**
1996-S Soccer clad Unc.	53,176	$10.50/$11.50[7]
1996-S Soccer clad Proof	123,860	$11.50/$12.50[7]
Games of the XXVI Olympiad, Atlanta silver dollar		**Jim Sharpe/ Thomas D. Rogers Sr.**
1996-D Tennis Unc,	16,693	$27.95/$31.95[7]
1996-S Tennis Proof	93,880	$30.95/$34.95[7]
Games of the XXVI Olympiad, Atlanta silver dollar		**Bart Forbes/Thomas D. Rogers Sr.**
1996-D Rowing Unc.	16,921	$27.95/$31.95[7]
1996-S Rowing Proof	155,543	$30.95/$34.95[7]
Games of the XXVI Olympiad, Atlanta silver dollar		**Calvin Massey/Thomas D. Rogers Sr.**
1996-D High Jump Unc.	16,485	$27.95/$31.95[7]
1996-S High Jump Proof	127,173	$30.95/$34.95[7]
Games of the XXVI Olympiad, Atlanta silver dollar		**Jim Sharpe/Thomas D. Rogers Sr.**
1996-D Paralympic, wheelchair athlete Unc.	15,325	$27.95/$31.95[7]
1996-S Paralympic, wheelchair athlete Proof	86,352	$30.95/$34.95[7]

Commemorative Date	Final Mintage	Designer Pre-Issue/ Regular Price
Games of the XXVI Olympiad, Atlanta gold half eagle		**Frank Gasparro/ William Krawczewicz**
1996-W Olympic Flame brazier Unc.	9,453	$229/$249[7]
1996-W Olympic Flame brazier Proof	38,871	$239/$259[7]
Games of the XXVI Olympiad, Atlanta gold half eagle		**Patricia L. Verani/ William Krawczewicz**
1996-W Flag Bearer Unc.	9,397	$229/$249[7]
1996-W Flag Bearer Proof	33,214	$239/$259[7]
National Community Service silver dollar		**Thomas D. Rogers Sr./William C. Cousins**
1996-P Unc.	23,463	$30/$32[3]
1996-S Proof	100,749	$33/$37[3]
Smithsonian 150th Anniversary silver dollar		**Thomas D. Rogers/John Mercanti**
1996-P Unc.	31,320	$30/$32[3]
1996-S Proof	129,152	$33/$37[3]
Smithsonian 150th Anniversary gold half eagle		**Alfred Maletsky/T. James Ferrell**
1996-W Unc.	9,068	$180/$205[3]
1996-W Proof	21,772	$195/$225[3]
Botanic Garden silver dollar		**Edgar Z. Steever IV/William C. Cousins**
1997-P Uncirculated	83,505	$30/32[3]
1997-P Proof	269,843	$33/37[3]
Franklin Delano Roosevelt gold half eagle		**T. James Ferrell/Jim Peed**
1996-W Unc.	29,417	$180/$205[3]
1996-W Proof	11,887	$195/$225[3]
National Law Enforcement Officers Memorial silver dollar		**Alfred Maletsky**
1997-P Uncirculated	28,575	$30/32[3]
1997-P Proof	110,428	$32/37[3]
Jackie Robinson silver dollar		**Al Maletsky/T. James Ferrell**
1997-S Uncirculated	30,180	$30/32[3]
1997-S Proof	110,002	$33/37[3]
Jackie Robinson gold half eagle		**William C. Cousins/Jim Peed**
1997-W Uncirculated	5,174	$180/205[3]
1997-W Proof	24,072	$195/225[3]
Robert F. Kennedy silver dollar		**Thomas D. Rogers/Jim Peed**
1998-S Uncirculated	106,422	$30/32[3]
1998-S Proof	99,020	$33/37[3]
Black Revolutionary War Patriots silver dollar		**John Mercanti/Ed Dwight**
1998-S Uncirculated	37,210	$30/32[3]
1998-S Proof	75,070	$33/37[3]
Dolley Madison silver dollar		**Tiffany & Co.**
1999-W Uncirculated	89,104	$30/32[3]
1999-W Proof	224,403	$33/37[3]
George Washington Death Bicentennial gold half eagle		**Laura Gardin Fraser[8]**
1999-W Uncirculated	22,511	$180/205[3]
1999-W Proof	41,693	$195/225[3]
Yellowstone National Park 125th Anniversary silver dollar		**Edgar Z. Steever IV/ William C. Cousins**
1999-P Uncirculated	23,614	$30/32[3]
1999-P Proof	128,646	$32/37[3]
Library of Congress Bicentennial silver dollar		**Thomas D. Rogers Sr./John Mercanti**
2000-P Uncirculated	52,771	$25/27[3]
2000-P Proof	196,900	$28/32[3]

Commemorative		Designer
Date	Final Mintage	Pre-Issue/ Regular Price
Library of Congress Bicentennial bimetallic $10 eagle		**John Mercanti/ Thomas D. Rogers Sr.**
2000-W Uncirculated	6,683	$380/405[3]
2000-W Proof	27,167	$395/425[3]
Leif Ericson Millennium silver dollar		**John Mercanti/T. James Ferrell**
2000-P Uncirculated	28,150	$30/32[3]
2000-P Proof	144,748	$32/37[3]
Capitol Visitor Center clad half dollar		**Elizabeth Jones**
2001-P Uncirculated	79,670	$8.75/9.75, $7.75/8.50[3,9]
2001-P Proof	77,240	$11.25/12, $10.75/11.50[3,9]
Capitol Visitor Center silver dollar		**Marika Somogyi/John Mercanti**
2001-P Uncirculated	35,500	$30/32, $27/29[3,9]
2001-P Proof	141,425	$33/37, $29/33[3,9]
Capitol Visitor Center $5 half eagle		**Dean McMullen/Alex Shagin and Marcel Jovine**
2001-W Uncirculated	6,750	$180/205, $175/200[3,9]
2001-W Proof	26,815	$195/225, $177/207[3,9]
American Buffalo silver dollar		**James Earle Fraser**
2001-D Uncirculated	227,080	$30/32[3]
2001-P Proof	272,785	$33/37[3]
U.S. Military Academy Bicentennial silver dollar		**T. James Ferrell/John Mercanti**
2002-W Uncirculated	103,201	$30/32[3]
2002-W Proof	288,293	$33/37[3]
Salt Lake City Olympic Games silver dollar		**John Mercanti/Donna Weaver**
2002-P Uncirculated	40,257	$30/32[3]
2002-P Proof	166,864	$33/37[3]
Salt Lake City Olympic Games $5 half eagle		**Donna Weaver/Norman E. Nemeth**
2002-W Uncirculated	10,585	$180/205[3]
2002-W Proof	32,877	$195/225[3]
First Flight Centennial half dollar		**John Mercanti/Donna Weaver**
2003-P Uncirculated	55,360[10]	$9.75/10.75[3]
2003-P Proof	109,671[10]	$12.50/13.50[3]
First Flight Centennial silver dollar		**T. James Ferrell/ Norman E. Nemeth**
2003-W Uncirculated	52,744[10]	$31/33[3]
2003-W Proof	190,739[10]	$33/37[3]
First Flight Centennial $10 eagle		**Donna Weaver**
2003-W Uncirculated	9,197[10]	$340/365[3]
2003-W Proof	21,442[10]	$350/375[3]
Thomas Alva Edison silver dollar		**Donna Weaver/John Mercanti**
2004-P Uncirculated	Pending	$31/33[3]
2004-P Proof	Pending	$33/37[3]
Lewis and Clark Expedition Bicentennial silver dollar		**Donna Weaver**
2004-P Uncirculated	Pending	$33/35[3]
2004-P Proof	Pending	$35/39[3]

Notes

1. Prices for 1982 George Washington half dollar are for 1982 and 1983-85.
2. Prices for 1983-84 Olympic coins in some cases are first prices charged and do not reflect higher prices charged later.
3. Prices since 1986 are pre-issue/regular issue of single coins only. Most modern commem programs have offered various packaging options and combinations.
4. Although produced and sold in 1993, none of these coins actually carries the year of issue in its legends, in apparent violation of law. The anniversary dates 1991-1995 refer to the 50th anniversaries of the beginning and ending of United States involvement in World War II. More clearly, it would have been stated "1941-1991/1945-1995."
5. Although produced and sold in 1994, the coin does not carry the year of issue in its legends, in apparent violation of law. 1743 is the year of Jefferson's birth; 1993 is the 250th anniversary of that date.
6. The Special Olympics World Games silver dollar was offered "encapsulated only" without the usual presentation case. The case option was also available, at a slightly higher price.
7. Price options for individual coins. The coins were offered on a subscription basis from Dec. 2, 1994, through Feb. 3, 1995. The coins were then to be released four at a time — one gold, two silver, one clad — in February 1995, July 1995, January 1996 and sometime in the spring of 1996. Pre-issue prices and options were to be offered during the first few weeks of each release.
8. The designs are based on Fraser's submissions in the design contest for the 1932 Washington quarter dollar. The Commission of Fine Art recommended Fraser's designs but was overruled by the secretary of the Treasury, who selected the designs used from 1932 to 1998. A popular movement supporting Fraser's 1932 quarter dollar designs led to them being used on the 1999 half eagle.
9. The Mint offered each coin in two packaging offerings (standard packaging with tray and sleeve for the gold and silver coins and Mylar and envelope for the half dollar, and encapsulated with mailer for all), each at pre-issue and regular prices. The different packaging options were designed to afford buyers a choice: the more elaborate and expensive package or the coin in less packaging at lower prices. Prices given here are, in this order: standard packaging pre-issue and regular, and mailer-only packaging at pre-issue and regular.
10. Sales program open as this edition was being edited; figures as of June 17, 2004.

Error and variety coins 13

What is an error coin? An error coin deviates from the norm because of a mishap in the minting processes; in effect, an error represents a "substandard" product of the Mint. However, some collectors prefer these items to normal coins.

Errors are in very short supply when compared to total mintages, especially in the 21st century. Mint officials have introduced equipment that has reduced the number of errors produced, and caught more of those that were made. Because of the reduced numbers of errors being made, prices for some 21st century errors are much higher than for older specimens of the same type of error. For example, older off-center cents are available for a few dollars each in quantity; a 2002 Lincoln cent struck off centered was bid to $500 in an auction before being withdrawn from sale. Other errors once considered common are very rarely encountered with 21st century dates. As the quantities of once common errors available on the market diminish as they enter collections, don't be surprised to see prices for these once-inexpensive items begin to rise.

Any discussion of error coins must include a discussion of varieties. A die variety is defined as a die that can be distinguished from other dies of the same design, year and Mint because of some difference that makes that die unique (for example, the placement of the four digits of the date may differ from die to die for 18th and 19th century coins, making each die a different variety). Among the 20th century coins considered varieties are such coins as the 1955, 1972 and 1995 Lincoln, Doubled Die cents, and the 1937-D Indian Head, Three-Legged Bison 5-cent coin.

Double-denomination mule

While some classify die varieties as errors, not all die varieties were produced by mistake. The scarcity of die steel in the late 18th century and early 19th century led Mint officials to practices their 21st century counterparts would reject. For example, a die with one date (1798, for example) might be repunched with another date (1800) and used

(1800/798 Draped Bust cents actually exist!). Such coins are a form of die variety called "overdates," and while it is possible that some overdates occurred by mistake, most of the early overdated dies likely were created deliberately. Deliberate die varieties were produced as recently as a half century ago, because of the temporary closing of the San Francisco Mint; reverse dies stamped with the San Francisco Mint's Mint mark purposely were restamped with the D Mint mark of the Denver Mint after the California facility was closed. The dies with the over Mint marks were placed into use at the Denver Mint and used to strike a series of 1955-D/S Jefferson 5-cent coins.

As with error coinage, the Mint has introduced technological changes that have made most of the significant forms of varieties impossible (or highly unlikely). Repunched Mint marks and over Mint marks (both defined later in this chapter) became impossible at the beginning of the 1990s. Doubled dies supposedly became impossible in the mid- to late 1990s due to other changes in the die-production process introduced in 1996 and 1997, but some discoveries announced in 2004 could belie claims by Mint officials that doubled dies are impossible. Some researchers have identified some 2001, 2003 and 2004 Lincoln cents, some Proof 1999-P Anthony dollars and some 2004-P Jefferson, Peace Medal 5-cent coins as being minor doubled dies, although there is no universal acceptance of these pieces as die varieties, and Mint officials continue to deny such pieces are possible. Even if these pieces are genuine doubled dies, the degree of doubling present is minor compared to that on classic varieties as the 1955 and 1972 Lincoln, Doubled Die Obverse cents.

One of the most significant U.S. error coins ever produced was struck sometime during the first six months of 2000 (or just possibly, late 1999). The coin is what collectors call a double-denomination mule—it was struck on a golden dollar planchet with an obverse die for a State quarter dollar and a reverse die for the Sacagawea golden dollar. This $1.25 coin is the first U.S. double-denomination mule authenticated.

As far as can be determined, the quarter dollar-dollar mule resulted when the obverse die of a Sacagawea dollar had to be replaced, possibly because of another error. The die setter installed an obverse quarter dollar die into the press rather than a new dollar obverse die. The coins are of a similar diameter.

The double-denomination mule has a quarter dollar obverse from one of the State quarters, meaning the denomination QUARTER DOLLAR appears on that side. The denomination ONE DOLLAR appears on the opposite side. The coin has no date, since the date on the quarter was moved to the reverse in 1999 with the advent of the State quarters program.

Authenticated specimens of the Washington quarter dollar-Sacagawea dollar mule have sold for prices ranging from $29,000 to more than $56,000.

Since the discovery of this mule, three other Mint-produced mules have been brought forward; each is unique as of July 2003. The most recent to be reported (in July 2003) is actually the first double-denomination U.S. mule to have been struck (that we know of). It is a 1993-D cent-dime mule struck on a cent planchet; it has a Lincoln cent obverse and Roosevelt dime reverse. Another is a 1995 cent-dime mule, with the obverse of a Lincoln cent and reverse of a Roosevelt dime, struck on a dime blank. A third is a 1999 cent-dime mule, with a cent obverse and dime reverse, struck on a cent blank.

While the double-denomination mules have brought high prices, most error coins are worth far less. Values for error coins depend on the same factors affecting normal numismatic merchandise: supply, demand and condition.

Some die variety coins, such as the 1955 Lincoln, Doubled Die cent (it's also considered a die variety, to be discussed in a few paragraphs), because of publicity and dealer promotion, "cross over" and become popular with general collectors; thus, demand is higher for a fixed supply, and values are correspondingly higher. Condition is important, although error collectors seem less concerned with "perfection" than other collectors.

Rare does not necessarily mean great value. Many older error coins struck in small quantities are available for a few dollars. Even errors that are considered unique are often available for several dollars. Sometimes, persons not familiar with errors, including some dealers, place uncharacteristically high values on error coins.

Error and variety coins can be found in circulation, unlike many other collector items. Some collectors go to banks and obtain large quantities of coins to search through (one of the more popular columns in *Coin World* magazine, "Found in Rolls," deals with searching through coins found in rolls purchased from banks and retailers); coins not bearing errors are returned to the bank. Many errors, particularly of the minor classification, can be discovered simply by going through pocket change. Major errors, particularly those that leave the coin misshapen, are generally acquired from individuals who work at private companies that receive large quantities of unsearched coins directly from the Mint (the employees find the coins while rolling them for banks and other customers; they purchase the coins at face value and sell them to dealers with whom they have regular contact). All it takes are sharp eyes and knowledge of what to look for.

Many error collectors are adept at what is called "cherry picking." They use their superior knowledge of errors and varieties when going through a dealer's stock to obtain scarcer pieces at prices less than what a specialist might charge.

Some of that knowledge comes from a clear understanding of the minting process. The minting of a coin is a manufacturing process and should be fully understood by anyone interested in collecting and studying error coins (see **Chapter 14, "How coins are made"**). Many forms of alteration and damage received outside the Mint resemble certain types of errors, but none precisely duplicate genuine Mint errors. Collectors who understand the minting process should be better able to distinguish between errors, damage and alteration.

The following section presents variety and error coins in three categories: die varieties and errors, planchet errors and striking errors. Our categorization of error types may differ from other references.

Die varieties or errors are those produced due to a change, difference or mishap involving the die or hub. Most categories of this error type involve the surface of the die that contacts the coin during striking. Several categories involve the placement or positioning of the die in the press during coining (some error specialists believe that these errors are actually striking errors; both camps have valid points). Still others involve the use of two dies not intended to be paired together (mules).

Planchet errors are the result of defective or improperly selected planchets.

Striking errors are created during the actual striking process. Among the errors found in this category are those in which the planchet was improperly positioned during striking, coins struck more times than intended and coins struck through some foreign matter or object.

Die varieties or errors

BIE: The term commonly used for minor errors or varieties affecting the letters of the word LIBERTY on Lincoln cents. A small break in the die between the letters, especially BE, often resembles the letter I, hence the BIE designation. Such errors are much more common on the coins of the 1950s and early 1960s than more recent issues. Collectors tend to be less interested in such errors in the early 21st century than they were 30 or 40 years ago.

Clashed dies: When during the striking process two dies come together without a planchet between them, the dies clash (come into direct contact). Depending on the force with which the dies come together and the nature of the designs, a portion of the obverse design is transferred to the reverse, and a portion of the reverse is transferred to the obverse. Coins struck from the clashed dies will show signs of the transferred designs; the transferred design elements are called clash marks. Although the cause of this type of error occurs during the striking process, the die is affected; thus, it is considered a die error.

Clashed dies

Design mule: The result of dies for two different design types of the same denomination being used to strike a coin. The only known example on a U.S. coin is a 1959-D Lincoln cent struck with the 1958-style Wheat Heads reverse rather than the 1959-style Lincoln Memorial reverse. The Secret Service has not determined this coin to be counterfeit, although grading services have been reluctant to authenticate the coin and some die variety specialists are skeptical. A convicted and imprisoned counterfeiter-murderer claims to have made this piece, although he has offered no proof of his claims. Design mules exist for the coins of other countries, including Canada.

Die breaks, chips, cracks, gouges, scratches: Dies, like any other piece of steel, are subject to all sorts of damage. Any incused mark on the die leaves raised areas on coins. Breaks and cracks are similar, appearing on coins as raised lines. A die break affects a larger area than the die crack, and breaks often result in pieces of the die falling out. A die chip occurs when a small portion of the die breaks away, while gouges and scratches generally occur when a foreign object scores the surface of the die.

Die crack

A major die break is often, though misleadingly, referred to as a "cud." It occurs when the die breaks at the rim and a piece of the die falls out of the press. The metal of coins struck from that die flows up into the missing area, resulting in a raised blob of metal bearing no image. The side of the coin opposite the raised blob is often weak and indistinct; this is because

Major die break

metal flows along the path of least resistance, flowing into the broken area of the damaged die and not the recesses of the normal die. A retained major die break occurs when the die breaks at the rim, but the piece does not fall out. Coins struck from these dies show the break, but also depict the image inside the break. The design element inside the broken area may have shifted position slightly because the chunk of broken die had moved.

Double-denomination mule: The result of dies for two different denominations being used to strike a coin. The only known double-denomination U.S. mules were struck from a Washington quarter dollar obverse die and Sacagawea dollar reverse die, on a Sacagawea dollar planchet; from a 1995-D Lincoln cent obverse die and Roosevelt dime reverse die, on a cent planchet; from a 1995 Lincoln cent obverse die and Roosevelt dime die, on a dime planchet; and from a 1999 cent obverse die and dime reverse die, on a cent planchet. They are similar in concept to the design mules (dissimilar dies being used to strike a coin).

Doubled dies: If during the hubbing and die making process, a misalignment between hub and partially completed die occurs, overlapping, multiple images may appear on the die. Coins struck from the die will show the overlapping images, like the doubled date, IN GOD WE TRUST and LIBERTY on the 1955 Lincoln, Doubled Die cent. Die doubling on coins with raised designs feature a rounded second image; on coins with incused designs, the second image is flat and shelf-like. At the corners of the overlapping images are distinct "notches" on coins with raised designs. A tripled or quadrupled die is caused by the same misalignment, but bears a tripled or quadrupled image. U.S. doubled dies have been largely considered impossible since 1996 to 1997 due to technological improvements at the Mint. Doubled dies generally can only occur when more than one impression of hub into die is required, and the alignment between hub and die shifts or distorts between hubbing operations. Mint officials claim the new single-hubbing equipment eliminates the possibility that doubled dies can be created. However, some die variety specialists have identified coins as minor doubled dies that were struck after the single-hubbing process was introduced, possibly of a class of doubled die that does not require double hubbing of the die.

Doubled die

Engraving varieties and errors: While more common on the dies of the 18th and 19th centuries, engraving errors and varieties have been made on modern dies. On the earlier dies, numerals and letters were often repunched to strengthen the design, punched in upside down or otherwise out of alignment, and sometimes, wrong letters or numbers were punched into the die. On more modern dies, engraving errors include the use of the wrong size Mint mark by mistake and Mint marks placed too close to design elements or otherwise too far from their intended locations. Other "engraving" errors, discussed in separate sections, include doubled dies, overdates and repunched Mint marks.

Repunched date

Misaligned dies: Although one side of the coin appears to have been struck off-center, the planchet was not off-centered during striking, as in an off-center coin. A misaligned die occurs when one die is horizontally displaced to the side, causing only a partial image to appear on that side of the coin. However, unlike the off-center coin that it resembles, only one side is affected. The other side is normal. Some specialists classify misaligned dies as striking errors.

Misplaced dates: A misplaced date is a relatively recently studied variety. Researchers have discovered numerous coins with numbers from the date punched well away from the region of the die where the date was punched. For example, coins have been found with a number or numbers punched into the dentils along the rim or into a major design element. While theories abound, no one is sure whether this punching was accidental or deliberate.

Overdates: When one or more numerals in the date are engraved, punched or hubbed over a different numeral or numerals, both the original date and the second date can be seen. Modern hubbed examples include the 1943/2-P Jefferson 5-cent coin and the 1942/1 Winged Liberty Head dime (both are also doubled dies). The traditional, pre-20th century overdate occurred when one date was punched over another date, as on the 1818/5 Capped Bust quarter dollar.

Overdate

Over Mint marks: A form of repunched Mint mark, but when punches of two different Mints are used. Examples include the 1944-D/S Lincoln cent and the 1938-D/S Indian Head 5-cent coin. These can occur accidentally or deliberately, as noted earlier.

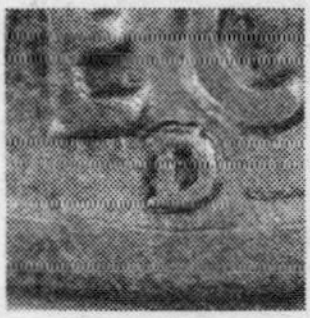
Over Mint mark

Polished dies: Mint employees polish dies to extend their working life and to remove such things as clash marks, die scratches, dirt and grease. If the die is polished too much, details may be erased or small raised lines may appear on the coins. Most over-polished errors have little value, but there are exceptions, most prominently the 1937-D Indian Head, Three-Legged Bison 5-cent coin.

Repunched

Repunched Mint marks: Mint marks were punched into each individual working die (for coins issued for circulation) by hand with mallet and punch until changes were made to the process in 1990 and 1991 (see **Chapter 14, "How Coins Are Made,"** and **Chapter 8, "Mints and Mint marks,"** for details). Under the old system, several blows to the punch were needed to properly sink the Mint mark into the working die. If the punch was not properly placed after the first blow, a multiple image could result. A coin identified as a 1960-D/D Lincoln cent has a repunched D Mint mark, for example.

Rotated dies: Most U.S. coins have the obverse and reverse sides oriented so each side is upright when rotated vertically. The alignment between the two is 180 degrees. However, if the dies are aligned at anything other than 180 degrees, the dies are considered rotated. The Mint considers coins rotated 5 degrees or less within tolerance. Some specialists consider rotated dies to be striking errors since the die's face is unchanged.

Worn dies: Dies have a limited life, based on the hardness of the coinage metal being struck and the striking pressures involved. When a die wears beyond a certain point, details around the rim tend to flow into the rim, while other details weaken. The surface of the die becomes scarred, as if heavily polished. Some design elements appear doubled. Coins struck from worn dies rarely have collector value as die errors.

Planchet errors

Alloy errors: All U.S. coins are produced from alloyed metals that are mixed when molten to strict specifications. If mixed incorrectly, the metals may cool in nonhomogeneous form, with streaks of different metals appearing on the surface of the coin.

Brass-plated cent: A post-1982 error is the brass-plated cent. Zinc planchets are plated with copper to form a copper-plated zinc planchet. Zinc planchets sometimes remain within the plating tanks and dissolve, contaminating the plating solution (electrolyte), adding their zinc content to the copper, thus forming brass. Subsequent planchets are plated with brass instead of pure copper. Brass-plated cents have a different color than copper-plated cents, although both can tone and may be difficult to distinguish.

Damaged planchets: Planchets are subject to various sorts of damage, including cracks (not to be confused with die cracks), holes and major breaks.

Damaged planchet

Fragments, scrap struck: Small pieces of coinage metal—fragments and scrap left over from the blanking process—sometimes fall between the dies and are struck. Fragments must be struck on both sides and weigh less than 25 percent of a normal coin's weight to qualify as struck fragments. Planchet scrap is generally larger than a fragment, and usually has straight or curved edges because of the blanking process.

Struck fragment

Incomplete planchets: Often, though erroneously, called a "clip," an incomplete planchet results from a mishap in the blanking process. If the planchet strip does not advance far enough after a bank of punches rams through the metal, producing planchets, the punches come down and overlap the holes where the planchets were already punched out. Where the overlapping takes place, a curved area appears to be "missing" from the planchet. The word "clip," commonly used, suggests a piece of the planchet was cut off, which is not the cause of the incomplete planchet. "Clip," when properly used, refers to the ancient process of cutting small pieces of metal from the edges of precious metal coins for the bullion; that is why U.S. gold and silver coins have lettered or reeded edges, to make it more difficult to clip a coin. Other incomplete planchets occur when the strip shifts to the side, causing the punches to overlap the strip's edge, or when the punches overlap the end of the strip. The missing area is represented by a straight edge, not curved. An "incomplete incomplete planchet" occurs when the punch does not completely punch out a planchet, but leaves a circular groove. If the strip advances improperly, planchets overlapping the incomplete punch will bear a curved groove; the groove remains visible after the coin is struck. It is often called an incomplete clip. Most but not all incomplete planchet errors have a "signature" known as the Blakesley effect. The area of the rim 180 degrees opposite the "clip" is

Incomplete planchet

weak or nonexistent since the "clip" negates the rim-making process in the upset mill. The lack of pressure in the upset mill at the clip results in improper formation of the rim on the opposite side.

Laminations: During the preparation of the planchet strip, foreign materials—grease, dirt, oil, slag or gas—may become trapped just below the surface of the metal. Coins struck from this strip later may begin to flake and peel since adhesion is poor in the location of the trapped material. The Jefferson, Wartime 5-cent coins are particularly susceptible to laminations, due to the poor mixing qualities of the metals used during the war metal emergency.

Split planchets: Planchets can split due to deep internal laminations or, in the case of clad coinage, because of poor adhesion of the copper-nickel outer layers to the copper core (these are also known as missing clad layer errors). Planchets may split before or after striking. On nonclad coins, the inner portion of the split shows parallel striations typical of the interior structure of coinage metal.

Split planchet

Thick and thin planchets: Planchets of the wrong thickness are produced from strip not properly rolled. Too little pressure can result in planchet stock that is too thick; too much pressure can result in thin planchets. Rollers out of alignment on one side create potential for tapered planchets—thicker in one area than another.

Unplated planchets: New in U.S. coinage, unplated planchets became possible in 1982 with the introduction of the copper-plated zinc cent (and similarly in 1943 with the zinc-coated steel cents). The zinc-copper alloy planchets are plated after they are punched from the strip but some planchets miss the plating process. Coins struck on the unplated planchets are grayish-white in color. Beware of cents that have had their plating removed or have been replated after leaving the Mint. Although beyond the ability of a neophyte to detect, any authentication service should be able to distinguish between a genuine piece and an altered version.

Wrong metal, planchet, stock: A wrong metal error is struck on a planchet intended for a denomination of a different composition. This includes 5-cent coins struck on cent planchets, cents on dime planchets, and higher denominations struck on cent and 5-cent planchets. A second type is the wrong planchet error, defined as a coin struck on a planchet of the correct composition, but the wrong denomination.

These include quarter dollars struck on dime planchets, half dollars struck on quarter dollar and dime planchets, and dollars struck on other clad planchets. Some specialists claim that wrong metal and wrong planchet errors are striking errors, not planchet errors. Their argument? The planchet is OK. It was just fed into the wrong coining press. A third type is the wrong planchet stock error. It occurs when clad coinage strip rolled to the thickness of one denomination is fed into the blanking press of another denomination; the diameter is correct, but the thickness is thicker or thinner than normal. The most common appears to be 1970-D Washington quarter dollars struck on planchet stock intended for dimes. A fourth, rarer, form is the double denomination. It occurs when a coin is struck on a previously struck coin, such as a cent struck over a dime. Since the U.S. Mint has struck coins for foreign governments in the past, it has been possible to find in circulation U.S. coins struck on planchets intended for foreign coins, as well as U.S. coins struck on previously struck foreign coins. Another rare type of wrong metal error is called the transitional error. It occurs as a coin's composition changes. Some 1965 coins are known struck on silver planchets of 1964 composition, while some 1964 coins were struck on clad planchets (1964 coins were struck through 1965, with planchets for both types of coins available side by side). Until 2000, it was thought impossible for a coin to be struck on a planchet larger than normal (the larger planchet, it was thought, would jam the feed mechanism of the press). However, several exceptions to this rule surfaced in 2000, including State quarter dollars struck on the slightly larger Sacagawea dollar planchets.

Wrong planchet

Striking errors

Broadstrikes: If the surrounding collar is pushed below the surface of the lower die during the moment of striking, the metal of the coin being struck is free to expand beyond the confines of the dies. The design of the coin is normal at center, but as it nears the periphery, becomes distorted due to the uncontrolled spread of metal.

Broadstrike

Brockage and capped die strikes: If a newly struck coin sticks to the surface of one of the dies, it acts as a die itself—called a die cap—and produces images on succeeding coins. The image produced by any die is the direct opposite on a coin, and brockages are no different. Since the image is raised on the coin adhering to the die, the image on the brockage is incused and reversed—a true mirror image. The first brockage strikes, perfect mirror images and undistorted, are most prized. As additional coins are struck from the capped die, the die cap begins to spread and is made thinner under the pressures of striking, distorting its image. Although the image is recognizable, the design expands, producing an image that can be several times the normal size. At some point, as the die cap becomes thinner and the brockage image disappears, the coins struck cease to be brockages and are known as capped die strikes. Capped die strikes are simply a form of struck-through coin. At first, few of the original design elements from the obscured die are visible, though as the cap becomes thinner, more and more of the original design elements are transferred from the obscured die through the die cap. Finally, the die cap breaks off or is pounded so thin it ceases to affect succeeding strikes. Sometimes, the die caps fall off early and in a relatively undistorted state. Die caps resemble bottle caps, with the metal wrapping around the shaft of the die. Die caps are very rare and collectible, much more so than capped die strikes.

Brockage

Double and multiple strikes: Double strikes are coins struck more than once. If the coin rotates slightly between strikes, but remains centered within the coining chamber, two images will appear on both sides of the coin. The first strike will be almost totally obliterated by the second strike, and the first strike will be flattened and have almost no relief. Sometimes, a struck coin will flip and fall upside down onto the surface of the die; thus, the second strike has an obverse image obliterating the original reverse, and a reverse image flattening the first obverse image. If the coin falls partially outside the dies after the first strike, the second image is only partial. The partial second strike obliterates the original image beneath it, but the rest of the first strike is undistorted, except in the immediate vicinity of the second strike. A saddle strike is generally not a

Double struck

true double strike, but usually the result of having a planchet fall partially between two pairs of dies on a multi-die press. Saddle strikes have two partial images and an expanse of unstruck planchet between the struck areas, resembling Mickey Mouse's head with the partial coin images representing his ears. Examples of coins struck three, four or more times are known, but are typically more rare than simple double-struck coins.

Filled dies: The Mint factory has its share of dirt, grease and other lubricants, and metal filings. The recessed areas of the dies sometimes fill with a combination of this foreign material, preventing the metal of the coins from flowing into the incused areas. This results in weak designs or missing design details, and is among the most common types of errors. Filled-die coins are a form of struck-through error. Filled-die coins rarely carry significant premiums.

Filled die

Indented errors: An indented error is a coin struck with another coin or planchet lying partially on its surface. The area covered by the planchet does not hit the die and thus is blank if indented by a planchet, or shows a partial brockage if indented by a struck coin. The most desirable of the indented errors are larger coins with the indentation of a smaller planchet centered on one side. Indented error coins are a form of struck-through error.

Indented error

Machine, mechanical or strike doubling: A form of doubling, this is among the most common types of Mint errors. Some do not consider it an error, but believe it to be a form of Mint-caused damage. Others, however, believe it a true form of error coin. The cause is a looseness of the die or other parts in the press that causes the die to twist or bounce across the surface of the newly struck coin. In twisting or bouncing, the die shoves the metal of the raised designs to one side, creating the doubled image. The doubling is flat, like a shelf. Machine-doubled coins are often mistaken for doubled die coins. However, the two forms of doubling have different causes and are distinct in appearance. Machine-doubled coins rarely carry significant premiums.

Strike doubling

Off-center coins: If a planchet lies partially outside of the dies during the striking, it receives an off-center strike. Each coin struck off center is unique. Off-center coins with dates are more valuable than coins without dates. Generally but not always, on dated coins, the greater the off-center strike, the more it is worth. Some collectors collect off-center coins by their "clock" positions. Hold the coin with portrait upright and look for the direction the strike lies. If it is at 90 degrees, the strike is at 3 o'clock; if it lies at 270 degrees, the strike is at 9 o'clock.

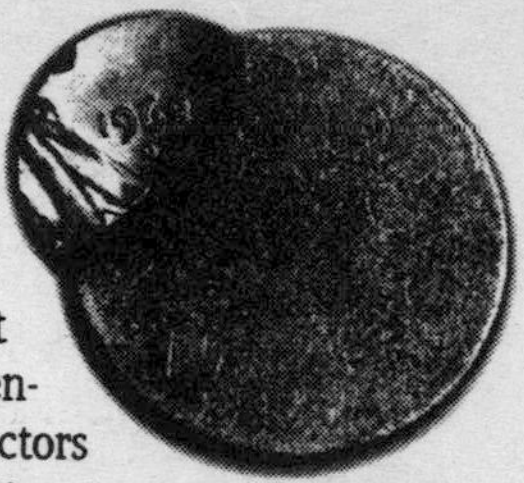

Off center

Partial collar: Often known as "railroad rim" errors, the edge, not the rim, is the portion of the coin affected. It occurs when the collar is pushed somewhat below the surface of the lower die, so that the upper portion of the coin is free to expand beyond the confines of the collar, while the lower portion is restrained. On coins struck from a reeded collar, partial reeding exists on the area restrained by the collar. The error gets the nickname "railroad rim" from its appearance—the coin, viewed edge-on, resembles the wheel from a railroad car.

Struck-through errors: Struck-through errors occur when foreign objects fall between die and planchet during striking. Pieces of cloth, metal fragments, wire, slivers of reeding, grease, oil, dirt, wire bristles (from wire brushes used to clean dies, resembling staples), die covers, a thin die cap, other coins, planchets and other objects may fall between the dies and the coin. The most collectible struck-through errors are those with the foreign object still embedded in the surface of the coin.

Struck through

Weak strikes: Weak strikes often resemble coins struck from grease-filled dies, but can be identified. They occur either when the press has been turned off—it tends to cycle through several strikings, each with less pressure than the previous—or when the press is being set up by the operators who test the placement of the dies at lower coining pressures. On reeded coins, weak strikes generally have poorly formed reeding (it is strong on filled dies). Depending on the pressure used, the image may be only slightly weak, practically nonexistent or any stage in between.

How coins are made 14

The various coining facilities of the United States Mint are factories, whose products happen to be coinage of the realm. Like any other metalworking factory, the U.S. Mint has a variety of presses, engraving and reducing machines, and metalworking equipment.

Like any metal product, coins don't "just happen." A number of intricate steps must be taken, from the preparation of the raw metal used in the coins to the striking of the coins. And before the coins can be struck, dies must be produced.

For a new design, the dies used for striking coins start out as an approved sketch in the Engraving Department at the Philadelphia Mint. Using the sketch, a sculptor-engraver makes a clay or wax model about 8¾ inches in diameter. When final approval of the design is received, a hard epoxy positive model is prepared.

The completed epoxy model is then mounted on a Janvier transfer engraving machine. This machine traces the exact details of the epoxy model, reduces them and cuts the design into soft tool steel, producing a positive replica that Mint officials call a "reduction hub" and collectors call a "master hub." The master hub, which has the exact dimensions of the coin, is then tempered and the steel hardened. The steel bar on which the master hub was engraved is trimmed and the shaft turned to a specific shape. The master hub then is placed in a hydraulic press and slowly pressed into a blank piece of soft die steel until a negative replica is made, called a master die. The die blank is cone shaped, which facilitates the process of creating the design details. Design details are first formed in the center, where the metal of the die blank is the highest and thus comes into contact with the hub first.

Work hubs (the Mint's term) or working hubs (the hobby's term) are made from the master die in the hydraulic press in the same way as the original, master die was impressed. Work dies (those used to strike coins) are made from the work hubs in the same way. (A single master die can make multiple work hubs, each of which can be used to make multiple work dies.)

Until the mid- to late 1990s, it took several hubbing operations to fully form the design on the hub or die being produced. Since the act of

Janvier reducing machine transfers image from large epoxy model at right to coin-sized steel hub at left

impressing a piece of blank die steel with a hub or die work hardens the metal, partially completed dies or hubs had to be removed from the hubbing press, placed into a furnace to be annealed (softened), allowed to cool and then reinstalled in the hubbing press for a second impression. This process would be repeated until the entire design was fully formed. (Any misalignment between hub and die during the subsequent hubbing operations, any distortion occurring to the partially completed die or hub during annealing and cooling, any wear to the hub or die being used to form the new die or hub, or the selection of a different die or hub to complete the hubbing operation, could result in doubling on the new die or hub where design details did not match exactly, creating what collectors call doubled dies.)

Since 1997, most dies produced at the Philadelphia and Denver Mints have been produced on newer equipment that permits single-impression hubbing, with the complete image formed during one impression of die into hub. That technology was introduced when a new die shop went into operation at the Denver Mint (the first there) on May 13, 1996. Half-dollar and other larger denomination dies continued to be produced throughout 1998 on older equipment requiring multiple impressions of hub into die to fully form the image. The two Mints began producing half dollar dies in a single hubbing operation in

1999. The dies for the 1999 Anthony dollars were made on the old multiple-hubbing press and required multiple hubbings.

No matter which equipment is used to make work dies, the final product needs to be tempered and hardened, and the shafts must be shaped on a lathe to permit their installation in the presses. Much of the equipment used in shaping the shaft of the die is new and computer controlled and monitored.

The Philadelphia Mint produces all master hubs and master dies for all coins: circulating, Uncirculated Mint set and Proofs.

The Philadelphia Mint also prepares all of the working hubs and working dies for circulating coins and Uncirculated Mint set coins to be produced at the Philadelphia Mint. The Denver Mint produces the working hubs and working dies for the coins it strikes.

The Philadelphia facility and the Denver Mint share die production duties for Proof coins struck at the San Francisco Mint, depending on workload production requirements. For the Proof 2004 coinage, for example, the Philadelphia Mint made the dies for the dollar (obverse and reverse), some of the quarter dollar obverses and all of the quarter dollar reverses. The Denver Mint made the dies for the Proof 2004 cent (both obverse and reverse), 5-cent coins (both designs, both sides), dime (both sides), some of the quarter dollar obverses and all of the half dollar dies (obverse and reverse).

The San Francisco Mint executes the chroming of the working dies to finish the process before the production of Proof coins.

The introduction of one design element to the die production process requires additional explanation. Mint marks—found on many U.S. coins since 1838 and all U.S. coins since 1980 except for the Lincoln cent struck at the Philadelphia Mint—have been added at various stages of the die-production process, depending on the era. Traditionally, beginning in the 1830s, Mint engravers placed the Mint mark by hand on each of the thousands of working dies.

That is no longer the case. Mint marks on commemorative coins and Proof coins are placed at the initial modeling stage and have been since the mid- to late 1980s. For the circulating coins, beginning in 1990, the Mint began placing the Mint mark on the master die for the cent and 5-cent coin. The other denominations—dime, quarter dollar and half dollar—followed in 1991.

Most recently, the S Mint mark appears at the earliest modeling stage, but not the other Mint marks. The master die from this master hub is used to produce two work hubs from which the S Mint mark is removed; a P Mint mark is added to one of these hubs and a D Mint mark to the other (creating, essentially, two new reduction hubs that can then be used to produce master dies for the Philadelphia and Denver Mints).

All of these changes lessen the possibility of producing Mint mark errors and varieties (see the chapter on error coins for details on the types of errors once possible).

Blanks and planchets

Modern United States coins have their beginnings in the private sector, where a number of companies process the raw metals from which coins are made, and produce some coinage blanks and planchets and all coils of strip metal the Mint purchases.

In preparing the raw metals used in coining, the coinage metals are assayed, mixed to the proper proportions, melted and formed into slabs that are heated and rolled to the correct thickness. For clad coinage, bonding operations are required to bond the two outer layers to the inner layer. The strip is then coiled and shipped to the Mint for blanking. The Mint once did all of its own metal processing, including melting, assaying and mixing different metals together to create alloys. However, the Mint closed its refining operations several decades ago because of environmental concerns and now relies on private companies to do all of this initial work. The Mint produced its own strip metal as late as Fiscal Year 1982 at the Philadelphia Mint, but the operations were closed officially in Fiscal 1983.

Once coinage strip is rolled to the proper thickness, blanks are punched from it (both at the Mint and at the private suppliers, depending on the denomination). Blanks and planchets are the unstruck, circular pieces of metal that become coins when struck between the dies. Blanks and planchets represent the same product at different stages of production, although sometimes the terms "blank" and "planchet" are used interchangeably. Blanks are unfinished planchets that haven't been through all of the processing steps necessary before they can be struck into coins. Once a blank has been through all of the processing steps, it becomes a planchet and is ready to be struck.

Blanks are produced on blanking presses, which are simply punch presses similar to those found in any machine shop. They have a bank of punches (or rams) that travel downward, just barely penetrating the strip of coinage metal. The blanks are partially sheared, partially torn from the strip each time the punches make their downward cycle and pass through the strip. At this stage, the blanks have rough edges where they were torn from the strip. Most of the rough edges (or burrs) are removed during succeeding operations.

The next step is to give most blanks a slightly raised rim. This is done in an upsetting mill.

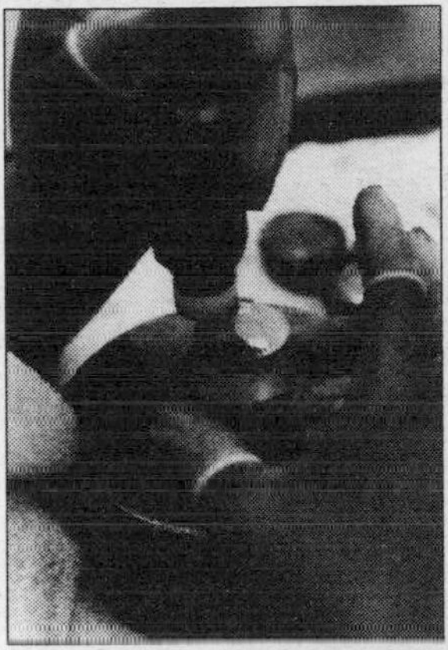

Die being polished for a Proof coin

The upsetting mill consists of a rotating wheel with V-shaped grooves on its edge. The grooved edge of the wheel fits into a curved section (or shoe) that has corresponding grooves. The distance between the wheel and the shoe gets progressively narrower so that, as the blank is rolled along the groove, it is compressed and a raised rim is formed on both sides of the blank. This raised rim serves several purposes. It sizes and shapes the blank to lower the stress on the dies in the coining press and facilitates the formation of the rim on the coin.

At times, the Mint has found it unnecessary to upset the rims of certain planchets, including, for at least part of the 1990s, those blanks intended for Jefferson 5-cent coins struck at the Denver Mint.

During the upsetting operation, the blanks have been "work-hardened" and must now be softened by being heated to controlled temperatures in a process called annealing. The blanks are heated in a rotating tubular furnace to approximately 1,400 degrees Fahrenheit, changing their crystal structure to a softer state. Planchets are cooled slowly. The annealing process prolongs the life of the coining dies by ensuring well-struck coins with lower striking pressures.

Despite a protective atmosphere, annealing causes some surface discoloration that must be removed from the blanks. The planchets (their status changes from blank to planchet with the addition of the rim) pass through a chemical bath, are tumble dried and then burnished (these last steps clean the planchets and shine them to a high luster).

The planchets are next passed over sorting screens, called "riddlers," that are supposed to eliminate all of the defective pieces. The screens separate too-large, too-small and incomplete planchets from the normal planchets. Rejected blanks are remelted.

The planchets are ready to be struck into coins on the Mint's coining presses. Conveyor belts or wheeled tote bins are used to move the planchets from the riddlers to the coining presses.

Coining presses are designed for any denomination of coin. Dies and collars can be removed and new ones for a different denomination installed. Striking pressures are adjustable for the various denominations and metals. A circular piece of hardened steel forms the collar, which acts as the wall of the coining chamber. The dies impress the various designs and devices on the obverse and reverse for the coin while the collar forms the edge of the coin, flat and smooth on cents, 5-cent coins and Sacagawea dollars and reeded on the dime, quarter dollar, half dollar and other dollar coins. The collar, which is five-thousandths of an inch larger in diameter than the dies, is mounted on springs that allow slight vertical movement.

Generally, the reverse die is the lower (or anvil) die while the obverse die is the upper (or hammer) die; however, there are exceptions. On some presses, dies are mounted horizontally so that they move parallel to the floor. Still, the terms anvil die and hammer die are appropriate on these latter presses.

Planchets are fed by gravity from a basin attached to the press through a cylindrical tube. This tube stacks 20 or so planchets. From this stack, the bottom planchet is fed into the press by one of several feed devices.

One device is called feed fingers: two parallel pieces of metal joined in such a way that they can open and close; on one end of the two pieces is a covered recessed slot and in the center is a hole. A second device is a dial feeder: a circular piece slotted with holes that transport the planchets to the coining chamber and then transport the newly struck coin from the dies.

No matter which feed device is used, the coining process is the same. The anvil die at this point is stationary. The hammer die moves toward the anvil die, the dies impress the designs of both sides into the planchet and then the hammer die completes its cycle by moving back to its original position. On presses using the dial feeder, the dial remains stationary so that the hole transporting the planchet remains centered over the anvil die, with the hammer die passing through the hole to strike the coin. Then, the anvil die moves above the collar, actuated by an eccentric cam, raising the struck coin out of the coining chamber. Depending on the feeder system used, one of two things happens.

As the anvil die moves, about the same time, the feeder fingers, in a closed position, start to move forward with a planchet lying in the center hole. At this time the anvil die reaches the top of its cycle, the recessed slot (ejection slot) in the feed fingers slides over the struck coin and pushes the coin away from the coining chamber. The struck coin's momentum carries it forward until it hits a shield that deflects it into the struck coin hopper. The feed fingers have completed their forward movement and now the center hole is above the coining chamber. The feed fingers open, allowing the planchet to fall into the coining chamber. Then the feed fingers reverse direction to return to their original position.

On presses using a dial feeder, the struck coin is pushed back up into the hole that had carried the planchet; the dial rotates, moving the coin away from the coining chamber while the next hole drops a new planchet onto the lower die. The cam action now causes the lower die to move to its stationary position.

Presses fed by dial feeders have sensors that automatically stop the press if a planchet is mispositioned, of the wrong size or incomplete, or is missing. The Mints have made good use of this feature to decrease production of many of the error coins that entice collectors.

Frequently, while a press is in operation, the press attendant may pick up a finished coin for inspection to catch some of the remaining varieties and errors that are still produced. The inspector examines the coin under a magnifier to search for any defects made in the die during operation.

Throughout the minting process, computers track such statistics as the productivity of each press operator, any repairs to a coining press, quantities of coins struck per press, plus installation, movement and destruction of the dies.

After the coins have been struck, they are counted automatically by machines or weighed, and are bagged or placed into shipping bins. The Mint has stopped using the canvas "Mint-sewn bags" for most denominations; instead, it uses much larger "ballistic" bags, which can hold hundreds or thousands of coins. Counters atop the mechanism that dumps coins into the ballistic bags remove most out-of-specification coins (errors), performing the functions that riddlers once did at the post-striking stage. The coins now are ready for shipment from the Mint to the Federal Reserve Banks or private money-handling firms for distribution.

Proof and Uncirculated coins

15

The United States Mint has had a longstanding relationship with American coin collectors, though not always a problem-free one. Although the primary business of the Mint is to produce sufficient coinage for use in commerce, it has produced special collectors' products for much of its existence. The Mint's most popular collectors' products, no doubt, have been Proof coins and sets and Uncirculated Mint sets, including since 1994 some low-mintage coins with a special Matte Finish. Limited edition sets of commemorative coins and rolls and mini-bags of State quarter dollars are other popular programs.

Proof coins are produced using special minting and processing techniques, resulting in coins with special finishes. They have been sold separately in the past, but since 1950, have been offered only in sets although Proof versions of recent commemorative coins, the American Eagle bullion coins and the 1999 Anthony dollars have been offered individually.

Uncirculated Mint sets contain coins produced under more or less standard conditions, packaged as a set and sold for a fee over the coins' face value. Recent sets contain coins of higher quality than those struck for circulation; older sets contain coins of the same quality as intended to circulate.

The sets provide collectors with Uncirculated examples of each coin struck for circulation that year, and in some cases, examples of coins struck for the Uncirculated Mint sets only (the three 1981 Anthony dollars, for example, and the 1970-D Kennedy half dollar).

The first Uncirculated Mint sets, with coins dated 1947, were offered in 1948. After the 1947 sets sold out, 1948-dated sets were offered to the public. Sets were again offered in 1949, but none were offered in 1950 due to a Treasury decision to conserve appropriations and manpower during the Korean War, and because Uncirculated coins were available from banks. From 1951 through 1964, sets were offered every year. The numbers of coins offered fluctuated from year to year, depending upon what denominations were being struck for circulation.

Before 1959, Uncirculated Mint sets were individually packaged in cardboard folders; each set contained two specimens of each coin struck that year. Beginning in 1959, sets were packaged in polyethylene packets and contained just one example of each coin struck that year.

No Uncirculated Mint sets or Proof sets were offered from 1965 to 1967 because the Mint focused almost all of its resources to meeting a major coin shortage sweeping the country, which was blamed in part (and mistakenly) on coin collectors and speculators. However, Mint officials did offer Special Mint sets, featuring coins not the quality of Proofs but better than those found in the pre-1964 Uncirculated Mint sets.

Production and sales of Uncirculated Mint sets resumed in 1968. From 1973 to 1978, Philadelphia and Denver Mint specimens of the Eisenhower dollar were contained in the set. In 1979, the Eisenhower dollar was replaced by the Anthony dollar, and a San Francisco Assay Office specimen was added; the Anthony dollars appeared in the sets through 1981. No Uncirculated Mint sets were offered in 1982 and 1983, with Mint officials blaming budgetary cutbacks for the decision to stop their production. Because of collector pressure, Congress passed a law in 1983 requiring annual sales of both Uncirculated Mint sets and Proof sets.

As noted earlier, some Uncirculated Mint sets contain coins not struck for circulation. This generally increases the value of the sets because collectors saving an example of each coin struck each year will be unable to find the needed coins in circulation. In 1970, no half dollars were struck for circulation; thus, the 1970-D Kennedy half dollar could only be found in the set. In 1973, no Eisenhower dollars were struck for circulation, but the dollars were included in the set. The only way to obtain the three 1981 Anthony dollars was to buy the Uncirculated Mint set of that year, and in 1987, no Kennedy half dollars were struck for circulation but they were included in the set. The 1996 Uncirculated sets include a 1996-W Roosevelt dime—available nowhere else—added at no charge to commemorate the 50th anniversary of the coin's introduction. The 2002 to 2004 Uncirculated Mint sets contain Kennedy half dollars and Sacagawea dollars, none of which were struck for circulation (although circulation-quality halves and dollars were struck each of those years for collector sales).

About the "mintages" given here: Figures for 2003 sets are unaudited as of mid-June 2004 and thus not final. Sales of the 2003 sets continued into 2004, generally until the 2004 editions became available. It takes Mint officials months after the close of sales of a particular set to audit the numbers and determine a final "mintage" or sales figure. Sales of the 2004 Silver State Quarters Proof set had closed as this edition was being prepared, but as with the 2003 sets, the sales figure had not been audited and thus is unofficial. Expect the figures for the 2003 sets and the

2004 silver quarter set listed to change in the 2006 edition of this book.

Proof coins and sets

While coins in Uncirculated Mint sets are little or no different from those struck for circulation, Proof coins are a special breed. A Proof coin is struck on specially prepared planchets, using special minting techniques, generally on a specialized coining press.

The term "Proof" means different things to many collectors, dealers and other hobbyists. Some believe Proof is the top level of preservation, or grade—it is not. Others believe Proof coins are particularly shiny coins destined for collectors rather than circulation—they are only partly correct.

"Proof" in numismatics refers to a special manufacturing process designed to result in coins of the highest quality produced especially for collectors. "Proof" is not a grade, as many beginning collectors think, although grading services, dealers and collectors generally assign Proof coins numerical grades such as Proof 63 or Proof 65.

Proof coins result from the same basic processes also required to make coins for circulation. However, Mint employees use special techniques in preparing the surfaces of the dies and planchets intended for Proof coins. Special presses and striking techniques are also used in the production of Proof coins.

Most of the Proof coins sold by the United States Mint today are Cameo Proofs. The flat fields are mirror-like, reflective and shiny. The raised devices, lettering and other points in relief are frosted, bearing a white, textured, nonreflective finish. The contrast between the frosted relief and mirrored fields give the coins their cameo appearance. Both the frosted and mirror finishes are the results of the special techniques used in preparing the dies.

All dies are produced at the Philadelphia Mint and Denver Mint die shops; the San Francisco Mint and West Point Mint have no die shops of their own. Remember that a die features a mirror-image, incused version of the finished coin's design. Points that are raised on the coin are incused on the die. Points incused on the coin are in relief on the die.

To prepare a Cameo Proof die, the entire die is sandblasted with an aluminum oxide and glass bead compound to create the frosted surfaces. The fields are then polished to a high sheen to achieve the mirrored effect.

Once the polishing is completed, the die receives a light plating of chrome, two- to three-thousandths of an inch thick. The chrome is then buffed. The finished die now has mirror-like fields and textured relief, and will impart the same finishes to the coins it strikes.

The planchets used to strike the Proof coins also receive special treatment. The planchets are burnished in a process that tumbles them in a media of carbon steel balls, water and an alkaline soap. The process cleans and polishes the planchets. The burnished planchets are rinsed in clear water and towel-dried by hand, then go through another cleaning and hand-drying process. Compressed air is used to blow lint and dust from the planchets.

Proof coins are struck on special presses that operate at slower speeds than the high-speed presses used for striking circulating coinage. While the Proof coining presses, like all presses, impress the design from the dies onto the planchet, the production of a business strike is a much more rapid, violent event. Each Proof coin is struck two or more times, depending on the size of the coin, the design and the composition of the metal. The multiple striking ensures that the detail is brought up fully on each coin. Business strikes are struck only once (although some U.S. business strikes in the past have been struck more than once, most notably the 1907 Saint-Gaudens, High Relief double eagle).

Proof coins are then sealed into plastic capsules or plastic holders to give their surfaces some protection (though not total) from potentially damaging environmental factors.

Although most collectors of modern U.S. Proof coins are familiar with the Frosted Proofs in vogue today, there are many other types of Proof finishes. Some used by the U.S. Mint include the Matte Proof, first used in the early 20th century; a similar Matte Finish was used on several special coins issued in the 1990s. The entire surface of the coin is uniformly dull or granular; the surface of the original Matte Proof coins results from the struck coin being pickled in acid. A Satin Finish Proof coin has a matte, satiny surface; the finishing process, used in the early 20th century, is currently unknown. A Sandblast Proof is a type of Matte Proof in which the surface of the coin is sandblasted, not pickled in acid. A Roman Finish Proof was used on gold Proofs of 1909 and 1910 and is similar to the Satin Finish Proof. A Brilliant Proof is one in which the entire surface is mirror-like; any frosted devices are accidental, found generally only on the first few strikes of the die. Brilliant Proofs were produced by the U.S. Mint until the late 1970s and early 1980s, when Mint officials began taking care to produce the Frosted Proofs.

The Philadelphia Mint struck its first true Proof coins in 1817, not for collectors but as presentation pieces. From 1817 to 1859, Proof coins were made in small batches whenever a number of orders had accumulated.

Proof coins were first offered to the public at large in 1858, the result of a decision by Mint Director John Ross Snowden. It was not until 1860, however, that mintages jumped as collector interest caught hold and the Mint began anticipating demand rather than striking the Proof coins to order.

Coins were sold individually and in complete sets, the latter in limited quantities. Sets were sometimes sold as separate sets of minor coins and gold coins in addition to the complete sets.

From 1907 to 1916, the Mint began experimenting with various Proof finishes, including the aforementioned Matte Proof, Sandblast Proof and Roman Finish Proof finishes.

The Mint stopped offering Proof coins in 1916. Walter Breen in his *Encyclopedia of United States and Colonial Proof Coins: 1722-1977* notes: "At first ostensibly because of the war, later more likely because of administration changes (there being no coin collectors in high office until William H. Woodin became secretary of the Treasury), no Proofs were publicly sold. The few made went to VIPs and most are controversial."

Proof coinage resumed in 1936 with the production of Brilliant Proofs. Coins were sold by the piece with five denominations making a complete set. Mintages of the Proof "sets" from 1936 through 1942 are based on the coin with the smallest mintage. Abandoned were the experiments with Matte Proofs and other Proof finishes. Proof production halted again at the end of 1942 because of World War II, and did not resume until 1950.

Beginning in 1950, customers could no longer purchase single coins. The five-coin sets were housed in individual cellophane envelopes, stapled together and placed into a cardboard box. The box and envelope combination was not meant to be a permanent holder for the coins, something collectors learned after the staple began to rust and threatened to damage the coins within the set. The Mint changed to new packaging in mid-1955 (the 1955 set is available each way): a plastic soft-pack inserted into an envelope. This packaging remained in use through 1964.

No Proof sets were struck in 1965 to 1967 because of the massive coin shortage haunting the nation. As noted earlier, Special Mint sets were sold in place of the Proof and Uncirculated Mint sets normally offered.

Proof set production resumed in 1968, but at a new location. Prior to 1968, most Proof coins were struck at the Philadelphia Mint. All earlier Branch Mint Proof coins were and are rare. Production was moved to the San Francisco Assay Office (the San Francisco Mint became an Assay Office in 1962, and a Mint again in 1988), and the S Mint mark was added to the coins. The coins were housed in a hard-plastic holder.

Proof sets have been struck every year since 1968, with a Proof version of the Eisenhower copper-nickel dollar first placed in the set in 1973. A 40 percent silver version of the Proof Eisenhower dollar was offered in a separate package from 1971 through 1974.

Special Proof and Uncirculated sets were offered in recognition of the 1976 Bicentennial of American Independence. The Bicentennial event was numismatically celebrated with changes in the reverse designs of the Washington quarter dollar, Kennedy half dollar and Eisenhower dollar. Copper-nickel versions of all three were issued for circulation and for the regular Proof set.

Collectors were offered two three-coin sets of the same coins struck in a 40 percent silver composition, in Proof and Uncirculated versions. The silver collectors' coins were first offered Nov. 15, 1974, at prices of $15 for the Proof set and $9 for the Uncirculated set. In the 12 years of sales for the two three-coin sets, from November 1974 to Dec. 31, 1986, prices for the three-coin sets were changed no less than five times due to rising and falling silver prices.

From 1976 to 1981, standard Proof sets were issued with either the Eisenhower dollar (through 1978) or Anthony dollar (beginning in 1979). With the resumption of commemorative coinage production in 1982, and the introduction of American Eagle bullion coins in 1986, Proof production was spread to all four coining facilities, in Philadelphia, Denver, San Francisco and West Point. The San Francisco Mint continues to strike the regular Proof set in addition to some Proof commemorative and bullion coins. Prestige Proof sets were offered beginning in 1983 in years when the Mint issued commemoratives. Prestige Proof sets contain the regular set and one or more Proof commemorative coins. The last Prestige Proof sets were produced in 1998.

Another change occurred in 1986 in the Proof die production process. Since Mint marks were first used in 1838, they had been punched into the individual working dies. However, the inadvertent release of a 1983 Proof dime with no S Mint mark prompted Mint officials to place the Mint mark on the master die in an attempt to prevent this type of error from occurring again. The same mistake also happened in 1968, 1970, 1971 and, according to some sources, 1975. In 1986, the Mint mark was included on the plasticene model stage for all Proof coins, including commemoratives; thus, the Mint mark appears at every stage of the modeling and die-making process of all collectors' coins.

Congress mandated annual sales of a Silver Proof set in 1990; it authorized a Proof set with 90 percent silver versions of all denominations of a dime or higher, the highest at that time the half dollar, since no dollar coins had been struck for circulation for about a decade. The Mint did not issue the first Silver Proof sets until 1992, citing 1991 production difficulties. The Mint offered two packaging versions of the new Proof set: a set in the same kind of holder as the standard Proof set marked with the word "silver," and a Premier Silver Proof set containing the same coins in a higher quality package.

More wrinkles in Proof coin production occurred in 1999 and 2000 because of changes in coinage designs and the need to strike new denominations.

The State quarter dollars program, introduced in 1999, is reflected in the Proof sets since 1999. The traditional Proof set contains all five quarters for nine coins total (in 1999) or 10 coins (in 2000). A second Proof set containing only the five State quarters is also offered.

The siphoning of 1979 and 1980 Anthony dollars from Treasury vaults throughout the end of the 1990s and the delay in production of the new Sacagawea dollar (introduced in 2000) resulted in the need to strike 1999-dated Anthony dollars for circulation. Mint officials announced that they would offer Proof and Uncirculated versions of the Anthony dollar later in the year in single-coin packaging. The decision to strike the coins came after Proof set production had begun, making it difficult to include them with the other Proof coins.

The Proof sets sold since 2000 contain a Proof version of the Sacagawea golden dollar, increasing the number of coins to 10. The addition of that new coin caused problems its first year because of the law requiring Silver Proof sets every year.

Mint officials delayed sales of the 2000 Silver Proof sets until Congress could amend the portion of the U.S. Code regulating their production. As noted earlier, the law required the Mint to produce 90 percent silver versions of all coins struck for circulation from the dime through the dollar. However, Mint officials did not want to strike a silver version of the coin it was marketing as the "golden dollar." The coin's golden color and new alloy were in complete opposition to a silver composition (unlike the dime, quarter dollar and half dollar, which had been composed of silver for most of their existence as denominations). Once Congress passed the necessary legislation and President Clinton signed it into law, the Mint could begin delivering the sets for which it had already accepted orders.

A new offering by the Mint generated a good deal of collector hostility in mid-2002. The Mint briefly reopened sales of sets it had previously reported as closed or sold out by offering a package of 1999, 2000 and 2001 Proof sets at coin market prices, not at their original prices. A majority of collectors objected to the program, saying that once a program is closed or reported as sold out, it should remain closed. The Mint stopped offering the packaged sets after a few weeks of sales; officials claimed that storage problems resulted in damage to some of the coins in the 1999 sets and made them unsaleable.

Mint officials, in announcing the closing of sales, also reported that Mint inventories did not contain other unsold coins that it would be offering later.

Matte Finish coins

As the United States Mint began offering more collector coin products in the 1980s and 1990s, officials began experimenting with special finishes to enhance some of the Uncirculated commemorative coins. By the early 1990s, for example, commemorative silver dollars were given a matte surface similar in appearance to the Matte Proof coins of the early 20th century mentioned earlier. Collectors took little note of this special finish, however, because the Mint referred to it as their Uncirculated finish (although it differed considerably from the Uncirculated finish given to coins in the standard Uncirculated Mint sets). In 1994, however, the special Uncirculated finish was applied to a noncommemorative denomination placed in a special limited-edition set.

Congress authorized a commemorative silver dollar celebrating the 250th anniversary of Thomas Jefferson's birth for release in 1994. The Mint offered the 1994 Jefferson silver dollar in Proof and Uncirculated versions, the latter bearing the special matte surfaces developed over the years. Mint officials also offered the dollar in a variety of purchasing options.

Among the special options was a Jefferson Coin and Currency set, which contained three monetary instruments bearing Jefferson's portrait: a 1994-P Jefferson silver dollar, a $2 Federal Reserve note and a 1994-P Jefferson 5-cent coin. While Mint officials intended to limit this set to 50,000 pieces, they forgot to mention that fact on any sales literature. Thus the Mint produced the set to order, selling 167,703 sets.

Mint officials also forgot to tell collectors that the Jefferson 5-cent coin in the set was given the same matte surfaces that had been given to the Jefferson silver dollar in the set, to give the two coins uniform finishes. A collector, however, noted the special finish and informed *Coin World* of that fact. That suddenly made the Jefferson Coin and Currency set a hot property. Many collectors collect Jefferson 5-cent coins, and many seek to acquire Proof and traditional Uncirculated specimens of each date and Mint mark. As collectors and dealers began referring to the coin as having a Matte Finish, many sought specimens of the special 5-cent coin to complete their collections of the denomination. Many Matte Finish 5-cent coins were probably removed from their original holders for placement into whatever holders the collectors were using to store their Jefferson 5-cent sets. Prices for this special 5-cent coin remain high, as much as $100.

Three years later, Mint officials offered a second Matte Finish Jefferson 5-cent coin (although Mint officials were still not using this terminology), this one dated 1997-P and housed in the Botanic Garden Coin and Currency set (also containing a Botanic Garden silver dollar and $1 Federal Reserve note). Production of the set was limited to 25,000 sets, meaning just 25,000 Matte Finish 1997-P Jefferson 5-cent coins would be offered, making this set an even hotter property than the Jefferson sets of three years earlier. In what became one of the most criticized offerings by the U.S. Mint in recent years, the Botanic Garden Coin and Currency set sold out in about a week, before many collectors even received their order forms in the mail. Dozens of irate collectors called *Coin World* to complain about being shut out of the offering because other collectors living closer to where the order forms were placed into the mail had an advantage over those living farther away. Few if any of the callers (including those lucky ones receiving the sets) wanted the sets for the Botanic Garden dollar. Most wanted the extremely limited, 25,000-mintage Matte Finish 1997-P Jefferson 5-cent coin for their collections. Today, these coins sell for as much as $275.

Mint officials learned from this experience, so in 1998, when it offered a Kennedy Collectors set bearing a 1998-P Robert F. Kennedy silver dollar and 1998-P John F. Kennedy half dollar, it limited sales to a specific ordering period, not to a specific number of sets. Sales totaled more than 63,000 sets. By this time, Mint officials had also accepted the terminology that had caught on in hobby circles, and noted that the half dollar in the set had been given the special Matte Finish. The same literature also noted that the dollar in the set was an Uncirculated specimen. However, it was clear to collectors that the finish was the same on both coins (which had been the intention in 1994 when the first Matte

Finish 5-cent coin was produced). *Coin World* began calling the RFK dollar a Matte Finish specimen, prompting a rival coin collector publication to contact Mint officials, who confirmed that the RFK had an Uncirculated surface, not a Matte Finish. *Coin World* persisted in calling both coins Matte Finish, and Mint officials eventually confirmed that yes, the finish on both coins is the identical Matte Finish. (As with the Botanic Garden set, many collectors bought the coin for the Matte Finish half dollar to keep their collections complete, not for the commemorative silver dollar.) The special 1998-P Kennedy half dollar today sells for $300 or more.

Will the popularity of the two Matte Finish 5-cent coins and half dollar prompt Mint officials to make similar offerings in the future? Stay tuned.

Proof sets

Year Minted	Note	Sets Sold	Prestige Commemorative	Selling Price	Face Value
1950		51,386		2.10	0.91
1951		57,500		2.10	0.91
1952		81,980		2.10	0.91
1953		128,800		2.10	0.91
1954		233,300		2.10	0.91
1955		378,200		2.10	0.91
1956		669,384		2.10	0.91
1957		1,247,952		2.10	0.91
1958		875,652		2.10	0.91
1959		1,149,291		2.10	0.91
1960	‹1›	1,691,602		2.10	0.91
1961		3,028,244		2.10	0.91
1962		3,218,019		2.10	0.91
1963		3,075,645		2.10	0.91
1964		3,950,762		2.10	0.91
Production suspended during 1965, 1966, 1967					
1968	‹2›	3,041,506		5.00	0.91
1969		2,934,631		5.00	0.91
1970	‹3›	2,632,810		5.00	0.91
1971	‹4›	3,220,733		5.00	0.91
1972		3,260,996		5.00	0.91
1973		2,760,339		7.00	1.91
1974		2,612,568		7.00	1.91

PROOF SETS (CONTINUED)

Year Minted	Note	Sets Sold	Prestige Commemorative	Selling Price	Face Value
1975	‹5›	2,845,450		7.00	1.91
1976	‹6›	4,123,056		7.00	1.91
1977		3,236,798		9.00	1.91
1978		3,120,285		9.00	1.91
1979	‹6›	3,677,175		9.00	1.91
1980		3,554,806		10.00	1.91
1981		4,063,083		11.00	1.91
1982	‹7›	3,857,479		11.00	0.91
1983	‹8›	3,138,765		11.00	0.91
1983 Prestige		140,361	1983-S Olympic silver dollar	59.00	1.91
1984		2,748,430		11.00	0.91
1984 Prestige		316,680	1984-S Olympic silver dollar	59.00	1.91
1985		3,362,821		11.00	0.91
1986		2,411,180		11.00	0.91
1986 Prestige		599,317	1986-S Immigrant half dollar, 1986-S Ellis Island silver dollar	48.50	2.41
1987		3,356,738		11.00	0.91
1987 Prestige		435,495	1987-S Constitution silver dollar	45.00	1.91
1988		3,031,287		11.00	0.91
1988 Prestige		231,661	1988-S Olympic silver dollar	45.00	1.91
1989		3,009,107		11.00	0.91
1989 Prestige		211,807	1989-S Congress half dollar 1989-S Congress silver dollar	52.00	2.41
1990	‹9›	2,793,433		11.00	0.91
1990 Prestige		506,126	1990-P Eisenhower silver dollar	46.00	1.91
1991		2,610,833		11.00	0.91
1991 Prestige		256,954	1991-S Mount Rushmore half dollar 1991-S Mount Rushmore silver dollar	55.00	2.41
1992	‹10›	2,675,618		11.00/12.50	0.91
1992 Prestige	‹11›	183,285	1992-S Olympic half dollar 1992-S Olympic silver dollar	49.00/56.00	2.41
1992 Silver	‹11, 12›	1,009,586		18.00/21.00	0.91
1992 Premiere	‹11,12›	308,055		29.50/37.00	0.91
1993		2,337,819		12.50	0.91
1993 Prestige	‹11›	232,063	1993-S James Madison half dollar 1993-S James Madison silver dollar	51.00/57.00	2.41
1993 Silver	‹11, 12›	589,712		18.00/21.00	0.91
1993 Premiere	‹11,12›	201,282		29.00/37.00	0.91
1994		2,308,701		12.50	0.91
1994 Prestige	‹11›	175,893	1994-P World Cup half dollar 1994-S World Cup silver dollar	49.00/56.00	2.41
1994 Silver	‹11, 12›	636,009		18.00/21.00	0.91
1994 Premiere	‹11,12›	149,320		29.00/37.00	0.91
1995		2,018,945		12.50	0.91
1995 Prestige	‹11›	105,845	1995-S Civil War Battlefields half dollar 1995-S Civil War Battlefields dollar	55.00/61.00	2.41
1995 Silver	‹11, 12›	537,374		18.00/21.00	0.91
1995 Premiere	‹11,12›	128,903		29.00/37.00	0.91
1996		2,085,191		12.50	0.91

Year Minted	Note	Sets Sold	Prestige Commemorative	Selling Price	Face Value
1996 Prestige	‹11›	59,886	1996-S Olympic Soccer half dollar 1996-P Olympic Rowing dollar	55.00/61.00	2.41
1996 Silver	‹11, 12›	623,264		18.00/21.00	0.91
1996 Premier	‹11,12›	151,817		29.00/37.00	0.91
1997		1,975,000		12.50	0.91
1997 Prestige		80,000	1997-S Botanic Garden dollar	44.00	1.91
1997 Silver	‹11,12›	605,289		18.00/21.00	0.91
1997 Premier	‹11,12›	135,905		29.00/37.00	0.91
1998		2,086,507		12.50	0.91
1998 Silver	‹11,12›	878,996		18.00/21.00	0.91
1999	‹19›	2,557,899		19.95	1.91
1999 State	‹20›	1,169,958		13.95	1.25
1999 Silver	‹12,19›	804,565		31.95	1.91
2000	‹19›	3,096,981		19.95	2.91
2000 State	‹20›	995,803		13.95	1.25
2000 Silver	‹12,19›	965,421		31.95	2.91
2001	‹19›	2,300,944		19.95	2.91
2001 State	‹20›	799,736		13.95	1.25
2001 Silver	‹12,19›	889,697		31.95	2.91
2002	‹19›	2,319,766		19.95	2.91
2002 State	‹20›	764,419		13.95	1.25
2002 Silver	‹12,19›	892,229		31.95	2.91
2003	‹19›	2,245,292		19.95	2.91
2003 State	‹20›	1,235,832		13.95	1.25
2003 Silver	‹12,19›	1,125,755		31.95	2.91
2004	‹23›	Pending		22.95	2.96
2004 State	‹20›	Pending		15.95	1.25
2004 Silver	‹12,19›	Pending		37.95	2.96
2004 Silver State	‹24›	601,671		23.95	1.25

40% silver clad dollars Struck in San Francisco

Year Minted	Uncirculated	Proof
1971	6,868,530	4,265,234
1972	2,193,056	1,811,631
1973	1,883,140	1,013,646
1974	1,900,156	1,306,579

Special Mint Sets

Year Minted	Sets Sold	Selling Price	Face Value
1965	2,360,000	4.00	0.91
1966	2,261,583	4.00	0.91
1967	1,863,344	4.00	0.91

Uncirculated sets

Year Minted	Note	Sets Sold	Selling Price	Face Value
1947		12,600	4.87	4.46
1948		17,000	4.92	4.46

UNCIRCULATED SETS (CONTINUED)

Year Minted	Note	Sets Sold	Selling Price	Face Value
1949		20,739	5.45	4.96
1951		8,654	6.75	5.46
1952		11,499	6.14	5.46
1953		15,538	6.14	5.46
1954		25,599	6.19	5.46
1955		49,656	3.57	2.86
1956		45,475	3.34	2.64
1957		34,324	4.40	3.64
1958		50,314	4.43	3.64
1959		187,000	2.40	1.82
1960		260,485	2.40	1.82
1961		223,704	2.40	1.82
1962		385,285	2.40	1.82
1963		606,612	2.40	1.82
1964		1,008,108	2.40	1.82
1965		2,360,000	4.00	0.91
1966		2,261,583	4.00	0.91
1967		1,863,344	4.00	0.91
1968		2,105,128	2.50	1.33
1969		1,817,392	2.50	1.33
1970		2,038,134	2.50	1.33
1971		2,193,396	3.50	1.83
1972		2,750,000	3.50	1.83
1973		1,767,691	6.00	3.83
1974		1,975,981	6.00	3.83
1975		1,921,488	6.00	3.82
1976		1,892,513	6.00	3.82
1977		2,006,869	7.00	3.82
1978		2,162,609	7.00	3.82
1979	‹13›	2,526,000	8.00	3.82
1980	‹13›	2,815,066	9.00	4.82
1981	‹13›	2,908,145	11.00	4.82
1984		1,832,857	7.00	1.82
1985		1,710,571	7.00	1.82
1986		1,153,536	7.00	1.82
1987		2,890,758	7.00	1.82
1988		1,447,100	7.00	1.82
1989		1,987,915	7.00	1.82
1990		1,809,184	7.00	1.82
1991		1,352,101	7.00	1.82
1992		1,500,098	7.00/8.00	1.82
1993		1,297,094	8.00	1.82
1994		1,234,813	8.00	1.82
1995		1,013,559	8.00	1.82
1995 Deluxe		24,166	12.00	1.82
1996	‹14›	1,450,440	8.00	1.92
1997		940,047	8.00	1.82
1998		1,188,487	8.00	1.82
1999	‹21›	1,421,625	14.95	3.82
2000	‹21›	1,490,160	14.95	5.82

UNCIRCULATED SETS (CONTINUED)

Year Minted	Note	Sets Sold	Selling Price	Face Value
2001	‹21›	1,113,623	14.95	5.82
2002	‹21›	1,139,388	14.95	5.82
2003	‹21›	1,002,555	14.95	5.82
2004	‹21›	Pending	16.95	5.92

Proof American Eagle issue prices ‹15›

Year	Note	Metal	1/10 oz	1/4 oz	1/2 oz	1 oz	Set
1986		Gold	—	—	—	550.	—
		Silver	—	—	—	21.00	—
1987		Gold	—	—	295.	585.	870.
		Silver	—	—	—	23.00	—
1988		Gold	65.00	150.	295.	585.	1065.
		Silver	—	—	—	23.00	—
1989		Gold	65.00	150.	295.	585.	1065.
		Silver	—	—	—	23.00	—
1990		Gold	70.00	150.	285.	570.	999.
		Silver	—	—	—	23.00	—
1991		Gold	70.00	150.	285.	570.	999.
		Silver	—	—	—	23.00	—
1992		Gold	70.00	150.	285.	570.	999.
		Silver	—	—	—	23.00	—
1993		Gold	70.00	150.	285.	570.	999.
		Silver	—	—	—	23.00	—
1993 Philadelphia set ‹16›			—	—	—	—	499.
1994		Gold	70.00	150.	285.	570.	999.
		Silver	—	—	—	23.00	—
1995		Gold	70.00	150.	285.	570.	999.
		Silver	—	—	—	23.00	—
1995 10th Anniv. set ‹17›			—	—	—	—	999.
1996		Gold	70.00/75.00	150./159.	285./299.	570./589.	999./1025.
		Silver	—	—	—	23.00	—
1997		Gold	75.00	159.	299.	589.	1,025.
		Silver	—	—	—	23.00	—
		Platinum	99.00	199.	395.	695.	1,350.
1997 Impressions of Liberty set ‹18›			—	—	—	—	1,499.
1998		Gold	70.00	150.	285.	570.	999.
		Silver	—	—	—	24.00	—
		Platinum	99.00	199.	395.	695.	1,350.
1999		Gold	70.00	150.	285.	570.	999.
		Silver	—	—	—	24.00	—
		Platinum	99.00	199.	395.	695.	1,350.
2000		Gold	70.00	150.	285.	570.	999.
		Silver	—	—	—	24.00	—
		Platinum	118.	227.	405.	740.	1,375.
2001		Gold	70.00	150.	285.	570.	999.
		Silver	—	—	—	24.00	—
		Platinum	118.	227.	405.	740.	1,375.
2001		Gold	70.00	150.	285.	570.	999.
		Silver	—	—	—	24.00	—
		Platinum	118.	227.	405.	740.	1,375.
2002		Gold	70.00	150.	285.	570.	999.

	Silver	—	—	—	24.00	—
	Platinum	118.	227.	405.	740.	1,375.
2003	Gold	85.00	165.	315.	630.	1,098.
	Silver	—	—	—	24.00	—
	Platinum	170.	329.	587.	1,073	1,995.
2004	Gold	90.	175.	335.	675.	1,175
	Silver	—	—	—	27.95	—
‹22›	Platinum	NA	NA	NA	NA	NA

Bicentennial sets

Final mintages are 3,998,621 for the Proof set, and 4,908,319 for the Uncirculated set.

Notes

1. Includes Large Date and Small Date cents. The Small Date is rarer.
2. Some Proof sets contain dimes struck from a Proof die missing the Mint mark, an engraver's oversight, not a filled die. Unofficially estimated that 20 specimens are known. Beware of sets opened and reclosed with "processed" P-Mint coins inserted. Check edge of case for signs of tampering.
3. An estimated 2,200 Proof sets contain dimes struck from Proof die missing the Mint mark, an engraver's oversight, not a filled die.
4. An estimated 1,655 Proof sets contain 5-cent coins struck from Proof die missing the Mint mark, an engraver's oversight, not a filled die.
5. Contains 1776-1976 dated Bicentennial quarter dollar, half dollar and dollar.
6. 1979 Proof set: The Anthony dollar replaced the Eisenhower dollar. During latter 1979, a new, clearer Mint mark punch was used on the dies. Sets with all six coins bearing the new Mint mark command a premium.
7. 1982 Proof set: A new Mint mark punch with serifs was introduced.
8. 1983 10-cent piece: Some 1983 sets were issued with dimes missing the S Mint mark, similar to errors on 1968, 1970, 1971 and 1975 Proof coins.
9. The Mint released an estimated 3,555 1990 Proof sets with a cent missing the S Mint mark. The die was for business strikes at Philadelphia, but was inadvertently sent to San Francisco, prepared as a Proof and placed into Proof production.
10. Price increased from $11 to $12.50 July 1, 1992.
11. Prices are pre-issue discount/regular price.
12. Beginning in 1992 a new type of Proof set was issued, consisting of a regular Proof cent and 5 cents, but with the dime, quarter dollar and half dollar struck on 90 percent silver planchets, rather than the copper-nickel clad planchets of the circulating and regular Proof coinage. A "Premiere" edition — essentially fancy packaging — was sold at an additional premium.
13. 1979-81 Uncirculated sets: While Anthony dollars were struck for circulation at the San Francisco Assay Office, the Unc. S dollar was not included in the 1979 Uncirculated Mint set, which has 12 coins and a face value of $3.82. The Anthony dollar was included in the 1980 and 1981 sets, which are 13-coin sets with a face value of $4.82.
14. 1996 Uncirculated set: A 1996-W Roosevelt dime, available only in these sets, was added at no additional cost to mark the 50th anniversary of the coin.
15. Prices are for single-coin or single-set purchase only; bulk discounts may apply; in 1996, a pre-issue discount was offered on gold coins.
16. Includes tenth-, quarter-, half-ounce gold, 1-ounce silver coin and 1-ounce silver medal.
17. Includes four gold coins and one silver, all with West Point Mint mark.
18. Includes one each Proof 1-ounce platinum, gold and silver bullion coin.
19. Includes one each of that year's State quarter dollars, plus Proof versions of other regular denominations.
20. Includes one each of that year's State quarter dollars only.
21. Includes one each of that year's State quarter dollars, plus examples of other regular denominations.
22. Mint officials had not released price information as of August 3, 2004.
23. Contains Peace Medal and Keelboat 5-cent coins.
24. Contains one of each 2004 State quarter dollar in 90 percent silver. Set offered for first time in 2004.

Glossary

16

Numismatics (pronounced nu-mis-mat-iks), like any science, has a language of its own spoken by its practitioners and students. New collectors unfamiliar with terms like obverse, reverse, Mint mark and double eagle may feel confused by a bewildering lexicon. However, the language need not be confusing.

The terms defined here are those that may be commonly encountered during the normal course of coin collecting. A more in-depth glossary can be found online at **www.coinworld.com**.

Alloy: Mixture of more than one metal.

Altered coin: A coin that has been deliberately changed to make it resemble a rare or more valuable piece, or to change its appearance for any reason.

American Buffalo silver dollar: Commemorative silver dollar struck in 2001, bearing revised versions of James Earle Fraser's designs for the Indian Head 5-cent coin ("Buffalo nickel").

American Eagle: A legal tender bullion coin struck and issued by the United States Mint. The Mint strikes four .9995 fine platinum coins, four .9167 fine gold coins and a .999 fine silver coin.

Bag marks: See Contact marks.

Bicentennial coins: Quarter dollar, half dollar and dollar struck in 1975 and 1976 with special reverse designs commemorating the 200th anniversary of the signing of the Declaration of Independence. Dated 1776-1976.

Buffalo nickel: Nickname given the Indian Head 5-cent coin. Nickname is commonly though incorrectly used; most U.S. coins are named after their obverse design; the creature on the reverse is a bison, not a buffalo; and no U.S. coin denomination is legally called a "nickel." See "American Buffalo silver dollar."

Clad: Composite coinage metal strip composed of a core, usually of a base metal such as copper, and surface layers of more valuable metal like copper-nickel. The U.S. dimes, quarter dollars, half dollars and dollars struck for circulation since 1965 are a clad coinage, including the Sacagawea "golden" dollar.

Coin: Usually a piece of metal, marked with a device, issued by a governing authority and intended to be used as money. Coins may or may not be legal tender. All U.S. coins are legal tender.

Colonial coins: Coins struck by one of the 13 British Colonies before the American Revolution. Few of the Colonial coins were struck with the authority of the British throne, which legally had all coinage rights in Great Britain and the Colonies.

Contact marks: Surface abrasions found on U.S. coins, because of coins striking the surfaces of other coins during bagging and shipping procedures. See chapter on "Grading," for details. Also called "bag marks," derived from the canvas bags coins were once shipped in from the Mint.

Coronet: A style of Liberty Head used on U.S. copper and gold coins for much of the 19th century. Liberty wears a coronet (usually marked with the word LIBERTY).

Denomination: The face value of a coin; the amount of money it is worth as legal tender.

Device: The principal design element, such as a portrait, shield or heraldic emblem, on the obverse or reverse of a coin.

Die: A hardened metal punch, the face of which carries an intaglio or incused mirror image to be impressed on one side of a planchet.

Disme: Original spelling of "dime," used into the 1830s in Mint documents. May have been pronounced "deem."

Double eagle: A $20 gold coin of the United States. Introduced into circulation in 1850; last struck in 1933.

Eagle: A $10 gold coin of the United States.

Edge: Often termed the third side of a coin, it is the surface perpendicular to the obverse and reverse. Not to be confused with the rim. Edges can be plain, reeded, lettered or carry other designs.

Fantasy piece: An object having the physical characteristics of a coin, issued by an agency other than a governing authority (or without official sanction) yet purporting to be issued by a real or imagined governing authority as a coin.

Field: The flat part of a surface of a coin surrounding and between the head, legend or other designs.

Flow lines: Microscopic striations in a coin's surface caused by the movement of metal under striking pressures. A coin's luster is caused by its flow lines; loss of luster is the result of wear to the flow lines.

Frost: Effect caused by striking a coin with sandblasted dies, often used in reference to Proof coins.

Half dimes, half dismes: A silver 5-cent coin of the United States. The Mint Act of April 2, 1792, authorized "half dismes," which was the standard spelling (rather than "half dime") until well into the 19th century. See disme.

Half eagle: A $5 gold coin of the United States.

Hub: A right-reading, positive punch used to impress incused, mirror-image dies.

Large cent: Refers to the U.S. cents of 1793 to 1857, with diameters between 26 and 29 millimeters, depending on the year.

Legal tender: Currency (coins or paper money) explicitly determined by a government to be acceptable in the discharge of debts.

Lettered edge: An incused or raised inscription on the edge of a coin.

Mint mark: A letter or other symbol indicating the Mint of origin. Also spelled Mintmark.

Money: A medium of exchange.

Mule: A coin struck from two designs not normally used together. Examples include a 1959 Lincoln cent with 1958-style Wheat Heads reverse and four double denomination mules (see the chapter on "error coins" for details on the latter).

Nickel: A silver-white metal widely used for coinage. It is factually incorrect to use "nickel" as a synonym for the copper-nickel 5-cent coin. In the mid-19th century, copper-nickel cents and 3-cent coins were also nicknamed "nickel," like the modern 5-cent coin. The U.S. Mint has never struck a coin officially called a "nickel."

Numismatics: The science, study or collecting of coins, medals, paper money, tokens, orders and decorations and similar objects.

Numismatist: A person knowledgeable in numismatics, with greater knowledge than a novice collector.

Obverse: The side of a coin that bears the principal design or device, often as prescribed by the issuing authority. In informal English, the "heads."

Pattern: Coin-like pieces designed to test coin designs, mottoes or denominations proposed for adoption as a regular issue and struck in the metal to be issued for circulation, but that were not adopted, at least in year of pattern issue. The 1856 Flying Eagle cent is a pattern; it was not authorized until 1857.

Penny: The nickname given the 1-cent coin. The United States Mint has never struck a penny for use in the United States. The nick-

name derives from the country's English origins; England still uses a denomination called a penny.

Pioneer gold coins: Gold coins, generally privately produced, struck in areas of the United States to meet the demands of a shortage of federally issued coins, generally in traditional U.S. coin denominations. Often called "private gold," which is correct for many but not all of the issues, and "territorial gold," which is incorrect since none of the coins were struck by a territorial government authority.

Planchet: The disc of metal that when placed between the dies and struck becomes a coin. Also called flan or blank.

Restrike: A numismatic item produced from original dies later. In the case of a coin, the restrike usually occurs to fulfill a collector demand and not a monetary requirement.

Reverse: The side opposite the obverse, usually but not always the side with the denomination (the denomination appears on the obverse of the State quarter dollars, for example). The side opposite the side containing the principal design. Informally, the "tails."

Ringed bimetallic coin: A coin composed of two parts: a holed ring into which is inserted a core. The two parts are often different colors and compositions. The only U.S. ringed bimetallic coin is a 2000 commemorative $10 coin honoring the Library of Congress, composed of a platinum core and gold ring.

Slab: A rigid plastic, sonically sealed holder, usually rectangular, especially those used by third-party grading services.

Series: Related coinage of the same denomination, design and type, including modifications and varieties.

Subtype: A modification of a basic design type that leaves the basic theme intact without major revision. Examples include the Bison on Plain and Bison on Mound reverses for the Indian Head 5-cent coin and the three reverse subtypes used on the Capped Bust half dollar from 1836 to 1838 (the same Eagle design was used with and without E PLURIBUS UNUM; the denomination appears as 50 C., 50 CENTS and HALF DOL.).

Type: A basic coin design, regardless of minor modifications. The Indian Head and Jefferson 5-cent coins are different types.

Variety: As in die variety. The difference between individual dies of the same basic design or type. A minute change in the positioning of the numerals of the date from one die to another results in different die varieties.

Index